PAST AND PRESENT

OXFORD
UNIVERSITY PRESS
AMEN HOUSE, E.C. 4
London Edinburgh Glasgow
New York Toronto Melbourne
Capetown Bombay Calcutta
Madras Shanghai
HUMPHREY MILFORD
PUBLISHER TO THE
UNIVERSITY

PAST AND PRESENT

By THOMAS CARLYLE

EDITED BY

A. M. D. HUGHES, M.A.

LATE SCHOLAR OF ST. JOHN'S COLLEGE, OXFORD

OXFORD
AT THE CLARENDON PRESS

NOTE

THE text of *Past and Present* here printed is that of the
edition of 1858, the first edition to which Carlyle added
a summary of contents and an index. A few obvious
misprints have been corrected.

FIRST PUBLISHED 1918
REPRINTED 1919, 1921, 1927, 1932, 1934
PRINTED IN GREAT BRITAIN

CONTENTS

BOOK III

THE MODERN WORKER

BOOK IV

HOROSCOPE

INTRODUCTION

1. POVERTY IN THE EARLY FORTIES.

The Industrial Revolution.

Past and Present was written in the first few weeks of 1843, when the state of the nation was troubled and anxious in the extreme.   Mr. Sidney Webb has written of the England of the forties [1] that 'in almost every respect the wage-earner was suffering from the surviving evils of the old order, while losing all its advantages ; and he was already exposed to many of the disadvantages of the new era, while enjoying but few of its benefits '.   The Industrial Revolution was only half-way through, and neither the economic nor the political order was adapted to the times.   The best date for the beginning of the period is, perhaps, 1785, when Watt finally elaborated his steam-engine ; whereupon, in conjunction with a great advance in the working of iron and steel, the newly harnessed power was set to the making of all kinds of other machines, of which the most important were Cartwright's power-loom, invented in 1785, and Crompton's mule for spinning cotton, invented in 1779. But the machines were slowly improved, and slowly won the field, and the agony of the Revolution was long.   The cotton industry was modernized, in respect of weaving, earlier than the woollen and the linen ; for while the power-

---

[1] See his *Labour in the Longest Reign.*

loom invaded the cotton factories in Lanark and Lancashire
about 1815, it was not applied to wool, even in Yorkshire,
until after 1839, and the hand-worked jenny held its own
in the weaving of linen for the same length of time.[1]   By
1840 mining, pottery, and chemicals were well in the hands
of the capitalist with his big plant; but hardware, silk-
weaving, hosiery-knitting, boot-making, were still carried on
to a large extent in small 'shops' or in the workers' homes.

In many cases, where the new engines came, their first
effect was to throw large numbers of men and women out
of work, and their second to tempt Capital to set up new
mills and to produce more goods than the market would
take.   For the dear food reduced the buying power of the
people, and in some trades the foreigner was astir and dis-
puting our lead.[2]   The new factories, therefore, were soon
half or wholly idle, and there was first less employment,
and then more, and then less again.   Meanwhile, the workman had still to learn the true strategy of Trade Unionism.
The Unions, driven underground by the coercive Acts of
1816 and 1820, were legally permitted in 1824 ; but their
crude aggressions in the thirties had ended in absolute dis-
comfiture,[3] and left labour to the mercy of the market.   At
the end of the thirties the railways were building apace ; but
it was only by slow degrees that they mobilized labour and
in that way levelled wages up.   And turning to Parliament,
the people found it in the hands of their masters, and even
its progressive elements in the grip of a creed that blessed
the struggle of all with all, and temporized for the struggle's
sake with the constant waste of life by accident and excessive hours of work, and with the nameless horrors of child
slavery.

Thus, while the wealth and population of the country

---

[1] S. J. Chapman, *The Lancashire Cotton Industry*, p. 47.
[2] See note to p. 165.   [3] See below, p. xl.

increased rapidly through the natural opportunities of its
trade, the masses of the people were miserable and poor.
The census of 1801 gave the population of England and
Wales as just below 9, that of Scotland as just above
1½, millions. The corresponding figures in millions for 1841
were 16 and 2½. The inhabitants of London in 1801
numbered approximately 865,000 ; in 1841, 1,900,000 ; and
between 1821 and 1831 the larger towns in the Midlands
and the North increased on an average by 50 per cent.
By 1850 the population of the towns had drawn level with
that of the rural districts. The value of real property
assessed to the income-tax for England and Wales in 1815
was £52,000,000 ; in 1843, £86,000,000. On the other
hand, wages at Queen Victoria's accession were generally
from 50 to 100 per cent. lower than at her death.[1] Thus
the standard wages of a Glasgow joiner rose in this period
from 21s. a week to 36s. ; of an engine-man in the Lothian
collieries from 11s. to 33s. ; of a Northumbrian miner from
3s. a day to nearly 7s. ; of a Leeds wool-spinner from 23s.
a week to 37s. 6d. ; of a cotton-spinner in the Manchester
mills by 30, of a cotton-weaver by more than 20, per cent.
And bread was dearer in the forties than before the recent
war ; the day's work longer ; and employment quite as
uncertain.

The Submerged.

Below the plane of tolerable wages there was a great
volume of severe distress, not greater absolutely than in our
own day, but a good deal greater in proportion. Such
of its aspects as meet us in *Past and Present* must be indicated here :

[1] Webb, *op. cit.* I take the ensuing figures from the same source,
or from Chapman, *op. cit.*, where the data are based on a paper in
Sir Robert Giffen's *Essays in Finance*, second series. I have also consulted Mr. A. L. Bowley's *Wages in the United Kingdom*.

(*a*) In Ireland the rural labourer earned 2*s*. 6*d*. a week, and the peasant's farm was not large enough, as a rule, to keep him in potatoes for a year. There was consequently a miserable Irish proletariate in England, and a flood of Irish harvesters in autumn (see *Chartism*, iv).

(*b*) In the last few years of the eighteenth century, when cotton was booming, the hand-loom weavers in the towns of Lancashire and Lanark and in the country cottages and farms were extremely prosperous. But the power-loom came about 1815, and ruined them. They loved their independence too much, and were too conservative, to yield to the times; so that in the lower grades of hand-loom labour wages 'fell as low sometimes as 5*s*. or 6*s*. a week'. 'The food in use was of the coarsest kind; it consisted mainly of water-porridge and potatoes,' and it was often only by charity that 'whole districts were preserved from the immediate horrors of famine'.[1] Moreover, for some years after 1836 there were bad times in the cotton trade, owing mainly to a surfeit of capital; and though the fully employed operatives in the mills were earning from 20*s*. to 30*s*. a week, large numbers were working half time, and many mills were shut down.[2]

(*c*) The great profits of agriculture during the war were of no advantage to the labourers. In the southern counties and the West wages were commonly from 6*s*. to 9*s*. a week, while cottage rent was costing 8*s*. 6*d*. a month, and wheat 8*s*. a bushel. The labouring population 'seldom saw meat or tasted milk'. In 1830 the men of the home counties had broken machines and fired ricks far and wide, and in 1839 the Anti-Corn-Law lecturers found the rural districts

[1] Chapman, *op. cit.*, ch. ii. He is quoting from Reports of Parliamentary Commissions during the thirties.

[2] Cf. *A Report of the Assistant Poor Law Commissioners on the State of the Population of Stockport* (1842), and see note to p. 154 on *over-production*.

'just as ready for pikes and pistols' as the industrial towns.[1]

(*d*) The state of things in Scotland was worse than in England, for in Scotland until 1845 there was no legal claim to relief for any but the disabled. In a pamphlet entitled *Observations on the Management of the Poor in Scotland and its Effects on the Health of the Great Towns* (1840), William Pulteney Alison, a medical professor at Edinburgh,[2] declared the 'ordinary diet and all the comforts of the lowest orders of society' to be 'much better' in the English towns than in Edinburgh and Glasgow, where the death-rate was twice as high as in London. A population fluctuating between 15,000 and 30,000 lived in the 'wynds' of Glasgow in such a way that one witness whom Alison quotes had never seen, in England or on the Continent, 'anything one half so bad either in intensity of pestilence, physical and moral, or in extent proportioned to the population.' The minister of the Old Church at Edinburgh gave evidence before a Commission, in 1836, of thickly-peopled houses in the city containing 'no bed and not even straw', and of families herded in cellars where 'it was impossible at noonday to distinguish the features of the face' and where beasts of burden were as well lodged as the human sharers of the room. 'It would almost make a heart of adamant bleed to see such an accumulation of misery in a country like this.' The country towns also were full of field-labourers, mostly women, who had grown feeble at fifty on hard work at 8*d*. a day. They had neither savings of their own nor claim to relief, and depended on casual charity. 'Habitual piety gives them resignation, occasionally even cheerfulness; but they live

---

[1] See Morley's *Life of Cobden*, ch. vi. On the condition of the home counties in 1830 and the labourers' revolt, see *The Village Labourer*, by J. L. Hammond and Barbara Hammond.

[2] See below, p. xvi, and the note on p. 3.

in a condition to which that of most domestic animals is a luxury.'[1]

The Crisis of 1842.

From 1826 to 1836 trade and harvests were predominantly good ; from 1837 to 1850 predominantly bad ; and a sharp phase of the distress came to a head in 1842. To take the expenditure under the Poor Law as an inverse barometer, it amounted for the year ending March 25, 1837, to a trifle over £4,000,000 ; to £4,500,000 in 1839–40 (with the same terminal date) ; to close on £5,000,000 in 1841–2 ; and to £5,200,000, or 6s. 6d. a head of the population, in 1842–3. (The strain was a little eased in 1843 and the two years following, but for 1847–8 the rate amounted to 7s. 1d. a head.) During the same period the price of wheat was on an average 66s. a quarter, and dearer by a third than in the earlier thirties ;[2] and foreign trade, through a combination of mischances, was standing still. The quantity of the exports did, indeed, increase ; but their market value fell by nearly £6,000,000 in the six years ; for 'in 1842 a yard of cotton cloth did not fetch much more than half its price in 1830 '. ' Much of this decrease was no doubt due to the ingenuity of inventors ; but much of it was also attributable to the continuous decrease in the wage-rate of the labouring classes. . . . A long apprenticeship had inured them to suffering ; but the misery which they endured in 1816 was as nothing compared with their wretchedness in 1842, when one

[1] These particulars are taken from Alison's own statements in the pamphlet or from evidence therein cited. As to the English towns, the reader should turn to the description of the Manchester cellars and courts in Mrs. Gaskell's *Mary Barton*. In the Parliamentary Report on the hand-loom weavers in 1841 it was stated that 175,000 persons in Liverpool depended on labour ; 86,000 of them lived in courts, and 38,000 in cellars.

[2] From figures given by the Commission of Enquiry at Stockport (quoted in foot-note p. x).

person out of every ten in the country was a pauper.'[1]
How serious the prospect was may be gathered from a speech
delivered in the House of Commons on July 8 of that year
by Richard Cobden :

'This might be said to be a Manchester question three
years ago ; but it is not so now. I see the hon. member
for Leeds in his place, and I challenge him to say whether
the condition of Leeds at this moment is not worse than that
of Stockport. We [in Stockport] have not 40,000 utterly
unemployed ; his borough must be one vast poor-house. . . .
But if I were to point to one place which is in the most
deplorable, the most hopeless state, I would say it is
Hinckley ; there there are 1,500 stocking frames, and only
21 fully employed. I apprehend that at no period of its
history was the pottery trade so severely depressed. Go to
the glass-cutters of Warrington, or the glovers of Yeovil,
and you will hear the same tale. Men and women have
subsisted only on boiled nettles ; and at Burnley the starving
people dug up the putrid carcase of a cow rather than die of
hunger. Is this state of things to be left till the winter ?
What was said yesterday by the Mayor of Stockport ?—that
he would not be responsible for the peace of the place. It
is my firm belief that within six months we shall have
populous districts in the North in a state of social dissolution.'

2.   BETWEEN AN OLD WORLD AND A NEW.

The Corn Law.

The most conspicuous factor in the misery of the people
was the tax on corn. The reform of the franchise in 1832
had only scotched the power of the landed interest in Parliament ; and the 'fair trade' in corn, introduced in 1815, was
continued until 1846. The policy was to assume a price of
wheat which should be favourable to the farmer and not

[1] Spencer Walpole, *History of England from the Conclusion of the Great
War in 1815*, new edition, 1890, vol. iv, p. 358.

too hard on the buyer, and to ensure, by a 'Sliding Scale' of
duties, that the market price should be near it. The law,
as modified in 1828, permitted the import of wheat at
a nominal duty when the price in the home market had
risen to 73s. a quarter, and increased the duty heavily as the
price sank ; and for twelve years this law was a sort of
palladium to either party. It was defended on many
grounds—as an aid without which the land could never be
farmed, as building a market for the manufactures,[1] as compensating the land for its 'peculiar burdens',[2] as keeping up
the breed of countrymen, and saving England from pre-
cariously depending on foreign food. It was assailed as
a parasitic impost that aided no one but the landlord, and
as not only a handicap on trade, but a positive spur to the
foreigner to start his own factories, instead of buying from
ours with his raw material and his corn. And the argument
culminated in hunger. It may be that the repealers over-
rated the effect of the tax ; but they spoke in good faith, and
stood at any rate on a moiety of the truth. 'At the very
lowest our bread tax has raised the price of bread full forty
per cent. . . . Forty per cent. out of 5s. which the labourer
spends every week for his family on bread, or 2s. out of
5s. ;—2s. out of 10s. is the income tax which the labouring
man pays for bread. Ascending till you come to the income
of a nobleman, he spends no more on bread than the poor
weaver, and to estimate the tax he pays for bread [in proportion to his income] you must go to a fractional coin less
than we can compute in this country.'[3]

In 1838, with wheat at 77s. and crowded workhouses,
Richard Cobden and his friends at Manchester founded the
Anti-Corn-Law League, and two years later were joined by

[1] See note to p. 155.   [2] See note to p. 221.
[3] Richard Cobden, in a speech to a congress of ministers of religion
at Manchester, August 1841.

John Bright. Their vast agitation and the force of the general discontent moved the Government to reconsider the Law. The Sliding Scale had tempted the seller to hold his stocks for higher prices, and greatly unsteadied the market. With a view to more steadiness and lower prices, and at the same time a modest protection of the land, Lord John Russell proposed, in May 1841, to abolish the Sliding Scale and impose a fixed duty of 8s. The Whigs had been in power for eleven years, and the country was tired of them. They had done much for reform, but not enough, and the new inclination to Free Trade was too sudden and too timid to conciliate any one. They were defeated on their budget, and in the General Election, in July, the Tories came in with a big majority. The great reform of the tariff in 1842, under the auspices of Peel and Gladstone, who then presided at the Board of Trade, swept away the duties on 750 articles, but the Corn Law remained, a little mitigated. In February of that year Sir Robert Peel announced his conviction that the ideal price should be, not 73s., as heretofore, but between 54s. and 58s., and the Sliding Scale was modified accordingly. To the Free Traders, who had hoped for much more than this, the new measure was ' a bitter insult to a suffering people '. To the extreme Tories it was the first act of the ' betrayal '. The busier trade and better harvests in the next three years preserved this law down to the Irish Famine of 1846, when Peel broke up his party to repeal it. Till then it clung to life like the leaves of autumn that wait for the first stress of weather to sweep them away.[1]

[1] See p. 164.

The Poor Law.

But the poor had to suffer not from abuse alone, but from the remedy of abuse. From 1601 to the present day the Law has given to every pauper in England and Wales a right to be maintained by the parish in which he or she resides. By an Act of 1722, parishes, or unions of parishes, were authorized to put up workhouses, and to withhold relief outside them. But under Acts passed in 1782 and 1796 it became the practice to reserve the workhouses for the aged and impotent, and to relieve the able-bodied in their homes. The result was that 'relief' was applied for and granted as a supplement to wages, and great numbers of the working classes were permanently pauperized. With the growth of the factory towns the evil became intolerable ; and in 1834 the 'wholesome surgery' of the Poor Law Amendment Act removed it. The Act provided that, except in cases of sickness or accident or under special circumstances, the able-bodied should be relieved in workhouses, and there only. By a notable change in the method of government the Justices in Quarter Sessions were superseded by Boards of Guardians, and these were strictly subordinated to a central Board of Commissioners sitting in London. For the next ten years the process of dispauperizing the people and building the workhouses went on steadily. The bitter anger of the working classes under this caustic remedy was the real fuel of Chartism ; and readers of *Oliver Twist* will hardly forget the picture of the new 'Bastilles' that hovered in the imagination of the times—the dismal abodes where man was separated from wife, and parent from child. The stringency of the Act gave Alison his chance in Scotland (see p. xi), where public relief was sternly reprobated as ruinous to self-help. In the pamphlet of 1840, already referred to, and in other publications, he pressed the need of a legal remedy against the vehement opposition of many of his countrymen, including, among others of note, the great Dr. Chalmers.   In the end he had his way, however ; for a Poor Law on the English model was made for Scotland in 1845.

Factories and Mines.

Under the fierce demand of the industries for cheap and manageable labour children became a very marketable commodity ; and the years down to 1833 in the factories, and to 1842 in the mines, are an era of child slavery that stains our history.   Hundreds of thousands of boys and girls, as young as five years or even less, were monstrously exploited ; many sold outright, and carted in gangs from London or the country to the North, to labour for fourteen hours in a day or night in crowded and fetid mills, ill fed and lodged, often brutally used, wholly untaught, stunted in body and mind, and frequently maimed or killed by the unfenced machines.   Unfortunate as were the children of independent parents, the waifs from the workhouses were in a still worse case, for the unions, only too glad to be rid of a burden, ' apprenticed ' them for long terms of years to factory masters or to individual workmen, who took their earnings, and whose chattels they became.   Three inquiries [1] were made into this state of things, and several Acts were passed to check it, before the remedy was found.   The first important measure, in 1802, forbade the working of children [2] at night, or for more than twelve hours a day (exclusive of mealtimes), and ordered that the apprentices should be decently treated and taught the rudiments of education, and that workrooms should be ventilated and cleaned.   The Justices

[1] By Parliamentary Committees in 1816 and 1831, and by a Royal Commission in 1833.

[2] It referred expressly to the apprentices only, however, and only to factories and mills, not to dwelling-houses used as ' shops '.

of the Peace were to visit and inspect the factories, and see that the law was obeyed. In a short time it was found that the Justices were shirking a disagreeable and indefinite duty, and leaving the law a dead letter. At length the Royal Commission of 1833 recommended that no one under nine be employed in any but silk factories, no one under thirteen for more than 48 hours in a week, no one under eighteen at night, and that the Home Office should enforce the law through permanent inspectors ; all which proposals were embodied in an Act of the same year. From 1833 to the time at which *Past and Present* was written the Factory Question is in two chapters: first, the constant battle of the inspectors to see the Act carried out ; and second, the vehement agitation among the operatives of the North to make ten hours, exclusive of meal-times, the statutory day's work in the mills.[1] The employers declared that ten hours a day was ruin, and, until Parliament ratified the proposal in 1847, resisted it tooth and nail.

But in all this only the factories were concerned.

In 1842 the Report of the Royal Commission on the children in the mines deepened the gloom of that gloomy year. It was a worse tale than the other—children and women dragging the coal in baskets to the shafts by chains from their girdles, on hands and knees, for twelve or fourteen hours at a time, often in passages scarcely two feet high, in moist heat and poisonous air, regularly exposed to accident, and frequently to outrage. It is hardly possible for the eye to catch one paragraph of the Report that is not painful. A mother has two children in a mine, and when they return home 'has often to lift them into bed'. A girl of eight 'traps' (i. e. opens doors) in solitude and darkness from three in the morning till five in the afternoon: 'I have

[1] The law they demanded was to apply to women and young persons, but under the conditions of work it would amount to a ten hours' day for all.

to trap without a light, and I'm scared.' 'A vast number of the women have dead children and false births.'

The battle of the factory children and the ten hours' day was fought by a small party of independent men on the spur of mercy and not as a party cause. Most of them, like Richard Oastler and Michael Sadler, were Tories ; some, unorthodox Radicals ; and one or two were Whigs. In 1833 Lord Ashley, afterwards Earl of Shaftesbury (1801–85),[1] took up the leadership of the group, and began his long service as a paladin in the war for the poor. In June 1842 he carried a Bill which forbade the employment in a mine of any girl or woman, or any boy under ten. In one respect it was a retrograde Act. The Home Secretary was empowered, if and when he should see fit, to appoint inspectors to visit any particular mine or mines ; but no system of permanent and organized inspection was instituted, as had been done for the factories, until 1850 : a conspicuous example of the reluctance of that generation to government ; for in the meanwhile the factory inspectors had proved themselves not only the hinge of the law, but a necessary organ of intelligence, and their Reports, issued twice yearly from 1836 onwards, had moulded the opinion by which alone such ordinances can fruitfully subsist.[2]

Education.

Since the children of the poor were elbowed out of the grammar schools in the sixteenth and seventeenth centuries, almost all the provision for their teaching was supplied by

[1] He nearly succeeded in carrying a Ten Hours' Bill in 1843. Other causes espoused by him during the forties were those of the boy chimney-sweeps, juvenile offenders, and 'ragged schools'. He knew the conditions of the poor not telescopically, but as a visitor in weavers' cellars and thieves' dens. See further, p. xxv.

[2] See *A History of Factory Legislation*, by B. L. Hutchins and A. Harrison.

an organization of Churchmen—the Society for Promoting Christian Knowledge, founded in 1699. At the close of the eighteenth century Andrew Bell and Joseph Lancaster started a new movement for primary education ; but unfortunately the two enthusiasts were enemies, and each enlisted in one of the two rival societies into which the effort was channelled—Bell in the National Society, representing the Church, and Lancaster in the British and Foreign School Society, representing the Dissenters. It was not until 1833 that the State 'interfered'. In that year a sum of £20,000 was voted to the Treasury to aid localities in building schools for the poor, the English share being given almost exclusively to one or the other of the two organizations above-named. It was a timid and slipshod beginning, for no care was taken that the schools should be well used or even well built. The grant was renewed in each of the next six years ; but its insufficiency became ever clearer. Far less than half the children in the towns ever came near a school, Sunday school or other ; and many of those who did were crowded in unwholesome rooms, and rather caged than taught by the casually recruited schoolmaster, who in many cases had taken to the task as the last shift of incompetence.[1]

At length, in 1839, a big step was taken by the appointment of a permanent Committee of the Privy Council to control the expenditure on education, with a staff of officers and inspectors, while the grant was increased to £30,000, and rose steadily as time went on. At the very outset the new Department collided violently with the religious difficulty that besets the matter to this day. The first requirements were a body of competent teachers and the substitution of something better for the so-called 'monitors'—the children set to teach children. But the Committee's plan for a State Training College, with full privileges for every denomination,

---

[1] Sir Henry Craik, *The State in its Relation to Education*, ch. i.

let loose an Anglican storm in which the government of
Lord Melbourne nearly foundered ; so that the scheme was
dropped, and has never since been realized. Warned by
this experience, the Committee endeavoured to carry on its
work through the two societies in such a manner as not to
aggravate the Dissenters and at the same time to humour
the Church. A most important measure had been taken by
the appointment of the inspectors, small as their powers
in the schools were meant to be. These inspectors were
to look into religious teaching; and by the so-called
Concordat of 1840 it was agreed upon that none should
be appointed without the approval of the Archbishop
of Canterbury. But the Concordat, and still more the
attempt by Sir James Graham, in 1843, to endow schools
for factory children on terms of Church predominance,
so embittered denominational jealousies that with many
men on both sides the whole principle of State agency fell
for a time into disrepute.

The Dissenters, it must be remembered, were poor, and
their schools few. In many districts they had to choose
between leaving their children untaught and sending them
to hear the Anglican doctrine.

As for the Church, her mind in the matter was somewhat
indefinite. In some Churchmen the idea still lingered that
the State was bound in duty to look upon Dissent as an evil,
and not to endow it in any way. Others thought that all
denominations should receive their proper share of State aid,
but that the Church had earned the right to special terms by
her extraordinary services ; for of the 1,270,000 children at
schools in 1833 only one twenty-fourth were in Dissenting
schools.[1] All Churchmen were agreed, however, in holding

[1] From a Parliamentary Return of 1833, quoted by the Bishop of
London in the House of Lords Debate of July 5, 1839. In this debate
the mixture of the two views shows clearly through the speeches of
the Archbishop of Canterbury and the Bishop of Exeter. The Whig

PAST AND PRESENT

that purely secular education was not to be tolerated, and
that to give knowledge, and not to mix it with Anglican
principles, would be in them a neglect of duty. They were
ready to confess that in their system the secular element
was purposely scanted. 'If', said one of the bishops, 'the
poor could make the Bible the corner-stone of all their
learning—if they could learn history to illustrate the
Bible—if they could learn the various sciences, to the extent
to which acquaintance with them is ordinarily carried by
that class, to illustrate the Bible'[1] . . . 'I know', asserted
another, 'that it will be said we devote too much time to the
Bible, and too little to instructing the children in secular
knowledge and those mechanical arts which may be useful
in after life. My lords, we are content to bear this imputa-
tion. We acknowledge that we hold the great object of
education to be the training up of immortal beings.'[2]
Unhappily, however, the critic might have said, not that
knowledge was restricted in their schools, but rather that
almost none was given at all. The children were drilled to
repeat the Catechism and creeds without understanding;
one-half left the schools unable to read, three-fourths unable
to write, and ninety-eight per cent. incapable of the rule of
three.[3]

leaders were always endeavouring to nail their opponents to a clear
declaration. 'He [Lord John Russell] asked hon. Gentlemen opposite
to state the truth openly, that the Government plan was opposed on
the ground that no system of education was hereafter to be supported
by the State, unless it was conducted under the exclusive direction of
the clergy. . . . They had at least advocated that policy by implication;
and although the rt. hon. Baronet [Sir Robert Peel] was willing to
allow toleration, he still considered that to aid the education of
Dissenters with the money of the State was inconsistent with the
principles of the Established Church' (June 20, 1839).

[1] The Bishop of Exeter, *loc. cit.*

[2] The Bishop of London, *loc. cit.*

[3] From a Report of the Midland Inspector in 1845, quoted by Craik,
op. cit.

Year by year, in view of these facts, the Committee pressed their policy of reform with a discreet persistence. In 1846 the monitorial system was swept away, and a great reform effected by the system of pupil teachers and (voluntary and aided) training colleges. The change brought with it a large increase in the power of the inspectors, and a considerable strengthening of the cords between the Committee and the localities. But not until 1870 were the vast numbers of children outside the schools compelled to come in, and not until 1886 were some of the schools above the primary included in the supervision. In 1837 Lord Brougham had tried in vain to carry a bill for a Ministry of Education, a Board of Commissioners, appointed for life, and only removable for misconduct, under a Minister.[1] But it was not until 1899 that the Committee of the Council was turned into a Board of Education under a President, with ampler powers than before and the dignity of a separate office of the State.

Sanitary Reform.

Of all the problems of the time none needed the hand of Government so urgently as that of Public Health. The mean dwellings around the new factories had been built at haphazard, with no law to regulate their building, and no authority to control it ; and, as a universal rule, they were unprovided with the two necessaries of a decent existence— water and drains. These are things that only a public service can supply ; but the industrial community had long left its infancy behind ere local government awoke to its duties in the matter and to the enormous element of preventible mortality in the big towns. The man to whom the

[1] The demand for a Ministry of Education was pressed from time to time. It was raised in the Commons, by William Smith O'Brien, on April 6, 1841 ; but opposed by the Government on the ground that the creation of a Ministry would set the denominations by the ears, and that the House at the moment was too empty to give its opinion.

conversion was especially due, Edwin Chadwick (1800-90), a
personal acquaintance of Carlyle's, is one of those faithful
servants whom England has forgotten. Born into the circle
of the big industrials in Manchester, and in early manhood
a chosen pupil of Bentham's, he became absorbed in the
hygiene of society, and spent his best years on boards and
commissions, the very image of that good official for whom
the eyes of the Socialists are longing—ardent, laborious,
severely rational, too thorough and too clear-minded to be
either liked or spared. As Secretary to the Factory Commission in 1833, as Assistant Commissioner in the Enquiry
into the Poor Law in 1834, and as Secretary for several
years to the Poor Law Board, he stood stoutly for expert and
unitary government—for a central office and paid officers,
to guide the blind localities and vitalize the law. He never
had so strong a case as in the movement for sanitary reform,
and never had to fight so hard. He started it (for he was
the leading spirit) by a Report from the Poor Law Commission, in August 1839, on the prevalence of typhus in London,
and by the formidable Report of the same Board in 1842
on the sanitary condition of Great Britain at large, proving
that the state of the big towns, in this respect, was 'almost
as bad as that of an encamped horde or undisciplined
soldiery', and that 'the [annual] slaughter in England and
Wales from preventible causes of typhus, which attacks
persons in the vigour of life, appears to be double the amount
of what was suffered by the allied armies in the battle of
Waterloo '.[1]   Stagnant filth in open gutters, all kinds of
refuse in close courts and corners, 'houses dirty beyond
description and extremely crowded', is the refrain of the
evidence.   Local government was not as mediaeval as before

[1] *Report of H.M.'s Principal Secretary of State for the Home Office from the
Poor Law Commissioners on an Enquiry into the Sanitary Condition of the
Labouring Population of Great Britain. Presented to both Houses by command
of Her Majesty, July 1842.*   3 volumes folio.

the Whigs reformed it in 1835 ; but a multitude of special
boards for special purposes cumbered and confused its action,
and it is not, therefore, surprising that, while many schemes
were already in being for draining houses and streets, most
of them had either languished or miscarried. The difficulty
of obtaining water had confirmed the poor in uncleanliness,
and all the noisomeness of their homes descended on the
community in a loss, as was reckoned, among large classes
of labourers, of eight or ten years of each man's working life
through intemperance or disease.[1] A gruesome chapter of
the story was the burying of the dead in the very midst of
populous areas and the habit of keeping bodies in crowded
tenements a long time before burial.

But each of the remedies proposed by Chadwick, and
by other Boards of Enquiry between 1840 and 1844, would
touch the quick of some prejudice or interest, and years
passed away before a step was taken. At length, in 1848,
a General Board of Health was created on the model of the
Poor Law Commission, to consist of a president and two
assessors, and to dispose of a staff of inspectors ; and it had
the power to appoint local boards wherever the death-rate
exceeded a certain figure to carry on the duties of a sanitary
police with domiciliary inquisition. Chadwick was one
member of the central board, Lord Ashley another ; and,
until it was dissolved, in 1854, and replaced by another body,
it pressed on its work in the teeth of a driving hail of public
wrath. 'An Englishman's home', the public clamoured, 'is
his castle.' 'If so,' returned Chadwick, 'it is undefended, for

---

[1] Sir Benjamin Richardson, *Health of Nations*, ii. 151, an account of
Chadwick's activities, with digests of his Reports. A short and
scholarly history of the subject of this section will be found in *The
Public Health Agitation*, 1833-48, by B. L. Hutchins. In one year half
the pauper population of Whitechapel, and 1,200 out of 1,400 of the
paupers in the parish of St. George the Martyr in London, were
attacked by typhus. (Parliamentary Report, 1840.)

disease may march in.' But he had now become impossible, and retired (1854) on a pension.

Emigration.

One medicine for the ills of England was looked upon by many of the doctors as the panacea. In 1819, and two or three times in the twenties, Government had obtained grants of money to settle emigrants at the Cape and in Canada, and a Select Committee, sitting in 1826 and 1827, projected a large policy to relieve the distress at home and people the empty lands oversea—an annual grant, advances to the emigrants from the Funds, and an Emigration Board. Something was done in 1829 by an Act to regulate the emigrant ships ; and the Colonial Land and Emigration Board was established in 1840 ; but the planting of the colonies was left, in the main, to unbidden causes and never taken thoroughly in hand. A great turning-point was reached when in 1838 the *Great Western* sailed under steam from Bristol to New York, and two years later Samuel Cunard crossed in his first ship, the *Britannia*, from Liverpool to Boston in fourteen days. Not only did steam lessen the terrors of the voyages, but it 'reduced the cost of an emigrant's passage from pounds to shillings'.[1] And now the stream of the exodus swelled to a river. In each of the six years ending 1840 the number of persons who left the country was on an average less than 68,000 ; in each of the next ten more than twice, and in each of the ten after that (1850-60) more than three times, as many.[2] There was also a happy conjuncture in imperial affairs. The first of the bigger Kaffir Wars (1834), the trek of the Boers to the Free

---

[1] Spencer Walpole, *History of England*, iv. 400.

[2] The pace was quickened by the discovery of gold in California (1848), and in Australia (1851). The figures are from Walpole, *op. cit.*, iv. 399, and from the *Encyclopaedia Britannica*, sub 'Migration'.

State (1836), and the British occupation of Natal (completed 1843) strengthened the Colony in S. Africa. New Zealand was annexed in 1839; and between 1825 and 1840 two Australian colonies—Western and Southern Australia—were added to New South Wales, and the first foundations laid at Melbourne. In 1840, again, the strife and sedition in the two Canadas were put to rest by the Act of Union.

Moreover, a new temper and style of thinking was appearing in England in regard to our kinsmen overseas. It began, like most good things in the nineteenth century, in the minds of Canning and Huskisson, and shone out in the amendment of the Navigation Laws in 1825, when the old view of the colonies as merely British markets was impressively cancelled. Their ports were to be open to all comers; they were to live for their own ends, and their prosperity would be ours.[1] In 1830 a small band of young men, each of whose lives, by some misfortune or other, was to come short of a splendid promise, united in the so-called 'Colonisation Society', in order to carry forward this doctrine in word and deed—among them Lord Durham (the saviour of Canada), William Molesworth, Charles Buller (Carlyle's own pupil and friend), and Edward Gibbon Wakefield. They were the far forerunners of the Liberal Imperialist whom we know to-day. Sworn champions of the right of self-government, they believed, however, that 'it was not the part either of prudence or of honour to abandon our countrymen, when our government of them has plunged them into disorder, or our territory, when we discover that we have not turned it to proper account'; that 'the experiment of keeping colonies and governing them well ought at least to have a trial'; and that, through the relief of the labour market, the British possessions might 'confer on the suffering classes of the mother country many

[1] This is the gist of Huskisson's great speech of March 21, 1825.

of the blessings which have hitherto been supposed to be peculiar to the New World'.[1] The need of the time, as Wakefield especially insisted, was a double policy: on the one hand, systematic colonization, the supply fitted to the demand, the sexes kept equal, the men and women well chosen, the empty lands sold at a fair price, and the emigrants aided with the money; and on the other, a free extension in all the British communities of all political rights—nay, a new valuation of the colonist as the full equal of the home-stayer and the vanguard of the host.[2]

And, apart from Lord Durham's influence on the fortunes of Canada, these men accomplished not a little. In 1832 the principle that colonial Crown lands should be sold, and not given away, and the proceeds devoted to aiding emigrants, was laid down, in respect of Australasia, by law, and great numbers were assisted in this manner to cross the seas. The idea of settling land by picked men and women of all classes of society was carried out in South Australia and in the early settlements in New Zealand. And Lord John Russell's Land and Emigration Commission, appointed in 1840, provided a service, in the colonies and at home, to inform, advise, and practically help the emigrant at every step of his venture. Nevertheless a feeling was abroad at the beginning of the forties that not enough was being done. On June 2, 1840, the Irish reformer, William Smith O'Brien, moved in the House of Commons for a system of free passages to the colonies at the public expense. Others thought that the pauper might be shipped oversea perforce, at the charge of the poor-rate; and in the first few weeks of 1843 the traveller James Silk

[1] From Lord Durham's *Report on British North America* (1838). It may be noted, by the by, that this great document was penned to a large extent by Buller, who went out as Durham's secretary.

[2] Wakefield's policy was first laid down in his *Letter from Sydney* 1829, and again in his *England and America*, 1833.

Buckingham suggested in a pamphlet[1] that a dead-lift effort should be made, with £15,000,000 from public sources and with the ships of the Navy, to settle a round million on colonial lands, and stock them with necessaries. At the same time Charles Buller, though in a far soberer vein, called on the Government for some more drastic measure to take the tide at the turn.[2] But the colonial reformers had come before their hour. The imperial idea, after the American experience, 'floated like a ship riddled with the enemy's guns and ready to sink in any troubled water'. The ascendant schools of Radicalism did their best to scuttle it. Colonies, they said, were drains on the revenue, fields of corruption, fruits that, as soon as ripe, would drop from the tree : make men homes in England rather. 'Did they ever go down to St. Catherine's Dock', said Cobden once, 'and see an emigrant ship about to start on its voyage? Had they seen the poor emigrants sitting till the moment of their departure on the stones of the quay, as if they would cling to the last to the land of their birth ? As the vessels departed from the Mersey, the last objects which met their gaze were the tall bonding-houses of Liverpool, where were shut up some hundreds of thousands of barrels of the finest flour of America—the only object that these poor wanderers were going in quest of.'[3] And indeed, if

[1] Cited and criticized by Lord Stanley in the House of Commons, April 6, 1843. The pamphlet was, apparently, an advance copy of the chapter on 'A National System of Colonisation' in Buckingham's book on Canada, published in the same year. In any case Buckingham had projected a similar plan in his *Eastern and Western States of America*, ii. 8 (1842). Its main features, especially that of the use of naval ships, were anticipated in 1839 in *Chartism*, x.

[2] See the debate, above referred to, on April 6, 1843, in which all the current views find expression from one speaker or another. The weakness of Buller's able speech was that he would not define what he wanted done.

[3] March 1843. In 1841 Sir George Cornewall Lewis advocated the abandoning of the Colonies in his *Enquiry into the Government of Dependencies*.

the Radicals only saw loss in emigration, the colonial reformers only saw gain. Yet more and more, as the Far West of the United States was penetrated, the tide of emigrants flowed to those territories. In the thirties double as many left our shores for Canada as for the States; in the last forties three times as many for the States as for Canada; in the fifties five times as many. But in 1840, save a comparatively small German element, almost all who crossed the Atlantic from Europe were Irish or British; and even patriots like Durham and his friends did not always see how much might depend on which home the wanderers should choose.[1] So unsure as yet was the emergent vision of the future overseas.

The Old Oligarchy.

Past and Present was written on the morrow of a great revolution that broke the political monopoly of the Upper Class, not only in Parliament by the Reform Act of 1832, but in the domain of local administration as well. The Municipal Corporations Act, carried through by the Whig Government in 1835, completely disestablished in 178 of the largest towns the little oligarchies hitherto ruling as close Corporations and as by immemorial right, and substituted Town Councils, elected by the whole body of ratepayers, with ample powers of local goverment. As the previous sections of this chapter will have shown, the great need of a central control had hardly dawned on the reformers of the day, or rather was generally repugnant to them, and not only did the Act fail to institute a Local Government Board, but it dissipated the authority and function properly

[1] See the introduction to Professor H. E. Egerton's *Select Speeches of Sir William Molesworth*, and on the whole subject of this section the same writer's chapter on 'The Colonial Reformers of 1830' in *King's College Lectures on Colonial Problems*, ed. Hearnshaw.

belonging to the Town Council by suffering the establishment of all manner of special boards for special purposes by
its side. It was, however, a long step, not only in administrative betterment, but in social revolution. 'It marshals all
the middle classes in all the towns of England in the ranks
of Reform,' writes an enthusiastic Whig,[1] 'aye, and gives
them monstrous power too. I consider it a much greater
blow to Toryism than the Reform Bill itself.' And the
blow followed on another, though not so complete, defeat in
the counties. Up to the end of the twenties the landed
gentry, as Justices of the Peace at Quarter Sessions, not
only administered the law in the county, but constituted its
supreme executive and, to no small extent, its legislature.
And if any measure were needed beyond their competence,
Parliament was 'a kind of federal league', where the gentry
'might obtain the sanction of their allies for any law
required in their own little sphere of influence'.[2] The Lord-
Lieutenant, who appointed the Justices, saw to it that
nothing but blue blood was admitted, nothing (save in the
case of the oldest Whig families) but Tory sentiment, and
certainly no Dissenter. In 1815 the oligarchy were almost
unchallenged in these fastnesses of their power ; twenty
years later a great wave of hostility swept them out of many
of its elements. For one thing, the growing needs of government forced the Justices continually to increase the county
rate, and thus to incense those who paid it. But they had
also misused their powers, grossly and vexatiously, in
respect of two sorts of cases that touched the country-side to
the quick—those under the Game Laws and those relating
to the public right of way. Characteristically, 'it was not
to the love of money that their judicial impartiality and

[1] Quoted from *The Creevey Papers* in *English Local Government : the Manor and the Borough,* by Sidney and Beatrice Webb, II. xi.
[2] *English Utilitarians*, i. 29.

intellectual integrity succumbed, but to their overmastering
desire to maintain their field sports and protect the amenity
of their country seats[1].' Up to 1831 it was illegal for any
but a landowner to kill game, and the restriction was not
greatly mitigated under the law of that year by the system
of permissive certificates. In 1843 night-poaching was still
punished by transportation, and the sanctity of rabbits,
hares, and feathered game was a burden to the farmer
amounting to a quarter of his rent.[2] Thanks, in the main,
to these causes, and to the trend of the times, a number of
Acts between 1828 and 1835 withdrew from the Justices
the control of the Poor Law, of the alehouses, and highway
repair; while in the administration of prisons and asylums,
and even to some extent of the police, they had lost their
autonomy, and were subject to the supervision of the central
government. And their prestige had suffered in proportion;
' they found themselves, individually and collectively,
denounced on every platform, and criticized in every newspaper.'[3] It is, nevertheless, another vivid sign of the incompetence of that period to admit the idea of systematic
government that, having acted so far, the hand of reform
was stayed, and until the Local Government Act of 1888
the Justices in Quarter Sessions were still the one authority
in many little areas of public life.

Thus the sap of the aristocracy was slowly withered.
The landlord, as such, had long ceased to be a military

[1] *English Local Government: the Parish and the County,* by Sidney and
Beatrice Webb, II. vi.

[2] A witness before the Committee on the Game Laws in 1846 stated
that he reckoned £1,000, if game were not preserved, a lower rent than
£800, if it were. Owing to the restrictions on the sale of game, and
its consequent high prices, poaching was a trade in which more could
be earned in two nights than by farm labour in a week, and the land
was thus burdened by a semi-criminal class who were generally
useless for farm work.

[3] See on the whole subject. Webb, *loc. cit.*

officer, and his civil functions were falling to others. Other
classes jostled his in Parliament, beat it in the fields of
ability, or enjoyed the fields to themselves. The usage of
his caste condemned him to fruitless leisure on his inherited
acres, and forbade his sons to emigrate or to trade. And
yet his rent-roll, since the war, was prodigously swollen,
and his legal privileges, though dropping one by one, were
still mighty. The law entailed his estate, larded it with
the tax on corn, and hedged it for his pleasure with a lively
survival of the mediaeval forest laws.

The Church.

'The Church, as she now is,' wrote Thomas Arnold in
1832, ' no human power can save.' In and about that year
a storm of hate broke upon her which ' stunned and
bewildered ' her leaders and friends, and ended her slum-
bers.[1] Many of the clergy, even of this date, were cousins,
not far removed, to Parson Trulliber; and the best, of
whom there were not a few,—the evangelical missioner, or
the High and Dry Divine of Trollope's novels—were
wanting either in the breadth of mind or the energy of
feeling, or in both, to renew the Church and set up her
battlements again. It was imperatively needful to reassert
her claims by rooting them in imaginations and hearts. To
one set of minds, which is represented by Arnold and his
Principles of Church Reform (1833), it seemed best in this
crisis to centre on the truth which is common to all
Christian societies, and to let in the whole body of English
Protestantism. To the Tractarians, on the other hand, the
world was marshalling for some stern encounter between
the spiritual and the natural man, and Liberalism was a
fatal compromise. They would fight in the whole armour
of the Primitive Church, and with all that was tried steel

[1] See Dean Church, *The Oxford Movement*, ch. i.

in the hand of the Mediaeval—with the doctrine of the
Catholic fold, and the Apostolic priesthood, and the supremacy of the Sacraments, and with the natural aids of ritual
and outward beauty which the Reformers threw away to
their cost. 'The age is moving towards something,' wrote
Newman, 'and most unhappily the one religious communion
among us which has of late years been practically in possession of this something is the Church of Rome. She alone,
amid all the errors and evils of her practical system, has
given free scope to the feelings of awe, mystery, tenderness, reverence, devotedness, and other feelings which may
especially be called Catholic. The question, then, is whether
we shall give them up to the Roman Church, or claim them
for ourselves.' When Carlyle was writing *Past and Present*
the Oxford Movement had come to a crisis and set the
country afire. It began with Keble's sermon on 'National
Apostasy' in 1833. It was greatly strengthened by the
accession of Pusey in 1834. In 1841 the trouble came with
Newman's *Tract No. XC*, and his secession followed in 1845.
It might appear in 1843 that the promise of revival was
being nipped, and a great disruption was setting in.

Meanwhile a series of corrective Acts had apparently discredited, but ultimately strengthened, the Church as a
political institution. In 1832 the Ecclesiastical Commission was appointed to inquire into her revenues and their
disposal, and the four Reports of 1835 and 1836 revealed
a state of wholesale simony. The office of a bishop was
often a small gold-mine, and was therefore almost a preserve for the sons or tutors of the great. Durham was
worth £18,000 a year, Canterbury £17,000, London
£12,000, Winchester nearly £11,000. Pluralism and
absenteeism were grievously rife, and the inequalities in
the values and burdens of benefices beyond reason. The
Commission, in its first Report, advised that 'where the
annual income of a bishop amounts to £4,500 it is not

necessary to make any addition, nor would we recommend
any diminution, unless it exceed £5,500; but we think
that the two Archbishoprics and the Bishoprics of London,
Durham, and Winchester ought to have a larger provision
than the rest'. On these lines the bishops' incomes were
distributed by the perpetual Ecclesiastical Commission incorporated in 1836. By a law of 1838 pluralism was mitigated in the present and forbidden in the future, and the
absentees heavily punished. In 1840 the capitular establishments were reduced in order to endow populous parishes;
and in the same year the axe was first laid to the Ecclesiastical Courts. But the political decline of the clergy was
evidenced in 1838 and the subsequent years during the
demand for 'Church Extension'. Church building had not
kept pace with the population. It was reckoned in 1818
that there were seats for only one inhabitant in five.[1] In
that year Lord Liverpool, believing that irreligion was the
root of Radicalism, obtained (with hardly a murmur of
dissent) a grant of £1,000,000 to build new churches, and
a further half-million in 1824. At the end of the thirties
the want was greater than ever, and an agitation led by
Sir Robert Inglis mildly fluttered the country in 1839 with
petitions to Parliament and counter-petitions for or against
a grant in aid. But when Inglis moved for an Address to
the Throne, June 30, 1840, he was defeated, and Sir Robert
Peel, on taking office, turned cautious, and the matter fell
to the ground.

Philanthropy.

Thus the currents of the time were bearing England fast
forward to the indiscernible future of opportunity and of
danger. In the few years of the Great War the nineteenth
century had burst into the eighteenth, and the whole fabric

---

[1] Spencer Walpole, *op. cit.*, i. 388.

of life needed rebuilding, whether on the old foundations
or from the bottom to the top. The government, local and
central, the franchise, the law, the commercial and civil
economy, and all other provisions of a modern State for
a modern people were to be called into being, and the
profound misery of millions of men and women menaced
the upper classes with either a short respite for reform or
else a short shrift. A succession of great ministers—Pitt,
Canning, Peel, Gladstone—led the nation on the road of
safety ; but the light was uncertain, the pace all too slow,
and disaster never far behind. Fortunately the statesmen
found to their hands a great volume of charity and social
sentiment. It was the day of the Evangelical crusades, of
Wilberforce, Clarkson, Buxton, Ashley. A crowd of societies,
of a strong Protestant grain, wrought up the temper in
which brutal sports were put down, animals and children
protected, the slave trade abolished (1807), the slaves set
free (1833), and the Bible carried all over the globe. A
critical witness has given a description[1] of the huge meetings
at Exeter Hall (opened in 1831) in which the Evangelical
spirit was voiced—the thousands of the middle and upper
classes, many in Quaker uniform, mostly women, 'all dieted
at home on Cowper, Fénelon, Wordsworth'—the 'loud
tongue and unctuous silkiness of profession' in the 'well-
paid agents' of this or that cause—the rapt look on multitudes of gentle faces, and the 'single thrill of the bonnets,
and deep long sigh', as the speaker made his stroke. In
Oliver Twist (1838), *Nicholas Nickleby* (1839), and *The Old
Curiosity Shop* (1840), Charles Dickens was swaying these
forces to Radical ends. But too often they spent themselves
far afield, as, for instance, in the Niger Expedition of 1841.
At the instigation of the 'Society for African Civilization',

[1] *Quarterly Review*, September, 1845, article on 'Poems by Alfred
Tennyson'.

three naval ships and three hundred men, leaving the
uncivilized at home, were sent out to bind the chiefs along
the river not to trade in slaves, and to establish model
farms that should teach the native to farm his land and
found a new British market by the way. In five months
the whole expedition succumbed to malaria, and returned
to the coast with every European sick, and a death-roll of
one in five,—to be a byword for those who felt towards the
philanthropists like Ebenezer Elliott:

> Their lofty souls have telescopic eyes,
> Which see the smallest speck of distant pain,
> While at their feet a world of agonies,
> Unseen, unheard, unheeded, writhes in vain.[1]

And Ashley complained that it was hard to get the Evan-
gelicals to lend a hand to the factory laws.

With all its caprice, however, philanthropy suffused the
age, and mellowed, broadened, and vivified its thought.
For a great energy of thought and imagination accompanied the humanitarian enthusiasm. In the thirties
and earliest forties Thomas Arnold, Frederick Denison
Maurice, Newman and Pusey, Tennyson, Charles Dickens,
Carlyle, John Stuart Mill, either made their marks or
laid in the mind to do so; and all were concerned, more
or less directly, with the state of England. 'The succeeding generation,' it has been said,[2] 'say from 1840 to
1870, practically lived on the thought and sentiment of
the seven or eight years immediately preceding the close
of the Liberal reign in 1841. It was during these years
that the schools were formed, and the principles shaped,
which have attracted to themselves all who were serious
enough to feel the need of a school or the use of a
principle.' It will be necessary here to give a rough

---

[1] The type is caricatured in Mrs. Jellyby in *Bleak House*.
[2] John Morley, *Life of Cobden*, iv.

sketch of the intellectual situation, as it had emerged in 1843.

3. The Attitude of the Working Classes.

Socialism.

The theory that the means and materials of labour should belong to the labourer was bound to come with the new conditions of industry, and it runs through the Utopian expectations of William Godwin in his momentous *Political Justice* (1793); but Godwin believed that all government was evil and hoped to see it disappear. There is a fragment of Socialism, however, in a paper read before a 'Philological Society' at Newcastle in 1775 by a local schoolmaster, Thomas Spence. Newcastle became too hot for Spence after his lecture was published, and for the rest of his life he propagated his doctrine from a bookshop in London. Its basis is that all men have a natural right to equal property in land. The few and rich have grabbed the land 'as if they had manufactured it and it was the work of their own hands'. That was the birth of tyranny. 'You are lost', he quotes Rousseau, 'if you forget that the produce belongs to all, the land to none.' In 1824, again, William Thompson, a landlord in Ireland, in his *Enquiry into the Principles of the Distribution of Wealth*, argued that, as all value is made by toil, there can be no property in land, but only in its produce under labour, and whose should that be but the labourers'? [1]

---

[1] When only rude hunters wandered over the American prairies, he says, those prairies were not even objects of desire, and even when pegged out and still uncultivated were not yet wealth. 'Labour was wanting to be superadded to mere desire, and in proportion as labour was bestowed upon them, they were transformed from mere objects of desire into objects of wealth. . . . What has nature done towards this conversion? Nothing. What has man, what has man's labour done? Everything.' *Enquiry*, ch. i, p. 11.

Lastly, Robert Owen (1771–1858) developed the notion of a commonwealth of co-operative communities, with rent and capital eliminated. Owen's voice is a sort of irrepressible drone in the music of the day, reiterating his plan for forty years, and scoring the co-operative idea on the general mind. The son of a village tradesman in Wales, he rose by integrity and business aptitude to be a cotton manufacturer and a rich man, without ceasing, however, to care for the poor. He was among the first to denounce child labour and 'the sacrifice of the living machinery to the dead'; and the experiments in paternal government which he carried on at his works at New Lanark by the Falls of the Clyde between 1800 and 1828 profoundly influenced public opinion and broke the path for the factory laws. His co-operative store, his infant school, his drilling-hall, dining-hall, dancing- and lecture-rooms, his fines on drunkenness, his 'silent monitors'—bits of paper affixed to the workmen's places and coloured so or so according to their conduct—resulted in a reign of thrift and sobriety and in a breed of children 'the happiest human beings he ever saw'. From this experience he drew the conclusion that character is formed by circumstance, and that the industrial conditions in England were the root of her evils. He would remedy them by eliminating competition, and setting up New Lanarks all over the country, minus the master and owner. Each trade should unite to form communistic settlements of its members, who would exchange goods with other trades in other settlements at rates fixed by the times spent in producing them. This done, man was saved. Owen put forth an outline of these opinions in *A New View of Society* in 1813, and gradually abandoned his business to preach his faith in the wilderness, and, artless, warmhearted, indomitable as he was, to blunder all his days in unpractical schemes for his decapitalized New Lanarks, whether in Britain or in the wilds of America, and to spoil his best beginnings by one naivety or another. The most stirring episode in his long Odyssey was his temporary capture of the Trade Unions and the attempted Revolution of 1834.

The Trade Unionism of the Thirties.

In 1833 he had come to believe that through a general strike the landlords and capitalists might be forced to surrender the sinews of industry, and he urged his plan on conventions of the Trade Unions with extraordinary results. Early in 1834 a federation of all the trades, the ' Grand National Consolidated Trades Union ', was formed to carry out the strike, and half a million men came in in a few weeks. Rumours of the strange ritual of admission which survived in most unions from the days of the Six Acts—the religious services, oaths of secrecy, symbolic skeletons, and battle-axes — shrouded the movement in terror, and when it spread to the country districts the governing classes were thoroughly alarmed. By a drastic use of the law and the lock-out they had altogether discomfited the conspirators by the autumn of 1834, and the Trade Unions lapsed for some years into ' general apathy '.[1]

Chartism.

Chartism, on the other hand, aimed chiefly at political change. From the very beginning it embraced two parties, one the advocates of physical force under Fergus O'Connor, the other the moral force section under William Lovett. O'Connor (1794–1855), the ' Lion of Freedom ', by origin an Irish barrister, owed his extraordinary power as a popular leader, not to his ideas, which were few and incoherent, but to an imposing presence and the gift of fiery speech. He

[1] *The History of Trade Unionism*, by Sidney and Beatrice Webb, ch. iii.

began his political career as a member of the Irish party in Parliament, quarrelled with O'Connell in 1835, and transferred his energies to the north of England.   Here he became the travelling organizer of discontent, and through his newspaper, *The Northern Star*, founded in 1837, advertised himself and his cause to great numbers of the working classes.   The 'five cardinal points', which he proposed to his Central Committee of the Radical Unions in 1836, were manhood suffrage, the ballot, annual Parliaments, payment of members of Parliament, and the abolition of the property qualification for the House of Commons.   In 1838 the 'People's Charter', in the guise of a Parliamentary Bill, was formulated by the 'Working Men's Association', a body of London artisans, of which Lovett was secretary ; and this programme, embodying O'Connor's ' five points ', and adding the sixth point of equal electoral districts, was adopted by the Radicals in enormous meetings throughout the country. In 1839 the deepening distress aided O'Connor and his party to overpower the moderates.   A comprehensive scheme of active and passive resistance, to culminate in a general strike, was drawn up at a great Convention in Birmingham, which ended in riot and bloodshed ; and until the easier months of 1843 the peace of the country was constantly menaced and frequently disturbed.

But Carlyle was right when he praised the British labourer for knowing the limits of force (p. 15).   The Trade Unions had sowed their wild oats in the Owenite adventure, and the steadier elements of the labouring world held aloof from the new insurrectionism.   The younger Unionists more and more cast in their lots with Cobden and Bright, or with the fruitful Co-operative Movement, which had sprung from Owen's example at New Lanark, and made its footing in 1844 through the 'Rochdale Pioneers'. Chartism subsided in 1843 and the two or three easier years that followed, and devoted itself mainly to O'Connor's ill-starred scheme for settling factory workers on the land. In 1848 the French Revolution revived the excitement of 1839 in England, and on the day (April 6) when O'Connor presided at the great Chartist march through London, and, as member for Nottingham, presented the Monster Petition to the House of Commons, the capital was fortified and manned with an army like a besieged town.   But it was the last flicker of the fire, and the free and buoyant trade after 1850 quenched it altogether.   'My belief is', said Peel to his party in 1849, 'that you have gained the confidence and goodwill of a powerful class in the country by parting with that [i. e. the Corn Tax] which was thought to be directly for the benefit of the landed interest.   I think it was that confidence in the generosity and justice of Parliament which in no small degree enabled you to pass triumphantly through the storm that convulsed other countries in the year 1848.'[1]

4. THE RADICALS OF THE MIDDLE CLASS.

The Utilitarians.

The dominant thinkers of the day, the so-called Utilitarians, were the theoretical allies of the industrial master, and dealt with the social situation in a clear and simple doctrine that came and conquered.   They, and they alone, had a precise policy, built on what was apparently a thorough analysis of the facts, and on a theory of man that seemed to unravel the whole perplexity of his government.   In 1843 they were, or had lately been, at the height of their power. Jeremy Bentham (1748–1832), the patriarch of the school, had spent his long life on a private fortune as a secluded thinker and the unseen fountain of reform.   A lawyer by

[1] Sir Spencer Walpole, in his *History*, assigns the eventual easement of the situation in England to : (*a*) Free Trade ; (*b*) the cessation of the Irish influx through the Irish exodus to America ; (*c*) the British emigration.

training and a lawyer's son, he devoted himself to the
elaborating of systems of government, and legal codes, and
'tables of the springs of action', and the methodic and the
dry are the marks of his school. His mantle fell at his
death on James Mill (1773–1836), a stern hard-thinking Scot,
and on James Mill's son John Stuart (1806–73), whose
endeavour for most of his life it was to 'build bridges', as he
once put it, between the beliefs of his early teachers and the
discoveries of a finer and larger mind than theirs. Bentham's
first book, the *Fragment on Government*, was published in
1776; his *Principles of Morals and Legislation* in 1789; his
Catechism of Parliamentary Reform in 1818. James Mill
began his propaganda in 1816, and his *Analysis of the Human
Mind* came out in 1829. The *Westminster Review*, the organ
of the school, was instituted in 1824. John Stuart Mill
contributed to it from the start; but the series of his more
important writings begins with the *Logic* in 1843, and the
Principles of Political Economy in 1848. It will be necessary
to enter some way into the Utilitarian system, since it is
continually referred to, directly or implicitly, in *Past and
Present*. For Carlyle came to his intellectual station on
a recoil from those doctrines, and of all that he regarded as
the mischief of the time they were the head and front.

The Standard of Pleasure and Pain.

'Nature has placed mankind under the governance of two
sovereign masters—pleasure and pain. It is for these alone
to point out what we ought to do, as well as to determine
what we shall do.' These, the opening sentences of
Bentham's *Principles of Morals and Legislation*, lay down
the corner-stone of his ethics. The main problem, with
him and his disciples, is to reconcile self-sacrifice with the
'principle of self-preference'[1]—with the postulate that,

[1] This is from the *Constitutional Code*, *Works*, ed. Bowring, ix. 5, where

when an action is perceived to promise more pleasure to the doer than if he abstained from it, he does not and should not abstain. The solution they found was to call in the law of the 'association of ideas'. The 'self-regarding' theory of morals is, of course, as old as human thought, and Mandeville, for instance, had set it forth in England long before. In the *Fable of the Bees* (1705) he had argued that men are moral, not by nature or any sort of grace, but because they fear each other, and the fear of others reins in a man's cupidities, and turns them to peaceable industry and to public benefits. Bentham's is the same argument with a difference. In the Utilitarian view the motives to good actions are more numerous, and the pleasure of other men's goodwill at least equal to the dread of their hate. And so firmly is the 'idea' or memory of the favour of our fellows 'associated' with this or that class of action, that the actions come to be pleasant in themselves; [1] the 'sanctions' or terrors of law and theology lend their aid; and prudence teaches that my own pleasure is insufficient, unless it conduces to other men's. The moral test, therefore, of any action or institution is, after all, its 'utility', or the degree of its consonance with 'the greatest happiness of the greatest number', [2] and egoism, if sufficiently far-sighted, will turn to altruism, which is only the plane of its highest success. [3] All this, to be sure, was an old philosophy,

he most explicitly lays down the 'superiority of egoism'. But he is not always clear on the matter. See Stephen, *English Utilitarians*, i. 312.

[1] See, for instance, chapters xxii and xxiii of James Mill's *Analysis*, a *locus classicus* in this regard.

[2] The formula was not new. Francis Hutcheson had used it in his *System of Moral Philosophy* (1755), and Bentham had found it in Joseph Priestley's *Essay on the First Principles of Government* (1768).

[3] ' "The project of Themistocles", said Aristides, "is very advantageous, but it is very unjust." Aristides should have said : "The project would be useful for a moment, and hurtful for ages; what it

but it came to the Utilitarians as a surprising light. Their metaphysic — their ' analysis of the human mind ' — was substantially that of Hume, and ended in the likelihood, as Carlyle used to say, that ' God was a myth, and the soul a gas, and the next world a coffin ' ; and the doctrine of Utility gave them a rule of conduct that seemed to stand by itself and without the mysterious conception of a transcendental conscience or a divine command. A science of government, they thought, could work only with a calculus of human motives, that would put them all in one line, and make of good and evil simply plus and minus. For themselves, they were far from being men of pleasure. ' In his views of life ', wrote John Stuart Mill of his father,[1] ' he partook of the character of the Stoic, the Epicurean, and the Cynic, not in the modern, but in the ancient sense of the word. In his personal qualities the Stoic predominated. His standard of morals was Epicurean. But he had (and this was the Cynic element) scarcely any belief in pleasure [i. e. divorced from utility]. Accordingly temperance, in the large sense intended by the Greek philosophers, was with him almost the central point of educational precept. He thought human life a poor thing at best, after the freshness of youth and of unsatisfied curiosity had gone by. He never varied in rating intellectual enjoyments above all others, even in their value as pleasures. The pleasures of the benevolent affections he placed high in the scale ; and used to say that he had never known a happy old man, except those who were able to live over again in the pleasures of the young. For passionate emotions of all sorts he

would bestow is nothing in comparison with what it would take away."—*Principles of Morals and Legislation*, ii. This was the state of the theory in 1843. In 1861, in his *Utilitarianism*, John Stuart Mill distinguished between ' qualities of pleasures ', thus introducing another standard, and giving the pure doctrine away.

[1] In the *Autobiography*.

professed the greatest contempt. "The intense" was with
him a byword of scornful disapprobation. No one prized
conscientiousness and rectitude of intention more highly,
or was more incapable of valuing any person in whom he
did not feel assurance of it.' 'Wintry' and 'sawdustish',
Carlyle would say of John Mill. 'Eh,' he would add, 'but
he 's a pure-minded man.'

The Atomic Sociology.

What, then, was the political result of these ethics?
Chiefly, the principle of 'the greatest happiness of the greatest
number' was a mighty plea for democracy and solvent of
privilege. It was the line and plummet which showed at
a glance that the English polity was all 'out of truth', and
by which a better might be built. That England, after the
War, began busily to set her house in order and discard her
anomalies was due, in the main, to the logic of the Utilitarians and their persistent propaganda. At the same time,
in reducing every pleasure to one kind, and making it the
one motive, they pitched the moral standard far too low for
their practice, and came to centre their view on the commoner desires of men, and to overlook the higher, as if
those were natural and these were not. 'The pursuit of
wealth,' said Nassau Senior in his Inaugural Lecture as
Professor of Political Economy at Oxford, 'that is, the
endeavour to accumulate the means of future subsistence
and enjoyment, is to the mass of mankind the great source
of moral improvement.' They said in effect : if we abstract
the selfish motives, and remember the others marginally,
like friction in a machine, we shall be some way out, but
not far ; and did not see that they were dropping stitches
without which the whole fabric would come to pieces. For
in the forgotten margin were all the religious loyalties that
make society a whole and not a crowd of atoms. Blind to

man's need of helping and being helped, or to the positive side of government, they resembled a surgeon who has cut the ulcer away, and is thenceforth powerless to continue the cure ; and the patient sinks from a bad complication into a worse.

Political Economy and Political Reform.

Utilitarian, it should be observed, is a vague term, and means either the stricter followers of Bentham or all those who, in public matters, were generally in sympathy with him and thought in his veins. In neither sense is it quite convertible with the term Radical, for many men whose caste of mind was Utilitarian were labelled in Parliament by the word Whig. Taking the Radicals, however, to include not only the good Benthamites, but those who marched in the same regiment, though in another company, their programme may be defined under the two headings of liberation and *laissez-faire*. Their Political Economy, starting from Adam Smith's *Wealth of Nations* (1776), resulted in the propositions, that, if poverty were to be cured, it could only be by the same combative instinct to which it was, in the first place, due ; and that, as the instinct was a good one and its own best guide, the duty and interest of the State were to give it room and stand aside. *Laissez-faire*, or 'let things alone', was not, however, an absolute rule. Even Bentham believed in a national system of education, and the rigorous centralism of the Poor Law Amendment Act was the work of his fervent disciples. It was a question of Utility. But the rule was at any rate a stubborn prejudice, and in economic matters barely admitted an exception.[1]

[1] It is strictly laid down by Bentham in his *Manual of Political Economy*, and adopted by James Mill, Malthus, Ricardo, and the rest. But the last chapter of John Stuart Mill's *Political Economy* (V. xi) allows of exceptions so far-reaching as to amount almost to a change of front.

The whole story of the trade of the period is of being
throttled by clumsy protection, by the exorbitancy of the
Exchequer, and the parasitism of the ruling class ; and all
the industries were fighting for breath.   Moreover, the
famous *Essay on Population* (first edition 1798), by Thomas
Robert Malthus, seemed to have shown that one sure means
of social betterment was very hunger.   Malthus teaches that
population is only checked by being starved, and, as a rule,
multiplies down to the limit of subsistence.   And this discovery was the first premiss of the science.   David Ricardo,
in his *Principles of Political Economy and Taxation* (1817)
had explained the operation of the three factors of English
industry, Land, Capital, and Labour, and pointed to the
inexorable limits of that portion of wealth which is paid in
wages.   Rent, he had argued, must necessarily beat down
Capital to a minimum profit, and Capital must beat down
Labour, disorganized as it then was, to the lowest rates.
As Malthus taught, the labourer's only hope was to
diminish his birth-rate and redress the balance of the
supply of labour and the demand ; but to that purpose his
present stock of prudence and temperance was altogether
inadequate.   And, as if to reinforce the misery of these
facts, there came the discovery of the ' law of diminishing
returns ', according to which land must yield ever less and
less the more it is solicited for food, and when the world's
virgin tracts have all been cultivated, not only will population press to the starvation line, but the line 'will press
back, and the labourer be left in a sadder plight than
the man in Poe's story of *The Pit and the Pendulum.*   To
look to Parliament to save him from this fact would be
putting his head in the sand ; the only way was to let the
fact work on, that terror might avail him.   Malthus, a
benevolent and amiable man, a Church of England clergy-
man, and a Professor at Haileybury, would not only have
repealed the old Poor Law, but made no other in its stead,

and left the people (for their own good) to die in the streets.[1] There were cases, and the Factory Laws were one, where the Radicals were forced to admit that the State might intervene; but they accepted even the Factory Laws with a bad grace, and stubbornly obstructed them. And when it came to a measure to protect men and women, instead of children—to the Ten Hours' Bill, for instance—they were unbending. 'Mine', wrote Cobden, 'is that masculine species of charity which would lead me to inculcate in the minds of the labouring classes the love of independence, the privilege of self-respect, the disdain of being patronized or petted, the desire to accumulate, and the ambition to rise. It is to themselves alone, individually, that they, as well as every other great section of the community, must trust for working out their own regeneration and happiness. Again I say to them, *Look not to Parliament, but look only to yourselves.*'[2]

But the rule of *laissez-faire* did not mean there was nothing to do. It meant only, 'give the combatant a chance', 'keep the ring'; and that amounted to a vast labour of liberation. So far as the machinery of freedom was concerned the canonical declaration of policy was contained in Bentham's *Catechism of Parliamentary Reform*, the book that blew in the defences of the old order for the great assault of 1832. Its argument is simple in the extreme. One governor or a few are bound to follow their own 'sinister interests'; tried by the test of Utility, all the factors of our Commonwealth—Crown, Peerage, Parliament, Law—are wanting; make the people their own governors, and the general good is automatic. Manhood suffrage, annual Parliaments, equal

---

[1] Ricardo shared this view (Leslie Stephen, *English Utilitarians*, iii. 167, 168). The same position was taken up against Alison by many of the leading men in Scotland.

[2] Cobden to W. C. Hunt on the Hours of Labour, October, 1836, quoted in Morley's *Life*.

constituencies, and the ballot are the evident requisites. In other respects Bentham in particular was devoted to the reform of the law and the criminal code, and the Radicals in general worked especially for two objects—Education and Free Trade. There were, however, two sections of Radicals, and they did not present the items of their policy in the same order. A small group of 'Philosophical Radicals', as they were called, men of culture and standing and good Benthamites—Grote, Roebuck, Buller, Molesworth, Hume —sat in Parliament from 1832 to 1837, and lent the sanction of intellect and gentility to the future demands of the Chartists and the Anti-Corn-Law League. Their ranks were sadly thinned at the ensuing election, and in their stead the 'Manchester Radicals' took up their causes— Cobden, more especially, who entered Parliament in 1841, and Bright, who entered it in 1843. These men were themselves industrial masters, and were not of the sort of mind to delve into metaphysics for their policy, which agreed, however, with that of the other group. Only they put commerce first. They saw, indeed, that the coming of the industries was fatal to the old political institutions as they then were; but the principal requirement seemed to them to be the physical well-being of the people. Without it public order and private virtue in such a community would be alike impossible; and to 'enlarge the circle of trade' by a peaceful policy towards other states, and by untaxing on all hands at home—and first and foremost untaxing bread— was to save the country and save souls. Unlike several of the prominent members of the other section, they cherished an intensive patriotism that grudged the flower of our manhood to foreign lands and to colonies which, as they believed, would soon fall away. They assumed that business would lead them right, and that whatever in politics was not good for business was not good at all. To Carlyle these Manchester Radicals and the class they represented were as much

the hope as they were also the misfortune of the age, for
practical doughtiness was one of the main things, and that
they had.   But he was oftener sensible of their defects, and
one reads without surprise that when, a few years after *Past
and Present,* he went to Rochdale and met John Bright,
'with his cocked nose and pugnacious eyes and Barclay-
Fox-Quaker collar', and Bright showed him over his mills,
'we discorded in our views not a little', so that 'I got occasionally to talking in the Annandale accent, and com-
municated large masses of my views'.

5.   CONSERVATISM.

The Romantic Influence.

In 1843 events were moving fast to the Tory disruption
after the repeal of the Corn Laws, and therewith to the long
predominance of the Whig or Liberal party, more and more
indoctrinated with radicalism.   Even when Disraeli carried
his followers into power, it was only by vying with the
Whigs in popular measures ; and democracy came steadily
in with good offices from either side.   But before the Tories
went with the stream there hovered before them, or before
their keenest minds, a dream of a grand reaction, a new
Conservatism, to restore the ancient vigour of the Crown,
the Land, and the Church, and bind them closer in the
leadership of the people.   Instead of recasting the Constitution, they would 'revive its torpid elements', and that
by moral rather than political change.   There was naturally
in this aspiration a touch of looking backward ; the old order
had come from the past, and the past would witness to its
worth.   Cardinal Newman once wrote that Scott and Wordsworth and Coleridge between them had made the way
straight for the Oxford movement, and the same influences
were telling also for some congenial endeavour in the

political world. In many men the devouter and deeper
instincts, chilled in the mercantile present, were twining
with the memory of whatever was great, beautiful, morally
sane, and humanly satisfying in the past. Many, in face
of the appalling state of the new towns, were wishing that
the wheels of Time would run back to some simpler and
wholesomer age, and there stay. When the Tory speakers
in Parliament denounced the factories and their trail of
mean streets as the pools of corruption, and contrasted with
them the cottage and garden of the rural labourer and the
incense-breathing fields, Cobden would ask bitterly how
much all that might profit at seven shillings a week. But
the Tory argument was not altogether mere flummery ;
there was an echo in it of a disgust and a longing that are
deep in modern man, and come down from the long
centuries of the ' natural life '—a sentiment that had spoken
already in Rousseau and in Wordsworth, and was soon to
speak again in John Ruskin.

Samuel Taylor Coleridge.

To these devout Conservatives the most troublesome fact,
both in the way of their own thoughts and in the armoury
of their opponents, was the amount of manifest failure in
the landed gentry to govern and in the Church to feed her
flock. There seemed to be a mortal sting in the constant
appeal of the Radicals to results,—in the argument: You
may know Aristocracy and Church Establishment by their
fruits, and there the fruits are. It was into this breach that
Coleridge stepped in 1830 with his *Constitution of Church
and State.* Coleridge, wrote John Stuart Mill in a famous
essay,[1] 'has been as truly as Bentham the great questioner
of things established. For a questioner need not necessarily
be an enemy. By Bentham above all others men have

---

[1] In the first volume of his *Dissertations and Discussions.*

been taught to ask themselves (with regard to any doctrine
or institution), Is it true? and by Coleridge, What is the
meaning of it? The one took his stand outside the received
opinion, and surveyed it as an entire stranger to it. The
other endeavoured to see it with the eyes of a believer in
it.' Accordingly, Coleridge's method is to look for the
'idea' of an institution, by which he means, not necessarily
the conception of those who carry it on, but the 'natural
want or requirement of human nature' to which it responds.
He finds, then, that in every society there is a 'Principle
of Permanence' and a 'Principle of Progression', each
corrective of the other, and the Constitution, even before
1832, gave expression to them both. It gave a voice to the
enterprise of the country, as embodied in the commercial,
manufacturing, and professional classes, in the House of
Commons; it committed the Principle of Permanence to the
Land and the House of Lords. Further, the Radicals, Coleridge was never tired of saying, had overlooked the vital
need of the sentiment that keeps a society together, and
this, the organic sense, is religious. It is natural, therefore,
that the State should cultivate it and the arts and sciences
that ought to league with it. It was a common practice,
accordingly, at any rate with ancient states, to set aside
some portion of the national wealth, or of the land, to
maintain a clergy or 'clerisy', not consisting only in priests,
but also in scholars, scientists, educators, and the practi-
tioners of the liberal arts, just as these were included in the
ecclesiastical order of the Middle Ages. Theology, however,
and the religious consciousness are always the centre of
gravity in knowledge and conduct; and the Church,
endowed and established in England, contracted as its
functions now are, is all the same a vital organ of our polity,
or rather its very heart. This was a timely and a welcome
argument, not so much for its precise terms as for its line
of attack. It ascribed to each of the main orders of the

commonwealth an indefeasible function, and made away
with the notion that any of these might be cast aside like
a worn-out coat. It parried the argument from results with
an argument for patience, and gave a licence, or a call
rather, to a policy of benevolent reform.

The Theory of the Permanent Superiority of the Land.

There are three other writers whom we must not pass
over, all of them high in Carlyle's esteem. Thomas
Chalmers (1780–1847), who led the great schism in the
Scottish Church in 1843, is mainly of account because the
peculiar point of his political theory seems to be adopted,
with a certain hesitation, in *Past and Present*.[1] In his
book on *Political Economy in Connexion with the Moral State
and Moral Prospects of Society* (1832) Chalmers rests the
ascendancy of the landed class on an economic doctrine or
heresy. He argues, like the French economists before him,[2]
that the only real and radical wealth is food; and that the
industries subsist by making luxuries for the men on the
land in return for its redundant produce. Agriculture, being
thus the only source of wealth, pays ultimately all the
expense of government; and Chalmers urges the landed
class for its own good to pay rather directly than indirectly,
that is, to suffer all the taxes to be commuted to a single
impost on their estates. They would lose nothing, would
disarm hostility, and take unchallenged their rightful
places in the seats of power. For by the very force of
economic facts, as the paymasters and taskmasters of
Industry, the landowners are 'naturally and properly the

[1] Cf. III. viii with the following, and see p. 221.
[2] The so-called Physiocrats of the school of Quesnay and Turgot.
Like Chalmers, they held that, as land was the one source of taxation,
it should also be the one object, and the *impôt unique* would simplify
half the problem of government.

lords of the ascendant'. True, if primogeniture were
abolished, the wealth of the country might be distributed
in small lots among a great number of freeholders ; but that
would mean no superfluity, and therefore no culture—no
art, no science, no manners. 'It is not for the sake of its
ornaments and its chivalry alone that we want the high
rank and fortune of our aristocracy to be upheld. It is
because we think there is a soul in chivalry which, though
nursed in the bosom of affluence, does not cloister there,
but lights up a certain glow of inspiration in the mass of
a community.'[1] Of these illuminators the Church was the
natural ally, and as necessarily rooted in the land ; and if,
as Chalmers believed, temperance in all senses, and in the
Malthusian first of all, was the great need of the working
classes, their best policy was to rest thankful that piety
and refinement were established and endowed.

If Chalmers trusted to right everything by the magic of
his 'single tax', there was no such hopefulness in the speculations of Robert Southey (1774–1843), who was the principal
mouthpiece of the Tory party. The substance of many
essays in the *Quarterly* is gathered in his *Colloquies on the
Progress and Prospects of Society* (1829), where the ghost of
Sir Thomas More sadly arraigns the state of the country,
and contrasts it with the far happier England of the early
Tudors. Southey is deeply convinced of two things—first,
that Industrialism is evil ; an irresponsible, unsocial power,
foreign to the true England and to all her traditions, and
illimitably dangerous ; and second, that the mass of men
need the guidance of their betters and are not fit to be let
alone. Under the Tudors, More is made to say, 'every
man had his place. If one class were treated in some
respects as cattle, they were at least taken care of; they
were trained, fed, sheltered, protected ; and there was an

[1] *Op. cit.*, chapter xii, 'On Primogeniture'. See Stephen, *English
Utilitarians*, ii. 242 f.

eye upon them when they strayed. But how large a part
of your population are like the dogs at Constantinople,
unowned, living by chance, subsisting in filth, mischief,
and wretchedness.' He writes always like a man in the
crater of a volcano. Co-operative Societies, state-aided emigration, and above all the influence of the Church may do
something to save England ; but her best hope is the mercy
of God. And the same vein of thinking, with a tinge of the
same desperation, comes out, as it were in an outlying reef,
in William Cobbett (1762–1835), more especially in his
History of the Protestant Reformation (1827). Cobbett was
the son of a Hampshire ploughman, and through all his
full-blooded career, as field-labourer, soldier, American
politician, Tory journalist, and Radical agitator, looked back
with passionate affection to the English country-side of the
days before the industries and the Great Public Debt, and
mourned that the gentlemen of England were leaving their
ancient homes and their pride of place to stock-jobbers and
cotton-spinners. The working-man was the heaviest loser
by the change, and the change was only the consummation
of that process by which the blessed order of the Middle
Ages was broken up. Our Catholic forefathers, he asserts,
' looked on bare bones and rags as indubitable marks of
slavery', and resisted all attempts to inflict them. In those
days there was 'fixedness' in the relations of men to men,
and the Church, with her great monasteries up and down
the country, was the Mother of the people, and fed the
hungry both in body and soul; an age not, perhaps,
enlightened, but not disgraced by any such sights as those
of ' the poor souls who are now eating sea-weed in Ireland,
who are detected robbing the pig-troughs in Yorkshire,
and harnessed like horses and drawing gravel in Hampshire
and Sussex '.[1]

[1] He is alluding to the notorious 'parish cart', drawn by paupers,
men and women.

Young England.

Finally, these wistful reminiscences of the ancient notions of government were embodied in the early forties in the programme of a small group of politicians, known as the 'Young Englanders', under the lead of Benjamin Disraeli, now at the first chapter of his career. They were young men of rank and culture, equally impressed by the religious movement at Oxford and by the teaching of Carlyle, and aspiring to be the saving salt of Toryism. By the end of 1842 they had begun to act together as a Parliamentary cave, and a little later Disraeli, at the request of the others, issued a manifesto of their principles in the form of his *Coningsby* (1844) and *Sybil* (1845)—two illuminative documents of the state and practice of Parliament at the time and of the conditions of the poor in the great towns. He too starts from the conviction that capitalism is an unstable and anti-social force, and that the natural governors of England are the landed men. They, if they acquired a conscience by consorting with the new spirit in the Church, might still redeem the country. For the one stable fact, he thought, in the political situation was the still unbroken loyalty of the people to the old order, and without extinguishing Parliament, a revolution was yet possible which should restore the Crown and the Peerage to their lost power and check the encroachment of that force, now vested in the House of Commons, before which 'the sceptre had become a pageant and the labourer a serf'. Once they had their own again, and were inwardly renewed, the appointed leaders of the nation would do against Capitalism what it would never do against itself,—would bring it under a moral control, and forbid the destitution of the people by protective law. Many years later, in the preface to *Lothair*, Disraeli declared that all these hopes were baffled by a lack of the religious energy to make them good. 'The writer, and those who acted with him, looked then upon the Anglican Church as a main machinery by which these results might be realized. There were few great things left in England, and the Church was one. Nor do I doubt that if, a quarter of a century ago, there had arisen a Churchman equal to the occasion, the position of ecclesiastical affairs in this country would have been very different from that which they now occupy. But these great matters fell into the hands of monks and schoolmen.'

6. CARLYLE AND POLITICS.

Dates.

1795. Carlyle born at Ecclefechan, Dumfriesshire.

1809. Entered the University of Edinburgh.

1814. Leaves the University, with the intention of entering the Presbyterian Ministry. Serves for a time as a schoolmaster at Annan and Kirkcaldy.

1818. Adopts literature as a profession. Lives for three years at hack work in Edinburgh.

1819. Begins learning German.

1821. The 'Everlasting No' (*Sartor*, II. vii). Becomes tutor to Charles Buller.

1823. *Life of Schiller.*

1824   Translation of *Wilhelm Meister.*

1825. Restful year at Hoddam Hill. His 're-birth' is accomplished (*Sartor*, II. ix).

1826. Marries Jane Baillie Welsh, and moves to Edinburgh.

1827. *German Romance* (translations).

1828. Removes to Craigenputtock.

1828–1834. Period (mainly) of the Literary and Biographical Essays.

1833–1834. *Sartor Resartus* appearing in *Fraser.*

1833. Moves from Craigenputtock to London.

1837. *The French Revolution.*

1839. *Chartism.*

1841. *Lectures on Heroes.*

1843. *Past and Present.*

1845. *Cromwell.*

1849. *Nigger Question.*

1850. *Latter-Day Pamphlets.*

The Ethical Premisses.

According to Carlyle's own story, as he tells it in three
chapters of *Sartor Resartus*, 'The Everlasting No', 'The
Centre of Indifference', and 'The Everlasting Yea', he went
through the experience of a ' new birth' in the years from
1821 to 1825 during his apprenticeship to the trade of
author. In 1821, being twenty-six years of age, and a literary
hack in Edinburgh, ill, solitary, unsuccessful, he suffered
under profound despondency and an almost total loss of
religious faith. The negative philosophy of the time, like
a ghost he could not lay, threatened to show him that in
the huge mechanism of the world he was a thing of no
account and altogether helpless. Suddenly the strange
trance which he describes as coming upon him one day
while walking in the city, brought him heart and hope.
In that hour he felt and knew that, however dismal his
worldly hap might be, and however vacant the heavens
might seem, he was always 'the master of his fate and the
captain of his soul'. It was not alone a great lift in moral
power, but the beginning of a new faith, for the revival
went on under the influence of the German poets and
philosophers, whose language he had begun to learn in
1819. And in the end 'I understood well', he writes
(*Reminiscences*, i. 288), 'what the old Christian people meant
by " conversion", by God's infinite mercy to them. I had
gained an immense victory, and for a number of years had,
in spite of nerves and chagrins, a constant inward happiness
that was quite royal and supreme, in which all temporal

evil was transient and insignificant, and which remains essentially with me still, though far oftener *eclipsed* and lying deeper *down* than then.'

What first of all he owed to the Germans, and principally to Fichte and to one or two passages in Goethe, as for instance the song of the Earth Spirit in *Faust*, was the conception of this indefeasible power, so vividly revealed in his own will, as not cloistered in himself, but one in kind and one in fellowship with a Will that moves in Nature and in the history of men—an old faith, indeed, but one which it was laid upon him to rediscover. It is true that, as a rule, he speaks of God in the way of his early creed as exterior to Nature and Man and definitely individual ; but the other conception stands, as it were, in reserve.[1] Further, this *anima mundi* is intensely active and formative. The world, as he sees it after his teachers, is the body or sphere of an ever-developing and creating energy, with some thought or intention within it, a 'glowing life', an 'ever-changing weft', the 'vital garment of the Divine'. And he was a flame of the fire ; he, or more especially the urgency in him to put himself out in work. For to work is truly to commune with God, to follow after order and truth, and submit the single will to that of society and that of the world.

Here, then, or nowhere is the mystery of conscience made clear ; it is the impulse of the divinity within. Conscience, said the Utilitarian, is the fear of punishment or the expectation of reward. You have the lure of an idea of pleasure, or the repulsion of an idea of pain, and action follows. ' No,' answers the idealist, ' you do not aim at the pleasure or the relief from pain, but you aim beyond or through that at the good. In choosing a pleasure you give it first a new value, a value which it has not in

[1] See the chapters on ' Natural Supernatural' and 'The Everlasting Yea' in *Sartor*, and the Essay on Diderot.

itself, but derives from you. You are not pushed by a
motive, that is to say, as by a casual and exterior thing,
but yourself are the mover, and yourself present the end.'[1]
Carlyle is not so much concerned, however, to argue the
matter in such terms, as to take up the answer at this
point and press it further. The more the mere pleasure
and pain enter into the account, he affirms, the less free
and authentic, the more 'mechanical', the action is. The
difference between the plane where these considerations tell,
and the plane where they are put aside—between pleasure,
as an end, and good, as an end—is infinite, for on the first
of these planes the man himself is not really in action at all.
True manhood sets in when the will ceases to register the
results of the weights and balances of different pleasures,
and becomes active or, in Carlyle's expression, dynamic—
flows free from sources that are deep in itself, and are also
the only springs of whatever is wonderful in man—love
and worship, and the enthusiasm of the beautiful or the
true.[2]

The Hero.

It is but a step from these premisses to the doctrine of
the hero. Of all the dynamic forces that issue in authentic
manliness the consummate force is the religious motive, or,
in plain words, the love of God. And the love of God is
nothing else than the joy and devotion of the weaker and

[1] 'That mysterious self-impulse of the whole man, heaven-inspired,
and in all senses partaking of the Infinite, is conceived as non-extant,
and only the outward Mechanism of it remains acknowledged; of
Volition, except as the synonym of Desire, we hear nothing; of
"Motives" without a Mover, more than enough.' Essay on
Characteristics.

[2] See the Essays on *Signs of the Times*, and *Characteristics.* Carlyle
never again made so clear and succinct a statement of his ethics
as in these Essays, where he develops the distinction between the
'mechanical' and the 'dynamic'.

baser in presence of the great and strong. How then do we rise to that sentiment as towards God, except by experiencing it as towards great men? Every great man is a revelation of the Divine, and if men are by Nature religious, they are by Nature in a perpetual quest of a true aristocracy or a true king. Given a state of spiritual health in a nation, one or other of those methods of government will spring from it with the same necessity as the flower from the root. And so far there is a sense in which the doctrine is not to be disputed,—the sense, that is to say, that good leadership is often a necessity and always a need. Where Carlyle is at issue with his time is on the relation of the leader to the led. Is he to lead by persuasion, or in virtue only of a blind consent? Are the people to be the partners or only the subjects of his will? And is there a virtue in taking the will of the people, whether or no that will be right or wrong? Once you admit that political freedom is in any way desirable, you are desiring the institutions to give it effect—a Parliament and a franchise, and desiring that your hero should work through these. The trouble with Carlyle is that he does not really know the answer to these questions, or what to make of the institutions. For from first to last he has in mind, as the type of perfection, those single-minded epochs in history, when great masses of men moved in unison and bent to one will. His Cromwell and his Frederick were leaders who did their work in far simpler conditions than those of to-day, and each in virtue of an exceptional unanimity in a whole or in a large part of the community he swayed. The result is that the value of political dissent, and of the institutions that voice it, was never clear to Carlyle, who was haunted from first to last by the idea of a dualism in the state of the body and the life.[1] He talks at times, with a certain

[1] This is the fallacy that is latent, for instance, in a great part of his striking Essay *Signs of the Times*.

simplicity, as if any system, whether of belief or of government, must be wrong,[1] as if it can only be there to silt
up the vital energy, and vanish in the dynamic wave; as
if the hero might always act like Frederick in his Prussia,
or Prospero on his isle.   And yet a large part of his argument consists of the proposition that social convention is
precious, and the law of historical continuity is not to be
defied.   In face of the levellers in France or England—the
Jacobins or the Radicals—he is a true Conservative.   In
face of the English Parliament he sighs for a strong man,
not indeed to extinguish it, but at any rate to extract its
powers.

There are, in fact, two versions of his theory, according
as he leans to democracy or leans away.   Both versions
mingle with each other at the very first; but in the earlier
books the democratic predominates, and in the later it pales
beside the other.   According to one a burning loyalty,
passing from highest and lowest and back again, is the
condition of a great state, and the fruit and the food of
wholesome living.   In this case a democratic Parliament
would be useful, or needful even, to foster the loyalty and
keep it sweet.   According to the other version, men are
most blessed when a strong man leads or drives them
aright, even though they follow not of choice, but in the
strength of a blind feeling that under his government it is
good to live; and in this case a Parliament is a superfluity.
The point at which the Prussian note comes on is marked
by the *Cromwell* in 1845; for the conviction that Cromwell
was right, and the nation wrong, over the plan of a compromise with the king—that the hero had saved the people
against themselves—wrenched, as it were, the whole frame
of his mind.[2]   In *Past and Present* you may easily find the
reactionary version: 'You do not allow a palpable madman

---

[1] 'All system-builders must be wrong' (to Sterling).

[2] See Froude, *Life in London*, I. xiii.

to leap over precipices; you violate his liberty.   Every
stupid, every cowardly and foolish man is but a less
palpable madman; his true liberty were that a wiser man
lay hold of him, and order and compel him to go a little
righter.   O, if thou do know better than I what is good
and right, I conjure thee, force me to do it; were it by
never such brass collars, whips and handcuffs, leave me
not to walk over precipices.'[1]   But this strain is altogether
dominated by the other.   'One of the worst kinds of waste
is that of irritating and exasperating men against each
other, by violence done; which is always sure to be injustice
done, for violence does even justice unjustly.'[2]   'No man is,
or can henceforth be, the brass-collar thrall of any man;
you will have to bind him by other, far nobler and cunninger methods.   Let him go abroad as a trusted one, as
a free one.   Gurth could only tend pigs; this one will
build cities, conquer waste worlds.—How, in conjunction
with inevitable Democracy, indispensable Sovereignty is to
exist: certainly it is the hugest question ever heretofore
propounded to Mankind.'[3]

Carlyle and the Radicals.

Put forth with ever greater power in the works and arts
of men, fostering and purifying the nations through kings
and poets and the grim sanctions of truth against untruth,
the God within us and without will not fail of His increasing
purpose.   Might and right in the long run are one; 'at
bottom there is nothing else but justice.'   The ages of
unfaith and decay do succeed to the religious and creative;

[1] p. 191 (abridged).   See quotation from Fichte in note.

[2] p. 14 (abridged).

[3] pp. 225, 226 (abridged).   Cf. *Heroes*, v : 'Printing, which comes
necessarily out of Writing, is equivalent to Democracy; invent Writing,
Democracy is inevitable.'   And *Sartor*, III. vii : 'Freedom, heavenborn,
and vitally essential for us all.'

but only to provoke the rebound and lead man higher by his very relapse.[1] Yet there is, if not inconstancy, at any rate much moodiness in Carlyle's view of evil. Is it a light matter, he often leaves us asking, a mere ' obstruction ', an ' outer coating ' over a kernel of good, a 'cross-current' that strives vainly to deflect the good from its path ?[2] Or is it 'perennial' and a 'fearful imperilment' of Nature ?[3] More particularly, is the nineteenth century, is Britain in the nineteenth century, 'hag-ridden', the prostrate victim of ' speciosities ', or is it true that ' the speciosity has no friend in the world ' ? These utterances are easy, perhaps, to reconcile on a fair view of Carlyle's philosophy ; and ultimately his optimism, his 'royal and supreme happiness ' remains ; but only ' in eclipse ' and ' deep down '. He was a great patriot, who thought of his country ' as a lover or a child ',—oftener of her than of the world in general, and oftener of her peril than of her strength. Gradually, as the state of England seemed to go from bad to worse, his solicitude for her future prevailed over all other questions. After 1850, when to other men's eyes the times were mending, he at best could only see a respite from the agony, and remained to the end of his life involved in politics. In *Sartor Resartus* his main purpose is to set forth the dynamic view of man, and had the state of Britain been less anxious, he might have continued on that theme, and dealt rather with the theologians than with the statesmen of the time. But ' the black aspect of Ruin and Decay ' fascinated him ; —' in every sinking heart a tragedy, less famous than that of the Sons of Atreus, wherein, however, if no "kingly

---

[1] See *Sartor Resartus*, II. iii ; *Heroes*, v, on the eighteenth century; and the Essay on Voltaire.

[2] See *Past and Present*, I. ii.

[3] ' Evil must ever exist while man exists. Evil is the dark disordered material out of which man's Freewill has to create an edifice of order and good.'—*Characteristics*.

house ", yet a manly house went to the dust. Must it grow
worse and worse till the last brave heart is broken in
England ? ' [1] In October 1830 we find him, in a letter to
Goethe, hinting a hope of the Saint-Simonians.[2] In that same
month, Jeffrey, after a visit to Craigenputtock, writes him
a sarcastic letter on his talk of taking from the rich to give
to the poor, and his enmity to the labour-saving machines.
Would he burn all the carts and spades, then, since spades
were machines ? [3]   And the passion that inspired these
conversational flings breaks out in *Sartor* in the grim chapter
on Helotage and the epitaph on Count Zaehdarm (III. iv,
II. iv). Moreover, all the main elements of his political
theory appear in that book, as it were, with their young
face. The general mould of the face is the same early and
late ; but the characteristic look of the after years is but
hinted now and then, and the features that afterwards
dominate are still unpronounced. The wickedness of *laissez-
faire*, the sacred need of government, the preciousness of
hero-worship, and the colonial destiny of the British race—
all this is set forth in the political chapters (Bk. III).   And
along with a profound sense of the poor man's oppressions
and of something sacrificial in his life—' our Conscript, on
whom the lot fell, and fighting our battles was so marred '—
there is also his characteristic scepticism of the franchise
and the ballot (III. vii).   It is not perdition he would bring
upon the old order, but chastisement and a change of heart.

Between *Sartor* and *Past and Present* there lies the *History
of the French Revolution*. The effect of writing that book
was to hasten his inward estrangement from the English
Radicals. From the first, indeed, he had pitched his tent on

[1] Essay on *Corn Law Rhymes* (1831); there is a similar passage in
that on *Characteristics* of the same year. In that on *Signs of the Times*
(1829) the political passion is not yet at this heat.

[2] See below, p. lxxvii.

[3] Froude, *Early Life*, ii. 137.

the very verge of their camp, eyeing his confederates, as they
eyed him, with much misgiving. They were right, he
thought—and this was the bond between them—in waging
war upon the anomalies and irredeemable survivals in
England; but they wanted a reconstructive policy; they
trusted that the State, when once reduced to rhyme and
reason, would go by itself, and the bulk of their programme
was such automatic machinery as the Chartists had demanded in their 'six points'. Carlyle too had welcomed
the Reform Bill, though he felt that all measures of that
sort would 'only burn the dry edges of the dunghill'. In
the story of the Revolution in France nothing was more
conspicuous than the failure of the Gironde to lay the storm
with academic theory and new-fangled mechanism. England
too had her Girondins, ' as barren as Sahara '.[1]   On the other
hand, the French Revolution had taught him how rash it
is to cut clean loose from the past,[2] and how calamitous to
let God's justice run to fire. For the wheat was burnt with
the tares, and much that was thrown down must needs be
built again. It led him, that is to say, on the road to
a doctrine like Coleridge's, of a natural order of ranks and
functions in a state, of which a revolution, if it change the
copy, will never change the type. What is more, the
history of 1789 and after bore in upon him the need of
the hero and of the spirit to use him; since the lack of the
one or the other was the radical disaster. This from 1837
onwards is his theme. He began to develop it in the
Lectures of 1841, and he designed his *Cromwell* (1845) as
a monumental proof.

[1] Froude, *Early Life*, ii. 424 : ' whom I heartily wish well to ', he
adds, however (1834). There is an almost comical discrepancy in
his letters at this time between his two sets of sentiments towards
the Radicals, and more especially towards John Stuart Mill.
[2] See especially the passage on France in *Chartism*, vi.

Chartism.

In the meanwhile, however, the terrible crisis of the beginning of the forties came and captured him, and in 1839 he gripped the situation in his pamphlet on *Chartism*,—'a thing that has been in my head and heart these ten, some of it these twenty, years'. It is significant that, when Mill had refused the article for the *Westminster Review*,[1] Carlyle sent it to Lockhart at the *Quarterly*, who returned it, 'seemingly not without reluctance, saying he dared not'. No political writing of that period had come 'more flamingly from the heart of a living man', or faced the problem with anything like this masterful catholicity, or so penetrated men's minds with the sense of voyaging in a strange sea, 'with the old lights extinguished and only the stars to steer by'. Its main argument is the failure of the Benthamite prescription for the social evil, and the necessity of a new Radicalism, with a workable theory of government and saner notions of the mind of man ; and in particular the urgency of national education, and the opportunity in the New World. 'Democracy, take it where you will in our Europe, is a regulated method of rebellion. It is the consummation of No-government.' And over against the needy philosophy of the 'cash-nexus' and the Poor Law and the Malthusian check he calls up a splendid vision of the great powers and destinies ice-bound, as he thinks, in the want of true government— a new English race on the empty prairies, and a redeemed Manchester in the 'Era of Labour' that is presently to be.

Emerson, on reading the pamphlet, wrote to him that 'we have a right to an answer less concise on a question so grave. It stands as a preliminary word, and you will one day write the second lesson.' It was full, indeed, of undeveloped thought, that went on working

[1] Mill afterwards offered to take it, but too late.

fiercely as the times grew worse. In September of 1842,
when riding through Cromwell's country to take notes for
his projected History, the stricken face of the country-side,
and in particular the sight of the paupers at St. Ives,
described on p. 2 of our text, poignantly impressed him.[1]
And as if to give an edge to these miseries, the Chronicles of
Eadmer and Jocelin fell into his hands on returning from
his excursion.[2] 'The whole ideal of Manhood', he had once
written,[3] 'has grown obsolete, and the new is still invisible.
For Contemplation and love of Wisdom no cloister now
opens its religious shades. Action, in those old days, was
easy, for the divine worth of human things lay acknowledged;
Speculation was wholesome, for it ranged itself as the hand-
maid of Action. Loyalty still hallowed obedience, and made
rule noble. The life of Man was encompassed and over-
canopied by a glory of Heaven. Truly may it be said
the Divinity has withdrawn from the Earth.' 'I found',
he writes to his mother, 'that I could not go on with
Cromwell or with anything else till I had disburdened my
heart.' And thus *Past and Present* was 'written off with
singular ease in the first weeks of 1843', and issued from
the press in the beginning of April.

Past and Present.

The plan of the book is not quite easy to discern. Carlyle
would seem to intend to begin with a declaration of the
truths on which the world is built and every nation must
depend (Bk. I). After this ethical preface comes the episode
of St. Edmund's Abbey to drive it home (Bk. II). Then,
an analysis of the disease of modern England (Bk. III);
and the horoscope of her future (Bk. IV). But at many

[1] *Life in London*, i. 280 f.
[2] He mentions his reading of them in the Diary on October 25.
[3] Essay on *Characteristics*.

points the first and the last two books overlap, and the scheme
is blurred with iteration. Much also of the intended effect
of the second book is carried off in the prolixity of the rest,
and the picture of the great Abbot and his great century
lapses to the state of an interlude. It is in virtue of the
interlude, however, that the book belongs to the classics of
our tongue. It has been said that Carlyle's Samson, like
many other of his portraits, is something of a *tour de force* ;
that the hands are the hands of a mediaeval monk, but the
voice is the writer's own.[1] It may be so. Carlyle wrote
history very much as a poet writes, leaving aside the
particular or minuter features of this or that age—the special
tissue of its institutions or ideas—in the quest of that which
is fundamentally human and perennially alive. Samson
is indeed the image of flesh and blood and moves in a vivid
scene. Were he accurately a Churchman of his time, we
might not understand him as now we do. It is one of those
cases where the part is greater than the whole.[2]

If the whole book suffers from a certain disjointedness,
so does its political programme. It is not, and does not
profess to be, a complete policy, but only a few jottings of
the main things required, of which a short summary may
here be given :

(a) As has been already said, we are still on the hither
side of that change in Carlyle by which his hero developed
into Frederick the Second. The hero of the second book is
not Samson, but the twelfth century ; and the labour of

[1] See Mr. Chesterton's Introduction in the 'World's Classics', and
the article on Carlyle in the *Dictionary of National Biography*.

[2] It may be added that, as Sir Ernest Clarke has pointed out in the
Introduction to his translation of the Chronicle, Carlyle is not quite
faithful to Jocelin. The Abbot's ways did not always please his
chronicler, who sometimes shared the feeling of the rest of the Abbey
that he was something of a tyrant. Carlyle says nothing of these
qualms of disapproval or of the two or three incidents that induced
them.

saving England is to fall, not so much on the heaven-sent
Minister, desirable as he is, as on an Aristocracy rooted in the
hearts of the people, and a people freely and intelligently
responsive.

(b) This Aristocracy, like the whole society of the future,
will be largely industrial. 'The leaders of Industry are
virtually the Captains of the World; if there be no nobleness in them, there will never be an Aristocracy more.' No
one venerated the Middle Ages more heartily than Carlyle;
but with that vein of wistful archaism that comes out in
Southey, and later in Ruskin—with the disposition to sit
down mournfully before the big towns, and wish back the
villages and castles—he had no sympathy whatever. The
future was with the industries, bigger in possibility than
any age of the past. At the same time the Aristocracy of
the land is not to lose its political predominance. For land,
as he agrees with Chalmers (III. viii), not without an appear-
ance of inconsistency, is the necessary basis of government
and carries with it the obligation to govern.[1] Further, with
these two aristocratic orders, however they may stand to
each other, there will be conjoined the 'didactic' and the
'gifted', or as Coleridge would call it, the 'clerisy'. And
the new society, as he hoped in spite of misgiving, would
develop peacefully from the old. 'Ah, how happy were it
if he (the English Aristocrat) would see his work and do it.
It is frightful seeking another to do it for him.' Nor does
he desire to dispense with Parliament, little as, in some
respects, he values it. Indeed his constant diatribes on the
'National Palaver' have obscured his real attitude towards
it. He hated it as having become the virtual executive, and
did not believe that any extension of the franchise would
enable it to do better what it should never do at all; but as

[1] See especially pp. 220, 221, where he seems to be inclining to
Chalmers's theory of the 'single tax'.

blessings of man, are not theirs.'[1] Whether Carlyle's policy
of permanence includes a plan of profit-sharing or not, it
amounts unmistakably to the plan of salaried workmen—
workmen paid, like soldiers, in brisk and in slack times
alike. And the military system of pay will bring with it
a military system of work. In the paper on ' New Downing
Street' in the *Latter-Day Pamphlets* (No. iv) the policy of
industrial permanence is more explicit. The Government is
to begin by organizing 'industrial regiments', and employing
them in a few trades—the beginning of a process ' which in
the course of generations will make us once more a Governed
Commonwealth'.   ' In the end . . . mill operatives, all
manner of free operatives, as yet unregimented, nomadic
under private masters, they, seeing such example and its
blessedness, will say : " Masters, you must regiment us
a little, make our interests with you permanent, we will
enlist with the State otherwise." Thus will all Masters of
Workmen, private Captains of Industry, be forced to incessantly co-operate with the State and its public Captains :
they regimenting in their way, the State in its way, with
ever-widening field ; till their fields *meet* and coalesce, and
there be no unregimented worker any more.' The reader
must remember in what year these opinions were pronounced,
if he would know how they sounded. In France they were
by then familiar ;[2] but to preach them in England in 1843
was bold indeed.

(*d*) At this point the objection naturally arises : ' Are you
not building in the air ? Would you not be killing your
industries, and expecting their golden eggs ? ' Carlyle's
answer is twofold. In the first place, he shrewdly mistrusts
the ancient protestation of all ' threatened trades' that this
or that burden spells ruin. ' Every noble thing is at first
impossible ; ' and the main and only question is, or should

---

[1] *Chartism*, iv.   [2] See below, p. lxxviii.

be : What are the irreducible conditions of manly living ?
And secondly, he trumps your argument with the lands
oversea. Greater Britain was not to him a matter of
political strategy, but a matter of life or death, and not
Fate's promise only but Fate's behest. It is a sort of
heaven-sent subsidy on which the whole of his reckoning
depends. For that lordly indifference to foreign competition, that absolute insistence on a minimum standard of
life, was only possible if the Malthusian problem could be
solved, and if an expansive market were somewhere secure.
Fiercely as Carlyle attacked the Malthusian school, he never
denied its facts ; [1] what he maintained against it was that
to talk of race suicide while Canada and Australia stood
empty was sheer sacrilege. Given only the due energy of
government, the due system of emigration, not only would
you ease the pressure at home, but the elastic market
would be made and won and ours for ever. There is
a far-sighted caution in his conception of the league of
the British nations dispersed throughout the world. Some
bond of sentiment would certainly unite them, like that
which drew the Ionians to the temple at Mycale, and were
the bond closer or looser in economic or in political terms,
the result in practice would be the same (p. 240). The
great tenth chapter of *Chartism* is the earliest note in our
imaginative literature of the second and more splendid
adventure in England's history overseas—the new dominion
that came to us when the old was lost. It was not until
the Epilogue was written to his *Idylls* in 1872 that Tennyson for the first time touched that theme.

(e) It is when we come to the immediate problem that
the fault in Carlyle's theory appears. How are we to set
about the reform ? Plainly by Parliament (pp. 232, 233).
But, as things now are, Parliament is useless and corrupt

---

[1] See p. 167, and *Chartism*, x.

(IV. ii), and Carlyle for one will never vote at a Parliamentary election, until a better sort of candidate come
forward than at present (p. 230). We must wait, then, for
a general change of heart. But how is the change to come?
By each man resolving within himself to be heroic (I. iv).
What is our particular hindrance to being heroic as it is?
Here he has a special and definite answer. The gate of
salvation, he always taught, is to be named not Goodness,
but Truth. It is in Truth that England fails, for her whole
life is involved in the half true, in beliefs and institutions
once vital and now moribund. 'Infidelity to fact is the
one sin.' We need, therefore, an English Illumination in
all the fields of life, but an Illumination prosecuted in the
spirit of Goethe, and not in the spirit of Voltaire. This,
and this only, would bring us the cleanness of mind and
the religious energy in which all great history is made,
and in which our institutions will conform, as it were by
some swift miracle, to heroic government. But how is the
Illumination to go forward in politics save by the very
channels that history has given it—Parliament, Platform,
and Press? And if the hero is brought in by the dry
light—by criticism and the conversion of minds—by debate,
whether in or out of Parliament—how will he maintain
himself, unless it be by these very means? Parliament, he
grants us (p. lxxi), is a needful check on power. But how
will it control, and not also co-operate? To all these
questions Carlyle has really no answer, because for him
democracy is too elaborate to be organic; and while the
forms and principles of a simpler society, like the mediaeval,
are indefeasible, vital, Nature's own work, and not to be
put aside by levellers and pedants, whatever is of later
development than these, and has given shape to the larger
needs of man, is something between a necessity and a
nuisance.

Carlyle and Saint-Simon.

Much has been said of Carlyle's debt to Fichte, the German absolutist.[1] But his mentor in *Past and Present* is not German, but French. Claude Henri, Comte de Saint-Simon (1760–1825), published his *Système industriel* in 1821, and his *Nouveau Christianisme* in the year of his death. His gospel did not fall to the ground, but a band of young men, including some of the keenest minds in France, continued to preach it. The story of the *Société Saint-Simonienne*, which they founded in 1830, was short and sad. It was broken up by the discord between its two leaders, Bazard and Enfantin, over the marriage question, and dissolved in 1832 under a cloud. But it had done its work ; its ideas had rooted, and are living to this hour. Carlyle was for some time keenly interested in these men, and in 1830, being impressed by his *Signs of the Times*, they sent him a bundle of their publications, which he read. In August of that year he wrote to Goethe to ask the sage about them, but received a curt admonition in reply to 'keep clear of the Saint-Simonians'.[2] 'They seem to me to be earnest, zealous, and nowise ignorant men,' Carlyle replies, 'but wandering in strange paths. I should say they have discovered and laid to heart this momentous and now almost forgotten truth : MAN IS STILL MAN ; and are already beginning to make false applications of it. I have every disposition to follow your advice and stand apart from them, looking on their Society and its progress nevertheless as a true and remarkable Sign of the Times.'[3] His interest

[1] See note to p. 191.

[2] October 17, 1830. *Correspondence of Goethe and Carlyle*, ed. Norton.

[3] Ibid., January 22, 1831. In *Sartor* (III. xii) Teufelsdröckh, on the eve of his mysterious disappearance, raises his glass to the St.-Simonians with the same words here written to Goethe : 'they have discovered the almost forgotten truth ', &c.

in the society continued lively throughout 1831. In
September of that year he was angry with an attack on
them by Southey in the *Quarterly*,[1] and during a short
stay in London was visited by some of their emissaries,
and 'exceedingly taken'.[2]   In November 1833 he has been
thinking of an article on the Saint-Simonian movement,
but concludes that the movement 'is not to be written of,
being in the fermenting state'.[3]   And that is, in fact, his
attitude from first to last.

Saint-Simon read history as an alternation of the periods
of 'social equipoise', in which every man is in his right
place, with those of 'oscillation' after the arrival of new
factors.   The Feudal Age was the last age of stability ; the
Revolution the welter of its disruption, but not the dis-
pensation to take its place.   Not Burke himself testified
against the 'vague and metaphysical idea of liberty' more
earnestly.   For liberty, as the Revolutionists preached it,
was the negation of the truth that 'society is an organic
body', and a menace, therefore, to society itself.   The era
that succeeds to Feudalism will be no less strictly articulated into governors and governed, but industry will be its
basis, and a new science of 'social hygiene'.   For, as things
now are, 'a nation is nothing but an industrial company',
and instead of the feudal system there will come the
industrial baron or king, and the 'organization of labour'
(*l'organisation industrielle*).   But to what end shall it be
organized ? The answer to this brings us to the last chapter of
Saint-Simon's development, that of *Le Nouveau Christianisme*.
If society be truly Christian it will reverse its purposes, and
exist not for the strong but for the weak ; it will impound
whatever wealth is made, and distribute it, not indeed in
equal shares, but according to a scientific humanity.   In

[1] Froude, *Early Life*, ii. 205.
[2] Letter by Jane Welsh Carlyle, ibid., ii. 231.
[3] Ibid., ii. 395.

Saint-Simon's Parliament there would be, besides the Industrials, a chamber of scientists to declare the hygienic laws,
and a chamber of 'artists'—the 'clerisy', as Coleridge would
call them—to represent the instincts of moral beauty, or
in other words a new Christian Church, professing not the
traditional creeds, but only the law of love. And that
Church, in the final form of Saint-Simon's theory, will be
the heart of the State. Here, again, the Revolution was
barren ; from the chaff of mere denial nothing good would
grow. 'La religion', said Saint-Simon in his dying words
to the little band of friends, 'ne peut disparaître du monde ;
elle ne fait que se transformer. Pour faire de grandes
choses il faut être passionné.' It is clear that the stricter
socialism developed by Saint-Simon's followers was the
vicious element of this system in the eyes of Carlyle ; but,
this point excepted, no theory then before the world agreed
so closely with his own.

Save for a few extra touches in the later writings, the
sum and substance of Carlyle's teaching in politics is contained in *Past and Present*. The later modifications were in
temper and in inclination. The final and definite breach
with John Stuart Mill and the Radicals, which came with
the *Discourse on the Nigger Question* in 1849, was long
overdue. Nor when he assaulted democracy by furious
onslaughts in the *Latter-Day Pamphlets* and *Shooting Niagara*,
and by immense battery in his *Frederick the Great*, was
anything said that is not foreshadowed in 1843 or earlier.
Nevertheless the difference in temper and in inclination
was much, and estranged many hearts. He had prophesied
(p. 167) that Free Trade, when it came, would bring only
a respite of ten or twenty years from the social agony.
The respite was longer than he thought, and this and other
causes delayed the harvest of our national faults till we
thought it had failed. Democracy went forward, and reform
with it. And if his policy of industrial 'permanence', in

the sense of salaried and disciplined service, is still a
possible or even a probable issue, the business of the labour
movement will have been until now to temper it, if and
when it shall come, with a liberty and elasticity such as
Carlyle, in his better mind, would certainly desire, but was
never careful to postulate. For his programme is a mere
sketch, and is far more strongly tinged with his fear of
anarchy than with his no less genuine love of the service
that is free. All this, and the real flaws in his thinking,
have made against him and weakened his influence. Yet
it is not too much to say of *Past and Present* that a new
spirit went out of it into English life. For along with
whatever dubious metal there is always the abundance of
gold,—the authentic voice of prophecy, the vision of eternal
law, the humanity of a great and pious heart, and a language
that stirs the pulse like battle-music. It was more especially
to the young and noble of the ruling classes that the book
appealed. John Ruskin, as a missioner of reform, lighted
his lamp at this flame, and many another worker and
thinker in that large movement which has scouted from our
midst the doctrine of the forties, and is bringing back the
faith of the greater times,—that 'we are members one of
another' and 'none of us liveth to himself', that riches are
a trust, and power a ministry, and the State for all its
children a family and a school.

BOOK I—PROEM

CHAPTER I

MIDAS

THE condition of England, on which many pamphlets are now in the course of publication, and many thoughts unpublished are going on in every reflective head, is justly regarded as one of the most ominous, and withal one of the strangest, ever seen in this world. England is full of wealth, of multifarious produce, supply for human want in every kind; yet England is dying of inanition. With unabated bounty the land of England blooms and grows; waving with yellow harvests; thick-studded with workshops, industrial implements, with fifteen millions of workers, understood to be the strongest, the cunningest and the willingest our Earth ever had; these men are here; the work they have done, the fruit they have realized is here, abundant, exuberant on every hand of us: and behold, some baleful fiat as of Enchantment has gone forth, saying, 'Touch it not, ye workers, ye master-workers, ye master-idlers; none of you can touch it, no man of you shall be the better for it; this is enchanted fruit!' On the poor workers such fiat falls first, in its rudest shape; but on the rich master-workers too it falls; neither can the rich master-idlers, nor any richest or highest man escape, but all are like to be brought low with it, and made 'poor' enough, in the money sense or a far fataller one.

Of these successful skilful workers some two millions, it is now counted, sit in Workhouses, Poor-law Prisons; or have 'out-door relief' flung over the wall to them,—the workhouse Bastille being filled to bursting, and the strong

Poor-law broken asunder by a stronger.[1] They sit there, these many months now; their hope of deliverance as yet small. In workhouses, pleasantly so named, because work cannot be done in them. Twelve hundred thousand workers in England alone; their cunning right-hand lamed, lying idle in their sorrowful bosom; their hopes, outlooks, share of this fair world, shut in by narrow walls. They sit there, pent up, as in a kind of horrid enchantment; glad to be imprisoned and enchanted, that they may not perish starved. The picturesque Tourist, in a sunny autumn day, through this bounteous realm of England, descries the Union Workhouse on his path. 'Passing by the Workhouse of St. Ives in Huntingdonshire, on a bright day last autumn,' says the picturesque Tourist, 'I saw sitting on wooden benches, in front of their Bastille and within their ring-wall and its railings, some half-hundred or more of these men. Tall robust figures, young mostly or of middle age; of honest countenance, many of them thoughtful and even intelligent-looking men. They sat there, near by one another; but in a kind of torpor, especially in a silence, which was very striking. In silence: for, alas, what word was to be said? An Earth all lying round, crying, Come and till me, come and reap me;—yet we here sit enchanted! In the eyes and brows of these men hung the gloomiest expression, not of anger, but of grief and shame and manifold inarticulate distress and weariness; they returned my glance with a glance that seemed to say, "Do not look at us. We sit enchanted here, we know not why. The Sun shines and the Earth calls; and, by the governing Powers and Impotences of this England, we are forbidden to obey. It is impossible, they tell us!" There was something that reminded me of Dante's Hell in the look of all this; and I rode swiftly away.'

So many hundred thousands sit in workhouses: and other hundred thousands have not yet got even workhouses; and in thrifty Scotland itself, in Glasgow or Edinburgh City, in their dark lanes, hidden from all but the eye of God, and of rare Benevolence the minister of God, there are scenes of

---

[1] The Return of Paupers for England and Wales, at Ladyday 1842, is, 'Indoor 221,687, Out-door 1,207,402, Total 1,429,089.'—(*Official Report.*)

woe and destitution and desolation, such as, one may hope,
the Sun never saw before in the most barbarous regions
where men dwelt. Competent witnesses, the brave and
humane Dr. Alison, who speaks what he knows, whose *1780-1859*
noble Healing Art in his charitable hands becomes once
more a truly sacred one, report these things for us: these
things are not of this year, or of last year, have no reference
to our present state of commercial stagnation, but only to
the common state. Not in sharp fever-fits, but in chronic
gangrene of this kind is Scotland suffering. A Poor-law,
any and every Poor-law, it may be observed, is but a temporary measure; an anodyne, not a remedy: Rich and Poor,
when once the naked facts of their condition have come into
collision, cannot long subsist together on a mere Poor-law.
True enough:—and yet, human beings cannot be left to die!
Scotland too, till something better come, must have a Poor-
law, if Scotland is not to be a byword among the nations. *1 1 S chap IX 7*
O, what a waste is there; of noble and thrice-noble national
virtues; peasant Stoicisms, Heroisms; valiant manful habits,
soul of a Nation's worth,—which all the metal of Potosi
cannot purchase back; to which the metal of Potosi, and all *silver mine in Bolivia*
you can buy with *it*, is dross and dust!

Why dwell on this aspect of the matter? It is too indisputable, not doubtful now to any one. Descend where you
will into the lower class, in Town or Country, by what
avenue you will, by Factory Inquiries, Agricultural Inquiries,
by Revenue Returns, by Mining-Labourer Committees, by
opening your own eyes and looking, the same sorrowful
result discloses itself: you have to admit that the working
body of this rich English Nation has sunk or is fast sinking
into a state, to which, all sides of it considered, there was
literally never any parallel. At Stockport Assizes,—and this
too has no reference to the present state of trade, being of
date prior to that,—a Mother and a Father are arraigned
and found guilty of poisoning three of their children, to
defraud a 'burial-society' of some £3 8s. due on the death of
each child: they are arraigned, found guilty; and the official
authorities, it is whispered, hint that perhaps the case is not
solitary, that perhaps you had better not probe farther into
that department of things. This is in the autumn of 1841;
the crime itself is of the previous year or season. 'Brutal
savages, degraded Irish,' mutters the idle reader of News-

papers; hardly lingering on this incident. Yet it is an incident worth lingering on; the depravity, savagery and degraded Irishism being never so well admitted. In the British land, a human Mother and Father, of white skin and professing the Christian religion, had done this thing; they, with their Irishism and necessity and savagery, had been driven to do it. Such instances are like the highest mountain apex emerged into view; under which lies a whole mountain region and land, not yet emerged. A human Mother and Father had said to themselves, What shall we do to escape starvation? We are deep sunk here, in our dark cellar; and help is far.—Yes, in the Ugolino Hunger-tower stern things happen; best-loved little Gaddo fallen dead on his Father's knees!—The Stockport Mother and Father think and hint: Our poor little starveling Tom, who cries all day for victuals, who will see only evil and not good in this world: if he were out of misery at once; he well dead, and the rest of us perhaps kept alive? It is thought, and hinted; at last it is done. And now Tom being killed, and all spent and eaten, Is it poor little starveling Jack that must go, or poor little starveling Will?— What a committee of ways and means!

In starved sieged cities, in the uttermost doomed ruin of old Jerusalem fallen under the wrath of God, it was prophe- sied and said, 'The hands of the pitiful women have sodden their own children.' The stern Hebrew imagination could conceive no blacker gulf of wretchedness; that was the ultimatum of degraded god-punished man. And we here, in modern England, exuberant with supply of all kinds, besieged by nothing if it be not by invisible Enchant- ments, are we reaching that?——How come these things? Wherefore are they, wherefore should they be?

Nor are they of the St. Ives workhouses, of the Glasgow lanes, and Stockport cellars, the only unblessed among us. This successful industry of England, with its plethoric wealth, has as yet made nobody rich; it is an enchanted wealth, and belongs yet to nobody. We might ask, Which of us has it enriched? We can spend thousands where we once spent hundreds; but can purchase nothing good with them. In Poor and Rich, instead of noble thrift and plenty, there is idle luxury alternating with mean scarcity and inability.

We have sumptuous garnitures for our Life, but have forgotten to *live* in the middle of them. It is an enchanted wealth; no man of us can yet touch it. The class of men who feel that they are truly better off by means of it, let them give us their name !

Many men eat finer cookery, drink dearer liquors,—with what advantage they can report, and their Doctors can : but in the heart of them, if we go out of the dyspeptic stomach, what increase of blessedness is there? Are they better, beautifuller, stronger, braver? Are they even what they call 'happier'? Do they look with satisfaction on more things and human faces in this God's-Earth; do more things and human faces look with satisfaction on them? Not so. Human faces gloom discordantly, disloyally on one another. Things, if it be not mere cotton and iron things, are growing disobedient to man. The Master Worker is enchanted, for the present, like his Workhouse Workman; clamours, in vain hitherto, for a very simple sort of ' Liberty ': the liberty ' to buy where he finds it cheapest, to sell where he finds it dearest '. With guineas jingling in every pocket, he was no whit richer; but now, the very guineas threatening to vanish, he feels that he is poor indeed. Poor Master Worker ! And the Master Unworker, is not he in a still fataller situation ? Pausing amid his game-preserves, with awful eye,—as he well may ! Coercing fifty-pound tenants ; coercing, bribing, cajoling; doing what he likes with his own. His mouth full of loud futilities, and arguments to prove the excellence of his Corn-law; and in his heart the blackest misgiving, a desperate half consciousness that his excellent Corn-law is *in*defensible, that his loud arguments for it are of a kind to strike men too literally *dumb*.

To whom, then, is this wealth of England wealth ? Who is it that it blesses ; makes happier, wiser, beautifuller, in any way better ? Who has got hold of it, to make it fetch and carry for him, like a true servant, not like a false mock-servant; to do him any real service whatsoever ? As yet no one. We have more riches than any Nation ever had before ; we have less good of them than any Nation ever had before. Our successful industry is hitherto unsuccessful ; a strange success, if we stop here ! In the midst of plethoric plenty, the people perish ; with gold walls, and full barns, no man feels himself safe or satisfied. Workers, Master Workers,

Unworkers, all men, come to a pause; stand fixed, and cannot farther. Fatal paralysis spreading inwards, from the extremities, in St. Ives workhouses, in Stockport cellars, through all limbs, as if towards the heart itself. Have we actually got enchanted, then; accursed by some god?—

Midas longed for gold, and insulted the Olympians. He got gold, so that whatsoever he touched became gold,—and he, with his long ears, was little the better for it. Midas had misjudged the celestial music-tones; Midas had insulted Apollo and the gods: the gods gave him his wish, and a pair of long ears, which also were a good appendage to it. What a truth in these old Fables!

CHAPTER II

THE SPHINX

How true, for example, is that other old Fable of the Sphinx, who sat by the wayside, propounding her riddle to the passengers, which if they could not answer she destroyed them! Such a Sphinx is this Life of ours, to all men and societies of men. Nature, like the Sphinx, is of womanly celestial loveliness and tenderness; the face and bosom of a goddess, but ending in claws and the body of a lioness. There is in her a celestial beauty,—which means celestial order, pliancy to wisdom; but there is also a darkness, a ferocity, fatality, which are infernal. She is a goddess, but one not yet disimprisoned; one still half-imprisoned,—the articulate, lovely still encased in the inarticulate, chaotic. How true! And does she not propound her riddles to us? Of each man she asks daily, in mild voice, yet with a terrible significance, 'Knowest thou the meaning of this Day? What thou canst do Today; wisely attempt to do?' Nature, Universe, Destiny, Existence, howsoever we name this grand unnamable Fact in the midst of which we live and struggle, is as a heavenly bride and con-

quest to the wise and brave, to them who can discern her
behests and do them ; a destroying fiend to them who cannot.
Answer her riddle, it is well with thee. Answer it not, pass
on regarding it not, it will answer itself ; the solution for
thee is a thing of teeth and claws ; Nature is a dumb lioness,
deaf to thy pleadings, fiercely devouring. Thou art not now
her victorious bridegroom ; thou art her mangled victim,
scattered on the precipices, as a slave found treacherous,
recreant, ought to be and must.

With Nations it is as with individuals : Can they rede the
riddle of Destiny ? This English Nation, will it get to know
the meaning of *its* strange new Today ? Is there sense
enough extant, discoverable anywhere or anyhow, in our
united twenty-seven million heads to discern the same ;
valour enough in our twenty-seven million hearts to dare
and do the bidding thereof ? It will be seen !—

The secret of gold Midas, which he with his long ears
never could discover, was, That he had offended the Supreme
Powers ;—that he had parted company with the eternal inner
Facts of this Universe, and followed the transient outer
Appearances thereof ; and so was arrived *here*. Properly it
is the secret of all unhappy men and unhappy nations. Had
they known Nature's right truth, Nature's right truth would
have made them free. They have become enchanted ; stagger
spell-bound, reeling on the brink of huge peril, because they
were not wise enough. They have forgotten the right Inner
True, and taken up with the Outer Shamtrue. They answer
the Sphinx's question *wrong*. Foolish men cannot answer
it aright ! Foolish men mistake transitory semblance for
eternal fact, and go astray more and more.

Foolish men imagine that because judgment for an evil
thing is delayed, there is no justice, but an accidental one,
here below. Judgment for an evil thing is many times
delayed some day or two, some century or two, but it is
sure as life, it is sure as death ! In the centre of the world-
whirlwind, verily now as in the oldest days, dwells and
speaks a God. The great soul of the world is *just*. O brother,
can it be needful now, at this late epoch of experience, after
eighteen centuries of Christian preaching for one thing, to
remind thee of such a fact ; which all manner of Mahometans,
old Pagan Romans, Jews, Scythians and heathen Greeks,
and indeed more or less all men that God made, have

managed at one time to see into; nay which thou thyself,
till 'redtape' strangled the inner life of thee, hadst once
some inkling of: That there *is* justice here below; and even,
at bottom, that there is nothing else but justice! Forget
that, thou hast forgotten all. Success will never more
attend thee: how can it now? Thou hast the whole Universe against thee. No more success: mere sham-success,
for a day and days; rising ever higher,—towards its Tarpeian Rock. Alas, how, in thy soft-hung Longacre vehicle,
of polished leather to the bodily eye, of redtape philosophy,
of expediencies, clubroom moralities, Parliamentary majorities
to the mind's eye, thou beautifully rollest: but knowest thou
whitherward? It is towards the *road's end.* Old use-and-
wont; established methods, habitudes, *once* true and wise;
man's noblest tendency, his perseverance, and man's ig-
noblest, his inertia; whatsoever of noble and ignoble Conservatism there is in men and Nations, strongest always in
the strongest men and Nations: all this is as a road to thee,
paved smooth through the abyss,—till all this *end.* Till
men's bitter necessities can endure thee no more. Till
Nature's patience with thee is done; and there is no road
or footing any farther, and the abyss yawns sheer!—

Parliament and the Courts of Westminster are venerable
to me; how venerable; grey with a thousand years of
honourable age! For a thousand years and more, Wisdom
and faithful Valour, struggling amid much Folly and greedy
Baseness, not without most sad distortions in the struggle,
have built them up; and they are as we see. For a thousand
years, this English Nation has found them useful or supportable; they have served this English Nation's want;
been a road to it through the abyss of Time. They are
venerable, they are great and strong. And yet it is good to
remember always that they are not the venerablest, nor the
greatest, nor the strongest! Acts of Parliament are venerable; but if they correspond not with the writing on the
'Adamant Tablet', what are they? Properly their one
element of venerableness, of strength or greatness, is, that
they at all times correspond therewith as near as by human
possibility they can. They are cherishing destruction in
their bosom every hour that they continue otherwise.

Alas, how many causes that can plead well for themselves
in the Courts of Westminster; and yet in the general

Court of the Universe, and free Soul of Man, have no word
to utter! Honourable Gentlemen may find this worth considering, in times like ours. And truly, the din of triumphant
Law-logic, and all shaking of horse-hair wigs and learned-
sergeant gowns having comfortably ended, we shall do well
to ask ourselves withal, What says that high and highest
Court to the verdict? For it is the Court of Courts, that
same; where the universal soul of Fact and very Truth sits
President;—and thitherward, more and more swiftly, with
a really terrible increase of swiftness, all causes do in these
days crowd for revisal,—for confirmation, for modification,
for reversal with costs. Dost thou know that Court; hast
thou had any Law-practice there? What, didst thou never
enter; never file any petition of redress, reclaimer, disclaimer
or demurrer, written as in thy heart's blood, for thy own
behoof or another's; and silently await the issue? Thou
knowest not such a Court? Hast merely heard of it by faint
tradition as a thing that was or had been? Of thee, I think,
we shall get little benefit.

For the gowns of learned-sergeants are good: parchment
records, fixed forms, and poor terrestrial Justice, with or
without horse-hair, what sane man will not reverence these?
And yet, behold, the man is not sane but insane, who considers these alone as venerable. Oceans of horse-hair, continents of parchment, and learned-sergeant eloquence, were
it continued till the learned tongue wore itself small in the
indefatigable learned mouth, cannot make unjust just. The
grand question still remains, Was the judgment just? If
unjust, it will not and cannot get harbour for itself, or continue to have footing in this Universe, which was made by
other than One Unjust. Enforce it by never such statuting,
three readings, royal assents; blow it to the four winds with
all manner of quilted trumpeters and pursuivants, in the rear
of them never so many gibbets and hangmen, it will not
stand, it cannot stand. From all souls of men, from all ends
of Nature, from the Throne of God above, there are voices
bidding it: Away, away! Does it take no warning; does it
stand, strong in its three readings, in its gibbets and artillery-
parks? The more woe is to it, the frightfuller woe. It will
continue standing for its day, for its year, for its century,
doing evil all the while; but it has One enemy who is
Almighty: dissolution, explosion, and the everlasting Laws

of Nature incessantly advance towards it; and the deeper its rooting, more obstinate its continuing, the deeper also and huger will its ruin and overturn be.

In this God's-World, with its wild-whirling eddies and mad foam-oceans, where men and nations perish as if without law, and judgment for an unjust thing is sternly delayed, dost thou think that there is therefore no justice? It is what the fool hath said in his heart. It is what the wise, in all times, were wise because they denied, and knew forever not to be. I tell thee again, there is nothing else but justice. One strong thing I find here below: the just thing, the true thing. My friend, if thou hadst all the artillery of Woolwich trundling at thy back in support of an unjust thing; and infinite bonfires visibly waiting ahead of thee, to blaze centuries long for thy victory on behalf of it,—I would advise thee to call halt, to fling down thy baton, and say, 'In God's name, No!' Thy 'success?' Poor devil, what will thy success amount to? If the thing is unjust, thou hast not succeeded; no, not though bonfires blazed from North to South, and bells rang, and editors wrote leading-articles, and the just thing lay trampled out of sight, to all mortal eyes an abolished and annihilated thing. Success? In few years thou wilt be dead and dark,—all cold, eyeless, deaf; no blaze of bonfires, ding-dong of bells or leading-articles visible or audible to thee again at all forever: What kind of success is that!—

It is true, all goes by approximation in this world; with any not insupportable approximation we must be patient. There is a noble Conservatism as well as an ignoble. Would to Heaven, for the sake of Conservatism itself, the noble alone were left, and the ignoble, by some kind severe hand, were ruthlessly lopped away, forbidden evermore to show itself! For it is the right and noble alone that will have victory in this struggle; the rest is wholly an obstruction, a postponement and fearful imperilment of the victory. Towards an eternal centre of right and nobleness, and of that only, is all this confusion tending. We already know whither it is all tending; what will have victory, what will have none! The Heaviest will reach the centre. The Heaviest, sinking through complex fluctuating media and vortices, has its deflexions, its obstructions, nay at times its

resiliences, its reboundings; whereupon some blockhead
shall be heard jubilating, 'See, your Heaviest ascends!'—
but at all moments it is moving centreward, fast as is convenient for it; sinking, sinking; and, by laws older than
the World, old as the Maker's first Plan of the World, it has
to arrive there.

Await the issue. In all battles, if you await the issue,
each fighter has prospered according to his right. His right
and his might, at the close of the account, were one and the
same. He has fought with all his might, and in exact proportion to all his right he has prevailed. His very death is
no victory over him. He dies indeed; but his work lives,
very truly lives. A heroic Wallace, quartered on the
scaffold, cannot hinder that his Scotland become, one day,
a part of England: but he does hinder that it become, on
tyrannous unfair terms, a part of it; commands still, as with
a god's voice, from his old Valhalla and Temple of the Brave,
that there be a just real union as of brother and brother,
not a false and merely semblant one as of slave and master.
If the union with England be in fact one of Scotland's chief
blessings, we thank Wallace withal that it was not the chief
curse. Scotland is not Ireland: no, because brave men rose
there, and said, 'Behold, ye must not tread us down like
slaves; and ye shall not,—and cannot!' Fight on, thou
brave true heart, and falter not, through dark fortune and
through bright. The cause thou fightest for, so far as it is
true, no farther, yet precisely so far, is very sure of victory.
The falsehood alone of it will be conquered, will be abolished,
as it ought to be: but the truth of it is part of Nature's own
Laws, coöperates with the World's eternal Tendencies, and
cannot be conquered.

The *dust* of controversy, what is it but the *falsehood* flying
off from all manner of conflicting true forces, and making
such a loud dust-whirlwind,—that so the truths alone may
remain, and embrace brother-like in some true resulting-
force! It is ever so. Savage fighting Heptarchies: their
fighting is an ascertainment, who has the right to rule
over whom; that out of such waste-bickering Saxondom a
peacefully coöperating England may arise. Seek through
this Universe; if with other than owl's eyes, thou wilt
find nothing nourished there, nothing kept in life, but
what has right to nourishment and life. The rest, look

at it with other than owl's eyes, is not living; is all
dying, all as good as dead! Justice was ordained from
the foundations of the world; and will last with the world
and longer.

From which I infer that the inner sphere of Fact, in this
present England as elsewhere, differs infinitely from the
outer sphere and spheres of Semblance. That the Temporary,
here as elsewhere, is too apt to carry it over the Eternal.
That he who dwells in the temporary Semblances, and does
not penetrate into the eternal Substance, will *not* answer the
Sphinx-riddle of Today, or of any Day. For the substance
alone is substantial; that *is* the law of Fact; if you discover
not that, Fact, who already knows it, will let you also know
it by and by!

What is Justice? that, on the whole, is the question of
the Sphinx to us. The law of Fact is, that Justice must
and will be done. The sooner the better; for the Time grows
stringent, frightfully pressing! 'What is Justice?' ask
many, to whom cruel Fact alone will be able to prove
responsive. It is like jesting Pilate asking, What is Truth?
Jesting Pilate had not the smallest chance to ascertain what
was Truth. He could not have known it, had a god shown
it to him. Thick serene opacity, thicker than amaurosis,
veiled those smiling eyes of his to Truth; the inner *retina*
of them was gone paralytic, dead. He looked at Truth; and
discerned her not, there where she stood. 'What is Justice?'
The clothed embodied Justice that sits in Westminster Hall,
with penalties, parchments, tipstaves, is very visible. But
the *un*embodied Justice, whereof that other is either an
emblem, or else is a fearful indescribability, is not so visible!
For the unembodied Justice is of Heaven; a Spirit, and
Divinity of Heaven,—*in*visible to all but the noble and pure
of soul. The impure ignoble gaze with eyes, and she is not
there. They will prove it to you by logic, by endless Hansard
Debatings, by bursts of Parliamentary eloquence. It is not
consolatory to behold! For properly, as many men as there
are in a Nation who *can* withal see Heaven's invisible Justice,
and know it to be on Earth also omnipotent, so many men
are there who stand between a Nation and perdition. So
many, and no more. Heavy-laden England, how many hast
thou in this hour? The Supreme Power sends new and ever

new, all *born* at least with hearts of flesh and not of stone ;—
and heavy Misery itself, once heavy enough, will prove
didactic !—

CHAPTER III

MANCHESTER INSURRECTION

BLUSTEROWSKI, Colacorde, and other Editorial prophets of
the Continental Democratic Movement, have in their leading-
articles shown themselves disposed to vilipend the late
Manchester Insurrection, as evincing in the rioters an extreme
backwardness to battle ; nay as betokening, in the English
People itself, perhaps a want of the proper animal-courage
indispensable in these ages. A million hungry operative
men started up, in utmost paroxysm of desperate protest
against their lot ; and, ask Colacorde and company, How
many shots were fired ? Very few in comparison ! Certain
hundreds of drilled soldiers sufficed to suppress this million-
headed hydra, and tread it down, without the smallest
appeasement or hope of such, into its subterranean settlements again, there to reconsider itself.   Compared with our
revolts in Lyons, in Warsaw and elsewhere, to say nothing
of incomparable Paris City past or present, what a lamb-like
Insurrection !—

The present Editor is not here, with his readers, to vindi-
cate the character of Insurrections ; nor does it matter to us
whether Blusterowski and the rest may think the English
a courageous people or not courageous.   In passing, however,
let us mention that, to our view, this was not an unsuccessful
Insurrection ; that as Insurrections go, we have not heard
lately of any that succeeded so well.

A million of hungry operative men, as Blusterowski says,
rose all up, came all out into the streets, and—stood there.
What other could they do ?   Their wrongs and griefs were
bitter, insupportable, their rage against the same was just :
but who are they that cause these wrongs, who that will
honestly make effort to redress them ?   Our enemies are we
know not who or what ; our friends are we know not where !
How shall we attack any one, shoot or be shot by any one ?
Oh, if the accursed invisible Nightmare, that is crushing out

the life of us and ours, would take a shape ; approach us
like the Hyrcanian tiger, the Behemoth of Chaos, the Arch-
fiend himself ; in any shape that we could see, and fasten
on !—A man can have himself shot with cheerfulness ; but
it needs first that he see clearly for what. Show him the
divine face of Justice, then the diabolic monster which is
eclipsing that : he will fly at the throat of such monster,
never so monstrous, and need no bidding to do it. Woolwich
grapeshot will sweep clear all streets, blast into invisibility
so many thousand men : but if your Woolwich grapeshot be
but eclipsing Divine Justice, and the God's-radiance itself
gleam recognizable athwart such grapeshot,—then, yes then
is the time come for fighting and attacking. All artillery-
parks have become weak, and are about to dissipate : in the
God's-thunder, their poor thunder slackens, ceases ; finding
that it is, in all senses of the term, a *brute* one !—

That the Manchester Insurrection stood still, on the
streets, with an indisposition to fire and bloodshed, was
wisdom for it even as an Insurrection. Insurrection, never
so necessary, is a most sad necessity ; and governors who
wait for that to instruct them, are surely getting into the
fatallest courses,—proving themselves Sons of Nox and Chaos,
of blind Cowardice, not of seeing Valour ! How can there
be any remedy in insurrection ? It is a mere announcement
of the disease,—visible now even to Sons of Night. Insurrection usually 'gains' little ; usually wastes how much !
One of its worst kinds of waste, to say nothing of the rest, is
that of irritating and exasperating men against each other,
by violence done ; which is always sure to be injustice done,
for violence does even justice unjustly.

Who shall compute the waste and loss, the obstruction of
every sort, that was produced in the Manchester region by
Peterloo alone ! Some thirteen unarmed men and women
cut down,—the number of the slain and maimed is very
countable : but the treasury of rage, burning hidden or
visible in all hearts ever since, more or less perverting the
effort and aim of all hearts ever since, is of unknown extent.
'How ye came among us, in your cruel armed blindness, ye
unspeakable County Yeomanry, sabres flourishing, hoofs
prancing, and slashed us down at your brute pleasure ; deaf,
blind to all *our* claims and woes and wrongs ; of quick sight
and sense to your own claims only ! There lie poor sallow

workworn weavers, and complain no more now; women
themselves are slashed and sabred, howling terror fills the
air; and ye ride prosperous, very victorious,—ye unspeakable: give *us* sabres too, and then come-on a little!' Such
are Peterloos.   In all hearts that witnessed Peterloo, stands
written, as in fire-characters, or smoke-characters prompt to
become fire again, a legible balance-account of grim vengeance; very unjustly balanced, much exaggerated, as is the
way with such accounts: but payable readily at sight, in full
with compound interest!   Such things should be avoided as
the very pestilence!   For men's hearts ought not to be set
against one another; but set *with* one another, and all
against the Evil Thing only.   Men's souls ought to be left
to see clearly; not jaundiced, blinded, twisted all awry, by
revenge, mutual abhorrence, and the like.   An Insurrection
that can announce the disease, and then retire with no such
balance-account opened anywhere, has attained the highest
success possible for it.

And this was what these poor Manchester operatives, with
all the darkness that was in them and round them, did
manage to perform.   They put their huge inarticulate
question, 'What do you mean to do with us?' in a manner
audible to every reflective soul in this kingdom; exciting
deep pity in all good men, deep anxiety in all men whatever;
and no conflagration or outburst of madness came to cloud
that feeling anywhere, but everywhere it operates unclouded.
All England heard the question: it is the first practical form
of *our* Sphinx-riddle.   England will answer it; or, on the
whole, England will perish;—one does not yet expect the
latter result!

For the rest, that the Manchester Insurrection could yet
discern no radiance of Heaven on any side of its horizon; but
feared that all lights, of the O'Connor or other sorts, hitherto
kindled, were but deceptive fish-oil transparencies, or bog
will-o'-wisp lights, and no dayspring from on high: for this
also we will honour the poor Manchester Insurrection, and
augur well of it.   A deep unspoken sense lies in these
strong men,—inconsiderable, almost stupid, as all they can
articulate of it is.   Amid all violent stupidity of speech,
a right noble instinct of what is doable and what is not
doable never forsakes them: the strong inarticulate men and
workers, whom *Fact* patronizes; of whom, in all difficulty

and work whatsoever, there is good augury! This work too
is to be done: Governors and Governing Classes that *can*
articulate and utter, in any measure, what the law of Fact
and Justice is, may calculate that here is a Governed Class
who will listen.

And truly this first practical form of the Sphinx-question,
inarticulately and so audibly put there, is one of the most
impressive ever asked in the world. 'Behold us here, so
many thousands, millions, and increasing at the rate of fifty
every hour. We are right willing and able to work; and
on the Planet Earth is plenty of work and wages for a million
times as many. We ask, If you mean to lead us towards
work; to try to lead us,—by ways new, never yet heard of
till this new unheard-of Time? Or if you declare that you
cannot lead us? And expect that we are to remain quietly
unled, and in a composed manner perish of starvation?
What is it you expect of us? What is it you mean to do
with us?' This question, I say, has been put in the hearing
of all Britain; and will be again put, and ever again, till
some answer be given it.

Unhappy Workers, unhappier Idlers, unhappy men and
women of this actual England! We are yet very far from
an answer, and there will be no existence for us without
finding one. 'A fair day's-wages for a fair day's-work': it
is as just a demand as Governed men ever made of Governing.
It is the everlasting right of man. Indisputable as Gospels,
as arithmetical multiplication-tables: it must and will have
itself fulfilled;—and yet, in these times of ours, with what
enormous difficulty, next-door to impossibility! For the
times are really strange; of a complexity intricate with all
the new width of the ever-widening world; times here of half-
frantic velocity of impetus, there of the deadest-looking
stillness and paralysis; times definable as showing two
qualities, Dilettantism and Mammonism;—most intricate
obstructed times! Nay, if there were not a Heaven's
radiance of Justice, prophetic, clearly of Heaven, discernible
behind all these confused world-wide entanglements, of
Landlord interests, Manufacturing interests, Tory-Whig
interests, and who knows what other interests, expediencies,
vested interests, established possessions, inveterate Dilettantisms, Midas-eared Mammonisms,—it would seem to every
one a flat impossibility, which all wise men might as well at

once abandon. If you do not know eternal Justice from
momentary Expediency, and understand in your heart of
hearts how Justice, radiant, beneficent, as the all-victorious
Light-element, is also in essence, if need be, an all-victorious
Fire-element, and melts all manner of vested interests, and
the hardest iron cannon, as if they were soft wax, and does
ever in the long-run rule and reign, and allows nothing else
to rule and reign,—you also would talk of impossibility !
But it is only difficult, it is not impossible.   Possible?   It
is, with whatever difficulty, very clearly inevitable.

Fair day's-wages for fair day's-work ! exclaims a sarcastic
man : Alas, in what corner of this Planet, since Adam first
awoke on it, was that ever realized ?   The day's-wages of
John Milton's day's-work, named *Paradise Lost* and *Milton's
Works*, were Ten Pounds paid by instalments, and a rather
close escape from death on the gallows.   Consider that : it
is no rhetorical flourish ; it is an authentic, altogether quiet
fact,—emblematic, quietly documentary of a whole world of
such, ever since human history began.   Oliver Cromwell
quitted his farming ; undertook a Hercules' Labour and lifelong wrestle with that Lernean Hydra-coil, wide as England,
hissing heaven-high through its thousand-crowned, coroneted,
shovel-hatted quack-heads ; and he did wrestle with it, the
truest and terriblest wrestle I have heard of ; and he wrestled
it, and mowed and cut it down a good many stages, so that
its hissing is ever since pitiful in comparison, and one can
walk abroad in comparative peace from it :— and his wages,
as I understand, were burial under the gallows-tree near
Tyburn Turnpike, with his head on the gable of Westminster
Hall, and two centuries now of mixed cursing and ridicule
from all manner of men.   His dust lies under the Edgware
Road, near Tyburn Turnpike, at this hour ; and his memory
is—Nay, what matters what his memory is?   His memory,
at bottom, is or yet shall be as that of a god: a terror and
horror to all quacks and cowards and insincere persons ; an
everlasting encouragement, new memento, battleword, and
pledge of victory to all the brave.   It is the natural course
and history of the Godlike, in every place, in every time.
What god ever carried it with the Tenpound Franchisers ;
in Open Vestry, or with any Sanhedrim of considerable
standing ?   When was a god found 'agreeable' to everybody ?

The regular way is to hang, kill, crucify your gods, and execrate and trample them under your stupid hoofs for a century or two ; till you discover that they are gods,—and then take to braying over them, still in a very long-eared manner!—So speaks the sarcastic man ; in his wild way, very mournful truths.

Day's-wages for day's-work ? continues he : The Progress of Human Society consists even in this same, The better and better apportioning of wages to work. Give me this, you have given me all. Pay to every man accurately what he has worked for, what he has earned and done and deserved,—to this man broad lands and honours, to that man high gibbets and treadmills : what more have I to ask? Heaven's Kingdom, which we daily pray for, *has* come ; God's will is done on Earth even as it is in Heaven! This *is* the radiance of celestial Justice ; in the light or in the fire of which all impediments, vested interests, and iron cannon, are more and more melting like wax, and disappearing from the pathways of men. A thing ever struggling forward ; irrepressible, advancing inevitably ; perfecting itself, all days, more and more,—never to be *perfect* till that general Doomsday, the ultimate Consummation, and Last of earthly Days.

True, as to 'perfection' and so forth, answer we ; true enough ! And yet withal we have to remark, that imperfect Human Society holds itself together, and finds place under the Sun, in virtue simply of some *approximation* to perfection being actually made and put in practice. We remark farther, that there are supportable approximations, and then likewise insupportable. With some, almost with any, supportable approximation men are apt, perhaps too apt, to rest indolently patient, and say, It will do. Thus these poor Manchester manual workers mean only, by day's-wages for day's-work, certain coins of money adequate to keep them living ;—in return for their work, such modicum of food, clothes and fuel as will enable them to continue their work itself ! They as yet clamour for no more ; the rest, still inarticulate, cannot yet shape itself into a demand at all, and only lies in them as a dumb wish ; perhaps only, still more inarticulate, as a dumb, altogether unconscious want. *This* is the supportable approximation they would rest patient with, That by their work they might be kept alive to work more! —*This* once grown unattainable, I think your approximation may consider itself to have reached the *in*supportable stage ; and may prepare, with whatever difficulty, reluctance and astonishment, for one of two things, for changing or perishing ! With the millions no longer able to live, how can the units keep living ? It is too clear the Nation itself is on the way to suicidal death.

Shall we say then, The world has retrograded in its talent of apportioning wages to work, in late days ? The world had always a talent of that sort, better or worse. Time was when the mere *hand*worker needed not announce his claim to the world by Manchester Insurrections !—The world, with its Wealth of Nations, Supply-and-demand and such like, has of late days been terribly inattentive to that question of work and wages. We will not say, the poor world has retrograded even here : we will say rather, the world has been rushing on with such fiery animation to get work and ever more work done, it has had no time to think of dividing the wages ; and has merely left them to be scrambled for by the Law of the Stronger, law of Supply-and-demand, law of Laissez-faire, and other idle Laws and Un-laws,—saying, in its dire haste to get the work done, That is well enough !

And now the world will have to pause a little, and take up that other side of the problem, and in right earnest strive for some solution of that. For it has become pressing. What is the use of your spun shirts ? They hang there by the million unsaleable ; and here, by the million, are diligent bare backs that can get no hold of them. Shirts are useful for covering human backs ; useless otherwise, an unbearable mockery otherwise. You have fallen terribly behind with that side of the problem ! Manchester Insurrections, French Revolutions, and thousandfold phenomena great and small, announce loudly that you must bring it forward a little again. Never till now, in the history of an Earth which to this hour nowhere refuses to grow corn if you will plough it, to yield shirts if you will spin and weave in it, did the mere manual two-handed worker (however it might fare with other workers) cry in vain for such 'wages' as *he* means by 'fair wages', namely food and warmth ! The Godlike could not and cannot be paid ; but the Earthly always could. Gurth, a mere swineherd, born thrall of Cedric the Saxon, tended pigs in the wood, and did get some parings of the pork. Why, the four-footed worker has already *got* all that this two-handed one is clamouring for! How often must I remind you? There is not a horse in England, able and willing to work, but *has* due food and lodging; and goes about sleek-coated, satisfied in heart. And you say, It is impossible. Brothers, I answer, if for you it be impossible, what is to become of you? It is impossible for us to believe it to be impossible. The human brain, looking at these sleek English horses, refuses to believe in such impossibility for English men. Do you depart quickly; clear the ways soon, lest worse befall. We for our share do purpose, with full view of the enormous difficulty, with total disbelief in the impossibility, to endeavour while life is in us, and to die endeavouring, we and our sons, till we attain it or have all died and ended.

Such a Platitude of a World, in which all working horses could be well fed, and innumerable working men should die starved, were it not best to end it; to have done with it, and restore it once for all to the *Jötuns*, Mud-giants, Frost-giants, and Chaotic Brute-gods of the Beginning? For the old Anarchic Brute-gods it may be well enough; but it is a Platitude which Men should be above countenancing by their presence in it. We pray you, let the word *impossible* disappear from your vocabulary in this matter. It is of awful omen; to all of us, and to yourselves first of all.

CHAPTER IV

MORRISON'S PILL

WHAT is to be done, what would you have us do? asks many a one, with a tone of impatience, almost of reproach; and then, if you mention some one thing, some two things, twenty things that might be done, turns round with a satirical tehee, and 'These are your remedies!' The state of mind indicated by such question, and such rejoinder, is worth reflecting on.

It seems to be taken for granted, by these interrogative philosophers, that there is some 'thing', or handful of 'things', which could be done; some Act of Parliament,

'remedial measure' or the like, which could be passed,
whereby the social malady were fairly fronted, conquered,
put an end to; so that, with your remedial measure in your
pocket, you could then go on triumphant, and be troubled no
farther. 'You tell us the evil', cry such persons, as if
justly aggrieved, 'and do not tell us how it is to be cured!'

How it is to be cured? Brothers, I am sorry I have got
no Morrison's Pill for curing the maladies of Society. It
were infinitely handier if we had a Morrison's Pill, Act of
Parliament, or remedial measure, which men could swallow,
one good time, and then go on in their old courses, cleared
from all miseries and mischiefs! Unluckily we have none
such; unluckily the Heavens themselves, in their rich
pharmacopœia, contain none such. There will no 'thing'
be done that will cure you. There will a radical universal
alteration of your regimen and way of life take place; there
will a most agonizing divorce between you and your
chimeras, luxuries and falsities, take place; a most toilsome,
all-but 'impossible' return to Nature, and her veracities and
her integrities, take place: that so the inner fountains of life
may again begin, like eternal Light-fountains, to irradiate
and purify your bloated, swollen, foul existence, drawing nigh,
as at present, to nameless death! Either death or else all
this will take place. Judge if, with such diagnosis, any
Morrison's Pill is like to be discoverable!

But the Life-fountain within you once again set flowing,
what innumerable 'things', whole sets and classes and continents of 'things', year after year, and decade after decade,
and century after century, will then be doable and done!
Not Emigration, Education, Corn-Law Abrogation, Sanitary
Regulation, Land Property-Tax; not these alone, nor
a thousand times as much as these. Good Heavens, there
will then be light in the inner heart of here and there a man,
to discern what is just, what is commanded by the Most
High God, what *must* be done, were it never so 'impossible'.
Vain jargon in favour of the palpably unjust will then
abridge itself within limits. Vain jargon, on Hustings, in
Parliaments or wherever else, when here and there a man
has vision for the essential God's-Truth of the things jargoned
of, will become very vain indeed. The silence of here and
there such a man, how eloquent in answer to such jargon!
Such jargon, frightened at its own gaunt echo, will unspeak-

ably abate; nay, for a while, may almost in a manner
disappear,—the wise answering it in silence, and even the
simple taking cue from them to hoot it down wherever heard.
It will be a blessed time; and many 'things' will become
doable,—and when the brains are out, an absurdity will die!
Not easily again shall a Corn-Law argue ten years for itself;
and shall talk and argue, when impartial persons have to
say with a sigh that, for so long back, they have heard no
'argument' advanced for it but such as might make the
angels and almost the very jackasses weep!—

Wholly a blessed time: when jargon might abate, and
here and there some genuine speech begin. When to the
noble opened heart, as to such heart they alone do, all noble
things began to grow visible; and the difference between
just and unjust, between true and false, between work and
sham-work, between speech and jargon, was once more,
what to our happier Fathers it used to be, *infinite*,—as
between a Heavenly thing and an Infernal: the one a thing
which you were *not* to do, which you were wise not to attempt
doing; which it were better for you to have a millstone tied
round your neck, and be cast into the sea, than concern
yourself with doing!—Brothers, it will not be a Morrison's
Pill, or remedial measure, that will bring all this about for us.

And yet, very literally, till, in some shape or other, it be
brought about, we remain cureless; till it begin to be
brought about, the cure does not begin. For Nature and
Fact, not Redtape and Semblance, are to this hour the basis
of man's life; and on those, through never such strata of
these, man and his life and all his interests do, sooner or
later, infallibly come to rest,—and to be supported or be
swallowed according as they agree with those. The question
is asked of them, not, How do you agree with Downing
Street and accredited Semblance? but, How do you agree
with God's Universe and the actual Reality of things? This
Universe *has* its Laws. If we walk according to the Law,
the Law-Maker will befriend us; if not, not. Alas, by no
Reform Bill, Ballot-box, Five-point Charter, by no boxes or
bills or charters, can you perform this alchemy: 'Given
a world of Knaves, to produce an Honesty from their united
action!' It is a distillation, once for all, not possible. You
pass it through alembic after alembic, it comes out still

a Dishonesty, with a new dress on it, a new colour to it.
' While we ourselves continue valets, how *can* any hero come
to govern us ? ' We are governed, very infallibly, by the
'sham-hero ', — whose name is Quack, whose work and
governance is Plausibility, and also is Falsity and Fatuity ;
to which Nature says, and must say when it comes to *her* to
speak, eternally No ! Nations cease to be befriended of the
Law-Maker, when they walk *not* according to the Law.
The Sphinx-question remains unsolved by them, becomes
ever more insoluble.

If thou ask again, therefore, on the Morrison's-Pill hypothesis, What is to be done ? allow me to reply : By thee, for
the present, almost nothing. Thou there, the thing for thee
to do is, if possible, to cease to be a hollow sounding-shell of
hearsays, egoisms, purblind dilettantisms ; and become, were
it on the infinitely small scale, a faithful discerning soul.
Thou shalt descend into thy inner man, and see if there be
any traces of a *soul* there ; till then there can be nothing
done ! O brother, we must if possible resuscitate some soul
and conscience in us, exchange our dilettantisms for sincerities, our dead hearts of stone for living hearts of flesh. Then
shall we discern, not one thing, but, in clearer or dimmer
sequence, a whole endless host of things that can be done.
Do the first of these; do it ; the second will already have
become clearer, doabler ; the second, third, and three-
thousandth will then have begun to be possible for us. Not
any universal Morrison's Pill shall we then, either as
swallowers or as vendors, ask after at all ; but a far different
sort of remedies : Quacks shall no more have dominion over
us, but true Heroes and Healers !

Will not that be a thing worthy of 'doing'; to deliver
ourselves from quacks, sham-heroes ; to deliver the whole
world more and more from such ? They are the one
bane of the world. Once clear the world of them, it
ceases to be a Devil's-world, in all fibres of it wretched,
accursed ; and begins to be a God's-world, blessed, and
working hourly towards blessedness. Thou for one wilt not
again vote for any quack, do honour to any edge-gilt vacuity
in man's shape : cant shall be known to thee by the sound
of it ;—thou wilt fly from cant with a shudder never felt
before ; as from the opened litany of Sorcerers' Sabbaths, the

true Devil-worship of this age, more horrible than any other blasphemy, profanity or genuine blackguardism elsewhere audible among men. It is alarming to witness,—in its present completed state ! And Quack and Dupe, as we must ever keep in mind, are upperside and under of the selfsame substance; convertible personages : turn up your dupe into the proper fostering element, and he himself can become a quack ; there is in him the due prurient insincerity, open voracity for profit, and closed sense for truth, whereof quacks too, in all their kinds, are made.

Alas, it is not to the hero, it is to the sham-hero that, of right and necessity, the valet-world belongs. 'What is to be done?' The reader sees whether it is like to be the seeking and swallowing of some 'remedial measure !'

CHAPTER V

ARISTOCRACY OF TALENT

WHEN an individual is miserable, what does it most of all behove him to do? To complain of this man or of that, of this thing or of that? To fill the world and the street with lamentation, objurgation? Not so at all; the reverse of so. All moralists advise him not to complain of any person or of any thing, but of himself only. He is to know of a truth that being miserable he has been unwise, he. Had he faithfully followed Nature and her Laws, Nature, ever true to her Laws, would have yielded fruit and increase and felicity to him : but he has followed other than Nature's Laws ; and now Nature, her patience with him being ended, leaves him desolate; answers with very emphatic significance to him : No. Not by this road, my son ; by another road shalt thou attain well-being: this, thou perceivest is the road to ill-being ; quit this !—So do all moralists advise : that the man penitently say to himself first of all, Behold I was not wise enough ; I quitted the laws of Fact, which are also called the Laws of God, and mistook for them the Laws of Sham and Semblance, which are called the Devil's Laws ; therefore am I here !

Neither with Nations that become miserable is it fundamentally otherwise. The ancient guides of Nations, Prophets,
Priests, or whatever their name, were well aware of this ;
and, down to a late epoch, impressively taught and inculcated
it. The modern guides of Nations, who also go under a great
variety of names, Journalists, Political Economists, Politicians, Pamphleteers, have entirely forgotten this, and are
ready to deny this. But it nevertheless remains eternally
undeniable : nor is there any doubt but we shall all be
taught it yet, and made again to confess it : we shall all be
striped and scourged till we do learn it ; and shall at last
either get to know it, or be striped to death in the process.
For it is undeniable ! When a Nation is unhappy, the old
Prophet was right and not wrong in saying to it : Ye have
forgotten God, ye have quitted the ways of God, or ye would
not have been unhappy. It is not according to the laws of
Fact that ye have lived and guided yourselves, but according
to the laws of Delusion, Imposture, and wilful and unwilful
Mistake of Fact ; behold therefore the Unveracity is worn
out ; Nature's long-suffering with you is exhausted ; and ye
are here !

Surely there is nothing very inconceivable in this, even to
the Journalist, to the Political Economist, Modern Pamphle-
teer, or any two-legged animal without feathers ! If a country
finds itself wretched, sure enough that country has been
*mis*guided : it is with the wretched Twenty-seven Millions,
fallen wretched, as with the Unit fallen wretched : they as
he have quitted the course prescribed by Nature and the
Supreme Powers, and so are fallen into scarcity, disaster,
infelicity ; and pausing to consider themselves, have to
lament and say : Alas, we were not wise enough ! We took
transient superficial Semblance for everlasting central Substance ; we have departed far away from the *Laws* of this
Universe, and behold now lawless Chaos and inane Chimera
is ready to devour us !—'Nature in late centuries,' says
Sauerteig, ' was universally supposed to be dead; an old
eight-day clock, made many thousand years ago, and still
ticking, but dead as brass,—which the Maker, at most, sat
looking at, in a distant, singular, and indeed incredible
manner : but now I am happy to observe, she is everywhere asserting herself to be not dead and brass at all, but
alive and miraculous, celestial-infernal, with an emphasis

that will again penetrate the thickest head of this Planet by and by!'——

Indisputable enough to all mortals now, the guidance of this country has not been sufficiently wise : men too foolish have been set to the guiding and governing of it, and have guided it *hither*; we must find wiser,—wiser, or else we perish! To this length of insight all England has now advanced ; but as yet no farther. All England stands wringing its hands, asking itself, nigh desperate, What farther? Reform Bill proves to be a failure ; Benthamee Radicalism, the gospel of 'Enlightened Selfishness', dies out, or dwindles into Five-point Chartism, amid the tears and hootings of men : what next are we to hope or try? Five-point Charter, Free-trade, Church-extension, Sliding-scale ; what, in Heaven's name, are we next to attempt, that we sink not in inane Chimera, and be devoured of Chaos?—— The case is pressing, and one of the most complicated in the world. A God's-message never came to thicker-skinned people ; never had a God's-message to pierce through thicker integuments, into heavier ears. It is Fact, speaking once more, in miraculous thunder-voice, from out of the centre of the world ;—how unknown its language to the deaf and foolish many ; how distinct, undeniable, terrible and yet beneficent, to the hearing few : Behold, ye shall grow wiser, or ye shall die! Truer to Nature's Fact, or inane Chimera will swallow you ; in whirlwinds of fire, you and your Mammonisms, Dilettantisms, your Midas-eared philosophies, double-barrelled Aristocracies, shall disappear!—— Such is the God's-message to *us*, once more, in these modern days.

We must have more Wisdom to govern us, we must be governed by the Wisest, we must have an Aristocracy of Talent! cry many. True, most true ; but how to get it? The following extract from our young friend of the *Houndsditch Indicator* is worth perusing : 'At this time', says he, 'while there is a cry everywhere, articulate or inarticulate, for an "Aristocracy of Talent", a Governing Class namely which did govern, not merely which took the wages of governing, and could not with all our industry be kept from misgoverning, corn-lawing, and playing the very deuce with us,—it may not be altogether useless to remind some of the greener-headed sort what a dreadfully difficult affair the getting of such an Aristocracy is! Do you expect, my friends, that your indispensable Aristocracy of Talent is to be enlisted straightway, by some sort of recruitment afore-thought, out of the general population; arranged in supreme regimental order; and set to rule over us? That it will be got sifted, like wheat out of chaff, from the Twenty-seven Million British subjects; that any Ballot-box, Reform Bill, or other Political Machine, with Force of Public Opinion never so active on it, is likely to perform said process of sifting? Would to Heaven that we had a sieve; that we could so much as fancy any kind of sieve, wind-fanners, or ne-plus-ultra of machinery, devisable by man, that would do it!

'Done nevertheless, sure enough, it must be; it shall and will be. We are rushing swiftly on the road to destruction; every hour bringing us nearer, until it be, in some measure, done. The doing of it is not doubtful; only the method and the costs! Nay I will even mention to you an infallible sifting-process whereby he that has ability will be sifted out to rule among us, and that same blessed Aristocracy of Talent be verily, in an approximate degree, vouchsafed us by and by: an infallible sifting-process; to which, however, no soul can help his neighbour, but each must, with devout prayer to Heaven, endeavour to help himself. It is, O friends, that all of us, that many of us, should acquire the true *eye* for talent, which is dreadfully wanting at present! The true eye for talent presupposes the true reverence for it,—O Heavens, presupposes so many things!

'For example, you Bobus Higgins, Sausage-maker on the great scale, who are raising such a clamour for this Aris-tocracy of Talent, what is it that you do, in that big heart of yours, chiefly in very fact pay reverence to? Is it to talent, intrinsic manly worth of any kind, you unfortunate Bobus? The manliest man that you saw going in a ragged coat, did you ever reverence him; did you so much as know that he was a manly man at all, till his coat grew better? Talent! I understand you to be able to worship the fame of talent, the power, cash, celebrity or other success of talent; but the talent itself is a thing you never saw with eyes. Nay what is it in yourself that you are proudest of, that you take most pleasure in surveying meditatively in thoughtful moments? Speak now, is it the bare Bobus stript of his very name and shirt, and turned loose upon society, that you admire and thank Heaven for; or Bobus with his cash-accounts and larders dropping fatness, with his respectabilities, warm garnitures, and pony-chaise, admirable in some measure to certain of the flunkey species? Your own degree of worth and talent, is it of *infinite* value to you; or only of finite,—measurable by the degree of currency, and conquest of praise or pudding, it has brought you to? Bobus, you are in a vicious circle, rounder than one of your own sausages; and will never vote for or promote any talent, except what talent or sham-talent has already *got* itself voted for!'—We here cut short the *Indicator*; all readers perceiving whither he now tends.

'More Wisdom' indeed: but where to find more Wisdom? We have already a Collective Wisdom, after its kind,—though 'class-legislation', and another thing or two, affect it somewhat! On the whole, as they say, Like people like priest; so we may say, Like people like king. The man gets himself appointed and elected who is ablest—to be appointed and elected. What can the incorruptiblest *Bobuses* elect, if it be not some *Bobissimus*, should they find such?

Or, again, perhaps there is not, in the whole Nation, Wisdom enough, 'collect' it as we may, to make an adequate Collective! That too is a case which may befall: a ruined man staggers down to ruin because there was not wisdom enough in him; so, clearly also, may Twenty-seven Million collective men!—But indeed one of the infalliblest fruits of Unwisdom in a Nation is that it cannot get the use of what Wisdom is actually in it: that it is not governed by the wisest it has, who alone have a divine right to govern in all Nations; but by the sham-wisest, or even by the openly not-so-wise if they are handiest otherwise! This is the infalliblest result of Unwisdom; and also the balefullest, immeasurablest,—not so much what we can call a poison-*fruit*, as a universal death-disease, and poisoning of the whole tree. For hereby are fostered, fed into gigantic bulk, all manner of Unwisdoms, poison-fruits; till, as we say, the life-tree everywhere is made a upas-tree, deadly Unwisdom overshadowing all things; and there is done what lies in human skill to stifle all Wisdom everywhere in the birth, to smite our poor world barren of Wisdom,— and make your utmost Collective Wisdom, were it collected and elected by Rhadamanthus, Aeacus and Minos, not to speak of drunken Tenpound Franchisers with their ballot-boxes, an inadequate Collective! The Wisdom is not now there: how will you 'collect' it? As well wash Thames mud, by improved methods, to find more gold in it.

Truly, the first condition is indispensable, That Wisdom be there: but the second is like unto it, is properly one with it; these two conditions act and react through every fibre of them, and go inseparably together. If you have much Wisdom in your Nation, you will get it faithfully collected; for the wise love Wisdom, and will search for it as for life and salvation. If you have little Wisdom, you will get even that little ill-collected, trampled under foot, reduced as near as possible to annihilation; for fools do not love Wisdom; they are foolish, first of all, because they have never loved Wisdom,—but have loved their own appetites, ambitions, their coroneted coaches, tankards of heavy-wet. Thus is your candle lighted at both ends, and the progress towards consummation is swift. Thus is fulfilled that saying in the Gospel: To him that hath shall be given; and from him that hath not shall be taken away even that which he hath. Very literally, in a very fatal manner, that saying is here fulfilled.

Our 'Aristocracy of Talent' seems at a considerable distance yet; does it not, O Bobus?

CHAPTER VI

HERO-WORSHIP

To the present Editor, not less than to Bobus, a Government of the Wisest, what Bobus calls an Aristocracy of Talent, seems the one healing remedy: but he is not so sanguine as Bobus with respect to the means of realizing it. He thinks that we have at once missed realizing it, and come to need it so pressingly, by departing far from the inner

eternal Laws, and taking up with the temporary outer
semblances of Laws. He thinks that 'enlightened Egoism',
never so luminous, is not the rule by which man's life can
be led. That 'Laissez-faire', 'Supply-and-demand', 'Cash-
payment for the sole nexus', and so forth, were not, are not,
and will never be, a practicable Law of Union for a Society
of Men. That Poor and Rich, that Governed and Governing,
cannot long live together on any such Law of Union. Alas,
he thinks that man has a soul in him, *different* from the
stomach in any sense of this word; that if said soul be
asphyxied, and lie quietly forgotten, the man and his affairs
are in a bad way. He thinks that said soul will have to be
resuscitated from its asphyxia; that if it prove irresuscitable,
the man is not long for this world. In brief, that Midas-
eared Mammonism, double-barrelled Dilettantism, and their
thousand adjuncts and corollaries, are *not* the Law by which
God Almighty has appointed this his Universe to go. That,
once for all, these are not the Law : and then farther that
we shall have to return to what *is* the Law,—not by smooth
flowery paths, it is like, and with ' tremendous cheers ' in
our throat ; but over steep untrodden places, through storm-
clad chasms, waste oceans, and the bosom of tornadoes ;
thank Heaven, if not through very Chaos and the Abyss !
The resuscitating of a soul that has gone to asphyxia
is no momentary or pleasant process, but a long and
terrible one.

To the present Editor, ' Hero-worship ', as he has elsewhere named it, means much more than an elected Parliament, or stated Aristocracy, of the Wisest ; for, in his
dialect, it is the summary, ultimate essence, and supreme
practical perfection of all manner of ' worship,' and true
worthships and noblenesses whatsoever. Such blessed Parliament and, were it once in perfection, blessed Aristocracy of
the Wisest, god-honoured and man-honoured, he does look
for, more and more perfected,—as the topmost blessed
practical apex of a whole world reformed from sham-worship,
informed anew with worship, with truth and blessedness !
He thinks that Hero-worship, done differently in every
different epoch of the world, is the soul of all social business
among men ; that the doing of it well, or the doing of it ill,
measures accurately what degree of well-being or of ill-being

there is in the world's affairs. He thinks that we, on the whole, do our Hero-worship worse than any Nation in this world ever did it before : that the Burns an Exciseman, the Byron a Literary Lion, are intrinsically, all things considered, a baser and falser phenomenon than the Odin a God, the Mahomet a Prophet of God. It is this Editor's clear opinion, accordingly, that we must learn to do our Hero-worship better ; that to do it better and better, means the awakening of the Nation's soul from its asphyxia, and the return of blessed life to us,—Heaven's blessed life, not Mammon's galvanic accursed one. To resuscitate the Asphyxied, apparently now moribund, and in the last agony if not resuscitated : such and no other seems the consummation.

'Hero-worship', if you will,—yes, friends ; but, first of all, by being ourselves of heroic mind. A whole world of Heroes ; a world not of Flunkeys, where no Hero-King *can* reign : that is what we aim at ! We, for our share, will put away all Flunkeyism, Baseness, Unveracity from us ; we shall then hope to have Noblenesses and Veracities set over us ; never till then. Let Bobus and Company sneer, 'That is your Reform !' Yes, Bobus, that is our Reform ; and except in that, and what will follow out of that, we have no hope at all. Reform, like Charity, O Bobus, must begin at home. Once well at home, how will it radiate outwards, irrepressible, into all that we touch and handle, speak and work; kindling ever new light, by incalculable contagion, spreading in geometric ratio, far and wide,— doing good only, wheresoever it spreads, and not evil.

By Reform Bills, Anti-Corn-Law Bills, and thousand other bills and methods, we will demand of our Governors, with emphasis, and for the first time not without effect, that they cease to be quacks, or else depart ; that they set no quackeries and blockheadisms anywhere to rule over us, that they utter or act no cant to us,—it will be better if they do not. For we shall now know quacks when we see them ; cant, when we hear it, shall be horrible to us ! We will say, with the poor Frenchman at the Bar of the Convention, though in wiser style than he, and 'for the space' not 'of an hour' but of a lifetime : '*Je demande l'arrestation des coquins et des lâches.*' 'Arrestment of the knaves and dastards': ah, we know what a work that is ; how long it will be before *they* are all or mostly got 'arrested':—but here is one; arrest him, in God's name; it is one fewer! We will, in all practicable ways, by word and silence, by act and refusal to act, energetically demand that arrestment,—'*je demande cette arrestation-là!*'—and by degrees infallibly attain it. Infallibly: for light spreads; all human souls, never so bedarkened, love light; light once kindled spreads, till all is luminous;—till the cry, '*Arrest* your knaves and dastards' rises imperative from millions of hearts, and rings and reigns from sea to sea. Nay, how many of them may we not 'arrest' with our own hands, even now; we! Do not countenance them, thou there: turn away from their lacquered sumptuosities, their belauded sophistries, their serpent graciosities, their spoken and acted cant, with a sacred horror, with an *Apage Satanas.*—Bobus and Company, and all men will gradually join us. We demand arrestment of the knaves and dastards, and begin by arresting our own poor selves out of that fraternity. There is no other reform conceivable. Thou and I, my friend, can, in the most flunkey world, make, each of us, *one* non-flunkey, one hero, if we like: that will be two heroes to begin with:—Courage! even that is a whole world of heroes to end with, or what we poor Two can do in furtherance thereof!

Yes, friends: Hero-kings, and a whole world not unheroic,—there lies the port and happy haven, towards which, through all these stormtost seas, French Revolutions, Chartisms, Manchester Insurrections, that make the heart sick in these bad days, the Supreme Powers are driving us. On the whole, blessed be the Supreme Powers, stern as they are! Towards that haven will we, O friends; let all true men, with what of faculty is in them, bend valiantly, incessantly, with thousandfold endeavour, thither, thither! There, or else in the Ocean-abysses, it is very clear to me, we shall arrive.

Well; here truly is no answer to the Sphinx-question; not the answer a disconsolate public, inquiring at the College of Health, was in hopes of! A total change of regimen, change of constitution and existence from the very centre of it; a new body to be got, with resuscitated soul,—not without convulsive travail-throes; as all birth and new-birth presupposes travail! This is sad news to a disconsolate discerning Public, hoping to have got off by some Morrison's Pill, some Saint-John's corrosive mixture and perhaps a little blistery friction on the back !—We were prepared to part with our Corn-Law, with various Laws and Unlaws : but this, what is this ?

Nor has the Editor forgotten how it fares with your ill-boding Cassandras in Sieges of Troy. Imminent perdition is not usually driven away by words of warning. Didactic Destiny has other methods in store ; or these would fail always. Such words should, nevertheless, be uttered, when they dwell truly in the soul of any man. Words are hard, are importunate ; but how much harder the importunate events they foreshadow ! Here and there a human soul may listen to the words,—who knows how many human souls ? whereby the importunate events, if not diverted and pre-vented, will be rendered *less* hard. The present Editor's purpose is to himself full of hope.

For though fierce travails, though wide seas and roaring gulfs lie before us, is it not something if a Lodestar, in the eternal sky, do once more disclose itself ; an everlasting light, shining through all cloud-tempests and roaring billows, ever as we emerge from the trough of the sea : the blessed beacon, far off on the edge of far horizons, towards which we are to steer incessantly for life ? Is it not something ; O Heavens, is it not all ? There lies the Heroic Promised Land ; under that Heaven's-light, my brethren, bloom the Happy Isles,—there, O there ! Thither will we ;

There dwells the great Achilles whom we knew.[1]

There dwell all Heroes, and will dwell: thither, all ye heroic-minded !—The Heaven's Lodestar once clearly in our eye, how will each true man stand truly to *his* work in the ship ; how, with undying hope, will all things be fronted, all be conquered. Nay, with the ship's prow once turned in that direction, is not all, as it were, already well ? Sick wasting misery has become noble manful effort with a goal in our eye. 'The choking Nightmare chokes us no longer ; for we *stir* under it ; the Nightmare has already fled.'—

Certainly, could the present Editor instruct men how to know Wisdom, Heroism, when they see it, that they might

---

[1] Tennyson's Poems (*Ulysses*).

do reverence to *it* only, and loyally make it ruler over them, —yes, he were the living epitome of all Editors, Teachers, Prophets, that now teach and prophesy ; he were an *Apollo*-Morrison, a Trismegistus and *effective* Cassandra ! Let no Able Editor hope such things. It is to be expected the present laws of copyright, rate of reward per sheet, and other considerations, will save him from that peril. Let no Editor hope such things: no ;—and yet let all Editors aim towards such things, and even towards such alone ! One knows not what the meaning of editing and writing is, if even this be not it.

Enough, to the present Editor it has seemed possible some glimmering of light, for here and there a human soul, might lie in these confused Paper-Masses now intrusted to him ; wherefore he determines to edit the same. Out of old Books, new Writings, and much Meditation not of yesterday, he will endeavour to select a thing or two ; and from the Past, in a circuitous way, illustrate the Present and the Future. The Past is a dim indubitable fact: the Future too is one, only dimmer ; nay properly it is the *same* fact in new dress and development. For the Present holds in it both the whole Past and the whole Future ;—as the LIFE-TREE IGDRASIL, wide-waving, many-toned, has its roots down deep in the Death-kingdoms, among the oldest dead dust of men, and with its boughs reaches always beyond the stars ; and in all times and places is one and the same Life-tree !

BOOK II—THE ANCIENT MONK

CHAPTER I

JOCELIN OF BRAKELOND

WE will, in this Second Portion of our Work, strive to penetrate a little, by means of certain confused Papers, printed and other, into a somewhat remote Century; and to look face to face on it, in hope of perhaps illustrating our own poor Century thereby. It seems a circuitous way; but it may prove a way nevertheless. For man has ever been a striving, struggling, and, in spite of wide-spread calumnies to the contrary, a veracious creature: the Centuries too are all lineal children of one another; and often, in the portrait of early grandfathers, this and the other enigmatic feature of the newest grandson shall disclose itself, to mutual elucidation. This Editor will venture on such a thing.

Besides, in Editors' Books, and indeed everywhere else in the world of Today, a certain latitude of movement grows more and more becoming for the practical man. Salvation lies not in tight lacing, in these times;—how far from that, in any province whatsoever! Readers and men generally are getting into strange habits of asking all persons and things, from poor Editors' Books up to Church Bishops and State Potentates, not, By what designation art thou called; in what wig and black triangle dost thou walk abroad? Heavens, I know thy designation and black triangle well enough! But, in God's name, what *art* thou? Not Nothing, sayest thou! Then, How much and what? This is the thing I would know; and even *must* soon know, such a pass am I come to!——What weather-symptoms,—not for the poor Editor of Books alone! The Editor of Books may understand withal that if, as is said, 'many kinds are permissible,' there is one kind not permissible, 'the kind that has nothing in it, *le genre ennuyeux*'; and go on his way accordingly.

A certain Jocelinus de Brakelonda, a natural-born Englishman, has left us an extremely foreign Book[1], which the labours of the Camden Society have brought to light in these days. Jocelin's Book, the ' Chronicle', or private Boswellean Notebook, of Jocelin, a certain old St. Edmundsbury Monk and Boswell, now seven centuries old, how remote is it from us; exotic, extraneous; in all ways, coming from far abroad! The language of it is not foreign only but dead: Monk-Latin lies across not the British Channel, but the ninefold Stygian Marshes, Stream of Lethe, and one knows not where! Roman Latin itself, still alive for us in the Elysian Fields of Memory, is domestic in comparison. And then the ideas, life-furniture, whole workings and ways of this worthy Jocelin; covered deeper than Pompeii with the lava-ashes and inarticulate wreck of seven hundred years!

Jocelin of Brakelond cannot be called a conspicuous literary character; indeed few mortals that have left so visible a work, or footmark, behind them can be more obscure. One other of those vanished Existences, whose work has not yet vanished;—almost a pathetic phenomenon, were not the whole world full of such! The builders of Stonehenge, for example:—or alas, what say we, Stonehenge and builders? The writers of the *Universal Review* and *Homer's Iliad*; the paviers of London streets;—sooner or later, the entire Posterity of Adam! It is a pathetic phenomenon; but an irremediable, nay, if well meditated, a consoling one.

By his dialect of Monk-Latin, and indeed by his name, this Jocelin seems to have been a Norman Englishman; the surname *de Brakelonda* indicates a native of St. Edmundsbury itself, *Brakelond* being the known old name of a street or quarter in that venerable Town. Then farther, sure enough, our Jocelin was a Monk of St. Edmundsbury Convent; held some '*obedientia*', subaltern officiality there, or

[1] *Chronica* JOCELINI DE BRAKELONDA, *de rebus gestis Samsonis Abbatis Monasterii Sancti Edmundi: nunc primum typis mandata, curante* JOHANNE GAGE ROKEWOOD. (Camden Society, London, 1840.)

rather, in succession several ; was, for one thing, 'chaplain to my Lord Abbot, living beside him night and day for the space of six years';—which last, indeed, is the grand fact of Jocelin's existence, and properly the origin of this present Book, and of the chief meaning it has for us now.   He was, as we have hinted, a kind of born *Boswell*, though an infinitesimally small one; neither did he altogether want his *Johnson* even there and then.   Johnsons are rare ; yet, as has been asserted, Boswells perhaps still rarer,—the more is the pity on both sides !   This Jocelin, as we can discern well, was an ingenious and ingenuous, a cheery-hearted, innocent, yet withal shrewd, noticing, quick-witted man ; and from under his monk's cowl has looked out on that narrow section of the world in a really *human* manner ; not in any *simial*, canine, ovine, or otherwise *in*human manner,—afflictive to all that have humanity !   The man is of patient, peaceable, loving, clear-smiling nature ; open for this and that.   A wise simplicity is in him ; much natural sense ; a *veracity* that goes deeper than words.   Veracity: it is the basis of all ; and, some say, means genius itself; the prime essence of all genius whatsoever.   Our Jocelin, for the rest, has read his classical manuscripts, his Virgilius, his Flaccus, Ovidius Naso ; of course still more, his Homilies and Breviaries, and if not the Bible, considerable extracts of the Bible.   Then also he has a pleasant wit; and loves a timely joke, though in mild subdued manner : very amiable to see.   A learned grown man, yet with the heart as of a good child ; whose whole life indeed has been that of a child, —St. Edmundsbury Monastery a larger kind of cradle for him, in which his whole prescribed duty was to *sleep* kindly, and love his mother well !   This is the Biography of Jocelin ; 'a man of excellent religion,' says one of his contemporary Brother Monks, '*eximiæ religionis, potens sermone et opere.*'

For one thing, he had learned to write a kind of Monk or Dog-Latin, still readable to mankind; and, by good luck for us, had bethought him of noting down thereby what things seemed notablest to him.   Hence gradually resulted a *Chronica Jocelini*; new Manuscript in the *Liber Albus* of St. Edmundsbury.   Which Chronicle, once written in its childlike transparency, in its innocent good humour, not without touches of ready pleasant wit and many kinds of worth, other men liked naturally to read : whereby it failed

not to be copied, to be multiplied, to be inserted in the
Liber Albus ; and so surviving Henry the Eighth, Putney
Cromwell, the Dissolution of Monasteries, and all accidents
of malice and neglect for six centuries or so, it got into the
Harleian Collection,—and has now therefrom, by Mr. Rokewood of the Camden Society, been deciphered into clear
print ; and lies before us, a dainty thin quarto, to interest
for a few minutes whomsoever it can.

Here too it will behove a just Historian gratefully to say
that Mr. Rokewood, Jocelin's Editor, has done his editorial
function well. Not only has he deciphered his crabbed
Manuscript into clear print ; but he has attended, what his
fellow editors are not always in the habit of doing, to the
important truth that the Manuscript so deciphered ought to
have a meaning for the reader. Standing faithfully by his
text, and printing its very errors in spelling, in grammar or
otherwise, he has taken care by some note to indicate that
they are errors, and what the correction of them ought to
be. Jocelin's Monk-Latin is generally transparent, as shallow
limpid water. But at any stop that may occur, of which
there are a few, and only a very few, we have the comfortable assurance that a meaning does lie in the passage,
and may by industry be got at ; that a faithful editor's
industry had already got at it before passing on. A com-
pendious useful Glossary is given ; nearly adequate to help
the uninitiated through : sometimes one wishes it had been
a trifle larger ; but, with a Spelman and Ducange at your
elbow, how easy to have made it far too large ! Notes are
added, generally brief ; sufficiently explanatory of most
points. Lastly, a copious correct Index ; which no such
Book should want, and which unluckily very few possess.
And so, in a word, the *Chronicle of Jocelin* is, as it professes
to be, unwrapped from its thick cerements, and fairly brought
forth into the common daylight, so that he who runs, and
has a smattering of grammar, may read.

We have heard so much of Monks ; everywhere, in real
and fictitious History, from Muratori Annals to Radcliffe
Romances, these singular two-legged animals, with their
rosaries and breviaries, with their shaven crowns, hair-
cilices, and vows of poverty, masquerade so strangely
through our fancy ; and they are in fact so very strange

an extinct species of the human family,—a veritable Monk of Bury St. Edmunds is worth attending to, if by chance made visible and audible.   Here he is; and in his hand a magical speculum, much gone to rust indeed, yet in fragments still clear; wherein the marvellous image of his existence does still shadow itself, though fitfully, and as with an intermittent light!   Will not the reader peep with us into this singular *camera lucida*, where an extinct species, though fitfully, can still be seen alive?   Extinct species, we say; for the live specimens which still go about under that character are too evidently to be classed as spurious in Natural History: the Gospel of Richard Arkwright once promulgated, no Monk of the old sort is any longer possible in this world.   But fancy a deep-buried Mastodon, some fossil Megatherion, Ichthyosaurus, were to begin to *speak* from amid its rock-swathings, never so indistinctly!   The most extinct fossil species of Men or Monks can do, and does, this miracle,—thanks to the Letters of the Alphabet, good for so many things.

Jocelin, we said, was somewhat of a Boswell; but unfortunately, by Nature, he is none of the largest, and distance has now dwarfed him to an extreme degree.   His light is most feeble, intermittent, and requires the intensest kindest inspection; otherwise it will disclose mere vacant haze.   It must be owned, the good Jocelin, spite of his beautiful childlike character, is but an altogether imperfect 'mirror' of these old-world things!   The good man, he looks on us so clear and cheery, and in his neighbourly soft-smiling eyes we see so well our *own* shadow,—we have a longing always to cross-question him, to force from him an explanation of much.   But no; Jocelin, though he talks with such clear familiarity, like a next-door neighbour, will not answer any question: that is the peculiarity of him, dead these six hundred and fifty years, and quite deaf to us, though still so audible!   The good man, he cannot help it, nor can we.

But truly it is a strange consideration this simple one, as we go on with him, or indeed with any lucid simple-hearted soul like him: Behold therefore, this England of the Year 1200 was no chimerical vacuity or dreamland, peopled with mere vaporous Fantasms, Rymer's Fœdera, and Doctrines of the Constitution; but a green solid place, that grew corn and several other things. The Sun shone on it; the vicissitude of seasons and human fortunes. Cloth was woven and worn; ditches were dug, furrow-fields ploughed, and houses built. Day by day all men and cattle rose to labour, and night by night returned home weary to their several lairs. In wondrous Dualism, then as now, lived nations of breathing men; alternating, in all ways, between Light and Dark; between joy and sorrow, between rest and toil,—between hope, hope reaching high as Heaven, and fear deep as very Hell. Not vapour Fantasms, Rymer's Fœdera at all! Cœur-de-Lion was not a theatrical popinjay with greaves and steel-cap on it, but a man living upon victuals,—*not* imported by Peel's Tariff. Cœur-de-Lion came palpably athwart this Jocelin at St. Edmundsbury; and had almost peeled the sacred gold '*Feretrum*', or St. Edmund Shrine itself, to ransom him out of the Danube Jail.

These clear eyes of neighbour Jocelin looked on the bodily presence of King John; the very John *Sansterre*, or Lackland, who signed *Magna Charta* afterwards in Runnymead. Lackland, with a great retinue, boarded once, for the matter of a fortnight, in St. Edmundsbury Convent; daily in the very eyesight, palpable to the very fingers of our Jocelin: O Jocelin, what did he say, what did he do; how looked he, lived he;—at the very lowest, what coat or breeches had he on? Jocelin is obstinately silent. Jocelin marks down what interests *him*; entirely deaf to *us*. With Jocelin's eyes we discern almost nothing of John Lackland. As through a glass darkly, we with our own eyes and appliances, intensely looking, discern at most: A blustering, dissipated human figure, with a kind of blackguard quality air, in cramoisy velvet, or other uncertain texture, uncertain cut, with much plumage and fringing; amid numerous other human figures of the like; riding abroad with hawks; talking noisy nonsense;—tearing out the bowels of St. Edmundsbury Convent (its larders namely and cellars) in the most ruinous way, by living at rack and manger there. Jocelin notes only, with a slight subacidity of manner, that the King's Majesty, *Dominus Rex*, did leave, as gift for our St. Edmund Shrine, a handsome enough silk cloak,—or rather pretended to leave, for one of his retinue borrowed it of us, and *we* never got sight of it again; and, on the whole, that the *Dominus Rex*, at departing, gave us 'thirteen *sterlingii*', one shilling and one penny, to say a mass for him ; and so departed,—like a shabby Lackland as he was ! 'Thirteen pence sterling,' this was what the Convent got from Lackland, for all the victuals he and his had made away with. We of course said our mass for him, having covenanted to do it,—but let impartial posterity judge with what degree of fervour !

And in this manner vanishes King Lackland ; traverses swiftly our strange intermittent magic-mirror, jingling the shabby thirteen pence merely ; and rides with his hawks into Egyptian night again. It is Jocelin's manner with all things ; and it is men's manner and men's necessity. How intermittent is our good Jocelin ; marking down, without eye to *us*, what *he* finds interesting ! How much in Jocelin, as in all History, and indeed in all Nature, is at once inscrutable and certain ; so dim, yet so indubitable ; exciting us to endless considerations. For King Lackland *was* there, verily he ; and did leave these *tredecim sterlingii*, if nothing more, and did live and look in one way or the other, and a whole world was living and looking along with him ! There, we say, is the grand peculiarity ; the immeasurable one ; distinguishing, to a really infinite degree, the poorest historical Fact from all Fiction whatsoever. Fiction, 'Imagination,' 'Imaginative Poetry,' &c., &c., except as the vehicle for truth, or *fact* of some sort,—which surely a man should first try various other ways of vehiculating, and conveying safe,—what is it ? Let the Minerva and other Presses respond !—

But it is time we were in St. Edmundsbury Monastery, and Seven good Centuries off. If indeed it be possible, by any aid of Jocelin, by any human art, to get thither, with a reader or two still following us ?

CHAPTER II

ST. EDMUNDSBURY

THE *Burg*, Bury, or 'Berry' as they call it, of St. Edmund is still a prosperous brisk Town; beautifully diversifying, with its clear brick houses, ancient clean streets, and twenty or fifteen thousand busy souls, the general grassy face of Suffolk; looking out right pleasantly, from its hill-slope, towards the rising Sun: and on the eastern edge of it, still runs, long, black and massive, a range of monastic ruins; into the wide internal spaces of which the stranger is admitted on payment of one shilling. Internal spaces laid out, at present, as a botanic garden. Here stranger or townsman, sauntering at his leisure amid these vast grim venerable ruins, may persuade himself that an Abbey of St. Edmundsbury did once exist; nay there is no doubt of it: see here the ancient massive Gateway, of architecture interesting to the eye of Dilettantism; and farther on, that other ancient Gateway, now about to tumble, unless Dilettantism, in these very months, can subscribe money to cramp it and prop it!

Here, sure enough, is an Abbey; beautiful in the eye of Dilettantism. Giant Pedantry also will step in, with its huge *Dugdale* and other enormous *Monasticons* under its arm, and cheerfully apprise you, That this was a very great Abbey, owner and indeed creator of St. Edmund's Town itself, owner of wide lands and revenues; nay that its lands were once a county of themselves; that indeed King Canute or Knut was very kind to it, and gave St. Edmund his own gold crown off his head, on one occasion: for the rest, that the Monks were of such and such a genus, such and such a number; that they had so many carucates of land in this hundred, and so many in that; and then farther that the large Tower or Belfry was built by such a one, and the smaller Belfry was built by &c., &c.—Till human nature can stand no more of it; till human nature desperately take refuge in forgetfulness, almost in flat disbelief of the whole business, Monks, Monastery, Belfries, Carucates and all! Alas, what mountains of dead ashes, wreck and burnt bones, does assiduous Pedantry dig up from the Past Time, and

name it History, and Philosophy of History; till, as we
say, the human soul sinks wearied and bewildered; till the
Past Time seems all one infinite incredible grey void, without sun, stars, hearth-fires, or candle-light; dim offensive
dust-whirlwinds filling universal Nature; and over your
Historical Library, it is as if all the Titans had written for
themselves: DRY RUBBISH SHOT HERE!

And yet these grim old walls are not a dilettantism and
dubiety; they are an earnest fact. It was a most real and
serious purpose they were built for! Yes, another world it
was, when these black ruins, white in their new mortar and
fresh chiselling, first saw the sun as walls, long ago. Gauge
not, with thy dilettante compasses, with that placid dilettante simper, the Heaven's-Watchtower of our Fathers, the
fallen God's-Houses, the Golgotha of true Souls departed!

Their architecture, belfries, land-carucates? Yes,—and
that is but a small item of the matter. Does it never give
thee pause, this other strange item of it, that men then had
a *soul*,—not by hearsay alone, and as a figure of speech;
but as a truth that they *knew*, and practically went upon!
Verily it was another world then. Their Missals have
become incredible, a sheer platitude, sayest thou? Yes,
a most poor platitude; and even, if thou wilt, an idolatry
and blasphemy, should any one persuade *thee* to believe
them, to pretend praying by them. But yet it is pity we
had lost tidings of our souls:—actually we shall have to go
in quest of them again, or worse in all ways will befall!
A certain degree of soul, as Ben Jonson reminds us, is
indispensable to keep the very body from destruction of the
frightfullest sort; to 'save us,' says he, 'the expense of
salt.' Ben has known men who had soul enough to keep
their body and five senses from becoming carrion, and save
salt:—men, and also Nations. You may look in Manchester
Hunger-mobs and Corn-law Commons Houses, and various
other quarters, and say whether either soul or else salt is not
somewhat wanted at present!—

Another world, truly: and this present poor distressed
world might get some profit by looking wisely into it,
instead of foolishly. But at lowest, O dilettante friend, let
us know always that it *was* a world, and not a void infinite
of grey haze with fantasms swimming in it. These old

St. Edmundsbury walls, I say, were not peopled with fantasms ; but with men of flesh and blood, made altogether as we are. Had thou and I then been, who knows but we ourselves had taken refuge from an evil Time, and fled to dwell here, and meditate on an Eternity, in such fashion as we could ? Alas, how like an old osseous fragment, a broken blackened shinbone of the old dead Ages, this black ruin looks out, not yet covered by the soil ; still indicating what a once gigantic Life lies buried there ! It is dead now, and dumb ; but was alive once, and spake. / For twenty generations, here was the earthly arena where painful living men worked out their life-wrestle,—looked at by Earth, by Heaven and Hell. Bells tolled to prayers ; and men, of many humours, various thoughts, chanted vespers, matins ; —and round the little islet of their life rolled forever (as round ours still rolls, though we are blind and deaf) the illimitable Ocean, tinting all things with *its* eternal hues and reflexes ; making strange prophetic music ! / How silent now ; all departed, clean gone. The World-Dramaturgist has written : *Exeunt.* The devouring Time-Demons have made away with it all : and in its stead, there is either nothing ; or what is worse, offensive universal dust-clouds, and grey eclipse of Earth and Heaven, from ' dry rubbish shot here !'—

Truly it is no easy matter to get across the chasm of Seven Centuries, filled with such material. But here, of all helps, is not a Boswell the welcomest ; even a small Boswell ? Veracity, true simplicity of heart, how valuable are these always ! He that speaks what *is* really in him, will find men to listen, though under never such impediments. Even gossip, springing free and cheery from a human heart, this too is a kind of veracity and *speech ;*—much preferable to pedantry and inane grey haze ! Jocelin is weak and garrulous, but he is human. Through the thin watery gossip of our Jocelin, we do get some glimpses of that deep-buried Time ; discern veritably, though in a fitful intermittent manner, these antique figures and their life-method, face to face ! Beautifully, in our earnest loving glance, the old centuries melt from opaque to partially translucent, transparent here and there ; and the void black Night, one finds, is but the summing-up of innumerable peopled luminous *Days.* Not parchment Chartularies, Doctrines of the Constitution, O Dryasdust; not altogether, my erudite friend!—

Readers who please to go along with us into this poor *Jocelini Chronica* shall wander inconveniently enough, as in wintry twilight, through some poor stript hazel-grove, rustling with foolish noises, and perpetually hindering the eyesight; but across which, here and there, some real human figure is seen moving: very strange; whom we could hail if he would answer;—and we look into a pair of eyes deep as our own, *imaging* our own, but all unconscious of us; to whom we for the time are become as spirits and invisible!

CHAPTER III

LANDLORD EDMUND

SOME three centuries or so had elapsed since *Beodric's-worth* [1] became St. Edmund's *Stow*, St. Edmund's *Town* and Monastery, before Jocelin entered himself a Novice there. 'It was', says he, 'the year after the Flemings were defeated at Fornham St. Genevieve.'

Much passes away into oblivion: this glorious victory over the Flemings at Fornham has, at the present date, greatly dimmed itself out of the minds of men. A victory and battle nevertheless it was, in its time: some thrice-

---

[1] Dryasdust puzzles and pokes for some biography of this Beodric; and repugns to consider him a mere East-Anglian Person of Condition, not in need of a biography,—whose þeopð, *weorth* or *worth,* that is to say, *Growth,* Increase, or as we should now name it, *Estate,* that same Hamlet and wood Mansion, now St. Edmund's Bury, originally was. For, adds our erudite Friend, the Saxon þeopðan, equivalent to the German *werden,* means to *grow,* to *become*; traces of which old vocable are still found in the North-country dialects, as, 'What is *word* of him?' meaning 'What is *become* of him?' and the like. Nay we in modern English still say, 'Woe *worth* the hour' (Woe *befall* the hour), and speak of the '*Weird* Sisters'; not to mention the innumerable other names of places still ending in *weorth* or *worth.* And indeed, our common noun *worth,* in the sense of *value,* does not this mean simply, What a thing has *grown* to, What a man has *grown* to, How much he amounts to,—by the Threadneedle-street standard or another!

renowned Earl of Leicester, not of the De Montfort breed
(as may be read in Philosophical and other Histories, could
any human memory retain such things), had quarrelled with
his sovereign, Henry Second of the name; had been worsted,
it is like, and maltreated, and obliged to fly to foreign parts;
but had rallied there into new vigour; and so, in the year
1173. returns across the German Sea with a vengeful army
of Flemings.   Returns, to the coast of Suffolk; to Fram-
lingham Castle, where he is welcomed; westward towards
St. Edmundsbury and Fornham Church, where he is met
by the constituted authorities with *posse comitatus*; and
swiftly cut in pieces, he and his, or laid by the heels; on
the right bank of the obscure river Lark,—as traces still
existing will verify.

For the river Lark, though not very discoverably, still
runs or stagnates in that country; and the battle-ground is
there; serving at present as a pleasure-ground to his Grace
of Northumberland.   Copper pennies of Henry II are still
found there;—rotted out from the pouches of poor slain
soldiers, who had not had *time* to buy liquor with them.   In
the river Lark itself was fished up, within man's memory,
an antique gold ring; which fond Dilettantism can almost
believe may have been the very ring Countess Leicester threw
away, in her flight, into that same Lark river or ditch.[1]
Nay, few years ago, in tearing out an enormous superannuated
ash-tree, now grown quite corpulent, bursten, superfluous,
but long a fixture in the soil, and not to be dislodged without revolution,—there was laid bare, under its roots, 'a circular mound of skeletons wonderfully complete,' all radiating
from a centre, faces upwards, feet inwards; a 'radiation'
not of Light, but of the Nether Darkness rather; and
evidently the fruit of battle; for 'many of the heads were
cleft, or had arrow-holes in them'.   The Battle of Fornham,
therefore, is a fact, though a forgotten one; no less obscure
than undeniable,—like so many other facts.

Like the St. Edmund's Monastery itself!   Who can doubt,
after what we have said, that there was a Monastery here at
one time?   No doubt at all there was a Monastery here; no
doubt, some three centuries prior to this Fornham Battle,

[1] Lyttelton's History of Henry II. (2nd Edition) v. 169, &c.

there dwelt a man in these parts of the name of Edmund,
King, Landlord, Duke, or whatever his title was, of the
Eastern Counties;—and a very singular man and landlord
he must have been.

For his tenants, it would appear, did not in the least complain of him; his labourers did not think of burning his
wheatstacks, breaking into his game-preserves; very far the
reverse of all that.   Clear evidence, satisfactory even to my
friend Dryasdust, exists that, on the contrary, they honoured,
loved, admired this ancient Landlord to a quite astonishing
degree,—and indeed at last to an immeasurable and inexpressible degree ; for, finding no limits or utterable words
for their sense of his worth, they took to beatifying and
adoring him! 'Infinite admiration,' we are taught, 'means
worship.'

Very singular,—could we discover it! What Edmund's
specific duties were; above all, what his method of dis-
charging them with such results was, would surely be
interesting to know ; but are *not* very discoverable now.
His Life has become a poetic, nay a religious *Mythus* ; though,
undeniably enough, it was once a prose Fact, as our poor
lives are ; and even a very rugged unmanageable one.   This
landlord Edmund did go about in leather shoes, with *femoralia* and bodycoat of some sort on him; and daily had his
breakfast to procure ; and daily had contradictory speeches,
and most contradictory facts not a few, to reconcile with
himself.   No man becomes a Saint in his sleep.   Edmund,
for instance, instead of *reconciling* those same contradictory
facts and speeches to himself,—which means *subduing*, and
in a manlike and godlike manner conquering them to himself,—might have merely thrown new contention into them,
new unwisdom into them, and so been conquered *by* them ;
much the commoner case ! In that way he had proved no
'Saint', or Divine-looking Man, but a mere Sinner, and
unfortunate, blameable, more or less Diabolic-looking man !
No landlord Edmund becomes infinitely admirable in his
sleep.

With what degree of wholesome rigour his rents were
collected, we hear not.   Still less by what methods he preserved his game, whether by 'bushing' or how,—and if the
partridge-seasons were 'excellent', or were indifferent.
Neither do we ascertain what kind of Corn-bill he passed, or

wisely-adjusted Sliding-scale :—but indeed there were few
spinners in those days ; and the nuisance of spinning, and
other dusty labour, was not yet so glaring a one.

How then, it may be asked, did this Edmund rise into
favour ; become to such astonishing extent a recognized
Farmer's Friend ? Really, except it were by doing justly
and loving mercy to an unprecedented extent, one does not
know. The man, it would seem, had 'walked', as they say,
'humbly with God' ; humbly and valiantly with God ;
struggling to make the Earth heavenly as he could : instead
of walking sumptuously and pridefully with Mammon,
leaving the Earth to grow hellish as it liked. Not sumptuously with Mammon ? How then could he 'encourage
trade',—cause Howel and James, and many wine-merchants
to bless him, and the tailor's heart (though in a very shortsighted manner) to sing for joy ? Much in this Edmund's
Life is mysterious.

That he could, on occasion, do what he liked with his own
is, meanwhile, evident enough. Certain Heathen Physical-
Force Ultra-Chartists, 'Danes' as they were then called,
coming into his territory with their 'five points', or rather
with their five-and-twenty thousand *points* and edges too, of
pikes namely and battle-axes ; and proposing mere Heathenism, confiscation, spoliation, and fire and sword,—Edmund
answered that he would oppose to the utmost such savagery.
They took him prisoner ; again required his sanction to said
proposals. Edmund again refused. Cannot we kill you ?
cried they.—Cannot I die ? answered he. My life, I think,
is my own to do what I like with ! And he died, under
barbarous tortures, refusing to the last breath ; and the
Ultra-Chartist Danes *lost* their propositions ;—and went with
their 'points' and other apparatus, as is supposed, to the
Devil, the Father of them. Some say, indeed, these Danes
were not Ultra-Chartists, but Ultra-Tories, demanding to
reap where they had not sown, and live in this world without working, though all the world should starve for it ;
which likewise seems a possible hypothesis. Be what they
might, they went, as we say, to the Devil ; and Edmund
doing what he liked with his own, the Earth was got cleared
of them.

Another version is, that Edmund on this and the like
occasions stood by his order ; the oldest, and indeed only

true order of Nobility known under the stars, that of Just
Men and Sons of God, in opposition to Unjust and Sons of
Belial,—which latter indeed are *second*-oldest, but yet a very
unvenerable order. This, truly, seems the likeliest hypothesis of all. Names and appearances alter so strangely, in
some half-score centuries; and all fluctuates chameleon-like,
taking now this hue, now that. Thus much is very plain,
and does not change hue : Landlord Edmund was seen and
felt by all men to have done verily a man's part in this life-
pilgrimage of his ; and benedictions, and outflowing love
and admiration from the universal heart, were his meed.
Well-done ! Well-done ! cried the hearts of all men. They
raised his slain and martyred body ; washed its wounds
with fast-flowing universal tears ; tears of endless pity, and
yet of a sacred joy and triumph. The beautifullest kind of
tears,—indeed perhaps the beautifullest kind of thing : like
a sky all flashing diamonds and prismatic radiance ; all
weeping, yet shone on by the everlasting Sun :—and *this* is
not a sky, it is a Soul and living Face ! Nothing liker the
Temple of the Highest, bright with some real effulgence of the
Highest, is seen in this world.

Oh, if all Yankee-land follow a small good 'Schnüspel the
distinguished Novelist' with blazing torches, dinner-invita-
tions, universal hep-hep-hurrah, feeling that he, though
small, *is* something ; how might all Angle-land once follow
a hero-martyr and great true Son of Heaven ! It is the very
joy of man's heart to admire, where he can ; nothing so lifts
him from all his mean imprisonments, were it but for
moments, as true admiration. Thus it has been said, 'all
men, especially all women, are born worshippers' ; and will
worship, if it be but possible. Possible to worship a Something, even a small one ; not so possible a mere loud-blaring
Nothing ! What sight is more pathetic than that of poor
multitudes of persons met to gaze at King's Progresses,
Lord Mayors' Shows, and other gilt-gingerbread phenomena
of the worshipful sort, in these times ; each so eager to
worship ; each, with a dim fatal sense of disappointment,
finding that he cannot rightly here ! These be thy gods,
O Israel ? And thou art so *willing* to worship,—poor Israel !

In this manner, however, did the men of the Eastern
Counties take up the slain body of their Edmund, where it
lay cast forth in the village of Hoxne ; seek out the severed

head, and reverently reunite the same. They embalmed him with myrrh and sweet spices, with love, pity, and all high and awful thoughts; consecrating him with a very storm of melodious adoring admiration, and sun-dyed showers of tears;—joyfully, yet with awe (as all deep joy has something of the awful in it), commemorating his noble deeds and god-like walk and conversation while on Earth. Till, at length, the very Pope and Cardinals at Rome were forced to hear of it; and they, summing up as correctly as they well could, with *Advocatus-Diaboli* pleadings and their other forms of process, the general verdict of mankind, declared : That he had, in very fact, led a hero's life in this world ; and being now *gone*, was gone, as they conceived, to God above, and reaping his reward *there*. Such, they said, was the best judgement they could form of the case ;—and truly not a bad judgement. Acquiesced in, zealously adopted, with full assent of ' private judgement', by all mortals.

The rest of St. Edmund's history, for the reader sees he has now become a *Saint*, is easily conceivable. Pious munificence provided him a *loculus*, a *feretrum* or shrine ; built for him a wooden chapel, a stone temple, ever widening and growing by new pious gifts ;—such the overflowing heart feels it a blessedness to solace itself by giving. St. Edmund's Shrine glitters now with diamond flowerages, with a plating of wrought gold. The wooden chapel, as we say, has become a stone temple. Stately masonries, long-drawn arches, cloisters, sounding aisles buttress it, begirdle it far and wide. Regimented companies of men, of whom our Jocelin is one, devote themselves, in every generation, to meditate here on man's Nobleness and Awfulness, and celebrate and show forth the same, as they best can,—thinking they will do it better here, in presence of God the Maker, and of the so Awful and so Noble made by Him. In one word, St. Edmund's Body has raised a Monastery round it. To such length, in such manner, has the Spirit of the Time visibly taken body, and crystallized itself here. New gifts, houses, farms, *katalla*[1]—come ever in. King Knut, whom men call Canute, whom the Ocean-tide would not be for-

---

[1] Goods, properties ; what we now call *chattels*, and still more singularly *cattle*, says my erudite friend !

bidden to wet,—we heard already of this wise King, with his crown and gifts; but of many others, Kings, Queens, wise men and noble loyal women, let Dryasdust and divine Silence be the record! Beodric's-Worth has become St. Edmund's *Bury;*—and lasts visible to this hour. All this that thou now seest, and namest Bury Town, is properly the Funeral Monument of Saint or Landlord Edmund. The present respectable Mayor of Bury may be said, like a Fakeer (little as he thinks of it), to have his dwelling in the extensive, many-sculptured Tombstone of St. Edmund; in one of the brick niches thereof dwells the present respectable Mayor of Bury.

Certain Times do crystallize themselves in a magnificent manner; and others, perhaps, are like to do it in rather a shabby one!—But Richard Arkwright too will have his Monument a thousand years hence: all Lancashire and Yorkshire, and how many other shires and countries, with their machineries and industries, for his monument! A true *pyra*mid or '*flame*-mountain', flaming with steam fires and useful labour over wide continents, usefully towards the Stars, to a certain height;—how much grander than your foolish Cheops Pyramids or Sakhara clay ones! Let us withal be hopeful, be content or patient.

CHAPTER IV

ABBOT HUGO

IT is true, all things have two faces, a light one and a dark. It is true, in three centuries much imperfection accumulates; many an Ideal, monastic or other, shooting forth into practice as it can, grows to a strange enough Reality; and we have to ask with amazement, Is this your Ideal! For, alas, the Ideal always has to grow in the Real, and to seek out its bed and board there, often in a very sorry way. No beautifullest Poet is a Bird-of-Paradise, living on perfumes; sleeping in the aether with outspread wings. The Heroic, *independent* of bed and board, is found in Drury-Lane Theatre only ; to avoid disappointments, let us bear this in mind.

By the law of Nature, too, all manner of Ideals have their fatal limits and lot ; their appointed periods, of youth, of maturity or perfection, of decline, degradation, and final death and disappearance. There is nothing born but has to die. Ideal monasteries, once grown real, do seek bed and board in this world ; do find it more and more successfully ; do get at length too intent on finding it, exclusively intent on that. They are then like diseased corpulent bodies fallen idiotic, which merely eat and sleep ; *ready* for ' dissolution ', by a Henry the Eighth or some other. Jocelin's St. Edmundsbury is still far from this last dreadful state : but here too the reader will prepare himself to see an Ideal not sleeping in the aether like a bird-of-paradise, but roosting as the common wood-fowl do, in an imperfect, uncomfortable, more or less contemptible manner !—

Abbot Hugo, as Jocelin, breaking at once into the heart of the business, apprises us, had in those days grown old, grown rather blind, and his eyes were somewhat darkened, *aliquantulum caligaverunt oculi ejus.* He dwelt apart very much, in his *Talamus* or peculiar Chamber ; got into the hands of flatterers, a set of mealy-mouthed persons who strove to make the passing hour easy for him,—for him easy, and for themselves profitable ; accumulating in the distance mere mountains of confusion. Old Dominus Hugo sat inaccessible in this way, far in the interior, wrapped in his warm flannels and delusions ; inaccessible to all voice of Fact ; and bad grew ever worse with us. Not that our worthy old *Dominus Abbas* was inattentive to the divine offices, or to the maintenance of a devout spirit in us or in himself ; but the Account-Books of the Convent fell into the frightfullest state, and Hugo's annual Budget grew yearly emptier, or filled with futile expectations, fatal deficit, wind and debts !

His one worldly care was to raise ready money ; sufficient for the day is the evil thereof. And how he raised it : From usurious insatiable Jews ; every fresh Jew sticking on him like a fresh horseleech, sucking his and our life out ; crying continually, Give, give ! Take one example instead of scores. Our *Camera* having fallen into ruin, William the

Sacristan received charge to repair it; strict charge, but no money; Abbot Hugo would, and indeed could, give him no fraction of money. The *Camera* in ruins, and Hugo penniless and inaccessible, Willelmus Sacrista borrowed Forty Marcs (some Seven-and-twenty Pounds) of Benedict the Jew, and patched up our Camera again. But the means of repaying him? There were no means. Hardly could *Sacrista*, *Cellerarius*, or any public officer, get ends to meet, on the indispensablest scale, with their shrunk allowances: ready money had vanished.

Benedict's Twenty-seven pounds grew rapidly at compound-interest; and at length, when it had amounted to a Hundred pounds, he, on a day of settlement, presents the account to Hugo himself. Hugo already owed him another Hundred of his own; and so here it has become Two Hundred! Hugo, in a fine frenzy, threatens to depose the Sacristan, to do this and do that; but, in the mean while, How to quiet your insatiable Jew? Hugo, for this couple of hundreds, grants the Jew his bond for Four hundred payable at the end of four years. At the end of four years there is, of course, still no money; and the Jew now gets a bond for Eight hundred and eighty pounds, to be paid by instalments, Fourscore pounds every year. Here was a way of doing business!

Neither yet is this insatiable Jew satisfied or settled with: he had papers against us of 'small debts fourteen years old'; his modest claim amounts finally to 'Twelve hundred pounds besides interest';—and one hopes he never got satisfied in this world; one almost hopes he was one of those beleagured Jews who hanged themselves in York Castle shortly afterwards, and had his usances and quittances and horseleech papers summarily set fire to! For approximate justice will strive to accomplish itself; if not in one way, then in another. Jews, and also Christians and Heathens, who accumulate in this manner, though furnished with never so many parchments, do, at times, 'get their grinder-teeth successively pulled out of their head, each day a new grinder,' till they consent to disgorge again. A sad fact,—worth reflecting on.

Jocelin, we see, is not without secularity: Our *Dominus Abbas* was intent enough on the divine offices; but then his

Account-Books — ? — One of the things that strike us most, throughout, in Jocelin's *Chronicle*, and indeed in Eadmer's *Anselm*, and other old monastic Books, written evidently by pious men, is this, That there is almost no mention whatever of 'personal religion' in them ; that the whole gist of their thinking and speculation seems to be the 'privileges of our order', 'strict exaction of our dues', 'God's honour' (meaning the honour of our Saint), and so forth. Is not this singular? A body of men, set apart for perfecting and purifying their own souls, do not seem disturbed about that in any measure : the 'Ideal' says nothing about its idea ; says much about finding bed and board for itself! How is this?

Why, for one thing, bed and board are a matter very apt to come to speech : it is much easier to *speak* of them than of ideas; and they are sometimes much more pressing with some! Nay, for another thing, may not this religious reticence, in these devout good souls, be perhaps a merit, and sign of health in them? Jocelin, Eadmer, and such religious men, have as yet nothing of 'Methodism'; no Doubt or even root of Doubt. Religion is not a diseased self-introspection, an agonizing inquiry : their duties are clear to them, the way of supreme good plain, indisputable, and they are travelling on it. Religion lies over them like an all-embracing heavenly canopy, like an atmosphere and life-element, which is not spoken of, which in all things is presupposed without speech. Is not serene or complete Religion the highest aspect of human nature; as serene Cant, or complete No-religion, is the lowest and miserablest? Between which two, all manner of earnest Methodisms, introspections, agonizing inquiries, never so morbid, shall play their respective parts, not without approbation.

But let any reader fancy himself one of the Brethren in St. Edmundsbury Monastery under such circumstances! How can a Lord Abbot, all stuck over with horseleeches of this nature, front the world? He is fast losing his life-blood, and the Convent will be as one of Pharaoh's lean kine. Old monks of experience draw their hoods deeper down ; careful what they say : the monk's first duty is obedience. Our Lord the king, hearing of such work, sends down his

Almoner to make investigations : but what boots it ? Abbot
Hugo assembles us in Chapter ; asks, ' If there is any complaint ?'   Not a soul of us dare answer, ' Yes, thousands ! '
but we all stand silent, and the Prior even says that things
are in a very comfortable condition.   Whereupon old Abbot
Hugo, turning to the royal messenger, says, ' You see ! '—
and the business terminates in that way. I, as a brisk-eyed,
noticing youth and novice, could not help asking of the
elders, asking of Magister Samson in particular : Why he,
well-instructed and a knowing man, had not spoken out, and
brought matters to a bearing ?   Magister Samson was
Teacher of the Novices, appointed to breed us up to the
rules, and I loved him well.   ' *Fili mi*,' answered Samson,
' the burnt child shuns the fire.   Dost thou not know, our
Lord the Abbot sent me once to Acre in Norfolk, to solitary
confinement and bread and water, already ?   The Hinghams,
Hugo and Robert, have just got home from banishment for
speaking.   This is the hour of darkness : the hour when
flatterers rule and are believed.   *Videat Dominus*, let the
Lord see, and judge.'
     In very truth, what could poor old Abbot Hugo do ?
A frail old man ; and the Philistines were upon him,—that
is to say, the Hebrews.   He had nothing for it but to shrink
away from them ; get back into his warm flannels, into his
warm delusions again.   Happily, before it was quite too
late, he bethought him of pilgriming to St. Thomas of
Canterbury.   He set out, with a fit train, in the autumn
days of the year 1180 ; near Rochester City, his mule threw
him, dislocated his poor kneepan, raised incurable inflam-
matory fever ; and the poor old man got his dismissal from
the whole coil at once.   St. Thomas à Becket, though in
a circuitous way, had *brought* deliverance !   Neither Jew
usurers, nor grumbling monks, nor other importunate
despicability of men or mud-elements afflicted Abbot Hugo
any more ; but he dropt his rosaries, closed his account-
books, closed his old eyes, and lay down into the long
sleep.   Heavy-laden hoary old Dominus Hugo, fare thee
well.
     One thing we cannot mention without a due thrill of
horror : namely, that, in the empty exchequer of Dominus
Hugo, there was not found one penny to distribute to the
Poor that they might pray for his soul !   By a kind of god-

send, Fifty shillings did, in the very nick of time, fall due,
or seem to fall due, from one of his Farmers (the *Firmarius*
de Palegrava), and he paid it, and the Poor had it ; though,
alas, this too only *seemed* to fall due, and we had it to
pay again afterwards. Dominus Hugo's apartments were
plundered by his servants, to the last portable stool, in a few
minutes after the breath was out of his body. Forlorn old
Hugo, fare thee well forever.

CHAPTER V

TWELFTH CENTURY

Our Abbot being dead, the *Dominus Rex*, Henry II, or
Ranulf de Glanvill *Justiciarius* of England for him, set
Inspectors or Custodiars over us ;—not in any breathless
haste to appoint a new Abbot, our revenues coming into his
own *Scaccarium*, or royal Exchequer, in the meanwhile.
They proceeded with some rigour, these Custodiars ; took
written inventories, clapt-on seals, exacted everywhere strict
tale and measure : but wherefore should a living monk
complain ? The living monk has to do his devotional
drill-exercise ; consume his allotted *pitantia*, what we call
pittance, or ration of victual ; and possess his soul in
patience.

Dim, as through a long vista of Seven Centuries, dim and
very strange looks that monk-life to us ; the ever-surprising
circumstance this, That it is a *fact* and no dream, that we
see it there, and gaze into the very eyes of it ! Smoke rises
daily from those culinary chimney-throats ; there are living
human beings there, who chant, loud-braying, their matins,
nones, vespers ; awakening *echoes*, not to the bodily ear
alone. St. Edmund's Shrine, perpetually illuminated, glows
ruddy through the Night, and through the Night of Centuries
withal ; St. Edmundsbury Town paying yearly Forty pounds
for that express end. Bells clang out ; on great occasions,
all the bells. We have Processions, Preachings, Festivals,
Christmas Plays, *Mysteries* shown in the Churchyard, at

which latter the Townsfolk sometimes quarrel.   Time was,
Time is, as Friar Bacon's Brass Head remarked ; and withal
Time will be.   There are three Tenses, *Tempora*, or Times ;
and there is one Eternity ; and as for us,

We are such stuff as Dreams are made of !

Indisputable, though very dim to modern vision, rests on
its hill-slope that same *Bury*, *Stow*, or Town of St. Edmund ;
already a considerable place, not without traffic, nay manufactures, would Jocelin only tell us what.   Jocelin is totally
careless of telling : but, through dim fitful apertures, we can
see *Fullones*, 'Fullers,' see cloth-making ; looms dimly
going, dye-vats, and old women spinning yarn.   We have
Fairs too, *Nundinae*, in due course ; and the Londoners give
us much trouble, pretending that they, as a metropolitan
people, are exempt from toll.   Besides there is Field-
husbandry, with perplexed settlement of Convent rents :
corn-ricks pile themselves within burgh, in their season ;
and cattle depart and enter ; and even the poor weaver has
his cow,—'dungheaps' lying quiet at most doors (*ante foras*,
says the incidental Jocelin), for the Town has yet no
improved police.   Watch and ward nevertheless we do keep,
and have Gates,—as what Town must not ; thieves so
abounding ; war, *werra*, such a frequent thing !   Our thieves,
at the Abbot's judgement-bar, deny ; claim wager of battle ;
fight, are beaten, and *then* hanged.   'Ketel, the thief,' took
this course ; and it did nothing for him,—merely brought
us, and indeed himself, new trouble !

Every way a most foreign Time.   What difficulty, for
example, has our *Cellerarius* to collect the *repselver*, 'reaping
silver,' or penny, which each householder is by law bound
to pay for cutting down the Convent grain !   Richer people
pretend that it is commuted, that it is this and the other ;
that, in short, they will not pay it.   Our *Cellerarius* gives
up calling on the rich.   In the houses of the poor, our
Cellerarius finding, in like manner, neither penny nor good
promise, snatches, without ceremony, what *vadium* (pledge,
wad) he can come at : a joint-stool, kettle, nay the very
house-door, '*hostium*' ; and old women, thus exposed to the
unfeeling gaze of the public, rush out after him with their
distaffs and the angriest shrieks : '*vetulae exibant cum colis
suis*,' says Jocelin, '*minantes et exprobrantes*.'

What a historical picture, glowing visible, as St. Edmund's
Shrine by night, after Seven long Centuries or so ! *Vetulae
cum colis:* My venerable ancient spinning grandmothers,—
ah, and ye too have to shriek, and rush out with your
distaffs ; and become Female Chartists, and scold all evening
with void doorway;—and in old Saxon, as we in modern,
would fain demand some Five-point Charter, could it be
fallen in with, the Earth being too tyrannous !—Wise Lord
Abbots, hearing of such phenomena, did in time abolish or
commute the reap-penny, and one nuisance was abated. But
the image of those justly offended old women, in their old
wool costumes, with their angry features, and spindles
brandished, lives forever in the historical memory. Thanks
to thee, Jocelin Boswell. Jerusalem was taken by the
Crusaders, and again lost by them ; and Richard Coeur-de-
Lion ' veiled his face ' as he passed in sight of it : but how
many other things went on, the while !

Thus, too, our trouble with the Lakenheath eels is very
great. King Knut, namely, or rather his Queen who also
did herself honour by honouring St. Edmund, decreed by
authentic deed yet extant on parchment, that the Holders
of the Town Fields, once Beodric's, should, for one thing,
go yearly and catch us four thousand eels in the marsh-
pools of Lakenheath. Well, they went, they continued to
go ; but, in later times, got into the way of returning with
a most short account of eels. Not the due six-score apiece ;
no, Here are two-score, Here are twenty, ten,—sometimes,
Here are none at all ; Heaven help us, we *could* catch no
more, they were not there ! What is a distressed *Cellerarius*
to do? We agree that each Holder of so many acres shall
pay one penny yearly, and let go the eels as too slippery.
But alas, neither is this quite effectual : the Fields, in my
time, have got divided among so many hands, there is no
catching of *them* either ; I have known our Cellarer get
seven-and-twenty pence formerly, and now it is much if he
get ten pence farthing (*vix decem denarios et obolum*). And
then their sheep, which they are bound to fold nightly in
our pens, for the manure's sake : and, I fear, do not always
fold : and their *aver-pennies,* and their *avragiums,* and their
fodercorns, and mill-and-market dues ! Thus, in its undeniable but dim manner, does old St. Edmundsbury spin and
till, and laboriously keep its pot boiling, and St. Edmund's

Shrine lighted, under such conditions and averages as it can.

How much is still alive in England; how much has not yet come into life! A Feudal Aristocracy is still alive, in the prime of life; superintending the cultivation of the land, and less consciously the distribution of the produce of the land, the adjustment of the quarrels of the land; judging, soldiering, adjusting; everywhere governing the people,— so that even a Gurth born thrall of Cedric lacks not his due parings of the pigs he tends. Governing;—and, alas, also game-preserving, so that a Robin Hood, a William Scarlet and others have, in these days, put on Lincoln coats, and taken to living, in some universal-suffrage manner, under the greenwood tree!

How silent, on the other hand, lie all Cotton-trades and such like; not a steeple-chimney yet got on end from sea to sea! North of the Humber, a stern Willelmus Conquestor burnt the Country, finding it unruly, into very stern repose. Wild fowl scream in those ancient silences, wild cattle roam in those ancient solitudes; the scanty sulky Norse-bred population all coerced into silence,—feeling that, under these new Norman Governors, their history has probably as good as *ended*. Men and Northumbrian Norse populations know little what has ended, what is but beginning! The Ribble and the Aire roll down, as yet unpolluted by dyers' chemistry; tenanted by merry trouts and piscatory otters; the sunbeam and the vacant wind's-blast alone traversing those moors. Side by side sleep the coal-strata and the iron-strata for so many ages; no Steam-Demon has yet risen smoking into being. Saint Mungo rules in Glasgow; James Watt still slumbering in the deep of Time. *Mancunium*, Manceaster, what we now call Manchester, spins no cotton,— if it be not *wool* 'cottons', clipped from the backs of mountain sheep. The Creek of the Mersey gurgles, twice in the four-and-twenty hours, with eddying brine, clangorous with sea-fowl; and is a *Lither*-Pool, a *lazy* or sullen Pool, no monstrous pitchy City, and Seahaven of the world! The Centuries are big; and the birth-hour is coming, not yet come. *Tempus ferax, tempus edax rerum.*

CHAPTER VI

MONK SAMSON

WITHIN doors, down at the hill-foot, in our Convent here, we are a peculiar people,—hardly conceivable in the Arkwright Corn-Law ages, of mere Spinning-Mills and Joe-Mantons! There is yet no Methodism among us, and we speak much of Secularities : no Methodism ; our Religion is not yet a horrible restless Doubt, still less a far horribler composed Cant ; but a great heaven-high Unquestionability, encompassing, interpenetrating the whole of Life. Imperfect as we may be, we are here, with our litanies, shaven crowns, vows of poverty, to testify incessantly and indisputably to every heart, That this Earthly Life and *its* riches and possessions, and good and evil hap, are not intrinsically a reality at all, but *are* a shadow of realities eternal, infinite ; that this Time-world, as an air-image, fearfully *emblematic*, plays and flickers in the grand still mirror of Eternity; and man's little Life has Duties that are great, that are alone great, and go up to Heaven and down to Hell. This, with our poor litanies, we testify and struggle to testify.

Which, testified or not, remembered by all men, or forgotten by all men, does verily remain the fact, even in Arkwright Joe-Manton ages! But it is incalculable, when litanies have grown obsolete ; when *fodercorns, avragiums,* and all human dues and reciprocities have been fully changed into one great due of *cash payment;* and man's duty to man reduces itself to handing him certain metal coins, or covenanted money-wages, and then shoving him out of doors ; and man's duty to God becomes a cant, a doubt, a dim inanity, a 'pleasure of virtue' or such like ; and the thing a man does infinitely fear (the real *Hell* of a man) is 'that he do not make money and advance himself,'—I say, it is incalculable what a change has introduced itself everywhere into human affairs ! How human affairs shall now circulate everywhere not healthy life-blood in them, but, as it were, a detestable copperas banker's ink ; and all is grown acrid, divisive, threatening dissolution ; and the huge tumultuous Life of Society is galvanic, devil-ridden, too truly possessed by a devil! For, in short, Mammon *is* not a god at all; but a devil, and even a very despicable devil. Follow the Devil faithfully, you are sure enough to *go* to the Devil: whither else can you go?—In such situations, men look back with a kind of mournful recognition even on poor limited Monk-figures, with their poor litanies; and reflect, with Ben Jonson, that soul is indispensable, some degree of soul, even to save you the expense of salt!—

For the rest, it must be owned, we Monks of St. Edmunds-bury are but a limited class of creatures, and seem to have a somewhat dull life of it. Much given to idle gossip; having indeed no other work, when our chanting is over. Listless gossip, for most part, and a mitigated slander; the fruit of idleness, not of spleen. We are dull, insipid men, many of us; easy-minded; whom prayer and digestion of food will avail for a life. We have to receive all strangers in our Convent, and lodge them gratis; such and such sorts go by rule to the Lord Abbot and his special revenues; such and such to us and our poor Cellarer, however straitened. Jews themselves send their wives and little ones hither in war-time, into our *Pitanceria*; where they abide safe, with due *pittances*,—for a consideration. We have the fairest chances for collecting news. Some of us have a turn for reading Books; for meditation, silence; at times we even write Books. Some of us can preach, in English-Saxon, in Norman-French, and even in Monk-Latin; others cannot in any language or jargon, being stupid.

Failing all else, what gossip about one another! This is a perennial resource. How one hooded head applies itself to the ear of another, and whispers—*tacenda*. Willelmus Sacrista, for instance, what does he nightly, over in that Sacristy of his? Frequent bibations, *'frequentes bibationes et quaedam tacenda,'*—eheu! We have *'tempora minutionis'*, stated seasons of blood-letting, when we are all let blood together; and then there is a general free-conference, a sanhedrim of clatter. Notwithstanding our vow of poverty, we can by rule amass to the extent of 'two shillings'; but it is to be given to our necessitous kindred, or in charity. Poor Monks! Thus too a certain Canterbury Monk was in the habit of 'slipping, *clanculo* from his sleeve', five shillings into the hand of his mother, when she came to see him, at the divine offices, every two months. Once, slipping the money clandestinely, just in the act of taking leave, he slipt it not into her hand but on the floor, and another had it; whereupon the poor Monk, coming to know it, looked mere despair for some days; till Lanfranc the noble Archbishop, questioning his secret from him, nobly made the sum *seven* shillings,[1] and said, Never mind!

One Monk of a taciturn nature distinguishes himself among these babbling ones: the name of him Samson; he that answered Jocelin, '*Fili mi*, a burnt child shuns the fire.' They call him 'Norfolk *Barrator*', or litigious person; for indeed, being of grave taciturn ways, he is not universally a favourite; he has been in trouble more than once. The reader is desired to mark this Monk. A personable man of seven-and-forty; stout-made, stands erect as a pillar; with bushy eyebrows, the eyes of him beaming into you in a really strange way; the face massive, grave, with 'a very eminent nose'; his head almost bald, its auburn remnants of hair, and the copious ruddy beard, getting slightly streaked with grey. This is Brother Samson; a man worth looking at.

He is from Norfolk, as the nickname indicates; from Tottington in Norfolk, as we guess; the son of poor parents there. He has told me, Jocelin, for I loved him much, That once in his ninth year he had an alarming dream;—as indeed we are all somewhat given to dreaming here. Little Samson, lying uneasily in his crib at Tottington, dreamed that he saw the Arch Enemy in person, just alighted in front of some grand building, with outspread bat-wings, and stretching forth detestable clawed hands to grip him, little Samson, and fly off with him: whereupon the little dreamer shrieked desperate to St. Edmund for help, shrieked and again shrieked; and St. Edmund, a reverend heavenly figure, did come,—and indeed poor little Samson's mother, awakened by his shrieking, did come; and the Devil and the Dream both fled away fruitless. On the morrow, his mother, pondering such an awful dream, thought it were good to take him over to St. Edmund's own Shrine, and pray with him there. See, said little Samson at sight of the Abbey-Gate; see, mother, this is the building I dreamed of! His

---

[1] Eadmeri Hist. p. 8.

poor mother dedicated him to St. Edmund,—left him there
with prayers and tears : what better could she do ? The
exposition of the dream, Brother Samson used to say, was
this : *Diabolus* with outspread bat-wings shadowed forth the
pleasures of this world, *voluptates hujus saeculi*, which were
about to snatch and fly away with me, had not St. Edmund
flung his arms round me, that is to say, made me a monk
of his. A monk, accordingly, Brother Samson is; and here
to this day where his mother left him. A learned man, of
devout grave nature ; has studied at Paris, has taught in the
Town Schools here, and done much else; can preach in three
languages, and, like Dr. Caius, ' has had losses ' in his time.
A thoughtful, firm-standing man ; much loved by some, not
loved by all ; his clear eyes flashing into you, in an almost
inconvenient way !

Abbot Hugo, as we said, had his own difficulties with him ;
Abbot Hugo had him in prison once, to teach him what
authority was, and how to dread the fire in future. For
Brother Samson, in the time of the Antipopes, had been
sent to Rome on business ; and, returning successful, was
too late,—the business had all misgone in the interim ! As
tours to Rome are still frequent with us English, perhaps
the reader will not grudge to look at the method of travelling
thither in those remote ages. We happily have, in small
compass, a personal narrative of it. Through the clear eyes
and memory of Brother Samson, one peeps direct into the
very bosom of that Twelfth Century, and finds it rather
curious. The actual *Papa*, Father, or universal President
of Christendom, as yet not grown chimerical, sat there ; think
of that only ! Brother Samson went to Rome as to the real
Light-fountain of this lower world ; we now— !—But let us
hear Brother Samson, as to his mode of travelling :

' You know what trouble I had for that Church of Woolpit ; how I was dispatched to Rome in the time of the
Schism between Pope Alexander and Octavian ; and passed
through Italy at that season, when all clergy carrying letters
for our Lord Pope Alexander were laid hold of, and some
were clapt in prison, some hanged ; and some, with nose and
lips cut off, were sent forward to our Lord the Pope, for the
disgrace and confusion of him (*in dedecus et confusionem ejus*).
I, however, pretended to be Scotch, and putting on the garb
of a Scotchman, and taking the gesture of one, walked along ;

and when anybody mocked at me, I would brandish my
staff in the manner of that weapon they call *gaveloc*,[1]
uttering comminatory words after the way of the Scotch. To
those that met and questioned me who I was, I made no
answer but: *Ride, ride Rome; turne Cantwereberei*.[2] Thus
did I, to conceal myself and my errand, and get safer to
Rome under the guise of a Scotchman.

 ' Having at last obtained a Letter from our Lord the Pope
according to my wishes, I turned homewards again. I had
to pass through a certain strong town on my road; and lo,
the soldiers thereof surrounded me, seizing me, and saying:
"This vagabond (*iste solivagus*), who pretends to be Scotch, is
either a spy, or has Letters from the false Pope Alexander."
And whilst they examined every stitch and rag of me, my
leggings (*caligas*), breeches, and even the old shoes that
I carried over my shoulder in the way of the Scotch,—I put
my hand into the leather scrip I wore, wherein our Lord the
Pope's Letter lay, close by a little jug (*ciffus*) I had for
drinking out of; and the Lord God so pleasing, and
St. Edmund, I got out both the Letter and the jug together;
in such a way that, extending my arm aloft, I held the Letter
hidden between jug and hand : they saw the jug, but the
Letter they saw not. And thus I escaped out of their hands
in the name of the Lord. Whatever money I had they took
from me ; wherefore I had to beg from door to door, without
any payment (*sine omni expensa*) till I came to England
again. But hearing that the Woolpit Church was already
given to Geoffry Ridell, my soul was struck with sorrow
because I had laboured in vain. Coming home, therefore,
I sat me down secretly under the Shrine of St. Edmund,
fearing lest our Lord Abbot should seize and imprison me,
though I had done no mischief ; nor was there a monk who
durst speak to me, nor a laic who durst bring me food except
by stealth.' [3]

Such resting and welcoming found Brother Samson, with
his worn soles, and strong heart ! He sits silent, revolving

---

 [1] Javelin, missile pike. *Gaveloc* is still the Scotch name for *crowbar*.
 [2] Does this mean, "Rome forever ; Canterbury *not* " (which claims
an unjust Supremacy over us) ! Mr. Rokewood is silent. Dryasdust
would perhaps explain it,—in the course of a week or two of talking;
did one dare to question him !
 [3] Jocelini Chronica, p. 36.

many thoughts, at the foot of St. Edmund's Shrine. In the wide Earth, if it be not Saint Edmund, what friend or refuge has he? Our Lord Abbot, hearing of him, sent the proper officer to lead him down to prison, and clap 'foot-gyves on him' there. Another poor official furtively brought him a cup of wine; bade him 'be comforted in the Lord'. Samson utters no complaint; obeys in silence. 'Our Lord Abbot, taking counsel of it, banished me to Acre, and there I had to stay long.'

Our Lord Abbot next tried Samson with promotions; made him Subsacristan, made him Librarian, which he liked best of all, being passionately fond of Books: Samson, with many thoughts in him, again obeyed in silence; discharged his offices to perfection, but never thanked our Lord Abbot, —seemed rather as if looking into him, with those clear eyes of his. Whereupon Abbot Hugo said, *Se nunquam vidisse*, He had never seen such a man; whom no severity would break to complain, and no kindness soften into smiles or thanks: —a questionable kind of man!

In this way, not without troubles, but still in an erect, clear-standing manner, has Brother Samson reached his forty-seventh year; and his ruddy beard is getting slightly grizzled. He is endeavouring, in these days, to have various broken things thatched in; nay perhaps to have the Choir itself completed, for he can bear nothing ruinous. He has gathered 'heaps of lime and sand'; has masons, slaters working, he and *Warinus monachus noster*, who are joint keepers of the Shrine; paying out the money duly,—furnished by charitable burghers of St. Edmundsbury, they say. Charitable burghers of St. Edmundsbury? To me Jocelin it seems rather, Samson and Warinus, whom he leads, have privily hoarded the oblations at the Shrine itself, in these late years of indolent dilapidation, while Abbot Hugo sat wrapped inaccessible; and are struggling, in this prudent way, to have the rain kept out![1]—Under what conditions, sometimes, has Wisdom to struggle with Folly; get Folly persuaded to so much as thatch out the rain from itself! For, indeed, if the Infant govern the Nurse, what dexterous practice on the Nurse's part will not be necessary!

[1] Jocelini Chronica, p. 7.

It is a new regret to us that, in these circumstances, our Lord the King's Custodiars, interfering, prohibited all building or thatching from whatever source; and no Choir shall be completed, and Rain and Time, for the present, shall have their way. Willelmus Sacrista, he of 'the frequent bibations and some things not to be spoken of;' he, with his red nose, I am of opinion, had made complaint to the Custodiars; wishing to do Samson an ill turn :—Samson his *Sub*-sacristan, with those clear eyes, could not be a prime favourite of his! Samson again obeys in silence.

CHAPTER VII

THE CANVASSING

Now, however, come great news to St. Edmundsbury: That there is to be an Abbot elected; that our interlunar obscuration is to cease; St. Edmund's Convent no more to be a doleful widow, but joyous and once again a bride! Often in our widowed state had we prayed to the Lord and St. Edmund, singing weekly a matter of 'one-and-twenty penitential Psalms, on our knees in the Choir', that a fit Pastor might be vouchsafed us. And, says Jocelin, had some known what Abbot we were to get, they had not been so devout, I believe!—Bozzy Jocelin opens to mankind the floodgates of authentic Convent gossip; we listen, as in a Dionysius' Ear, to the inanest hubbub, like the voices at Virgil's Horn-Gate of Dreams. Even gossip, seven centuries off, has significance. List, list, how like men are to one another in all centuries:

'*Dixit quidam de quodam*, A certain person said of a certain person, "He, that *Frater*, is a good monk, *probabilis persona;* knows much of the order and customs of the church; and though not so perfect a philosopher as some others, would make a very good Abbot. Old Abbot Ording, still famed among us, knew little of letters. Besides, as we read in Fables, it is better to choose a log for king, than a serpent, never so wise, that will venomously hiss and bite his subjects."

—"Impossible!" answered the other: "How can such a man make a sermon in the Chapter, or to the people on festival days, when he is without letters? How can he have the skill to bind and to loose, he who does not understand the Scriptures? How—?"'

And then 'another said of another, *alius de alio*, "That *Frater* is a *homo literatus*, eloquent, sagacious; vigorous in discipline; loves the Convent much, has suffered much for its sake." To which a third party answers, "From all your great clerks good Lord deliver us! From Norfolk barrators, and surly persons, That it would please thee to preserve us, We beseech thee to hear us, good Lord!"' Then another *quidam* said of another *quodam*, "That *Frater* is a good manager (*husebondus*); "but was swiftly answered, "God forbid that a man who can neither read nor chant, nor celebrate the divine offices, an unjust person withal, and grinder of the faces of the poor, should ever be Abbot!"' One man, it appears, is nice in his victuals. Another is indeed wise; but apt to slight inferiors; hardly at the pains to answer, if they argue with him too foolishly. And so each *aliquis* concerning his *aliquo*,—through whole pages of electioneering babble. 'For,' says Jocelin, 'So many men, as many minds.' Our Monks 'at time of blood-letting, *tempore minutionis*', holding their sanhedrim of babble, would talk in this manner: Brother Samson, I remarked, never said anything; sat silent, sometimes smiling; but he took good note of what others said, and would bring it up, on occasion, twenty years after. As for me Jocelin, I was of opinion that 'some skill in Dialectics, to distinguish true from false', would be good in an Abbot. I spake, as a rash Novice in those days, some conscientious words of a certain benefactor of mine; 'and behold, one of those sons of Belial' ran and reported them to him, so that he never after looked at me with the same face again! Poor Bozzy!—

Such is the buzz and frothy simmering ferment of the general mind and no-mind; struggling to 'make itself up', as the phrase is, or ascertain what *it* does really want: no easy matter, in most cases. St. Edmundsbury, in that Candlemas season of the year 1182, is a busily fermenting place. The very clothmakers sit meditative at their looms; asking, Who shall be Abbot? The *sochemanni* speak of it, driving their ox-teams afield; the old women with their spindles: and none yet knows what the days will bring forth.

The Prior, however, as our interim chief, must proceed to work ; get ready 'Twelve Monks', and set off with them to his Majesty at Waltham, there shall the election be made. An election, whether managed directly by ballot-box on public hustings, or indirectly by force of public opinion, or were it even by open alehouses, landlords' coercion, popular club-law, or whatever electoral methods, is always an interesting phenomenon. A mountain tumbling in great travail, throwing up dustclouds and absurd noises, is visibly there ; uncertain yet what mouse or monster it will give birth to.

Besides it is a most important social act ; nay, at bottom, the one important social act. Given the men a People choose, the People itself, in its exact worth and worthlessness, is given. A heroic people chooses heroes, and is happy ; a valet or flunkey people chooses sham-heroes, what are called quacks, thinking them heroes, and is not happy. The grand summary of a man's spiritual condition, what brings out all his herohood and insight, or all his flunkeyhood and horn-eyed dimness, is this question put to him, What man dost thou honour ? Which is thy ideal of a man ; or nearest that ? So too of a People : for a People too, every People, *speaks* its choice,—were it only by silently obeying, and not revolting,—in the course of a century or so. Nor are electoral methods, Reform Bills and such like, unimportant. A People's electoral methods are, in the long-run, the express image of its electoral *talent;* tending and gravitating perpetually, irresistibly, to a conformity with that: and are, at all stages, very significant of the People. Judicious readers, of these times, are not disinclined to see how Monks elect their Abbot in the Twelfth Century : how the St. Edmundsbury mountain manages its midwifery ; and what mouse or man the outcome is.

CHAPTER VIII

THE ELECTION

ACCORDINGLY our Prior assembles us in Chapter; and, we adjuring him before God to do justly, nominates, not by our selection, yet with our assent, Twelve Monks, moderately satisfactory. Of whom are Hugo Third-Prior, Brother Dennis a venerable man, Walter the *Medicus*, Samson *Subsacrista*, and other esteemed characters,—though Willelmus *Sacrista*, of the red nose, too is one. These shall proceed straightway to Waltham; and there elect the Abbot as they may and can. Monks are sworn to obedience; must not speak too loud, under penalty of foot-gyves, limbo, and bread and water: yet monks too would know what it is they are obeying. The St. Edmundsbury Community has no hustings, ballot-box, indeed no open voting: yet by various vague manipulations, pulse-feelings, we struggle to ascertain what its virtual aim is, and succeed better or worse.

This question, however, rises; alas, a quite preliminary question: Will the *Dominus Rex* allow us to choose freely? It is to be hoped! Well, if so, we agree to choose one of our own Convent. If not, if the *Dominus Rex* will force a stranger on us, we decide on demurring, the Prior and his Twelve shall demur: we can appeal, plead, remonstrate; appeal even to the Pope, but trust it will not be necessary. Then there is this other question, raised by Brother Samson: What if the Thirteen should not themselves be able to agree? Brother Samson *Subsacrista*, one remarks, is ready oftenest with some question, some suggestion, that has wisdom in it. Though a servant of servants, and saying little, his words all tell, having sense in them; it seems by his light mainly that we steer ourselves in this great dimness.

What if the Thirteen should not themselves be able to agree? Speak, Samson, and advise.—Could not, hints Samson, Six of our venerablest elders be chosen by us, a kind of electoral committee, here and now: of these, 'with their hand on the Gospels, with their eye on the *Sacrosancta*,' we take oath that they will do faithfully; let these, in secret and as before God, agree on Three whom they reckon fittest ; write their names in a Paper, and deliver the same sealed, forthwith, to the Thirteen : one of those Three the Thirteen shall fix on, if permitted. If not permitted, that is to say, if the *Dominus Rex* force us to demur,—the Paper shall be brought back unopened, and publicly burned, that no man's secret bring him into trouble.

So Samson advises, so we act ; wisely, in this and in other crises of the business. Our electoral committee, its eye on the *Sacrosancta*, is soon named, soon sworn ; and we striking up the Fifth Psalm, ' *Verba mea,*

> Give ear unto my words, O Lord,
> My meditation weigh,'

march out chanting, and leave the Six to their work in the Chapter here. Their work, before long, they announce as finished : they, with their eye on the Sacrosancta, imprecating the Lord to weigh and witness their meditation, have fixed on Three Names, and written them in this Sealed Paper. Let Samson Subsacrista, general servant of the party, take charge of it. On the morrow morning, our Prior and his Twelve will be ready to get under way.

This then is the ballot-box and electoral winnowing-machine they have at St. Edmundsbury : a mind fixed on the Thrice Holy, an appeal to God on high to witness their meditation : by far the best, and indeed the only good electoral winnowing-machine,—if men have souls in them. Totally worthless, it is true, and even hideous and poisonous, if men have no souls. But without soul, alas what winnowing-machine in human elections, can be of avail ? We cannot get along without soul ; we stick fast, the mournfullest spectacle ; and salt itself will not save us !

On the morrow morning, accordingly, our Thirteen set forth ; or rather our Prior and Eleven ; for Samson, as general servant of the party, has to linger, settling many things. At length he too gets upon the road ; and, ' carrying the sealed Paper in a leather pouch hung round his neck ; and *froccum bajulans in ulnis* ' (thanks to thee Bozzy Jocelin), ' his frock-skirts looped over his elbow,' showing substantial stern-works, tramps stoutly along. Away across the Heath, not yet of Newmarket and horse-jockeying ; across your

Fleam-dike and Devil's-dike, no longer useful as a Mercian East-Anglian boundary or bulwark : continually towards Waltham, and the Bishop of Winchester's House there, for his Majesty is in that. Brother Samson, as purse-bearer, has the reckoning always, when there is one, to pay ; ' delays are numerous,' progress none of the swiftest.

But, in the solitude of the Convent, Destiny thus big and in her birthtime, what gossiping, what babbling, what dreaming of dreams ! The secret of the Three our electoral elders alone know : some Abbot we shall have to govern us ; but which Abbot, O which ! One Monk discerns in a vision of the night-watches, that we shall get an Abbot of our own body, without needing to demur : a prophet appeared to him clad all in white, and said, ' Ye shall have one of yours, and he will rage among you like a wolf, *saeviet ut lupus.*' Verily ! —then which of ours ? Another Monk now dreams : he has seen clearly which ; a certain Figure taller by head and shoulders than the other two, dressed in alb and *pallium*, and with the attitude of one about to fight ;—which tall Figure a wise Editor would rather not name at this stage of the business ! Enough that the vision is true : that St. Edmund himself, pale and awful, seemed to rise from his Shrine, with naked feet, and say audibly, ' He, *ille*, shall veil my feet ' ; which part of the vision also proves true. Such guessing, visioning, dim perscrutation of the momentous future : the very clothmakers, old women, all townsfolk speak of it, ' and more than once it is reported in St. Edmundsbury, This one is elected ; and then, This one and That other.' Who knows ?

But now, sure enough, at Waltham ' on the Second Sunday of Quadragesima ', which Dryasdust declares to mean the 22d day of February, year 1182, Thirteen St. Edmundsbury Monks are, at last, seen processioning towards the Winchester Manorhouse ; and in some high Presence-chamber, and Hall of State, get access to Henry II in all his glory. What a Hall,—not imaginary in the least, but entirely real and indisputable, though so extremely dim to us ; sunk in the deep distances of Night ! The Winchester Manorhouse has fled bodily, like a Dream of the old Night ; not Dryasdust himself can show a wreck of it. House and people, royal and episcopal, lords and varlets, where are they ? Why *there*, I say, Seven Centuries off ; sunk *so* far in the Night, there they *are* ; peep through the blankets of the old Night, and thou will see ! King Henry himself is visibly there, a vivid, noble-looking man, with grizzled beard, in glittering uncertain costume ; with earls round him, and bishops and dignitaries, in the like. The Hall is large, and has for one thing an altar near it,—chapel and altar adjoining it ; but what gilt seats, carved tables, carpeting of rush-cloth, what arras-hangings, and huge fire of logs :—alas, it has Human Life in it ; and is not that the grand miracle, in what hangings or costume soever ?—

The *Dominus Rex*, benignantly receiving our Thirteen with their obeisance, and graciously declaring that he will strive to act for God's honour, and the Church's good, commands, 'by the Bishop of Winchester and Geoffrey the Chancellor,'—*Galfridus Cancellarius*, Henry's and the Fair Rosamond's authentic Son present here !—commands, 'That they, the said Thirteen, do now withdraw, and fix upon Three from their own Monastery.' A work soon done ; the Three hanging ready round Samson's neck, in that leather pouch of his. Breaking the seal, we find the names,—what think *ye* of it, ye higher dignitaries, thou indolent Prior, thou Willelmus *Sacrista* with the red bottle-nose ?—the names, in this order: of Samson *Subsacrista*, of Roger the distressed Cellarer, of Hugo *Tertius-Prior*.

The higher dignitaries, all omitted here, 'flush suddenly red in the face' ; but have nothing to say. One curious fact and question certainly is, How Hugo Third-Prior, who was of the electoral committee, came to nominate *himself* as one of the Three ? A curious fact, which Hugo Third-Prior has never yet entirely explained, that I know of !—However, we return, and report to the King our Three names ; merely altering the order ; putting Samson last, as lowest of all. The King, at recitation of our Three, asks us : 'Who are they ? Were they born in my domain ? Totally unknown to me ! You must nominate three others.' Whereupon Willelmus Sacrista says, 'Our Prior must be named, *quia caput nostrum est*, being already our head.' And the Prior responds, ' Willelmus Sacrista is a fit man, *bonus vir est,*'— for all his red nose. Tickle me, Toby, and I'll tickle thee ! Venerable Dennis too is named ; none in his conscience can say nay. There are now Six on our List. 'Well', said the

King, 'they have done it swiftly, they! *Deus est cum eis.*'
The Monks withdraw again ; and Majesty revolves, for
a little, with his *Pares* and *Episcopi*, Lords or ' *Law-wards* '
and Soul-Overseers, the thoughts of the royal breast.   The
Monks wait silent in an outer room.

In short while, they are next ordered, To add yet another
three ; but not from their own Convent ; from other Con-
vents, 'for the honour of my kingdom.'   Here,—what is to
be done here?   We will demur, if need be!   We do name
three, however, for the nonce: the Prior of St. Faith's,
a good Monk of St. Neot's, a good Monk of St. Alban's ;
good men all ; all made abbots and dignitaries since, at this
hour.   There are now Nine upon our List.   What the
thoughts of the Dominus Rex may be farther ?   The Dominus
Rex, thanking graciously, sends out word that we shall now
strike off three.   The three strangers are instantly struck
off.   Willelmus Sacrista adds, that he will of his own
accord decline,—a touch of grace and respect for the *Sacrosancta*, even in Willelmus !   The King then orders us to
strike off a couple more ; then yet one more: Hugo Third-
Prior goes, and Roger *Cellerarius*, and venerable Monk
Dennis ;—and now there remain on our List two only,
Samson Subsacrista and the Prior.

Which of these two?   It were hard to say,—by Monks
who may get themselves foot-gyved and thrown into limbo,
for speaking!   We humbly request that the Bishop of
Winchester and Geoffrey the Chancellor may again enter,
and help us to decide.   ' Which do you want?' asks the
Bishop.   Venerable Dennis made a speech, 'commending
the persons of the Prior and Samson ; but always in the
corner of his discourse, *in angulo sui sermonis*, brought
Samson in.'   'I see!' said the Bishop: 'We are to understand that your Prior is somewhat remiss ; that you want
to have him you call Samson for Abbot.'   'Either of them
is good,' said venerable Dennis, almost trembling ; ' but we
would have the better, if it pleased God '.   'Which of the
two *do* you want?' inquires the Bishop pointedly.   ' Samson !'
answered Dennis ; 'Samson !' echoed all of the rest that durst
speak or echo anything: and Samson is reported to the King
accordingly.   His Majesty, advising of it for a moment,
orders that Samson be brought in with the other Twelve.

The King's Majesty, looking at us somewhat sternly, then

says: 'You present to me Samson; I do not know him: had it been your Prior, whom I do know, I should have accepted him: however, I will now do as you wish. But have a care of yourselves. By the true eyes of God, *per veros oculos Dei*, if you manage badly, I will be upon you!' Samson, therefore, steps forward, kisses the King's feet; but swiftly rises erect again, swiftly turns towards the altar, uplifting with the other Twelve, in clear tenor-note, the Fifty-first Psalm, '*Miserere mei Deus*,

> After thy loving-kindness, Lord,
> Have mercy upon *me*;'

with firm voice, firm step and head, no change in his countenance whatever. 'By God's eyes,' said the King, 'that one, I think, will govern the Abbey well.' By the same oath (charged to your Majesty's account), I too am precisely of that opinion! It is some while since I fell in with a likelier man anywhere than this new Abbot Samson. Long life to him, and may the Lord *have* mercy on him as Abbot!

Thus, then, have the St. Edmundsbury Monks, without express ballot-box or other good winnowing-machine, contrived to accomplish the most important social feat a body of men can do, to winnow out the man that is to govern them: and truly one sees not that, by any winnowing-machine whatever, they could have done it better. O ye kind Heavens, there is in every Nation and Community *a fittest*, a wisest, bravest, best; whom could we find and make King over us, all were in very truth well;—the best that God and Nature had permitted *us* to make it! By what art discover him? Will the Heavens in their pity teach us no art; for our need of him is great!

Ballot-boxes, Reform Bills, winnowing-machines: all these are good, or are not so good;—alas, brethren, how *can* these, I say, be other than inadequate, be other than failures, melancholy to behold? Dim all souls of men to the divine, the high and awful meaning of Human Worth and Truth, we shall never, by all the machinery in Birmingham, discover the True and Worthy. It is written, 'if we are ourselves valets, there shall exist no hero for us; we shall not know the hero when we see him';—we shall take the quack for a hero; and cry, audibly through all ballot-boxes and machinery whatsoever, Thou art he; be thou King over us! What boots it? Seek only deceitful Speciosity, money with gilt carriages, 'fame' with newspaper-paragraphs, whatever name it bear, you will find only deceitful Speciosity; godlike Reality will be forever far from you. The Quack shall be legitimate inevitable King of you; no earthly machinery able to exclude the Quack. Ye shall be born thralls of the Quack, and suffer under him, till your hearts are near broken, and no French Revolution or Manchester Insurrection, or partial or universal volcanic combustions and explosions, never so many, can do more than 'change the *figure* of your Quack'; the essence of him remaining, for a time and times.—'How long, O Prophet?' say some, with a rather melancholy sneer. Alas, ye *un*prophetic, ever till this come about: Till deep misery, if nothing softer will, have driven you out of your Speciosities *into* your Sincerities; and you find that there either is a Godlike in the world, or else ye are an unintelligible madness; that there is a God, as well as a Mammon and a Devil, and a Genius of Luxuries and canting Dilettantisms and Vain Shows! How long that will be, compute for yourselves. My unhappy brothers!—

CHAPTER IX

ABBOT SAMSON

So then the bells of St. Edmundsbury clang out one and all, and in church and chapel the organs go: Convent and Town, and all the west side of Suffolk, are in gala; knights, viscounts, weavers, spinners, the entire population, male and female, young and old, the very sockmen with their chubby infants,—out to have a holiday, and see the Lord Abbot arrive! And there is 'stripping barefoot' of the Lord Abbot at the Gate, and solemn leading of him in to the High Altar and Shrine; with sudden 'silence of all the bells and organs', as we kneel in deep prayer there; and again with outburst of all the bells and organs, and loud *Te*

Deum from the general human windpipe ; and speeches by the leading viscount, and giving of the kiss of brotherhood ; the whole wound up with popular games, and dinner within doors of more than a thousand strong, *plus quam mille comedentibus in gaudio magno.*

In such manner is the selfsame Samson once again returning to us, welcomed on *this* occasion. He that went away with his frock-skirts looped over his arm, comes back riding high ; suddenly made one of the dignitaries of this world. Reflective readers will admit that here was a trial for a man. Yesterday a poor mendicant, allowed to possess not above two shillings of money, and without authority to bid a dog run for him, this man today finds himself a *Dominus Abbas,* mitred Peer of Parliament, Lord of manorhouses, farms, manors, and wide lands ; a man with ' Fifty Knights under him ', and dependent, swiftly obedient multitudes of men. It is a change greater than Napoleon's ; so sudden withal. As if one of the Chandos day-drudges had, on awakening some morning, found that *he* overnight was become Duke ! Let Samson with his clear-beaming eyes see into that, and discern it if he can. We shall now get the measure of him by a new scale of inches, considerably more rigorous than the former was. For if a noble soul is rendered tenfold beautifuller by victory and prosperity, springing now radiant as into his own due element and sun-throne ; an ignoble one is rendered tenfold and hundredfold uglier, pitifuller. Whatsoever vices, whatsoever weaknesses were in the man, the parvenu will show us them enlarged, as in the solar microscope, into frightful distortion. Nay, how many mere seminal principles of vice, hitherto all wholesomely kept latent, may we now see unfolded, as in the solar hothouse, into growth, into huge universally-conspicuous luxuriance and development !

But is not this, at any rate, a singular aspect of what political and social capabilities, nay let us say what depth and opulence of true social vitality, lay in those old barbarous ages, That the fit Governor could be met with under such disguises, could be recognized and laid hold of under such ? Here he is discovered with a maximum of two shillings in his pocket, and a leather scrip round his neck ; trudging along the highway, his frock-skirts looped over his arm.

They think this is he nevertheless, the true Governor; and he proves to be so. Brethren, have we no need of discovering true Governors, but will sham ones forever do for us? These were absurd superstitious blockheads of Monks; and we are enlightened Tenpound Franchisers, without taxes on knowledge! Where, I say, are our superior, are our similar or at all comparable discoveries? We also have eyes, or ought to have; we have hustings, telescopes; we have lights, link-lights and rush-lights of an enlightened free Press, burning and dancing everywhere, as in a universal torch-dance; singeing your whiskers as you traverse the public thoroughfares in town and country. Great souls, true Governors, go about under all manner of disguises now as then. Such telescopes, such enlightenment,—and such discovery! How comes it, I say; how comes it? Is it not lamentable; is it not even, in some sense, amazing?

Alas, the defect, as we must often urge and again urge, is less a defect of telescopes than of some eyesight. Those superstitious blockheads of the Twelfth Century had no telescopes, but they had still an eye; not ballot-boxes; only reverence for Worth, abhorrence of Unworth. It is the way with all barbarians. Thus Mr. Sale informs me, the old Arab Tribes would gather in liveliest *gaudeamus*, and sing, and kindle bonfires, and wreathe crowns of honour, and solemnly thank the gods that, in their Tribe too, a Poet had shown himself. As indeed they well might; for what usefuller, I say not nobler and heavenlier thing could the gods, doing their very kindest, send to any Tribe or Nation, in any time or circumstances? I declare to thee, my afflicted quack-ridden brother, in spite of thy astonishment, it is very lamentable! We English find a Poet, as brave a man as has been made for a hundred years or so anywhere under the Sun; and do we kindle bonfires, or thank the gods? Not at all. We, taking due counsel of it, set the man to gauge ale-barrels in the Burgh of Dumfries; and pique ourselves on our 'patronage of genius'.

Genius, Poet: do we know what these words mean? An inspired Soul once more vouchsafed us, direct from Nature's own great fire-heart, to see the Truth, and speak it, and do it; Nature's own sacred voice heard once more athwart the dreary boundless element of hearsaying and canting, of twaddle and poltroonery, in which the bewildered Earth,

nigh perishing, has *lost its way.* Hear once more, ye
bewildered benighted mortals ; listen once again to a voice
from the inner Light-sea and Flame-sea, Nature's and Truth's
own heart ; know the Fact of your Existence what it is, put
away the Cant of it which it is *not;* and knowing, do, and
let it be well with you !—

George the Third is Defender of something we call 'the
Faith' in those years ; George the Third is head charioteer
of the Destinies of England, to guide them through the gulf
of French Revolutions, American Independences ; and Robert
Burns is Gauger of ale in Dumfries. It is an Iliad in a nut-
shell. The physiognomy of a world now verging towards
dissolution, reduced now to spasms and death-throes, lies
pictured in that one fact,—which astonishes nobody, except
at me for being astonished at it. The fruit of long ages of
confirmed Valethood, entirely confirmed as into a Law of
Nature ; cloth-worship and quack-worship : entirely *confirmed*
Valethood,—which will have to *un*-confirm itself again ; God
knows, with difficulty enough !—

Abbot Samson had found a Convent all in dilapidation ;
rain beating through it, material rain and metaphorical, from
all quarters of the compass. Willelmus Sacrista sits drinking
nightly, and doing mere *tacenda.* Our larders are reduced
to leanness, Jew harpies and unclean creatures our pur-
veyors ; in our basket is no bread. Old women with their
distaffs rush out on a distressed Cellarer in shrill Chartism.
'You cannot stir abroad but Jews and Christians pounce
upon you with unsettled bonds' ; debts boundless seemingly
as the National Debt of England. For four years our new
Lord Abbot never went abroad but Jew creditors and
Christian, and all manner of creditors, were about him ;
driving him to very despair. Our Prior is remiss ; our
Cellarers, officials are remiss, our monks are remiss : what
man is not remiss ? Front this, Samson, thou alone art there
to front it ; it is thy task to front and fight this, and to die
or kill it. May the Lord have mercy on thee !

To our antiquarian interest in poor Jocelin and his Convent, where the whole aspect of existence, the whole dialect,
of thought, of speech, of activity, is so obsolete, strange,
long-vanished, there now superadds itself a mild glow of
human interest for Abbot Samson ; a real pleasure, as at

sight of man's work, especially of governing, which is man's highest work, done *well*. Abbot Samson had no experience in governing; had served no apprenticeship to the trade of governing,—alas, only the hardest apprenticeship to that of obeying. He had never in any court given *vadium* or *plegium*, says Jocelin; hardly ever seen a court, when he was set to preside in one. But it is astonishing, continues Jocelin, how soon he learned the ways of business; and, in all sort of affairs, became expert beyond others. Of the many persons offering him their service, 'he retained one Knight skilled in taking *vadia* and *plegia*'; and within the year was himself well skilled. Nay, by and by, the Pope appoints him Justiciary in certain causes; the King one of his new Circuit Judges: official Osbert is heard saying, 'That Abbot is one of your shrewd ones, *disputator est*; if he go on as he begins, he will cut out every lawyer of us!'[1]

Why not? What is to hinder this Samson from governing? There is in him what far transcends all apprenticeships; in the man himself there exists a model of governing, something to govern by! There exists in him a heart-abhorrence of whatever is incoherent, pusillanimous, unveracious,—that is to say, chaotic, *un*governed; of the Devil, not of God. A man of this kind cannot help governing! He has the living ideal of a governor in him; and the incessant necessity of struggling to unfold the same out of him. Not the Devil or Chaos, for any wages, will he serve; no, this man is the born servant of Another than them. Alas, how little avail all apprenticeships, when there is in your governor himself what we may well call *nothing* to govern by: nothing;— a general grey twilight, looming with shapes of expediencies, parliamentary traditions, division-lists, election-funds, lead-ing-articles; this, with what of vulpine alertness and adroit-ness soever, is not much!

But indeed what say we, apprenticeship? Had not this Samson served, in his way, a right good apprenticeship to governing; namely, the harshest slave-apprenticeship to obeying! Walk this world with no friend in it but God and St. Edmund, you will either fall into a ditch, or learn a good many things. To learn obeying is the fundamental art of governing. How much would many a Serene High-

---

[1] Jocelini Chronica, p. 25

ness have learned, had he travelled through the world with
water-jug and empty wallet, *sine omni expensa ;* and, at his
victorious return, sat down not to newspaper-paragraphs and
city-illuminations, but at the foot of St. Edmund's Shrine to
shackles and bread and water ! He that cannot be servant
of many, will never be master, true guide and deliverer of
many ;—that is the meaning of true mastership. Had not
the Monk-life extraordinary 'political capabilities' in it ; if
not imitable by us, yet enviable ? Heavens, had a Duke of
Logwood, now rolling sumptuously to his place in the
Collective Wisdom, but himself happened to plough daily,
at one time, on seven-and-sixpence a week, with no out-door
relief,—what a light, unquenchable by logic and statistic
and arithmetic, would it have thrown on several things
for him !

In all cases, therefore, we will agree with the judicious
Mrs. Glass : 'First catch your hare !' First get your man ;
all is got : he can learn to do all things, from making boots,
to decreeing judgements, governing communities ; and will
do them like a man. Catch your no-man,—alas, have you
not caught the terriblest Tartar in the world ! Perhaps all
the terribler, the quieter and gentler he looks. For the
mischief that one blockhead, that every blockhead does, in
a world so feracious, teeming with endless results as ours, no
ciphering will sum up. The quack bootmaker is considerable ; as corn-cutters can testify, and desperate men reduced
to buckskin and list-shoes. But the quack priest, quack
high-priest, the quack king ! Why do not all just citizens
rush, half-frantic, to stop him, as they would a conflagration ?
Surely a just citizen *is* admonished by God and his own
Soul, by all silent and articulate voices of this Universe, to
do what in *him* lies towards relief of this poor blockhead-
quack, and of a world that groans under him. Run swiftly ;
relieve him,—were it even by extinguishing him ! For all
things have grown so old, tinder-dry, combustible ; and he is
more ruinous than conflagration. Sweep him *down*, at least ;
keep him strictly within the hearth : he will then cease to
be conflagration ; he will then become useful, more or less,
as culinary fire. Fire is the best of servants ; but what
a master ! This poor blockhead too is born for uses : why,
elevating him to mastership, will you make a conflagration,
a parish-curse or world-curse of him ?

CHAPTER X

GOVERNMENT

How Abbot Samson, giving his new subjects seriatim the kiss of fatherhood in the St. Edmundsbury chapter-house, proceeded with cautious energy to set about reforming their disjointed distracted way of life ; how he managed with his Fifty rough *Milites* (Feudal Knights), with his lazy Farmers, remiss refractory Monks, with Pope's Legates, Viscounts, Bishops, Kings ; how on all sides he laid about him like a man, and putting consequence on premiss, and everywhere the saddle on the right horse, struggled incessantly to educe organic method out of lazily fermenting wreck,—the careful reader will discern, not without true interest, in these pages of Jocelin Boswell. In most antiquarian quaint costume, not of garments alone, but of thought, word, action, outlook and position, the substantial figure of a man with eminent nose, bushy brows and clear-flashing eyes, his russet beard growing daily greyer, is visible, engaged in true governing of men. It is beautiful how the chrysalis governing-soul, shaking off its dusty slough and prison, starts forth winged, a true royal soul ! Our new Abbot has a right honest unconscious feeling, without insolence as without fear or flutter, of what he is and what others are. A courage to quell the proudest, an honest pity to encourage the humblest. Withal there is a noble reticence in this Lord Abbot : much vain unreason he hears ; lays up without response. He is not there to expect reason and nobleness of others ; he is there to give them of his own reason and nobleness. Is he not their servant, as we said, who can suffer from them, and for them ; bear the burden their poor spindle-limbs totter and stagger under ; and in virtue *thereof* govern them, lead them out of weakness into strength, out of defeat into victory !

One of the first Herculean Labours Abbot Samson undertook, or the very first, was to institute a strenuous review and radical reform of his economics. It is the first labour of every governing man, from *Paterfamilias* to *Dominus Rex.*

To get the rain thatched out from you is the preliminary of whatever further, in the way of speculation or of action, you may mean to do. Old Abbot Hugo's budget, as we saw, had become empty, filled with deficit and wind. To see his account-books clear, be delivered from those ravening flights of Jew and Christian creditors, pouncing on him like obscene harpies wherever he showed face, was a necessity for Abbot Samson.

On the morrow after his instalment, he brings in a load of money-bonds, all duly stamped, sealed with this or the other Convent Seal: frightful, unmanageable, a bottomless confusion of Convent finance. There they are;—but there at least they all are; all that shall be of them. Our Lord Abbot demands that all the official seals in use among us be now produced and delivered to him. Three-and-thirty seals turn up; are straightway broken, and shall seal no more: the Abbot only, and those duly authorized by him shall seal any bond. There are but two ways of paying debt: increase of industry in raising income, increase of thrift in laying it out. With iron energy, in slow but steady undeviating perseverance, Abbot Samson sets to work in both directions. His troubles are manifold: cunning *milites*, unjust bailiffs, lazy sockmen, he an inexperienced Abbot; relaxed lazy monks, not disinclined to mutiny in mass: but continued vigilance, rigorous method, what we call the 'eye of the master', work wonders. The clear-beaming eyesight of Abbot Samson, steadfast, severe, all-penetrating,—it is like *Fiat lux* in that inorganic waste whirl-pool; penetrates gradually to all nooks, and of the chaos makes a *kosmos* or ordered world !

He arranges everywhere, struggles unweariedly to arrange, and place on some intelligible footing, the 'affairs and dues, *res ac redditus*', of his dominion. The Lakenheath eels cease to breed squabbles between human beings; the penny of *reap-silver* to explode into the streets the Female Chartism of St. Edmundsbury. These and innumerable greater things. Wheresoever Disorder may stand or lie, let it have a care; here is the man that has declared war with it, that never will make peace with it. Man is the Missionary of Order; he is the servant not of the Devil and Chaos, but of God and the Universe ! Let all sluggards and cowards, remiss, false-spoken, unjust, and otherwise diabolic persons have a care:

this is a dangerous man for them. He has a mild grave
face ; a thoughtful sternness, a sorrowful pity : but there is
a terrible flash of anger in him too ; lazy monks often have
to murmur, '*Saevit ut lupus,* He rages like a wolf ; was not
our Dream true !' 'To repress and hold-in such sudden
anger he was continually careful,' and succeeded well:—right,
Samson ; that it may become in thee as noble central heat,
fruitful, strong, beneficent ; not blaze out, or the seldomest
possible blaze out, as wasteful volcanoism to scorch and
consume !

'We must first creep, and gradually learn to walk,' had
Abbot Samson said of himself, at starting. In four years
he has become a great walker ; striding prosperously along ;
driving much before him. In less than four years, says
Jocelin, the Convent Debts were all liquidated : the harpy
Jews not only settled with, but banished, bag and baggage,
out of the *Bannaleuca* (Liberties, *Banlieue*) of St. Edmundsbury,—so has the King's Majesty been persuaded to permit.
Farewell to *you,* at any rate ; let us, in no extremity, apply
again to you ! Armed men march them over the borders,
dismiss them under stern penalties,—sentence of excommunication on all that shall again harbour them here : there
were many dry eyes at their departure.

New life enters everywhere, springs up beneficent, the
Incubus of Debt once rolled away. Samson hastes not ; but
neither does he pause to rest. This of the Finance is a lifelong business with him ;—Jocelin's anecdotes are filled to
weariness with it. As indeed to Jocelin it was of very
primary interest.

But we have to record also, with a lively satisfaction, that
spiritual rubbish is as little tolerated in Samson's Monastery
as material. With due rigour, Willelmus Sacrista, and his
bibations and *tacenda* are, at the earliest opportunity, softly,
yet irrevocably put an end to. The bibations, namely, had
to end ; even the building where they used to be carried on
was razed from the soil of St. Edmundsbury, and 'on its
place grow rows of beans': Willelmus himself, deposed
from the Sacristy and all offices, retires into obscurity, into
absolute taciturnity unbroken thenceforth to this hour.
Whether the poor Willelmus did not still, by secret channels,
occasionally get some slight wetting of vinous or alcoholic

liquor,—now grown, in a manner, indispensable to the poor man? Jocelin hints not; one knows not how to hope, what to hope! But if he did, it was in silence and darkness; with an ever-present feeling that teetotalism was his only true course. Drunken dissolute Monks are a class of persons who had better keep out of Abbot Samson's way. *Saevit ut lupus:* was not the Dream true! murmured many a Monk. Nay Ranulf de Glanville, Justiciary in Chief, took umbrage at him, seeing these strict ways; and watched farther with suspicion: but discerned gradually that there was nothing wrong, that there was much the opposite of wrong.

CHAPTER XI

THE ABBOT'S WAYS

ABBOT SAMSON showed no extraordinary favour to the Monks who had been his familiars of old; did not promote them to offices,—*nisi essent idonei,* unless they chanced to be fit men! Whence great discontent among certain of these, who had contributed to make him Abbot: reproaches, open and secret, of his being 'ungrateful, hard-tempered, unsocial, a Norfolk *barrator* and *paltenerius*'.

Indeed, except it were for *idonei,* 'fit men', in all kinds, it was hard to say for whom Abbot Samson had much favour. He loved his kindred well, and tenderly enough acknowledged the poor part of them; with the rich part, who in old days had never acknowledged him, he totally refused to have any business. But even the former he did not promote into offices; finding none of them *idonei.* 'Some whom he thought suitable he put into situations in his own household, or made keepers of his country places: if they behaved ill, he dismissed them without hope of return.' In his promotions, nay almost in his benefits, you would have said there was a certain impartiality. 'The official person who had, by Abbot Hugo's order, put the fetters on him at his return from Italy, was now supported with food and clothes to the end of his days at Abbot Samson's expense.'

Yet he did not forget benefits ; far the reverse, when an opportunity occurred of paying them at his own cost. How pay them at the public cost ;—how, above all, by *setting fire* to the public, as we said ; clapping 'conflagrations' on the public, which the services of blockheads, *non-idonei*, intrinsically are! He was right willing to remember friends, when it could be done. Take these instances : 'A certain chaplain who had maintained him at the Schools of Paris by the sale of holy water, *quaestu aquae benedictae ;*—to this good chaplain he did give a vicarage, adequate to the comfortable sustenance of him.' 'The Son of Elias, too, that is, of old Abbot Hugo's Cupbearer, coming to do homage for his Father's land, our Lord Abbot said to him in full court: "I have, for these seven years, put off taking thy homage for the land which Abbot Hugo gave thy Father, because that gift was to the damage of Elmswell, and a questionable one: but now I must profess myself overcome ; mindful of the kindness thy Father did me when I was in bonds; because he sent me a cup of the very wine his master had been drinking, and bade me be comforted in God."'

'To Magister Walter, son of Magister William de Dice, who wanted the vicarage of Chevington, he answered : "Thy Father was Master of the Schools ; and when I was an indigent *clericus*, he granted me freely and in charity an entrance to his School, and opportunity of learning ; wherefore I now, for the sake of God, grant to thee what thou askest."' Or lastly, take this good instance,—and a glimpse, along with it, into long-obsolete times: 'Two *Milites* of Risby, Willelm and Norman, being adjudged in Court to come under his mercy, *in misericordia ejus,*' for a certain very considerable fine of twenty shillings, 'he thus addressed them publicly on the spot: "When I was a Cloister-monk, I was once sent to Durham on business of our Church ; and coming home again, the dark night caught me at Risby, and I had to beg a lodging there. I went to Dominus Norman's, and he gave me a flat refusal. Going then to Dominus Willelm's, and begging hospitality, I was by him honourably received. The twenty shillings therefore of *mercy*, I, without mercy, will exact from Dominus Norman ; to Dominus Willelm, on the other hand, I, with thanks, will wholly remit the said sum." ' Men know not always to whom they refuse lodgings ; men have lodged Angels unawares !—

It is clear Abbot Samson had a talent ; he had learned to judge better than Lawyers, to manage better than bred Bailiffs :—a talent shining out indisputable, on whatever side you took him. 'An eloquent man he was,' says Jocelin, 'both in French and Latin ; but intent more on the substance and method of what was to be said, than on the ornamental way of saying it. He could read English Manuscripts very elegantly, *elegantissime* : he was wont to preach to the people in the English tongue, though according to the dialect of Norfolk, where he had been brought up ; wherefore indeed he had caused a Pulpit to be erected in our Church both for ornament of the same, and for the use of his audiences '. There preached he, according to the dialect of Norfolk : a man worth going to hear.

That he was a just clear-hearted man, this, as the basis of all true talent, is presupposed. How can a man, without clear vision in his heart first of all, have any clear vision in the head ? It is impossible ! Abbot Samson was one of the justest of judges ; insisted on understanding the case to the bottom, and then swiftly decided without feud or favour. For which reason, indeed, the Dominus Rex, searching for such men, as for hidden treasure and healing to his distressed realm, had made him one of the new Itinerant Judges,—such as continue to this day. 'My curse on that Abbot's court,' a suitor was heard imprecating, ' *Maledicta sit curia istius Abbatis*, where neither gold nor silver can help me to confound my enemy !' And old friendships and all connexions forgotten, when you go to seek an office from him ! 'A kinless loon,' as the Scotch said of Cromwell's new judges,—intent on mere indifferent fair-play !

Eloquence in three languages is good ; but it is not the best. To us, as already hinted, the Lord Abbot's eloquence is less admirable than his *in*eloquence, his great invaluable 'talent of silence ' ! ' " *Deus, Deus,*" said the Lord Abbot to me once, when he heard the Convent were murmuring at some act of his, " I have much need to remember that Dream they had of me, that I was to rage among them like a wolf. Above all earthly things I dread their driving me to do it. How much do I hold in, and wink at ; raging and shuddering

in my own secret mind, and not outwardly at all!" He
would boast to me at other times: "This and that I have
seen, this and that I have heard; yet patiently stood it."
He had this way, too, which I have never seen in any other
man, that he affectionately loved many persons to whom he
never or hardly ever showed a countenance of love. Once
on my venturing to expostulate with him on the subject, he
reminded me of Solomon: "Many sons I have; it is not fit
that I should smile on them." He would suffer faults,
damage from his servants, and know what he suffered, and
not speak of it; but I think the reason was, he waited
a good time for speaking of it, and in a wise way amending
it. He intimated, openly in chapter to us all, that he would
have no eavesdropping: "Let none", said he, "come to me
secretly accusing another, unless he will publicly stand to
the same; if he come otherwise, I will openly proclaim the
name of him. I wish, too, that every Monk of you have
free access to me, to speak of your needs or grievances when
you will."'

The kinds of people Abbot Samson liked worst were these
three: '*Mendaces, ebriosi, verbosi*, Liars, drunkards, and
wordy or windy persons';—not good kinds, any of them!
He also much condemned 'persons given to murmur at their
meat or drink, especially Monks of that disposition'. We
remark, from the very first, his strict anxious order to his
servants to provide handsomely for hospitality, to guard
'above all things that there be no shabbiness in the matter
of meat and drink; no look of mean parsimony, *in novitate
mea*, at the beginning of my Abbotship'; and to the last
he maintains a due opulence of table and equipment for
others: but he is himself in the highest degree indifferent to
all such things.

'Sweet milk, honey, and other naturally sweet kinds of
food, were what he preferred to eat: but he had this
virtue,' says Jocelin, 'he never changed the dish (*ferculum*)
you set before him, be what it might. Once when I, still
a novice, happened to be waiting table in the refectory, it
came into my head' (rogue that I was!) 'to try if this were
true; and I thought I would place before him a *ferculum*
that would have displeased any other person, the very platter
being black and broken. But he, seeing it, was as one that
saw it not: and now some little delay taking place, my

heart smote me that I had done this; and so, snatching up the platter (*discus*), I changed both it and its contents for a better, and put down that instead; which emendation he was angry at, and rebuked me for,'—the stoical monastic man! 'For the first seven years he had commonly four sorts of dishes on his table; afterwards only three, except it might be presents, or venison from his own parks, or fishes from his ponds. And if, at any time, he had guests living in his house at the request of some great person, or of some friend, or had public messengers, or had harpers (*citharoedos*), or any one of that sort, he took the first opportunity of shifting to another of his Manor-houses, and so got rid of such superfluous individuals,'[1]—very prudently, I think.

As to his parks, of these, in the general repair of buildings, general improvement and adornment of the St. Edmund Domains, 'he had laid out several, and stocked them with animals, retaining a proper huntsman with hounds: and, if any guest of great quality were there, our Lord Abbot with his Monks would sit in some opening of the woods, and see the dogs run; but he himself never meddled with hunting, that I saw.'[2]

'In an opening of the woods';—for the country was still dark with wood in those days; and Scotland itself still rustled shaggy and leafy, like a damp black American Forest, with cleared spots and spaces here and there. Dryasdust advances several absurd hypotheses as to the insensible but almost total disappearance of these woods; the thick wreck of which now lies as *peat*, sometimes with huge heart-of-oak timber logs imbedded in it, on many a height and hollow. The simplest reason doubtless is, that by increase of husbandry, there was increase of cattle; increase of hunger for green spring food; and so, more and more, the new seedlings got yearly eaten out in April; and the old trees, having only a certain length of life in them, died gradually, no man heeding it, and disappeared into *peat*.

A sorrowful waste of noble wood and umbrage! Yes,—but a very common one; the course of most things in this world. Monachism itself, so rich and fruitful once, is now

---

[1] Jocelini Chronica, p. 31.　　　　[2] Ibid., p. 21.

all rotted into *peat*; lies sleek and buried,—and a most
feeble bog-grass of Dilettantism all the crop we reap from it!
That also was frightful waste; perhaps among the saddest
our England ever saw. Why will men destroy noble Forests,
even when in part a nuisance, in such reckless manner;
turning loose four-footed cattle and Henry-the-Eighths into
them! The fifth part of our English soil, Dryasdust com-
putes, lay consecrated to 'spiritual uses', better or worse;
solemnly set apart to foster spiritual growth and culture of
the soul, by the methods then known: and now—it too,
like the four-fifths, fosters what? Gentle shepherd, tell me
what!

CHAPTER XII

THE ABBOT'S TROUBLES

THE troubles of Abbot Samson, as he went along in this
abstemious, reticent, rigorous way, were more than tongue
can tell. The Abbot's mitre once set on his head, he knew
rest no more. Double, double toil and trouble; that is the
life of all governors that really govern: not the spoil of
victory, only the glorious toil of battle can be theirs.
Abbot Samson found all men more or less headstrong, irrational, prone to disorder; continually threatening to prove
*un*governable.

His lazy Monks gave him most trouble. 'My heart
is tortured', said he, 'till we get out of debt, *cor meum
cruciatum est.*' Your heart, indeed;—but not altogether
ours! By no devisable method, or none of three or four
that he devised, could Abbot Samson get these Monks of his
to keep their accounts straight; but always, do as he might,
the Cellerarius at the end of the term is in a coil, in a flat
deficit,—verging again towards debt and Jews. The Lord
Abbot at last declares sternly he will keep our accounts too
himself; will appoint an officer of his own to see our
Cellerarius keep them. Murmurs thereupon among us:
Was the like ever heard? Our Cellerarius a cipher; the

very Townsfolk know it: *subsannatio et derisio sumus,* we have become a laughingstock to mankind. The Norfolk barrator and paltener!

And consider, if the Abbot found such difficulty in the mere economic department, how much in more complex ones, in spiritual ones perhaps! He wears a stern calm face; raging and gnashing teeth, *fremens* and *frendens,* many times, in the secret of his mind. Withal, however, there is a noble slow perseverance in him; a strength of 'subdued rage' calculated to subdue most things: always, in the long-run, he contrives to gain his point.

Murmurs from the Monks, meanwhile, cannot fail; ever deeper murmurs, new grudges accumulating. At one time, on slight cause, some drop making the cup run over, they burst into open mutiny: the Cellarer will not obey, prefers arrest on bread and water to obeying; the Monks thereupon strike work; refuse to do the regular chanting of the day, at least the younger part of them with loud clamour and uproar refuse:—Abbot Samson has withdrawn to another residence, acting only by messengers: the awful report circulates through St. Edmundsbury that the Abbot is in danger of being murdered by the Monks with their knives! How wilt thou appease this, Abbot Samson! Return; for the Monastery seems near catching fire!

Abbot Samson returns; sits in his *Thalamus* or inner room, hurls out a bolt or two of excommunication: lo, one disobedient Monk sits in limbo, excommunicated, with foot-shackles on him, all day; and three more our Abbot has gyved 'with the lesser sentence, to strike fear into the others'! Let the others think with whom they have to do. The others think; and fear enters into them. 'On the morrow morning we decide on humbling ourselves before the Abbot, by word and gesture, in order to mitigate his mind. And so accordingly was done. He, on the other side, replying with much humility, yet always alleging his own justice and turning the blame on us, when he saw that we were conquered, became himself conquered. And bursting into tears, *perfusus lachrymis,* he swore that he had never grieved so much for anything in the world as for this, first on his own account, and then secondly and chiefly for the public scandal which had gone abroad, that St. Edmund's

Monks were going to kill their Abbot. And when he had narrated how he went away on purpose till his anger should cool, repeating this word of the philosopher, "I would have taken vengeance on thee, had not I been angry," he arose weeping, and embraced each and all of us with the kiss of peace. He wept; we all wept':[1]—what a picture! Behave better, ye remiss Monks, and thank Heaven for such an Abbot; or know at least that ye must and shall obey him.

Worn down in this manner, with incessant toil and tribulation, Abbot Samson had a sore time of it; his grizzled hair and beard grew daily greyer. Those Jews, in the first four years, had 'visibly emaciated him': Time, Jews, and the task of Governing, will make a man's beard very grey! 'In twelve years', says Jocelin, 'our Lord Abbot had grown wholly white as snow, *totus efficitur albus sicut nix.*' White atop, like the granite mountains:—but his clear-beaming eyes still look out, in their stern clearness, in their sorrow and pity; the heart within him remains unconquered.

Nay sometimes there are gleams of hilarity too; little snatches of encouragement granted even to a Governor. 'Once my Lord Abbot and I, coming down from London through the Forest, I inquired of an old woman whom we came up to, Whose wood this was, and of what manor; who the master, who the keeper?'—All this I knew very well beforehand, and my Lord Abbot too, Bozzy that I was! But 'the old woman answered, The wood belonged to the new Abbot of St. Edmund's, was of the manor of Harlow, and the keeper of it was one Arnald. How did he behave to the people of the manor? I asked farther. She answered that he used to be a devil incarnate, *daemon vivus,* an enemy of God, and flayer of the peasants' skins',—skinning them like live eels, as the manner of some is: 'but that now he dreads the new Abbot, knowing him to be a wise and sharp man, and so treats the people reasonably, *tractat homines pacifice.*' Whereat the Lord Abbot *factus est hilaris,*—could not but take a triumphant laugh for himself; and determines to leave that Harlow manor yet unmeddled with, for a while.[2]

A brave man, strenuously fighting, fails not of a little

---

[1] Jocelini Chronica, p. 85.   [2] Ibid., p. 24.

triumph, now and then, to keep him in heart. Everywhere we try at least to give the adversary as good as he brings ; and, with swift force or slow watchful manœuvre, extinguish this and the other solecism, leave one solecism less in God's Creation ; and so *proceed* with our battle, not slacken or surrender in it ! The Fifty feudal Knights, for example, were of unjust greedy temper, and cheated us, in the Installation-day, of ten knights'-fees ;—but they know now whether that has profited them aught, and I Jocelin know. Our Lord Abbot for the moment had to endure it, and say nothing ; but he watched his time.

Look also how my Lord of Clare, coming to claim his *un*due ' debt' in the Court at Witham, with barons and apparatus, gets a Rowland for his Oliver ! Jocelin shall report : ' The Earl, crowded round (*constipatus*) with many barons and men-at-arms, Earl Alberic and others standing by him, said, "That his bailiffs had given him to understand they were wont annually to receive for his behoof, from the Hundred of Risebridge and the bailiffs thereof, a sum of five shillings, which sum was now unjustly held back" ; and he alleged farther that his predecessors had been infeft, at the Conquest, in the lands of Alfric son of Wisgar, who was Lord of that Hundred, as may be read in Domesday Book by all persons.—The Abbot, reflecting for a moment, without stirring from his place, made answer : "A wonderful deficit, my Lord Earl, this that thou mentionest ! King Edward gave to St. Edmund that entire Hundred, and confirmed the same with his Charter ; nor is there any mention there of those five shillings. It will behove thee to say, for what service, or on what ground, thou exactest those five shillings." Whereupon the Earl, consulting with his followers, replied, That he had to carry the Banner of St. Edmund in wartime, and for this duty the five shillings were his. To which the Abbot : " Certainly, it seems inglorious, if so great a man, Earl of Clare no less, receive so small a gift for such a service. To the Abbot of St. Edmund's it is no unbearable burden to give five shillings. But Roger Earl Bigot holds himself duly seised, and asserts that he by such seisin has the office of carrying St. Edmund's Banner ; and he did carry it when the Earl of Leicester and his Flemings were beaten at Fornham. Then again Thomas de Mendham says that the right is his. When you have made out with one another, that this right is thine, come then and claim the five shillings, and I will promptly pay them!" Whereupon the Earl said, He would speak with Earl Roger his relative; and so the matter *cepit dilationem,*' and lies undecided to the end of the world. Abbot Samson answers by word or act, in this or the like pregnant manner, having justice on his side, innumerable persons: Pope's Legates, King's Viscounts, Canterbury Archbishops, Cellarers, *Sochemanni* ;—and leaves many a solecism extinguished.

On the whole, however, it is and remains sore work. ' One time, during my chaplaincy, I ventured to say to him: "*Domine*, I heard thee, this night after matins, wakeful, and sighing deeply, *valde suspirantem,* contrary to thy usual wont." He answered: "No wonder. Thou, son Jocelin, sharest in my good things, in food and drink, in riding and such like; but thou little thinkest concerning the manage-ment of House and Family, the various and arduous busi-nesses of the Pastoral Care, which harass me, and make my soul to sigh and be anxious." Whereto I, lifting up my hands to Heaven: "From such anxiety, Omnipotent Merciful Lord deliver me!"—I have heard the Abbot say, If he had been as he was before he became a Monk, and could have anywhere got five or six marcs of income,' some three pound ten of yearly revenue, ' whereby to support himself in the schools, he would never have been Monk nor Abbot. Another time he said with an oath, If he had known what a business it was to govern the Abbey, he would rather have been Almoner, how much rather Keeper of the Books, than Abbot and Lord. That latter office he said he had always longed for, beyond any other. *Quis talia crederet,*' concludes Jocelin, ' Who can believe such things?'

Three pound ten, and a life of Literature, especially of quiet Literature, without copyright, or world-celebrity of literary-gazettes,—yes, thou brave Abbot Samson, for thyself it had been better, easier, perhaps also nobler! But then, for thy disobedient Monks, unjust Viscounts ; for a Domain of St. Edmund overgrown with Solecisms, human and other, it had not been so well. Nay neither could *thy* Literature, never so quiet, have been easy. Literature, when noble, is not easy ; but only when ignoble. Literature too is a quarrel, and internecine duel, with the whole World of Darkness that lies without one and within one ;—rather a hard fight at times, even with the three pound ten secure. Thou, there where thou art, wrestle and duel along, cheerfully to the end ; and make no remarks !

CHAPTER XIII

IN PARLIAMENT

OF Abbot Samson's public business we say little, though that also was great. He had to judge the people as Justice Errant, to decide in weighty arbitrations and public controversies ; to equip his *milites*, send them duly in war-time to the King ;—strive every way that the Commonweal, in his quarter of it, take no damage.

Once, in the confused days of Lackland's usurpation, while Cœur-de-Lion was away, our brave Abbot took helmet himself, having first excommunicated all that should favour Lackland ; and led his men in person to the siege of *Windleshora*, what we now[*] call Windsor ; where Lackland had entrenched himself, the centre of infinite confusions ; some Reform Bill, then as now, being greatly needed. There did Abbot Samson 'fight the battle of reform ',—with other ammunition, one hopes, than 'tremendous cheering' and such like ! For these things he was called 'the magnanimous Abbot'.

He also attended duly in his place in Parliament *de arduis regni;* attended especially, as in *arduissimo,* when 'the news reached London that King Richard was a captive in Germany '. Here 'while all the barons sat to consult ', and many of them looked blank enough, 'the Abbot started forth, *prosiliit coram omnibus,* in his place in Parliament, and said, That *he* was ready to go and seek his Lord the King, either clandestinely by subterfuge (*in tapinagio*), or by any other method ; and search till he found him, and got certain notice of him ; he for one ! By which word,' says Jocelin, 'he acquired great praise for himself,'—unfeigned commendation from the Able Editors of that age.

By which word ;—and also by which *deed :* for the Abbot

actually went 'with rich gifts to the King in Germany';[1] Usurper Lackland being first rooted out from Windsor, and the King's peace somewhat settled.

As to these 'rich gifts', however, we have to note one thing: In all England, as appeared to the Collective Wisdom, there was not like to be treasure enough for ransoming King Richard; in which extremity certain Lords of the Treasury, *Justiciarii ad Scaccarium*, suggested that St. Edmund's Shrine, covered with thick gold, was still untouched. Could not it, in this extremity, be peeled off, at least in part; under condition, of course, of its being replaced, when times mended? The Abbot, starting plumb up, *se erigens*, answered: 'Know ye for certain, that I will in nowise do this thing; nor is there any man who could force me to consent thereto. But I will open the doors of the Church: Let him that likes enter; let him that dares come forward!' Emphatic words, which created a sensation round the woolsack. For the Justiciaries of the *Scaccarium* answered, 'with oaths, each for himself: "I won't come forward, for my share; nor will I, nor I! The distant and absent who offended him, Saint Edmund has been known to punish fearfully; much more will he those close by, who lay violent hands on his coat, and would strip it off!" These things being said, the Shrine was not meddled with, nor any ransom levied for it.'[2]

For Lords of the Treasury have in all times their impassable limits, be it by 'force of public opinion' or otherwise; and in those days a Heavenly Awe overshadowed and encompassed, as it still ought and must, all earthly Business whatsoever.

---

[1] Jocelini Chronica, pp. 39, 40.   [2] Ibid., p. 71.

CHAPTER XIV

HENRY OF ESSEX

OF St. Edmund's fearful avengements have they not the remarkablest instance still before their eyes? He that will go to Reading Monastery may find there, now tonsured into a mournful penitent Monk, the once proud Henry Earl of Essex; and discern how St. Edmund punishes terribly, yet with mercy! This Narrative is too significant to be omitted as a document of the Time. Our Lord Abbot, once on a visit at Reading, heard the particulars from Henry's own mouth; and thereupon charged one of his monks to write it down;—as accordingly the Monk has done, in ambitious rhetorical Latin; inserting the same, as episode, among Jocelin's garrulous leaves. Read it here; with ancient yet with modern eyes.

Henry Earl of Essex, standard-bearer of England, had high places and emoluments; had a haughty high soul, yet with various flaws, or rather with one many-branched flaw and crack, running through the texture of it. For example, did he not treat Gilbert de Cereville in the most shocking manner? He cast Gilbert into prison; and, with chains and slow torments, wore the life out of him there. And Gilbert's crime was understood to be only that of innocent Joseph: the Lady Essex was a Potiphar's Wife, and had accused poor Gilbert! Other cracks, and branches of that widespread flaw in the Standard-bearer's soul we could point out: but indeed the main stem and trunk of all is too visible in this, That he had no right reverence for the Heavenly in Man,—that far from showing due reverence to St. Edmund, he did not even show him common justice. While others in the Eastern Counties were adorning and enlarging with rich gifts St. Edmund's resting-place, which had become a city of refuge for many things, this Earl of Essex flatly defrauded him, by violence or quirk of law, of five shillings yearly, and converted said sum to his own poor uses! Nay, in another case of litigation, the unjust Standard-bearer, for his own profit, asserting that the cause

belonged not to St. Edmund's Court, but to *his* in Lailand
Hundred, 'involved us in travellings and innumerable expenses, vexing the servants of St. Edmund for a long tract
of time.' In short, he is without reverence for the Heavenly,
this Standard-bearer; reveres only the Earthly, Gold-coined;
and has a most morbid lamentable flaw in the texture of
him. It cannot come to good.

Accordingly, the same flaw, or St.-Vitus' *tic*, manifests
itself ere long in another way. In the year 1157, he went
with his Standard to attend King Henry, our blessed
Sovereign (whom *we* saw afterwards at Waltham), in his
War with the Welsh. A somewhat disastrous War; in
which while King Henry and his force were struggling to
retreat Parthian-like, endless clouds of exasperated Welsh-
men hemming them in, and now we had come to the 'difficult pass of Coleshill', and as it were to the nick of
destruction,—Henry Earl of Essex shrieks out on a sudden
(blinded doubtless by his inner flaw, or 'evil genius' as
some name it), That King Henry is killed, That all is lost,—
and flings down his Standard to shift for itself there! And,
certainly enough, all *had* been lost, had all men been as he;
—had not brave men, without such miserable jerking *tic-
douloureux* in the souls of them, come dashing up, with
blazing swords and looks, and asserted That nothing was
lost yet, that all must be regained yet. In this manner
King Henry and his force got safely retreated, Parthian-like,
from the pass of Coleshill and the Welsh War.[1] But, once
home again, Earl Robert de Montfort, a kinsman of this
Standard-bearer's, rises up in the King's Assembly to declare
openly that such a man is unfit for bearing English Stan-
dards, being in fact either a special traitor, or something
almost worse, a coward namely, or universal traitor. Wager
of Battle in consequence; solemn Duel, by the King's
appointment, 'in a certain Island of the Thames-stream at
Reading, *apud Radingas*, short way from the Abbey there.'
King, Peers, and an immense multitude of people, on such
scaffoldings and heights as they can come at, are gathered
round, to see what issue the business will take. The business takes this bad issue, in our Monk's own words faithfully
rendered:

[1] See Lyttelton's Henry II, ii. 384.

'And it came to pass, while Robert de Montfort thundered on him manfully (*viriliter intonâsset*) with hard and frequent strokes, and a valiant beginning promised the fruit of victory, Henry of Essex, rather giving way, glanced round on all sides; and lo, at the rim of the horizon, on the confines of the River and land, he discerned the glorious King and Martyr Edmund, in shining armour, and as if hovering in the air; looking towards him with severe countenance, nodding his head with a mien and motion of austere anger. At St. Edmund's hand there stood also another Knight, Gilbert de Cereville, whose armour was not so splendid, whose stature was less gigantic; casting vengeful looks at him. This he seeing with his eyes, remembered that old crime brings new shame. And now wholly desperate, and changing reason into violence, he took the part of one blindly attacking, not skilfully defending. Who while he struck fiercely was more fiercely struck; and so, in short, fell down vanquished, and it was thought, slain. As he lay there for dead, his kinsmen, Magnates of England, besought the King, that the Monks of Reading might have leave to bury him. However, he proved not to be dead, but got well again among them; and now, with recovered health, assuming the Regular Habit, he strove to wipe out the stain of his former life, to cleanse the long week of his dissolute history by at least a purifying sabbath, and cultivate the studies of Virtue into fruits of eternal Felicity.' [1]

Thus does the Conscience of man project itself athwart whatsoever of knowledge or surmise, of imagination, understanding, faculty, acquirement, or natural disposition he has in him; and, like light through coloured glass, paint strange pictures 'on the rim of the horizon' and elsewhere! Truly, this same 'sense of the Infinite nature of Duty' is the central part of all with us; a ray as of Eternity and Immortality, immured in dusky many-coloured Time, and its deaths and births. Your 'coloured glass' varies so much from century to century;—and, in certain money-making, game-preserving centuries, it gets so terribly opaque! Not a Heaven with cherubim surrounds you then, but a kind of vacant leaden-coloured Hell. One day it will again cease to

[1] Jocelini Chronica, p. 52.

be *opaque*, this 'coloured glass'. Nay, may it not become at once translucent and *un*coloured? Painting no Pictures more for us, but only the everlasting Azure itself? That will be a right glorious consummation!—

Saint Edmund from the horizon's edge, in shining armour, threatening the misdoer in his hour of extreme need: it is beautiful, it is great and true. So old, yet so modern, actual; true yet for every one of us, as for Henry the Earl and Monk! A glimpse as of the Deepest in Man's Destiny, which is the same for all times and ages. Yes, Henry my brother, there in thy extreme need, thy soul is *lamed ;* and behold thou canst not so much as fight! For Justice and Reverence *are* the everlasting central Law of this Universe; and to forget them, and have all the Universe against one, God and one's own Self for enemies, and only the Devil and the Dragons for friends, is not that a 'lameness' like few? That some shining armed St. Edmund hang minatory on thy horizon, that infinite sulphur-lakes hang minatory, or do not now hang,—this alters no whit the eternal fact of the thing. I say, thy soul is lamed, and the God and all Godlike in it marred: lamed, paralytic, tending towards baleful eternal death, whether thou know it or not;—nay hadst thou never known it, that surely had been worst of all!—

Thus, at any rate, by the heavenly Awe that over-shadows earthly Business, does Samson, readily in those days, save St. Edmund's Shrine, and innumerable still more precious things.

CHAPTER XV

PRACTICAL-DEVOTIONAL

HERE indeed, perhaps, by rule of antagonisms, may be the place to mention that, after King Richard's return, there was a liberty of tourneying given to the fighting-men of England: that a Tournament was proclaimed in the Abbot's domain, 'between Thetford and St. Edmundsbury,'—perhaps in the Euston region, on Fakenham Heights, midway

between these two localities : that it was publicly prohibited
by our Lord Abbot ; and nevertheless was held in spite of
him,—and by the parties, as would seem, considered ' a
gentle and free passage of arms '.

Nay, next year, there came to the same spot four-and-
twenty young men, sons of Nobles, for another passage of
arms ; who, having completed the same, all rode into
St. Edmundsbury to lodge for the night. Here is modesty !
Our Lord Abbot, being instructed of it, ordered the Gates
to be closed ; the whole party shut in. The morrow was
the Vigil of the Apostles Peter and Paul ; no outgate on the
morrow. Giving their promise not to depart without permission, those four-and-twenty young bloods dieted all that
day (*manducaverunt*) with the Lord Abbot, waiting for trial
on the morrow. ' But after dinner,'—mark it, posterity !—
' the Lord Abbot retiring into his *Thalamus*, they all started
up, and began carolling and singing (*carolare et cantare*) ;
sending into the Town for wine ; drinking, and afterwards
howling (*ululantes*) ;—totally depriving the Abbot and Convent of their afternoon's nap ; doing all this in derision of
the Lord Abbot, and spending in such fashion the whole
day till evening, nor would they desist at the Lord Abbot's
order ! Night coming on, they broke the bolts of the Town-
Gates, and went off by violence ! '[1] Was the like ever heard
of ? The roysterous young dogs ; carolling, howling, breaking the Lord Abbot's sleep,—after that sinful chivalry cock-
fight of theirs ! They too are a feature of distant centuries,
as of near ones. St. Edmund on the edge of your horizon,
or whatever else there, young scamps, in the dandy state,
whether cased in iron or in whalebone, begin to caper and
carol on the green Earth ! Our Lord Abbot excommunicated
most of them ; and they gradually came in for repentance.

Excommunication is a great recipe with our Lord Abbot ;
the prevailing purifier in those ages. Thus when the Townsfolk and Monks-menials quarrelled once at the Christmas
Mysteries in St. Edmund's Churchyard, and ' from words it
came to cuffs, and from cuffs to cuttings and the effusion of
blood ',—our Lord Abbot excommunicates sixty of the rioters,
with bell, book and candle (*accensis candelis*), at one stroke[2].
Whereupon they all come suppliant, indeed nearly naked,

[1] Jocelini Chronica, p. 40.   [2] Ibid., p. 68.

'nothing on but their breeches, *omnino nudi praeter femoralia*, and prostrate themselves at the Church-door.' Figure
that!

In fact, by excommunication or persuasion, by impetuosity
of driving or adroitness in leading, this Abbot, it is now
becoming plain everywhere, is a man that generally remains
master at last. He tempers his medicine to the malady,
now hot, now cool; prudent though fiery, an eminently
practical man. Nay sometimes in his adroit practice there
are swift turns almost of a surprising nature! Once, for
example, it chanced that Geoffrey Riddell Bishop of Ely,
a Prelate rather troublesome to our Abbot, made a request
of him for timber from his woods towards certain edifices
going on at Glemsford. The Abbot, a great builder himself,
disliked the request; could not however give it a negative.
While he lay, therefore, at his Manorhouse of Melford not
long after, there comes to him one of the Lord Bishop's men
or monks, with a message from his Lordship, 'That he now
begged permission to cut down the requisite trees in Elmswell wood,'—so said the monk: Elms*well*, where there are
no trees but scrubs and shrubs, instead of Elm*set*, our true
nemus, and high-towering oak-wood, here on Melford Manor!
Elmswell? The Lord Abbot, in surprise, inquires privily
of Richard his Forester; Richard answers that my Lord of
Ely has already had his *carpentarii* in Elm*set*, and marked
out for his own use all the best trees in the compass of it.
Abbot Samson thereupon answers the Monk: 'Elmswell?
Yes surely, be it as my Lord Bishop wishes.' The successful
monk, on the morrow morning, hastens home to Ely; but,
on the morrow morning, 'directly after mass,' Abbot Samson
too was busy! The successful monk, arriving at Ely, is
rated for a goose and an owl; is ordered back to say that
Elmset was the place meant. Alas, on arriving at Elmset,
he finds the Bishop's trees, they 'and a hundred more', all
felled and piled, and the stamp of St. Edmund's Monastery
burnt into them,—for roofing of the great tower we are
building there! Your importunate Bishop must seek wood
for Glemsford edifices in some other *nemus* than this. A
practical Abbot!

We said withal there was a terrible flash of anger in
him: witness his address to old Herbert the Dean, who
in a too thrifty manner has erected a windmill for himself

on his glebe-lands at Haberdon. On the morrow, after mass, our Lord Abbot orders the Cellerarius to send off his carpenters to demolish the said structure *brevi manu*, and lay up the wood in safe keeping. Old Dean Herbert, hearing what was toward, comes tottering along hither, to plead humbly for himself and his mill. The Abbot answers: 'I am obliged to thee as if thou hadst cut off both my feet! By God's face, *per os Dei*, I will not eat bread till that fabric be torn in pieces. Thou art an old man, and shouldst have known that neither the King nor his Justiciary dare change aught within the Liberties without consent of Abbot and Convent: and thou hast presumed on such a thing? I tell thee, it will *not* be without damage to my mills; for the Townsfolk will go to thy mill, and grind their corn (*bladum suum*) at their own good pleasure; nor can I hinder them, since they are free men. I will allow no new mills on such principle. Away, away; before thou gettest home again, thou shalt see what thy mill has grown to!'[1]—The very reverend the old Dean totters home again, in all haste; tears the mill in pieces by his own *carpentarii*, to save at least the timber; and Abbot Samson's workmen, coming up, find the ground already clear of it.

Easy to bully down poor old rural Deans, and blow their windmills away: but who is the man that dare abide King Richard's anger; cross the Lion in his path, and take him by the whiskers! Abbot Samson too; he is that man, with justice on his side. The case was this. Adam de Cokefield, one of the chief feudatories of St. Edmund, and a principal man in the Eastern Counties, died, leaving large possessions, and for heiress a daughter of three months; who by clear law, as all men know, became thus Abbot Samson's ward; whom accordingly he proceeded to dispose of to such person as seemed fittest. But now King Richard has another person in view, to whom the little ward and her great possessions were a suitable thing. He, by letter, requests that Abbot Samson will have the goodness to give her to this person. Abbot Samson, with deep humility, replies that she is already given. New letters from Richard, of severer tenor; answered with new deep humilities, with

---

[1] Jocelini Chronica, p. 43.

gifts and entreaties, with no promise of obedience. King Richard's ire is kindled ; messengers arrive at St. Edmundsbury, with emphatic message to obey or tremble! Abbot Samson, wisely silent as to the King's threats, makes answer : 'The King can send if he will, and seize the ward : force and power he has to do his pleasure, and abolish the whole Abbey. But I, for my part, never can be bent to wish this that he seeks, nor shall it by me be ever done. For there is danger lest such things be made a precedent of, to the prejudice of my successors. *Videat Altissimus*, Let the Most High look on it. Whatsoever thing shall befall I will patiently endure.'

Such was Abbot Samson's deliberate decision. Why not ? Cœur-de-Lion is very dreadful, but not the dreadfullest. *Videat Altissimus.* I reverence Cœur-de-Lion to the marrow of my bones, and will in all right things be *homo suus;* but it is not, properly speaking, with terror, with any fear at all. On the whole, have I not looked on the face of 'Satan with outspread wings'; steadily into Hellfire these seven-and-forty years ;—and was not melted into terror even at that, such the Lord's goodness to me ? Cœur-de-Lion !

Richard swore tornado oaths, worse than our armies in Flanders, To be revenged on that proud Priest. But in the end he discovered that the Priest was right; and forgave him, and even loved him. 'King Richard wrote, soon after, to Abbot Samson, That he wanted one or two of the St. Edmundsbury dogs, which he heard were good.' Abbot Samson sent him dogs of the best ; Richard replied by the present of a ring, which Pope Innocent the Third had given him. Thou brave Richard, thou brave Samson ! Richard too, I suppose, 'loved a man,' and knew one when he saw him.

No one will accuse our Lord Abbot of wanting worldly wisdom, due interest in worldly things. A skilful man ; full of cunning insight, lively interests; always discerning the road to his object, be it circuit, be it short-cut, and victoriously travelling forward thereon. Nay rather it might seem, from Jocelin's Narrative, as if he had his eye all but exclusively directed on terrestrial matters, and was much too secular for a devout man. But this too, if we examine it, was right. For it is *in* the world that a man, devout or other, has his

life to lead, his work waiting to be done. The basis of
Abbot Samson's, we shall discover, was truly religion, after
all. Returning from his dusty pilgrimage, with such welcome
as we saw, 'he sat down at the foot of St. Edmund's Shrine.'
Not a talking theory that; no, a silent practice: Thou,
St. Edmund, with what lies in thee, thou now must help me,
or none will!

This also is a significant fact: the zealous interest our
Abbot took in the Crusades. To all noble Christian hearts
of that era, what earthly enterprise so noble? 'When
Henry II, having taken the cross, came to St. Edmund's, to
pay his devotions before setting out, the Abbot secretly made
for himself a cross of linen cloth: and, holding this in one
hand and a threaded needle in the other, asked leave of the
King to assume it.' The King could not spare Samson out
of England;—the King himself indeed never went. But the
Abbot's eye was set on the Holy Sepulchre, as on the spot
of this Earth where the true cause of Heaven was deciding
itself. 'At the retaking of Jerusalem by the Pagans, Abbot
Samson put on a cilice and hair-shirt, and wore under-
garments of hair-cloth ever after; he abstained also from
flesh and flesh-meats (*carne et carneis*) thenceforth to the end
of his life.' Like a dark cloud eclipsing the hopes of
Christendom, those tidings cast their shadow over St. Edmundsbury too: Shall Samson Abbas take pleasure while
Christ's Tomb is in the hands of the Infidel? Samson, in
pain of body, shall daily be reminded of it, daily be admonished to grieve for it.

The great antique heart: how like a child's in its simplicity, like a man's in its earnest solemnity and depth!
Heaven lies over him wheresoever he goes or stands on the
Earth; making all the Earth a mystic Temple to him, the
Earth's business all a kind of worship. Glimpses of bright
creatures flash in the common sunlight; angels yet hover
doing God's messages among men: that rainbow was set in
the clouds by the hand of God! Wonder, miracle encom-
pass the man; he lives in an element of miracle; Heaven's
splendour over his head, Hell's darkness under his feet.
A great Law of duty, high as these two Infinitudes, dwarfing
all else, annihilating all else,—making royal Richard as
small as peasant Samson, smaller if need be!—The 'imaginative faculties'? 'Rude poetic ages'? The 'primaeval

poetic element'?   O for God's sake, good reader, talk no
more of all that !   It was not a Dilettantism this of Abbot
Samson.   It was a Reality, and it is one.   The garment
only of it is dead ; the essence of it lives through all Time
and all Eternity !—

And truly, as we said above, is not this comparative
silence of Abbot Samson as to his religion, precisely the
healthiest sign of him and of it?   'The Unconscious is the
alone Complete.'   Abbot Samson all·along a busy working
man, as all men are bound to be, his religion, his worship
was like his daily bread to him ;—which he did not take the
trouble to talk much about ; which he merely ate at stated
intervals, and lived and did his work upon !   This is Abbot
Samson's Catholicism of the Twelfth Century ;—something
like the *Ism* of all true men in all true centuries, I fancy !
Alas, compared with any of the *Isms* current in these poor
days, what a thing !   Compared with the respectablest,
morbid, struggling Methodism, never so earnest ; with the
respectablest, ghastly, dead or galvanized Dilettantism, never
so spasmodic !

Methodism with its eye forever turned on its own navel ;
asking itself with torturing anxiety of Hope and Fear, ' Am
I right, am I wrong?   Shall I be saved, shall I not be
damned ?'—what is this, at bottom, but a new phasis of
Egoism, stretched out into the Infinite ; not always the
heavenlier for its infinitude !   Brother, so soon as possible,
endeavour to rise above all that.   ' Thou *art* wrong ; thou
art like to be damned ': consider that as the fact, reconcile
thyself even to that, if thou be a man ;—then first is the
devouring Universe subdued under thee, and from the black
murk of midnight and noise of greedy Acheron, dawn as of
an everlasting morning, how far above all Hope and all Fear,
springs for thee, enlightening thy steep path, awakening in
thy heart celestial Memnon's music !

But of our Dilettantisms, and galvanized Dilettantisms ;
of Puseyism—O Heavens, what shall we say of Puseyism, in
comparison to Twelfth-Century Catholicism?   Little or
nothing ; for indeed it is a matter to strike one dumb.

The Builder of this Universe was wise,
He plann'd all souls, all systems, planets, particles:
The Plan He shap'd all Worlds and Aeons by,
Was——Heavens!—Was thy small Nine-and-thirty Articles?

That certain human souls, living on this practical Earth, should think to save themselves and a ruined world by noisy theoretic demonstrations and laudations of *the* Church, instead of some unnoisy, unconscious, but *practical*, total, heart-and-soul demonstration of *a* Church : this, in the circle of revolving ages, this also was a thing we were to see. A kind of penultimate thing, precursor of very strange consummations ; last thing but one ? If there is no atmosphere, what will it serve a man to demonstrate the excellence of lungs ? How much profitabler when you can, like Abbot Samson, breathe ; and go along your way !

CHAPTER XVI

ST. EDMUND

ABBOT SAMSON built many useful, many pious edifices ; human dwellings, churches, church-steeples, barns ;—all fallen now and vanished, but useful while they stood. He built and endowed ' the Hospital of Babwell ' ; built ' fit houses for the St. Edmundsbury Schools '. Many are the roofs once ' thatched with reeds ' which he ' caused to be covered with tiles ' ; or if they were churches, probably ' with lead '. For all ruinous incomplete things, buildings or other, were an eye-sorrow to the man. We saw his ' great tower of St. Edmund's ' ; or at least the roof-timbers of it, lying cut and stamped in Elmset Wood. To change combustible decaying reed-thatch into tile or lead ; and material, still more, moral wreck into rain-tight order, what a comfort to Samson !

One of the things he could not in any wise but rebuild was the great Altar, aloft on which stood the Shrine itself; the great Altar, which had been damaged by fire, by the careless rubbish and careless candle of two somnolent Monks, one night,—the Shrine escaping almost as if by miracle ! Abbot Samson read his Monks a severe lecture : ' A Dream one of us had, that he saw St. Edmund naked and in

lamentable plight.   Know ye the interpretation of that
Dream ?   St. Edmund proclaims himself naked, because ye
defraud the naked Poor of your old clothes, and give with
reluctance what ye are bound to give them of meat and
drink : the idleness moreover and negligence of the Sacristan
and his people is too evident from the late misfortune by
fire.   Well might our Holy Martyr seem to lie cast out from
his Shrine, and say with groans that he was stript of his
garments, and wasted with hunger and thirst ! '

This is Abbot Samson's interpretation of the Dream ;—
diametrically the reverse of that given by the Monks themselves, who scruple not to say privily, ' It is *we* that are the
naked and famished limbs of the Martyr ; we whom the
Abbot curtails of all our privileges, setting his own official
to control our very Cellarer ! '   Abbot Samson adds, that
this judgement by fire has fallen upon them for murmuring
about their meat and drink.

Clearly enough, meanwhile, the Altar, whatever the
burning of it mean or foreshadow, must needs be re-edified.
Abbot Samson re-edifies it, all of polished marble ; with the
highest stretch of art and sumptuosity, re-embellishes the
Shrine for which it is to serve as pediment.   Nay farther, as
had ever been among his prayers, he enjoys, he sinner, a glimpse
of the glorious Martyr's very Body in the process ; having
solemnly opened the *Loculus*, Chest or sacred Coffin, for that
purpose.   It is the culminating moment of Abbot Samson's
life.   Bozzy Jocelin himself rises into a kind of Psalmist
solemnity on this occasion ; the laziest monk ' weeps ' warm
tears, as *Te Deum* is sung.

Very strange ;—how far vanished from us in these unworshipping ages of ours !   The Patriot Hampden, best
beatified man we have, had lain in like manner some two
centuries in his narrow home, when certain dignitaries of us,
' and twelve grave-diggers with pulleys,' raised him also up,
under cloud of night, cut off his arm with penknives, pulled
the scalp off his head,—and otherwise worshipped our Hero
Saint in the most amazing manner ! [1]   Let the modern eye
look earnestly on that old midnight hour in St. Edmundsbury Church, shining yet on us, ruddy-bright, through the

[1] Annual Register (year 1828, Chronicle, p. 93), Gentleman's
Magazine, &c., &c.

depths of seven hundred years; and consider mournfully
what our Hero-worship once was, and what it now is! We
translate with all the fidelity we can:

' The Festival of St. Edmund now approaching, the marble
blocks are polished, and all things are in readiness for lifting
of the Shrine to its new place. A fast of three days was
held by all the people, the cause and meaning thereof being
publicly set forth to them. The Abbot announces to the
Convent that all must prepare themselves for transferring of
the Shrine, and appoints time and way for the work.
Coming therefore that night to matins, we found the great
Shrine (*feretrum magnum*) raised upon the Altar, but empty;
covered all over with white doeskin leather, fixed to the
wood with silver nails; but one pannel of the Shrine was
left down below, and resting thereon, beside its old column
of the Church, the Loculus with the Sacred Body yet lay
where it was wont. Praises being sung, we all proceeded to
commence our disciplines (*ad disciplinas suscipiendas*). These
finished, the Abbot and certain with him are clothed in their
albs; and, approaching reverently, set about uncovering the
Loculus. There was an outer cloth of linen, enwrapping
the Loculus and all; this we found tied on the upper side
with strings of its own: within this was a cloth of silk, and
then another linen cloth, and then a third; and so at last
the Loculus was uncovered, and seen resting on a little tray
of wood, that the bottom of it might not be injured by the
stone. Over the breast of the Martyr, there lay, fixed to the
surface of the Loculus, a Golden Angel about the length of
a human foot; holding in one hand a golden sword, and in the
other a banner: under this there was a hole in the lid of the
Loculus, on which the ancient servants of the Martyr had
been wont to lay their hands for touching the Sacred Body.
And over the figure of the Angel was this verse inscribed:

' *Martiris ecce zoma servat Michaelis agalma*.[1]

At the head and foot of the Loculus were iron rings whereby
it could be lifted.

' Lifting the Loculus and Body, therefore, they carried it
to the Altar; and I put-to my sinful hand to help in carrying, though the Abbot had commanded that none should

---

[1] This is the Martyr's Garment, which Michael's Image guards.

approach except called.   And the Loculus was placed in the
Shrine ; and the pannel it had stood on was put in its place,
and the Shrine for the present closed.   We all thought that
the Abbot would show the Loculus to the people ; and bring
out the Sacred Body again, at a certain period of the
Festival.   But in this we were woefully mistaken, as the
sequel shows.

' For in the fourth holiday of the Festival, while the Convent were all singing *Completorium,* our Lord Abbot spoke
privily with the Sacristan and Walter the Medicus; and order
was taken that twelve of the Brethren should be appointed
against midnight who were strong for carrying the pannel-
planks of the Shrine, and skilful in unfixing them, and
putting them together again.   The Abbot then said that it
was among his prayers to look once upon the Body of his
Patron ; and that he wished the Sacristan and Walter the
Medicus to be with him.   The Twelve appointed Brethren
were these : The Abbot's two Chaplains, the two Keepers of
the Shrine, the two Masters of the Vestry ; and six more,
namely, the Sacristan Hugo, Walter the Medicus, Augustin,
William of Dice, Robert, and Richard.   I, alas, was not of
the number.

' The Convent therefore being all asleep, these Twelve,
clothed in their albs, with the Abbot, assembled at the
Altar ; and opening a pannel of the Shrine, they took out
the Loculus ; laid it on a table, near where the Shrine used
to be ; and made ready for unfastening the lid, which was
joined and fixed to the Loculus with sixteen very long nails.
Which when, with difficulty, they had done, all except the
two forenamed associates are ordered to draw back.   The
Abbot and they two were alone privileged to look in.   The
Loculus was so filled with the Sacred Body that you could
scarcely put a needle between the head and the wood, or
between the feet and the wood : the head lay united to the
body, a little raised with a small pillow.   But the Abbot,
looking close, found now a silk cloth veiling the whole Body,
and then a linen cloth of wondrous whiteness ; and upon the
head was spread a small linen cloth, and then another small
and most fine silk cloth, as if it were the veil of a nun.
These coverings being lifted off, they found now the Sacred
Body all wrapped in linen ; and so at length the lineaments
of the same appeared.   But here the Abbot stopped ; saying

he durst not proceed farther, or look at the sacred flesh naked. Taking the head between his hands, he thus spake groaning: "Glorious Martyr, holy Edmund, blessed be the hour when thou wert born. Glorious Martyr, turn it not to my perdition that I have so dared to touch thee, I miserable and sinful; thou knowest my devout love, and the intention of my mind." And proceeding, he touched the eyes; and the nose, which was very massive and prominent (*valde grossum et valde eminentem*); and then he touched the breast and arms; and raising the left arm he touched the fingers, and placed his own fingers between the sacred fingers. And proceeding he found the feet standing stiff up, like the feet of a man dead yesterday; and he touched the toes, and counted them (*tangendo numeravit*).

'And now it was agreed that the other Brethren should be called forward to see the miracles; and accordingly those ten now advanced, and along with them six others who had stolen in without the Abbot's assent, namely, Walter of St. Alban's, Hugh the Infirmirarius, Gilbert brother of the Prior, Richard of Henham, Jocellus our Cellarer, and Turstan the Little; and all these saw the Sacred Body, but Turstan alone of them put forth his hand, and touched the Saint's knees and feet. And that there might be abundance of witnesses, one of our Brethren, John of Dice, sitting on the roof of the Church, with the servants of the Vestry, and looking through, clearly saw all these things.'

What a scene; shining luminous effulgent, as the lamps of St. Edmund do, through the dark Night; John of Dice, with vestry-men, clambering on the roof to look through; the Convent all asleep, and the Earth all asleep,—and since then, Seven Centuries of Time mostly gone to sleep! Yes, there, sure enough, is the martyred Body of Edmund landlord of the Eastern Counties, who, nobly doing what he liked with his own, was slain three hundred years ago: and a noble awe surrounds the memory of him, symbol and promoter of many other right noble things.

But have not we now advanced to strange new stages of Hero-worship, now in the little Church of Hampden, with our penknives out, and twelve grave-diggers with pulleys? The manner of men's Hero-worship, verily it is the innermost fact of their existence, and determines all the rest,—at public hustings, in private drawing-rooms, in church, in market, and wherever else. Have true reverence, and what indeed is inseparable therefrom, reverence the right man, all is well ; have sham-reverence, and what also follows, greet with it the wrong man, then all is ill, and there is nothing well. Alas, if Hero-worship become Dilettantism, and all except Mammonism be a vain grimace, how much, in this most earnest Earth, has gone and is evermore going to fatal destruction, and lies wasting in quiet lazy ruin, no man regarding it ! Till at length no heavenly *Ism* any longer coming down upon us, *Isms* from the other quarter have to mount up. For the Earth, I say, is an earnest place ; Life is no grimace, but a most serious fact. And so, under universal Dilettantism much having been stripped bare, not the souls of men only, but their very bodies and bread-cupboards having been stripped bare, and life now no longer possible,—all is reduced to desperation, to the iron law of Necessity and very Fact again ; and to temper Dilettantism, and astonish it, and burn it up with infernal fire, arises Chartism, *Bare-back-ism*, Sansculottism so-called ! May the gods, and what of unworshipped heroes still remain among us, avert the omen.—

But however this may be, St. Edmund's Loculus, we find, has the veils of silk and linen reverently replaced, the lid fastened down again with its sixteen ancient nails ; is wrapt in a new costly covering of silk, the gift of Hubert Archbishop of Canterbury : and through the sky-window John of Dice sees it lifted to its place in the Shrine, the pannels of this latter duly refixed, fit parchment documents being introduced withal ;—and now John and his vestrymen can slide down from the roof, for all is over, and the Convent wholly awakens to matins. 'When we assembled to sing matins', says Jocelin, 'and understood what had been done, grief took hold of all that had not seen these things, each saying to himself, "Alas, I was deceived." Matins over, the Abbot called the Convent to the great Altar ; and briefly recounting the matter, alleged that it had not been in his power, nor was it permissible or fit, to invite us all to the sight of such things. At hearing of which, we all wept, and with tears sang *Te Deum laudamus ;* and hastened to toll the bells in the Choir.'

Stupid blockheads, to reverence their St. Edmund's dead Body in this manner? Yes, brother;—and yet, on the whole, who knows how to reverence the Body of a Man? It is the most reverend phenomenon under this Sun. For the Highest God dwells visible in that mystic unfathomable Visibility, which calls itself 'I' on the Earth. 'Bending before men,' says Novalis, 'is a reverence done to this Revelation in the Flesh. We touch Heaven when we lay our hand on a human Body.' And the Body of one Dead;—a temple where the Hero-soul once was and now is not: Oh, all mystery, all pity, all mute *awe* and wonder; *Super*-naturalism brought home to the very dullest; Eternity laid open, and the nether Darkness and the upper Light-Kingdoms,—do conjoin there, or exist nowhere! Sauerteig used to say to me, in his peculiar way: 'A Chancery Lawsuit; justice, nay justice in mere money, denied a man, for all his pleading, till twenty, till forty years of his Life are gone seeking it: and a Cockney Funeral, Death reverenced by hatchments, horsehair, brass-lacker, and unconcerned bipeds carrying long poles and bags of black silk:—are not these two reverences, this reverence for Death and that reverence for Life, a notable pair of reverences among you English?'

Abbot Samson, at this culminating point of his existence, may, and indeed must, be left to vanish with his Life-scenery from the eyes of modern men. He had to run into France, to settle with King Richard for the military service there of his St. Edmundsbury Knights; and with great labour got it done. He had to decide on the dilapidated Coventry Monks; and with great labour, and much pleading and journeying, got them reinstated; dined with them all, and with the 'Masters of the Schools of Oxneford,'—the veritable Oxford *Caput* sitting there at dinner, in a dim but undeniable manner, in the City of Peeping Tom! He had, not without labour, to controvert the intrusive Bishop of Ely, the intrusive Abbot of Cluny. Magnanimous Samson, his life is but a labour and a journey; a bustling and a justling, till the still Night come. He is sent for again, over sea, to advise King Richard touching certain Peers of England, who had taken the Cross, but never followed it to Palestine; whom the Pope is inquiring after. The magnanimous Abbot makes preparation for departure; departs,

and——. And Jocelin's Boswellean Narrative, suddenly
shorn through by the scissors of Destiny, *ends*. There are
no words more ; but a black line, and leaves of blank paper.
Irremediable : the miraculous hand that held all this theatric-
machinery suddenly quits hold ; impenetrable Time-Curtains
rush down ; in the mind's eye all is again dark, void ; with
loud dinning in the mind's ear, our real-phantasmagory of
St. Edmundsbury plunges into the bosom of the Twelfth
Century again, and all is over. Monks, Abbot, Hero-worship, Government, Obedience, Cœur-de-Lion and St. Edmund's Shrine, vanish like Mirza's Vision ; and there is
nothing left but a mutilated black Ruin amid green botanic
expanses, and oxen, sheep and dilettanti pasturing in their
places.

CHAPTER XVII

THE BEGINNINGS

WHAT a singular shape of a Man, shape of a Time, have
we in this Abbot Samson and his history ; how strangely do
modes, creeds, formularies, and the date and place of a man's
birth, modify the figure of the man !

Formulas too, as we call them, have a *reality* in Human
Life. They are real as the very *skin* and *muscular tissue* of
a Man's Life ; and a most blessed indispensable thing, so
long as they have *vitality* withal, and are a *living* skin and
tissue to him ! No man, or man's life, can go abroad and do
business in the world without skin and tissues. No ; first
of all, these have to fashion themselves,—as indeed they
spontaneously and inevitably do. Foam itself, and this is
worth thinking of, can harden into oyster-shell ; all living
objects do by necessity form to themselves a skin.

And yet, again, when a man's Formulas become *dead ;* as
all Formulas, in the progress of living growth, are very
sure to do ! When the poor man's integuments, no longer
nourished from within, become dead skin, mere adscititious
leather and callosity, wearing thicker and thicker, uglier and

uglier; till no *heart* any longer can be felt beating through them, so thick, callous, calcified are they; and all over it has now grown mere calcified oyster-shell, or were it polished mother-of-pearl, inwards almost to the very heart of the poor man:—yes then, you may say, his usefulness once more is quite obstructed; once more, he cannot go abroad and do business in the world; it is time that *he* take to bed, and prepare for departure, which cannot now be distant!

Ubi homines sunt modi sunt. Habit is the deepest law of human nature. It is our supreme strength; if also, in certain circumstances, our miserablest weakness.—From Stoke to Stowe is as yet a field, all pathless, untrodden: from Stoke where I live, to Stowe where I have to make my merchandises, perform my businesses, consult my heavenly oracles, there is as yet no path or human footprint; and I, impelled by such necessities, must nevertheless undertake the journey. Let me go once, scanning my way with any earnestness of outlook, and successfully arriving, my footprints are an invitation to me a second time to go by the same way. It is easier than any other way: the industry of 'scanning' lies already invested in it for me; I can go this time with less of scanning, or without scanning at all. Nay the very sight of my footprints, what a comfort for me; and in a degree, for all my brethren of mankind! The footprints are trodden and retrodden; the path wears ever broader, smoother, into a broad highway, where even wheels can run; and many travel it;—till—till the Town of Stowe disappear from that locality (as towns have been known to do), or no merchandising, heavenly oracle, or real business any longer exist for one there: then why should anybody travel the way?—Habit is our primal, fundamental law; Habit and Imitation, there is nothing more perennial in us than these two. They are the source of all Working and all Apprenticeship, of all Practice and all Learning, in this world.

Yes, the wise man too speaks, and acts, in Formulas; all men do so. And in general, the more completely cased with Formulas a man may be, the safer, happier is it for him. Thou who, in an All of rotten Formulas, seemest to stand nigh bare, having indignantly shaken off the superannuated rags and unsound callosities of Formulas,—consider how thou too art still clothed! This English Nationality, whatsoever from uncounted ages is genuine and a fact among thy native People, in their words and ways: all this, has it not made for thee a skin or second-skin, adhesive actually as thy natural skin? This thou hast not stript off, this thou wilt never strip off: the humour that thy mother gave thee has to show itself through this. A common, or it may be an uncommon Englishman thou art: but good Heavens, what sort of Arab, Chinaman, Jew-Clothes-man, Turk, Hindoo, African Mandingo, wouldst thou have been, *thou* with those mother-qualities of thine!

It strikes me dumb to look over the long series of faces, such as any full Church, Courthouse, London-Tavern Meeting, or miscellany of men will show them. Some score or two of years ago, all these were little red-coloured pulpy infants; each of them capable of being kneaded, baked into any social form you chose: yet see now how they are fixed and hardened,—into artisans, artists, clergy, gentry, learned serjeants, unlearned dandies, and can and shall now be nothing else henceforth!

Mark on that nose the colour left by too copious port and viands; to which the profuse cravat with exorbitant breast-pin, and the fixed, forward, and as it were menacing glance of the eyes correspond. That is a 'Man of Business'; prosperous manufacturer, house-contractor, engineer, law-manager; his eye, nose, cravat have, in such work and fortune, got such a character: deny him not thy praise, thy pity. Pity him too, the Hard-handed, with bony brow, rudely combed hair, eyes looking out as in labour, in difficulty and uncertainty; rude mouth, the lips coarse, loose, as in hard toil and lifelong fatigue they have got the habit of hanging:—hast thou seen aught more touching than the rude intelligence, so cramped, yet energetic, unsubduable, true, which looks out of that marred visage? Alas, and his poor wife, with her own hands, washed that cotton neck-cloth for him, buttoned that coarse shirt, sent him forth creditably trimmed as she could. In such imprisonment lives he, for his part; man cannot now deliver him: the red pulpy infant has been baked and fashioned *so.*

Or what kind of baking was it that this other brother-mortal got, which has baked him into the genus Dandy? Elegant Vacuum; serenely looking down upon all Plenums and Entities, as low and poor to his serene Chimeraship and

*Non*entity laboriously attained! Heroic Vacuum; inexpugnable, while purse and present condition of society hold out; curable by no hellebore. The doom of Fate was, Be thou a Dandy! Have thy eye-glasses, opera-glasses, thy Long-Acre cabs with white-breeched tiger, thy yawning impassivities, pococurantisms; *fix* thyself in Dandyhood, undeliverable; it is thy doom.

And all these, we say, were red-coloured infants; of the same pulp and stuff, few years ago; now irretrievably shaped and kneaded as we see! Formulas? There is no mortal extant, out of the depths of Bedlam, but lives all skinned, thatched, covered over with Formulas; and is, as it were, held in from delirium and the Inane by his Formulas! They are withal the most beneficent, indispensable of human equipments: blessed he who has a skin and tissues, so it be a living one, and the heart-pulse everywhere discernible through it. Monachism, Feudalism, with a real King Plantagenet, with real Abbots Samson, and their other living realities, how blessed!—

Not without a mournful interest have we surveyed that authentic image of a Time now wholly swallowed. Mournful reflections crowd on us;—and yet consolatory. How many brave men have lived before Agamemnon! Here is a brave governor Samson, a man fearing God, and fearing nothing else; of whom as First Lord of the Treasury, as King, Chief Editor, High Priest, we could be so glad and proud; of whom nevertheless Fame has altogether forgotten to make mention! The faint image of him, revived in this hour, is found in the gossip of one poor Monk, and in Nature nowhere else. Oblivion had so nigh swallowed him altogether, even to the echo of his ever having existed. What regiments and hosts and generations of such has Oblivion already swallowed! Their crumbled dust makes up the soil our life-fruit grows on. Said I not, as my old Norse Fathers taught me, The Life-tree Igdrasil, which waves round thee in this hour, whereof thou in this hour art portion, has its roots down deep in the oldest Death-Kingdoms; and grows; the Three Nornas, or *Times*, Past, Present, Future, watering it from the Sacred Well!

For example, who taught thee to *speak*? From the day when two hairy-naked or fig-leaved Human Figures began,

as uncomfortable dummies, anxious no longer to be dumb,
but to impart themselves to one another ; and endeavoured,
with gaspings, gesturings, with unsyllabled cries, with
painful pantomine and interjections, in a very unsuccessful
manner,—up to the writing of this present copyright Book,
which also is not very successful ! Between that day and
this, I say, there has been a pretty space of time ; a pretty
spell of work, which *somebody* has done ! Thinkest thou
there were no poets till Dan Chaucer ? No heart burning with
a thought, which it could not hold, and had no word for ;
and needed to shape and coin a word for,—what thou callest
a metaphor, trope, or the like ? For every word we have,
there was such a man and poet. The coldest word was once
a glowing new metaphor, and bold questionable originality.
' Thy very ATTENTION, does it not mean an *attentio*, a
STRETCHING-TO ? ' Fancy that act of the mind, which all were
conscious of, which none had yet named,—when this new
' poet ' first felt bound and driven to name it ! His questionable originality, and new glowing metaphor, was found
adoptable, intelligible ; and remains our name for it to
this day.

Literature :—and look at Paul's Cathedral, and the
Masonries and Worships and Quasi-Worships that are
there ; not to speak of Westminster Hall and its wigs !
Men had not a hammer to begin with, not a syllabled
articulation : they had it all to make ;—and they have made
it. What thousand thousand articulate, semi-articulate,
earnest-stammering *Prayers* ascending up to Heaven, from
hut and cell, in many lands, in many centuries, from the
fervent kindled souls of innumerable men, each struggling
to pour itself forth incompletely as it might, before the
incompletest *Liturgy* could be compiled ! The Liturgy, or
adoptable and generally adopted Set of Prayers and Prayer-
Method, was what we can call the Select Adoptabilities,
' Select Beauties ' well-edited (by Oecumenic Councils and
other Useful-Knowledge Societies) from that wide waste
imbroglio of Prayers already extant and accumulated, good
and bad. The good were found adoptable by men ; were
gradually got together, well-edited, accredited : the bad,
found inappropriate, unadoptable, were gradually forgotten,
disused and burnt. It is the way with human things. The
first man who, looking with opened soul on this august

Heaven and Earth, this Beautiful and Awful, which we name Nature, Universe and such like, the essence of which remains forever UNNAMEABLE ; he who first, gazing into this, fell on his knees awestruck, in silence as is likeliest,—he, driven by inner necessity, the 'audacious original' that he was, had done a thing, too, which all thoughtful hearts saw straightway to be an expressive, altogether adoptable thing ! To bow the knee was ever since the attitude of supplication. Earlier than any spoken Prayers, *Litanias*, or *Leitourgias ;* the beginning of all Worship,—which needed but a beginning, so rational was it. What a poet he ! Yes, this bold original was a successful one withal. The well-head this one, hidden in the primeval dusks and distances, from whom as from a Nile-source all *Forms of Worship* flow :—such a Nile-river (somewhat muddy and malarious now !) of Forms of Worship sprang there, and flowed, and flows, down to Puseyism, Rotatory Calabash, Archbishop Laud at St. Catherine Creed's, and perhaps lower !

Things rise, I say, in that way. The *Iliad* Poem, and indeed most other poetic, especially epic things, have risen as the Liturgy did. The great *Iliad* in Greece, and the small *Robin Hood's Garland* in England, are each, as I understand, the well-edited 'Select Beauties' of an immeasurable waste imbroglio of Heroic Ballads in their respective centuries and countries. Think what strumming of the seven-stringed heroic lyre, torturing of the less heroic fiddle-catgut, in Hellenic Kings' Courts, and English wayside Public Houses; and beating of the studious Poetic brain, and gasping here too in the semi-articulate windpipe of Poetic men, before the Wrath of a Divine Achilles, the Prowess of a Will Scarlet or Wakefield Pindar, could be adequately sung ! Honour to you, ye nameless great and greatest ones, ye long-forgotten brave !

Nor was the Statute *De Tallagio non concedendo*, nor any Statute, Law-method, Lawyer's-wig, much less were the Statute-Book and Four Courts, with Coke upon Lyttelton and Three Estates of Parliament in the rear of them, got together without human labour,—mostly forgotten now ! From the time of Cain's slaying Abel by swift head-breakage, to this time of killing your man in Chancery by inches, and slow heart-break for forty years,— there too is an interval ! Venerable Justice herself began by Wild-Justice ; all Law is as a tamed furrowfield, slowly worked out, and rendered arable, from the waste jungle of Club-Law. Valiant Wisdom tilling and draining; escorted by owl-eyed Pedantry, by owlish and vulturish and many other forms of Folly;—the valiant husbandman assiduously tilling; the blind greedy enemy *too* assiduously sowing tares! It is because there is yet in venerable wigged Justice some wisdom, amid such mountains of wiggeries and folly, that men have not cast her into the River; that she still sits there, like Dryden's Head in the *Battle of the Books*,—a huge helmet, a huge mountain of greased parchment, of unclean horsehair, first striking the eye; and then in the innermost corner, visible at last, in size as a hazel-nut, a real fraction of God's Justice, perhaps not yet unattainable to some, surely still indispensable to all;—and men know not what to do with her! Lawyers were not all pedants, voluminous voracious persons; Lawyers too were poets, were heroes,—or their Law had been past the Nore long before this time. Their Owlisms, Vulturisms, to an incredible extent, will disappear by and by, their Heroisms only remaining, and the helmet be reduced to something like the size of the head, we hope!—

It is all work and forgotten work, this peopled, clothed, articulate-speaking, high-towered, wide-acred World. The hands of forgotten brave men have made it a World for us; they,—honour to them; they, in *spite* of the idle and the dastard. This English Land, here and now, is the summary of what was found of wise, and noble, and accordant with God's Truth, in all the generations of English Men. Our English Speech is speakable because there were Hero-Poets of our blood and lineage; speakable in proportion to the number of these. This Land of England has its conquerors, possessors, which change from epoch to epoch, from day to day; but its real conquerors, creators, and eternal proprietors are these following, and their representatives if you can find them: All the Heroic Souls that ever were in England, each in their degree; all the men that ever cut a thistle, drained a puddle out of England, contrived a wise scheme in England, did or said a true and valiant thing in England. I tell thee, they had not a hammer to begin with; and yet Wren built St. Paul's: not an articulated syllable; and yet there have come English Literatures, Elizabethan Literatures, Satanic-School, Cockney-School and other Literatures;—once more, as in the old time of the *Leitourgia*, a most waste imbroglio, and world-wide jungle and jumble; waiting terribly to be 'well-edited' and 'well-burnt!' Arachne started with forefinger and thumb, and had not even a distaff; yet thou seest Manchester, and Cotton Cloth, which will shelter naked backs, at twopence an ell.

Work? The quantity of done and forgotten work that lies silent under my feet in this world, and escorts and attends me, and supports and keeps me alive, wheresoever I walk or stand, whatsoever I think or do, gives rise to reflections! Is it not enough, at any rate, to strike the thing called 'Fame' into total silence for a wise man? For fools and unreflective persons, she is and will be very noisy, this 'Fame', and talks of her 'immortals' and so forth: but if you will consider it, what is she? Abbot Samson was not nothing because nobody *said* anything of him. Or thinkest thou, the Right Honourable Sir Jabesh Windbag can be made something by Parliamentary Majorities and Leading Articles? Her 'immortals'! Scarcely two hundred years back can Fame recollect articulately at all; and there she but maunders and mumbles. She manages to recollect a Shakespeare or so; and prates, considerably like a goose, about him;—and in the rear of that, onwards to the birth of Theuth, to Hengst's Invasion, and the bosom of Eternity, it was all blank; and the respectable Teutonic Languages, Teutonic Practices, Existences, all came of their own accord, as the grass springs, as the trees grow; no Poet, no work from the inspired heart of a Man needed there; and Fame has not an articulate word to say about it! Or ask her, What, with all conceivable appliances and mnemonics, including apotheosis and human sacrifices among the number, she carries in her head with regard to a Wodan, even a Moses, or other such? She begins to be uncertain as to what they were, whether spirits or men of mould,—gods, charlatans; begins sometimes to have a misgiving that they were mere symbols, ideas of the mind; perhaps nonentities, and Letters of the Alphabet! She is the noisiest, inarticulately babbling, hissing, screaming, foolishest, unmusicallest of fowls that fly; and needs no 'trumpet', I think, but her own enormous goose-throat,—measuring several degrees of celestial latitude, so to speak. Her 'wings', in these days, have grown far swifter than ever; but her goose-throat hitherto seems only larger, louder and foolisher than ever. *She* is transitory, futile, a goose-goddess:—if she were not transitory, what would become of us! It is a chief comfort that she forgets us all; all, even to the very Wodans; and grows to consider us, at last, as probably nonentities and Letters of the Alphabet.

Yes, a noble Abbot Samson resigns himself to Oblivion too; feels *it* no hardship, but a comfort; counts it as a still resting-place, from much sick fret and fever and stupidity, which in the night-watches often made his strong heart sigh. Your most sweet voices, making one enormous goose-voice, O Bobus and Company, how can they be a guidance for any Son of Adam? In *silence* of you and the like of you, the 'small still voices' will speak to him better; in which does lie guidance.

My friend, all speech and rumour is short-lived, foolish, untrue. Genuine WORK alone, what thou workest faithfully, that is eternal, as the Almighty Founder and World-Builder himself. Stand thou by that; and let 'Famo' and the rest of it go prating.

> Heard are the Voices,
> Heard are the Sages,
> The Worlds and the Ages:
> 'Choose well, your choice is
> Brief and yet endless.
>
> Here eyes do regard you,
> In Eternity's stillness;
> Here is all fulness,
> Ye brave, to reward you;
> Work, and despair not.'[1]

     [1] Goethe.

BOOK III—THE MODERN WORKER

CHAPTER I

PHENOMENA

But, it is said, our religion is gone: we no longer believe in St. Edmund, no longer see the figure of him 'on the rim of the sky', minatory or confirmatory! God's absolute Laws, sanctioned by an eternal Heaven and an eternal Hell, have become Moral Philosophies, sanctioned by able computations of Profit and Loss, by weak considerations of Pleasures of Virtue and the Moral Sublime.

It is even so. To speak in the ancient dialect, we 'have forgotten God';—in the most modern dialect and very truth of the matter, we have taken up the Fact of this Universe as it *is not*. We have quietly closed our eyes to the eternal Substance of things, and opened them only to the Shows and Shams of things. We quietly believe this Universe to be intrinsically a great unintelligible PERHAPS; extrinsically, clear enough, it is a great, most extensive Cattlefold and Workhouse, with most extensive Kitchen-ranges, Dining-tables,—whereat he is wise who can find a place! All the truth of this Universe is uncertain; only the profit and loss of it, the pudding and praise of it, are and remain very visible to the practical man.

There is no longer any God for us! God's Laws are become a Greatest-Happiness Principle, a Parliamentary Expediency: the Heavens overarch us only as an Astronomical Time-keeper; a butt for Herschel-telescopes to shoot science at, to shoot sentimentalities at:—in our and old Jonson's dialect, man has lost the *soul* out of him; and now, after the due period,—begins to find the want of it! This is verily the plague-spot; centre of the universal Social

Gangrene, threatening all modern things with frightful death. To him that will consider it, here is the stem, with its roots and taproot, with its world-wide upas-boughs and accursed poison-exudations, under which the world lies writhing in atrophy and agony. You touch the focal-centre of all our disease, of our frightful nosology of diseases, when you lay your hand on this. There is no religion; there is no God; man has lost his soul, and vainly seeks antiseptic salt. Vainly : in killing Kings, in passing Reform Bills, in French Revolutions, Manchester Insurrections, is found no remedy. The foul elephantine leprosy, alleviated for an hour, reappears in new force and desperateness next hour.

For actually this is *not* the real fact of the world ; the world is not made so, but otherwise!—Truly, any Society setting out from this No-God hypothesis will arrive at a result or two. The *Un*veracities, escorted, each Unveracity of them by its corresponding Misery and Penalty; the Phantasms, and Fatuities, and ten-years Corn-Law Debatings, that shall walk the Earth at noonday,—must needs be numerous. The Universe *being* intrinsically a Perhaps, being too probably an ‘infinite Humbug’, why should any minor Humbug astonish us? It is all according to the order of Nature ; and Phantasms riding with huge clatter along the streets, from end to end of our existence, astonish nobody. Enchanted St. Ives’ Workhouses and Joe-Manton Aristocracies ; giant Working Mammonism near strangled in the partridge-nets of giant-looking Idle Dilettantism,—this, in all its branches, in its thousand thousand modes and figures, is a sight familiar to us.

The Popish Religion, we are told, flourishes extremely in these years ; and is the most vivacious looking religion to be met with at present. ‘ *Elle a trois cents ans dans le ventre*’, counts M. Jouffroy ; ‘ *c’est pourquoi je la respecte !* ’—The old Pope of Rome, finding it laborious to kneel so long while they cart him through the streets to bless the people on *Corpus-Christi* Day, complains of rheumatism ; whereupon his Cardinals consult ;—construct him, after some study, a stuffed cloaked figure, of iron and wood, with wool or baked hair ; and place it in a kneeling posture. Stuffed figure, or rump of a figure ; to this stuffed rump he, sitting at his ease on a lower level, joins, by the aid of cloaks and

drapery, his living head and outspread hands: the rump
with its cloaks kneels, the Pope looks, and holds his hands
spread; and so the two in concert bless the Roman population on *Corpus-Christi* Day, as well as they can.

I have considered this amphibious Pope, with the wool-
and-iron back, with the flesh head and hands; and endeavoured to calculate his horoscope. I reckon him the
remarkablest Pontiff that has darkened God's daylight, or
painted himself in the human retina, for these several
thousand years. Nay, since Chaos first shivered, and
' sneezed ', as the Arabs say, with the first shaft of sunlight
shot through it, what stranger product was there of Nature
and Art working together? Here is a Supreme Priest who
believes God to be—What, in the name of God, *does* he believe God to be?—and discerns that all worship of God is a
scenic phantasmagory of wax-candles, organ-blasts, Gregorian
Chants, mass-brayings, purple monsignori, wool-and-iron
rumps, artistically spread out,—to save the ignorant from
worse.

O reader, I say not who are Belial's elect. This poor
amphibious Pope too gives loaves to the Poor; has in him
more good latent than he is himself aware of. His poor
Jesuits, in the late Italian Cholera, were, with a few German
Doctors, the only creatures whom dastard terror had not
driven mad: they descended fearless into all gulfs and
bedlams; watched over the pillow of the dying, with help,
with counsel and hope; shone as luminous fixed stars, when
all else had gone out in chaotic night: honour to them!
This poor Pope,—who knows what good is in him? In
a Time otherwise too prone to forget, he keeps up the
mournfulest ghastly memorial of the Highest, Blessedest,
which once was; which, in new fit forms, will again partly
have to be. Is he not as a perpetual death's-head and
cross-bones, with their *Resurgam*, on the grave of a Universal
Heroism,—grave of a Christianity? Such Noblenesses, purchased by the world's best heart's-blood, must not be lost;
we cannot afford to lose them, in what confusions soever.
To all of us the day will come, to a few of us it has already
come, when no mortal, with his heart yearning for a ' Divine
Humility ', or other ' Highest form of Valour ', will need to
look for it in death's-heads, but will see it round him in here
and there a beautiful living head.

Besides, there is in this poor Pope, and his practice of the Scenic Theory of Worship, a frankness which I rather honour. Not half and half, but with undivided heart does *he* set about worshipping by stage-machinery; as if there were now, and could again be, in Nature no other. He will ask you, What other? Under this my Gregorian Chant, and beautiful wax-light Phantasmagory, kindly hidden from you is an Abyss, of Black Doubt, Scepticism, nay Sansculottic Jacobinism; an Orcus that has no bottom. Think of that. ' Groby Pool *is* thatched with pancakes,'—as Jeannie Deans's Innkeeper defied it to be! The Bottomless of Scepticism, Atheism, Jacobinism, behold, it is thatched over, hidden from your despair, by stage-properties judiciously arranged. This stuffed rump of mine saves not me only from rheumatism, but you also from what other *isms!* In this your Life-pilgrimage Nowhither, a fine Squallacci marching-music, and Gregorian Chant, accompanies you, and the hollow Night of Orcus is well hid!

Yes truly, few men that worship by the rotatory Calabash of the Calmucks do it in half so great, frank or effectual a way. Drury-Lane, it is said, and that is saying much, might learn from him in the dressing of parts, in the arrangement of lights and shadows. He is the greatest Play-actor that at present draws salary in this world. Poor Pope; and I am told he is fast growing bankrupt too; and will, in a measurable term of years (a great way *within* the ' three hundred '), not have a penny to make his pot boil! His old rheumatic back will then get to rest; and himself and his stage-properties sleep well in Chaos forevermore.

Or, alas, why go to Rome for Phantasms walking the streets? Phantasms, ghosts, in this midnight hour, hold jubilee, and screech and jabber; and the question rather were, What high Reality anywhere is yet awake? Aristocracy has become Phantasm-Aristocracy, no longer able to *do* its work, not in the least conscious that it has any work longer to do. Unable, totally careless to *do* its work; careful only to clamour for the *wages* of doing its work,—nay for higher, and *palpably* undue wages, and Corn-Laws and *increase* of rents; the old rate of wages not being adequate now! In hydra-wrestle, giant ' *Millo*cracy ' so-called, a real giant, though as yet a blind one and but half-awake, wrestles and wrings in choking nightmare, 'like to be strangled in the partridge-nets of Phantasm-Aristocracy,' as we said, which fancies itself still to be a giant. Wrestles, as under nightmare, till it do awaken; and gasps and struggles thousandfold, we may say, in a truly painful manner, through all fibres of our English Existence, in these hours and years! Is our poor English Existence wholly becoming a Nightmare; full of mere Phantasms?—

The Champion of England, cased in iron or tin, rides into Westminster Hall, 'being lifted into his saddle with little assistance,' and there asks, If in the four quarters of the world, under the cope of Heaven, is any man or demon that dare question the right of this King? Under the cope of Heaven no man makes intelligible answer,—as several men ought already to have done. Does not this Champion too know the world; that it is a huge Imposture, and bottomless Inanity, thatched over with bright cloth and other ingenious tissues? Him let us leave there, questioning all men and demons.

Him we have left to his destiny; but whom else have we found? From this the highest apex of things, downwards through all strata and breadths, how many fully awakened Realities have we fallen in with:—alas, on the contrary, what troops and populations of Phantasms, not God-Veracities but Devil-Falsities, down to the very lowest stratum,—which now, by such superincumbent weight of Unveracities, lies enchanted in St. Ives' Workhouses, broad enough, helpless enough! You will walk in no public thoroughfare or remotest byway of English Existence but you will meet a man, an interest of men, that has given up hope in the Everlasting, True, and placed its hope in the Temporary, half or wholly False. The Honourable Member complains unmusically that there is 'devil's-dust' in Yorkshire cloth. Yorkshire cloth,—why, the very Paper I now write on is made, it seems, partly of plaster-lime well-smoothed, and obstructs my writing! You are lucky if you can find now any good Paper,—any work really *done*; search where you will, from highest Phantasm apex to lowest Enchanted basis.

Consider, for example, that great Hat seven-feet high, which now perambulates London Streets; which my Friend Sauerteig regarded justly as one of our English notabilities·

'the topmost point as yet,' said he, 'would it were your culminating and returning point, to which English Puffery has been observed to reach!'—The Hatter in the Strand of London, instead of making better felt-hats than another, mounts a huge lath-and-plaster Hat, seven-feet high, upon wheels; sends a man to drive it through the streets; hoping to be saved *thereby*. He has not attempted to *make* better hats, as he was appointed by the Universe to do, and as with this ingenuity of his he could very probably have done; but his whole industry is turned to *persuade* us that he has made such! He too knows that the Quack has become God. Laugh not at him, O reader; or do not laugh only. He has ceased to be comic; he is fast becoming tragic. To me this all-deafening blast of Puffery, of poor Falsehood grown necessitous, of poor Heart-Atheism fallen now into Enchanted Workhouses, sounds too surely like a Doom's-blast! I have to say to myself in old dialect: ' God's blessing is not written on all this; His curse is written on all this!' Unless perhaps the Universe *be* a chimera;—some old totally deranged eightday clock, dead as brass; which the Maker, if there ever was any Maker, has long ceased to meddle with?—To my Friend Sauerteig this poor seven-feet Hat-manufacturer, as the topstone of English Puffery, was very notable.

Alas, that we natives note him little, that we view him as a thing of course, is the very burden of the misery. We take it for granted, the most rigorous of us, that all men who have made anything are expected and entitled to make the loudest possible proclamation of it, and call on a discerning public to reward them for it. Every man his own trumpeter; that is, to a really alarming extent, the accepted rule. Make loudest possible proclamation of your Hat: true proclamation if that will do; if that will not do, then false proclamation,—to such extent of falsity as will serve your purpose; as will not seem too false to be credible!—I answer, once for all, that the fact is not so. Nature requires no man to make proclamation of his doings and hat-makings; Nature forbids all men to make such. There is not a man or hat-maker born into the world but feels, or has felt, that he is degrading himself if he speak of his excellencies and prowesses, and supremacy in his craft: his inmost heart says to him, ' Leave thy friends to speak of these; if possible, thy enemies to speak of these; but at all events, thy friends!'

He feels that he is already a poor braggart; fast hastening to be a falsity and speaker of the Untruth.

Nature's Laws, I must repeat, are eternal: her small still voice, speaking from the inmost heart of us, shall not, under terrible penalties, be disregarded. No one man can depart from the truth without damage to himself; no one million of men; no Twenty-seven Millions of men. Show me a Nation fallen everywhere into this course, so that each expects it, permits it to others and himself, I will show you a Nation travelling with one assent on the broad way. The broad way, however many Banks of England, Cotton-Mills and Duke's Palaces it may have. Not at happy Elysian fields, and everlasting crowns of victory, earned by silent Valour, will this Nation arrive; but at precipices, devouring gulfs, if it pause not. Nature has appointed happy fields, victorious laurel-crowns; but only to the brave and true: *Un*nature, what we call Chaos, holds nothing in it but vacuities, devouring gulfs. What are Twenty-seven Millions, and their unanimity? Believe them not: the Worlds and the Ages, God and Nature and All Men say otherwise.

'Rhetoric all this'? No, my brother, very singular to say, it is Fact all this. Cocker's Arithmetic is not truer. Forgotten in these days, it is old as the foundations of the Universe, and will endure till the Universe cease. It is forgotten now; and the first mention of it puckers thy sweet countenance into a sneer: but it will be brought to mind again,—unless indeed the Law of Gravitation chance to cease, and men find that they *can* walk on vacancy. Unanimity of the Twenty-seven Millions will do nothing; walk not thou with them; fly from them as for thy life. Twenty-seven Millions travelling on such courses, with gold jingling in every pocket, with vivats heaven-high, are incessantly advancing, let me again remind thee, towards the *firmland's end*,—towards the end and extinction of what Faithfulness, Veracity, real Worth, was in their way of life. Their noble ancestors have fashioned for them a 'life-road';—in how many thousand senses, this! There is not an old wise Proverb on their tongue, an honest Principle articulated in their hearts into utterance, a wise true method of doing and dispatching any work or commerce of men, but helps yet to carry them forward. Life is still possible to them, because all is not yet Puffery, Falsity, Mammon-worship and Un-nature; because somewhat is yet Faithfulness, Veracity and Valour. With a certain very considerable finite quantity of Unveracity and Phantasm, social life is still possible; not with an infinite quantity! Exceed your certain quantity, the seven-feet Hat, and all things upwards to the very Champion cased in tin, begin to reel and flounder,— in Manchester Insurrections, Chartisms, Sliding-scales; the Law of Gravitation not forgetting to act. You advance incessantly towards the land's end; you are, literally enough, 'consuming the way.' Step after step, Twenty-seven Million unconscious men;—till you are *at* the land's end; till there is not Faithfulness enough among you any more: and the next step now is lifted *not* over land, but into air, over ocean-deeps and roaring abysses:—unless perhaps the Law of Gravitation have forgotten to act?

O, it is frightful when a whole Nation, as our Fathers used to say, has 'forgotten God'; has remembered only Mammon, and what Mammon leads to! When your self-trumpeting Hatmaker is the emblem of almost all makers, and workers, and men, that make anything,—from soul-overseerships, body-overseerships, epic poems, acts of parliament, to hats and shoe-blacking! Not one false man but does uncountable mischief: how much, in a generation or two, will Twenty-seven Millions, mostly false, manage to accumulate? The sum of it, visible in every street, market-place, senate-house, circulating-library, cathedral, cotton-mill, and union-workhouse, fills one *not* with a comic feeling!

CHAPTER II

GOSPEL OF MAMMONISM

READER, even Christian Reader as thy title goes, hast thou any notion of Heaven and Hell? I rather apprehend, not. Often as the words are on our tongue, they have got a fabulous or semi-fabulous character for most of us, and pass on like a kind of transient similitude, like a sound signifying little.

Yet it is well worth while for us to know, once and always, that they are not a similitude, nor a fable nor semi-fable ; that they are an everlasting highest fact !   'No Lake of Sicilian or other sulphur burns now anywhere in these ages,' sayest thou?   Well, and if there did not !   Believe that there does not ; believe it if thou wilt, nay hold by it as a real increase, a rise to higher stages, to wider horizons and empires.   All this has vanished, or has not vanished; believe as thou wilt as to all this.   But that an Infinite of Practical Importance, speaking with strict arithmetical exactness, an *Infinite*, has vanished or can vanish from the Life of any Man : this thou shalt not believe !   O brother, the Infinite of Terror, of Hope, of Pity, did it not at any moment disclose itself to thee, indubitable, unnameable ?   Came it never, like the gleam of *preter*-natural eternal Oceans, like the voice of old Eternities, far-sounding through thy heart of hearts ?   Never?   Alas, it was not thy Libe-ralism then ; it was thy Animalism !   The Infinite is more sure than any other fact.   But only men can discern it ; mere building beavers, spinning arachnes, much more the predatory vulturous and vulpine species, do not discern it well !—

'The word Hell', says Sauerteig, 'is still frequently in use among the English People : but I could not without difficulty ascertain what they meant by it.   Hell generally signifies the Infinite Terror, the thing a man *is* infinitely afraid of, and shudders and shrinks from, struggling with his whole soul to escape from it.   There is a Hell therefore, if you will consider, which accompanies man, in all stages of his history, and religious or other development : but the Hells of men and Peoples differ notably.   With Christians it is the infinite terror of being found guilty before the Just Judge.   With old Romans, I conjecture, it was the terror not of Pluto, for whom probably they cared little, but of doing unworthily, doing unvirtuously, which was their word for un*man*fully.   And now what is it, if you pierce through his Cants, his oft-repeated Hearsays, what he calls his Wor-ships and so forth,—what is it that the modern English soul does, in very truth, dread infinitely, and contemplate with entire despair ?   What *is* his Hell, after all these reputable, oft-repeated Hearsays, what is it ?   With hesita-tion, with astonishment, I pronounce it to be : The terror

K 2

of " Not succeeding "; of not making money, fame, or some other figure in the world,—chiefly of not making money! Is not that a somewhat singular Hell ?'

Yes, O Sauerteig, it is very singular. If we do not 'succeed', where is the use of us ? We had better never have been born. 'Tremble intensely,' as our friend the Emperor of China says: *there* is the black Bottomless of Terror ; what Sauerteig calls the 'Hell of the English !'— But indeed this Hell belongs naturally to the Gospel of Mammonism, which also has its corresponding Heaven. For there *is* one Reality among so many Phantasms ; about one thing we are entirely in earnest : The making of money. Working Mammonism does divide the world with idle game-preserving Dilettantism:—thank Heaven that there is even a Mammonism, *any*thing we are in earnest about ! Idleness is worst, Idleness alone is without hope : work earnestly at anything, you will by degrees learn to work at almost all things. There is endless hope in work, were it even work at making money.

True, it must be owned, we for the present, with our Mammon-Gospel, have come to strange conclusions. We call it a Society ; and go about professing openly the totallest separation, isolation. Our life is not a mutual helpfulness ; but rather, cloaked under due laws-of-war, named 'fair competition' and so forth, it is a mutual hostility. We have profoundly forgotten everywhere that *Cash-payment* is not the sole relation of human beings ; we think, nothing doubting, that *it* absolves and liquidates all engagements of man. 'My starving workers?' answers the rich Millowner : 'Did not I hire them fairly in the market ? Did I not pay them, to the last sixpence, the sum covenanted for ? What have I to do with them more ?'—Verily Mammon-worship is a melancholy creed. When Cain, for his own behoof, had killed Abel, and was questioned, 'Where is thy brother ?' he too made answer, 'Am I my brother's keeper ?' Did I not pay my brother *his* wages, the thing he had merited from me ?

O sumptuous Merchant-Prince, illustrious game-preserving Duke, is there no way of 'killing' thy brother but Cain's rude way ! 'A good man by the very look of him, by his very presence with us as a fellow wayfarer in this Life-pilgrimage, *promises* so much': woe to him if he forget all such promises, if he never know that they were given! To a deadened soul, seared with the brute Idolatry of Sense, to whom going to Hell is equivalent to not making money, all 'promises', and moral duties, that cannot be pleaded for in Courts of Requests, address themselves in vain. Money he can be ordered to pay, but nothing more. I have not heard in all Past History, and expect not to hear in all Future History, of any Society anywhere under God's Heaven supporting itself on such Philosophy. The Universe is not made so; it is made otherwise than so. The man or nation of men that thinks it is made so, marches forward nothing doubting, step after step; but marches—whither we know! In these last two centuries of Atheistic Government (near two centuries now, since the blessed restoration of his Sacred Majesty, and Defender of the Faith, Charles Second), I reckon that we have pretty well exhausted what of 'firm earth' there was for us to march on;—and are now, very ominously, shuddering, reeling, and let us hope trying to recoil, on the cliff's edge!—

For out of this that we call Atheism come so many other *isms* and falsities, each falsity with its misery at its heels!— A SOUL is not like wind (*spiritus*, or breath) contained within a capsule; the ALMIGHTY MAKER is not like a Clockmaker that once, in old immemorial ages, having *made* his Horologe of a Universe, sits ever since and sees it go! Not at all. Hence comes Atheism; come, as we say, many other *isms*; and as the sum of all, comes Valetism, the *reverse* of Heroism; sad root of all woes whatsoever. For indeed, as no man ever saw the above-said wind-element enclosed within its capsule, and finds it at bottom more deniable than conceivable; so too he finds, in spite of Bridgewater Bequests, your Clockmaker Almighty an entirely questionable affair, a deniable affair;—and accordingly denies it, and along with it so much else. Alas, one knows not what and how much else! For the faith in an Invisible, Unnameable, Godlike, present everywhere in all that we see and work and suffer, is the essence of all faith whatsoever; and that once denied, or still worse, asserted with lips only, and out of bound prayerbooks only, what other thing remains believable? That Cant well-ordered is marketable Cant; that Heroism means gas-lighted Histrionism; that seen with 'clear eyes' (as they call Valet-eyes), no man is

a Hero, or ever was a Hero, but all men are Valets and
Varlets. The accursed practical quintessence of all sorts of
Unbelief! For if there be now no Hero, and the Histrio
himself begin to be seen into, what hope is there for the
seed of Adam here below? We are the doomed everlasting
prey of the Quack; who, now in this guise, now in that, is
to filch us, to pluck and eat us, by such modes as are convenient for him. For the modes and guises I care little.
The Quack once inevitable, let him come swiftly, let him
pluck and eat me;—swiftly, that I may at least have done
with him; for in his Quack-world I can have no wish to
linger. Though he slay me, yet will I *not* trust in him.
Though he conquer nations, and have all the Flunkeys of
the Universe shouting at his heels, yet will I know well
that *he* is an Inanity; that for him and his there is no
continuance appointed, save only in Gehenna and the Pool.
Alas, the Atheist world, from its utmost summits of Heaven
and Westminster Hall, downwards through poor seven-feet
Hats and 'Unveracities fallen hungry', down to the lowest
cellars and neglected hunger-dens of it, is very wretched.

One of Dr. Alison's Scotch facts struck us much.[1] A poor
Irish Widow, her husband having died in one of the Lanes
of Edinburgh, went forth with her three children, bare of
all resource, to solicit help from the Charitable Establishments of that City. At this Charitable Establishment and
then at that she was refused; referred from one to the
other, helped by none;—till she had exhausted them all;
till her strength and heart failed her: she sank down in
typhus-fever; died, and infected her Lane with fever, so
that 'seventeen other persons' died of fever there in consequence. The humane Physician asks thereupon, as with
a heart too full for speaking, Would it not have been *economy*
to help this poor Widow? She took typhus-fever, and killed
seventeen of you!—Very curious. The forlorn Irish Widow
applies to her fellow-creatures, as if saying, 'Behold I am
sinking, bare of help: ye must help me! I am your sister,
bone of your bone; one God made us: ye must help me!'
They answer, 'No; impossible; thou art no sister of ours.'
But she proves her sisterhood; her typhus-fever kills *them* :

[1] Observations on the Management of the Poor in Scotland: By
William Pulteney Alison, M.D. (Edinburgh, 1840.)

they actually were her brothers, though denying it! Had human creature ever to go lower for a proof?

For, as indeed was very natural in such case, all government of the Poor by the Rich has long ago been given over to Supply-and-demand, Laissez-faire and such like, and universally declared to be 'impossible'. 'You are no sister of ours; what shadow of proof is there? Here are our parchments, our padlocks, proving indisputably our money-safes to be *ours*, and you to have no business with them. Depart! It is impossible!'—Nay, what wouldst thou thyself have us do? cry indignant readers. Nothing, my friends,—till you have got a soul for yourselves again. Till then all things are 'impossible'. Till then I cannot even bid you buy, as the old Spartans would have done, two-pence worth of powder and lead, and compendiously shoot to death this poor Irish Widow: even that is 'impossible' for you. Nothing is left but that she prove her sisterhood by dying, and infecting you with typhus. Seventeen of you lying dead will not deny such proof that she *was* flesh of your flesh; and perhaps some of the living may lay it to heart.

'Impossible': of a certain two-legged animal with feathers it is said if you draw a distinct chalk-circle round him, he sits imprisoned, as if girt with the iron ring of Fate; and will die there, though within sight of victuals,—or sit in sick misery there, and be fatted to death. The name of this poor two-legged animal is—Goose; and they make of him, when well fattened, *Pâté de foie gras*, much prized by some!

CHAPTER III

GOSPEL OF DILETTANTISM

But after all, the Gospel of Dilettantism, producing a Governing Class who do not govern, nor understand in the least that they are bound or expected to govern, is still mournfuller than that of Mammonism. Mammonism, as we said, at least works; this goes idle. Mammonism has seized some portion of the message of Nature to man ; and seizing that, and following it, will seize and appropriate more and more of Nature's message : but Dilettantism has missed it wholly. 'Make money': that will mean withal, 'Do work in order to make money.' But, 'Go gracefully idle in Mayfair,' what does or can that mean ? An idle, game-preserving and even corn-lawing Aristocracy, in such an England as ours: has the world, if we take thought of it, ever seen such a phenomenon till very lately ? Can it long continue to see such ?

Accordingly the impotent, insolent Donothingism in Practice, and Saynothingism in Speech, which we have to witness on that side of our affairs, is altogether amazing. A Corn-Law demonstrating itself openly, for ten years or more, with 'arguments' to make the angels, and some other classes of creatures, weep ! For men are not ashamed to rise in Parliament and elsewhere, and speak the things they do *not* think. 'Expediency,' 'Necessities of Party,' &c. &c. ! It is not known that the Tongue of Man is a sacred organ ; that Man himself is definable in Philosophy as an 'Incarnate *Word';* the Word not there, you have no Man there either, but a Phantasm instead ! In this way it is that Absurdities may live long enough,—still walking, and talking for themselves, years and decades after the brains are quite out ! How are 'the knaves and dastards' ever to be got 'arrested' at that rate ?—

'No man in this fashionable London of yours,' friend Sauerteig would say, 'speaks a plain word to me. Every man feels bound to be something more than plain ; to be pungent withal, witty, ornamental. His poor fraction of sense has to be perked into some epigrammatic shape, that it may prick into me ;—perhaps (this is the commonest) to be topsyturvied, left standing on its head, that I may remember it the better ! Such grinning inanity is very sad to the soul of man. Human faces should not grin on one like masks ; they should look on one like faces ! I love honest laughter, as I do sunlight ; but not dishonest : most kinds of dancing too ; but the St.-Vitus kind not at all ! A fashionable wit, *ach Himmel,* if you ask, Which, he or a Death's-head, will be the cheerier company for me ? pray send *not* him !'

Insincere Speech, truly, is the prime material of insincere

Action. Action hangs, as it were, *dissolved* in Speech, in Thought whereof Speech is the shadow ; and precipitates itself therefrom. The kind of Speech in a man betokens the kind of Action you will get from him. Our Speech, in these modern days, has become amazing. Johnson complained, 'Nobody speaks in earnest, Sir ; there is no serious conversation.' To us all serious speech of men, as that of Seventeenth-Century Puritans, Twelfth-Century Catholics, German Poets of this Century, has become jargon, more or less insane. Cromwell was mad and a quack ; Anselm, Becket, Goethe, *ditto ditto.*

Perhaps few narratives in History or Mythology are more significant than that Moslem one, of Moses and the Dwellers by the Dead Sea. A tribe of men dwelt on the shores of that same Asphaltic Lake ; and having forgotten, as we are all too prone to do, the inner facts of Nature, and taken up with the falsities and outer semblances of it, were fallen into sad conditions,—verging indeed towards a certain far deeper Lake. Whereupon it pleased kind Heaven to send them the Prophet Moses, with an instructive word of warning, out of which might have sprung 'remedial measures' not a few. But no : the men of the Dead Sea discovered, as the valet-species always does in heroes or prophets, no comeliness in Moses ; listened with real tedium to Moses, with light grinning, or with splenetic sniffs and sneers, affecting even to yawn ; and signified, in short, that they found him a humbug, and even a bore. Such was the candid theory these men of the Asphalt Lake formed to themselves of Moses, That probably he was a humbug, that certainly he was a bore.

Moses withdrew ; but Nature and her rigorous veracities did not withdraw. The men of the Dead Sea, when we next went to visit them, were all 'changed into Apes'[1]; sitting on the trees there, grinning now in the most *un*affected manner ; gibbering and chattering very genuine nonsense ; finding the whole Universe now a most indisputable Humbug ! The Universe has *become* a Humbug to these Apes who thought it one. There they sit and chatter, to this hour : only, I believe, every Sabbath there returns to them

---

[1] Sale's Koran (*Introduction*).

a bewildered half-consciousness, half-reminiscence ; and they sit, with their wizened smoke-dried visages, and such an air of supreme tragicality as Apes may ; looking out through those blinking smoke-bleared eyes of theirs, into the wonderfullest universal smoky Twilight and undecipherable disordered Dusk of Things ; wholly an Uncertainty, Unintelligibility, they and it ; and for commentary thereon, here and there an unmusical chatter or mew :—truest, tragicallest Humbug conceivable by the mind of man or ape ! They made no use of their souls ; and so have lost them. Their worship on the Sabbath now is to roost there, with unmusical screeches, and half-remember that they had souls.

Didst thou never, O Traveller, fall in with parties of this tribe ? Meseems they are grown somewhat numerous in our day.

CHAPTER IV

HAPPY

ALL work, even cotton-spinning, is noble ; work is alone noble : be that here said and asserted once more. And in like manner too all dignity is painful ; a life of ease is not for any man, nor for any god. The life of all gods figures itself to us as a Sublime Sadness,—earnestness of Infinite Battle against Infinite Labour. Our highest religion is named the 'Worship of Sorrow'. For the son of man there is no noble crown, well worn, or even ill worn, but is a crown of thorns !—These things, in spoken words, or still better, in felt instincts alive in every heart, were once well known.

Does not the whole wretchedness, the whole *Atheism* as I call it, of man's ways, in these generations, shadow itself for us in that unspeakable Life-philosophy of his : The pretension to be what he calls 'happy' ? Every pitifullest whipster that walks within a skin has his head filled with the notion that he is, shall be, or by all human and divine laws ought to be, 'happy.' His wishes, the pitifullest whipster's, are to be fulfilled for him ; his days, the pitifullest whipster's, are to flow on in ever-gentle current of enjoyment, impossible even for the gods. The prophets preach to us, Thou shalt be happy; thou shalt love pleasant things, and find them. The people clamour, Why have we not found pleasant things?

We construct our theory of Human Duties, not on any Greatest-Nobleness Principle, never so mistaken; no, but on a Greatest-Happiness Principle. 'The word *Soul* with us, as in some Slavonic dialects, seems to be synonymous with *Stomach*.' We plead and speak, in our Parliaments and elsewhere, not as from the Soul, but from the Stomach;— wherefore, indeed, our pleadings are so slow to profit. We plead not for God's Justice; we are not ashamed to stand clamouring and pleading for our own 'interests', our own rents and trade-profits; we say, They are the 'interests' of so many; there is such an intense desire in us for them! We demand Free-Trade, with much just vociferation and benevolence, That the poorer classes, who are terribly ill-off at present, may have cheaper New-Orleans bacon. Men ask on Free-trade platforms, How can the indomitable spirit of Englishmen be kept up without plenty of bacon? We shall become a ruined Nation!—Surely, my friends, plenty of bacon is good and indispensable: but, I doubt, you will never get even bacon by aiming only at that. You are men, not animals of prey, well-used or ill-used! Your Greatest-Happiness Principle seems to me fast becoming a rather unhappy one.—What if we should cease babbling about 'happiness', and leave *it* resting on its own basis, as it used to do!

A gifted Byron rises in his wrath; and feeling too surely that he for his part is not 'happy', declares the same in very violent language, as a piece of news that may be interesting. It evidently has surprised him much. One dislikes to see a man and poet reduced to proclaim on the streets such tidings: but on the whole, as matters go, that is not the most dislikable. Byron speaks the *truth* in this matter. Byron's large audience indicates how true it is felt to be.

'Happy', my brother? First of all, what difference is it whether thou art happy or not! Today becomes Yesterday so fast, all Tomorrows become Yesterdays; and then there is no question whatever of the 'happiness', but quite another question. Nay, thou hast such a sacred pity left at least for thyself, thy very pains, once gone over into Yesterday, becomes joys to thee. Besides, thou knowest not what heavenly blessedness and indispensable sanative virtue was in them; thou shalt only know it after many days, when thou art wiser!—A benevolent old Surgeon sat once in our company, with a Patient fallen sick by gourmandizing, whom he had just, too briefly in the Patient's judgement, been examining. The foolish Patient still at intervals continued to break in on our discourse, which rather promised to take a philosophic turn : 'But I have lost my appetite,' said he, objurgatively, with a tone of irritated pathos; 'I have no appetite ; I can't eat!'—'My dear fellow,' answered the Doctor in mildest tone, 'it isn't of the slightest consequence';—and continued his philosophical discoursings with us!

Or does the reader not know the history of that Scottish iron Misanthrope? The inmates of some town-mansion, in those Northern parts, were thrown into the fearfullest alarm by indubitable symptoms of a ghost inhabiting the next house, or perhaps even the partition-wall! Ever at a certain hour, with preternatural gnarring, growling and screeching, which attended as running bass, there began, in a horrid, semi-articulate, unearthly voice, this song: 'Once I was hap-hap-happy, but now I'm *mees*-erable! Clack-clack-clack, gnarr-r-r, whuz-z: Once I was hap-hap-happy, but now I'm *mees*-erable!'—Rest, rest, perturbed spirit ;—or indeed, as the good old Doctor said: My dear fellow, it isn't of the slightest consequence! But no ; the perturbed spirit could not rest; and to the neighbours, fretted, affrighted, or at least insufferably bored by him, it *was* of such consequence that they had to go and examine in his haunted chamber. In his haunted chamber, they find that the perturbed spirit is an unfortunate—Imitator of Byron? No, is an unfortunate rusty Meat-jack, gnarring and creaking with rust and work ; and this, in Scottish dialect, is *its* Byronian musical Life-philosophy, sung according to ability!

Truly, I think the man who goes about pothering and uproaring for his 'happiness',—pothering, and were it ballot-boxing, poem-making, or in what way soever fussing and exerting himself,—he is not the man that will help us to 'get our knaves and dastards arrested'! No ; he rather is on the way to increase the number,—by at least one unit and his tail! Observe, too, that this is all a modern affair; belongs not to the old heroic times, but to these dastard new times. 'Happiness our being's end and aim', all that very paltry speculation, is at bottom, if we will count well, not yet two centuries old in the world.

The only happiness a brave man ever troubled himself with asking much about was, happiness enough to get his work done. Not 'I can't eat!' but 'I can't work!' that was the burden of all wise complaining among men. It is, after all, the one unhappiness of a man. That he cannot work; that he cannot get his destiny as a man fulfilled. Behold, the day is passing swiftly over, our life is passing swiftly over; and the night cometh, wherein no man can work. The night once come, our happiness, our unhappiness,—it is all abolished; vanished, clean gone; a thing that has been: 'not of the slightest consequence' whether we were happy as eupeptic Curtis, as the fattest pig of Epicurus, or unhappy as Job with potsherds, as musical Byron with Giaours and sensibilities of the heart; as the unmusical Meat-jack with hard labour and rust! But our work,—behold that is not abolished, that has not vanished: our work, behold, it remains, or the want of it remains;— for endless Times and Eternities, remains; and that is now the sole question with us for evermore! Brief brawling Day, with its noisy phantoms, its poor paper-crowns tinsel-gilt, is gone; and divine everlasting Night, with her star-diadems, with her silences and her veracities, is come! What hast thou done, and how? Happiness, unhappiness: all that was but the *wages* thou hadst; thou hast spent all that, in sustaining thyself hitherward; not a coin of it remains with thee, it is all spent, eaten: and now thy work, where is thy work? Swift, out with it, let us see thy work!

Of a truth, if man were not a poor hungry dastard, and even much of a blockhead withal, he would cease criticizing his victuals to such extent; and criticize himself rather, what he does with his victuals!

CHAPTER V

THE ENGLISH

AND yet, with all thy theoretic platitudes, what a depth of practical sense in thee, great England! A depth of sense, of justice, and courage; in which, under all emergencies and world-bewilderments, and under this most complex of emergencies we now live in, there is still hope, there is still assurance!

The English are a dumb people. They can do great acts, but not describe them. Like the old Romans, and some few others, *their* Epic Poem is written on the Earth's surface: England her Mark! It is complained that they have no artists: one Shakspeare indeed; but for Raphael only a Reynolds; for Mozart nothing but a Mr. Bishop: not a picture, not a song. And yet they did produce one Shakspeare: consider how the element of Shakspearean melody does lie imprisoned in their nature; reduced to unfold itself in mere Cotton-mills, Constitutional Governments, and such like;—all the more interesting when it does become visible, as even in such unexpected shapes it succeeds in doing! Goethe spoke of the Horse, how impressive, almost affecting it was that an animal of such qualities should stand obstructed so; its speech nothing but an inarticulate neighing, its handiness mere *hoof*iness, the fingers all constricted, tied together, the finger-nails coagulated into a mere hoof, shod with iron. The more significant, thinks he, are those eye-flashings of the generous noble quadruped; those prancings, curvings of the neck clothed with thunder.

A Dog of Knowledge has free utterance; but the War-horse is almost mute, very far from free! It is even so. Truly, your freest utterances are not by any means always the best: they are the worst rather; the feeblest, trivialest; their meaning prompt, but small, ephemeral. Commend me to the silent English, to the silent Romans. Nay, the silent Russians too I believe to be worth something: are they not even now drilling, under much obloquy, an immense semi-barbarous half-world from Finland to

Kamtschatka, into rule, subordination, civilization,—really in an old Roman fashion ; speaking no word about it ; quietly hearing all manner of vituperative Able Editors speak ! While your ever-talking, ever-gesticulating French, for example, what are they at this moment drilling?—Nay, of all animals, the freest of utterance, I should judge, is the genus *Simia :* go into the Indian woods, say all Travellers, and look what a brisk, adroit, unresting Ape-population it is!

The spoken Word, the written Poem, is said to be an epitome of the man ; how much more the done Work. Whatsoever of morality and of intelligence; what of patience, perseverance, faithfulness, or method, insight, ingenuity, energy ; in a word, whatsoever of Strength the man had in him will lie written in the Work he does. To work : why, it is to try himself against Nature, and her everlasting unerring Laws ; these will tell a true verdict as to the man. So much of virtue and of faculty did *we* find in him ; so much and no more ! He had such capacity of harmonizing himself with *me* and my unalterable ever-veracious Laws ; of co-operating and working as *I* bade him ;—and has prospered, and has not prospered, as you see !—Working as great Nature bade him : does not that mean virtue of a kind ; nay, of all kinds ? Cotton can be spun and sold, Lancashire operatives can be got to spin it, and at length one has the woven webs and sells them, by following Nature's regulations in that matter : by not following Nature's regulations, you have them not. You have them not ;—there is no Cotton-web to sell : Nature finds a bill against you ; your 'Strength' is not Strength, but Futility ! Let faculty be honoured, so far as it is faculty. A man that can succeed in working is to me always a man.

How one loves to see the burly figure of him, this thick-skinned, seemingly opaque, perhaps sulky, almost stupid Man of Practice, pitted against some light adroit Man of Theory, all equipt with clear logic, and able anywhere to give you Why for Wherefore ! The adroit Man of Theory, so light of movement, clear of utterance, with his bow full-bent and quiver full of arrow-arguments,—surely he will strike down the game, transfix everywhere the heart of the matter ; triumph everywhere, as he proves that he shall and must do ? To your astonishment, it turns out oftenest

No. The cloudy-browed, thick-soled, opaque Practicality, with no logic utterance, in silence mainly, with here and there a low grunt or growl, has in him what transcends all logic-utterance: a Congruity with the Unuttered. The Speakable, which lies atop, as a superficial film, or outer skin, is his or is not his: but the Doable, which reaches down to the World's centre, you find him there !

The rugged Brindley has little to say for himself; the rugged Brindley, when difficulties accumulate on him, retires silent, 'generally to his bed'; retires 'sometimes for three days together to his bed, that he may be in perfect privacy there', and ascertain in his rough head how the difficulties can be overcome. The ineloquent Brindley, behold he *has* chained seas together; his ships do visibly float over valleys, invisibly through the hearts of mountains; the Mersey and the Thames, the Humber and the Severn have shaken hands: Nature most audibly answers, Yea ! The man of Theory twangs his full-bent bow: Nature's Fact ought to fall stricken, but does not: his logic-arrow glances from it as from a scaly dragon, and the obstinate Fact keeps walking its way. How singular ! At bottom, you will have to grapple closer with the dragon; take it home to you, by real faculty, not by seeming faculty; try whether you are stronger or it is stronger. Close with it, wrestle it : sheer obstinate toughness of muscle; but much more, what we call toughness of heart, which will mean persistence hopeful and even desperate, unsubduable patience, composed candid openness, clearness of mind : all this shall be 'strength' in wrestling your dragon; the whole man's real strength is in this work, we shall get the measure of him here.

Of all the Nations in the world at present the English are the stupidest in speech, the wisest in action. As good as a 'dumb' Nation, I say, who cannot speak, and have never yet spoken,—spite of the Shakespeares and Miltons who show us what possibilities there are !—O Mr. Bull, I look in that surly face of thine with a mixture of pity and laughter, yet also with wonder and veneration. Thou complainest not, my illustrious friend; and yet I believe the heart of thee is full of sorrow, of unspoken sadness, serious-ness,—profound melancholy (as some have said) the basis of thy being. Unconsciously, for thou speakest of nothing, this great Universe is great to thee. Not by levity of floating, but by stubborn force of swimming, shalt thou make thy way. The Fates sing of thee that thou shalt many times be thought an ass and a dull ox, and shalt with a godlike indifference believe it. My friend,—and it is all untrue, nothing ever falser in point of fact! Thou art of those great ones whose greatness the small passer-by does not discern. Thy very stupidity is wiser than their wisdom. A grand *vis inertiae* is in thee; how many grand qualities unknown to small men! Nature alone knows thee, acknowledges the bulk and strength of thee: thy Epic, unsung in words, is written in huge characters on the face of this Planet,—sea-moles, cotton-trades, railways, fleets and cities, Indian Empires, Americas, New-Hollands; legible throughout the Solar System!

But the dumb Russians too, as I said, they, drilling all wild Asia and wild Europe into military rank and file, a terrible yet hitherto a prospering enterprise, are still dumber. The old Romans also could not *speak*, for many centuries:—not till the world was theirs; and so many speaking Greekdoms, their logic-arrows all spent, had been absorbed and abolished. The logic-arrows, how they glanced futile from obdurate thick-skinned Facts; Facts to be wrestled down only by the real vigour of Roman thews!—As for me, I honour, in these loud-babbling days, all the Silent rather. A grand Silence that of Romans;—nay the grandest of all, is it not that of the gods! Even Triviality, Imbecility, that can sit silent, how respectable is it in comparison! The 'talent of silence' is our fundamental one. Great honour to him whose Epic is a melodious hexameter Iliad; not a jingling Sham-Iliad, nothing true in it but the hexameters and forms merely. But still greater honour, if his Epic be a mighty Empire slowly built together, a mighty Series of Heroic Deeds,—a mighty Conquest over Chaos; *which* Epic the 'Eternal Melodies' have, and must have, informed and dwelt in, as *it* sung itself! There is no mistaking that latter Epic. Deeds are greater than Words. Deeds have such a life, mute but undeniable, and grow as living trees and fruit-trees do; they people the vacuity of Time, and make it green and worthy. Why should the oak prove logically that it ought to grow, and will grow? Plant it, try it; what gifts of diligent judicious assimilation and secretion it has, of progress and resistance, of *force* to grow, will then declare themselves. My much-honoured, illustrious, extremely inarticulate Mr. Bull!—

Ask Bull his spoken opinion of any matter,—oftentimes the force of dullness can no farther go. You stand silent, incredulous, as over a platitude that borders on the Infinite. The man's Churchisms, Dissenterisms, Puseyisms, Benthamisms, College Philosophies, Fashionable Literatures, are unexampled in this world. Fate's prophecy is fulfilled; you call the man an ox and an ass. But set him once to work,— respectable man! His spoken sense is next to nothing, ninetenths of it palpable *non*sense: but his unspoken sense, his inner silent feeling of what is true, what does agree with fact, what is doable and what is not doable,—this seeks its fellow in the world. A terrible worker; irresistible against marshes, mountains, impediments, disorder, incivilization; everywhere vanquishing disorder, leaving it behind him as method and order. He 'retires to his bed three days', and considers!

Nay withal, stupid as he is, our dear John,—ever, after infinite tumblings, and spoken platitudes innumerable from barrel-heads and parliament-benches, he does settle down somewhere about the just conclusion; you are certain that his jumblings and tumblings will end, after years or centuries, in the stable equilibrium. Stable equilibrium, I say; centre-of-gravity lowest;—not the unstable, with centre-of-gravity highest, as I have known it done by quicker people! For indeed, do but jumble and tumble sufficiently, you avoid that worse fault, of settling with your centre-of-gravity highest; your centre-of-gravity is certain to come lowest, and to stay there. If slowness, what we in our impatience call 'stupidity', be the price of stable equilibrium over unstable, shall we grudge a little slowness? Not the least admirable quality of Bull is, after all, that of remaining insensible to logic; holding out for considerable periods, ten years or more, as in this of the Corn-Laws, after all arguments and shadow of arguments have faded away from him, till the very urchins on the street titter at the arguments he brings. Logic,—Λογική, the 'Art of Speech',—does indeed speak so and so; clear enough: nevertheless Bull still shakes his head; will see whether nothing else *illogical*, not yet 'spoken', not yet able to be 'spoken', do not lie in the business, as there so often does!—My firm belief is, that, finding himself now enchanted, hand-shackled, foot-shackled, in Poor-Law Bastilles and elsewhere, he will retire three days to his bed, and *arrive* at a conclusion or two! His three-years 'total stagnation of trade', alas, is not that a painful enough 'lying in bed to consider himself'? Poor Bull!

Bull is a born Conservative ; for this too I inexpressibly honour him.   All great Peoples are conservative ; slow to believe in novelties; patient of much error in actualities ; deeply and forever certain of the greatness that is in LAW, in Custom once solemnly established, and now long recognized as just and final.—True, O Radical Reformer, there is no Custom that can, properly speaking, be final ; none.   And yet thou seest *Customs* which, in all civilized countries, are accounted final ; nay, under the Old-Roman name of *Mores*, are accounted *Morality*, Virtue, Laws of God Himself.   Such, I assure thee, not a few of them are ; such almost all of them once were.   And greatly do I respect the solid character,— a blockhead, thou wilt say; yes, but a well-conditioned blockhead, and the best-conditioned,—who esteems all 'Customs once solemnly acknowledged' to be ultimate, divine, and the rule for a man to walk by, nothing doubting, not inquiring farther.   What a time of it had we, were all men's life and trade still, in all parts of it, a problem, a hypothetic seeking, to be settled by painful Logics and Baconian Inductions ! The Clerk in Eastcheap cannot spend the day in verifying his Ready-Reckoner ; he must take it as verified, true and indisputable ; or his Book-keeping by Double Entry will stand still.   'Where is your Posted Ledger?' asks the Master at night.—'Sir,' answers the other, ' I was verifying my Ready-Reckoner, and find some errors.   The Ledger is— !'—Fancy such a thing !

True, all turns on your Ready-Reckoner being moderately correct, — being *not* insupportably incorrect !   A Ready-Reckoner which has led to distinct entries in your Ledger such as these : ' *Creditor* an English People by fifteen hundred years of good Labour ; and *Debtor* to lodging in enchanted Poor-Law Bastilles: *Creditor* by conquering the largest Empire the Sun ever saw ; and *Debtor* to Donothingism and "Impossible" written on all departments of the government thereof : *Creditor* by mountains of gold ingots earned ; and

Debtor to No Bread purchasable by them':—*such* Ready-Reckoner, methinks, is beginning to be suspect; nay is ceasing, and has ceased, to be suspect! Such Ready-Reckoner is a Solecism in Eastcheap; and must, whatever be the press of business, and will and shall be rectified a little. Business can go on no longer with *it*. The most Conservative English People, thickest-skinned, most patient of Peoples, is driven alike by its Logic and its Unlogic, by things 'spoken', and by things not yet spoken or very speakable, but only felt and very unendurable, to be wholly a Reforming People. Their Life as it is has ceased to be longer possible for them.

Urge not this noble silent People: rouse not the Berserkir-rage that lies in them! Do you know their Cromwells, Hampdens, their Pyms and Bradshaws? Men very peaceable, but men that can be made very terrible! Men who, like their old Teutsch Fathers in Agrippa's days, 'have a soul that despises death'; to whom 'death', compared with falsehoods and injustices, is light;—'in whom there is a rage unconquerable by the immortal gods!' Before this, the English People have taken very preternatural-looking Spectres by the beard; saying virtually: 'And if thou *wert* "preternatural"? Thou with thy "divine-rights" grown diabolic wrongs? Thou,—not even "natural"; decapitable; totally extinguishable!'——Yes, just so godlike as this People's patience was, even so godlike will and must its impatience be. Away, ye scandalous Practical Solecisms, children actually of the Prince of Darkness; ye have near broken our hearts; we can and will endure you no longer. Begone, we say; depart, while the play is good! By the Most High God, whose sons and born missionaries true men are, ye shall not continue here! You and we have become incompatible; can inhabit one house no longer. Either you must go, or we. Are ye ambitious to try *which* it shall be?

O my Conservative friends, who still specially name and struggle to approve yourselves 'Conservative', would to Heaven I could persuade you of this world-old fact, than which Fate is not surer, That Truth and Justice alone are *capable* of being 'conserved' and preserved! The thing which is unjust, which is *not* according to God's Law, will you, in a God's Universe, try to conserve that? It is so old, say you? Yes, and the hotter haste ought *you*, of all others, to be in to let it grow no older! If but the faintest whisper in your hearts intimate to you that it is not fair,— hasten, for the sake of Conservatism itself, to probe it rigorously, to cast it forth at once and forever if guilty. How will or can you preserve *it*, the thing that is not fair? 'Impossibility' a thousandfold is marked on that. And ye call yourselves Conservatives, Aristocracies:—ought not honour and nobleness of mind, if they had departed from all the Earth elsewhere, to find their last refuge with you? Ye unfortunate!

The bough that is dead shall be cut away, for the sake of the tree itself. Old? Yes, it is too old. Many a weary winter has it swung and creaked there, and gnawed and fretted, with its dead wood, the organic substance and still living fibre of this good tree; many a long summer has its ugly naked brown defaced the fair green umbrage; every day it has done mischief, and that only: off with it, for the tree's sake, if for nothing more; let the Conservatism that would preserve cut *it* away. Did no wood-forester apprise you that a dead bough with its dead root left sticking there is extraneous, poisonous; is as a dead iron spike, some horrid rusty ploughshare driven into the living substance;—nay is far worse; for in every windstorm ('commercial crisis' or the like), it frets and creaks, jolts itself to and fro, and cannot lie quiet as your dead iron spike would.

If I were the Conservative Party of England (which is another bold figure of speech), I would not for a hundred thousand pounds an hour allow those Corn-Laws to continue! Potosi and Golconda put together would not purchase my assent to them. Do you count what treasuries of bitter indignation they are laying up for you in every just English heart? Do you know what questions, not as to Corn-prices and Sliding-scales alone, they are *forcing* every reflective Englishman to ask himself? Questions insoluble, or hitherto unsolved; deeper than any of our Logic-plummets hitherto will sound: questions deep enough,—which it were better that we did not name even in thought! You are forcing us to think of them, to begin uttering them. The utterance of them is begun; and where will it be ended, think you? When two millions of one's brother-men sit in Workhouses, and five millions, as is insolently said, 'rejoice in potatoes,' there are various things that must be begun, let them end where they can.

CHAPTER VI

TWO CENTURIES

THE Settlement effected by our ' Healing Parliament' in the Year of Grace 1660, though accomplished under universal acclamations from the four corners of the British Dominions, turns out to have been one of the mournfullest that ever took place in this land of ours. It called and thought itself a Settlement of brightest hope and fulfilment, bright as the blaze of universal tar-barrels and bonfires could make it: and we find it now, on looking back on it with the insight which trial has yielded, a Settlement as of despair. Considered well, it was a settlement to govern henceforth without God, with only some decent Pretence of God.

Governing by the Christian Law of God had been found a thing of battle, convulsion, confusion, an infinitely difficult thing: wherefore let us now abandon it, and govern only by so much of God's Christian Law as—as may prove quiet and convenient for us. What is the end of Government? To guide men in the way wherein they should go; towards their true good in this life, the portal of infinite good in a life to come? To guide men in such way, and ourselves in such way, as the Maker of men, whose eye is upon us, will sanction at the Great Day ?—Or alas, perhaps at bottom *is* there no Great Day, no sure outlook of any life to come ; but only this poor life, and what of taxes, felicities, Nell-Gwyns and entertainments we can manage to muster here ? In that case, the end of Government will be, To suppress all noise and disturbance, whether of Puritan preaching, Cameronian psalm-singing, thieves'-riot, murder, arson, or what noise soever, and—be careful that supplies do not fail ! A very notable conclusion, if we will think of it, and not

without an abundance of fruits for us.   Oliver Cromwell's
body hung on the Tyburn-gallows, as the type of Puritanism
found futile, inexecutable, execrable,—yes, that gallows-tree
has been a fingerpost into very strange country indeed.
Let earnest Puritanism die ; let decent Formalism, whatsoever cant it be or grow to, live !   We have had a pleasant
journey in that direction ; and are—arriving at our inn ?

To support the Four Pleas of the Crown, and keep Taxes
coming in : in very sad seriousness, has not this been, ever
since, even in the best times, almost the one admitted end
and aim of Government ?   Religion, Christian Church, Moral
Duty ; the fact that man had a soul at all ; that in man's
life there was any eternal truth or justice at all,—has been
as good as left quietly out of sight.   Church indeed,—alas,
the endless talk and struggle we have had of High-Church,
Low-Church, Church-Extension, Church-in-Danger : we invite the Christian reader to think whether it has not been
a too miserable screech-owl phantasm of talk and struggle,
as for a ' Church ',—which one had rather not define at
present !

But now in these godless two centuries, looking at
England and her efforts and doings, if we ask, What of
England's doings the Law of Nature had accepted, Nature's
King had actually furthered and pronounced to have truth
in them,—where is our answer ?   Neither the ' Church ' of
Hurd and Warburton, nor the Antichurch of Hume and
Paine ; not in any shape the Spiritualism of England : all
this is already seen, or beginning to be seen, for what it is ;
a thing that Nature does *not* own.   On the one side is
dreary Cant, with a *reminiscence* of things noble and divine ;
on the other is but acrid Candour, with a *prophecy* of things
brutal, infernal.   Hurd and Warburton are sunk into the   Bishop of
Gloucester
sere and yellow leaf ; no considerable body of true-seeing
men looks thitherward for healing : the Paine-and-Hume
Atheistic theory, of ' things well let alone ', with Liberty,
Equality and the like, is also in these days declaring itself
naught, unable to keep the world from taking fire.

The theories and speculations of both these parties, and,
we may say, of all intermediate parties and persons, prove
to be things which the Eternal Veracity did not accept ;
things superficial, ephemeral, which already a near Posterity,
finding them already dead and brown-leafed, is about to

suppress and forget. The Spiritualism of England, for those godless years, is, as it were, all forgettable. Much has been written : but the perennial Scriptures of Mankind have had small accession : from all English Books, in rhyme or prose, in leather binding or in paper wrappage, how many verses have been added to these ? Our most melodious Singers have sung as from the throat outwards: from the inner Heart of Man, from the great Heart of Nature, through no Pope or Philips, has there come any tone. The Oracles have been dumb. In brief, the Spoken Word of England has not been true. The Spoken Word of England turns out to have been trivial ; of short endurance ; not valuable, not available as a Word, except for the passing day. It has been accordant with transitory Semblance ; discordant with eternal Fact. It has been unfortunately not a Word, but a Cant ; a helpless involuntary Cant, nay too often a cunning voluntary one : either way, a very mournful Cant ; the Voice not of Nature and Fact, but of something other than these.

With all its miserable shortcomings, with its wars, controversies, with its trades-unions, famine-insurrections,—it is her Practical Material Work alone that England has to show for herself ! This, and hitherto almost nothing more ; yet actually this. The grim inarticulate veracity of the English People, unable to speak its meaning in words, has turned itself silently on things ; and the dark powers of Material Nature have answered, ' Yes, this at least is true, this is not false !' So answers Nature. 'Waste desert-shrubs of the Tropical swamps have become Cotton-trees ; and here, under my furtherance, are verily woven shirts,— hanging unsold, undistributed, but capable to be distributed, capable to cover the bare backs of my children of men. Mountains, old as the Creation, I have permitted to be bored through ; bituminous fuel-stores, the wreck of forests that were green a million years ago,—I have opened them from my secret rock-chambers, and they are yours, ye English. Your huge fleets, steamships, do sail the sea ; huge Indias do obey you ; from huge *New* Englands and Antipodal Australias comes profit and traffic to this Old England of mine !' So answers Nature. The Practical Labour of England is *not* a chimerical Triviality : it is a Fact, acknowledged by all the Worlds ; which no man and no demon will contradict. It is, very audibly, though very

inarticulately as yet, the one God's Voice we have heard in
these two atheistic centuries.

And now to observe with what bewildering obscurations
and impediments all this as yet stands entangled, and is yet
intelligible to no man !   How, with our gross Atheism, we
hear it not to be the Voice of God to us, but regard it merely
as a Voice of earthly Profit-and-Loss.   And have a Hell in
England,—the Hell of not making money.   And coldly see
the all-conquering valiant Sons of Toil sit enchanted, by the
million, in their Poor-Law Bastille, as if this were Nature's
Law ;—mumbling to ourselves some vague janglement of
Laissez-faire, Supply-and-demand, Cash-payment the one
nexus of man to man : Free-trade, Competition, and Devil
take the hindmost, our latest Gospel yet preached !

As if, in truth, there were no God of Labour; as if
godlike Labour and brutal Mammonism were convertible
terms.   A serious, most earnest Mammonism grown Midas-
eared ; an unserious Dilettantism, earnest about nothing,
grinning with inarticulate incredulous incredible jargon
about all things, as the *enchanted* Dilettanti do by the Dead
Sea !   It is mournful enough, for the present hour ; were
there not an endless hope in it withal.   Giant LABOUR,
truest emblem there is of God the World-Worker, Demiurgus, and Eternal Maker ; noble LABOUR, which is yet to
be the King of this Earth, and sit on the highest throne,—
staggering hitherto like a blind irrational giant, hardly
allowed to have his common place on the street-pavements ;
idle Dilettantism, Dead-Sea Apism crying out, ' Down with
him, he is dangerous !'

Labour must become a seeing rational giant, with a *soul*
in the body of him, and take his place on the throne of
things,—leaving his Mammonism, and several other adjuncts,
on the lower steps of said throne.

CHAPTER VII

OVER-PRODUCTION

But what will reflective readers say of a Governing Class, such as ours, addressing its Workers with an indictment of 'Over-production!' Over-production: runs it not so? 'Ye miscellaneous, ignoble manufacturing individuals, ye have produced too much! We accuse you of making above two-hundred thousand shirts for the bare backs of mankind. Your trousers too, which you have made, of fustian, of cassimere, of Scotch-plaid, of jane, nankeen and woollen broadcloth, are they not manifold? Of hats for the human head, of shoes for the human foot, of stools to sit on, spoons to eat with—Nay, what say we hats or shoes? You produce gold-watches, jewelleries, silver-forks and epergnes, commodes, chiffoniers, stuffed sofas—Heavens, the Commercial Bazaar and multitudinous Howel-and-Jameses cannot contain you. You have produced, produced ;—he that seeks your indictment, let him look around. Millions of shirts, and empty pairs of breeches, hang there in judgement against you. We accuse you of over-producing: you are criminally guilty of producing shirts, breeches, hats, shoes and commodities, in a frightful over-abundance. And now there is a glut, and your operatives cannot be fed!'

Never surely, against an earnest Working Mammonism was there brought, by Game-preserving aristocratic Dilettantism, a stranger accusation, since this world began. My lords and gentlemen,—why, it was *you* that were appointed, by the fact and by the theory of your position on the Earth, to 'make and administer Laws',—that is to say, in a world such as ours, to guard against 'gluts'; against honest operatives, who had done their work, remaining unfed! I say, *you* were appointed to preside over the Distribution and Apportionment of the Wages of Work done ; and to see well that there went no labourer without his hire, were it of money-coins, were it of hemp gallows-ropes: that function was yours, and from immemorial time has been; yours, and as yet no other's. These poor shirt-spinners have forgotten much, which by the virtual unwritten law of their position they should have remembered : but by any written recognized law of their position, what have they forgotten ? They were set to make shirts. The Community with all its voices commanded them, saying, ' Make shirts'; —and there the shirts are ! Too many shirts ? Well, that is a novelty, in this intemperate Earth, with its nine-hundred millions of bare backs ! But the Community commanded you, saying, ' See that the shirts are well apportioned, that our Human Laws be emblem of God's Laws' ;—and where is the apportionment? Two million shirtless or ill-shirted workers sit enchanted in Workhouse Bastilles, five million more (according to some) in Ugolino Hunger-cellars ; and for remedy, you say,—what say you ?— ' Raise *our* rents !' I have not in my time heard any stranger speech, not even on the Shores of the Dead Sea. You continue addressing those poor shirt-spinners and over-producers, in really a *too* triumphant manner :

' Will you bandy accusations, will you accuse *us* of over-production ? We take the Heavens and the Earth to witness that we have produced nothing at all. Not from us proceeds this frightful overplus of shirts. In the wide domains of created Nature circulates no shirt or thing of our producing. Certain fox-brushes nailed upon our stable-door, the fruit of fair audacity at Melton Mowbray ; these we have produced, and they are openly nailed up there. He that accuses us of producing, let him show himself, let him name what and when. We are innocent of producing ;—ye ungrateful, what mountains of things have we not, on the contrary, had to 'consume', and make away with ! Mountains of those your heaped manufactures, wheresoever edible or wearable, have they not disappeared before us, as if we had the talent of ostriches, or cormorants, and a kind of divine faculty to eat ? Ye ungrateful !—and did you not grow under the shadow of our wings ? Are not your filthy mills built on these fields of ours ; on this soil of England, which belongs to—whom think you ? And we shall not offer you our own wheat at the price that pleases us, but that partly pleases you ? A precious notion ! What would become of you, if we chose, at any time, to decide on growing no wheat more ? '

Yes, truly, *here* is the ultimate rock-basis of all Corn-

Laws ; whereon, at the bottom of much arguing, they rest, as securely as they can : What would become of you, if we decided, some day, on growing no more wheat at all? If we chose to grow only partridges henceforth, and a modicum of wheat for our own uses ? Cannot we do what we like with our own ?—Yes, indeed ! For my share, if I could melt Gneiss Rock, and create Law of Gravitation ; if I could stride out to the Doggerbank, some morning, and striking down my trident there into the mud-waves, say, 'Be land, be fields, meadows, mountains and fresh-rolling streams !' by Heaven, I should incline to have the letting of *that* land in perpetuity, and sell the wheat of it, or burn the wheat of it, according to my own good judgement ! My Corn-Lawing friends, you affright me.

To the 'Millo-cracy' so-called, to the Working Aristocracy, steeped too deep in mere ignoble Mammonism, and as yet all unconscious of its noble destinies, as yet but an irrational or semi-rational giant, struggling to awake some soul in itself,—the world will have much to say, reproachfully, reprovingly, admonishingly. But to the Idle Aristocracy, what will the world have to say? Things painful and not pleasant !

To the man who *works*, who attempts, in never so ungracious barbarous a way, to get forward with some work, you will hasten out with furtherances, with encouragements, corrections; you will say to him : 'Welcome ; thou art ours ; our care shall be of thee.' To the Idler, again, never so gracefully going idle, coming forward with never so many parchments, you will not hasten out : you will sit still, and be disinclined to rise. You will say to him : 'Not welcome, O complex Anomaly ; would thou hadst stayed out of doors : for who of mortals knows what to do with thee? Thy parchments : yes, they are old, of venerable yellowness ; and we too honour parchment, old-established settlements, and venerable use and wont. Old parchments in very truth :—yet on the whole, if thou wilt remark, they are young to the Granite Rocks, to the Groundplan of God's Universe ! We advise thee to put up thy parchments ; to go home to thy place, and make no needless noise whatever. Our heart's wish is to save thee : yet there as thou art, hapless Anomaly, with nothing but thy yellow parchments, noisy futilities, and shotbelts and fox-brushes, who of gods or men can avert dark Fate ? Be counselled, ascertain if no work exist for thee on God's Earth ; if thou find no com-manded-duty there but that of going gracefully idle ? Ask, inquire earnestly, with a half-frantic earnestness ; for the answer means Existence or Annihilation to thee. We apprise thee of the world-old fact, becoming sternly disclosed again in these days, That he who cannot work in this Universe cannot get existed in it : had he parchments to thatch the face of the world, these, combustible fallible sheepskin, can-not avail him. Home, thou unfortunate ; and let us have at least no noise from thee !'

Suppose the unfortunate Idle Aristocracy, as the un-fortunate Working one has done, were to 'retire three days to *its* bed ', and consider itself there, what o'clock it had become ?—

How have we to regret not only that men have 'no religion ', but that they have next to no reflection ; and go about with heads full of mere extraneous noises, with eyes wide-open but visionless,—for most part, in the somnam-bulist state !

CHAPTER VIII

UNWORKING ARISTOCRACY

It is well said, ' Land is the right basis of an Aristocracy '; whoever possesses the Land, he, more emphatically than any other, is the Governor, Viceking of the people on the Land. It is in these days as it was in those of Henry Plantagenet and Abbot Samson; as it will in all days be. The Land is *Mother* of us all ; nourishes, shelters, gladdens, lovingly enriches us all ; in how many ways, from our first wakening to our last sleep on her blessed mother-bosom, does she, as with blessed mother-arms, enfold us all !

The Hill I first saw the Sun rise over, when the Sun and I and all things were yet in their auroral hour, who can divorce me from it ? Mystic, deep as the world's centre, are the roots I have struck into my Native Soil ; no *tree* that grows is rooted so. From noblest Patriotism to humblest industrial Mechanism ; from highest dying for your country, to lowest quarrying and coal-boring for it, a Nation's Life depends upon its Land. Again and again we have to say, there can be no true Aristocracy but must possess the Land.

Men talk of 'selling' Land. Land, it is true, like Epic Poems and even higher things, in such a trading world, has to be presented in the market for what it will bring, and as we say be 'sold': but the notion of 'selling', for certain bits of metal, the *Iliad* of Homer, how much more the *Land* of the World-Creator, is a ridiculous impossibility! We buy what is saleable of it ; nothing more was ever buyable. Who can, or could, sell it to us? Properly speaking, the Land belongs to these two : To the Almighty God ; and to all His Children of Men that have ever worked well on it, or that shall ever work well on it. No generation of men can or could, with never such solemnity and effort, sell Land on any other principle : it is not the property of any generation, we say, but that of all the past generations that have worked on it, and of all the future ones that shall work on it.

Again, we hear it said, The soil of England, or of any country, is properly worth nothing, except 'the labour bestowed on it'. This, speaking even in the language of Eastcheap, is not correct. The rudest space of country equal in extent to England, could a whole English Nation, with all their habitudes, arrangements, skills, with whatsoever they do carry within the skins of them and cannot be stript of, suddenly take wing and alight on it,—would be worth a very considerable thing! Swiftly, within year and day, this English Nation, with its multiplex talents of ploughing, spinning, hammering, mining, road-making and trafficking, would bring a handsome value out of such a space of country. On the other hand, fancy what an English Nation, once 'on the wing', could have done with itself, had there been simply no soil, not even an inarable one, to alight on ? Vain all its talents for ploughing, hammering, and whatever else; there is no Earth-room for this Nation with its talents: this Nation will have to *keep* hovering on the wing, dolefully shrieking to and fro ; and perish piecemeal ; burying itself, down to the last soul of it, in the waste unfirmamented seas. Ah yes, soil, with or without ploughing, is the gift of God. The soil of all countries belongs evermore, in a very considerable degree, to the Almighty Maker! The last stroke of labour bestowed on it is not the making of its value, but only the increasing thereof.

It is very strange, the degree to which these truisms are forgotten in our days ; how, in the ever-whirling chaos of Formulas, we have quietly lost sight of Fact,—which it is so perilous not to keep forever in sight. Fact, if we do not see it, will make us *feel* it by and by !—From much loud controversy and Corn-Law debating there rises, loud though inarticulate, once more in these years, this very question among others, Who made the Land of England? Who made it, this respectable English Land, wheat-growing, metalliferous, carboniferous, which will let readily hand over head for seventy millions or upwards, as it here lies: who did make it?—'We!' answer the much-*consuming* Aristocracy ; 'We!' as they ride in, moist with the sweat of Melton Mowbray : 'It is we that made it ; or are the heirs, assigns and representatives of those who did !'—My brothers, You ? Everlasting honour to you, then ; and Corn-Laws as many as you will, till your own deep stomachs cry Enough, or some voice of Human pity for our famine bids you Hold ! Ye are as gods, that can create soil. Soil-creating gods there is no withstanding. They have the might to sell wheat at what price they list ; and the right, to all lengths, and famine-lengths,—if they be pitiless infernal gods ! Celestial gods, I think, would stop short of the famine-price ; but no infernal nor any kind of god can be bidden stop !— Infatuated mortals, into what questions are you driving every thinking man in England ?

I say, you did *not* make the Land of England ; and, by the possession of it, you *are* bound to furnish guidance and governance to England ! That is the law of your position on this God's-Earth ; an everlasting act of Heaven's Parliament, not repealable in St. Stephen's or elsewhere! True govern-ment and guidance ; not no-government and Laissez-faire ; how much less, *mis*-government and Corn-Law! There is not an imprisoned Worker looking out from these Bastilles but appeals, very audibly in Heaven's High Courts, against you, and me, and every one who is not imprisoned, 'Why am I here ?' His appeal is audible in Heaven ; and will become audible enough on Earth too, if it remain unheeded here. His appeal is against you, foremost of all ; you stand in the front-rank of the accused ; you, by the very place you hold, have first of all to answer him and Heaven!

What looks maddest, miserablest in these mad and miserable Corn-Laws is independent altogether of their 'effect on wages', their effect on 'increase of trade', or any other such effect: it is the continual maddening proof they protrude into the faces of all men, that our Governing Class, called by God and Nature and the inflexible law of Fact, either to do something towards governing, or to die and be abolished,—have not yet learned even to sit still and do no mischief! For no Anti-Corn-Law League yet asks more of them than this ;—Nature and Fact, very imperatively, asking so much more of them. Anti-Corn-Law League asks not, Do something ; but, Cease your destructive misdoing, Do ye nothing !

Nature's message will have itself obeyed: messages of mere Free-Trade, Anti-Corn-Law League and Laissez-faire, will then need small obeying !—Ye fools, in name of Heaven, work, work, at the Ark of Deliverance for yourselves and us, while hours are still granted you ! No : instead of working at the Ark, they say, ' We cannot get our hands kept rightly warm ' ; and *sit obstinately burning the planks*. No madder spectacle at present exhibits itself under this Sun.

The Working Aristocracy ; Mill-owners, Manufacturers, Commanders of Working Men : alas, against them also much shall be brought in accusation ; much,—and the freest Trade in Corn, total abolition of Tariffs, and uttermost 'Increase of Manufactures' and 'Prosperity of Commerce', will permanently mend no jot of it. The Working Aristocracy must strike into a new path ; must understand that money alone is *not* the representative either of man's success in the world, or of man's duties to man ; and reform their own selves from top to bottom, if they wish England reformed. England will not be habitable long, unreformed.

The Working Aristocracy—Yes, but on the threshold of all this, it is again and again to be asked, What of the Idle Aristocracy ? Again and again, what shall we say of the Idle Aristocracy, the Owners of the Soil of England ; whose recognized function is that of handsomely consuming the rents of England, shooting the partridges of England, and as an agreeable amusement (if the purchase-money and other conveniences serve), dilettante-ing in Parliament and Quarter-Sessions for England? We will say mournfully, in the presence of Heaven and Earth,—that we stand speech-less, stupent, and know not what to say! That a class of men entitled to live sumptuously on the marrow of the earth ; permitted simply, nay entreated, and as yet entreated in vain, to do nothing at all in return, was never heretofore seen on the face of this Planet. That such a class is tran-sitory, exceptional, and, unless Nature's Laws fall dead, can-not continue. That it has continued now a moderate while ; has, for the last fifty years, been rapidly attaining its state of perfection. That it will have to find its duties and do them ; or else that it must and will cease to be seen on the face of this Planet, which is a Working one, not an Idle one.

Alas, alas, the Working Aristocracy, admonished by Trades-unions, Chartist conflagrations, above all by their own shrewd sense kept in perpetual communion with the fact of things, will assuredly reform themselves, and a working world will still be possible:—but the fate of the Idle Aris-tocracy, as one reads its horoscope hitherto in Corn-Laws and such like, is an abyss that fills one with despair. Yes, my rosy fox-hunting brothers, a terrible *Hippocratic look* reveals itself (God knows, not to my joy) through those fresh buxom countenances of yours. Through your Corn-Law Majorities, Sliding-Scales, Protecting-Duties, Bribery-Elec-tions, and triumphant Kentish-fire, a thinking eye discerns ghastly images of ruin, too ghastly for words ; a hand-writing as of MENE, MENE. Men and brothers, on your Sliding-scale you seem sliding, and to have slid,—you little know whither! Good God! did not a French Donothing Aristocracy, hardly above half a century ago, declare in like manner, and in its featherhead believe in like manner, ' We cannot exist, and continue to dress and parade ourselves, on the just rent of the soil of France ; but we must have farther payment than rent of the soil, we must be exempted from taxes too,'—we must have a Corn-Law to extend our rent ? This was in 1789 : in four years more—Did you look into the Tanneries of Meudon, and the long-naked making for themselves breeches of human skins! May the merciful Heavens avert the omen ; may we be wiser, that so we be less wretched.

A High Class without duties to do is like a tree planted on precipices; from the roots of which all the earth has been crumbling. Nature owns no man who is not a Martyr withal. Is there a man who pretends to live luxuriously housed up; screened from all work, from want, danger, hardship, the victory over which is what we name work;— he himself to sit serene, amid down-bolsters and appliances, and have all his work and battling done by other men? And such man calls himself a *noble*-man? His fathers worked for him, he says; or successfully gambled for him: here *he* sits; professes, not in sorrow but in pride, that he and his have done no work, time out of mind. It is the law of the land, and is thought to be the law of the Universe, that he, alone of recorded men, shall have no task laid on him, except that of eating his cooked victuals, and not flinging himself out of window. Once more I will say, there was no stranger spectacle ever shown under this Sun. A veritable fact in our England of the Nineteenth Century. His victuals he does eat: but as for keeping in the inside of the window,— have not his friends, like me, enough to do? Truly, looking at his Corn-Laws, Game-Laws, Chandos-Clauses, Bribery-Elections and much else, you do shudder over the tumbling and plunging he makes, held back by the lapelles and coat-skirts; only a thin fence of window-glass before him,—and in the street mere horrid iron spikes! My sick brother, as in hospital-maladies men do, thou dreamest of Paradises and Eldorados, which are far from thee. 'Cannot I do what I like with my own?' Gracious Heaven, my brother, this that thou seest with those sick eyes is no firm Eldorado, and Corn-Law Paradise of Donothings, but a dream of thy own fevered brain. It is a glass-window, I tell thee, so many stories from the street; where are iron spikes and the law of gravitation!

What is the meaning of nobleness, if this be 'noble'? In a valiant suffering for others, not in a slothful making others suffer for us, did nobleness ever lie. The chief of men is he who stands in the van of men; fronting the peril which frightens back all others; which, if it be not van-quished, will devour the others. Every noble crown is, and on Earth will forever be, a crown of thorns. The Pagan Hercules, why was he accounted a hero? Because he had slain Nemean Lions, cleansed Augean Stables, undergone

Twelve Labours only not too heavy for a god. In modern, as in ancient and all societies, the Aristocracy, they that assume the functions of an Aristocracy, doing them or not, have taken the post of honour; which is the post of difficulty, the post of danger,—of death, if the difficulty be not overcome. *Il faut payer de sa vie.* Why was our life given us, if not that we should manfully give it? Descend, O Do-nothing Pomp; quit thy down-cushions; expose thyself to learn what wretches feel, and how to cure it! The Czar of *Peter the* Russia became a dusty toiling shipwright; worked with *Great* his axe in the Docks of Saardam; and his aim was small to *1672-1725* thine. Descend thou: undertake this horrid 'living chaos of Ignorance and Hunger' weltering round thy feet; say, ' I will heal it, or behold I will die foremost in it.' Such is verily the law. Everywhere and everywhen a man has to '*pay* with his life'; to do his work, as a soldier does, at the expense of life. In no Piepowder earthly Court can you sue an Aristocracy to do its work, at this moment: but in the Higher Court, which even *it* calls 'Court of Honour', and which is the Court of Necessity withal, and the eternal Court of the Universe, in which all Fact comes to plead, and every Human Soul is an apparitor,—the Aristocracy is answerable, and even now answering, *there.*

Parchments? Parchments are venerable: but they ought at all times to represent, as near as they by possibility can, the writing of the Adamant Tablets; otherwise they are not so venerable! Benedict the Jew in vain pleaded parchments; his usuries were too many. The King said, ' Go to, for all thy parchments, thou shalt pay just debt; down with thy dust, or observe this tooth-forceps!' Nature, a far juster Sovereign, has far terribler forceps. Aristocracies, actual and imaginary, reach a time when parchment pleading does not avail them. 'Go to, for all thy parchments, thou shalt pay due debt!' shouts the Universe to them, in an emphatic manner. They refuse to pay, confidently pleading parchment: their best grinder-tooth, with horrible agony, goes out of their jaw. Wilt thou pay now? A second grinder, again in horrible agony, goes: a second, and a third, and if need be, all the teeth and grinders, and the life itself with them;— and *then* there is free payment, and an anatomist-subject into the bargain!

Reform Bills, Corn-Law Abrogation Bills, and then Land-Tax Bill, Property-Tax Bill, and still dimmer list of *etceteras;* grinder after grinder:—my lords and gentlemen, it were better for you to arise, and begin doing your work, than sit there and plead parchments !

We write no Chapter on the Corn-Laws, in this place ; the Corn-Laws are too mad to have a Chapter. There is a certain immorality, when there is not a necessity, in speaking about things finished ; in chopping into small pieces the already slashed and slain. When the brains are out, why does not a Solecism die ? It is at its own peril if it refuse to die ; it ought to make all conceivable haste to die, and get itself buried ! The trade of Anti-Corn-Law Lecturer in these days, still an indispensable, is a highly tragic one.

The Corn-Laws will go, and even soon go : would we were all as sure of the Millennium as they are of going! They go swiftly in these present months ; with an increase of velocity, an ever-deepening, ever-widening sweep of momentum, truly notable. It is at the Aristocracy's own damage and peril, still more than at any other's whatsoever, that the Aristocracy maintains them ;—at a damage, say only, as above computed, of a ' hundred thousand pounds an hour ' ! The Corn-Laws keep all the air hot: fostered by their fever-warmth, much that is evil, but much also, how much that is good and indispensable, is rapidly coming to life among us !

CHAPTER IX

WORKING ARISTOCRACY

A POOR Working Mammonism getting itself 'strangled in the partridge-nets of an Unworking Dilettantism', and bellowing dreadfully, and already black in the face, is surely a disastrous spectacle ! But of a Midas-eared Mammonism, which indeed at bottom all pure Mammonisms are, what better can you expect ? No better ;—if not this, then some-

thing other equally disastrous, if not still more disastrous.
Mammonisms, grown asinine, have to become human again,
and rational; they have, on the whole, to cease to be
Mammonisms, were it even on compulsion, and pressure of
the hemp round their neck!—My friends of the Working
Aristocracy, there are now a great many things which you
also, in your extreme need, will have to consider.

The Continental people, it would seem, are 'exporting
our machinery, beginning to spin cotton and manufacture
for themselves, to cut us out of this market and then out of
that'! Sad news indeed; but irremediable ;—by no means
the saddest news. The saddest news is, that we should find
our National Existence, as I sometimes hear it said, depend
on selling manufactured cotton at a farthing an ell cheaper
than any other People. A most narrow stand for a great
Nation to base itself on ! A stand which, with all the Corn-
Law Abrogations conceivable, I do not think will be capable
of enduring.

My friends, suppose we quitted that stand; suppose we
came honestly down from it, and said: 'This is our minimum of cotton-prices. We care not, for the present, to
make cotton any cheaper. Do you, if it seem so blessed to
you, make cotton cheaper. Fill your lungs with cotton-fuz,
your hearts with copperas-fumes, with rage and mutiny;
become ye the general gnomes of Europe, slaves of the
lamp!'—I admire a Nation which fancies it will die if it do
not undersell all other Nations, to the end of the world.
Brothers, we will cease to *under*sell them; we will be content to *equal*-sell them; to be happy selling equally with
them ! I do not see the use of underselling them. Cotton-
cloth is already two-pence a yard or lower; and yet bare
backs were never more numerous among us. Let inventive
men cease to spend their existence incessantly contriving
how cotton can be made cheaper; and try to invent, a little,
how cotton at its present cheapness could be somewhat justlier divided among us. Let inventive men consider, Whether
the Secret of this Universe, and of Man's Life there, does,
after all, as we rashly fancy it, consist in making money?
There is One God, just, supreme, almighty: but is Mammon
the name of him ?—With a Hell which means ' Failing to
make money ', I do not think there is any Heaven possible

that would suit one well ; nor so much as an Earth that can be habitable long! In brief, all this Mammon-Gospel, of Supply-and-demand, Competition, Laissez-faire, and Devil take the hindmost, begins to be one of the shabbiest Gospels ever preached ; or altogether the shabbiest. Even with Dilettante partridge-nets, and at a horrible expenditure of pain, who shall regret to see the entirely transient, and at best somewhat despicable life strangled out of *it*? At the best, as we say, a somewhat despicable, unvenerable thing, this same ' Laissez-faire '; and now, at the *worst*, fast growing an altogether detestable one!

'But what is to be done with our manufacturing popula- tion, with our agricultural, with our ever-increasing popu- lation ?' cry many.—Aye, what? Many things can be done with them, a hundred things, and a thousand things,—had we once got a soul, and begun to try. This one thing, of doing for them by ' underselling all people ', and filling our own bursten pockets and appetites by the road ; and turning over all care for any ' population ', or human or divine con- sideration except cash only, to the winds, with a ' Laissez- faire ' and the rest of it: this is evidently not the thing. Farthing cheaper per yard? No great Nation can stand on the apex of such a pyramid ; screwing itself higher and higher ; balancing itself on its great-toe! Can England not subsist without being *above* all people in working ? England never deliberately purposed such a thing. If England work better than all people, it shall be well. England, like an honest worker, will work as well as she can ; and hope the gods may allow her to live on that basis. Laissez-faire and much else being once well dead, how many ' impossibles ' will become possible! They are impossible, as cotton-cloth at two-pence an ell was—till men set about making it. The inventive genius of great England will not for ever sit patient with mere wheels and pinions, bobbins, straps and billy-rollers whirring in the head of it. The inventive genius of England is not a Beaver's, or a Spinner's or Spider's genius: it is a *Man's* genius, I hope, with a God over him!

Laissez-faire, Supply-and-demand,—one begins to be weary of all that. Leave all to egoism, to ravenous greed of money, of pleasure, of applause:—it is the Gospel of Despair! Man *is* a Patent-Digester, then: only give him Free Trade, Free digesting-room; and each of us digest what he can come at, leaving the rest to Fate! My unhappy brethren of the Working Mammonism, my unhappier brethren of the Idle Dilettantism, no world was ever held together in that way for long. A world of mere Patent-Digesters will soon have nothing to digest: such world ends, and by Law of Nature must end, in 'over-population'; in howling universal famine, 'impossibility,' and suicidal madness, as of endless dog-kennels run rabid. Supply-and-demand shall do its full part, and Free Trade shall be free as air;—thou of the shot-belts, see thou forbid it not, with those paltry, *worse* than Mammonish swindleries and Sliding-scales of thine, which are seen to be swindleries for all thy canting, which in times like ours are very scandalous to see! And Trade never so well freed, and all Tariffs settled or abolished, and Supply-and-demand in full operation,—let us all know that we have yet done nothing; that we have merely cleared the ground for doing.

Yes, were the Corn-Laws ended to-morrow, there is nothing yet ended; there is only room made for all manner of things beginning. The Corn-Laws gone, and Trade made free, it is as good as certain this paralysis of industry will pass away. We shall have another period of commercial enterprise, of victory and prosperity; during which, it is likely, much money will again be made, and all the people may, by the extant methods, still for a space of years, be kept alive and physically fed. The strangling band of Famine will be loosened from our necks; we shall have room again to breathe; time to bethink ourselves, to repent and consider! A precious and thrice-precious space of years; wherein to struggle as for life in reforming our foul ways; in alleviating, instructing, regulating our people; seeking, as for life, that something like spiritual food be imparted them, some real governance and guidance be provided them! It will be a priceless time. For our new period or paroxysm of commercial prosperity will and can, on the old methods of 'Competition and Devil take the hindmost', prove but a paroxysm: a new paroxysm,—likely enough, if we do not use it better, to be our *last*. In this, of itself, is no salvation. If our Trade in twenty years, 'flourishing' as never Trade flourished, could double itself; yet then also, by the old Laissez-faire method, our Population is doubled: we shall be as we are, only twice as many of us, twice and ten times as unmanageable!

All this dire misery, therefore; all this of our poor Workhouse Workmen, of our Chartisms, Trades-strikes, Corn-Laws, Toryisms, and the general downbreak of Laissez-faire in these days,—may we not regard it as a voice from the dumb bosom of Nature, saying to us: 'Behold! Supply-and-demand is not the one Law of Nature; Cash-payment is not the sole nexus of man with man,—how far from it! Deep, far deeper than Supply-and-demand, are Laws, Obligations sacred as Man's Life itself: these also, if you will continue to do work, you shall now learn and obey. He that will learn them, behold Nature is on his side, he shall yet work and prosper with noble rewards. He that will not learn them, Nature is against him, he shall not be able to do work in Nature's empire,—not in hers. Perpetual mutiny, contention, hatred, isolation, execration shall wait on his footsteps, till all men discern that the thing which he attains, however golden it look or be, is not success, but the want of success.'

Supply-and-demand,—alas! For what noble work was there ever yet any audible 'demand' in that poor sense? The man of Macedonia, speaking in vision to an Apostle Paul, 'Come over and help us,' did not specify what rate of wages he would give! Or was the Christian Religion itself accomplished by Prize-Essays, Bridgwater Bequests, and a 'minimum of Four thousand five hundred a year'? No demand that I heard of was made then, audible in any Labour-market, Manchester Chamber of Commerce, or other the like emporium and hiring establishment; silent were all these from any whisper of such demand;—powerless were all these to 'supply' it, had the demand been in thunder and earthquake, with gold Eldorados and Mahometan Paradises for the reward. Ah me, into what waste latitudes, in this Time-Voyage, have we wandered; like adventurous Sindbads;—where the men go about as if by galvanism, with meaningless glaring eyes, and have no soul, but only a beaver-faculty and stomach! The haggard despair of Cotton-factory, Coal-mine operatives, Chandos Farm-labourers, in these days, is painful to behold; but not so painful, hideous to the inner sense, as that brutish godforgetting Profit-and-Loss Philosophy and Life-theory, which we hear jangled on all hands of us, in senate-houses, spouting-clubs, leading-articles, pulpits and platforms, everywhere as the Ultimate Gospel and candid Plain-English of Man's Life, from the throats and pens and thoughts of all-but all men!—

Enlightened Philosophies, like Molière Doctors, will tell you: ' Enthusiasms, Self-sacrifice, Heaven, Hell and such like : yes, all that was true enough for old stupid times ; all that used to be true : but we have changed all that, *nous avons changé tout cela!*' Well ; if the heart be got round now into the right side, and the liver to the left ; if man have no heroism in him deeper than the wish to eat, and in his soul there dwell now no Infinite of Hope and Awe, and no divine Silence can become imperative because it is not Sinai Thunder, and no tie will bind if it be not that of Tyburn gallows-ropes,—then verily you have changed all that ; and for it, and for you, and for me, behold the Abyss and nameless Annihilation is ready. So scandalous a beggarly Universe deserves indeed nothing else ; I cannot say I would save it from Annihilation. Vacuum, and the serene Blue, will be much handsomer ; easier too for all of us. I, for one, decline living as a Patent-Digester. Patent-Digester, Spinning-Mule, Mayfair Clothes-Horse: many thanks, but your Chaosships will have the goodness to excuse me!

CHAPTER X

PLUGSON OF UNDERSHOT

ONE thing I do know: Never, on this Earth, was the relation of man to man long carried on by Cash-payment alone. If, at any time, a philosophy of Laissez-faire, Competition and Supply-and-demand, start up as the exponent of human relations, expect that it will soon end.

Such philosophies will arise: for man's philosophies are usually the ' supplement of his practice' ; some ornamental Logic-varnish, some outer skin of Articulate Intelligence, with which he strives to render his dumb Instinctive Doings presentable when they are done. Such philosophies will arise ; be preached as Mammon-Gospels, the ultimate Evangel of the World ; be believed, with what is called belief, with much superficial bluster, and a kind of shallow satisfaction real in its way :—but they are ominous gospels ! They are the sure, and even swift, forerunner of great changes. Expect that the old System of Society is done, is dying and fallen into dotage, when it begins to rave in that fashion. Most Systems that I have watched the death of, for the last three thousand years, have gone just so. The Ideal, the True and Noble that was in them having faded out, and nothing now remaining but naked Egoism, vul-turous Greediness, they cannot live ; they are bound and inexorably ordained by the oldest Destinies, Mothers of the Universe, to die. Curious enough : they thereupon, as I have pretty generally noticed, devise some light com-fortable kind of ' wine-and-walnuts philosophy' for them-selves, this of Supply-and-demand or another ; and keep saying, during hours of mastication and rumination, which they call hours of meditation : ' Soul, take thy ease, it is all *well* that thou art a vulture-soul ' ;—and pangs of dissolution come upon them, oftenest before they are aware !

Cash-payment never was, or could except for a few years be, the union-bond of man to man. Cash never yet paid one man fully his deserts to another ; nor could it, nor can it, now or henceforth to the end of the world. I invite his Grace of Castle-Rackrent to reflect on this ;—does he think that a Land Aristocracy when it becomes a Land Auctioneer-ship can have long to live ? Or that Sliding-scales will increase the vital stamina of it ? The indomitable Plugson too, of the respected Firm of Plugson, Hunks and Company, in St. Dolly Undershot, is invited to reflect on this ; for to him also it will be new, perhaps even newer. Book-keeping by double entry is admirable, and records several things in an exact manner. But the Mother-Destinies also keep their Tablets ; in Heaven's Chancery also there goes on a recording ; and things, as my Moslem friends say, are ' written on the iron leaf '.

Your Grace and Plugson, it is like, go to Church occa-sionally : did you never in vacant moments, with perhaps a dull parson droning to you, glance into your New Testament, and the cash-account stated four times over, by a kind of quadruple entry,—in the Four Gospels there? I consider that a cash-account, and balance-statement of work done and wages paid, worth attending to. Precisely *such*, though on a smaller scale, go on at all moments under this Sun; and the statement and balance of them in the Plugson Ledgers and on the Tablets of Heaven's Chancery are discrepant exceedingly;—which ought really to teach, and to have long since taught, an indomitable common-sense Plugson of Undershot, much more an unattackable *un*common-sense Grace of Rackrent, a thing or two!—In brief, we shall have to dismiss the Cash-Gospel rigorously into its own place: we shall have to know, on the threshold, that either there is some infinitely deeper Gospel, subsidiary, explanatory and daily and hourly corrective, to the Cash one; or else that the Cash one itself and all others are fast travelling!

For all human things do require to have an Ideal in them; to have some Soul in them, as we said, were it only to keep the Body unputrefied. And wonderful it is to see how the Ideal or Soul, place it in what ugliest Body you may, will irradiate said Body with its own nobleness; will gradually, incessantly, mould, modify, new-form or reform said ugliest Body, and make it at last beautiful, and to a certain degree divine!—O, if you could dethrone that Brute-god Mammon, and put a Spirit-god in his place! One way or other, he must and will have to be dethroned.

Fighting, for example, as I often say to myself, Fighting with steel murder-tools is surely a much uglier operation than Working, take it how you will. Yet even of Fighting, in religious Abbot Samson's days, see what a Feudalism there had grown,—a ' glorious Chivalry', much besung down to the present day. Was not that one of the ' impossiblest ' things? Under the sky is no uglier spectacle than two men with clenched teeth, and hellfire eyes, hacking one another's flesh; converting precious living bodies, and priceless living souls, into nameless masses of putrescence, useful only for turnip-manure. How did a Chivalry ever come out of that; how anything that was not hideous, scandalous, infernal? It will be a question worth considering by and by.

I remark, for the present, only two things: first, that the Fighting itself was not, as we rashly suppose it, a

Fighting without cause, but more or less with cause. Man is created to fight; he is perhaps best of all definable as a born soldier; his life 'a battle and a march', under the right General. It is for ever indispensable for a man to fight: now with Necessity, with Barrenness, Scarcity, with Puddles, Bogs, tangled Forests, unkempt Cotton;—now also with the hallucinations of his poor fellow Men. Hallucinatory visions rise in the head of my poor fellow man; make him claim over me rights which are not his. All Fighting, as we noticed long ago, is the dusty conflict of strengths, each thinking itself the strongest, or, in other words, the justest;—of Mights which do in the long-run, and for ever will in this just Universe in the long-run, mean Rights. In conflict the perishable part of them, beaten sufficiently, flies off into dust: this process ended, appears the imperishable, the true and exact.

And now let us remark a second thing: how, in these baleful operations, a noble devout-hearted Chevalier will comfort himself, and an ignoble godless Bucanier and Chactaw Indian. Victory is the aim of each. But deep in the heart of the noble man it lies forever legible, that, as an Invisible Just God made him, so will and must God's Justice and this only, were it never so invisible, ultimately prosper in all controversies and enterprises and battles whatsoever. What an Influence; ever-present,—like a Soul in the rudest Caliban of a body; like a ray of Heaven, and illuminative creative *Fiat-Lux*, in the wastest terrestrial Chaos! Blessed divine Influence, traceable even in the horror of Battlefields and garments rolled in blood: how it ennobles even the Battlefield; and, in place of a Chactaw Massacre, makes it a Field of Honour! A Battlefield too is great. Considered well, it is a kind of Quintessence of Labour; Labour distilled into its utmost concentration; the significance of years of it compressed into an hour. Here too thou shalt be strong, and not in muscle only, if thou wouldst prevail. Here too thou shalt be strong of heart, noble of soul; thou shalt dread no pain or death, thou shalt not love ease or life; in rage, thou shalt remember mercy, justice;—thou shalt be a Knight and not a Chactaw, if thou wouldst prevail! It is the rule of all battles, against hallucinating fellow Men, against unkempt Cotton, or whatsoever battles they may be which a man in this world has to fight.

Edward

Howel Davies dyes the West Indian Seas with blood, piles his decks with plunder; approves himself the expertest Seaman, the daringest Seafighter: but he gains no lasting victory, lasting victory is not possible for him. Not, had he fleets larger than the combined British Navy all united with him in bucaniering. He, once for all, cannot prosper in his duel. He strikes down his man: yes; but his man, or his man's representative, has no notion to lie struck down; neither, though slain ten times, will he keep so lying;—nor has the Universe any notion to keep him so lying! On the contrary, the Universe and he have, at all moments, all manner of motives to start up again, and desperately fight again. Your Napoleon is flung out, at last, to St. Helena; the latter end of him sternly compensating the beginning. The Bucanier strikes down a man, a hundred or a million men: but what profits it? He has one enemy never to be struck down; nay two enemies: Mankind and the Maker of Men. On the great scale or on the small, in fighting of men or fighting of difficulties, I will not embark my venture with Howel Davies: it is not the Bucanier, it is the Hero only that can gain victory, that can do more than *seem* to succeed. These things will deserve meditating; for they apply to all battle and soldiership, all struggle and effort whatsoever in this Fight of Life. It is a poor Gospel, Cash-Gospel or whatever name it have, that does not, with clear tone, uncontradictable, carrying conviction to all hearts, forever keep men in mind of these things.

Unhappily, my indomitable friend Plugson of Undershot has, in a great degree, forgotten them;—as, alas, all the world has; as, alas, our very Dukes and Soul-Overseers have, whose special trade it was to remember them! Hence these tears.—Plugson, who has indomitably spun Cotton merely to gain thousands of pounds, I have to call as yet a Bucanier and Chactaw; till there come something better, still more indomitable from him. His hundred Thousand-pound Notes, if there be nothing other, are to me but as the hundred Scalps in a Chactaw wigwam. The blind Plugson: he was a Captain of Industry, born member of the Ultimate genuine Aristocracy of this Universe, could he have known it! These thousand men that span and toiled round him, they were a regiment whom he had enlisted, man by man;

to make war on a very genuine enemy: Bareness of back, and disobedient Cotton-fibre, which will not, unless forced to it, consent to cover bare backs.   Here is a most genuine enemy; over whom all creatures will wish him victory. He enlisted his thousand men; said to them, 'Come, brothers, let us have a dash at Cotton!' They follow with cheerful shout; they gain such a victory over Cotton as the Earth has to admire and clap hands at: but, alas, it is yet only of the Bucanier or Chactaw sort,—as good as no victory! Foolish Plugson of St. Dolly Undershot: does he hope to become illustrious by hanging up the scalps in his wigwam, the hundred thousands at his banker's, and saying, Behold my scalps? Why, Plugson, even thy own host is all in mutiny: Cotton is conquered; but the 'bare backs'—are worse covered than ever! Indomitable Plugson, thou must cease to be a Chactaw; thou and others; thou thyself, if no other!

Did William the Norman Bastard, or any of his Taillefers, *Ironcutters*, manage so? Ironcutter, at the end of the campaign, did not turn off his thousand fighters, but said to them: 'Noble fighters, this is the land we have gained; be I Lord in it,—what we will call *Law-ward*, maintainer and *keeper* of Heaven's *Laws*: be I *Law-ward*, or in brief orthoepy *Lord* in it, and be ye Loyal Men around me in it: and we will stand by one another, as soldiers round a captain, for again we shall have need of one another!' Plugson, bucanier-like, says to them: 'Noble spinners, this is the Hundred Thousand we have gained, wherein I mean to dwell and plant vineyards; the hundred thousand is mine, the three and sixpence daily was yours: adieu, noble spinners; drink my health with this groat each, which I give you over and above!' The entirely unjust Captain of Industry, say I; not Chevalier, but Bucanier! 'Commercial Law' does indeed acquit him; asks, with wide eyes, What else? So too Howel Davies asks, Was it not according to the strictest Bucanier Custom? Did I depart in any jot or tittle from the Laws of the Bucaniers?

After all, money, as they say, is miraculous.   Plugson wanted victory; as Chevaliers and Bucaniers, and all men alike do. He found money recognized, by the whole world with one assent, as the true symbol, exact equivalent and synonym of victory ;—and here we have him, a grimbrowed, indomitable Bucanier, coming home to us with a 'victory', which the whole world is *ceasing* to clap hands at! The whole world, taught somewhat impressively, is beginning to recognize that such victory is but half a victory; and that now, if it please the Powers, we must—have the other half!

Money is miraculous. What miraculous facilities has it yielded, will it yield us; but also what never-imagined confusions, obscurations has it brought in; down almost to total extinction of the moral-sense in large masses of mankind! 'Protection of property', of what is '*mine*', means with most men protection of money,—the thing which, had I a thousand padlocks over it, is least of all *mine;* is, in a manner, scarcely worth calling mine! The symbol shall be held sacred, defended everywhere with tipstaves, ropes and gibbets; the thing signified shall be composedly cast to the dogs. A human being who has worked with human beings clears all scores with them, cuts himself with triumphant completeness for over loose from them, by paying down certain shillings and pounds. Was it not the wages I promised you? There they are, to the last sixpence,—according to the Laws of the Bucaniers!—Yes, indeed;—and, at such times, it becomes imperatively necessary to ask all persons, bucaniers and others, Whether these same respectable Laws of the Bucaniers are written on God's eternal Heavens at all, on the inner Heart of Man at all; or on the respectable Bucanier Logbook merely, for the convenience of bucaniering merely? What a question;— whereat Westminster Hall shudders to its driest parchment; and on the dead wigs each particular horsehair stands on end!

The Laws of Laissez-faire, O Westminster, the laws of industrial Captain and industrial Soldier, how much more of idle Captain and industrial Soldier, will need to be remodelled, and modified, and rectified in a hundred and a hundred ways,—and *not* in the Sliding-scale direction, but in the totally opposite one! With two million industrial Soldiers already sitting in Bastilles, and five million pining on potatoes, methinks Westminster cannot begin too soon! —A man has other obligations laid on him, in God's Universe, than the payment of cash: these also Westminster, if it will continue to exist and have board-wages, must contrive to take some charge of:—by Westminster or by another, they must and will be taken charge of; be, with whatever difficulty, got articulated, got enforced, and to a certain approximate extent put in practice. And, as I say, it cannot be too soon! For Mammonism, left to itself, has become Midas-eared; and with all its gold mountains, sits starving for want of bread: and Dilettantism with its partridge-nets, in this extremely earnest Universe of ours, is playing somewhat too high a game. 'A man by the very look of him promises so much': yes; and by the rent-roll of him does he promise nothing?—

Alas, what a business will this be, which our Continental friends, groping this long while somewhat absurdly about it and about it, call ' Organization of Labour ';—which must be taken out of the hands of absurd windy persons, and put into the hands of wise, laborious, modest and valiant men, to begin with it straightway: to proceed with it, and succeed in it more and more, if Europe, at any rate if England, is to continue habitable much longer. Looking at the kind of most noble Corn-law Dukes or Practical *Duces* we have, and also of right reverend Soul-Overseers, Christian Spiritual *Duces* 'on a minimum of four thousand five hundred', one's hopes are a little chilled. Courage, nevertheless; there are many brave men in England! My indomitable Plugson,— nay is there not even in thee some hope? Thou art hitherto a Bucanier, as it was written and prescribed for thee by an evil world: but in that grim brow, in that indomitable heart which *can* conquer Cotton, do there not perhaps lie other ten times nobler conquests?

CHAPTER XI

LABOUR

FOR there is a perennial nobleness, and even sacredness, in Work. Were he never so benighted, forgetful of his high calling, there is always hope in a man that actually and earnestly works: in Idleness alone is there perpetual

The Landed. Chapter VI

The man with a thousand pounds a day could do a great deal of good. — could be a strong worker. At the end of a year what has he done? — kept himself alive in comfort and helped no one else. Will he find his soul and help his fellow men once more? — Compare the Duke of Weimar to the present English Dukes. he was a spiritual man with spiritual men under him — Wieland Herder Schiller Goethe. — he has done more than all the Dukes since Henry VIII

These men must help their fellow creatures and not sit in Idleness

There are exceptions like Ashley Earl of Shaftesbury 1842 Mines Act. — no women at all and no boys under 10.

Men cannot sit idle albeit. — they are bound together and must help one another.

Sham superiors must be rejected and real superiors put in their place.

The Gifted Chapter VII

Chaos and disaster can be calmed down and put into order if it has a soul.

Mammonism like fire, a great servant but a dreadful master. — must gold be man's main desire? The yellow guinea is not omnipotent.

There is a man who is not a slave. — nothing can touch or affect him — he is brightening a new against power — he cannot be bribed and do not try to infect him. — he is God's Justice — Human Nobleness and Veracity. What a Man of Genius is. Maecenas Twiddledee has no idea. — Genius is the clearer presence of God.

Chapter VIII The Dialectic
Nothing I can say will help — it is Destiny that counts. — Light will appear when it is dark enough. What has the Capitalist mill owner. against — money yet surrounded by squalor — he will say 'let me try something else, Thé money' Christianity will fail and the Mammon Empire crack. — Men love light, and 'impossible' will be finished with.

Book IV   Horoscope.
Chapter I - Aristocracies,

despair. Work, never so Mammonish, mean, *is* in communication with Nature; the real desire to get Work done
will itself lead one more and more to truth, to Nature's
appointments and regulations, which are truth.

The latest Gospel in this world is, Know thy work and
do it. 'Know thyself': long enough has that poor 'self'
of thine tormented thee; thou wilt never get to 'know' it,
I believe! Think it not thy business, this of knowing thyself; thou art an unknowable individual: know what thou
canst work at; and work at it, like a Hercules! That will
be thy better plan.

It has been written, 'an endless significance lies in
Work'; a man perfects himself by working. Foul jungles
are cleared away, fair seedfields rise instead, and stately
cities; and withal the man himself first ceases to be a jungle
and foul unwholesome desert thereby. Consider how, even
in the meanest sorts of Labour, the whole soul of a man is
composed into a kind of real harmony, the instant he sets
himself to work! Doubt, Desire, Sorrow, Remorse, Indignation, Despair itself, all these like helldogs lie beleaguering
the soul of the poor dayworker, as of every man: but he
bends himself with free valour against his task, and all these
are stilled, all these shrink murmuring far off into their
caves. The man is now a man. The blessed glow of
Labour in him, is it not as purifying fire, wherein all poison
is burnt up, and of sour smoke itself there is made bright
blessed flame!

Destiny, on the whole, has no other way of cultivating
us. A formless Chaos, once set it *revolving*, grows round
and ever rounder; ranges itself, by mere force of gravity,
into strata, spherical courses; is no longer a Chaos, but
a round compacted World. What would become of the
Earth, did she cease to revolve? In the poor old Earth, so
long as she revolves, all inequalities, irregularities disperse
themselves; all irregularities are incessantly becoming
regular. Hast thou looked on the Potter's wheel,—one of
the venerablest objects; old as the Prophet Ezekiel and far
older? Rude lumps of clay, how they spin themselves up,
by mere quick whirling, into beautiful circular dishes. And
fancy the most assiduous Potter, but without his wheel;
reduced to make dishes, or rather amorphous botches, by
mere kneading and baking! Even such a Potter were

Destiny, with a human soul that would rest and lie at ease, that would not work and spin! Of an idle unrevolving man the kindest Destiny, like the most assiduous Potter without wheel, can bake and knead nothing other than a botch; let her spend on him what expensive colouring, what gilding and enamelling she will, he is but a botch. Not a dish; no, a bulging, kneaded, crooked, shambling, squint-cornered, amorphous botch,—a mere enamelled vessel of dishonour! Let the idle think of this.

Blessed is he who has found his work; let him ask no other blessedness. He has a work, a life-purpose; he has found it, and will follow it! How, as a free-flowing channel, dug and torn by noble force through the sour mud-swamp of one's existence, like an ever-deepening river there, it runs and flows;—draining off the sour festering water, gradually from the root of the remotest grass-blade; making, instead of pestilential swamp, a green fruitful meadow with its clear-flowing stream. How blessed for the meadow itself, let the stream and *its* value be great or small! Labour is Life: from the inmost heart of the Worker rises his god-given Force, the sacred celestial Life-essence breathed into him by Almighty God; from his inmost heart awakens him to all nobleness,—to all knowledge, 'self-knowledge' and much else, so soon as Work fitly begins. Knowledge? The knowledge that will hold good in working, cleave thou to that; for Nature herself accredits that, says Yea to that. Properly thou hast no other knowledge but what thou hast got by working: the rest is yet all a hypothesis of knowledge; a thing to be argued of in schools, a thing floating in the clouds, in endless logic-vortices, till we try it and fix it. 'Doubt, of whatever kind, can be ended by Action alone.'

And again, hast thou valued Patience, Courage, Perseverance, Openness to light; readiness to own thyself mistaken, to do better next time? All these, all virtues, in wrestling with the dim brute Powers of Fact, in ordering of thy fellows in such wrestle, there and elsewhere not at all, thou wilt continually learn. Set down a brave Sir Christopher in the middle of black ruined Stone-heaps, of foolish unarchitectural Bishops, redtape Officials, idle Nell-Gwyn Defenders of the Faith; and see whether he will ever

raise a Paul's Cathedral out of all that, yea or no! Rough,
rude, contradictory are all things and persons, from the
mutinous masons and Irish hodmen, up to the idle Nell-
Gwyn Defenders, to blustering redtape Officials, foolish
unarchitectural Bishops. All these things and persons are
there not for Christopher's sake and his Cathedral's; they
are there for their own sake mainly! Christopher will have
to conquer and constrain all these,—if he be able. All these
are against him. Equitable Nature herself, who carries her
mathematics and architectonics not on the face of her, but
deep in the hidden heart of her,—Nature herself is but
partially for him; will be wholly against him, if he constrain her not! His very money, where is it to come from?
The pious munificence of England lies far-scattered, distant,
unable to speak, and say, ' I am here';—must be spoken to
before it can speak. Pious munificence, and all help, is so
silent, invisible like the gods; impediment, contradictions
manifold are so loud and near! O brave Sir Christopher,
trust thou in those, notwithstanding, and front all these;
understand all these; by valiant patience, noble effort,
insight, by man's-strength, vanquish and compel all these,—
and, on the whole, strike down victoriously the last topstone of that Paul's Edifice; thy monument for certain
centuries, the stamp ' Great Man' impressed very legibly
on Portland-stone there!—

Yes, all manner of help, and pious response from Men or
Nature, is always what we call silent; cannot speak or come
to light, till it be seen, till it be spoken to. Every noble
work is at first 'impossible'. In very truth, for every
noble work the possibilities will lie diffused through
Immensity; inarticulate, undiscoverable except to faith.
Like Gideon thou shalt spread out thy fleece at the door of
thy tent; see whether under the wide arch of Heaven there
be any bounteous moisture, or none. Thy heart and life-
purpose shall be as a miraculous Gideon's fleece, spread out
in silent appeal to Heaven; and from the kind Immensities,
what from the poor unkind Localities and town and country
Parishes there never could, blessed dew-moisture to suffice
thee shall have fallen!

Work is of a religious nature:—work is of a *brave* nature;
which it is the aim of all religion to be. All work of man
is as the swimmer's: a waste ocean threatens to devour

him ; if he front it not bravely, it will keep its word. By incessant wise defiance of it, lusty rebuke and buffet of it, behold how it loyally supports him, bears him as its conqueror along. 'It is so', says Goethe, 'with all things that man undertakes in this world.'

Brave Sea-captain, Norse Sea-king,—Columbus, my hero, royallest Sea-king of all ! it is no friendly environment this of thine, in the waste deep waters; around thee mutinous discouraged souls, behind thee disgrace and ruin, before thee the unpenetrated veil of Night. Brother, these wild water-mountains, bounding from their deep bases (ten miles deep, I am told), are not entirely there on thy behalf ! Meseems *they* have other work than floating thee forward :—and the huge Winds, that sweep from Ursa Major to the Tropics and Equators, dancing their giant-waltz through the kingdoms of Chaos and Immensity, they care little about filling rightly or filling wrongly the small shoulder-of-mutton sails in this cockle-skiff of thine ! Thou art not among articulate-speaking friends, my brother ; thou art among immeasurable dumb monsters, tumbling, howling wide as the world here. Secret, far off, invisible to all hearts but thine, there lies a help in them : see how thou wilt get at that. Patiently thou wilt wait till the mad South-wester spend itself, saving thyself by dexterous science of defence, the while : valiantly, with swift decision, wilt thou strike in, when the favouring East, the Possible, springs up. Mutiny of men thou wilt sternly repress ; weakness, despondency, thou wilt cheerily encourage : thou wilt swallow down complaint, unreason, weariness, weakness of others and thyself ;—how much wilt thou swallow down ! There shall be a depth of Silence in thee, deeper than this Sea, which is but ten miles deep : a Silence unsoundable ; known to God only. Thou shalt be a Great Man. Yes, my World-Soldier, thou of the World Marine-service,—thou wilt have to be *greater* than this tumultuous unmeasured World here round thee is : thou, in thy strong soul, as with wrestler's arms, shalt embrace it, harness it down ; and make it bear thee on,—to new Americas, or whither God wills !

CHAPTER XII

REWARD

'RELIGION,' I said; for, properly speaking, all true Work is Religion: and whatsoever Religion is not Work may go and dwell among the Brahmins, Antinomians. Spinning Dervishes, or where it will; with me it shall have no harbour. Admirable was that of the old Monks, '*Laborare est Orare*, Work is Worship.'

Older than all preached Gospels was this unpreached, inarticulate, but ineradicable, forever-enduring Gospel: Work, and therein have wellbeing. Man, Son of Earth and of Heaven, lies there not, in the innermost heart of thee, a Spirit of active Method, a Force for Work;—and burns like a painfully smouldering fire, giving thee no rest till thou unfold it, till thou write it down in beneficent Facts around thee! What is immethodic, waste, thou shalt make methodic, regulated, arable; obedient and productive to thee. Wheresoever thou findest Disorder, there is thy eternal enemy; attack him swiftly, subdue him; make Order of him, the subject not of Chaos, but of Intelligence, Divinity and Thee! The thistle that grows in thy path, dig it out, that a blade of useful grass, a drop of nourishing milk, may grow there instead. The waste cotton-shrub, gather its waste white down, spin it, weave it; that, in place of idle litter, there may be folded webs, and the naked skin of man be covered.

But above all, where thou findest Ignorance, Stupidity, Brute-mindedness,—yes, there, with or without Church-tithes and Shovel-hat, with or without Talfourd-Mahon Copyrights, or were it with mere dungeons and gibbets and crosses, attack it, I say; smite it wisely, unweariedly, and rest not while thou livest and it lives; but smite, smite, in the name of God! The Highest God, as I understand it, does audibly so command thee; still audibly, if thou have ears to hear. He, even He, with his *un*spoken voice, awfuller than any Sinai thunders or syllabled speech of Whirlwinds; for the SILENCE of deep Eternities, of Worlds from beyond the morning-stars, does it not speak to thee?

The unborn Ages; the old Graves, with their long-mouldering
dust, the very tears that wetted it now all dry,—do not these
speak to thee, what ear hath not heard ?   The deep Death-
kingdoms, the Stars in their never-resting courses, all Space
and all Time, proclaim it to thee in continual silent admonition.   Thou too, if ever man should, shalt work while it
is called Today.   For the Night cometh, wherein no man
can work.

All true Work is sacred ; in all true Work, were it but
true hand-labour, there is something of divineness.   Labour,
wide as the Earth, has its summit in Heaven.   Sweat of
the brow ; and up from that to sweat of the brain, sweat of
the heart ; which includes all Kepler calculations, Newton
meditations, all Sciences, all spoken Epics, all acted
Heroisms, Martyrdoms,—up to that 'Agony of bloody
sweat', which all men have called divine!   O brother, if
this is not 'worship', then I say, the more pity for worship;
for this is the noblest thing yet discovered under God's sky.
Who art thou that complainest of thy life of toil ?   Complain not.   Look up, my wearied brother ; see thy fellow
Workmen there, in God's Eternity ; surviving there, they
alone surviving : sacred Band of the Immortals, celestial
Bodyguard of the Empire of Mankind.   Even in the weak
Human Memory they survive so long, as saints, as heroes,
as gods; they alone surviving ; peopling, they alone, the
unmeasured solitudes of Time !   To thee Heaven, though
severe, is *not* unkind ; Heaven is kind,—as a noble Mother ;
as that Spartan Mother, saying while she gave her son his
shield, 'With it, my son, or upon it !'   Thou too shalt
return *home* in honour ; to thy far-distant Home, in honour ;
doubt it not,—if in the battle thou keep thy shield !   Thou,
in the Eternities and deepest Death-kingdoms, are not an
alien ; thou everywhere art a denizen !   Complain not; the
very Spartans did not *complain*.

And who art thou that braggest of thy life of Idleness ;
complacently showest thy bright gilt equipages ; sumptuous
cushions ; appliances for folding of the hands to mere sleep ?
Looking up, looking down, around, behind or before, dis-
cernest thou, if it be not in Mayfair alone, any *idle* hero,
saint, god, or even devil ?   Not a vestige of one.   In the
Heavens, in the Earth, in the Waters under the Earth, is
none like unto thee.   Thou art an original figure in this

Creation ; a denizen in Mayfair alone, in this extraordinary
Century or Half-Century alone ! One monster there is in
the world : the idle man. What is his 'Religion'? That
Nature is a Phantasm, where cunning beggary or thievery
may sometimes find good victual. That God is a lie ; and
that Man and his Life are a lie.—Alas, alas, who of us *is*
there that can say, I have worked ? The faithfullest of us
are unprofitable servants ; the faithfullest of us know that
best. The faithfullest of us may say, with sad and true old
Samuel, 'Much of my life has been trifled away !' But he
that has, and except 'on public occasions' professes to have,
no function but that of going idle in a graceful or graceless
manner ; and of begetting sons to go idle ; and to address
Chief Spinners and Diggers, who at least *are* spinning and
digging, 'Ye scandalous persons who produce too much'—
My Corn-Law friends, on what imaginary still richer
Eldorados, and true iron-spikes with law of gravitation, are
ye rushing !

As to the Wages of Work there might innumerable things
be said ; there will and must yet innumerable things be said
and spoken, in St. Stephen's and out of St. Stephen's ; and
gradually not a few things be ascertained and written, on
Law-parchment, concerning this very matter :—' Fair day's-
wages for a fair day's-work' is the most unrefusable
demand ! Money-wages 'to the extent of keeping your
worker alive that he may work more' ; these, unless you
mean to dismiss him straightway out of this world, are
indispensable alike to the noblest Worker and to the least
noble !

One thing only I will say here, in special reference to the
former class, the noble and noblest ; but throwing light on
all the other classes and their arrangements of this difficult
matter: The 'wages' of every noble Work do yet lie in
Heaven or else Nowhere. Not in Bank-of-England bills, in
Owen's Labour-bank, or any the most improved establishment of banking and money-changing, needest thou, heroic
soul, present thy account of earnings. Human banks and
labour-banks know thee not ; or know thee after generations and centuries have passed away, and thou art clean
gone from 'rewarding',—all manner of bank-drafts, shop-
tills, and Downing-street Exchequers lying very invisible,

so far from thee! Nay, at bottom, dost thou need any reward? Was it thy aim and life-purpose to be filled with good things for thy heroism; to have a life of pomp and ease, and be what men call 'happy', in this world, or in any other world? I answer for thee deliberately, No. The whole spiritual secret of the new epoch lies in this, that thou canst answer for thyself, with thy whole clearness of head and heart, deliberately, No!

My brother, the brave man has to give his Life away. Give it, I advise thee;—thou dost not expect to *sell* thy Life in an adequate manner? What price, for example, would content thee? The just price of thy LIFE to thee,—why, God's entire Creation to thyself, the whole Universe of Space, the whole Eternity of Time, and what they hold: that is the price which would content thee; that, and if thou wilt be candid, nothing short of that! It is thy all; and for it thou wouldst have all. Thou art an unreasonable mortal;—or rather thou art a poor *infinite* mortal, who, in thy narrow clay-prison here, *seemest* so unreasonable! Thou wilt never sell thy Life, or any part of thy Life, in a satisfactory manner. Give it, like a royal heart; let the price be Nothing: thou *hast* then, in a certain sense, got All for it! The heroic man,—and is not every man, God be thanked, a potential hero?—has to do so, in all times and circumstances. In the most heroic age, as in the most unheroic, he will have to say, as Burns said proudly and humbly of his little Scottish Songs, little dewdrops of Celestial Melody in an age when so much was unmelodious: 'By Heaven, they shall either be invaluable or of no value; I do not need your guineas for them!' It is an element which should, and must, enter deeply into all settlements of wages here below. They never will be 'satisfactory' otherwise; they cannot, O Mammon Gospel, they never can! Money for my little piece of work ' to the extent that will allow me to keep working'; yes, this,—unless you mean that I shall go my ways *before* the work is all taken out of me: but as to 'wages'—!—

On the whole, we do entirely agree with those old Monks, *Laborare est Orare*. In a thousand senses, from one end of it to the other, true Work *is* Worship. He that works, whatsoever be his work, he bodies forth the form of Things Unseen; a small Poet every Worker is. The idea,

were it but of his poor Delf Platter, how much more of his
Epic Poem, is as yet 'seen', half-seen, only by himself; to
all others it is a thing unseen, impossible ; to Nature herself
it is a thing unseen, a thing which never hitherto was ;—
very 'impossible', for it is as yet a No-thing ! The Unseen
Powers had need to watch over such a man ; he works in
and for the Unseen. Alas, if he look to the Seen Powers
only, he may as well quit the business ; his No-thing will
never rightly issue as a Thing, but as a Deceptivity, a Sham-
thing,—which it had better not do !

Thy No-thing of an Intended Poem, O Poet who hast
looked merely to reviewers, copyrights, booksellers, popularities, behold it has not yet become a Thing ; for the truth
is not in it ! Though printed, hotpressed, reviewed, celebrated, sold to the twentieth edition: what is all that?
The Thing, in philosophical uncommercial language, is
still a No-thing, mostly semblance, and deception of the
sight ;—benign Oblivion incessantly gnawing at it, impatient
till Chaos, to which it belongs, do reabsorb it !—

He who takes not counsel of the Unseen and Silent, from
him will never come real visibility and speech. Thou must
descend to the *Mothers*, to the *Manes*, and Hercules-like long
suffer and labour there, wouldst thou emerge with victory
into the sunlight. As in battle and the shock of war,—
for is not this a battle ?—thou too shalt fear no pain or
death, shalt love no ease or life ; the voice of festive Lubber-
lands, the noise of greedy Acheron shall alike lie silent under
thy victorious feet. Thy work, like Dante's, shall 'make
thee lean for many years'. The world and its wages, its
criticisms, counsels, helps, impediments, shall be as a waste
ocean-flood ; the chaos through which thou art to swim and
sail. Not the waste waves and their weedy gulf-streams,
shalt thou take for guidance: thy star alone,—' *Se tu segui
lua stella !* ' Thy star alone, now clear-beaming over Chaos,
nay now by fits gone out, disastrously eclipsed : this only
shalt thou strive to follow. O, it is a business, as I fancy,
that of weltering your way through Chaos and the murk
of Hell ! Green-eyed dragons watching you, three-headed
Cerberuses,—not without sympathy of *their* sort ! ' *Eccovi
l' uom ch' è stato all' Inferno.* ' For in fine, as Poet Dryden
says, you do walk hand in hand with sheer Madness, all the
way,—who is by no means pleasant company ! You look

fixedly into Madness, and *her* undiscovered, boundless, bottomless Night-empire ; that you may extort new Wisdom out of it, as an Eurydice from Tartarus. The higher the Wisdom, the closer was its neighbourhood and kindred with mere Insanity ; literally so ;—and thou wilt, with a speechless feeling, observe how highest Wisdom, struggling up into this world, has oftentimes carried such tinctures and adhesions of Insanity still cleaving to it hither !

All Works, each in their degree, are a making of Madness sane ;—truly enough a religious operation ; which cannot be carried on without religion. You have not work otherwise ; you have eye-service, greedy grasping of wages, swift and ever swifter manufacture of semblances to get hold of wages. Instead of better felt-hats to cover your head, you have bigger lath-and-plaster hats set travelling the streets on wheels. Instead of heavenly and earthly Guidance for the souls of men, you have 'Black or White Surplice' Controversies, stuffed hair-and-leather Popes ;—terrestrial *Lawwards*, Lords and Law-bringers, ' organizing Labour ' in these years, by passing Corn-Laws. With all which, alas, this distracted Earth is now full, nigh to bursting. Semblances most smooth to the touch and eye ; most accursed nevertheless to body and soul. Semblances, be they of Sham-woven Cloth or of Dilettante Legislation, which are *not* real wool or substance, but Devil's-dust, accursed of God and man ! No man has worked, or can work, except religiously ; not even the poor day-labourer, the weaver of your coat, the sewer of your shoes. All men, if they work not as in a Great Taskmaster's eye, will work wrong, work unhappily for themselves and you.

Industrial work, still under bondage to Mammon, the rational soul of it not yet awakened, is a tragic spectacle. Men in the rapidest motion and self-motion ; restless, with convulsive energy, as if driven by Galvanism, as if possessed by a Devil ; tearing asunder mountains,—to no purpose, for Mammonism is always Midas-eared ! This is sad, on the face of it. Yet courage : the beneficent Destinies, kind in their sternness, are apprising us that this cannot continue. Labour is not a devil, even while encased in Mammonism ; Labour is ever an imprisoned god, writhing unconsciously or consciously to escape out of Mammonism ! Plugson of Undershot, like Taillefer of Normandy, wants victory; how much happier will even Plugson be to have a Chivalrous victory than a Chactaw one. The unredeemed ugliness is that of a slothful People. Show me a People energetically busy; heaving, struggling, all shoulders at the wheel; their heart pulsing, every muscle swelling, with man's energy and will; —I will show you a People of whom great good is already predicable; to whom all manner of good is yet certain, if their energy endure. By very working, they will learn; they have, Antaeus-like, their foot on Mother Fact: how can they but learn?

The vulgarest Plugson of a Master-Worker, who can command Workers, and get work out of them, is already a considerable man. Blessed and thrice-blessed symptoms I discern of Master-Workers who are not vulgar men; who are Nobles, and begin to feel that they must act as such: all speed to these, they are England's hope at present! But in this Plugson himself, conscious of almost no nobleness whatever, how much is there! Not without man's faculty, insight, courage, hard energy, is this rugged figure. His words none of the wisest; but his actings cannot be altogether foolish. Think, how were it, stoodst thou suddenly in his shoes! He has to command a thousand men. And not imaginary commanding; no, it is real, incessantly practical. The evil passions of so many men (with the Devil in them, as in all of us) he has to vanquish; by manifold force of speech and of silence, to repress or evade. What a force of silence, to say nothing of the others, is in Plugson! For these his thousand men he has to provide raw-material, machinery, arrangement, house-room; and ever at the week's end, wages by due sale. No Civil-List, or Goulburn-Baring Budget has he to fall back upon, for paying of his regiment; he has to pick his supplies from this confused face of the whole Earth and Contemporaneous History, by his dexterity alone. There will be dry eyes if he fail to do it!—He exclaims, at present, 'black in the face,' near strangled with Dilettante Legislation: 'Let me have elbow-room, throat-room, and I will not fail! No, I will spin yet, and conquer like a giant: what "sinews of war" lie in me, untold resources towards the Conquest of this Planet, if instead of hanging me, you husband them, and help me!'—My indomitable friend, it is *true*; and thou shalt and must be helped.

This is not a man I would kill and strangle by Corn-Laws, even if I could! No, I would fling my Corn-Laws and Shotbelts to the Devil; and try to help this man. I would teach him, by noble precept and law-precept, by noble example most of all, that Mammonism was not the essence of his or of my station in God's Universe; but the adscititious excrescence of it; the gross, terrene, godless embodiment of it; which would have to become, more or less, a godlike one. By noble *real* legislation, by true *noble's*-work, by unwearied, valiant, and were it wageless effort, in my Parliament and in my Parish, I would aid, constrain, encourage him to effect more or less this blessed change. I should know that it would have to be effected; that unless it were in some measure effected, he and I and all of us, I first and soonest of all, were doomed to perdition!— Effected it will be; unless it were a Demon that made this Universe; which I, for my own part, do at no moment, under no form, in the least believe.

May it please your Serene Highnesses, your Majesties, Lordships and Law-wardships, the proper Epic of this world is not now 'Arms and the Man'; how much less, 'Shirt-frills and the Man': no, it is now 'Tools and the Man': that, henceforth to all time is now our Epic;—and you, first of all others, I think, were wise to take note of that!

CHAPTER XIII

DEMOCRACY

IF the Serene Highnesses and Majesties do not take note of that, then, as I perceive, *that* will take note of itself! The time for levity, insincerity, and idle babble and play-acting, in all kinds, is gone by; it is a serious, grave time. Old long-vexed questions, not yet solved in logical words or parliamentary laws, are fast solving themselves in facts, somewhat unblessed to behold! This largest of questions, this question of Work and Wages, which ought, had we heeded Heaven's voice, to have begun two generations ago or more, cannot be delayed longer without hearing Earth's

voice. ' Labour' will verily need to be somewhat ' organized', as they say,—God knows with what difficulty.   Man
will actually need to have his debts and earnings a little
better paid by man ; which, let Parliaments speak of them,
or be silent of them, are eternally his due from man, and
cannot, without penalty and at length not without death-
penalty, be withheld.   How much ought to cease among us
straightway ; how much ought to begin straightway, while
the hours yet are !

Truly they are strange results to which this of leaving all
to ' Cash '; of quietly shutting up the God's Temple, and
gradually opening wide-open the Mammon's Temple, with
' Laissez-faire, and Every man for himself',—have led us in
these days !   We have Upper, speaking Classes, who indeed
do ' speak' as never man spake before ; the withered flimsi-
ness, the godless baseness and barrenness of whose Speech
might of itself indicate what kind of Doing and practical
Governing went on under it !   For Speech is the gaseous
element out of which most kinds of Practice and Performance, especially all kinds of moral Performance, condense
themselves, and take shape ; as the one is, so will the other
be.   Descending, accordingly, into the Dumb Class in its
Stockport Cellars and Poor-Law Bastilles, have we not to
announce that they also are hitherto unexampled in the
History of Adam's Posterity ?

Life was never a May-game for men : in all times the lot
of the dumb millions born to toil was defaced with manifold
sufferings, injustices, heavy burdens, avoidable and unavoid-
able ; not play at all, but hard work that made the sinews
sore and the heart sore.   As bond-slaves, *villani, bordarii,
sochemanni*, nay indeed as dukes, earls and kings, men were
oftentimes made weary of their life ; and had to say, in the
sweat of their brow and of their soul, Behold it is not sport,
it is grim earnest, and our back can bear no more !   Who
knows not what massacrings and harryings there have been ;
grinding, long-continuing, unbearable injustices,—till the
heart had to rise in madness, and some ' *Eu Sachsen, nimith
euer sachses,* You Saxons, out with your gully-knives then ! '
You Saxons, some ' arrestment', partial ' arrestment of the
Knaves and Dastards ' has become indispensable !—The page
of Dryasdust is heavy with such details.

And yet I will venture to believe that in no time, since

the beginnings of Society, was the lot of those same dumb
millions of toilers so entirely unbearable as it is even in the
days now passing over us.   It is not to die, or even to die of
hunger, that makes a man wretched ; many men have died ;
all men must die,—the last exit of us all is in a Fire-Chariot
of Pain.   But it is to live miserable we know not why ; to
work sore and yet gain nothing; to be heart-worn, weary,
yet isolated, unrelated, girt-in with a cold universal Laissez-
faire : it is to die slowly all our life long, imprisoned in
a deaf, dead, Infinite Injustice, as in the accursed iron belly
of a Phalaris' Bull !   This is and remains forever intolerable
to all men whom God has made.   Do we wonder at French
Revolutions, Chartisms, Revolts of Three Days ?   The times,
if we will consider them, are really unexampled.

Never before did I hear of an Irish Widow reduced to
' prove her sisterhood by dying of typhus-fever and infecting
seventeen persons ',—saying in such undeniable way, ' You
see, I was your sister ! '   Sisterhood, brotherhood was often
forgotten ; but not till the rise of these ultimate Mammon
and Shotbelt Gospels did I ever see it so expressly denied.
If no pious Lord or *Law-ward* would remember it, always
some pious Lady ('*Hlaf dig*', Benefactress, ' *Loaf-giveress*,'
they say she is,—blessings on her beautiful heart !) was there,
with mild mother-voice and hand, to remember it ; some
pious thoughtful *Elder*, what we now call ' Prester ', *Presbyter*
or ' Priest ', was there to put all men in mind of it, in the
name of the God who had made all.

Not even in Black Dahomey was it ever, I think, forgotten
to the typhus-fever length.   Mungo Park, resourceless, had
sunk down to die under the Negro Village-Tree, a horrible
White object in the eyes of all.   But in the poor Black
Woman, and her daughter who stood aghast at him, whose
earthly wealth and funded capital consisted of one small
calabash of rice, there lived a heart richer than ' *Laissez-
faire*' : they, with a royal munificence, boiled their rice for
him ; they sang all night to him, spinning assiduous on their
cotton distaffs, as he lay to sleep: ' Let us pity the poor
white man ; no mother has he to fetch him milk, no sister
to grind him corn ! '   Thou poor black Noble One,—thou
Lady too: did not a God make thee too ; was there not in
thee too something of a God !—

Gurth, born thrall of Cedric the Saxon, has been greatly pitied by Dryasdust and others. Gurth, with the brass collar round his neck, tending Cedric's pigs in the glades of the wood, is not what I call an exemplar of human felicity: but Gurth, with the sky above him, with the free air and tinted boscage and umbrage round him, and in him at least the certainty of supper and social lodging when he came home; Gurth to me seems happy, in comparison with many a Lancashire and Buckinghamshire man, of these days, not born thrall of anybody! Gurth's brass collar did not gall him: Cedric *deserved* to be his Master. The pigs were Cedric's, but Gurth too would get his parings of them. Gurth had the inexpressible satisfaction of feeling himself related indissolubly, though in a rude brass-collar way, to his fellow-mortals in this Earth. He had superiors, inferiors, equals.—Gurth is now 'emancipated' long since; has what we call 'Liberty'. Liberty, I am told, is a Divine thing. Liberty when it becomes the 'Liberty to die by starvation' is not so divine!

Liberty? The true liberty of a man, you would say, consisted in his finding out, or being forced to find out, the right path, and to walk thereon. To learn, or to be taught, what work he actually was able for; and then by permission, persuasion, and even compulsion, to set about doing of the same! That is his true blessedness, honour, 'liberty' and maximum of wellbeing: if liberty be not that, I for one have small care about liberty. You do not allow a palpable madman to leap over precipices; you violate his liberty, you that are wise; and keep him, were it in strait-waistcoats, away from the precipices! Every stupid, every cowardly and foolish man is but a less palpable madman: his true liberty were that a wiser man, that any and every wiser man, could, by brass collars, or in whatever milder or sharper way, lay hold of him when he was going wrong, and order and compel him to go a little righter. Or, if thou really art my *Senior*, Seigneur, my *Elder*, Presbyter or Priest,—if thou art in very deed my *Wiser*, may a beneficent instinct lead and impel thee to 'conquer' me, to command me! If thou do know better than I what is good and right, I conjure thee in the name of God, force me to do it; were it by never such brass collars, whips and handcuffs, leave me not to walk over precipices! That I have been called, by

guidance and the right man to do it is what is needed.— even by compulsion all the Newspapers, a 'free man' will avail me little, if my pilgrimage have ended in death and wreck. O that the Newspapers had called me slave, coward, fool, or what it pleased their sweet voices to name me, and I had attained not death, but life!—Liberty requires new definitions.

A conscious abhorrence and intolerance of Folly, of Baseness, Stupidity, Poltroonery and all that brood of things, dwells deep in some men : still deeper in others an *un*conscious abhorrence and intolerance, clothed moreover by the beneficent Supreme Powers in what stout appetites, energies, egoisms so-called, are suitable to it ;—these latter are your Conquerors, Romans, Normans, Russians, Indo-English ; Founders of what we call Aristocracies. Which indeed have they not the most 'divine right' to found ;—being themselves very truly Ἄριστοι, BRAVEST, BEST ; and conquering generally a confused rabble of WORST, or at lowest, clearly enough, of WORSE ? I think their divine right, tried, with affirmatory verdict, in the greatest Law-Court known to me, was good ! A class of men who are dreadfully exclaimed against by Dryasdust; of whom nevertheless beneficent Nature has oftentimes had need ; and may, alas, again have need.

When, across the hundredfold poor scepticisms, trivialisms, and constitutional cobwebberies of Dryasdust, you catch any glimpse of a William the Conqueror, a Tancred of Hauteville or such like,—do you not discern veritably some rude outline of a true God-made King ; whom not the Champion of England cased in tin, but all Nature and the Universe were calling to the throne ? It is absolutely necessary that he get thither. Nature does not mean her poor Saxon children to perish, of obesity, stupor or other malady, as yet : a stern Ruler and Line of Rulers therefore is called in,—a stern but most beneficent *perpetual House-Surgeon* is by Nature herself called in, and even the appropriate *fees* are provided for him ! Dryasdust talks lamentably about Hereward and the Fen Counties ; fate of Earl Waltheof; Yorkshire and the North reduced to ashes ; all of which is undoubtedly lamentable. But even Dryasdust apprises me of one fact: 'A child, in this William's reign, might have carried a purse of gold from end to end of England.' My erudite friend, it is a fact which outweighs a thousand ! Sweep away thy constitutional, sentimental, and other cobwebberies ; look eye to eye, if thou still have any eye, in the face of this big burly

William Bastard: thou wilt see a fellow of most flashing discernment, of most strong lion-heart;—in whom, as it were, within a frame of oak and iron, the gods have planted the soul of 'a man of genius'! Dost thou call that nothing? I call it an immense thing!—Rage enough was in this Willelmus Conquestor, rage enough for his occasions;—and yet the essential element of him, as of all such men, is not scorching *fire*, but shining illuminative *light*. Fire and light are strangely interchangeable; nay, at bottom, I have found them different forms of the same most godlike 'elementary substance' in our world: a thing worth stating in these days. The essential element of this Conquestor is, first of all, the most sun-eyed perception of what *is* really what on this God's-Earth;—which, thou wilt find, does mean at bottom 'Justice', and 'Virtues' not a few: *Conformity* to what the Maker has seen good to make; that, I suppose, will mean Justice and a Virtue or two?—

Dost thou think Willelmus Conquestor would have tolerated ten years' jargon, one hour's jargon, on the propriety of killing Cotton-manufactures by partridge Corn-Laws? I fancy, this was not the man to knock out of his night's-rest with nothing but a noisy bedlamism in your mouth! 'Assist us still better to bush the partridges; strangle Plugson who spins the shirts?'—'*Par la Splendeur de Dieu !*'——Dost thou think Willelmus Conquestor, in this new time, with Steam-engine Captains of Industry on one hand of him, and Joe-Manton Captains of Idleness on the other, would have doubted which *was* really the BEST; which did deserve strangling, and which not?

I have a certain indestructible regard for Willelmus Conquestor. A resident House-Surgeon, provided by Nature for her beloved English People, and even furnished with the requisite fees, as I said; for he by no means felt himself doing Nature's work, this Willelmus, but his own work exclusively! And his own work withal it was; informed '*par la Splendeur de Dieu*'.—I say, it is necessary to get the work out of such a man, however harsh that be! When a world, not yet doomed for death, is rushing down to ever-deeper Baseness and Confusion, it is a dire necessity of Nature's to bring in her ARISTOCRACIES, her BEST, even by forcible methods. When their descendants or representatives cease entirely to *be* the Best, Nature's poor world will very

soon rush down again to Baseness; and it becomes a dire
necessity of Nature's to cast them out.   Hence French
Revolutions, Five-point Charters, Democracies, and a mournful list of *Etceteras*, in these our afflicted times.

To what extent Democracy has now reached, how it
advances irresistible with ominous, ever-increasing speed, he
that will open his eyes on any province of human affairs
may discern.   Democracy is everywhere the inexorable
demand of these ages, swiftly fulfilling itself. From the
thunder of Napoleon battles, to the jabbering of Open-vestry
in St. Mary Axe, all things announce Democracy.   A distinguished man, whom some of my readers will hear again with
pleasure, thus writes to me what in these days he notes from
the Wahngasse of Weissnichtwo, where our London fashions
seem to be in full vogue.   Let us hear the Herr Teufelsdröckh again, were it but the smallest word!

'Democracy, which means despair of finding any Heroes
to govern you, and contented putting up with the want of
them,—alas, thou too, *mein Lieber*, seest well how close it
is of kin to *Atheism*, and other sad *Isms*: he who discovers
no God whatever, how shall he discover Heroes, the visible
Temples of God?—Strange enough meanwhile it is, to
observe with what thoughtlessness, here in our rigidly Conservative Country, men rush into Democracy with full cry.
Beyond doubt, his Excellenz the Titular-Herr Ritter Kauder-
wälsch von Pferdefuss-Quacksalber, he our distinguished
Conservative Premier himself, and all but the thicker-headed
of his Party, discern Democracy to be inevitable as death,
and are even desperate of delaying it much!

'You cannot walk the streets without beholding Democracy announce itself: the very Tailor has become, if not
properly Sansculottic, which to him would be ruinous, yet
a Tailor unconsciously symbolizing, and prophesying with
his scissors, the reign of Equality.   What now is our
fashionable coat?   A thing of superfinest texture, of deeply
meditated cut; with Malines-lace cuffs; quilted with gold;
so that a man can carry, without difficulty, an estate of land
on his back?   *Keineswegs*, By no manner of means!   The
Sumptuary Laws have fallen into such a state of desuetude
as was never before seen.   Our fashionable coat is an amphibium between barn-sack and drayman's doublet.   The
cloth of it is studiously coarse; the colour a speckled soot-

black or rust-brown grey ;—the nearest approach to a Peasant's. And for shape,—thou shouldst see it! The last
consummation of the year now passing over us is definable
as Three Bags ; a big bag for the body, two small bags for
the arms, and by way of collar a hem! The first Antique
Cheruscan who, of felt-cloth or bear's-hide, with bone or
metal needle, set about making himself a coat, before Tailors
had yet awakened out of Nothing,—did not he make it even
so ? A loose wide poke for body, with two holes to let out
the arms ; this was his original coat: to which holes it was
soon visible that two small loose pokes, or sleeves, easily
appended, would be an improvement.

'Thus has the Tailor-art, so to speak, overset itself, like
most other things ; changed its centre-of-gravity ; whirled
suddenly over from zenith to nadir. Your Stulz, with huge
somerset, vaults from his high shopboard down to the depths
of primal savagery,—carrying much along with him! For
I will invite thee to reflect that the Tailor, as topmost
ultimate froth of Human Society, is indeed swift-passing,
evanescent, slippery to decipher ; yet significant of much,
nay of all. Topmost evanescent froth, he is churned up
from the very lees, and from all intermediate regions of the
liquor. The general outcome he, visible to the eye, of what
men aimed to do, and were obliged and enabled to do, in this
one public department of symbolizing themselves to each
other by covering of their skins. A smack of all Human
Life lies in the Tailor: its wild struggles towards beauty,
dignity, freedom, victory ; and how, hemmed in by Sedan
and Huddersfield, by Nescience, Dullness, Prurience, and
other sad necessities and laws of Nature, it has attained just
to this: Gray savagery of Three Sacks with a hem !

'When the very Tailor verges towards Sansculottism, is
it not ominous ? The last Divinity of poor mankind de-
throning himself; sinking *his* taper too, flame downmost,
like the Genius of Sleep or of Death ; admonitory that Tailor
time shall be no more !—For, little as one could advise
Sumptuary Laws at the present epoch, yet nothing is clearer
than that where ranks do actually exist, strict division of
costumes will also be enforced ; that if we ever have a new
Hierarchy and Aristocracy, acknowledged veritably as such,
for which I daily pray Heaven, the Tailor will re-awaken ;
and be, by volunteering and appointment, consciously and

unconsciously, a safeguard of that same.'—Certain farther observations, from the same invaluable pen, on our never-ending changes of mode, our 'perpetual nomadic and even ape-like appetite for change and mere change' in all the equipments of our existence, and the 'fatal revolutionary character' thereby manifested, we suppress for the present. It may be admitted that Democracy, in all meanings of the word, is in full career; irresistible by any Ritter Kauder-wälsch or other Son of Adam, as times go. 'Liberty' is a thing men are determined to have.

But truly, as I had to remark in the meanwhile, 'the liberty of not being oppressed by your fellow man' is an indispensable, yet one of the most insignificant fractional parts of Human Liberty. No man oppresses thee, can bid thee fetch or carry, come or go, without reason shown. True; from all men thou art emancipated: but from Thyself and from the Devil—? No man, wiser, unwiser, can make thee come or go : but thy own futilities, bewilderments, thy false appetites for Money, Windsor Georges and such like? No man oppresses thee, O free and independent Franchiser: but does not this stupid Porter-pot oppress thee? No Son of Adam can bid thee come or go; but this absurd Pot of Heavy-wet, this can and does! Thou art the thrall not of Cedric the Saxon, but of thy own brutal appetites, and this scoured dish of liquor. And thou pratest of thy 'liberty'? Thou entire blockhead!

Heavy-wet and gin: alas, these are not the only kinds of thraldom. Thou who walkest in a vain show, looking out with ornamental dilettante sniff and serene supremacy at all Life and all Death; and amblest jauntily; perking up thy poor talk into crotchets, thy poor conduct into fatuous somnambulisms;—and *art* as an 'enchanted Ape' under God's sky, where thou mightest have been a man, had proper Schoolmasters and Conquerors, and Constables with cat-o'-nine tails, been vouchsafed thee: dost thou call that 'liberty'? Or your unreposing Mammon-worshipper, again, driven, as if by Galvanisms, by Devils and Fixed-Ideas, who rises early and sits late, chasing the impossible ; straining every faculty to 'fill himself with the east wind',—how merciful were it, could you, by mild persuasion or by the severest tyranny so-called, check him in his mad path, and turn him into

a wiser one! All painful tyranny, in that case again, were
but mild 'surgery'; the pain of it cheap, as health and life,
instead of galvanism and fixed-idea, are cheap at any price.

Sure enough, of all paths a man could strike into, there
is, at any given moment, a *best path* for every man ; a thing
which, here and now, it were of all things *wisest* for him to
do ;—which could he be but led or driven to do, he were
then doing 'like a man', as we phrase it; all men and gods
agreeing with him, the whole Universe virtually exclaiming
Well-done to him ! His success, in such case, were complete ;
his felicity a maximum. This path, to find this path and
walk in it, is the one thing needful for him. Whatsoever
forwards him in that, let it come to him even in the shape
of blows and spurnings, is liberty : whatsoever hinders him,
were it wardmotes, open-vestries, poll-booths, tremendous
cheers, rivers of heavy-wet, is slavery.

The notion that a man's liberty consists in giving his vote
at election-hustings, and saying, 'Behold now I too have my
twenty-thousandth part of a Talker in our National Palaver ;
will not all the gods be good to me ?'—is one of the
pleasantest! Nature nevertheless is kind at present; and
puts it into the heads of many, almost of all. The liberty
especially which has to purchase itself by social isolation,
and each man standing separate from the other, having 'no
business with him' but a cash-account : this is such a liberty
as the Earth seldom saw ;—as the Earth will not long put
up with, recommend it how you may. This liberty turns
out, before it have long continued in action, with all men
flinging up their caps round it, to be, for the Working
Millions, a liberty to die by want of food ; for the Idle
Thousands and Units, alas, a still more fatal liberty to live
in want of work ; to have no earnest duty to do in this
God's-World any more. What becomes of a man in such
predicament ? Earth's Laws are silent ; and Heaven's
speak in a voice which is not heard. No work, and the
ineradicable need of work, give rise to new very wondrous
life-philosophies, new very wondrous life-practices! Dilettantism, Pococurantism, Beau-Brummelism, with perhaps an
occasional, half-mad, protesting burst of Byronism, establish
themselves : at the end of a certain period,—if you go back
to 'the Dead Sea', there is, say our Moslem friends, a very
strange 'Sabbath-day' transacting itself there !—Brethren,

we know but imperfectly yet, after ages of Constitutional Government, what Liberty and Slavery are.

Democracy, the chase of Liberty in that direction, shall go its full course ; unrestrained by him of Pferdefuss-Quacksalber, or any of *his* household. The Toiling Millions of Mankind, in most vital need and passionate instinctive desire of Guidance, shall cast away False-Guidance ; and hope, for an hour, that No-Guidance will suffice them : but it can be for an hour only. The smallest item of human Slavery is the oppression of man by his Mock-Superiors ; the palpablest, but I say at bottom the smallest. Let him shake off such oppression, trample it indignantly under his feet ; I blame him not, I pity and commend him. But oppression by your Mock-Superiors well shaken off, the grand problem yet remains to solve : That of finding government by your Real-Superiors ! Alas, how shall we ever learn the solution of that, benighted, bewildered, sniffing, sneering, godforgetting unfortunates as we are ? It is a work for centuries ; to be taught us by tribulations, confusions, insurrections, obstructions ; who knows if not by conflagration and despair ! It is a lesson inclusive of all other lessons ; the hardest of all lessons to learn.

One thing I do know : Those Apes, chattering on the branches by the Dead Sea, never got it learned ; but chatter there to this day. To them no Moses need come a second time ; a thousand Moseses would be but so many painted Phantasms, interesting Fellow-Apes of new strange aspect,— whom they would 'invite to dinner', be glad to meet with in lion-soirées. To them the voice of Prophecy, of heavenly monition, is quite ended. They chatter there, all Heaven shut to them, to the end of the world. The unfortunates ! Oh, what is dying of hunger, with honest tools in your hand, with a manful purpose in your heart, and much real labour lying round you done, in comparison ? You honestly quit your tools ; quit a most muddy confused coil of sore work, short rations, of sorrows, dispiritments and contradictions, having now honestly done with it all ;— and await, not entirely in a distracted manner, what the Supreme Powers, and the Silences and the Eternities may have to say to you.

A second thing I know : This lesson will have to be learned,—under penalties ! England will either learn it, or

England also will cease to exist among Nations. England will either learn to reverence its Heroes, and discriminate them from its Sham-Heroes and Valets and gaslighted Histrios; and to prize them as the audible God's-voice, amid all inane jargons and temporary market-cries, and say to them with heart-loyalty, ' Be ye King and Priest, and Gospel and Guidance for us ': or else England will continue to worship now and ever-new forms of Quackhood,—and so, with what resiliences and reboundings matters little, go down to the Father of Quacks! Can I dread such things of England? Wretched, thick-eyed, gross-hearted mortals, why will ye worship lies, and ' Stuffed Clothes-suits, created by the ninth-parts of men !' It is not your purses that suffer ; your farm-rents, your commerces, your mill-revenues, loud as ye lament over these ; no, it is not these alone, but a far deeper than these : it is your souls that lie dead, crushed down under despicable Nightmares, Atheisms, Brain-fumes ; and are not souls at all, but mere succedanea for *salt* to keep your bodies and their appetites from putrefying! Your cotton-spinning and thrice-miraculous mechanism, what is this too, by itself, but a larger kind of Animalism? Spiders can spin, Beavers can build and show contrivance ; the Ant lays up accumulation of capital, and has, for aught I know, a Bank of Antland. If there is no soul in man higher than all that, did it reach to sailing on the cloud-rack and spinning sea-sand ; then I say, man is but an animal, a more cunning kind of brute : he has no soul, but only a succedaneum for salt. Whereupon, seeing himself to be truly of the beasts that perish, he ought to admit it, I think ;—and also straightway universally to kill himself; and so, in a manlike manner, at least, *end*, and wave these brute-worlds *his* dignified farewell !—

CHAPTER XIV

SIR JABESH WINDBAG

OLIVER CROMWELL, whose body they hung on their Tyburn Gallows because he had found the Christian Religion inexecutable in this country, remains to me by far the remarkablest Governor we have had here for the last five centuries or so. For the last five centuries, there has been no Governor among us with anything like similar talent ; and for the last two centuries, no Governor, we may say, with the possibility of similar talent,—with an idea in the heart of him capable of inspiring similar talent, capable of co-existing therewith. When you consider that Oliver believed in a God, the difference between Oliver's position and that of any subsequent Governor of this Country becomes, the more you reflect on it, the more immeasurable !

Oliver, no volunteer in Public Life, but plainly a balloted soldier strictly ordered thither, enters upon Public Life ; comports himself there like a man who carried his own life in his hand ; like a man whose Great Commander's eye was always on him. Not without results. Oliver, well-advanced in years, finds now, by Destiny and his own Deservings, or as he himself better phrased it, by wondrous successive 'Births of Providence', the Government of England put into his hands. In senate-house and battle-field, in counsel and in action, in private and in public, this man has proved himself a man : England and the voice of God, through waste awful whirlwinds and environments, speaking to his great heart, summon him to assert formally, in the way of solemn Public Fact and as a new piece of English Law, what informally and by Nature's eternal Law needed no asserting, That he, Oliver, was the Ablest-Man of England, the King of England ; that he, Oliver, would undertake governing England. His way of making this same 'assertion', the one way he had of making it, has given rise to immense criticism : but the assertion itself, in what way soever 'made', is it not somewhat of a solemn one, somewhat of a tremendous one !

And now do but contrast this Oliver with my right honourable friend Sir Jabesh Windbag, Mr. Facing-both-ways, Viscount Mealymouth, Earl of Windlestraw, or what other Cagliostro, Cagliostrino, Cagliostraccio, the course of Fortune and Parliamentary Majorities has constitutionally guided to that dignity, any time during these last sorrowful hundred-and-fifty years! Windbag, weak in the faith of a God, which he believes only at Church on Sundays, if even then; strong only in the faith that Paragraphs and Plausibilities bring votes; that Force of Public Opinion, as he calls it, is the primal Necessity of Things, and highest God we have :— Windbag, if we will consider him, has a problem set before him which may be ranged in the impossible class. He is a Columbus minded to sail to the indistinct country of No-WHERE, to the indistinct country of WHITHERWARD, by the *friendship* of those same waste-tumbling Water-Alps and howling waltz of All the Winds ; not by conquest of them and in spite of them, but by friendship of them, when once *they* have made up their mind! He is the most original Columbus I ever saw. Nay, his problem is not an impossible one: he will infallibly *arrive* at that same country of NOWHERE ; his indistinct Whitherward will be a *Thither*ward! In the Ocean Abysses and Locker of Davy Jones, there certainly enough do he and *his* ship's company, and all their cargo and navigatings, at last find lodgement.

Oliver knew that his America lay THERE, Westward Ho ; —and it was not entirely by *friendship* of the Water-Alps, and yeasty insane Froth-Oceans, that he meant to get thither! He sailed accordingly; had compass-card, and Rules of Navigation,—older and greater than these Froth-Oceans, old as the Eternal God! Or again, do but think of this. Windbag in these his probable five years of office has to prosper and get Paragraphs: the Paragraphs of these five years must be his salvation, or he is a lost man ; redemption nowhere in the Worlds or in the Times discoverable for him. Oliver too would like his Paragraphs; successes, popularities in these five years are not undesirable to him: but mark, I say, this enormous circumstance: *after* these five years are gone and done, comes an Eternity for Oliver! Oliver has to appear before the Most High Judge: the utmost flow of Paragraphs, the utmost ebb of them, is now, in

strictest arithmetic, verily no matter at all; its exact value
zero; an account altogether erased! Enormous;—which
a man, in these days, hardly fancies with an effort! Oliver's
Paragraphs are all done, his battles, division-lists, successes
all summed: and now in that awful unerring Court of Review, the real question first rises, Whether he has succeeded
at all; whether he has not been defeated miserably for evermore? Let him come with world-wide *Io-Paeans*, these
avail him not. Let him come covered over with the world's
execrations, gashed with ignominious death-wounds, the
gallows-rope about his neck: what avails that? The word
is, Come thou brave and faithful; the word is, Depart thou
quack and accursed!

O Windbag, my right honourable friend, in very truth
I pity thee. I say, these Paragraphs, and low or loud
votings of thy poor fellow-blockheads of mankind, will
never guide thee in any enterprise at all. Govern a country
on such guidance? Thou canst not make a pair of shoes,
sell a pennyworth of tape, on such. No, thy shoes are
vamped up falsely to meet the market; behold, the leather
only *seemed* to be tanned; thy shoes melt under me to rub-
bishy pulp, and are not veritable mud-defying shoes, but
plausible vendible similitudes of shoes,—thou unfortunate,
and I! O my right honourable friend, when the Paragraphs flowed in, who was like Sir Jabesh? On the swelling tide he mounted; higher, higher, triumphant, heaven-
high. But the Paragraphs again ebbed out, as unwise
Paragraphs needs must: Sir Jabesh lies stranded, sunk and
forever sinking in ignominious ooze; the Mud-nymphs, and
ever-deepening bottomless Oblivion, his portion to eternal
time. 'Posterity?' Thou appealest to Posterity, thou?
My right honourable friend, what will Posterity do for thee!
The voting of Posterity, were it continued through centuries
in thy favour, will be quite inaudible, extra-forensic, without any effect whatever. Posterity can do simply nothing
for a man; nor even seem to do much, if the man be not
brainsick. Besides, to tell thee truth, the bets are a thousand to one, Posterity will not hear of thee, my right honourable friend! Posterity, I have found, has generally his
own Windbags sufficiently trumpeted in all market-places,
and no leisure to attend to ours. Posterity, which has made
of Norse Odin a similitude, and of Norman William a brute

monster, what will or can it make of English Jabesh ?   O
Heavens, 'Posterity'!—

'These poor persecuted Scotch Covenanters', said I to my
inquiring Frenchman, in such stinted French as stood at
command, '*ils s'en appelaient à*'—'*A la Postérité*,' inter-
rupted he, helping me out.—'*Ah, Monsieur, non, mille fois
non!* They appealed to the Eternal God; not to Posterity
at all! *C'était différent.*'

CHAPTER XV

MORRISON AGAIN

NEVERTHELESS, O Advanced Liberal, one cannot promise
thee any 'New Religion', for some time ; to say truth, I do
not think we have the smallest chance of any ! Will the
candid reader, by way of closing this Book Third, listen to
a few transient remarks on that subject ?

Candid readers have not lately met with any man who
had less notion to interfere with their Thirty-Nine, or other
Church-Articles ; wherewith, very helplessly as is like, they
may have struggled to form for themselves some not inconceivable hypothesis about this Universe, and their own
Existence there. Superstition, my friend, is far from me ;
Fanaticism, for any *Fanum* likely to arise soon on this
Earth, is far. A man's Church-Articles are surely articles
of price to him ; and in these times one has to be tolerant
of many strange 'Articles', and of many still stranger 'No-
articles', which go about placarding themselves in a very
distracted manner,—the numerous long placard-poles, and
questionable infirm paste-pots, interfering with one's peaceable thoroughfare sometimes !

Fancy a man, moreover, recommending his fellow men to
believe in God, that so Chartism might abate, and the
Manchester Operatives be got to spin peaceably ! The idea
is more distracted than any placard-pole seen hitherto in
a public thoroughfare of men ! My friend, if thou ever do
come to believe in God, thou wilt find all Chartism, Manchester riot, Parliamentary incompetence, Ministries of

Windbag, and the wildest Social Dissolutions, and the burning up of this entire Planet, a most small matter in comparison. Brother, this Planet, I find, is but an inconsiderable sandgrain in the continents of Being: this Planet's poor temporary interests, thy interests and my interests there, when I look fixedly into that eternal Light-Sea and Flame-Sea with *its* eternal interests, dwindle literally into Nothing; my speech of it is—silence for the while. I will as soon think of making Galaxies and Star-Systems to guide little herring-vessels by, as of preaching Religion that the Constable may continue possible. Oh my Advanced-Liberal friend, this new second progress, of proceeding 'to invent God', is a very strange one! Jacobinism unfolded into Saint-Simonism bodes innumerable blessed things; but the thing itself might draw tears from a Stoic!—As for me, some twelve or thirteen New Religions, heavy Packets, most of them unfranked, having arrived here from various parts of the world, in a space of six calendar months, I have instructed my invaluable friend the Stamped Postman to introduce no more of them, if the charge exceeded one penny.

Henry of Essex, duelling in that Thames Island, 'near to Reading Abbey,' had a religion. But was it in virtue of his seeing armed Phantasms of St. Edmund 'on the rim of the horizon', looking minatory on him? Had that, intrinsically, anything to do with his religion at all? Henry of Essex's religion was the Inner Light or Moral Conscience of his own soul; such as is vouchsafed still to all souls of men;—which Inner Light shone here 'through such intellectual and other media' as there were; producing 'Phantasms', Kircherean Visual-Spectra, according to circumstances! It is so with all men. The clearer my Inner Light may shine, through the *less* turbid media; the *fewer* Phantasms it may produce,—the gladder surely shall I be, and not the sorrier! Hast thou reflected, O serious reader, Advanced-Liberal or other, that the one end, essence, use of all religion past, present and to come, was this only: To keep that same Moral Conscience or Inner Light of ours alive and shining;—which certainly the 'Phantasms' and the 'turbid media' were not essential for! All religion was here to remind us, better or worse, of what we already

know better or worse, of the quite *infinite* difference there is
between a Good man and a Bad ; to bid us love infinitely
the one, abhor and avoid infinitely the other,—strive infinitely to *be* the one, and not to be the other. 'All religion
issues in due Practical Hero-worship.' He that has a soul
unasphyxied will never want a religion ; he that has a soul
asphyxied, reduced to a succedaneum for salt, will never
find any religion, though you rose from the dead to preach
him one.

But indeed, when men and reformers ask for 'a religion',
it is analogous to their asking, 'What would you have us to
do ?' and such like. They fancy that their religion too
shall be a kind of Morrison's Pill, which they have only to
swallow once, and all will be well. Resolutely once gulp
down your Religion, your Morrison's Pill, you have it all
plain sailing now: you can follow your affairs, your no-
affairs, go along money-hunting, pleasure-hunting, dilettante-
ing, dangling, and miming and chattering like a Dead-Sea
Ape : your Morrison will do your business for you. Men's
notions are very strange !—Brother, I say there is not, was
not, nor will ever be, in the wide circle of Nature, any Pill
or Religion of that character. Man cannot afford thee such ;
for the very gods it is impossible. I advise thee to renounce
Morrison ; once for all, quit hope of the Universal Pill.
For body, for soul, for individual or society, there has not
any such article been made. *Non extat.* In Created Nature
it is not, was not, will not be. In the void imbroglios of
Chaos only, and realms of Bedlam, does some shadow of it
hover, to bewilder and bemock the poor inhabitants *there.*

Rituals, Liturgies, Creeds, Hierarchies : all this is not
religion ; all this, were it dead as Odinism, as Fetishism,
does not kill religion at all ! It is Stupidity alone, with
never so many rituals, that kills religion. Is not this still
a World ? Spinning Cotton under Arkwright and Adam
Smith ; founding Cities by the Fountain of Juturna, on the
Janiculum Mount ; tilling Canaan under Prophet Samuel
and Psalmist David, man is ever man ; the missionary of
Unseen Powers ; and great and victorious, while he continues true to his mission ; mean, miserable, foiled, and at
last annihilated and trodden out of sight and memory, when
he proves untrue. Brother, thou art a Man, I think ; thou
art not a mere building Beaver, or two-legged Cotton-Spider ;

thou hast verily a Soul in thee, asphyxied or otherwise!
Sooty Manchester,—it too is built on the infinite Abysses;
overspanned by the skyey Firmaments; and there is birth
in it, and death in it;—and it is every whit as wonderful,
as fearful, unimaginable, as the oldest Salem or Prophetic
City. Go or stand, in what time, in what place we will,
are there not Immensities, Eternities over us. around us,
in us:

> Solemn before us,
> Veiled, the dark Portal,
> Goal of all mortal :—
> Stars silent rest o'er us,
> Graves under us silent!

Between *these* two great Silences, the hum of all our spinning cylinders, Trades-Unions, Anti-Corn-Law Leagues and
Carlton Clubs goes on. Stupidity itself ought to pause a
little and consider that. I tell thee, through all thy Ledgers,
Supply-and-demand Philosophies, and daily most modern
melancholy Business and Cant, there does shine the presence of a Primaeval Unspeakable; and thou wert wise to
recognize, not with lips only, that same!

The Maker's Laws, whether they are promulgated in
Sinai Thunder, to the ear or imagination, or quite otherwise
promulgated, are the Laws of God; transcendent, everlasting, imperatively demanding obedience from all men.
This, without any thunder, or with never so much thunder,
thou, if there be any soul left in thee, canst know of a truth.
The Universe, I say, is made by Law; the great Soul of the
World is just and not unjust. Look thou, if thou have eyes
or soul left, into this great shoreless Incomprehensible: in
the heart of its tumultous Appearances, Embroilments, and
mad Time-vortexes, is there not, silent, eternal, an All-just,
an All-beautiful; sole Reality and ultimate controlling
Power of the whole? This is not a figure of speech; this
is a fact. The fact of Gravitation known to all animals, is
not surer than this inner Fact, which may be known to all
men. He who knows this, it will sink, silent, awful, unspeakable, into his heart. He will say with Faust: 'Who *dare*
name HIM?' Most rituals or 'namings' he will fall in with
at present, are like to be 'namings'—which shall be nameless! In silence, in the Eternal Temple, let him worship,
if there be no fit word. Such knowledge, the crown of his

whole spiritual being, the life of his life, let him keep and sacredly walk by. He has a religion. Hourly and daily, for himself and for the whole world, a faithful, unspoken, but not ineffectual prayer rises, 'Thy will be done.' His whole work on Earth is an emblematic spoken or acted prayer, Be the will of God done on Earth,—not the Devil's will, or any of the Devil's servants' wills! He has a re-ligion, this man; an everlasting Loadstar that beams the brighter in the Heavens, the darker here on Earth grows the night around him. Thou, if thou know not this, what are all rituals, liturgies, mythologies, mass-chantings, turn-ings of the rotatory calabash? They are as nothing; in a good many respects they are as *less*. Divorced from this, getting half-divorced from this, they are a thing to fill one with a kind of horror; with a sacred inexpressible pity and fear. The most tragical thing a human eye can look on. It was said to the Prophet, 'Behold, I will show thee worse things than these: women weeping to Thammuz.' That was the acme of the Prophet's vision,—then as now.

Rituals, Liturgies, Credos, Sinai Thunder: I know more or less the history of these; the rise, progress, decline and fall of these. Can thunder from all the thirty-two azimuths, repeated daily for centuries of years, make God's Laws more godlike to me? Brother, No. Perhaps I am grown to be a man now; and do not need the thunder and the terror any longer! Perhaps I am above being frightened; perhaps it is not Fear, but Reverence alone, that shall now lead me! — Revelations, Inspirations? Yes: and thy own god-created Soul; dost thou not call that a 'revelation'? Who made THEE? Where didst Thou come from? The Voice of Eternity, if thou be not a blasphemer and poor asphyxied mute, speaks with that tongue of thine! *Thou* art the latest Birth of Nature; it is 'the Inspiration of the Almighty' that giveth *thee* understanding! My brother, my brother!—

Under baleful Atheisms, Mammonisms, Joe-Manton Dilet-tantisms, with their appropriate Cants and Idolisms, and whatsoever scandalous rubbish obscures and all but extin-guishes the soul of man,—religion now is; its Laws, written if not on stone tables, yet on the Azure of Infinitude, in the inner heart of God's Creation, certain as Life, certain as Death! I say the Laws are there, and thou shalt not disobey them. It were better for thee not. Better a hundred deaths

than yes. Terrible 'penalties' withal, if thou still need
'penalties', are there for disobeying. Dost thou observe,
O redtape Politician, that fiery infernal Phenomenon, which
men name FRENCH REVOLUTION, sailing, unlooked-for, unbidden ; through thy inane Protocol Dominion :—far-seen, with
splendour not of Heaven ? Ten centuries will see it. There
were Tanneries at Meudon for human skins. And Hell, very
truly Hell, had power over God's upper Earth for a season.
The cruellest Portent that has risen into created Space these
ten centuries : let us hail it, with awestruck repentant
hearts, as the voice once more of a God, though of one in
wrath. Blessed be the God's-voice ; for *it* is true, and
Falsehoods have to cease before it ! But for that same preternatural quasi-infernal Portent, one could not know what
to make of this wretched world, in these days, at all. The
deplorablest quack-ridden, and now hunger-ridden, down-
trodden Despicability and *Flebile Ludibrium*, of redtape
Protocols, rotatory Calabashes, Poor-Law Bastilles : who is
there that could think of *its* being fated to continue ?—

Penalties enough, my brother ! This penalty inclusive of
all : Eternal Death to thy own hapless Self, if thou heed no
other. Eternal Death, I say,—with many meanings old and
new, of which let this single one suffice us here : The eternal
impossibility for thee to be aught but a Chimera, and
swift-vanishing deceptive Phantasm, in God's Creation ;—
swift-vanishing, never to reappear : why should *it* reappear !
Thou hadst one chance, thou wilt never have another.
Everlasting ages will roll on, and no other be given thee.
The foolishest articulate-speaking soul now extant, may not
he say to himself : 'A whole Eternity I waited to be born ;
and now I have a whole Eternity waiting to see what I will
do when born !' This is not Theology, this is Arithmetic.
And thou but half-discernest this ; thou but half-believest it ?
Alas, on the shores of the Dead Sea on Sabbath, there goes
on a Tragedy !—

But we will leave this of 'Religion'; of which, to say
truth, it is chiefly profitable in these unspeakable days to
keep silence. Thou needest no 'New Religion'; nor art
thou like to get any. Thou hast already more 'religion'
than thou makest use of. This day, thou knowest ten commanded duties, seest in thy mind ten things which should
be done, for one that thou doest ! *Do* one of them ; this of

itself will show thee ten others which can and shall be done. 'But my future fate?' Yes, thy future fate, indeed? Thy future fate, while thou makest *it* the chief question, seems to me—extremely questionable! I do not think it can be good. Norse Odin, immemorial centuries ago, did not he, though a poor Heathen, in the dawn of Time, teach us that for the Dastard there was, and could be, no good fate; no harbour anywhere, save down with Hela, in the pool of Night! Dastards, Knaves, are they that lust for Pleasure, that tremble at Pain. For this world and for the next, Dastards are a class of creatures made to be 'arrested'; they are good for nothing else, can look for nothing else. A greater than Odin has been here. A greater than Odin has taught us—not a greater Dastardism, I hope! My brother, thou must pray for a *soul*; struggle, as with life-and-death energy, to get back thy soul! Know that 'religion' is no Morrison's Pill from without, but a reawakening of thy own Self from within:—and, above all, leave me alone of thy 'religions' and 'new religions' here and elsewhere! I am weary of this sick croaking for a Morrison's-Pill religion; for any and for every such. I want none such; and discern all such to be impossible. The resuscitation of old liturgies fallen dead; much more, the manufacture of new liturgies that will never be alive: how hopeless! Stylitisms, eremite fanaticisms and fakeerisms; spasmodic agonistic posture-makings, and narrow, cramped, morbid, if for ever noble wrestlings: all this is not a thing desirable to me. It is a thing the world *has* done once,—when its beard was not grown as now!

And yet there is, at worst, one Liturgy which does remain forever unexceptionable: that of *Praying* (as the old Monks did withal) *by Working*. And indeed the Prayer which accomplished itself in special chapels at stated hours, and went not with a man, rising up from all his Work and Action, at all moments sanctifying the same,—what was it ever good for? 'Work is Worship': yes, in a highly considerable sense,—which, in the present state of all 'worship', who is there that can unfold! He that understands it well, understands the Prophecy of the whole Future; the last Evangel, which has included all others. *Its* cathedral the Dome of Immensity,—hast thou seen it? coped with the

star-galaxies ; paved with the green mosaic of land and
ocean ; and for altar, verily, the Star-throne of the Eternal !
Its litany and psalmody the noble acts, the heroic work and
suffering, and true heart-utterance of all the Valiant of the
Sons of Men. Its choir-music the ancient Winds and Oceans,
and deep-toned, inarticulate, but most speaking voices of
Destiny and History,—supernal ever as of old. Between
two great Silences :

> 'Stars silent rest o'er us,
> Graves under us silent.'

Between which two great Silences, do not, as we said, all
human Noises, in the naturallest times, most *preter*naturally
march and roll ?—

I will insert this also, in a lower strain, from Sauerteig's
Aesthetische Springwurzeln. 'Worship ?' says he : 'Before
that inane tumult of Hearsay filled men's heads, while the
world lay yet silent, and the heart true and open, many
things were Worship ! To the primaeval man whatsoever
good came, descended on him (as, in mere fact, it ever does)
direct from God ; whatsoever duty lay visible for him, this
a Supreme God had prescribed. To the present hour I ask
thee, Who else ? For the primaeval man, in whom dwelt
Thought, this Universe was all a Temple ; Life everywhere
a Worship.

'What Worship, for example, is there not in mere Washing ! Perhaps one of the most moral things a man, in
common cases, has it in his power to do. Strip thyself, go
into the bath, or were it into the limpid pool and running
brook, and there wash and be clean ; thou wilt step out
again a purer and a better man. This consciousness of
perfect outer pureness, that to thy skin there now adheres
no foreign speck of imperfection, how it radiates in on thee,
with cunning symbolic influences, to thy very soul ! Thou
hast an increase of tendency towards all good things whatsoever. The oldest Eastern Sages, with joy and holy gratitude,
had felt it so,—and that it was the Maker's gift and will.
Whose else *is* it ? It remains a religious duty, from oldest
times, in the East.—Nor could Herr Professor Strauss, when
I put the question, deny that for us at present it is still such
here in the West ! To that dingy fuliginous Operative,
emerging from his soot-mill, what is the first duty I will

prescribe, and offer help towards ? That he clean the skin of him. *Can* he pray, by any ascertained method ? One knows not entirely :—but with soap and a sufficiency of water, he can wash. Even the dull English feel something of this ; they have a saying, " Cleanliness is near of kin to Godliness ":—yet never, in any country, saw I operative men worse washed, and, in a climate drenched with the softest cloud-water, such a scarcity of baths !'—Alas, Sauerteig, our ' operative men ' are at present short even of potatoes: what ' duty ' can you prescribe to them !

Or let us give a glance at China. Our new friend, the Emperor there, is Pontiff of three hundred million men ; who do all live and work, these many centuries now ; authentically patronized by Heaven so far ; and therefore must have some ' religion ' of a kind. This Emperor-Pontiff has, in fact, a religious belief of certain Laws of Heaven ; observes, with a religious rigour, his 'three thousand punctualities', given out by men of insight, some sixty generations since, as a legible transcript of the same,—the Heavens do seem to say, not totally an incorrect one. He has not much of a ritual, this Pontiff-Emperor ; believes, it is likest, with the old Monks, that ' Labour is Worship'. His most public Act of Worship, it appears, is the drawing solemnly at a certain day, on the green bosom of our Mother Earth, when the Heavens, after dead black winter, have again with their vernal radiances awakened her, a distinct red Furrow with the Plough,—signal that all the Ploughs of China are to begin ploughing and worshipping ! It is notable enough. He, in sight of the Seen and Unseen Powers, draws his distinct red Furrow there ; saying, and praying, in mute symbolism, so many most eloquent things !

If you ask this Pontiff, ' Who made him ? What is to become of him and us ?' he maintains a dignified reserve ; waves his hand and pontiff-eyes over the unfathomable deep of Heaven, the 'Tsien', the azure kingdoms of Infinitude ; as if asking, ' Is it doubtful that we are right *well* made ? Can aught that is *wrong* become of us ?'—He and his three hundred millions (it is their chief ' punctuality ') visit yearly the Tombs of their Fathers ; each man the Tomb of his Father and his Mother : alone there, in silence, with what of ' worship ' or of other thought there may be, pauses solemnly each man ; the divine Skies all silent over him; the divine Graves, and this divinest Grave, all silent under him; the pulsings of his own soul, if he have any soul, alone audible. Truly it may be a kind of worship! Truly, if a man cannot get some glimpse into the Eternities, looking through this portal,—through what other need he try it?

Our friend the Pontiff-Emperor permits cheerfully, though with contempt, all manner of Buddhists, Bonzes, Talapoins and such like, to build brick Temples, on the voluntary principle; to worship with what of chantings, paper-lanterns and tumultuous brayings, pleases them; and make night hideous, since they find some comfort in so doing. Cheerfully, though with contempt. He is a wiser Pontiff than many persons think! He is as yet the one Chief Potentate or Priest in this Earth who has made a distinct systematic attempt at what we call the ultimate result of all religion, 'Practical Hero-worship': he does incessantly, with true anxiety, in such way as he can, search and sift (it would appear) his whole enormous population for the Wisest born among them; by which Wisest, as by born Kings, these three hundred million men are governed. The Heavens, to a certain extent, do appear to countenance him. These three hundred millions actually make porcelain, souchong tea, with innumerable other things; and fight, under Heaven's flag, against Necessity;—and have fewer Seven-Years Wars, Thirty-Years Wars, French-Revolution Wars, and infernal fightings with each other, than certain millions elsewhere have!

Nay, in our poor distracted Europe itself, in these newest times, have there not religious voices risen,—with a religion new and yet the oldest; entirely indisputable to all hearts of men? Some I do know, who did not call or think themselves 'Prophets', far enough from that; but who were, in very truth, melodious Voices from the eternal Heart of Nature once again; souls forever venerable to all that have a soul. A French Revolution is one phenomenon; as complement and spiritual exponent thereof, a Poet Goethe and German Literature is to me another. The old Secular or Practical World, so to speak, having gone up in fire, is not here the prophecy and dawn of a new Spiritual World, parent of far nobler, wider, new Practical Worlds? A Life of Antique devoutness, Antique veracity and heroism, has again become possible, is again *seen* actual there, for the most modern man. A phenomenon, as quiet as it is, comparable for greatness to no other! 'The great event for the world is, now as always, the arrival in it of a new Wise Man.' Touches there are, be the Heavens ever thanked, of new Sphere-melody; audible once more, in the infinite jargoning discords and poor scrannel-pipings of the thing called Literature;—priceless there, as the voice of new Heavenly Psalms! Literature, like the old Prayer-Collections of the first centuries, were it 'well selected from and burnt', contains precious things. For Literature, with all its printing-presses, puffing-engines and shoreless deafening triviality, *is* yet 'the Thought of Thinking Souls'. A sacred 'religion', if you like the name, does live in the heart of that strange froth-ocean, not wholly froth, which we call Literature; and will more and more disclose itself therefrom;—not now as scorching Fire: the red smoky scorching Fire has purified itself into white sunny Light. Is not Light grander than Fire? It is the same element in a state of purity.

My ingenuous readers, we will march out of this Third Book with a rhythmic word of Goethe's on our lips; a word which perhaps has already sung itself, in dark hours and in bright, through many a heart. To me, finding it devout yet wholly credible and veritable, full of piety yet free of cant; to me, joyfully finding much in it, and joyfully missing so much in it, this little snatch of music, by the greatest German Man, sounds like a stanza in the grand *Road-Song* and *Marching-Song* of our great Teutonic Kindred, wending, wending, valiant and victorious, through the undiscovered Deeps of Time! He calls it *Mason-Lodge*,—not Psalm or Hymn:

> The Mason's ways are
> A type of Existence,
> And his persistence
> Is as the days are
> Of men in this world.
>
> The Future hides in it
> Gladness and sorrow;
> We press still thorow,
> Naught that abides in it
> Daunting us,—onward.

And solemn before us,
Veiled, the dark Portal,
Goal of all mortal:—
Stars silent rest o'er us,
Graves under us silent.

While earnest thou gazest,
Comes boding of terror,
Comes phantasm and error,
Perplexes the bravest
With doubt and misgiving.

But heard are the Voices,—
Heard are the Sages,
The Worlds and the Ages:
'Choose well, your choice is
Brief and yet endless:

Here eyes do regard you,
In Eternity's stillness;
Here is all fullness,
Ye brave, to reward you;
Work, and despair not.'

BOOK IV—HOROSCOPE

CHAPTER I

ARISTOCRACIES

To predict the Future, to manage the Present, would not be so impossible, had not the Past been so sacrilegiously mishandled; effaced, and what is worse, defaced! The Past cannot be seen; the Past, looked at through the medium of 'Philosophical History' in these times, cannot even be *not* seen: it is misseen; affirmed to have existed,—and to have been a godless Impossibility. Your Norman Conquerors, true royal souls, crowned kings as such, were vulturous irrational tyrants: your Becket was a noisy egoist and hypocrite; getting his brains spilt on the floor of Canterbury Cathedral, to secure the main chance,—somewhat uncertain how! 'Policy, Fanaticism'; or say 'Enthusiasm', even 'honest Enthusiasm',—ah yes, of course:

> 'The Dog, to gain his private ends,
> *Went* mad, and bit the Man!'—

For in truth, the eye sees in all things 'what it brought with it the means of seeing'. A godless century, looking back on centuries that were godly, produces portraitures more miraculous than any other. All was inane discord in the Past; brute Force bore rule everywhere; Stupidity, savage Unreason, fitter for Bedlam than for a human World! Whereby indeed it becomes sufficiently natural that the like qualities, in new sleeker habiliments, should continue in our time to rule. Millions enchanted in Bastille Workhouses; Irish Widows proving their relationship by typhus-fever: what would you have? It was ever so, or worse. Man's History, was it not always even this: The cookery and eating up of imbecile Dupedom by successful Quackhood;

the battle, with various weapons, of vulturous Quack and Tyrant against vulturous Tyrant and Quack ?   No God was in the Past Time ; nothing but Mechanisms and Chaotic Brute-Gods:—how shall the poor ' Philosophic Historian ', to whom his own century is all godless, see any God in other centuries ?

Men believe in Bibles, and disbelieve in them : but of all Bibles the frightfullest to disbelieve in is this 'Bible of Universal History'.   This is the Eternal Bible and God's-Book, ' which every born man' till once the soul and eye-sight are extinguished in him, 'can and must, with his own eyes, see the God's-Finger writing ! '   To discredit this, is an *infidelity* like no other.   Such infidelity you would punish, if not by fire and faggot, which are difficult to manage in our times, yet by the most peremptory order, To hold its peace till it got something wiser to say.   Why should the blessed Silence be broken into noises, to communicate only the like of this ?   If the Past have no God's-Reason in it, nothing but Devil's-Unreason, let the Past be eternally forgotten : mention *it* no more ;—we whose ancestors were all hanged, why should we talk of ropes !

It is, in brief, not true that men ever lived by Delirium, Hypocrisy, Injustice, or any form of Unreason, since they came to inhabit this Planet.   It is not true that they ever did, or ever will, live except by the reverse of these.   Men will again be taught this.   Their acted History will then again be a Heroism ; their written History, what it once was, an Epic.   Nay, forever it is either such, or else it virtually is—Nothing.   Were it written in a thousand volumes, the Unheroic of such volumes hastens incessantly to be forgotten ; the net content of an Alexandrian Library of Un-heroics is, and will ultimately show itself to be, *zero*.   What man is interested to remember *it* ; have not all men, at all times, the liveliest interest to forget it ?—' Revelations ', if not celestial, then infernal, will teach us that God is ; we shall then, if needful, discern without difficulty that He has always been !   The Dryasdust Philosophisms and enlight-ened Scepticisms of the Eighteenth Century, historical and other, will have to survive for a while with the Physiolo-gists, as a memorable *Nightmare-Dream*.   All this haggard epoch, with its ghastly Doctrines, and death's-head Philoso-phies ' teaching by example ' or otherwise, will one day have become, what to our Moslem friends their godless ages are, 'the Period of Ignorance.'

If the convulsive struggles of the last Half-Century have taught poor struggling convulsed Europe any truth, it may perhaps be this as the essence of innumerable others : That Europe requires a real Aristocracy, a real Priesthood, or it cannot continue to exist. Huge French Revolutions, Napoleonisms, then Bourbonisms with their corollary of Three Days, finishing in very unfinal Louis-Philippisms : all this ought to be didactic ! All this may have taught us, That False Aristocracies are insupportable ; that No-Aristocracies, Liberty-and-Equalities are impossible ; that True Aristocracies are at once indispensable and not easily attained.

Aristocracy and Priesthood, a Governing Class and a Teaching Class : these two, sometimes separate, and endeavouring to harmonize themselves, sometimes conjoined as one, and the King a Pontiff-King :—there did no Society exist without these two vital elements, there will none exist. It lies in the very nature of man : you will visit no remotest village in the most republican country of the world, where virtually or actually you do not find these two powers at work. Man, little as he may suppose it, is necessitated to obey superiors. He is a social being in virtue of this necessity ; nay he could not be gregarious otherwise. He obeys those whom he esteems better than himself, wiser, braver ; and will forever obey such ; and even be ready and delighted to do it.

The Wiser, Braver : these, a Virtual Aristocracy everywhere and everywhen, do in all Societies that reach any articulate shape, develop themselves into a ruling class, an Actual Aristocracy, with settled modes of operating, what are called laws and even *private-laws* or privileges, and so forth ; very notable to look upon in this world.—Aristocracy and Priesthood, we say, are sometimes united. For indeed the Wiser and the Braver are properly but one class ; no wise man but needed first of all to be a brave man, or he never had been wise. The noble Priest was always a noble *Aristos* to begin with, and something more to end with. Your Luther, your Knox, your Anselm, Becket, Abbot Samson, Samuel Johnson, if they had not been brave

enough, by what possibility could they ever have been wise ?
—If, from accident or forethought, this your Actual Aristocracy have got discriminated into Two Classes, there can
be no doubt but the Priest Class is the more dignified ;
supreme over the other, as governing head is over active
hand.   And yet in practice again, it is likeliest the reverse
will be found arranged ;—a sign that the arrangement is
already vitiated ; that a split is introduced into it, which
will widen and widen till the whole be rent asunder.

In England, in Europe generally, we may say that these
two Virtualities have unfolded themselves into Actualities,
in by far the noblest and richest manner any region of the
world ever saw.   A spiritual Guideship, a practical Gover-
norship, fruit of the grand conscious endeavours, say rather
of the immeasurable unconscious instincts and necessities of
men, have established themselves ; very strange to behold.
Everywhere, while so much has been forgotten, you find
the King's Palace, and the Viceking's Castle, Mansion,
Manorhouse ; till there is not an inch of ground from sea to
sea but has both its King and Viceking, long due series of
Vicekings, its Squire, Earl, Duke or whatever the title of
him,—to whom you have given the land, that he may govern
you in it.

More touching still, there is not a hamlet where poor
peasants congregate, but by one means and another a Church-
Apparatus has been got together,—roofed edifice, with
revenues and belfries ; pulpit, reading-desk, with Books and
Methods : possibility in short, and strict prescription, That
a man stand there and speak of spiritual things to men.   It
is beautiful ;—even in its great obscuration and decadence,
it is among the beautifullest, most touching objects one sees
on the Earth.   This Speaking Man has indeed, in these
times, wandered terribly from the point ; has, alas, as it
were totally lost sight of the point : yet, at bottom, whom
have we to compare with him ?   Of all public functionaries
boarded and lodged on the Industry of Modern Europe, is
there one worthier of the board he has?   A man even professing, and never so languidly making still some endeavour,
to save the souls of men : contrast him with a man professing to do little but shoot the partridges of men !   I wish he
could find the point again, this Speaking One ; and stick to
it with tenacity, with deadly energy ; for there is need of

him yet! The Speaking Function, this of Truth coming to
us with a living voice, nay in a living shape, and as a con-
crete practical exemplar: this, with all our Writing and
Printing Functions, has a perennial place. Could he but
find the point again,—take the old spectacles off his nose,
and looking up discover, almost in contact with him, what
the *real* Satanas, and soul-devouring, world-devouring *Devil*,
now is! Original Sin and such like are bad enough, I doubt
not: but distilled Gin, dark Ignorance, Stupidity, dark
Corn-Law, Bastille and Company, what are they! *Will* he discover our new real Satan, whom he has to fight; or go on
droning through his old nose-spectacles about old extinct
Satans; and never see the real one, till he *feel* him at his
own throat and ours? That is a question, for the world!
Let us not intermeddle with it here.

Sorrowful, phantasmal as this same Double Aristocracy
of Teachers and Governors now looks, it is worth all men's
while to know that the purport of it is and remains noble
and most real. Dryasdust, looking merely at the surface, is
greatly in error as to those ancient Kings. William Conqueror, William Rufus or Redbeard, Stephen Curthose himself, much more Henry Beauclerc and our brave Plantagenet
Henry: the life of these men was not a vulturous Fighting;
it was a valorous Governing,—to which occasionally Fighting did, and alas must yet, though far seldomer now, super-
add itself as an accident, a distressing impedimental adjunct.
The fighting too was indispensable, for ascertaining who had
the might over whom, the right over whom. By much
hard fighting, as we once said, ' the unrealities, beaten into
dust, flew gradually off'; and left the plain reality and fact,
' Thou stronger than I; thou wiser than I; thou king, and
subject I,' in a somewhat clearer condition.

Truly we cannot enough admire, in those Abbot-Samson
and William-Conqueror times, the arrangement they had
made of their Governing Classes. Highly interesting to
observe how the sincere insight, on their part, into what
did, of primary necessity, behove to be accomplished, had
led them to the way of accomplishing it, and in the course
of time to get it accomplished! No imaginary Aristocracy
would serve their turn; and accordingly they attained
a real one. The Bravest men, who, it is ever to be repeated
and remembered, are also on the whole the Wisest, Strong-

est, everyway Best, had here, with a respectable degree of accuracy, been got selected ; seated each on his piece of territory, which was lent him, then gradually given him, that he might govern it. These Vicekings, each on his portion of the common soil of England, with a Head King over all, were a 'Virtuality perfected into an Actuality' really to an astonishing extent.

For those were rugged stalwart ages ; full of earnestness, of a rude God's-truth :—nay, at any rate, their *quilting* was so unspeakably *thinner* than ours ; Fact came swiftly on them, if at any time they had yielded to Phantasm ! 'The Knaves and Dastards' had to be 'arrested' in some measure ; or the world, almost within year and day, found that it could not live. The Knaves and Dastards accordingly were got arrested. Dastards upon the very throne had to be got arrested, and taken off the throne,—by such methods as there were ; by the roughest method, if there chanced to be no smoother one ! Doubtless there was much harshness of operation, much severity ; as indeed government and surgery are often somewhat severe. Gurth born thrall of Cedric, it is like, got cuffs as often as pork-parings, if he misdemeaned himself ; but Gurth did belong to Cedric : no human creature then went about connected with nobody ; left to go his way into Bastilles or worse, under *Laissez-faire* ; reduced to prove his relationship by dying of typhus-fever !—Days come when there is no King in Israel, but every man is his own king, doing that which is right in his own eyes ;—and tarbarrels are burnt to 'Liberty', 'Ten-pound Franchise' and the like, with considerable effect in various ways !—

That Feudal Aristocracy, I say, was no imaginary one. To a respectable degree, its *Jarls*, what we now call Earls, were *Strong-Ones* in fact as well as etymology; its Dukes *Leaders*; its Lords *Law-wards*. They did all the Soldiering and Police of the country, all the Judging, Law-making, even the Church-Extension ; whatsoever in the way of Governing, of Guiding and Protecting could be done. It was a Land Aristocracy ; it managed the Governing of this English People, and had the reaping of the Soil of England in return. It is, in many senses, the Law of Nature, this same Law of Feudalism ;—no right Aristocracy but a Land one ! The curious are invited to meditate upon it in these days. Soldiering, Police and Judging, Church-Extension, nay real Government and Guidance, all this was actually *done* by the Holders of the Land in return for their Land. How much of it is now done by them ; done by anybody ? Good Heavens, 'Laissez-faire, Do ye nothing, eat your wages and sleep,' is everywhere the passionate half-wise cry of this time ; and they will not so much as do nothing, but must do mere Corn-Laws ! We raise Fifty-two millions, from the general mass of us, to get our Governing done—or, alas, to get ourselves persuaded that it is done : and the 'peculiar burden of the Land' is to pay, not all this, but to pay, as I learn, one twenty-fourth part of all this. Our first Chartist Parliament, or Oliver *Redivivus*, you would say, will know where to lay the new taxes of England !— Or, alas, taxes ? If we made the Holders of the Land pay every shilling still of the expense of Governing the Land, what were all that ? The Land, by mere hired Governors, cannot be got governed. You cannot hire men to govern the Land : it is by a mission not contracted for in the Stock-Exchange, but felt in their own hearts as coming out of Heaven, that men can govern a Land. The mission of a Land Aristocracy is a *sacred* one, in both the senses of that old word. The footing it stands on, at present, might give rise to thoughts other than of Corn-Laws !—

But truly a 'Splendour of God', as in William Conqueror's rough oath, did dwell in those old rude veracious ages ; did inform, more and more, with a heavenly nobleness, all departments of their work and life. Phantasms could not yet walk abroad in mere Cloth Tailorage ; they were at least Phantasms 'on the rim of the horizon', pencilled there by an eternal Light-beam from within. A most 'practical' Hero-worship went on, unconsciously or half-consciously, everywhere. A Monk Samson, with a maximum of two shillings in his pocket, could, without ballot-box, be made a Viceking of, being seen to be worthy. The difference between a good man and a bad man was as yet felt to be, what it forever is, an immeasurable one. Who *durst* have elected a Pandarus Dogdraught, in those days, to any office, Carlton Club, Senatorship, or place whatsoever ? It was felt that the arch Satanas and no other had a clear right of property in Pandarus ; that it were better for you to have no hand in Pandarus, to keep out of Pandarus his neighbourhood! Which is, to this hour, the mere fact; though for the present, alas, the forgotten fact. I think they were comparatively blessed times those, in their way! 'Violence,' 'war,' 'disorder': well, what is war, and death itself, to such a perpetual life-in-death, and 'peace, peace, where there is no peace!' Unless some Hero-worship, in its new appropriate form, can return, this world does not promise to be very habitable long.

Old Anselm, exiled Archbishop of Canterbury, one of the purest-minded 'men of genius', was travelling to make his appeal to Rome against King Rufus, —a man of rough ways, in whom the 'inner Lightbeam' shone very fitfully. It is beautiful to read, in Monk Eadmer, how the Continental populations welcomed and venerated this Anselm, as no French population now venerates Jean-Jacques or giant-killing Voltaire; as not even an American population now venerates a Schnüspel the distinguished Novelist! They had, by phantasy and true insight, the intensest conviction that a God's-Blessing dwelt in this Anselm,—as is my conviction too. They crowded round, with bent knees and enkindled hearts, to receive his blessing, to hear his voice, to see the light of his face. My blessings on them and on him !—But the notablest was a certain necessitous or covetous Duke of Burgundy, in straitened circumstances we shall hope,—who reflected that in all likelihood this English Archbishop, going towards Rome to appeal, must have taken store of cash with him to bribe the Cardinals. Wherefore he of Burgundy, for his part, decided to lie in wait and rob him. 'In an open space of a wood', some 'wood' then green and growing, eight centuries ago, in Burgundian Land,—this fierce Duke, with fierce steel followers, shaggy, savage, as the Russian bear, dashes out on the weak old Anselm ; who is riding along there, on his small quiet-going pony; escorted only by Eadmer and another poor Monk on ponies; and, except small modicum of roadmoney, not a gold coin in his possession. The steelclad Russian bear emerges, glaring: the old white-bearded man starts not,— paces on unmoved, looking into him with those clear old earnest eyes, with that venerable sorrowful time-worn face ; of whom no man or thing need be afraid, and who also is afraid of no created man or thing. The fire-eyes of his Burgundian Grace meet these clear eye-glances, convey them swift to his heart: he bethinks him that probably this feeble, fearless, hoary Figure has in it something of the Most High God; that probably he shall be damned if he meddle with it,—that, on the whole, he had better not. He plunges, the rough savage, from his war-horse, down to his knees; embraces the feet of old Anselm: he too begs his blessing; orders men to escort him, guard him from being robbed, and under dread penalties see him safe on his way. *Per os Dei*, as his Majesty was wont to ejaculate!

Neither is this quarrel of Rufus and Anselm, or Henry and Becket, uninstructive to us. It was, at bottom, a great quarrel. For, admitting that Anselm was full of divine blessing, he by no means included in him all forms of divine blessing:—there were far other forms withal, which he little dreamed of; and William Redbeard was unconsciously the representative and spokesman of these. In truth, could your divine Anselm, your divine Pope Gregory have had their way, the results had been very notable. Our Western World had all become a European Thibet, with one Grand Lama sitting at Rome; our one honourable business that of singing mass, all day and all night. Which would not in the least have suited us! The Supreme Powers willed it not so.

It was as if King Redbeard unconsciously, addressing Anselm, Becket and the others, had said: 'Right Reverend, your Theory of the Universe is indisputable by man or devil. To the core of our heart we feel that this divine thing, which you call Mother Church, does fill the whole world hitherto known, and is and shall be all our salvation and all our desire. And yet—and yet—Behold, though it is an unspoken secret, the world is *wider* than any of us think, Right Reverend! Behold, there are yet other immeasurable Sacrednesses in this that you call Heathenism, Secularity! On the whole, I, in an obscure but most rooted manner, feel that I cannot comply with you. Western Thibet and perpetual mass-chanting,—No. I am, so to speak, in the family-way; with child, of I know not what,— certainly of something far different from this! I have—*Per os Dei*, I have Manchester Cotton-trades, Bromwicham Iron-trades, American Commonwealths, Indian Empires, Steam Mechanisms and Shakspeare Dramas, in my belly; and cannot do it, Right Reverend!'—So accordingly it was

decided: and Saxon Becket spilt his life in Canterbury
Cathedral, as Scottish Wallace did on Tower-hill, and as
generally a noble man and martyr has to do,—not for
nothing ; no, but for a divine something, other than *he* had
altogether calculated. We will now quit this of the hard,
organic, but limited Feudal Ages ; and glance timidly into
the immense Industrial Ages, as yet all inorganic, and in
a quite pulpy condition, requiring desperately to harden
themselves into some organism !

Our Epic having now become *Tools and the Man*, it is
more than usually impossible to prophesy the Future. The
boundless Future does lie there, predestined, nay already
extant though unseen ; hiding, in its Continents of Darkness, 'gladness and sorrow': but the supremest intelligence
of man cannot prefigure much of it :—the united intelligence
and effort of All Men in all coming generations, this alone
will gradually prefigure it, and figure and form it into a seen
fact ! Straining our eyes hitherto, the utmost effort of intelligence sheds but some most glimmering dawn, a little way
into its dark enormous Deeps : only huge outlines loom
uncertain on the sight ; and the ray of prophecy, at a short
distance, expires. But may we not say, here as always,
Sufficient for the day is the evil thereof ! To shape the whole
Future is not our problem ; but only to shape faithfully
a small part of it, according to rules already known. It is
perhaps possible for each of us, who will with due earnestness inquire, to ascertain clearly what he, for his own part,
ought to do : this let him, with true heart, do, and continue
doing. The general issue will, as it has always done, rest
well with a Higher Intelligence than ours.

One grand 'outline', or even two, many earnest readers
may perhaps, at this stage of the business, be able to prefigure for themselves,—and draw some guidance from. One
prediction, or even two, are already possible. For the Life-
tree Igdrasil, in all its new developments, is the selfsame
world-old Life-tree : having found an element or elements
there, running from the very roots of it in Hela's Realms, in
the Well of Mimer and of the Three Nornas or TIMES, up to
this present hour of it in our own hearts, we conclude that
such will have to continue. A man has, in his own soul, an
Eternal ; can read something of the Eternal there, if he will

look ! He already knows what will continue ; what cannot, by any means or appliance whatsoever, be made to continue !

One wide and widest 'outline' ought really, in all ways, to be becoming clear to us; this namely: That a 'Splendour of God', in one form or other, will have to unfold itself from the heart of these our Industrial Ages too ; or they will never get themselves 'organized'; but continue chaotic, distressed, distracted evermore, and have to perish in frantic suicidal dissolution. A second 'outline' or prophecy, narrower, but also wide enough, seems not less certain: That there will again *be* a King in Israel; a system of Order and Government ; and every man shall, in some measure, see himself constrained to do that which is right in the King's eyes. This too we may call a sure element of the Future ; for this too is of the Eternal;—this too is of the Present, though hidden from most ; and without it no fibre of the Past ever was. An actual new Sovereignty, Industrial Aristocracy, real not imaginary Aristocracy, is indispensable and indubitable for us.

But what an Aristocracy ; on what new, far more complex and cunningly devised conditions than that old Feudal fighting one ! For we are to bethink us that the Epic verily is not *Arms and the Man*, but *Tools and the Man*,—an infinitely wider kind of Epic. And again we are to bethink us that men cannot now be bound to men by *brass-collars*,—not at all : that this brass-collar method, in all figures of it, has vanished out of Europe for evermore! Huge Democracy, walking the streets everywhere in its Sack Coat, has asserted so much ; irrevocably, brooking no reply! True enough, man *is* forever the 'born thrall' of certain men, born master of certain other men, born equal of certain others, let him acknowledge the fact or not. It is unblessed for him when he cannot acknowledge this fact ; he is in the chaotic state, ready to perish, till he do get the fact acknowledged. But no man is, or can henceforth be, the brass-collar thrall of any man ; you will have to bind him by other, far nobler and cunninger methods. Once for all, he is to be loose of the brass-collar, to have a scope *as* wide as his faculties now are :— will he not be all the usefuller to you, in that new state? Let him go abroad as a trusted one, as a free one ; and return home to you with rich earnings at night ! Gurth could only tend pigs ; this one will build cities,

conquer waste worlds.—How, in conjunction with inevitable
Democracy, indispensable Sovereignty is to exist : certainly
it is the hugest question ever heretofore propounded to
Mankind ! The solution of which is work for long years and
centuries. Years and centuries, of one knows not what
complexion ;—blessed or unblessed, according as they shall,
with earnest valiant effort, make progress therein, or, in
slothful unveracity and dilettantism, only talk of making
progress. For either progress therein, or swift and
ever swifter progress towards dissolution, is henceforth
a necessity.

It is of importance that this grand reformation were
begun ; that Corn-Law Debatings and other jargon, little
less than delirious in such a time, had fled far away, and
left us room to begin ! For the evil has grown practical,
extremely conspicuous ; if it be not seen and provided for,
the blindest fool will have to feel it ere long. There is
much that can wait ; but there is something also that
cannot wait. With millions of eager Working Men imprisoned in 'Impossibility' and Poor-Law Bastilles, it is
time that some means of dealing with them were trying to
become 'possible' ! Of the Government of England, of all
articulate-speaking functionaries, real and imaginary Aristocracies, of me and of thee, it is imperatively demanded,
'How do you mean to manage these men ? Where are they
to find a supportable existence ? What is to become of
them,—and of you ! '

CHAPTER II

BRIBERY COMMITTEE

In the case of the late Bribery Committee, it seemed to
be the conclusion of the soundest practical minds that
Bribery could not be put down ; that Pure Election was
a thing we had seen the last of, and must now go on
without, as we best could. A conclusion not a little startling ; to which it requires a practical mind of some seasoning

to reconcile yourself at once! It seems, then, we are henceforth to get ourselves constituted Legislators not according
to what merit we may have, or even what merit we may
seem to have, but according to the length of our purse, and
our frankness, impudence and dexterity in laying out the
contents of the same. Our theory, written down in all
books and law-books, spouted forth from all barrel-heads, is
perfect purity of Tenpound Franchise, absolute sincerity of
question put and answer given;—and our practice is irremediable bribery; irremediable, unpunishable, which you
will do more harm than good by attempting to punish!
Once more, a very startling conclusion indeed; which,
whatever the soundest practical minds in Parliament may
think of it, invites all British men to meditations of various
kinds.

A Parliament, one would say, which proclaims itself
elected and eligible by bribery, tells the Nation that is
governed by it a piece of singular news. Bribery: have we
reflected what bribery is? Bribery means not only length
of purse, which is neither qualification nor the contrary for
legislating well; but it means dishonesty, and even impudent
dishonesty;—brazen insensibility to lying and to making
others lie; total oblivion, and flinging overboard, for the
nonce, of any real thing you can call veracity, morality;
with dexterous putting on the cast-clothes of that real
thing, and strutting about in them! What Legislating can
you get out of a man in that fatal situation? None that will
profit much, one would think! A Legislator who has left
his veracity lying on the door-threshold, he, why verily *he*—
ought to be sent out to seek it again!

Heavens, what an improvement, were there once fairly in
Downing-street an Election-Office opened, with a Tariff of
Boroughs! Such and such a population, amount of property-
tax, ground-rental, extent of trade; returns two Members,
returns one Member, for so much money down: Ipswich so
many thousands, Nottingham so many,—as they happened,
one by one, to fall into this new Downing-street Schedule A!
An incalculable improvement, in comparison: for now at
least you have it fairly by length of purse, and leave the
dishonesty, the impudence, the unveracity all handsomely
aside. Length of purse and desire to be a Legislator ought
to get a man into Parliament, not *with*, but if possible

without the unveracity, the impudence and the dishonesty ! Length of purse and desire, these are, as intrinsic qualifications, correctly equal to zero ; but they are not yet *less* than zero,—as the smallest addition of that latter sort will make them !

And is it come to this? And does our venerable Parliament announce itself elected and eligible in this manner ? Surely such a Parliament promulgates strange horoscopes of itself. What is to become of a Parliament elected or eligible in this manner ? Unless Belial and Beelzebub have got possession of the throne of this Universe, such Parliament is preparing itself for new Reform-bills. We shall have to try it by Chartism, or any conceivable *ism*, rather than put up with this ! There is already in England 'religion' enough to get six hundred and fifty-eight Consulting Men brought together who do *not* begin work with a lie in their mouth. Our poor old Parliament, thousands of years old, is still good for something, for several things ;—though many are beginning to ask, with ominous anxiety, in these days : For what thing ? But for whatever thing and things Parliament be good, indisputably it must start with other than a lie in its mouth ! On the whole, a Parliament working with a lie in its mouth, will have to take itself away. To no Parliament or thing, that one has heard of, did this Universe ever long yield harbour on that footing. At all hours of the day and night, some Chartism is advancing, some armed Cromwell is advancing, to apprise such Parliament : 'Ye are no Parliament. In the name of God,—go ! '

In sad truth, once more, how is our whole existence, in these present days, built on Cant, Speciosity, Falsehood, Dilettantism ; with this one serious Veracity in it : Mammonism ! Dig down where you will, through the Parliament-floor or elsewhere, how infallibly do you, at spade's depth below the surface, come upon this universal *Liars*-rock substratum ! Much else is ornamental ; true on barrel-heads, in pulpits, hustings, Parliamentary benches ; but this is forever true and truest : 'Money does bring money's worth ; Put money in your purse.' Here, if nowhere else, is the human soul still in thorough earnest ; sincere with a prophet's sincerity : and 'the Hell of the English', as Sauerteig said, 'is the infinite terror of Not getting on, especially of Not making money.' With results !

To many persons the horoscope of Parliament is more interesting than to me : but surely all men with souls must admit that sending members to Parliament by bribery is an infamous solecism ; an act entirely immoral, which no man can have to do with, more or less, but he will soil his fingers more or less. No Carlton Clubs, Reform Clubs, nor any sort of clubs or creatures, or of accredited opinions or practices, can make a Lie Truth, can make Bribery a Propriety. The Parliament should really either punish and put away Bribery, or legalize it by some Office in Downing-street. As I read the Apocalypses, a Parliament that can do neither of these things is not in a good way.—And yet, alas, what of Parliaments and their Elections ? Parliamentary Elections are but the topmost ultimate outcome of an electioneering which goes on at all hours, in all places, in every meeting of two or more men. It is *we* that vote wrong, and teach the poor ragged Freemen of Boroughs to vote wrong. We pay respect to those worthy of no respect.

Is not Pandarus Dogdraught a member of select clubs, and admitted into the drawingrooms of men ? Visibly to all persons he is of the offal of Creation ; but he carries money in his purse, due lacquer on his dog-visage, and it is believed will not steal spoons. The human species does not with one voice, like the Hebrew Psalmist, 'shun to sit' with Dogdraught, refuse totally to dine with Dogdraught ; men called of honour are willing enough to dine with him, his talk being lively, and his champagne excellent. We say to ourselves, 'The man is in good society,'— others have already voted for him ; why should not I ? We *forget* the indefeasible right of property that Satan has in Dogdraught, —we are not afraid to be near Dogdraught ! It is we that vote wrong ; blindly, nay, with falsity prepense ! It is we that no longer know the difference between Human Worth and Human Unworth ; or feel that the one is admirable and alone admirable, the other detestable, damnable ! How shall *we* find out a Hero and Viceking Samson with a maximum of two shillings in his pocket ? We have no chance to do such a thing. We have got out of the Ages of Heroism, deep into the Ages of Flunkeyism,—and must return or die. What a noble set of mortals are we, who, because there is no Saint Edmund threatening us at the rim of the horizon, are not afraid to be whatever, for the day and hour, is smoothest for us!

And now, in good sooth, why should an indigent discerning Freeman give his vote without bribes? Let us rather honour the poor man that he does discern clearly wherein lies, for him, the true kernel of the matter. What is it to the ragged grimy Freeman of a Tenpound-Franchise Borough, whether Aristides Rigmarole, Esq. of the Destructive, or the Hon. Alcides Dolittle of the Conservative Party, be sent to Parliament;— much more, whether the two-thousandth part of them be sent, for that is the amount of his faculty in it? Destructive or Conservative, what will either of them destroy or conserve of vital moment to this Freeman? Has he found either of them care, at bottom, a sixpence for him or his interests, or those of his class or of his cause, or of any class or cause that is of much value to God or to man? Rigmarole and Dolittle have alike cared for themselves hitherto; and for their own clique, and self-conceited crotchets,—their greasy dishonest interests of pudding, or windy dishonest interests of praise; and not very perceptibly for any other interest whatever. Neither Rigmarole nor Dolittle will accomplish any good or any evil for this grimy Freeman, like giving him a five-pound note, or refusing to give it him. It will be smoothest to vote according to value received. That is the veritable fact; and he indigent, like others that are not indigent, acts conformably thereto.

Why, reader, truly, if they asked thee or me, Which way we meant to vote?—were it not our likeliest answer: Neither way! I, as a Tenpound Franchiser, will receive no bribe; but also I will not vote for either of these men. Neither Rigmarole nor Dolittle shall, by furtherance of mine, go and make laws for this country. I will have no hand in such a mission. How dare I! If other men cannot be got in England, a totally other sort of men, different as light is from dark, as star-fire is from street-mud, what is the use of votings, or of Parliaments in England? England ought to resign herself; there is no hope or possibility for England. If England cannot get her Knaves and Dastards 'arrested', in some degree, but only get them 'elected', what is to become of England?

I conclude, with all confidence, that England will verily

have to put an end to briberies on her Election Hustings and elsewhere, at what cost soever ;—and likewise that we, Electors and Eligibles, one and all of us, for our own behoof and hers, cannot too soon begin, at what cost soever, to put an end to *bribe-abilities* in ourselves. The death-leprosy, attacked in this manner, by purifying lotions from without and by rallying of the vital energies and purities from within, will probably abate somewhat ! It has otherwise no chance to abate.

CHAPTER III

THE ONE INSTITUTION

WHAT our Government can do in this grand Problem of the Working Classes of England ? Yes, supposing the insane Corn-Laws totally abolished, all speech of them ended, and 'from ten to twenty years of new possibility to live and find wages' conceded us in consequence : What the English Government might be expected to accomplish or attempt towards rendering the existence of our Labouring Millions somewhat less anomalous, somewhat less impossible, in the years that are to follow those 'ten or twenty', if either 'ten' or 'twenty' there be ?

It is the most momentous question. For all this of the Corn-Law Abrogation, and what can follow therefrom, is but as the shadow on King Hezekiah's Dial : the shadow has gone back twenty years ; but will again, in spite of Free-Trades and Abrogations, travel forward its old fated way. With our present system of individual Mammonism, and Government by Laissez-faire, this Nation cannot live. And if, in the priceless interim, some new life and healing be not found, there is no second respite to be counted on. The shadow on the Dial advances thenceforth without pausing. What Government can do ? This that they call ' Organizing of Labour ' is, if well understood, the Problem of the whole Future, for all who will in future pretend to govern men. But our first preliminary stage of it, How to deal with the Actual Labouring Millions of England ? this is the imperatively pressing Problem of the Present, pressing with a truly fearful intensity and imminence in

these very years and days. No Government can longer
neglect it : once more, what can our Government do in it ?

Governments are of very various degrees of activity : some,
altogether Lazy Governments, in 'free countries' as they
are called, seem in these times almost to profess to do, if
not nothing, one knows not at first what. To debate in
Parliament, and gain majorities ; and ascertain who shall
be, with a toil hardly second to Ixion's, the Prime Speaker
and Spoke-holder, and keep the Ixion's-Wheel going, if not
forward, yet round ? Not altogether so :—much, to the
experienced eye, is not what it seems ! Chancery and certain other Law-Courts seem nothing ; yet in fact they are,
the worst of them, something : chimneys for the devilry and
contention of men to escape by ;—a very considerable something ! Parliament too has its tasks, if thou wilt look ; fit
to wear-out the lives of toughest men. The celebrated
Kilkenny Cats, through their tumultuous congress, cleaving
the ear of Night, could they be said to do nothing ? Hadst
thou been of them, thou hadst seen ! The feline heart
laboured, as with steam up—to the bursting point ; and
death-doing energy nerved every muscle : they had a work
there ; and did it ! On the morrow, two tails were found
left, and peaceable annihilation ; a neighbourhood *delivered*
from despair.

Again, are not Spinning-Dervishes an eloquent emblem,
significant of much ? Hast thou noticed him, that solemn-
visaged Turk, the eyes shut ; dingy wool mantle circularly
hiding his figure ;—bell-shaped ; like a dingy bell set spinning on the *tongue* of it ? By centrifugal force the dingy
wool mantle heaves itself ; spreads more and more, like
upturned cup widening into upturned saucer : thus spins
he, to the praise of Allah and advantage of mankind, fast
and faster, till collapse ensue, and sometimes death !—

A Government such as ours, consisting of from seven to
eight hundred Parliamentary Talkers, with their escort of
Able Editors and Public Opinion ; and for head, certain
Lords and Servants of the Treasury, and Chief Secretaries
and others, who find themselves at once Chiefs and No-
Chiefs, and often commanded rather than commanding,—
is doubtless a most complicate entity, and none of the alert-
est for getting on with business ! Clearly enough, if the

Chiefs be not self-motive and what we call men, but mere
patient lay-figures without self-motive principle, the Government will not move anywhither; it will tumble disastrously,
and jumble, round its own axis, as for many years past we
have seen it do.—And yet a self-motive man who is not a
lay-figure, place him in the heart of what entity you may,
will make it move more or less! The absurdest in Nature
he will make a little *less* absurd, he. The unwieldiest he
will make to move;—that is the use of his existing there.
He will at least have the manfulness to depart out of it, if
not; to say: 'I cannot move in thee, and be a man; like
a wretched drift-log dressed in man's clothes and minister's
clothes, doomed to a lot baser than belongs to man, I will
not continue with thee, tumbling aimless on the Mother of
Dead Dogs here:—Adieu!'

For, on the whole, it is the lot of Chiefs everywhere, this
same. No Chief in the most despotic country but was a
Servant withal; at once an absolute commanding General,
and a poor Orderly-Sergeant, ordered by the very men in
the ranks,—obliged to collect the vote of the ranks too,
in some articulate or inarticulate shape, and weigh well the
same. The proper name of all Kings is Minister, Servant.
In no conceivable Government can a lay-figure get forward!
This Worker, surely he above all others has to 'spread out
his Gideon's Fleece', and collect the monitions of Immensity;
the poor Localities, as we said, and Parishes of Palace-yard
or elsewhere, having no due monition in them. A Prime
Minister, even here in England, who shall dare believe the
heavenly omens, and address himself like a man and hero to
the great dumb-struggling heart of England; and speak out
for it, and act out for it, the God's-Justice it is writhing to
get uttered and perishing for want of,—yes, he too will see
awaken round him, in passionate burning all-defiant loyalty,
the heart of England, and such a 'support' as no Division-
List or Parliamentary Majority was ever yet known to yield
a man! Here as there, now as then, he who can and dare
trust the heavenly Immensities, all earthly Localities are
subject to him. We will pray for such a Man and First-
Lord;—yes, and far better, we will strive and incessantly
make ready, each of us, to be worthy to serve and second
such a First-Lord! We shall then be as good as sure of
his arriving; sure of many things, let him arrive or not.

Who can despair of Governments that passes a Soldier's Guardhouse, or meets a redcoated man on the streets! That a body of men could be got together to kill other men when you bade them: this, *a priori*, does it not seem one of the impossiblest things? Yet look, behold it: in the stolidest of Donothing Governments, that impossibility is a thing done. See it there, with buff-belts, red coats on its back; walking sentry at guardhouses, brushing white breeches in barracks; an indisputable palpable fact. Out of grey Antiquity, amid all finance-difficulties, *scaccarium*-tallies, ship-moneys, coat - and - conduct moneys, and vicissitudes of Chance and Time, there, down to the present blessed hour, it is.

Often, in these painfully decadent and painfully nascent Times, with their distresses, inarticulate gaspings and 'impossibilities'; meeting a tall Lifeguardsman in his snow-white trousers, or seeing those two statuesque Lifeguardsmen in their frowning bearskins, pipe-clayed buckskins, on their coal-black sleek-fiery quadrupeds, riding sentry at the Horse-Guards,—it strikes one with a kind of mournful interest, how, in such universal down-rushing and wrecked impotence of almost all old institutions, this oldest Fighting Institution is still so young! Fresh-complexioned, firm-limbed, six feet by the standard, this fighting-man has verily been got up, and can fight. While so much has not yet got into being; while so much has gone gradually out of it, and become an empty Semblance or Clothes-suit; and highest king's-cloaks, mere chimeras parading under them so long, are getting unsightly to the earnest eye, unsightly, almost offensive, like a costlier kind of scarecrow's-blanket,—here still is a reality!

The man in horsehair wig advances, promising that he will get me 'justice': he takes me into Chancery Law-Courts, into decades, half-centuries of hubbub, of distracted jargon; and does *get* me—disappointment, almost desperation; and one refuge: that of dismissing him and his 'justice' altogether out of my head. For I have work to do; I cannot spend my decades in mere arguing with other men about the exact wages of my work: I will work cheerfully with no wages, sooner than with a ten-years gangrene or Chancery Lawsuit in my heart! He of the horsehair wig is a sort of failure; no substance, but a fond imagination of the mind. He of the shovel-hat, again, who comes forward professing that he will save my soul—O ye Eternities, of him in this place be absolute silence!—But he of the red coat, I say, is a success and no failure! He will veritably, if he get orders, draw out a long sword and kill me. No mistake there. He is a fact and not a shadow. Alive in this Year Forty-three, able and willing to do *his* work. In dim old centuries, with William Rufus, William of Ipres, or far earlier, he began ; and has come down safe so far. Catapult has given place to cannon, pike has given place to musket, iron mail-shirt to coat of red cloth, saltpetre rope-match to percussion cap ; equipments, circumstances have all changed, and again changed : but the human battle-engine, in the inside of any or of each of these, ready still to do battle, stands there, six feet in standard size. There are Pay-Offices, Woolwich Arsenals, there is a Horse-Guards, War-Office, Captain-General ; persuasive Sergeants, with tap of drum, recruit in market-towns and villages ;—and, on the whole, I say, here is your actual drilled fighting-man ; here are your actual Ninety-thousand of such, ready to go into any quarter of the world and fight !

Strange, interesting, and yet most mournful to reflect on. Was this, then, of all the things mankind had some talent for, the one thing important to learn well, and bring to perfection ; this of successfully killing one another ? Truly you have learned it well, and carried the business to a high perfection. It is incalculable what, by arranging, command-ing and regimenting, you can make of men. These thousand straight-standing firm-set individuals, who shoulder arms, who march, wheel, advance, retreat ; and are, for your behoof, a magazine charged with fiery death, in the most perfect condition of potential activity : few months ago, till the persuasive sergeant came, what were they ? Multiform ragged losels, runaway apprentices, starved weavers, thievish valets ; an entirely broken population, fast tending towards the treadmill. But the persuasive sergeant came ; by tap of drum enlisted, or formed lists of them, took heartily to drill-ing them ;—and he and you have made them this ! Most potent, effectual for all work whatsoever, is wise planning, firm combining and commanding among men. Let no man despair of Governments who looks on these two sentries at the Horse-Guards, and our United-Service Clubs ! I could conceive an Emigration Service, a Teaching Service, considerable varieties of United and Separate Services, of the due thousands strong, all effective as this Fighting Service is; all doing *their* work, like it;—which work, much more than fighting, is henceforth the necessity of these New Ages we are got into! Much lies among us, convulsively, nigh desperately *struggling to be born.*

But mean Governments, as mean-limited individuals do, have stood by the physically indispensable; have realized that and nothing more. The Soldier is perhaps one of the most difficult things to realize; but Governments, had they not realized him, could not have existed: accordingly he is here. O Heavens, if we saw an army ninety-thousand strong, maintained and fully equipt, in continual real action and battle against Human Starvation, against Chaos, Necessity, Stupidity, and our real 'natural enemies', what a business were it! Fighting and molesting not 'the French', who, poor men, have a hard enough battle of their own in the like kind, and need no additional molesting from us; but fighting and incessantly spearing down and destroying Falsehood, Nescience, Delusion, Disorder, and the Devil and his Angels! Thou thyself, cultivated reader, hast done something in that alone true warfare; but, alas, under what circumstances was it? Thee no beneficent drill-sergeant, with any effectiveness, would rank in line beside thy fellows; train, like a true didactic artist, by the wit of all past experience, to do thy soldiering; encourage thee when right, punish thee when wrong, and everywhere with wise word-of-command say, Forward on this hand, Forward on that! Ah, no: thou hadst to learn thy small-sword and platoon exercise where and how thou couldst; to all mortals but thyself it was indifferent whether thou shouldst ever learn it. And the rations, and shilling a day, were they provided thee,—reduced as I have known brave Jean-Pauls, learning their exercise, to live on 'water *without* the bread'? The rations; or any furtherance of promotion to corporalship, lance-corporalship, or due cat-o'-nine tails, with the slightest reference to thy deserts, were not provided. Forethought, even as of a pipe-clayed drill-sergeant, did not preside over thee. To corporalship, lance-corporalship, thou didst attain; alas, also to the halberts and cat: but thy rewarder and punisher seemed blind as the Deluge: neither lance-corporalship, nor even drummer's cat, because both appeared delirious, brought thee due profit.

It was well, all this, we know;—and yet it was not well! Forty soldiers, I am told, will disperse the largest Spital-fields mob: forty to ten-thousand, that is the proportion between drilled and undrilled. Much there is which cannot yet be organized in this world ; but somewhat also which can, somewhat also which must. When one thinks, for example, what Books are become and becoming for us, what Operative Lancashires are become ; what a Fourth Estate, and innumerable Virtualities not yet got to be Actualities are become and becoming,—one sees Organisms enough in the dim huge Future ; and 'United Services' quite other than the redcoat one ; and much, even in these years, struggling to be born !

Of Time-Bill, Factory-Bill and other such Bills the present Editor has no authority to speak. He knows not, it is for others than he to know, in what specific ways it may be feasible to interfere, with Legislation, between the Workers and the Master-Workers ;—knows only and sees, what all men are beginning to see, that Legislative interference, and interferences not a few are indispensable ; that as a lawless anarchy of supply-and-demand, on market-wages alone, this province of things cannot longer be left. Nay interference has begun: there are already Factory Inspectors,—who seem to have no *lack* of work. Perhaps there might be Mine-Inspectors too :—might there not be Furrowfield Inspectors withal, and ascertain for us how on seven and sixpence a week a human family does live ! Interference has begun ; it must continue, must extensively enlarge itself, deepen and sharpen itself. Such things cannot longer be idly lapped in darkness, and suffered to go on unseen: the Heavens do see them ; the curse, not the blessing of the Heavens is on an Earth that refuses to see them.

Again, are not Sanitary Regulations possible for a Legis-lature ? The old Romans had their Ædiles ; who would, I think, in direct contravention to supply-and-demand, have rigorously seen rammed up into total abolition many a foul cellar in our Southwarks, Saint-Gileses, and dark poison-lanes ; saying sternly, 'Shall a Roman man dwell there ?' The Legislature, at whatever cost of consequences, would

have had to answer, 'God forbid!'—The Legislature, even
as it now is, could order all dingy Manufacturing Towns to
cease from their soot and darkness; to let-in the blessed
sunlight, the blue of Heaven, and become clear and clean;
to burn their coal-smoke, namely, and make flame of it. Baths,
free air, a wholesome temperature, ceilings twenty feet high,
might be obtained, by Act of Parliament, in all establishments licensed as Mills. There are such Mills already extant;—honour to the builders of them! The Legislature can
say to others: Go ye and do likewise; better if you can.

Every toiling Manchester, its smoke and soot all burnt,
ought it not, among so many world-wide conquests, to have
a hundred acres or so of free greenfield, with trees on it,
conquered, for its little children to disport in; for its all-
conquering workers to take a breath of twilight air in?
You would say so! A willing Legislature could say so
with effect. A willing Legislature could say very many
things! And to whatsoever 'vested interest', or such like,
stood up, gainsaying merely, 'I shall lose profits',— the
willing Legislature would answer, 'Yes, but my sons and
daughters will gain health, and life, and a soul.'—'What is
to become of our Cotton-trade?' cried certain Spinners,
when the Factory Bill was proposed; 'What is to become
of our invaluable Cotton-trade?' The Humanity of England answered steadfastly: 'Deliver me these rickety perishing souls of infants, and let your Cotton-trade take its chance.
God Himself commands the one thing; not God especially
the other. We cannot have prosperous Cotton-trades at the
expense of keeping the Devil a partner in them!'—

Bills enough, were the Corn-Law Abrogation Bill once
passed, and a Legislature willing! Nay this one Bill, which
lies yet unenacted, a right Education Bill, is not this of
itself the sure parent of innumerable wise Bills,—wise
regulations, practical methods and proposals, gradually ripen-
ing towards the state of Bills? To irradiate with intelligence, that is to say, with order, arrangement and all
blessedness, the Chaotic, Unintelligent: how, except by
educating, *can* you accomplish this? That thought, reflection, articulate utterance and understanding be awakened
in these individual million heads, which are the atoms of
your Chaos: there is no other way of illuminating any
Chaos! The sum-total of intelligence that is found in it,

determines the extent of order that is possible for your
Chaos,—the feasibility and rationality of what your Chaos
will dimly demand from you, and will gladly obey when
proposed by you! It is an exact equation; the one accurately measures the other.—If the whole English People,
during these 'twenty years of respite', be not educated, with
at least schoolmaster's educating, a tremendous responsi-
bility, before God and men, will rest somewhere! How
dare any man, especially a man calling himself minister of
God, stand up in any Parliament or place, under any pretext
or delusion, and for a day or an hour forbid God's Light to
come into the world, and bid the Devil's Darkness continue
in it one hour more! For all light and science, under all
shapes, in all degrees of perfection, is of God; all darkness,
nescience, is of the Enemy of God. 'The schoolmaster's
creed is somewhat awry?' Yes, I have found few creeds
entirely correct; few light-beams shining *white*, pure of
admixture: but of all creeds and religions now or ever
before known, was not that of thoughtless thriftless
Animalism, of Distilled Gin, and Stupor and Despair, unspeakably the least orthodox? We will exchange *it* even
with Paganism, with Fetishism; and, on the whole, must
exchange it with something.

An effective 'Teaching Service' I do consider that there
must be; some Education Secretary, Captain-General of
Teachers, who will actually contrive to get us *taught*. Then
again, why should there not be an 'Emigration Service',
and Secretary, with adjuncts, with funds, forces, idle Navy-
ships, and ever-increasing apparatus; in fine an *effective
system* of Emigration; so that, at length, before our twenty
years of respite ended, every honest willing Workman who
found England too strait, and the 'Organization of Labour'
not yet sufficiently advanced, might find likewise a bridge
built to carry him into new Western Lands, there to
'organize' with more elbow-room some labour for himself?
There to be a real blessing, raising new corn for us, purchasing new webs and hatchets from us; leaving us at
least in peace;—instead of staying here to be a Physical-
Force Chartist, unblessed and no blessing! Is it not
scandalous to consider that a Prime Minister could raise
within the year, as I have seen it done, a Hundred and
Twenty Millions Sterling to shoot the French; and we are

stopped short for want of the hundredth part of that to keep the English living? The bodies of the English living, and the souls of English living:—these two 'Services', an Education Service and an Emigration Service, these with others will actually have to be organized!

A free bridge for Emigrants: why, we should then be on a par with America itself, the most favoured of all lands that have no government; and we should have, besides, so many traditions and mementos of priceless things which America has cast away. We could proceed deliberately to 'organize Labour', not doomed to perish unless we effected it within year and day;—every willing Worker that proved superfluous, finding a bridge ready for him. This verily will have to be done; the Time is big with this. Our little Isle is grown too narrow for us; but the world is wide enough yet for another Six Thousand Years. England's sure markets will be among new Colonies of Englishmen in all quarters of the Globe. All men trade with all men, when mutually convenient; and are even bound to do it by the Maker of men. Our friends of China, who guiltily refused to trade, in these circumstances,—had we not to argue with them, in cannon-shot at last, and convince them that they ought to trade! 'Hostile Tariffs' will arise, to shut us out; and then again will fall, to let us in: but the Sons of England, speakers of the English language were it nothing more, will in all times have the ineradicable predisposition to trade with England. Mycale was the *Pan-Ionion*, rendezvous of all the Tribes of Ion, for old Greece: why should not London long continue the *All-Saxon-home*, rendezvous of all the 'Children of the Harz-Rock', arriving, in select samples, from the Antipodes and elsewhere, by steam and otherwise, to the 'season' here!—What a Future; wide as the world, if we have the heart and heroism for it,—which, by Heaven's blessing, we shall:

> Keep not standing fixed and rooted,
> Briskly venture, briskly roam;
> Head and hand, where'er thou foot it,
> And stout heart are still at home.
>
> In what land the sun does visit,
> Brisk are we, whate'er betide:
> To give space for wandering is it
> That the world was made so wide.[1]

[1] Goethe, *Wilhelm Meister.*

Fourteen hundred years ago, it was by a considerable 'Emigration Service', never doubt it, by much enlistment, discussion and apparatus, that we ourselves arrived in this remarkable Island,—and got into our present difficulties among others!

It is true the English Legislature, like the English People, is of slow temper; essentially conservative. In our wildest periods of reform, in the Long Parliament itself, you notice always the invincible instinct to hold fast by the Old; to admit the *minimum* of New; to expand, if it be possible, some old habit or method, already found fruitful, into new growth for the new need. It is an instinct worthy of all honour; akin to all strength and all wisdom. The Future hereby is not dissevered from the Past, but based continuously on it; grows with all the vitalities of the Past, and is rooted down deep into the beginnings of us. The English Legislature is entirely repugnant to believe in 'new epochs'. The English Legislature does not occupy itself with epochs; has, indeed, other business to do than looking at the Time-Horologe and hearing it tick! Nevertheless new epochs do actually come; and with them new imperious peremptory necessities; so that even an English Legislature has to look up, and admit, though with reluctance, that the hour has struck. The hour having struck, let us not say 'impossible':—it will have to be possible! 'Contrary to the habits of Parliament, the habits of Government'? Yes: but did any Parliament or Government ever sit in a Year Forty-three before? One of the most original, unexampled years and epochs; in several important respects, totally unlike any other! For Time, all-edacious and all-feracious, does run on: and the Seven Sleepers, awakening hungry after a hundred years, find that it is not their old nurses who can now give them suck!

For the rest, let not any Parliament, Aristocracy, Millocracy, or Member of the Governing Class, condemn with much triumph this small specimen of 'remedial measures'; or ask again, with the least anger, of this Editor, What is to be done, How that alarming problem of the Working Classes is to be managed? Editors are not here, foremost of all, to say How. A certain Editor thanks the gods that nobody pays him three hundred thousand pounds a year, two hundred thousand, twenty thousand, or any similar sum of cash for saying How ;—that his wages are very different, his work somewhat fitter for him. An Editor's stipulated work is to apprise *thee* that it must be done. The 'way to do it', is to try it, knowing that thou shalt die if it be not done. There is the bare back, there is the web of cloth ; thou shalt cut me a coat to cover the bare back, thou whose trade it is. 'Impossible'? Hapless Fraction, dost thou discern Fate there, half unveiling herself in the gloom of the future, with her gibbet-cords, her steel-whips, and very authentic Tailor's Hell ; waiting to see whether it is 'possible'? Out with thy scissors, and cut that cloth or thy own windpipe !

CHAPTER IV

CAPTAINS OF INDUSTRY

IF I believed that Mammonism with its adjuncts was to continue henceforth the one serious principle of our existence, I should reckon it idle to solicit remedial measures from any Government, the disease being insusceptible of remedy. Government can do much, but it can in no wise do all. Government, as the most conspicuous object in Society, is called upon to give signal of what shall be done ; and, in many ways, to preside over, further, and command the doing of it. But the Government cannot do, by all its signalling and commanding, what the Society is radically indisposed to do. In the long-run every Government is the exact symbol of its People, with their wisdom and unwisdom ; we have to say, Like People like Government.— The main substance of this immense Problem of Organizing Labour, and first of all of Managing the Working Classes, will, it is very clear, have to be solved by those who stand practically in the middle of it ; by those who themselves work and preside over work. Of all that can be enacted by any Parliament in regard to it, the germs must already lie potentially extant in those two Classes, who are to obey such enactment. A Human Chaos *in* which there is no light, you vainly attempt to irradiate by light shed *on* it: order never can arise there.

But it is my firm conviction that the 'Hell of England' will *cease* to be that of 'not making money'; that we shall get a nobler Hell and a nobler Heaven! I anticipate light *in* the Human Chaos, glimmering, shining more and more; under manifold true signals from without That light shall shine. Our deity no longer being Mammon,—O Heavens, each man will then say to himself: 'Why such deadly haste to make money? I shall not go to Hell, even if I do not make money! There is another Hell, I am told!' Competition, at railway-speed, in all branches of commerce and work will then abate:—good felt-hats for the head, in every sense, instead of seven-feet lath-and-plaster hats on wheels, will then be discoverable! Bubble-periods, with their panics and commercial crises, will again become infrequent; steady modest industry will take the place of gambling speculation. To be a noble Master, among noble Workers, will again be the first ambition with some few; to be a rich Master only the second. How the Inventive Genius of England, with the whirr of its bobbins and billy-rollers shoved somewhat into the backgrounds of the brain, will contrive and devise, not cheaper produce exclusively, but fairer distribution of the produce at its present cheapness! By degrees, we shall again have a Society with something of Heroism in it, something of Heaven's Blessing on it; we shall again have, as my German friend asserts, 'instead of Mammon-Feudalism with unsold cotton-shirts and Preservation of the Game, noble just Industrialism and Government by the Wisest!'

It is with the hope of awakening here and there a British man to know himself for a man and divine soul, that a few words of parting admonition, to all persons to whom the Heavenly Powers have lent power of any kind in this land, may now be addressed. And first to those same Master-Workers, Leaders of Industry; who stand nearest, and in fact powerfullest, though not most prominent, being as yet in too many senses a Virtuality rather than an Actuality.

The Leaders of Industry, if Industry is ever to be led, are virtually the Captains of the World; if there be no nobleness in them, there will never be an Aristocracy more. But let the Captains of Industry consider: once again, are they

born of other clay than the old Captains of Slaughter;
doomed forever to be not Chivalry, but a mere gold-plated
Doggery,—what the French well name *Canaille*, ' Doggery '
with more or less gold carrion at its disposal? Captains of
Industry are the true Fighters, henceforth recognizable as
the only true ones: Fighters against Chaos, Necessity and
the Devils and Jötuns; and lead on Mankind in that great,
and alone true, and universal warfare; the stars in their
courses fighting for them, and all Heaven and all Earth saying audibly, Well done! Let the Captains of Industry
retire into their own hearts, and ask solemnly, If there is
nothing but vulturous hunger for fine wines, valet reputation and gilt carriages, discoverable there? Of hearts made
by the Almighty God I will not believe such a thing. Deep-
hidden under wretchedest godforgetting Cants, Epicurisms,
Dead-Sea Apisms; forgotten as under foullest fat Lethe mud
and weeds, there is yet, in all hearts born into this God's-
World, a spark of the Godlike slumbering. Awake, O
nightmare sleepers; awake, arise, or be forever fallen! This
is not playhouse poetry; it is sober fact. Our England, our
world cannot live as it is. It will connect itself with a God
again, or go down with nameless throes and fire-consumma-
tion to the Devils. Thou who feelest aught of such a Godlike stirring in thee, any faintest intimation of it as through
heavy-laden dreams, follow *it*, I conjure thee. Arise, save
thyself, be one of those that save thy country.

Bucaniers, Chactaw Indians, whose supreme aim in fighting is that they may get the scalps, the money, that they
may amass scalps and money; out of such came no Chivalry,
and never will! Out of such came only gore and wreck,
infernal rage and misery; desperation quenched in annihilation. Behold it, I bid thee, behold there, and consider!
What is it that thou have a hundred thousand-pound bills
laid up in thy strong-room, a hundred scalps hung up in thy
wigwam? I value not them or thee. Thy scalps and thy
thousand-pound bills are as yet nothing, if no nobleness
from within irradiate them; if no Chivalry, in action, or in
embryo ever struggling towards birth and action, be there.

Love of men cannot be bought by cash-payment: and
without love, men cannot endure to be together. You
cannot lead a Fighting World without having it regimented,
chivalried: the thing, in a day, becomes impossible; all

men in it, the highest at first, the very lowest at last, discern consciously, or by a noble instinct, this necessity. And can you any more continue to lead a Working World unregimented, anarchic ? I answer, and the Heavens and Earth are now answering, No ! The thing becomes not ' in a day' impossible ; but in some two generations it does. Yes, when fathers and mothers, in Stockport hunger-cellars, begin to eat their children, and Irish widows have to prove their relationship by dying of typhus-fever ; and amid Governing ' Corporations of the Best and Bravest', busy to preserve their game by ' bushing ', dark millions of God's human creatures start up in mad Chartisms, impracticable Sacred-Months, and Manchester Insurrections ;—and there is a virtual Industrial Aristocracy as yet only half-alive, spell-bound amid money-bags and ledgers ; and an actual Idle Aristocracy seemingly near dead in somnolent delusions, in trespasses and double-barrels ; 'sliding,' as on inclined-planes, which every new year they *soap* with new Hansard's-jargon under God's sky, and so are ' sliding' ever faster, towards a ' scale ' and balance-scale whereon is written *Thou art found Wanting* :—in such days, after a generation or two, I say, it does become, even to the low and simple, very palpably impossible ! No Working World, any more than a Fighting World, can be led on without a noble Chivalry of Work, and laws and fixed rules which follow out of that,—far nobler than any Chivalry of Fighting was. As an anarchic multitude on mere Supply-and-demand, it is becoming inevitable that we dwindle in horrid suicidal convulsion, and self-abrasion, frightful to the imagination, into *Chactaw* Workers.   With wigwams and scalps, —with palaces and thousand-pound bills ; with savagery, depopulation, chaotic desolation ! Good Heavens, will not one French Revolution and Reign of Terror suffice us, but must there be two ? There will be two if needed ; there will be twenty if needed ; there will be precisely as many as are needed.   The Laws of Nature will have themselves fulfilled.   That is a thing certain to me.

Your gallant battle-hosts and work-hosts, as the others did, will need to be made loyally yours ; they must and will be regulated, methodically secured in their just share of conquest under you ;—joined with you in veritable brotherhood, sonhood, by quite other and deeper ties than those of temporary day's wages! How would mere redcoated regiments, to say nothing of chivalries, fight for you, if you could discharge them on the evening of the battle, on payment of the stipulated shillings,—and they discharge you on the morning of it! Chelsea Hospitals, pensions, promotions, rigorous lasting covenant on the one side and on the other, are indispensable even for a hired fighter. The Feudal Baron, much more,—how could he subsist with mere temporary mercenaries round him, at sixpence a day ; ready to go over to the other side, if sevenpence were offered? He could not have subsisted ;—and his noble instinct saved him from the necessity of even trying ! The Feudal Baron had a Man's Soul in him ; to which anarchy, mutiny, and the other fruits of temporary mercenaries, were intolerable : he had never been a Baron otherwise, but had continued a Chactaw and Bucanier. He felt it precious, and at last it became habitual, and his fruitful enlarged existence included it as a necessity, to have men round him who in heart loved him ; whose life he watched over with rigour yet with love ; who were prepared to give their life for him, if need came. It was beautiful ; it was human ! Man lives not otherwise, nor can live contented, anywhere or anywhen. Isolation is the sum-total of wretchedness to man. To be cut off, to be left solitary : to have a world alien, not your world ; all a hostile camp for you ; not a home at all, of hearts and faces who are yours, whose you are ! It is the frightfullest enchantment ; too truly a work of the Evil One. To have neither superior, nor inferior, nor equal, united manlike to you. Without father, without child, without brother. Man knows no sadder destiny. 'How is each of us,' exclaims Jean Paul, 'so lonely in the wide bosom of the All !' Encased each as in his transparent 'ice-palace' ; our brother visible in his, making signals and gesticulations to us ;—visible, but forever unattainable : on his bosom we shall never rest, nor he on ours. It was not a God that did this ; no !

Awake, ye noble Workers, warriors in the one true war : all this must be remedied. It is you who are already half-alive, whom I will welcome into life ; whom I will conjure in God's name to shake off your enchanted sleep, and live wholly ! Cease to count scalps, gold-purses ; not in these lies your or our salvation. Even these, if you count only these, will not be left. Let bucaniering be put far from you ; alter, speedily abrogate all laws of the bucaniers, if you would gain any victory that shall endure. Let God's justice, let pity, nobleness and manly valour, with more gold-purses or with fewer, testify themselves in this your brief Life-transit to all the Eternities, the Gods and Silences. It is to you I call ; for ye are not dead, ye are already half-alive : there is in you a sleepless dauntless energy, the prime-matter of all nobleness in man. Honour to you in your kind. It is to you I call : ye know at least this, That the mandate of God to His creature man is : Work ! The future Epic of the World rests not with those that are near dead, but with those that are alive, and those that are coming into life.

Look around you. Your world-hosts are all in mutiny, in confusion, destitution ; on the eve of fiery wreck and madness ! They will not march farther for you, on the sixpence a day and supply-and-demand principle : they will not ; nor ought they, nor can they. Ye shall reduce them to order, begin reducing them. To order, to just sub-ordination ; noble loyalty in return for noble guidance. Their souls are driven nigh mad ; let yours be sane and ever saner. Not as a bewildered bewildering mob ; but as a firm regimented mass, with real captains over them, will these men march any more. All human interests, combined human endeavours, and social growths in this world, have, at a certain stage of their development, required organizing : and Work, the grandest of human interests, does now require it.

God knows, the task will be hard : but no noble task was ever easy. This task will wear away your lives, and the lives of your sons and grandsons : but for what purpose, if not for tasks like this, were lives given to men ? Ye shall cease to count your thousand-pound scalps, the noble of you shall cease ! Nay, the very scalps, as I say, will not long be left if you count only these. Ye shall cease wholly to be barbarous vulturous Chactaws, and become noble European Nineteenth-Century Men. Ye shall know that Mammon, in never such gigs and flunkey ' respectabilities ', is not the alone God ; that of himself he is but a Devil, and even a Brute-god.

Difficult ? Yes, it will be difficult. The short-fibre cotton ;

that too was difficult. The waste cotton-shrub, long useless, disobedient, as the thistle by the wayside,—have ye not conquered it ; made it into beautiful bandana webs ; white woven shirts for men ; bright-tinted air-garments wherein flit goddesses ? Ye have shivered mountains asunder, made the hard iron pliant to you as soft putty: the Forest-giants, Marsh-jötuns bear sheaves of golden grain ; Ægir the Sea-demon himself stretches his back for a sleek highway to you, and on Firehorses and Windhorses ye career. Ye are most strong. Thor red-bearded, with his blue sun-eyes, with his cheery heart and strong thunder-hammer, he and you have prevailed. Ye are most strong, ye Sons of the icy North, of the far East,—far marching from your rugged Eastern Wildernesses, hitherward from the grey Dawn of Time! Ye are Sons of the *Jötun*-land ; the land of Difficulties Conquered. Difficult ? You must try this thing. Once try it with the understanding that it will and shall have to be done. Try it as ye try the paltrier thing, making of money ! I will bet on you once more, against all Jötuns, Tailor-gods, Double-barrelled Law-wards, and Denizens of Chaos whatsoever !

CHAPTER V

PERMANENCE

STANDING on the threshold, nay as yet outside the threshold, of a ' Chivalry of Labour ', and an immeasurable Future which it is to fill with fruitfulness and verdant shade ; where so much has not yet come even to the rudimental state, and all speech of positive enactments were hazardous in those who know this business only by the eye,— let us here hint at simply one widest universal principle, as the basis from which all organization hitherto has grown up among men, and all henceforth will have to grow: The principle of Permanent Contract instead of Temporary.

Permanent not Temporary :—you do not hire the mere redcoated fighter by the day, but by the score of years! Permanence, persistence is the first condition of all fruitfulness in the ways of men. The 'tendency to persevere', to persist in spite of hindrances, discouragements and 'impossibilities': it is this that in all things distinguishes the strong soul from the weak ; the civilized burgher from the nomadic savage,—the Species Man from the Genus Ape! The Nomad has his very house set on wheels ; the Nomad, and in a still higher degree the Ape, are all for 'liberty', the privilege to flit continually is indispensable for them. Alas, in how many ways does our humour, in this swift-rolling self-abrading Time, show itself nomadic, apelike ; mournful enough to him that looks on it with eyes! This humour will have to abate ; it is the first element of all fertility in human things, that such 'liberty' of apes and nomads do by freewill or constraint abridge itself, give place to a better. The civilized man lives not in wheeled houses. He builds stone castles, plants lands, makes lifelong marriage-contracts ;—has long-dated hundred-fold possessions, not to be valued in the money-market ; has pedigrees, libraries, law-codes ; has memories and hopes, even for this Earth, that reach over thousands of years. Lifelong marriage-contracts : how much preferable were year-long or month-long—to the nomad or ape!

Month-long contracts please me little, in any province where there can by possibility be found virtue enough for more. Mcnth-long contracts do not answer well even with your house-servants ; the liberty on both sides to change every month is growing very apelike, nomadic ;—and I hear philosophers predict that it will alter, or that strange results will follow : that wise men, pestered with nomads, with unattached ever-shifting spies and enemies rather than friends and servants, will gradually, weighing substance against semblance, with indignation, dismiss such, down almost to the very shoeblack, and say, 'Begone ; I will serve myself rather, and have peace!' Gurth was hired for life to Cedric, and Cedric to Gurth. O Anti-Slavery Convention, loud-sounding long-eared Exeter-Hall— But in thee too is a kind of instinct towards justice, and I will complain of nothing. Only black Quashee over the seas being once sufficiently attended to, wilt thou not perhaps open thy dull sodden eyes to the 'sixty-thousand valets in London itself who are yearly dismissed to the streets, to be what they can, when the season ends';—or to the hungerstricken,

pallid, *yellow*-coloured 'Free Labourers' in Lancashire,
Yorkshire, Buckinghamshire, and all other shires! These
Yellow-coloured, for the present, absorb all my sympathies:
if I had a Twenty Millions, with Model-Farms and Niger
Expeditions, it is to these that I would give it! Quashee has
already victuals, clothing; Quashee is not dying of such
despair as the yellow-coloured pale man's. Quashee, it must
be owned, is hitherto a kind of blockhead. The Haiti Duke
of Marmalade, educated now for almost half a century,
seems to have next to no sense in him. Why, in one of
those Lancashire Weavers, dying of hunger, there is more
thought and heart, a greater arithmetical amount of misery
and desperation, than in whole gangs of Quashees. It must
be owned, thy eyes are of the sodden sort; and with thy
emancipations, and thy twenty-millionings and long-eared
clamourings, thou, like Robespierre with his pasteboard
Être Suprême, threatenest to become a bore to us: *Avec ton
Être Suprême tu commences m'embéter!*—

In a Printed Sheet of the assiduous, much-abused, and
truly useful Mr. Chadwick's, containing queries and responses
from far and near, as to this great question, 'What is the
effect of Education on working-men, in respect of their value
as mere workers?' the present Editor, reading with satisfaction a decisive unanimous verdict as to Education, reads
with inexpressible interest this special remark, put in by
way of marginal incidental note, from a practical manufacturing Quaker, whom, as he is anonymous, we will call
Friend Prudence. Prudence keeps a thousand workmen;
has striven in all ways to attach them to him; has provided
conversational soirées; playgrounds, bands of music for the
young ones; went even 'the length of buying them a drum';
all which has turned out to be an excellent investment. For
a certain person, marked here by a black stroke, whom we
shall name Blank, living over the way,—he also keeps
somewhere about a thousand men; but has done none of
these things for them, nor any other thing, except due payment of the wages by supply-and-demand. Blank's workers
are perpetually getting into mutiny, into broils and coils:
every six months, we suppose, Blank has a strike; every
one month, every day and every hour, they are fretting and
obstructing the shortsighted Blank; pilfering from him,

wasting and idling for him, omitting and committing for
him. ' I would not,' says Friend Prudence, ' exchange my
workers for his *with seven thousand pounds to boot.*'[1]

Right, O honourable Prudence ; thou art wholly in the
right : Seven thousand pounds even as a matter of profit for
this world, nay for the mere cash-market of this world !
And as a matter of profit not for this world only, but for
the other world and all worlds, it outweighs the Bank of
England ! Can the sagacious reader descry here, as it were
the outmost inconsiderable rock-ledge of a universal rock-
foundation, deep once more as the Centre of the World,
emerging so, in the experience of this good Quaker, through
the Stygian mud-vortexes and general Mother of Dead Dogs,
whereon, for the present, all sways and insecurely hovers,
as if ready to be swallowed ?

Some Permanence of Contract is already almost possible;
the principle of Permanence, year by year, better seen into
and elaborated, may enlarge itself, expand gradually on
every side into a system. This once secured, the basis of
all good results were laid. Once permanent, you do not
quarrel with the first difficulty on your path, and quit it in
weak disgust ; you reflect that it cannot be quitted, that
it must be conquered, a wise arrangement fallen on with
regard to it. Ye foolish Wedded Two, who have quarrelled,
between whom the Evil Spirit has stirred up transient strife
and bitterness, so that ' incompatibility ' seems almost nigh,
ye are nevertheless the Two who, by long habit, were it
by nothing more, do best of all others suit each other : it is
expedient for your own two foolish selves, to say nothing of
the infants, pedigrees and public in general, that ye agree
again ; that ye put away the Evil Spirit, and wisely on both
hands struggle for the guidance of a Good Spirit !

The very horse that is permanent, how much kindlier do
his rider and he work, than the temporary one, hired on any
hack principle yet known ! I am for permanence in all
things, at the earliest possible moment, and to the latest
possible. Blessed is he that continueth where he is. Here
let us rest, and lay out seedfields ; here let us learn to dwell.
Here, even here, the orchards that we plant will yield us
fruit ; the acorns will be wood and pleasant umbrage, if we

[1] Report on the Training of Pauper Children (1841), p. 18.

wait. How much grows everywhere, if we do but wait! Through the swamps we will shape causeways, force purifying drains; we will learn to thread the rocky inaccessibilities; and beaten tracks, worn smooth by mere travelling of human feet, will form themselves. Not a difficulty but can transfigure itself into a triumph; not even a deformity but, if our own soul have imprinted worth on it, will grow dear to us. The sunny plains and deep indigo transparent skies of Italy are all indifferent to the great sick heart of a Sir Walter Scott: on the back of the Apennines, in wild spring weather, the sight of bleak Scotch firs, and snow-spotted heath and desolation, brings tears into his eyes.[1]

O unwise mortals that for ever change and shift, and say, Yonder, not Here! Wealth richer than both the Indies lies everywhere for man, if he will endure. Not his oaks only and his fruit-trees, his very heart roots itself wherever he will abide;—roots itself, draws nourishment from the deep fountains of Universal Being! Vagrant Sam-Slicks, who rove over the Earth doing 'strokes of trade', what wealth have they? Horseloads, shiploads of white or yellow metal: in very sooth, what *are* these? Slick rests nowhere, he is homeless. He can build stone or marble houses; but to continue in them is denied him. The wealth of a man is the number of things which he loves and blesses, which he is loved and blessed by! The herdsman in his poor clay shealing, where his very cow and dog are friends to him, and not a cataract but carries memories for him, and not a mountain-top but nods old recognition: his life, all encircled as in blessed mother's-arms, is it poorer than Slick's with the ass-loads of yellow metal on his back? Unhappy Slick! Alas, there has so much grown nomadic, apelike, with us: so much will have, with whatever pain, repugnance and 'impossibility', to alter itself, to fix itself again,—in some wise way, in any not delirious way!'

A question arises here: Whether, in some ulterior, perhaps some not far-distant stage of this 'Chivalry of Labour', your Master-Worker may not find it possible, and needful, to grant his Workers permanent *interest* in his enterprise and theirs? So that it become, in practical result, what in essential fact and justice it ever is, a joint enterprise; all

[1] Lockhart's *Life of Scott.*

men, from the Chief Master down to the lowest Overseer and Operative, economically as well as loyally concerned for it ?—Which question I do not answer. The answer, near or else far, is perhaps, Yes ;—and yet one knows the difficulties. Despotism is essential in most enterprises ; I am told, they do not tolerate ' freedom of debate ' on board a Seventy-four ! Republican senate and *plebiscita* would not answer well in Cotton-Mills. And yet observe there too : Freedom, not nomad's or ape's Freedom, but man's Freedom ; this is indispensable. We must have it, and will have it ! To reconcile Despotism with Freedom :—well, is that such a mystery ? Do you not already know the way ? It is to make your Despotism *just*. Rigorous as Destiny ; but just too, as Destiny and its Laws. The Laws of God : all men obey these, and have no ' Freedom ' at all but in obeying them. The way is already known, part of the way ;—and courage and some qualities are needed for walking on it !

CHAPTER VI

THE LANDED

A MAN with fifty, with five hundred, with a thousand pounds a day, given him freely, without condition at all,— on condition, as it now runs, that he will sit with his hands in his pockets and do no mischief, pass no Corn-Laws or the like,—he too, you would say, is or might be a rather strong Worker ! He is a Worker with such tools as no man in this world ever before had. But in practice, very astonishing, very ominous to look at, he proves not a strong Worker ;— you are too happy if he will prove but a No-worker, do nothing, and not be a Wrong-worker.

You ask him, at the year's end : ' Where is your three-hundred thousand pound ; what have you realized to us with that ? ' He answers, in indignant surprise : ' Done with it ? Who are you that ask ? I have eaten it ; I and my flunkeys, and parasites, and slaves two-footed and four-footed, in an ornamental manner ; and I am here alive by it ; *I* am realized by it to you ! '—It is, as we have often said, such an answer as was never before given under this Sun. An answer that fills me with boding apprehension, with foreshadows of despair. O stolid Use-and-wont of an atheistic Half-century, O Ignavia, Tailor-godhood, soul-killing Cant, to what passes art thou bringing us!—Out of the loud-piping whirlwind, audibly to him that has ears, the Highest God is again announcing in these days: 'Idleness shall not be.' God has said it, man cannot gainsay.

Ah, how happy were it, if he this Aristocrat Worker would, in like manner, see *his* work and do it! It is frightful seeking another to do it for him. Guillotines, Meudon Tanneries, and half-a-million men shot dead, have already been expended in that business; and it is yet far from done. This man too is something; nay he is a great thing. Look on him there: a man of manful aspect; something of the 'cheerfulness of pride' still lingering in him. A free air of graceful stoicism, of easy silent dignity sits well on him; in his heart, could we reach it, lie elements of generosity, self-sacrificing justice, true human valour. Why should he, with such appliances, stand an incumbrance in the Present; perish disastrously out of the Future! From no section of the Future would we lose these noble courtesies, impalpable yet all-controlling; these dignified reticences, these kingly simplicities;—lose aught of what the fruitful Past still gives us token of, memento of, in this man. Can we not save him:—can he not help us to save him! A brave man he too; had not undivine Ignavia, Hearsay, Speech without meaning,—had not Cant, thousandfold Cant within him and around him, enveloping him like choke-damp, like thick Egyptian darkness, thrown his soul into asphyxia, as it were extinguished his soul; so that he sees not, hears not, and Moses and all the Prophets address him in vain.

Will he awaken, be alive again, and have a soul; or is this death-fit very death? It is a question of questions, for himself and for us all! Alas, is there no noble work for this man too? Has he not thick-headed ignorant boors; lazy, enslaved farmers; weedy lands? Lands! Has he not weary heavy-laden ploughers of land; immortal souls of men, ploughing, ditching, day-drudging; bare of back, empty of stomach, nigh desperate of heart; and none peaceably to help them but he, under Heaven? Does he find, with his three hundred thousand pounds, no noble

thing trodden down in the thoroughfares, which it were
godlike to help up ?   Can he do nothing for his Burns but
make a Gauger of him ; lionize him, bedinner him, for a
foolish while ; then whistle him down the wind, to desperation and bitter death ?—His work too is difficult, in these
modern, far-dislocated ages.   But it may be done ; it may
be tried ;—it must be done.

A modern Duke of Weimar, not a god he either, but *Karl August*
a human duke, levied, as I reckon, in rents and taxes and *(1757-1828)*
all incomings whatsoever, less than several of our English
Dukes do in rent alone.   The Duke of Weimar, with these
incomings, had to govern, judge, defend, everyway administer *his* Dukedom.   He does all this as few others did :
and he improves lands besides all this, makes river embank-
ments, maintains not soldiers only but Universities and
Institutions ;—and in his Court were these four men :
Wieland, Herder, Schiller, Goethe.   Not as parasites, which
was impossible ; not as table-wits and poetic Katerfeltoes ;
but as noble Spiritual Men working under a noble Practical
Man.   Shielded by him from many miseries ; perhaps from
many shortcomings, destructive aberrations.   Heaven had
sent, once more, heavenly Light into the world ; and this
man's honour was that he gave it welcome.   A new noble
kind of Clergy, under an old but still noble kind of King !
I reckon that this one Duke of Weimar did more for the
Culture of his Nation than all the English Dukes and *Duces*
now extant, or that were extant since Henry the Eighth
gave them the Church Lands to eat, have done for theirs !—
I am ashamed, I am alarmed for my English Dukes : what
word have I to say ?

If our Actual Aristocracy, appointed 'Best-and-Bravest',
will be wise, how inexpressibly happy for us !   If not,—the
voice of God from the whirlwind is very audible to me.
Nay, I will thank the great God, that He has said, in whatever fearful ways, and just wrath against us, ' Idleness shall
be no more !'   Idleness ?   The awakened soul of man, all
but the asphyxied soul of man, turns from it as from worse
than death.   It is the life-in-death of Poet Coleridge.   That
fable of the Dead-Sea Apes ceases to be a fable.   The poor
Worker starved to death is not the saddest of sights.   He
lies there, dead on his shield ; fallen down into the bosom
of his old Mother ; with haggard pale face, sorrow-worn,

but stilled now into divine peace, silently appeals to the
Eternal God and all the Universe,—the most silent, the
most eloquent of men.

Exceptions,—ah yes, thank Heaven, we know there are
exceptions. Our case were too hard, were there not exceptions, and partial exceptions not a few, whom we know,
and whom we do not know. Honour to the name of Ashley,
—honour to this and the other valiant Abdiel, found faithful
still; who would fain, by work and by word, admonish their
Order not to rush upon destruction! These are they who
will, if not save their Order, postpone the wreck of it;—
by whom, under blessing of the Upper Powers, 'a quiet
euthanasia spread over generations, instead of a swift torture-
death concentred into years,' may be brought about for
many things. All honour and success to these. The noble
man can still strive nobly to save and serve his Order;—at
lowest, he can remember the precept of the Prophet: 'Come
out of her, my people; come out of her!'

To sit idle aloft, like living statues, like absurd Epicurus'-
gods, in pampered isolation, in exclusion from the glorious
fateful battlefield of this God's-World: it is a poor life for
a man, when all Upholsterers and French-Cooks have done
their utmost for it!—Nay, what a shallow delusion is this
we have all got into, That any man should or can keep himself apart from men, have 'no business' with them, except
a cash-account 'business!' It is the silliest tale a distressed
generation of men ever took to telling one another. Men
cannot live isolated: we *are* all bound together, for mutual
good or else for mutual misery, as living nerves in the same
body. No highest man can disunite himself from any lowest.
Consider it. Your poor 'Werter blowing out his distracted
existence because Charlotte will not have the keeping thereof': this is no peculiar phasis; it is simply the highest
expression of a phasis traceable wherever one human creature
meets another! Let the meanest crookbacked Thersites
teach the supremest Agamemnon that he actually does not
reverence him, the supremest Agamemnon's eyes flash fire
responsive; a real pain, and partial insanity, has seized
Agamemnon. Strange enough: a many-counselled Ulysses
is set in motion by a scoundrel-blockhead; plays tunes, like
a barrel-organ, at the scoundrel-blockhead's touch,—has to

snatch, namely, his sceptre-cudgel, and weal the crooked back with bumps and thumps! Let a chief of men reflect well on it. Not in having 'no business' with men, but in having no unjust business with them, and in *having* all manner of true and just business, can either his or their blessedness be found possible, and this waste world become, for both parties, a home and peopled garden.

Men do reverence men. Men do worship in that 'one temple of the world', as Novalis calls it, the Presence of a Man! Hero-worship, true and blessed, or else mistaken, false and accursed, goes on everywhere and everywhen. In this world there is one godlike thing, the essence of all that was or ever will be of godlike in this world : the veneration done to Human Worth by the hearts of men. Hero-worship, in the souls of the heroic, of the clear and wise,— it is the perpetual presence of Heaven in our poor Earth : when it is not there, Heaven is veiled from us ; and all is under Heaven's ban and interdict, and there is no worship, or worth-ship, or worth or blessedness in the Earth any more !—

Independence, 'lord of the lion-heart and eagle-eye,'— alas, yes, he is one we have got acquainted with in these late times : a very indispensable one, for spurning off with due energy innumerable sham-superiors, Tailor-made : honour to him, entire success to him! Entire success is sure to him. But he must not stop there, at that small success, with his eagle-eye. He has now a second far greater success to gain : to seek out his real superiors, whom not the Tailor but the Almighty God has made superior to him, and see a little what he will do with these! Rebel against these also ? Pass by with minatory eagle-glance, with calm-sniffing mockery, or even without any mockery or sniff, when these present themselves ? The lion-hearted will never dream of such a thing. Forever far be it from him! His minatory eagle-glance will veil itself in softness of the dove : his lion-heart will become a lamb's ; all its just indignation changed into just reverence, dissolved in blessed floods of noble humble love, how much heavenlier than any pride, nay, if you will, how much prouder! I know him, this lion-hearted, eagle-eyed one ; have met him, rushing on, ' with bosom bare,' in a very distracted dishevelled manner, the times being hard ;—and can say, and guarantee on my life,

That in him is no rebellion ; that in him is the reverse of rebellion, the needful preparation for obedience. For if you do mean to obey God-made superiors, your first step is to sweep out the Tailor-made ones ; order them, under penalties, to vanish, to make ready for vanishing !

Nay, what is best of all, he cannot rebel, if he would. Superiors whom God has made for us we cannot order to withdraw ! Not in the least. No Grand-Turk himself, thickest-quilted tailor-made Brother of the Sun and Moon can do it : but an Arab Man, in cloak of his own clouting ; with black beaming eyes, with flaming sovereign-heart direct from the centre of the Universe ; and also, I am told, with terrible ' horse-shoe vein ' of swelling wrath in his brow, and lightning (if you will not have it as light) tingling through every vein of him,—he rises ; says authoritatively : ' Thickest-quilted Grand-Turk, tailor-made Brother of the Sun and Moon, No :—*I* withdraw not ; thou shalt obey me or withdraw !' And so accordingly it is : thickest-quilted Grand-Turks and all their progeny, to this hour, obey that man in the remarkablest manner ; preferring *not* to withdraw.

O brother, it is an endless consolation to me, in this disorganic, as yet so quack-ridden, what you may well call hagridden and hell-ridden world, to find that disobedience to the Heavens, when they send any messenger whatever, is and remains impossible. It cannot be done ; no Turk grand or small can do it. ' Show the dullest clodpole,' says my invaluable German friend, ' show the haughtiest featherhead, that a soul higher than himself is here ; were his knees stiffened into brass, he must down and worship.'

CHAPTER VII

THE GIFTED

Yes, in what tumultuous huge anarchy soever a Noble human Principle may dwell and strive, such tumult is in the way of being calmed into a fruitful sovereignty. It is inevitable. No Chaos can continue chaotic with a soul in it. Besouled with earnest human Nobleness, did not slaughter, violence and fire-eyed fury, grow into a Chivalry; into a blessed Loyalty of Governor and Governed? And in Work, which is of itself noble, and the only true fighting, there shall be no such possibility? Believe it not; it is incredible; the whole Universe contradicts it. Here too the Chactaw Principle will be subordinated; the Man Principle will, by degrees, become superior, become supreme.

I know Mammon too; Banks-of-England, Credit-Systems, world-wide possibilities of work and traffic; and applaud and admire them. Mammon is like Fire; the usefullest of all servants, if the frightfullest of all masters! The Cliffords, Fitzadelms and Chivalry Fighters 'wished to gain victory', never doubt it: but victory, unless gained in a certain spirit, was no victory; defeat, sustained in a certain spirit, was itself victory. I say again and again, had they counted the scalps alone, they had continued Chactaws, and no Chivalry or lasting victory had been. And in Industrial Fighters and Captains is there no nobleness discoverable? To them, alone of men, there shall forever be no blessedness but in swollen coffers? To see beauty, order, gratitude, loyal human hearts around them, shall be of no moment; to see fuliginous deformity, mutiny, hatred and despair, with the addition of half a million guineas, shall be better? Heaven's blessedness not there; Hell's cursedness, and your half-million bits of metal, a substitute for that! Is there no profit in diffusing Heaven's blessedness, but only in gaining gold?—If so, I apprise the Mill-owner and Millionaire, that he too must prepare for vanishing; that neither is *he* born to be of the sovereigns of this world; that he will have to be trampled and chained down in whatever terrible ways, and brass-collared safe, among the born thralls of this world! We cannot have *Canailles* and Doggeries that will not make some Chivalry of themselves: our noble Planet is impatient of such; in the end, totally intolerant of such!

For the Heavens, unwearying in their bounty, do send other souls into this world, to whom yet, as to their forerunners, in Old Roman, in Old Hebrew and all noble times, the omnipotent guinea is, on the whole, an impotent guinea. Has your half-dead avaricious Corn-Law Lord, your half-alive avaricious Cotton-Law Lord, never seen one such? Such are, not one, but several; are, and will be, unless the

gods have doomed this world to swift dire ruin. These are
they, the elect of the world ; the born champions, strong
men, and liberatory Samsons of this poor world : whom the
poor Delilah-world will not always shear of their strength
and eyesight, and set to grind in darkness at *its* poor gin-
wheel ! Such souls are, in these days, getting somewhat
out of humour with the world. Your very Byron, in these
days, is at least driven mad ; flatly refuses fealty to the
world. The world with its injustices, its golden brutalities,
and dull yellow guineas, is a disgust to such souls : the ray
of Heaven that is in them does at least predoom them to be
very miserable here. Yes:—and yet all misery is faculty
misdirected, strength that has not yet found its way. The
black whirlwind is mother of the lightning. No *smoke,* in
any sense, but can become flame and radiance ! Such soul,
once graduated in Heaven's stern University, steps out
superior to your guinea.

Dost thou know, O sumptuous Corn-Lord, Cotton-Lord,
O mutinous Trades-Unionist, gin-vanquished, undeliverable;
O much-enslaved World,—this man is not a slave with
thee ! None of thy promotions is necessary for him. His
place is with the stars of Heaven: to thee it may be
momentous, to thee it may be life or death, to him it is
indifferent, whether thou place him in the lowest hut, or
forty feet higher at the top of thy stupendous high tower,
while here on Earth. The joys of Earth that are precious,
they depend not on thee and thy promotions. Food and
raiment, and, round a social hearth, souls who love him,
whom he loves: these are already his. He wants none of
thy rewards ; behold also, he fears none of thy penalties.
Thou canst not answer even by killing him : the case of
Anaxarchus thou canst kill ; but the self of Anaxarchus,
the word or act of Anaxarchus, in no wise whatever. To
this man death is not a bugbear ; to this man life is already
as earnest and awful, and beautiful and terrible, as death.

Not a May-game is this man's life ; but a battle and
a march, a warfare with principalities and powers. No
idle promenade through fragrant orange-groves and green
flowery spaces, waited on by the choral Muses and the rosy
Hours: it is a stern pilgrimage through burning sandy
solitudes, through regions of thick-ribbed ice. He walks
among men ; loves men, with inexpressible soft pity,—as

they *cannot* love him: but his soul dwells in solitude, in the uttermost parts of Creation. In green oases by the palm-tree wells, he rests a space ; but anon he has to journey forward, escorted by the Terrors and the Splendours, the Archdemons and Archangels. All Heaven, all Pandemonium are his escort. The stars keen-glancing, from the Immensities, send tidings to him ; the graves, silent with their dead, from the Eternities. Deep calls for him unto Deep.

Thou, O World, how wilt thou secure thyself against this man ? Thou canst not hire him by thy guineas ; nor by thy gibbets and law-penalties restrain him. He eludes thee like a Spirit. Thou canst not forward him, thou canst not hinder him. Thy penalties, thy poverties, neglects, contumelies : behold, all these are good for him. Come to him as an enemy ; turn from him as an unfriend ; only do not this one thing,—infect him not with thy own delusion : the benign Genius, were it by very death, shall guard him against this !—What wilt thou do with him ? He is above thee, like a god. Thou, in thy stupendous three-inch pattens, art under him. He is thy born king, thy conqueror and supreme lawgiver : not all the guineas and cannons, and leather and prunella, under the sky can save thee from him. Hardest thick-skinned Mammon-world, ruggedest Caliban shall obey him, or become not Caliban but a cramp. Oh, if in this man, whose eyes can flash Heaven's lightning, and make all Calibans into a cramp, there dwelt not, as the essence of his very being, a God's justice, human Nobleness, Veracity and Mercy,—I should tremble for the world. But his strength, let us rejoice to understand, is even this : The quantity of Justice, of Valour and Pity that is in him. To hypocrites and tailored quacks in high places, his eyes are lightning ; but they melt in dewy pity softer than a mother's to the downpressed, maltreated ; in his heart, in his great thought, is a sanctuary for all the wretched. This world's improvement is forever sure.

'Man of Genius'? Thou hast small notion, meseems, O Maecenas Twiddledee, of what a Man of Genius is. Read in thy New Testament and elsewhere,—if, with floods of mealy-mouthed inanity, with miserable froth-vortices of Cant now several centuries old, thy New Testament is not all bedimmed for thee. *Canst* thou read in thy New Testament at all? The Highest Man of Genius, knowest thou him; Godlike and a God to this hour? His crown a Crown of Thorns? Thou fool, with *thy* empty Godhoods, Apotheoses *edge-gilt*; the Crown of Thorns made into a poor jewel-room crown, fit for the head of blockheads; the bearing of the Cross changed to a riding in the Long-Acre Gig! Pause in thy mass-chantings, in thy litanyings, and Calmuck prayings by machinery; and pray, if noisily, at least in a more human manner. How with thy rubrics and dalmatics, and clothwebs and cobwebs, and with thy stupidities and grovelling baseheartedness, hast thou hidden the Holiest into all but invisibility!—

'Man of Genius': O Maecenas Twiddledee, hast thou any notion what a Man of Genius is? Genius is 'the inspired gift of God'. It is the clearer presence of God Most High in a man. Dim, potential in all men; in this man it has become clear, actual. So says John Milton, who ought to be a judge; so answer him the Voices of all Ages and all Worlds. Wouldst thou commune with such a one?—*Be* his real peer then: does that lie in thee? Know thyself and thy real and thy apparent place, and know him and his real and his apparent place, and act in some noble conformity with all that. What! The star-fire of the Empyrean shall eclipse itself, and illuminate magic-lanterns to amuse grown children? He, the god-inspired, is to twang harps for thee, and blow through scrannel-pipes, to soothe thy sated soul with visions of new, still wider Eldorados, Houri Paradises, richer Lands of Cockaigne? Brother, this is not he; this is a counterfeit, this twangling, jangling, vain, acrid, scrannel-piping man. Thou dost well to say with sick Saul, 'It is naught, such harping!'—and in sudden rage, to grasp thy spear, and try if thou canst pin such a one to the wall. King Saul was mistaken in his man, but thou art right in thine. It is the due of such a one: nail him to the wall, and leave him there. So ought copper shillings to be nailed on counters; copper geniuses on walls, and left there for a sign!—

I conclude that the Men of Letters too may become a 'Chivalry', an actual instead of a virtual Priesthood, with result immeasurable,—so soon as there is nobleness in themselves for that. And, to a certainty, not sooner! Of intrinsic Valetisms you cannot, with whole Parliaments to help you, make a Heroism. Doggeries never so gold-plated, Doggeries never so escutcheoned, Doggeries never so diplomaed, bepuffed, gas-lighted, continue Doggeries, and must take the fate of such.

CHAPTER VIII

THE DIDACTIC

CERTAINLY it were a fond imagination to expect that any preaching of mine could abate Mammonism ; that Bobus of Houndsditch will love his guineas less, or his poor soul more, for any preaching of mine ! But there is one Preacher who does preach with effect, and gradually persuade all persons : his name is Destiny, is Divine Providence, and his Sermon the inflexible Course of Things. Experience does take dreadfully high school-wages ; but he teaches like no other !

I revert to Friend Prudence the good Quaker's refusal of ' seven thousand pounds to boot '. Friend Prudence's practical conclusion will, by degrees, become that of all rational practical men whatsoever. On the present scheme and principle, Work cannot continue. Trades' Strikes, Trades' Unions, Chartisms ; mutiny, squalor, rage and desperate revolt, growing ever more desperate, will go on their way. As dark misery settles down on us, and our refuges of lies fall in pieces one after one, the hearts of men, now at last serious, will turn to refuges of truth. The eternal stars shine out again, so soon as it is dark *enough*.

Begirt with desperate Trades' Unionism and Anarchic Mutiny, many an Industrial *Law-ward*, by and by, who has neglected to make laws and keep them, will be heard saying to himself : ' Why have I realized five hundred thousand pounds ? I rose early and sat late, I toiled and moiled, and in the sweat of my brow and of my soul I strove to gain this money, that I might become conspicuous, and have some honour among my fellow-creatures. I wanted them to honour me, to love me. The money is here, earned with my best lifeblood : but the honour ? I am encircled with

The Capitalist will wonder what he has gained

squalor, with hunger, rage, and sooty desperation. Not honoured, hardly even envied; only fools and the flunkey-species so much as envy me. I am conspicuous,—as a mark for curses and brickbats. What good is it? My five hundred scalps hang here in my wigwam: would to Heaven I had sought something else than the scalps; would to Heaven I had been a Christian Fighter, not a Chactaw one! To have ruled and fought not in a Mammonish but in a Godlike spirit; to have had the hearts of the people bless me, as a true ruler and captain of my people; to have felt my own heart bless me, and that God above instead of Mammon below was blessing me,—this had been something. Out of my sight, ye beggarly five hundred scalps of banker's-thousands: I will try for something other, or account my life a tragical futility!'

bids to change his life.

Friend Prudence's 'rock-ledge', as we called it, will gradually disclose itself to many a man; to all men. Gradually, assaulted from beneath and from above, the Stygian mud-deluge of Laissez-faire, Supply-and-demand, Cash-payment the one Duty, will abate on all hands; and the everlasting mountain-tops, and secure rock-foundations that reach to the centre of the world, and rest on Nature's self, will again emerge, to found on, and to build on. When Mammon-worshippers here and there begin to be God-worshippers, and bipeds-of-prey become men, and there is a Soul felt once more in the huge-pulsing elephantine mechanic Animal-ism of this Earth, it will be again a blessed Earth.

'Men cease to regard money?' cries Bobus of Houndsditch: 'What else do all men strive for? The very Bishop informs me that Christianity cannot get on without a minimum of Four thousand five hundred in its pocket. Cease to regard money? That will be at Doomsday in the afternoon!'— O Bobus, my opinion is somewhat different. My opinion is, that the Upper Powers have not yet determined on destroy-ing this Lower World. A respectable, ever-increasing minority, who do strive for something higher than money, I with confidence anticipate; ever-increasing, till there be a sprinkling of them found in all quarters, as salt of the Earth once more. The Christianity that cannot get on without a minimum of Four thousand five hundred, will give place to something better that can. Thou wilt not join our small minority, thou? Not till Doomsday in the afternoon? Well; *then*, at least, thou wilt join it, thou and the majority in mass!

But truly it is beautiful to see the brutish empire of Mammon cracking everywhere; giving sure promise of dying, or of being changed. A strange, chill, almost ghastly day-spring strikes up in Yankeeland itself: my Transcendental friends announce there, in a distinct, though somewhat lankhaired, ungainly manner, that the Demiurgus Dollar is dethroned; that new unheard-of Demiurgus-ships, Priest-hoods, Aristocracies, Growths and Destructions, are already visible in the grey of coming Time. Chronos is dethroned by Jove; Odin by St. Olaf: the Dollar cannot rule in Heaven forever. No; I reckon, not. Socinian Preachers quit their pulpits in Yankeeland, saying, 'Friends, this is all gone to coloured cobweb, we regret to say!'—and retire into the fields to cultivate onion-beds, and live frugally on vegetables. It is very notable. Old godlike Calvinism declares that its old body is now fallen to tatters, and done; and its mournful ghost, disembodied, seeking new embodiment, pipes again in the winds;—a ghost and spirit as yet, but heralding new Spirit-worlds, and better Dynasties than the Dollar one.

Yes, here as there, light is coming into the world; men love not darkness, they do love light. A deep feeling of the eternal nature of Justice looks out among us everywhere,— even through the dull eyes of Exeter Hall; an unspeakable religiousness struggles, in the most helpless manner, to speak itself, in Puseyisms and the like. Of our Cant, all condemnable, how much is not condemnable without pity; we had almost said, without respect! The *in*articulate worth and truth that is in England goes down yet to the Foundations.

Some 'Chivalry of Labour', some noble Humanity and practical Divineness of Labour, will yet be realized on this Earth. Or why *will*; why do we pray to Heaven, without setting our own shoulder to the wheel? The Present, if it will have the Future accomplish, shall itself commence. Thou who prophesiest, who believest, begin thou to fulfil. Here or nowhere, now equally as at any time! That outcast help-needing thing or person, trampled down under vulgar feet or hoofs, no help 'possible' for it, no prize offered for the saving of it,—canst not thou save it, then, without prize? Put forth thy hand, in God's name; know that 'impossible',

impossible will be furnished with

where Truth and Mercy and the everlasting Voice of Nature order, has no place in the brave man's dictionary. That when all men have said 'Impossible', and tumbled noisily elsewhither, and thou alone art left, then first thy time and possibility have come. It is for thee now; do thou that, and ask no man's counsel, but thy own only and God's. Brother, thou hast possibility in thee for much : the possibility of writing on the eternal skies the record of a heroic life. That noble downfallen or yet unborn 'Impossibility', thou canst lift it up, thou canst, by thy soul's travail, bring it into clear being. That loud inane Actuality, with millions in its pocket, too 'possible' that, which rolls along there, with quilted trumpeters blaring round it, and all the world escorting it as mute or vocal flunkey,—escort it not thou ; say to it, either nothing, or else deeply in thy heart : 'Loud-blaring Nonentity, no force of trumpets, cash, Long-Acre art, or universal flunkeyhood of men, makes thee an Entity ; thou art a *Non*entity, and deceptive Simulacrum, more accursed than thou seemest. Pass on in the Devil's name, unworshipped by at least one man, and leave the thorough-fare clear !'

Not on Ilion's or Latium's plains; on far other plains and places henceforth can noble deeds be now done. Not on Ilion's plains ; how much less in Mayfair's drawing rooms! Not in victory over poor brother French or Phrygians ; but in victory over Frost-jötuns, Marsh-giants, over demons of Discord, Idleness, Injustice, Unreason, and Chaos come again. None of the old Epics is longer possible. The Epic of French and Phrygians was comparatively a small Epic : but that of Flirts and Fribbles, what is that ? A thing that vanishes at cock-crowing,—that already begins to scent the morning air ! Game-preserving Aristocracies, let them 'bush' never so effectually, cannot escape the Subtle Fowler. Game seasons will be excellent, and again will be indifferent, and by and by they will not be at all. The Last Partridge of England, of an England where millions of men can get no corn to eat, will be shot and ended. Aristocracies with beards on their chins will find other work to do than amuse themselves with trundling-hoops.

Aristocr021
will work

But it is to you, ye Workers, who do already work, and are as grown men, noble and honourable in a sort, that the whole world calls for new work and nobleness. Subdue mutiny, discord, widespread despair, by manfulness, justice, mercy and wisdom. Chaos is dark, deep as Hell; let light be, and there is instead a green flowery World. O, it is great, and there is no other greatness. To make some nook of God's Creation a little fruitfuller, better, more worthy of God; to make some human hearts a little wiser, manfuller, happier,—more blessed, less accursed! It is work for a God. Sooty Hell of mutiny and savagery and despair can, by man's energy, be made a kind of Heaven; cleared of its soot, of its mutiny, of its need to mutiny; the everlasting arch of Heaven's azure overspanning *it* too, and its cunning mechanisms and tall chimney-steeples, as a birth of Heaven; God and all men looking on it well pleased.

Unstained by wasteful deformities, by wasted tears or heart's-blood of men, or any defacement of the Pit, noble fruitful Labour, growing ever nobler, will come forth,—the grand sole miracle of Man; whereby Man has risen from the low places of this Earth, very literally, into divine Heavens. Ploughers, Spinners, Builders; Prophets, Poets, Kings; Brindleys and Goethes, Odins and Arkwrights; all martyrs, and noble men, and gods are of one grand Host; immeasurable; marching ever forward since the Beginnings of the World. The enormous, all-conquering, flame-crowned Host, noble every soldier in it; sacred, and alone noble. Let him who is not of it hide himself; let him tremble for himself. Stars at every button cannot make him noble; sheaves of Bath-garters, nor bushels of Georges; nor any other contrivance but manfully enlisting in it, valiantly taking place and step in it. O Heavens, will he not bethink himself; he too is so needed in the Host! It were so blessed, thrice-blessed, for himself and for us all! In hope of the Last Partridge, and some Duke of Weimar among our English Dukes, we will be patient yet a while.

> 'The Future hides in it
> Gladness and sorrow;
> We press still thorow,
> Naught that abides in it
> Daunting us,—onward.'

NOTES

BOOK I. CHAPTER I

PAGE 1. *fifteen millions.* See Introduction, p. ix.

the workhouse Bastille being filled. See Introduction, p. xvi. In the years in which the Poor Law Amendment Act was coming into operation there were many more able-bodied paupers than the workhouses could hold, and in 1841 there were still 33 unions unprovided with workhouses. The undersized workhouses were conspicuously frequent in the manufacturing districts of the North (Nicholls, *History of the Poor Law*, ii. 355).

PAGE 2. *because work cannot be done in them.* Workhouses were originally started in the seventeenth century, to help the destitute to earn wages and to compete with outside industries; but they soon ceased to be self-supporting. Moreover, the plan was opposed from outside in the interests of the free labourer, among others by Daniel Defoe in *Giving Alms no Charity*. In Carlyle's time the task-work at the workhouses consisted of a set amount of exertion in stone-breaking, bone-crushing, or oakum-picking.

The picturesque Tourist. See Introduction, p. lxix.

PAGES 2–3. *in thrifty Scotland ... Dr. Alison.* See Introduction, pp. xi, xvii. William Pulteney Alison (1790–1859), brother of Sir Archibald Alison the historian, was physician to the New Town Dispensary at Edinburgh for a few years from 1815 onwards, and his reports on epidemic ailments laid much stress on the connexion between disease and poverty. From 1820 to 1856 he held various Chairs of Medicine at the University; was the author of medical text-books; and for a long time the leading member of his profession in Scotland, and universally beloved.

PAGE 3. *our present state of commercial stagnation.* See Introduction, p. xii.

Scotland must have a Poor Law. Introduction, pp. xi, xvii. A number of private charities subsisted in the great towns to take the place of a Poor Law, but quite ineffectually. The law, as it was, required the Ministers of parishes and bailiffs of boroughs to levy a rate to maintain 'all aged poor and impotent persons'; but the expression was narrowly interpreted, and the duty consistently shirked.

a byword among the nations. 1 Kings ix. 7.

metal of Potosi. Potosi is a province in the south-west of

Bolivia famous for its silver mines on the slopes of the Andes. The capital, also named Potosi, is built on the side of the so-called 'silver mountain', which is honeycombed with mining shafts, and was once the richest source of silver in the world.

Factory Inquiries. See Introduction, pp. xviii, xix. *Agricultural Inquiries.* A Select Committee to inquire into the state of Agriculture presented reports in 1833 and 1836. A Select Committee of the House of Lords on the same subject in 1837. *Mining Labourer Committees.* There was a Select Committee on Accidents in Mines in 1833. See further Introduction, p. xviii.

Stockport Assizes. The circumstances of the crime are reported at length in *The Times* of October 20, 1840, and the trial from August 4 to August 6, 1841. Three children, all of them girls, were believed to have met their death by poisoning. The Coroner's Jury found that Robert and Ann Sandys were guilty of poisoning two of their children, and George Sandys (Robert's brother) and his wife of murdering a child of their own in the same way and abetting the murder of one of the others. At the Assizes Robert Sandys was convicted of poisoning one of his children by arsenic in order to obtain a burial fee of £3 8s. 6d. All the accused were Irish living in Stockport cellars. The case excited an immense sensation. Throughout 1842 the distress in Stockport was frequently referred to in Parliament, and on a motion of the House of Commons an inquiry into it was held by the Poor Law Commissioners, who drew up a lengthy Report.

PAGE 4. *Ugolino Hunger-tower.* Count Ugolino made himself master of Pisa in the year 1284. He belonged to the old and powerful family of the Gherardesca, and was the owner of great estates in Tuscany. After taking sides with the Ghibellines he deserted them in 1275, and joined the Guelfs, by whose aid he ruled in Pisa. In 1288 the Ghibelline faction in the town revolted against him in his absence. On returning to Pisa he was invited to a parley, and treacherously set upon and captured. With his two sons, Gaddo and Uguccione, and two grandsons, he was shut up in the tower of Gualandi, where they were all starved. The room was entered a few days after they died, and the bodies were found to have been bitten by rats. Two chroniclers assert that they ate one another in their hunger, and Dante, in his poignant story of their deaths (*Inferno* xxxiii), is taken by some commentators to accept this view.

committee of ways and means. The term is applied in Parliament to a Committee of the House of Commons concerned with the raising of money.

'*The hands of the pitiful women*', &c. Lamentations iv. 10.

ultimatum. The word in this sense is either peculiar or exceedingly rare. There is an instance in the Essay *Signs of the Times*: 'His (Cabanis') book may be regarded as the ultimatum of mechanical metaphysics.'

PAGE 5. *gloom.* Common in dialect; and there are many examples of its literary use in the *N. E. D.*

'*to buy where he finds it cheapest*'. . . . 'The interest of a nation in its commercial relations to foreign nations is, like that of a merchant with regard to the different people with whom he deals, to buy as cheap and to sell as dear as possible.'—Adam Smith on the freedom of trade, *Wealth of Nations,* IV. ii.

fifty-pound tenants. The Reform Act of 1832 enlarged the franchise for county constituencies by conferring it on all occupiers of tenements or lands liable to a yearly rent of not less than £50.

doing what he likes with his own. In 1829 the electors of Newark rejected a nominee of the Duke of Newcastle's; whereupon the Duke evicted every one of the hostile voters who was his tenant. He defended his action by asking : 'Have I not the right to do what I like with my own ?'

Corn-law. See Introduction, p. xiii.

PAGE 6. *Midas.* He was king of Phrygia. Carlyle seems to be mixing two stories about him: (*a*) Midas showed hospitality to Silenus, the companion of Dionysus, when Silenus had been found wandering in the king's gardens in an intoxicated state. As a reward for this kindness Dionysus promised to grant the king any favour he might ask. Midas asked that whatsoever he touched might be turned to gold ; but, finding that even his food became gold, prevailed on the God to revoke his gift. (*b*) Midas was umpire in a musical match between Pan and Apollo, and 'insulted the Olympians' by awarding the prize to Pan ; whereupon Apollo gave him ass's ears.

BOOK I. CHAPTER II

PAGE 6. *the Sphinx.* A she-monster, who sat on a rock by Thebes propounding a riddle to the passers-by, and flung from the rock all that could not solve it. Oedipus, King of Thebes, solved it ; whereupon the Sphinx killed herself. She had the winged body of a lion, but her breast and face were a woman's. For the metaphorical use of the fable, cf. *Sartor,* II. iv.

unnameable Fact. Cf. *Heroes and Hero-Worship,* Lecture I : 'It is a poor science that would hide from us the great deep sacred infinitude of Nescience. . . . That great mystery of Time . . . on which we and all the Universe swim like exhalations . . . is very literally a miracle ; a thing to strike us dumb,—for we have no word to speak about it.' See the passage from *Faust,* quoted in a note to p. 206, on the Unnameable God, Who is the heart of the mystery.

PAGE 7. *her victorious bridegroom.* An allusion to Brunhild, the Queen of Issland, in the *Nibelungen Lied,* who vowed to wed no man but him who should excel her in hurling the spear, throwing a stone, and leaping. Siegfried overcame her in these feats after disguising himself as Gunther, and Brunhild consented to marry her supposed conqueror. The classical legend of Atalanta is closely analogous.

Scattered on the precipices. This may allude to the Sphinx throwing her victims from the rock, or to the Tarpeian Rock which dropped sheer for 80 feet on the south-east side of the Capitol at Rome, and from which in early times traitors and state criminals were thrown.

rede the riddle. The verb is the same as the verb to read, and when used in this form generally means to counsel or advise. For the sense in the text the *N. E. D.* gives Ramsay, *Gentle Shepherd*: ' Nor come I to redd fortunes for reward '. Carlyle uses it in *Sartor Resartus*, I. viii : ' The secret of Man's being is still a riddle that he cannot rede '; and in *The French Revolution*, V. iii. His use of it is either dialect or archaism.

our united twenty-seven millions. In 1841 the figures of the Census were : England and Wales just under 16 millions ; Scotland just over 2½ ; Ireland just over 8.

In the centre of the world-whirlwind. Ezekiel i. 4 f.

Scythians, i. e., in classical writers, the nomad tribes to the north and north-east of the Black Sea, of whose customs and religion a full account is given by Herodotus (iv. 1–142). Carlyle is possibly referring to the supreme honours which they paid to Ares and to their use of the sword as a divine symbol. Cf. Colossians iii. 11.

PAGE 8. *red tape* : i. e. convention.

Tarpeian Rock. See note to *Scattered on the precipices*, p. 7.

Longacre vehicle. Long Acre was a favourite seat of the carriage-building trade in the eighteenth century and in Carlyle's day. Two famous coachbuilders, and great improvers of the art, John Hatchett (from 1770 to 1790) and Jacob Hobson (for many years from 1815 onwards), had their premises here (G. A. Thrupp, *The History of Coaches*). At the accession of Queen Victoria the coaches of the wealthy had become as splendid and comfortable as they could be, and were one of the peculiar attractions of a London season.

Courts of Westminster. From Edward the Confessor downwards the principal courts of law were in the precincts of the Palace of Westminster. William Rufus built his great Hall for a seat of Justice and ' wore his crown ' in it (i. e. held a court) for the first time at Whitsuntide, 1099. By a clause in *Magna Charta* it was provided that the hearing of common pleas, i.e. suits between subject and subject, was not to take place wherever the king might happen to go, but in ' a fixed place ', which meant the Hall. The King's Bench and the Exchequer continued to follow the king about, but in the fourteenth century these, as well as the Chancellor's Court (see note to p. 118), became settled at Westminster. Through all its architectural transformations that famous building roofed the Courts, sitting at its ends and along its walls, until in 1822 a number of separate chambers were erected for them wall to wall with its western side. These survived the fire of 1834, and justice was administered in them until the Royal Courts in the Strand were opened in 1882, and they were swept away. There is a plan of the Hall, with the positions of the different Courts in 1795, in Inderwick's *The King's Peace*, facing p. 233.

'*Adamant Tablet*'. In the ancient world laws and oracles were often engraved on tablets of bronze. So in Sophocles, *Trachiniae* 683, Deianeira says that she kept the precepts of the Centaur χαλκῆς ὅπως δύσνιπτον ἐκ δέλτου γραφήν, 'like words written indelibly on a bronze tablet'. Jebb cites a number of parallels, including Cicero, *Philippics*, i. 26 'Quod ita erit gestum, id lex erit? Et in aes incidi iubebitis?' The word 'adamant' originally meant any hard metal.

PAGE 9. *learned-sergeant*. A 'sergeant (or serjeant) at law' (*serviens ad legem*) was a member of a superior order of barristers, from whom the judges of the Common Law were always chosen. The order was abolished in 1880.

reclaimer. Carlyle coins the word on the analogy of 'disclaimer'. *disclaimer*. A term in law for the act of repudiating or renouncing a legal claim. *demurrer*. Lat. *demorari*, to delay. 'A pleading which, admitting for the moment the facts as stated in the opponent's pleading, denies that he is legally entitled to relief, and thus stops the action until this point be determined by the Court' (*N. E. D.*).

parchment records. The great majority of the documents at the Record Office, as for instance the 'rolls' of the Common Law Courts, are of parchment.

PAGE 10. *the fool hath said in his heart*. Psalms xiv. 1.

One strong thing I find, &c. Compare with these pages *Chartism*, ch. v; and a passage on Napoleon in 'The Hero as King' (*Heroes and Hero-Worship*) beginning, 'The Duke of Weimar told his friends always, To be of courage. . . .' For dubious applications of the theory, see Carlyle's remarks on the Prussian invasion of Silesia in *Frederick the Great*, XI. ix, and on the Partition of Poland, *ibid.*, XXI. iv. Cf. a passage on p. 171 f.

PAGE 11. *Valhalla*, i. e. in Old Norse, Valhöll, the 'Hall of the Slain', where the spirits of those who fall in battle are received by Odin, and live for ever fighting and feasting.

semblant. The word is rare, and only used in poetry after the seventeenth century, in the sense of 'similar'. For its present use the *N. E. D.* gives only one quotation (1840) besides instances from Carlyle.

waste-bickering. Poetic diction for 'unproductively quarrelling'. In the Essay *On History* he quotes Milton's comparison of the Heptarchy to 'the flocking and fighting of kites and crows'.

jesting Pilate. ' " What is Truth ? ", said jesting Pilate, and would not stay for an answer.'—Bacon, *Essays*, ' Of Truth '.

PAGE 12. *Hansard Debatings.* Luke Hansard (1752–1828) was originally a compositor in the office of the Printer to the House of Commons. He became the manager of the business in 1774, and ultimately its sole proprietor (1800), and printed the *Journals of the House of Commons* from 1774 to his death. The business was carried on after him by his sons, one of whom, Thomas Curson Hansard, set up a press of his own in 1803, and began publishing the *Parliamentary Debates.*

BOOK I. CHAPTER III

PAGE 13. *Blusterowski, Colacorde.* The names are fictitious. The meaning of ' Blusterowski ' is clear. ' Colacorde ' will have been suggested by ' Le cou (' col ' when euphony requires it) à la corde ',—' the neck to the halter '; the usual proposition of the Parisian insurrectionary.

vilipend. Fr. *vilipender,* Lat. *vilipendere,* to hold cheap.

Manchester Insurrection. This was the ' Great Turn-out ' of August 1842, and not Peterloo. Peterloo took place on August 16, 1819, on an open space, now the site of the Free Trade Hall, by St. Peter's Church. A meeting in favour of the reform of Parliament was appointed for this day, and was attended by large numbers of men, accompanied by women and children, who marched to St. Peter's Field from Manchester and the adjacent towns and villages in more or less of military order. To call it a ' million-headed meeting ' is to adopt the language of ' Blusterowski '. The estimates of its size vary from 20,000 to 80,000 ; Castlereagh, on the reports furnished to Government, put it at ' over 40,000 '. There were mild hints at insurrection in some devices on the banners, such as ' Equal Representation or Death ' ; but the leaders exhorted the processionists to be orderly, and to leave their sticks or other weapons behind, which they generally did. No sooner had ' Orator ' Hunt begun to speak than the Magistrates present declared the meeting dangerous and so illegal, and ordered his arrest. The Chief Constable of Manchester reported that he could not effect the arrest without military aid ; and forty of the Manchester Yeomanry were ordered to assist, and rode at the hustings brandishing their swords. It was stated afterwards on the one hand that these men were violently assaulted, on the other that they were only wedged fast in an unresisting crowd ; in any case they were altogether powerless. There were two other bodies of Cavalry on the field—some 400 of the Cheshire Yeomanry and part of the 15th Hussars. The Hussars now charged with drawn swords to the help of the distressed Yeomanry ; and the defenceless multitude was scattered in all directions in a few minutes. The soldiers did not fire. The figures of killed in the reports vary from six to fourteen. Most of the killed and wounded were trampled or bruised in the panic. Peterloo whetted the agitation for Reform, and served the reformers as a signal demonstration of the issue at stake. (Mainly from the account by an officer of the Hussars in Dean Pellew's *Life of Lord Sidmouth*.) The 'Great Turn-out' was a general strike with processions, in Lancashire especially, against the Corn Law. It peacefully collapsed after a few days. (See Trevelyan, *Life of John Bright*, pp. 79 f.)

Lyons. In July 1793, Lyons, a centre of Girondist and Royalist sentiment, revolted from the Convention after 'rabid fighting' (in Carlyle's words) against its own Jacobins ; and stood a siege of seven weeks (August–October) by a Jacobin army. It was compelled to surrender, and the surrender was followed by a massacre of the insurgents with the guillotine and grape-shot. On the fall of Robespierre the defeated party again mastered their enemies in the town and requited the massacre in kind.

Warsaw. Warsaw was the centre of the Polish insurrection of November 1830, and was captured by the Russians after great bloodshed in September 1831. It remained until 1856 under military law.

invisible Nightmare. In popular mythology the Nightmare is a female monster or goblin that besets men and animals in the dark, and sits upon their bodies.

PAGE 14. *Hyrcanian tiger.* *Macbeth*, III. iv. 101, 'the Hyrcan tiger'; and *Hamlet*, II. ii. 481, 'Pyrrhus like the Hyrcanian beast'. Hyrcania was an ancient district bordering on the Caspian Sea (*Hyrcanum Mare*) and the river Oxus.

Behemoth. Job xl. 15–24 ; the commentators refer it either to the hippopotamus or the elephant. The word is the plural form of the Hebrew *b'hemah*, meaning 'beast'.

a brute one. The Latin *brutus* is contracted from *barutus* (Gk. βαρύs) and means 'heavy', 'unwieldy', and so 'stupid', 'irrational'. In English it is applied (rarely) to sound, meaning 'inarticulate'. *N. E. D.* quotes a note of Cowley's to his *Davideis*, iv. 154, 'Thunders from which the Ancients could collect no Prognostications were called *Brute Thunders*'.

Sons of Nox and Chaos. One of Carlyle's frequent references to Scandinavian Mythology, which suited the dualism in his thought. 'The dark hostile Powers of Nature they figure to themselves as "*Jötuns*", Giants, huge shaggy beings of a demonic character. Frost, Fire, Sea-tempest ; these are Jötuns. The friendly Powers again, as Summer-heat, the Sun, are Gods. The empire of the Universe is divided between these two ; they dwell apart in perennial internecine feud. The Gods dwell above in Asgard, the Garden of the Asen, or Divinities ; Jötunheim, a distant dark chaotic land, is the home of the Jötuns'. On 'The Hero as Divinity', in *Heroes and Hero-Worship*.

Some thirteen unarmed men and women. On the figures of killed and injured, see note above on *Manchester Insurrection.*

PAGE 15. *O'Connor.* See Introduction, pp. xl, xli.

dayspring from on high. St. Luke i. 78.

PAGE 16. *increasing at the rate of fifty every hour.* If this is meant for the net increase of population in England or in Great Britain in any decade from 1801 to 1841, the calculation is a good way out. If it refers to births alone it is approximately right. In 1831 the population of Great Britain in round numbers was 16,366,000 ; in 1841, 18,664,000 ; an increase of a little over $2\frac{1}{4}$ million in the ten years ; of 225,000 in a year ; of 616 in 24 hours; and of some 25 in an hour. According to the Registrar-General's Return for England for 1841 there were 512,158 births in that year, or an increase of 55·3 an hour ; there were also, however, 343,847 deaths.

Dilettantism and Mammonism. In Carlyle, the first of these terms is frequently used for the landed gentry, the second for the Industrial Masters.

Midas-eared Mammonisms. See p. 6.

PAGE 17. *the all-victorious Light-element.* Carlyle was fond of dualistic philosophies and their myths. He is thinking here partly of the religion of Zoroaster as professed by the Parsees, according to which the Good Power (Ormuzd) is opposed by the Evil (Ahriman). Ormuzd is the origin of Light and Fire, and these are his symbols, and held sacred. The Scandinavian Mythology, to which he often refers, fables that in the beginning there were two worlds, Niflheim, the world of mist and darkness, and Muspelheim, the fire world ; the Giants and Gods were born from the contact of these two ; and in Ragnarok, the last battle between the Upper and Nether Powers, the fire from Muspelheim consumes the great ash Ygdrasil, the tree of life, and with it all the world ; whereupon a new world arises, with a brighter sun, and nothing beneath it but beauty, plenty, and happiness.

a sarcastic man. This is none other, of course, than Carlyle himself.

wages of John Milton's day's work. Carlyle means that the reward for *Paradise Lost* was £10, and the reward for Milton's Works a close escape from the gallows. Milton sold the copyright of his great epic to Samuel Simmons in 1667 for £5 down and £5 after the sale of each of the first three editions of 1300 copies. He received the £5 down, and £5 for the first edition in 1669. At the Restoration he lay concealed in a friend's house in Bartholomew Close, while on June 16, 1660, it was ordered by the House of Commons that his *Pro Populo Anglicano Defensio* should be burnt by the hangman, and himself be arrested, and indicted by the Attorney-General. He was actually arrested, and then released, and finally relieved of anxiety by the Indemnity Act in August of the same year. It has been doubted if he was in real danger ; but according to Bishop Burnet it was a narrow escape.

Lernean Hydra-coil. Hercules, or Heracles, was the son of Zeus and Alcmene, and therefore hated by Hera, the wife of Zeus. By Hera's doing, he was bidden by the Delphic Oracle to submit to the behests of Eurystheus, King of Mycenae, who laid on him twelve labours. One of the twelve was to overcome the Hydra, or water-snake, of the marsh of Lerna by Argos, whose very breath was fatal. It had nine heads, and for every head cut off two arose in its place.

His dust lies under the Edgware Road. His body was hung on the gallows on January 30, 1661. Tyburn was the name of a brook running from Hampstead into the Thames by Westminster Palace. Oxford Street was originally known as Tyburn Road, and the turnpike gate stood opposite to the entrance of the Edgware Road. The gallows, under which it was the custom to bury the criminals executed, and where Cromwell was buried, was near this spot ; but its exact site has been a matter of dispute (Chambers, *Book of Days*, ii. 557).

Tenpound Franchise. The Parliamentary Reform Act of 1832 conferred the right of voting in boroughs on all ratepayers occupying premises of the annual value of £10 and upwards.

Open Vestry. 'Vestry' means a body of the ratepayers of a parish assembled on parish business in the vestry of the church, the incumbent being *ex officio* the chairman. Until 1894 it carried out most of the functions which were committed to Parish Councils by the Local Government Act of that year. Its business is now only ecclesiastical. An 'open vestry' means the whole body of the ratepayers, as distinct from a 'select vestry', or a chosen number of them ; which is the rule in some parishes, either by custom or by the Vestries Act of 1831.

Sanhedrim. The supreme tribunal of the Jews established under the Maccabees and consisting of 71 members of the priestly and the learned *classes*. It came to control a great deal of the internal administration of the land.

PAGE 18. *in the light or in the fire of which*, &c. Carlyle seems to be thinking of the fire of Muspelheim burning the worse world to bring in the better. See note to p. 17.

PAGE 19. *Wealth of Nations.* Adam Smith's *Wealth of Nations* (1776) was the starting-point of the Political Economy of the time.

Supply-and-demand. Carlyle, in his scorn of this formula, is thinking in the first place of its application to Labour, and the assumption underlying it that labour is a commodity and nothing more. Adam Smith taught (*Wealth of Nations*, Bk. I, ch. viii) that the price of labour, as of other commodities, was fixed by the proportion of the supply to the demand. In Ricardo supply and demand determines the fluctuations in a labourer's wages, but the cost of his subsistence determines their minimum point.

Laissez-faire. See Introduction, p. xlvii f. The use of the term as a political maxim originated with the French free-trade economists of the eighteenth century.

Gurth ... Cedric. These are characters from Scott's *Ivanhoe*.

PAGE 20. *Platitude*, i. e. 'absurdity'. *N. E. D.* quotes two or three instances, from about 1820, in which the word verges on this sense or may be taken to bear it. From the (hypothetic) late Latin *plattus*, Gk. πλατύς = 'flat', 'smooth', and so 'dull', 'plain', 'insipid'.

Jötuns. See note to p. 14.

Mud-giants. As, for instance, the Midgard-serpent, who lived at the bottom of the sea and encircled the earth, or the God Hoene, the 'lord of the ooze'.

BOOK I. CHAPTER IV

PAGE 20. *Morrison's Pill.* James Morrison, the 'Hygeist', died in the year 1840. He was for a long time in business in the West Indies, where, at the age of fifty, he 'renewed his youth' by concocting and taking vegetable pills. He put the pills on the English market, and in the first two years they brought in £60,000 to Government in duty. The headquarters of the business were the 'British College of Health' in the New Road, London (Chambers, *Book of Days*, i. 587).

PAGE 21. *Light-fountains.* He is alluding to the use of light as a curative agency for such diseases as lupus and ulcer, or for obesity.

Emigration. See Introduction, p. xxvi. *Education.* See Introduction, p. xix. *Corn-Law Abrogation.* See Introduction, p. xiii. *Sanitary Regulation.* See Introduction, p. xxiii.

Land Property Tax. The English Land Tax dates from 1692, when Parliament voted a subsidy of 4*s*. in the pound on personal estate, offices, land, and tenements. In a few years personal property was suffered to escape by evading assessment, and the brunt of the tax fell upon land. For convenience' sake it was determined (1697) to appoint a definite sum to be raised in a year on the basis of the valuation of 1692, and according to the proportion of liability then fixed between the counties and certain named towns. From that time forward for 100 years the proportion of liability, as well as the valuation, remained the same, the rate varying according to the needs of the Exchequer from 1*s*. to 4*s*. in the pound, but never exceeding 4*s*. That is to say, however much the value of land might rise, it was taxed on its value in 1692; and at the maximum rate of 4*s*. did not yield more than £2,000,000. An Act introduced by Pitt in 1797 enabled such landowners as chose to do so to redeem their land from what was virtually a rent-charge by cancelling so much Government stock; but less than half the land liable was so redeemed. Naturally the lowness of the charge was an offence to other classes of the community (see p. 221), and a new tax was advocated which should bring in to the state the unearned increment in land values. This idea was favoured by Adam Smith (*Wealth of Nations*, V. ii), discouraged by Ricardo (*Principles*, ch. xii), and strongly supported by John Stuart Mill (*Principles*, v. ii, ed. 1848). To some extent the demand was met by the Income Tax imposed by Pitt in 1798, and applied to the yield of land as well as to that of all other property. It was repealed in 1816, and from that repeal flowed all the difficulties of English finance for the next five-and-twenty years. The authorities of the day (Sir Henry Parnell, *Financial Reform*, 1830; B. Sayer, *The Income Tax*, 1833) declared the tax to be necessary, and in 1842 Sir Robert Peel re-imposed it, since when it has been the corner-stone of our revenue and a great means of reform. Thus there were two imposts on land: one, that assessed in 1692, and the other the Income, or as it was then called, the Property Tax. (Bastable, *Public Finance*, IV. iv; and Dowell, *History of Taxation and Taxes in England*.)

PAGE 22. *when the brains are out.* Cf. *Macbeth*, III. iv. 78:

> the times have been
> That, when the brains were out, the man would die.

argue ten years. i. e. since the reform of Parliament in 1832. For dates, see Introduction, p. xiii f.

difference between just and unjust ... infinite. Cf. *Signs of the Times*: 'In true dignity of soul and character we are perhaps inferior to most civilized ages. . . . The infinite, absolute character of Virtue has passed into a finite, conditional one; it is no longer a worship of the Beautiful and Good: but a calculation of the Profitable.' And *The Hero as Poet*: 'Dante felt Good and Evil to be the two polar elements of this Creation; that these two differ not by *preferability* of the one to the other, but by incompatibility absolute and infinite.'

millstone tied round your neck. St. Matthew xviii. 6; St. Mark ix. 42; St. Luke xvii. 2.

Downing Street. This street in Whitehall contains the Colonial and Foreign Offices and (since 1735) the official residence of the First Lord of the Treasury, where Cabinet Councils are often held.

Five-point Charter. The People's Charter embraced six points; but see Introduction, p. xli, on O'Connor's 'five points of radicalism'.

'*Given a world of knaves*', &c. The equation of the idea that 'private vices are public benefits' (see Introduction, p. xliv), or that self-seeking is public spirit.

PAGE 23. *edge-gilt vacuity.* Gilt-edged writing paper passes for an instance of a thing of high value and a thing extravagantly dear; hence we talk of 'gilt-edged securities', and the *N. E. D.* quotes 'gilt-edged butter'.

litany of Sorcerer's Sabbaths. St. Walpurga was an English
Saint who converted the Saxons in the eighth century. Her day
is May 1. It was an ancient superstition in Germany that on the
eve of this day (*Walpurgisnacht*) the witches rode to the Harz
mountains on broomsticks and goats to hold revel with Satan.
The highest point of the Harz, the Brocken, was especially favoured
for this purpose, and is the scene of the Sorcerer's Sabbath in
Goethe's *Faust.*

BOOK I. CHAPTER V

PAGE 25. *the old Prophet was right.* Isaiah xvii. 10; Jeremiah
iii. 21, and xiii. 25.

two-legged animal without feathers. Plato's description (*Definitions* 415 A): ἄνθρωπος ζῷον δίπουν ἄπτερον, *animal implume bipes.*
Cf. Dryden, *Absalom and Achitophel,* i. 169:

> And all to leave what with his toil he won
> To that unfeather'd two-legged thing, a son.

Sauerteig. Carlyle is in the habit of putting his own sentiments into the mouths of imaginary philosophers—Smelfungus,
Sauerteig, Teufelsdröckh—in order the more freely to have his
fling. There is never any difference, however, between one of his
voices and another. 'Sauerteig' is German for 'leaven'. See
note to p. 210. The allusion in this passage is to the characteristic
Theology of the eighteenth century, which supposed either that
God sat apart from His work after the act of Creation, or interfered only exceptionally. The metaphor of the Clockmaker and
the Clock was employed by Paley in the opening of his *Natural
Theology* (1802); but it has a great number of literary precedents
reaching back, in a slightly different form, to Cicero (see Leslie
Stephen, *English Thought in the Eighteenth Century,* i. 409). Paley
sees God as an Engineer working with Gravity and Matter, the
materials He found given, and revealed to the natural man by His
ingenuity. Remaining outside His Creation, He can only be a part
of the Universe, the supervisor of Nature, and not her life and soul.
After the Christian Revelation, Paley says, 'the seed, being sown,
was left to vegetate . . . according to the laws of nature. . . . And
in this Christianity is analogous to most other provisions for
happiness. The provision is made, and being made is left to
act' . . . (from the *Evidences* cited by Stephen). Carlyle was in
agreement with the general mind of his age in rejecting this
externalism. See, among many passages, the chapter on 'Natural
Supernatural' in *Sartor Resartus.* A similar figure for the
mechanical theory occurs in the opening lines of Goethe's poem
Gott und Welt, lines which Carlyle has more than once quoted:

> Was wär' ein Gott, der nur von aussen stiesse,
> Im Kreis das All am Finger laufen liesse !

'What sort of a God were He who should simply push the world from outside and let it spin by a string from His finger?'

PAGE 26. *Benthamee Radicalism* . . . '*Enlightened Selfishness*'. See Introduction, p. xliii.

Five-point Chartism. See note to p. 22.

Church-extension. See Introduction, p. xxxv.

Sliding-scale. See Introduction, p. xiii.

speaking once more in miraculous thunder-voice from out the centre of the world. The Sibyl delivered the oracles of Phoebus in a thunderous voice from the depths of a vast cave. See *Aeneid* vi. 42 f.

double-barrelled. With double surnames.

our young friend of the Houndsditch Indicator. Houndsditch is a street in the City long known as the seat of usurers and sellers of cast-off clothes. It is so mentioned by Anthony Munday, in his edition of Stow's *Survey of London* (cited in *Notes and Queries*, 9th series, ix. 348); and Mr. Percy Simpson has kindly referred me to Fletcher, *The Woman's Prize*, II. ii: 'More knavery, and usury, And foolery, and brokery than in Dog's-Ditch'; and Jonson, *Every Man in his Humour*, III. v:

WEL. Where got'st thou this coat, I marl'e?

BRAY. Of a Hounds-ditch man, sir. One of the deuil's neere kinsmen, a broker.

Hence the name passes for anything second-hand, antiquated, or shoddy. In addition to this, it is associated in Carlyle's mind with the idea of Jews as vendors of such articles; and he looked upon the Jews as the conspicuous instance of a people that had thrown in its lot with speciosity rather than truth, i. e. with the Pharisees rather than with Christ. Thus all antiquated or unvital beliefs and usages, and more especially that part of Christianity that had fallen, as he thought, out of touch with truth, were of Houndsditch. Hence his frequent metaphor of 'old clothes': 'Well, they got Barabbas; and they got such guidance as Barabbas could give them; and at this hour, after eighteen centuries of sad fortune, they prophetically sing "Ou' clo'!" in all the cities of the world' (*Latter-Day Pamphlets*, i). 'If it please Heaven, we shall all yet make our *Exodus* from Houndsditch, and bid the sordid continents, of once rich apparel now grown poisonous *Ou' clo'* a mild farewell. Exodus into wider horizons, into God's daylight once more' (*ibid.*, viii). The 'young friend' of the *Indicator* is, of course, a fictitious personage. The *Indicator* may be supposed to be a book or a journal the aim of which is to point out whatsoever is of Houndsditch.

PAGE 27. *Twenty-seven Million.* See note to p. 7.

Bobus Higgins, Sausage-maker. The ignoble type of the commercial world, otherwise called 'Bobus of Houndsditch' (p. 264). Cf. *Latter-Day Pamphlets*, vii: 'What think you of "Bobus of

Houndsditch"? He, sausage-maker on the great scale, knows the art of cutting fat bacon, and exposing it seasoned with grey pepper to advantage . . . gains by the universal suffrage of men's souls and stomachs *ten* thousand a year by it. A poor art, and worth no such recompense. Judges pronounce his sausages bad, and at the cheap price even dear; and finer palates have detected alarming symptoms of horseflesh, or worse, under that cunningly devised grey pepper spice of his.'

PAGE 28. *dropping fatness.* Psalm lxv. 11.

Like people like priest. Hosea iv. 9.

the life-tree everywhere is made a upas-tree. On the 'life-tree', see note to p. 34. 'Upas' is a Malay word for poison, and is applied especially to the poison exuded by the Antjar or Anchar tree, the scent of which, when felled or peeled, is strong enough to cause cutaneous eruptions. Hence among other fables, it is said that the air around the tree is fatal to animal life. Erasmus Darwin treats of the legends belonging to it in his *Loves of the Plants.*

PAGE 29. *Rhadamanthus, Aeacus, and Minos.* The three judges of the shades in Hades, sons and friends of Zeus, renowned in life for piety and wisdom. Minos was King of Cnossos in Crete, Rhadamanthus his brother. Aeacus ruled over the Myrmidons in Aegina.

BOOK I. CHAPTER VI

PAGE 30. '*enlightened Egoism*'. See Introduction, p. xliv.

'*Cash-payment for the sole nexus*'. Carlyle is quoting himself. See *Chartism*, ch. vi: '*Cash payment* had not then grown to be the universal sole nexus of man to man [i. e. in the Feudal Ages]; it was something other than money that the high then expected from the low, and could not live without getting from the low.'

PAGE 31. *Burns an Exciseman, Byron a Literary Lion.* See note to p. 255. Carlyle elaborates the contrast between these two poets in his Essay on Burns: 'Surely all these stormful agonies [of Byron's], this volcanic heroism . . . and moody desperation . . . is more like the brawling of a player . . . than the bearing of a man in the business of life.' Burns, on the other hand, is 'an honest man, and an honest writer . . . clear, simple, true, and glitters with no lustre but his own'. See further the chapter on 'The Everlasting Yea' in *Sartor* on the Byronic despair, with the conclusion, 'Close thy Byron; open thy Goethe'; and pp. 139, 260. Carlyle, however, was too great a critic not to see the 'ray of heaven' in Byron: 'A change from inward imprisonment, doubt, and discontent into freedom, belief, and clear activity will seldom take place without bitter conflicts, in which the character itself is too often maimed and impoverished. . . . Among our own poets Byron was almost the only man we saw faithfully and manfully struggling to the end in this cause; and he died while the victory was still doubtful, or at best only beginning to be gained '— Essay on Goethe. Cf. further a passage on Moore's *Life of Byron* in the Essay on Sir Walter Scott, and another in the Essay on *The State of German Literature*: 'All things were to have been hoped for from Byron; for he loved truth in his inmost heart, and would have discovered that his Corsairs and Harolds were not true.'

a baser and falser phenomenon than the Odin a God. Cf. *Heroes*, 'The Hero as Divinity': 'That men should have worshipped their poor fellow-men as a God ... is strange ... but quackery was never the originating influence in such things. ... I find Grand Lamaism itself to have a kind of truth in it. They have their belief, these poor Thibet people, that Providence sends down always an Incarnation of Himself unto every generation. ... We shall begin to have a chance of understanding Paganism when we first admit that to its followers it was, at one time, earnestly true.'

the poor Frenchman at the bar of the Convention. See *French Revolution*, VII. v.

PAGE 32. *Apage Satanas.* 'Avaunt, Satan!' St. Matthew iv. 10.

There, or else in the Ocean-abysses. Carlyle is thinking of Tennyson's 'Ulysses', from which he quotes a line on the next page:

> Come, my friends,
> 'Tis not too late to seek a newer world.
> Push off, and, sitting well in order, smite
> The sounding furrows; for my purpose holds
> To sail beyond the sunset, and the baths
> Of all the western stars, until I die.
> It may be that the gulfs will wash us down:
> It may be we shall touch the Happy Isles,
> And see the great Achilles whom we knew.

' Ulysses ' appeared in Tennyson's *Poems* of 1842; and Lord Tennyson's *Memoir* of his father contains a letter from Carlyle in which the poem is heartily praised.

College of Health. See note to p. 20 on *Morrison's Pill.*

PAGE 33. *Cassandra.* Daughter of Priam, King of Troy. Apollo, being enamoured of her, granted her the prescience of future events, but, when she refused his addresses, ordained furthermore that no one should believe her prophecies. Thus her prophecy of the downfall of Troy was disregarded.

' *The choking Nightmare* ', &c. This is from Jean Paul Richter's autobiographical reminiscences, quoted in the Essay *On Richter Again*.

PAGE 34. *a Trismegistus,* i. e. 'thrice-greatest'. The name 'Hermes Trismegistus' was given by the Greeks to the Egyptian God Thoth, the inventor of writing, art, science, and religion.

The 'Hermetic Books', an encyclopaedia in forty-two volumes, the sacred canon of the Egyptians, was supposed to be his work.

the present laws of copy-right. The Law of Copyright was amended by 'Talfourd's Act' in 1842. Under it the term of copyright in a book was to be forty-two years, or the life of the author and seven years, whichever of these two terms was the longer. Previously the term had been twenty-eight years or the author's life. In 1839 Carlyle wrote a Petition to the House of Commons, in which he pleaded that, in strict justice, no one but himself or his had any right to the proceeds of his works 'now, henceforth, or forever': failing strict justice, he prayed that publishers or booksellers might be forbidden to 'steal his small winnings for a space of sixty years at shortest'.

it is the same fact. See the whole chapter on 'Organic Filaments' in *Sartor Resartus* (iii. 7) : ' How shall we domesticate ourselves in this spectral Necropolis, or rather City both of the Dead and of the Unborn, where the Present seems little other than an inconsiderable Film, dividing the Past and the Future ? '

LIFE-TREE IGDRASIL. See *Heroes*, 'The Hero as Divinity'. In the Scandinavian Mythology, 'Igdrasil, the Ash-tree of Existence, has its roots deep down in the Kingdoms of Hela or Death; its trunk reaches up heaven-high, spreads its boughs over the whole Universe. At the foot of it, in the Death-kingdom, sit three *Nornas*, Fates,—the Past, Present, Future; watering its roots from the Sacred Well. Its "boughs" with their buddings and disleafings—events, things suffered, things done, catastrophes,—stretch through all lands and times. Is not every leaf of it a biography, every fibre there an act or word? Its boughs are Histories of Nations. . . . It is the past, the present, and the future ; what was done, what is doing, what will be done.'

BOOK II

INTRODUCTORY NOTE

St. Edmund.

A FEW lines in the Anglo-Saxon Chronicle and in Asser's *Life of Alfred* is all the contemporary reference to St. Edmund ; but Abbo, Abbot of Fleury, who for two years presided over a monastery at Ramsay in Huntingdonshire, and died in 1004, wrote a short account of Edmund and his death (*Passio Sti Eadmundi*, in *Memorials of St. Edmund's Abbey*, vol. i, ed. Arnold, Rolls Series), based, as he tells us, on what he once heard St. Dunstan relate to the Bishop of Rochester, and St. Dunstan had himself known an armour-bearer of the royal Martyr's. After Abbo, and up to the middle of the fifteenth century, a circumstantial legend was gradually created, and the likeliest inferences from all the accounts are these: Edmund came of a royal family in Old Saxony, and was born in 841. He emigrated to England, and had a house at Hunstanton. In terror of the Danish pirates the men of East Anglia chose him as their king, and he ruled them justly and piously. About the year 870 the Danes made a terrible descent on East Anglia, in which Edmund was taken prisoner, either unresistingly, as Abbo and others aver, or after 'stout fighting', according to the Anglo-Saxon Chronicle and Asser. Hinguar, the Danish leader, demanded of the prisoner that he should hold the kingdom of East Anglia as his (Hinguar's) vassal. But Edmund felt that, as a Christian king and responsible for the Christianity of his subjects, he could not rule as the servant of a heathen. He refused the demand, therefore, unless Hinguar should adopt the faith. Thereupon the Danes bound him to a tree, scourged him, made him a target for their arrows, and cut off his head. They left the body where it lay and hid the head in the wood of Hoxne, where the Christians subsequently found it, and buried head and body in a tomb at Hoxne, and built a chapel. See Arnold, Introduction, *op. cit.*

St. Edmund's Abbey.

After a length of time, which is variously computed in the accounts, the body was removed to Beodricsworth, the place afterwards named St. Edmundsbury, where in 945 Edmund, son of Edward the Elder, granted the lands round the town to the 'family' of four priests and two deacons who ministered in the large wooden church containing the tomb. The sudden death of Sweyn in 1014 is stated by Florence of Worcester and William of Malmesbury to have been inflicted by the Saint in requital of an attempt to rob his shrine. Anyhow, Canute thought it well to conciliate him; for in 1028, in a charter which is still extant (Arnold, *Memorials*, i. 342), he ordained that the *fundus* or 'farm' of St. Edmund was to be for ever in the possession of monks (not, i. e., as hitherto, of secular clergy), who should be free of episcopal authority, should have the right of taxing their tenants and hearing their suits, and should take over certain of the king's privileges with regard to fisheries. The clerks were now turned out of Beodricsworth and replaced by a college of twenty Benedictine monks, and a stone church (consecrated 1032) was built by Canute instead of the wooden one. The piety of Edward the Confessor greatly enriched the monastery in lands and privileges, and the wisdom and energy of Abbot Baldwin (Abbot from 1065 to 1097) raised it to that degree of honour and power in which it continued down to its dissolution in 1539, when it was second only to Glastonbury among English abbeys. Baldwin signally defeated the Bishop of Elmham, when he claimed authority over the monastery, and secured for it the special protection of the Pope;

and, since grants of land had long been pouring in, and the assessment for taxes had risen by as much again, was able to build a great abbey church, to which the remains of the Saint were translated with much pomp in 1095. A new refectory, a dormitory, a chapter-house, a house for the Abbot were added soon afterwards. The abbacy of Hugo (1156–1180) was a period of grave decline. A bull of Alexander III in 1172 established the independence of the Abbey by making it directly subject to Rome; but the lax and disorderly administration almost buried it in debt, and debased the standard of its life.

Abbot Samson.

It was at this juncture that, after a vacancy of two years, Samson became Abbot in 1182. There are one or two material facts known of him which Carlyle does not mention. He was author, or part author, of a treatise entitled *De Miraculis Sti Eadmundi*, written, says Mr. Arnold, 'in a massive and manly style'. He died at the age of seventy-seven on Dec. 30, 1211, his death being thus recorded by the unknown author of the *Annales Sti Eadmundi* (Arnold, Vol. II). 'On the 30th December, at St. Edmund's, died Samson of pious memory, the venerable Abbot of that place. Who, after he had prosperously ruled the Abbey committed to him for thirty years,—had enriched it with privileges, liberties, possessions, and spacious buildings, and restored the worship of the Church both internally and externally in the most ample manner, bidding his last farewell to his sons by whom the blessed man deserved to be blest for evermore, while they all were standing by, and gazing with awe at a death which was a cause for admiration, not for pity ('non miserabilem sed mirabilem'), in the fourth year of the Interdict, rested in peace.' As he died during the Interdict (1208–1214) his body was buried in unconsecrated earth. On Aug. 9, 1214, immediately after the Interdict was removed, the body was exhumed, and reburied in the chapter-house, after the Sacrist had opposed a motion to rebury it in the church (*Super Electione Hugonis*, ed. Arnold, II. 85). A coffin supposed to be his was discovered on the site of the Chapter House in 1903.

Jocelin of Brakelond.

The Preface to the Camden Society's edition of the Chronicle says: 'Jocelin de Brakelond, the writer, a native of St. Edmundsbury [see note to p. 36], dates his Chronicle from the year when the Flemings were taken prisoner without the town (alluding to the battle of Fornham in 1173), in which year, he tells us, that he took the habit at St. Edmund's, having made his noviciate under Samson, then Master of the Novices, to whose charge he had been specially committed [*Chronicle*, p. 3]. According to Bale [*Script. Illust.* 1559, p. 259] he studied at Cambridge; but for this we have not seen any authority. At the time of the election of Abbot Samson Jocelin was the Prior's chaplain; and within four months was promoted to be chaplain to the Abbot [*Chron.* p. 19], with whom he lived, to use his own language, day and night for six years [*Chron.* p. 27]. In 1198 and 1200 he did the honours of the Abbey as guest-master, perhaps still continuing one of the Abbot's chaplains; and was afterwards almoner, an office which he filled at the death of Samson in 1211. A contemporary monk of St. Edmund's has recorded the character of our Chronicler [in the story *De Henrico de Esexia,* incorporated in the Chronicle] in these simple words: "Dominus Jocelinus, elemosinarius noster, vir religionis eximie, potens in sermone et opere". Jocelin de Brakelond wrote on the miracles of St. Robert, the boy martyred by the Jews at St. Edmundsbury in 1181 [*Chron.* p. 12; but the work is not extant]. Bale, and later bibliographers, also ascribe to him the *Chronica Super Electione Hugonis Abbatis* [Samson's successor]; but the part which our author took on the occasion of that election is spoken of in the same Chronicle in such a manner as to leave no doubt that it was the work of another.' From the *Super Electione Hugonis* (*Memorials,* ed. Arnold, Vol. II.) we learn that Jocelin was a prominent member of the party supporting Robert of Gravelee the Sacrist. They wished the King to appoint the new Abbot out of a list of three names submitted by the Monastery, instead of confirming an election already made; which was also King John's wish. The Pope appointed a Commission to inquire into the case, and the Commission supported the majority of the monks who had elected Hugh. We learn further that Hugh, after his election, consulted Jocelin on the appointment of certain officials to keep custody of Abbey manors.

Bibliography.

The manuscript of the Chronicle is one among a large number of documents relating to the Abbey in a thick quarto volume, written on vellum, and known as the *Liber Albus.* The *Liber Albus* was once in the library of the Abbey; then it belonged to the family of Bacon of Redgrave, then to Bishop Stillingfleet of Worcester, and now to the British Museum, where it is preserved among the Harleian Manuscripts (Harl. MS. 1005). The writing of the Chronicle is of the end of the 13th or beginning of the 14th century, says the Camden Society's editor, 'and at first sight would seem to be executed by more than one scribe, but perhaps it is the same handwriting throughout'. The only other complete copy known to have existed was in one of the Cottonian MSS., and burnt in the fire of 1731 ; but there are two Bodleian MSS. containing the portion of the Chronicle on the examining of the relics in 1198, and a separate text in the Harleian MS. of the portion referring to the payment of dues, by the town to the monastery. The episode of the duel between Henry of Essex and Robert de Montford (*Chron.* pp. 50 ff.) is by another monk of St. Edmund's, who once accompanied Samson to Reading and heard the story from Henry himself, then in the cloister at that town. And at the end of the Chronicle a page is added with evidence of the lands held of St. Edmund's by the family of Cokefield, which became the subject of a suit mentioned by Jocelin. This short appendix purports to be written by William de Dice (Diss), then one of Abbot Samson's chaplains.

The Chronicle was first printed for the Camden Society in 1840, the editor being John Gage Rokewode, F.R.S. (1786–1842), a learned genealogist and Director of the Society of Antiquaries. The volume, a thin quarto of 171 pages, contains three facsimiles of portions of the MS., and its other merits are described by Carlyle on pp. 44, 45. Again, between 1890 and 1896 Thomas Arnold, a brother of Matthew Arnold, edited for the Rolls Series his *Memorials of St. Edmund's Abbey*, already referred to :—three volumes of documents and histories, the Chronicle of Jocelin, with notes and a revised text, being in the first. A translation by Thomas Edlyne Tomlins was published in 1844. Another translation with editor's preface, notes, and index, by Sir Ernest Clarke was published in 'The King's Classics' (Alexander Moring, the De La More Press) in 1903 ; and yet another by L. C. Jane, with similar editorial matter, in the same series (Chatto & Windus) in 1907. The quotations of the Chronicle in my notes are from the Camden Society's text, and the page references are to the same edition. I have added the sign (R) to the quotations from the notes by Rokewode.

The Government of an Abbey.

The following particulars of the customs of a mediaeval abbey are taken mainly from Abbot Gasquet's *English Monastic Life*:

The title *Abbas* (Father), borne by the superior of most Benedictine and Cistercian houses, indicates his paternal authority. He was the absolute governor of the monastery, and, as the Rule of St. Benedict says, 'is considered to represent the person of Christ, seeing that he is called by His name'. An elaborate code of observances was in force to secure for his person the most meticulous respect ; his commands were to be obeyed 'as if they came from God'. If he were a Benedictine, as at St. Edmundsbury, the Rule enjoined on him to consult certain of the senior members of the community on certain questions, but not to follow their advice. The officers of the Convent, from the Prior downwards, were appointed by him, and all acts whatsoever of business or government were his or by his authority. At his death the King was held to step into the place of the original founder. It was the King, accordingly, who took over the temporalities of the Abbey during the interregnum, who gave permission to the brethren of the community to exercise their right of electing his successor, and confirmed the choice they made ; the King's confirmation being ratified again by the proper Bishop or, in the case of privileged abbeys, by the Pope.

The Prior, the second Superior, was concerned above all with the discipline of the house. He was the Abbot's lieutenant in his absence and next in honour after him. He was a very important person, for the peace of the Abbey depended in a large degree on him. According to one rule he is 'the mother of the family ', standing between the Abbot and his sons, and he must manifest, says one writer, 'the patience of holy Job '. He was assisted by a sub-prior, and sometimes by third and fourth priors. Under the Abbot and the Prior a large number of subordinate officers or 'obedientiaries' *(obedientes,* holding an *obedientia)* carried on the work of the place, and were often charged with the care of the estates or dues assigned to them for the maintenance of their offices. The chief of them were usually in priest's orders. The following are named in Jocelin's Chronicle :

The Cantor or Precentor, who was also the Librarian, and the first of the obedientiaries in rank. In many monasteries he was also charged to teach the boys of the cloister-school to read.

Next in rank came the Sacrist. To him was assigned the up-keep of the Church and the charge of the relics, the sacred vessels, the ornaments and vestments. He got ready the Altars, the Choir, and the robes for the services, and the bread and wine for Mass ; he kept the cemetery ; and he looked to the lighting, not of the Church only, but of the entire house. He had usually four assistants—the sub-sacrist, and three others, one or more of them being named *vestiarius,* or keeper of the vestry, and one the treasurer. A great amount of business connected with building and repairs passed through the hands of the Sacrist or his subordinates.

The Cellarer was the caterer for the community both for food and fuel; and his duties continually took him abroad to granges, markets, and fairs. He was a supervisor of the Abbey servants, whom he alone, under the Abbot, could punish or dismiss. There was also a sub-cellarer.

The Infirmarian *(Infirmarius)* kept the Infirmary, and nursed the sick. He also conducted the operation of blood-letting (see note to p. 61).

The Almoner not only distributed the alms of the Abbey to the poor, but visited the aged and bedridden in their homes, and took general measures to relieve poverty on the domains. He had charge of any schools belonging to the Abbey, other than the cloister school for the young religious.

The Guest-master *(hospitarius)* was appointed to entertain the guests, rich and poor, whose coming and going were daily events in a great abbey. 'Hospites tamquam Christus suscipiantur' are the words of St. Benedict's Rule.

The Daily Routine.

The daily life of a Monastery may be said to have begun at midnight, when the monks, who had been three hours in their beds, were awakened, and repaired to the Church for the night office or Vigils. This was immediately followed by Matins, and Matins by Lauds, so called because it consisted mainly of three psalms (cxlviii, cxlix, cl) in which the word *laudate* frequently occurs. The term Matins (*matutinae horae, matutinum tempus*) was sometimes extended to Lauds, or even to Vigils, and might therefore include the entire service of three parts, which lasted about an hour and a half. Lauds having been sung, the monks retired once more to bed for some five hours of rest.

From 6 a.m. to 6 p.m. the day was divided into four quarters of three hours each, the names of the third, sixth, and ninth hours (terce, sext, and none) being applied also, in the case of each of them, to the whole quarter of the day to which it belonged. The day's devotions began with the Hour of Prime at half-past six or seven, immediately followed by the *missa familiaris* for the servants of the Convent, and the private masses at the different altars. After this the order of the chief events was as follows:

8 a.m. Breakfast.

8.30 a.m. Morning Mass and Hour of Terce.

9 a.m. The daily Chapter, or meeting of the whole community in the Chapter House, the Abbot presiding. After a reading from the Martyrology, and short prayer, the Abbot pronounced the words, 'Loquamur de Ordine nostro,' all strangers and novices retired, and matters of business and discipline were then discussed. It was at this meeting that any deed or charter affecting the Abbey was publicly sealed. The Chapter would generally last less than half an hour, and some time was left over, which was passed in conversation in the cloisters, and in discussions or 'Parliaments' between the officials.

10 a.m. High Mass.

11 a.m. Dinner, followed after a longer or shorter interval by the Office of None.

Afternoon. Recreation, an hour's sleep in the dormitory (in summer), and work.

5 p.m. in winter, or 6 in summer. Vespers, followed immediately by supper.

5.30 or 6.30. Collation, or public reading.

7 or 8. Compline (*Completorium*).

7.30 or 8.30. Bed.

BOOK II. CHAPTER I

PAGE 35. *confused Papers, printed and other.* This plainly means that Carlyle consulted manuscript sources. It seems likely that he read the text of Abbo's *Passio Sancti Eadmundi* (see note to p. 49 on *they raised his body*), which was first printed in Mr. Thomas Arnold's *Memorials* (1890). There is a manuscript copy of the *Passio* in the Cottonian collection, and another in the Lambeth Library. Other minor sources which afford a detail here and there for Book II are Lyttleton's *History of Henry II*, Dugdale's *Monasticon*, and Dr. Yates's *History of the Town and Abbey of St. Edmund's, Bury* (1805), who remarks on the need of a public subscription for propping the ruined Gateway of the Abbey (see p. 42).

black triangle. The 'triangle' is apparently the coat or gown, spreading at the skirts and tapering upwards.

many kinds are permissible . . . le genre ennuyeux. 'Tous les genres sont bons, hors le genre ennuyeux.' The saying is Voltaire's, and is quoted as his in Littré, without any further reference.

PAGE 36. *ninefold Stygian Marshes.* The Styx was one of the four rivers of Hades, and fringed it with a great marsh through which it ran in nine bends ('novies ... interfusa', Vergil, *Aeneid* vi. 439). The souls of the dead on entering Hades drank of another river — Lethe, the river of Forgetfulness.

Elysian Fields. See note to p. 129.

Universal Review. A reference, probably, to Jean Leclerc's *Bibliothèque universelle et historique* (1686–93), one of the earliest of the French literary reviews. Or it may refer to the earlier title of *The Times*, between 1785 and 1788 — *The Daily Universal Register*.

de Brakelonda. 'The Long Braklond, leading from the North Gate to the Market Place, and the Little Braklond, are ancient streets of St. Edmundsbury, mentioned in deeds 33 Edw. I.' (R.)

obedientia. See p. 289.

PAGE 37. *and, some say, means genius itself.* 'Das Erste und Letzte, was vom Genie gefordert wird, ist Wahrheitsliebe' — 'The first and last thing required of genius is the love of truth '.— Goethe.

Breviares. From L. *breviarium*, summary. A book with the offices for each day to be recited by the ordained.

says one of his contemporary Brother Monks. See Introductory Note, p. 287.

Dog-Latin. i. e. bad Latin; so 'dog Greek', and 'dog-logic'.

PAGE 38. *Putney Cromwell.* Thomas Cromwell, Earl of Essex (1485–1540), who as the King's Vicar-General under the Act of Supremacy executed the spoliation of the monasteries between 1534 and 1540, was the son of a man who carried on the trades of blacksmith, fuller, and innkeeper at Putney.

Harleian Collection. Robert Harley (1661–1724), Earl of Oxford, Queen Anne's Lord High Treasurer, was a friend of scholars, and founded the collection of MSS. known by his name in the British Museum. It was purchased by Government in 1754. It is rich in illuminated MSS., in early English poetry, in civil and ecclesiastical records, and in classical texts.

Mr. Rokewood. See Prefatory Note, p. 288.

Camden Society. William Camden (1551–1623), scholar and antiquary, is best known by his *Britannia* (1586), a survey of the British Isles. The Camden Society for the publication of early historical records was founded in his honour in 1838.

Spelman. Sir Henry Spelman (? 1564–1641), antiquary and ecclesiastical historian, published the first volume of his Glossary of Mediaeval Latin (*Archaeologus in modum Glossarii ad rem antiquam posteriorem, continentis Latina Barbara, peregrina, obsoleta . . . quae in Ecclesiasticis, profanis Scriptoribus, legibus, antiquis chartis et formulis occurrunt*) in 1626. The second volume, edited by Dugdale, appeared posthumously in 1664.

Ducange. Charles Dufresne, Sieur Du Cange (1610–68), one of the greatest of French scholars, published his *Glossarium ad Scriptores Mediae et Infimae Latinitatis* in three volumes in 1678. The work has been much enlarged since his time by Benedictine Scholars, and is now in ten volumes.

Muratori Annals. Luigi Antonio Muratori (1671–1759), librarian in Modena, compiled among other works a *corpus* of the sources for the history of Italy in twenty-eight folio volumes, published between 1723 and 1751, under the title: *Rerum italicarum Scriptores ab anno 500 ad annum 1500.*

Radcliffe Romances. Ann Radcliffe (1764–1823) was the authoress of several novels, chief among them *The Mysteries of Udolpho* (1794), which commanded an enormous public in their day. They are novels of mystery and intrigue, with mediaeval castles, secret chambers, Italian scenery, and strange and terrorizing monks and assassins to achieve the effect.

hair-cilices. Lat. *cilicium*, a hair-cloth, originally made of Cilician goats-hair, and worn by seamen and soldiers.

PAGE 39. *speculum.* A mirror.

camera lucida. Lat. = 'light chamber', a photographic apparatus for tracing an image of a distant object on paper. Cf. ' camera obscura '.

Gospel of Richard Arkwright. See note to p. 205.

Mastodon. 'Large extinct mammal like elephant, with nipple-shaped tubercles on crowns of molar teeth.' (Gk. μαστός, breast, and ὀδούς, ὀδόντος, tooth.) (*Concise Oxford Dictionary.*)

Megatherion. Extinct genus of a huge kind of sloth, the fossils of which are found in South America (Gk. μέγα, large, + θηρίον, animal).

Ichthyosaurus. 'Extinct marine animal with huge head,

tapering body, four paddles, and long tail.' (Gk. ἰχθύς, fish, + σαῦρος, lizard.) (*Concise Oxford Dictionary.*)

Rymer's Foedera. i. e. Thomas Rymer (1641–1713), Historiographer Royal to William III. His *Foedera,* a collection of the public conventions of Great Britain with other powers in twenty volumes, came out, in part posthumously, between 1704 and 1735. The latest edition, undertaken by the Record Commission, and incomplete, between 1816 and 1830.

PAGE 40. *Peel's Tariff.* See Introduction, p. xv.

Feretrum. In Latin the word means a bier; in med. Lat. a sarcophagus; also a Pyx, in which the sacrament was reserved.

to ransom him out of the Danube Jail. See pp. 94, 95. In *Chron.,* p. 34, Jocelin mentions that, as in the case of all other monasteries in the kingdom, 'our treasure was carried to London for the ransom of King Richard'. This was in 1193. Richard was arrested in Germany when returning from his Crusade, and held to ransom. He was first imprisoned by Leopold of Austria in the castle of Dürrenstein; then handed over to the Emperor Henry VI, who kept him in the stronghold of Trifels.

King John. The visit took place immediately after his coronation.

cramoisy. Crimson; It. *chermisì,* Arab. *qirmiz,* the Scarlet Grain insect.

for one of his retinue borrowed it of us. The *Chronicle* says (p. 85) that the King's servants borrowed the cloth from the sacrist without paying for it, and the King then offered it to the Saint.

thirteen sterlingii. Text, 'xiij sterlingos'. The word was first applied to a penny, and in later times to other coins. The original meaning is perhaps 'little star' or 'starling', with reference to a star or bird represented on the coin. The only coin in use at this period was the silver penny or *denarius;* but accounts were reckoned in *solidi* (shillings = 12 *denarii*) and *librae* (= 20 *solidi,* pounds), though no coins corresponded to these amounts. Mr. Joseph Jacobs in *The Jews of Angevin England,* Appendix, p. 316 f., has an elaborate calculation of the value of money at that time in comparison with its value when he was writing, and concludes that one *denarius* went as far as two shillings in 1885.

PAGE 41. *Minerva and other Presses.* A publishing firm established in Leadenhall Street about the year 1800, and famous for trashy and ultra-sentimental novels.

BOOK II. CHAPTER II

PAGE 42. *The Burg.* The original meaning is a fortress or walled town.

venerable ruins. 'The actual remains of the church, once 505 feet in length, and of the vast monastic buildings are very scanty. Chief amongst the actual existing ruins is the tower,

86 feet high, formerly the great gate of the cemetery. It stands exactly opposite to the spot where the great western door of the church was, and it is still in good preservation. . . . Somewhat farther to the north is the church of St. James, built as a parochial church by the monks in the twelfth century, and farther on again there still stands the beautiful decorated gateway, built in the period from 1327–40. . . . Within it the remains of the Abbot's house are not inconsiderable, but of the extensive western front, with its great central tower, and its two lower octagonal towers, which in size and beauty must have rivalled the front of Ely, nothing whatever is now left.'—Abbot Gasquet, *The Greater Abbeys of England*, p. 44. John Leland describes the place in its magnificence: 'The sun hath not shone on a goodlier abbey. . . . He that saw it would say, verily, that it was a city, so many gates are there in it, and some of brass, and so many towers, and a most stately church, upon which attend three others, also, standing gloriously in one and the same churchyard, all of passing fine and curious workmanship' (quoted by Gasquet, *loc. cit.*).

Dugdale and other Monasticons. Sir William Dugdale (1605–86), Garter King-at-arms, published the first volume of his *Monasticon Anglicanum* in 1655, the second in 1661, both volumes conjointly with Roger Dodsworth. The third, by Dugdale alone, came out in 1673. The standard edition is that in six volumes, edited chiefly by Sir Henry Ellis (1817–30). The work consists of charters of foundation, donations, &c. granted to the monasteries in England, and is a mine of information on the history, biography, and architecture of the Church before the Reformation.

gave St. Edmund his own gold crown. This is stated in Dugdale iii. 99, on the authority of John Brompton, who adds that thenceforth it was the custom of the English kings to offer their crowns at the shrine. If so, King John, coming fresh from his coronation, as described on p. 40, was doubtless expected to offer his.

carucates. As much land as can be ploughed in a year by one plough with the ordinary team of eight oxen; in modern English 'a plough-land'. The area varies with the quality of the soil.

PAGE 43. *Philosophy of History.* See note to p. 215.

Golgotha of true souls. i. e. the dead relics.

Missals. Mass-books (Lat. *missale*, from *missa*, mass).

A certain degree of soul, as Ben Jonson reminds us. . . . Mr. Percy Simpson has kindly given me the following references:—*Bartholomew Fair*, IV. ii: 'Talke of him to have a soule? 'heart, if hee have any more than a thing giuen him in stead of salt, onely to keepe him from stinking, I'le be hang'd afore my time, presently. *The Diuell is an Asse*, I. vi:

That you are the wife
To so much blasted flesh, as scarce hath soule,
In stead of salt, to keepe it sweete, I thinke,
Will aske no witnesses, to proue.

Cf. Cicero, *De Natura Deorum*, ii, § 160 'Sus vero quid habet practer escam? cui quidem, ne putresceret, animam ipsam pro sale datam dicit esse Chrysippus'.

PAGE 44. *For twenty generations.* Reckoning, presumably, from the first charter in 945 (see p. 285) to the dissolution in 1539.

men of many humours. The word is used in the same sense as in the title of Jonson's play *Every Man in his Humour*, as meaning a man's physical and mental qualities, determined by the predominance in him of one of the four fluids of the body,—blood, phlegm, choler, melancholy.

PAGE 45. *Chartularies.* Lat. *cartularium*, diminutive of *c(h)arta*, collection of records, register.

Doctrines of the Constitution. Referring, probably, to the theory of the Constitution (as a balance of political powers or principles) advanced in Sir William Blackstone's *Commentaries on the Laws of England* (1765-69), for many years the authoritative exposition of the subject.

Dryasdust. 'Dr. Jonas Dryasdust' is a fictitious person to whom Sir Walter Scott pretends to dedicate some of his novels, e. g. *Ivanhoe, Fortunes of Nigel*. The name signifies a dull and plodding scholar.

BOOK II. CHAPTER III

PAGE 45. *Beodricsworth.* According to Hermannus the Archdeacon (*De miraculis Sti Eadmundi* in *Memorials*, ed. Arnold, vol. i) this Beodric was of the blood-royal of East Anglia. The change in the name of the town first occurs in the charters of Edward the Confessor.

Fornham St. Genevieve. Hardly four miles north of St. Edmundsbury. There is another hamlet close by called Fornham St. Martin. The river Lark flows by the hill on which the town of Bury stands on its course to the Ouse and the North Sea, and is joined at this point by the Linnet, which comes from the West close under the southern foot of the hill, past the site of the Monastery. Robert de Beaumont, Earl of Leicester, was in league with the King's three sons Henry, Richard, and Geoffrey, supported by the Kings of France and Scotland and the Count of Flanders, and by several English noblemen, in the attempt to wrest from their father a large portion of his power and territory. Leicester was accompanied on the invasion and at the battle by his Countess. He was met by a superior army under Richard de Lucy, the Justiciary, and Humphrey de Bohun, the Constable. A full account will be found in Miss Kate Norgate's *England under the Angevin Kings*, ii. 150 f. Carlyle has taken several particulars, including that of the ring of bodies, from Rokewode's notes.

PAGE 46. *posse comitatus.* *Posse*, 'to be able', is med. Lat. for 'power', = the force of the county, or body of men over fifteen years of age whom the Sheriff may summon to suppress riot or invasion.

PAGE 47. '*Infinite admiration*', &c. : ' Worship, that is, admire without limit '—*Heroes*, i.

femoralia. Thigh-armour; also breeches.

'*bushing*'. The verb means to set ground with bushes to frustrate net-poaching.

PAGE 48. *Farmer's Friend.* See note to p. 168, on the Duke of Buckingham and Chandos.

'*walked humbly with God*'. Micah vi. 8.

Howel and James. Warehousemen, 9 Regent Street (*Post Office Directory*, 1843).

do what he liked with his own. See note to p. 5.

'*five points*'. See Introduction, p. xli.

PAGE 49. *They raised his body.* Abbo says (*Passio*, x–xiv) that, when the Danes had departed, the Christians emerged from their hiding-places, and searched for the head (see pp. 49, 50) 'in great numbers' ('plurima multitudine'); and, having found it, brought it to Hoxne ' with tears of gladness ' ('profusis prae gaudio lacrimarum imbribus ').

Temple of the Highest. See note to p. 257.

' *Schnüspel the Distinguished Novelist*'. Probably an allusion to Charles Dickens's visit to America in 1842.

' *all men, especially all women, are born worshippers*'. This is, perhaps, not a quotation, but the summary of a passage in the Essay on *Goethe's Works*, beginning: ' Women are born worshippers '. . . .

gilt-gingerbread phenomena. In former times gingerbread was frequently gilded.

These be thy Gods. Exodus xxxii. 4.

Hoxne. This village is two miles from Ipswich.

PAGE 50. *Advocatus Diaboli.* The process of canonization resembles a prolonged law-suit ; in which the claims of the candidate are severely tested, and are upheld or impugned before a sort of Jury, chosen from the College of Rites at Rome, by counsel on either side. The counsel whose task it is to put forward all the objections to the proposed canonization is termed 'Advocatus Diaboli', his opponent is the 'Advocatus Dei '.

loculus. Any shrine or consecrated receptacle in which the body of a dead person is deposited.

feretrum. See note to p. 40.

a wooden chapel, a stone temple. See p. 285.

katalla = movable goods, chattels. *Chron.* p. 33 'Data est ergo licentia, ut eos (i. e. the Jews) eiceret, ita tamen quod haberent omnia katalla '.

PAGE 51. *Like a Fakeer.* From the Arabic *faqir*, poor man, = religious mendicant or devotee, Mohammedan or Hindu.

pyramid. Carlyle would derive it from the Greek $\pi\hat{v}\rho$ = fire, the Gk. form being πυραμίς; which is an old explanation. The word is, however, of Egyptian origin.

Cheops Pyramids or Sakhara clay ones. Kinglake's *Eöthen,* xix. The Great Pyramid, the burying-place of Cheops, second King of the Fourth Dynasty (about 3733–3666) is at Gizeh or Giza, near Memphis. There are eleven pyramids at Sakhara (usually Sakkara or Sakara), fifteen miles south-west of Cairo, as well as a vast necropolis. 'The usual construction of pyramids is a mass of masonry composed of horizontal layers of rough-hewn blocks, with a small amount of mortar ; and this mass in the later forms became more and more rubbly, until in the Sixth Dynasty it was merely a cellular system of retaining walls of rough stone and mud, filled up with loose chips, and in the Twelfth Dynasty the bulk was of mud bricks ' (*Encycl. Brit., sub* 'Pyramid '). Of the ruined Sakkara pyramids several are of brick, the largest of the kind being the Pyramid of Teta.

BOOK II. CHAPTER IV

PAGE 51. *a Bird-of-Paradise . . . with outspread wings.* Before the bird was known in Europe it was reported to float perpetually in the air, being without feet, and to live only on dew or scent. The fable that it lacked feet is explained by the custom among the Papuans of cutting off its legs, when they kill it, before disposing of the body. A passage in Lydekker's *Royal Natural History* mentions that Linnaeus first described the bird from a skin prepared in this manner by the Papuans. Cf. Tennyson, *Day Dream,* 275 :

> Like long-tail'd birds of Paradise,
> That float thro' Heaven, and cannot light.

Talamus. Gk. θάλαμος, chamber.

PAGE 52. *crying continually, Give, give.* Proverbs xxx. 15.

Camera, i. e. the Abbot's House.

PAGE 53. *William the Sacristan,* or Sacrist, see p. 289. Afterwards a rival candidate for the Abbacy. He was removed from his office on the ground of bad conduct by Samson when Abbot.

Benedict the Jew. 'Benedicto, iudeo de Norwico' (i. e. Norwich)—*Chron.* p. 2. His name occurs in the Pipe Rolls for Norfolk and Suffolk under the year 1171, when he was fined for taking certain sacred vestments in pawn (R).

Cellararius. See p. 289.

beleagured Jews who hanged themselves in York Castle. The Jews occupied an extraordinary position at this time ; they were the King's 'chattels', exempt from any jurisdiction but his, and living apart from the rest of the community in their quarters or Jewries. The prejudice of the Church against usury made them monopolists of the trade of money-lending, and they became ' the

masters of a large portion of the wealth of the realm', so that
without their loans wars, ventures in trade, and even the building
of churches could not be undertaken. The kings reined in the
popular hatred against them as well as they could, but it broke
loose in 1190 in a series of massacres, one at St. Edmundsbury, and
the worst at York. 'The principal Jews of that city, in dread of
a popular attack, had sought and obtained shelter in one of the
towers of the castle, under the protection of its constable and the
sheriff of Yorkshire. Once there, they refused to give it up again;
whereupon the constable and sheriff called out all the forces of
city and shire to dislodge them. After twenty-four hours' siege
the Jews offered to ransom themselves by a heavy fine; but the
blood of the citizens was up, and they rejected the offer. The
Jews resolved to die by their own hands; the women and children
were slaughtered by their husbands and fathers, who flung the
corpses over the battlements, or piled them up in the tower, which
they fired. Nearly five hundred Jews perished in the massacre or
the flames.'—Miss Kate Norgate, *England under the Angevin Kings*,
ii. 289. Carlyle may have read in William of Newbury (ed.
Howlett, i. 312), where he describes the massacre, that one of the
two chief Jews of York was named Benedict.

usances. A usance is a commercial term, meaning the time
allowed for the payment of foreign bills of exchange.

grinder-teeth pulled out. This happened in the case of a Jew
of Bristol in 1210, when King John was levying a heavy tallage on
the Jews, and is described in Holinshed's *Chronicle, ad. loc.* The
victim had eight teeth, and resisted until only one was left.

PAGE 54. *Eadmer's Anselm.* See note to p. 222.

PAGE 55. *sent me once to Acre in Norfolk.* 'At Castle Acre
William Earl Warren founded a Priory as a cell to the Cluniac Monks
of St. Pancras, Lewes. At West Acre was a Priory of Austin Canons.
It was doubtless to one of these Priories that Samson was sent for
correction' (R). The monks of St. Edmund were Benedictines,
and the Cluniacs a stricter derivation from that order; so that
Castle Acre is the likelier place (Clarke). It appears that Samson
was twice imprisoned at Acre. First, in the time of the Anti-
Popes in 1161, because, being sent to Rome to make good the
claim of the Abbey to the vacant benefice at Woolpit, he accomplished the business too slowly, so that Woolpit was conferred
by the King on Geoffrey Ridell (afterwards Archdeacon of Canterbury, and a thorn in the side of Becket there, and then Bishop of
Ely) during his absence. (See pp. 63-6.) The second imprisonment occurred during Jocelin's noviciate for withstanding the
Abbot to the face.

The Hinghams. Hugo and Roger de Hingham or Hengeham
are again mentioned, at *Chron.* p. 36, as brothers. Roger accompanied Samson on his visit to Rome. A Richard de Hengeham
intrudes into the Church at the inspection of St. Edmund's body

'without the Abbot's leave' (see p. 110). 'Robert' is probably a mistake ; the text says : ' Dionysius et H. et R. de Hingham '.

men or mud-elements. The allusion is to the mud-gods, representing the Nether Powers, in Scandinavian Mythology. See p. 20, and note on *Mud-giants.*

BOOK II.   CHAPTER V

PAGE 56. *Ranulf de Glanvill, Justiciarius of England.* As Justiciar (1180-9) was the King's right-hand man. Author of the classical treatise *De legibus et consuetudinibus regni.* Took the Cross and died at the siege of Acre in 1190. 'Justiciar' is the title applied to the Chief Minister of the Norman and Angevin Kings, who presided under the King in the Court of Exchequer and was in supreme charge of the business afterwards conducted in the Courts of Common Pleas and of King's Bench. He represented the King during his absence from England, and the office became so important as almost to threaten the monarchy, so that after the fall of Hubert de Burgh (1231) it was never again entrusted to a single man, but put into commission.

Scaccarium. The word means a chess-board (med. Lat. pl. *scacci,* chess). The chamber of the Exchequer was so called from the pattern on the cloth covering the table on which the money was counted. Each square on the cloth had a numerical value, beginning with pence and ending with thousands of pounds. The barons and clerks of the court sat round the table, with the Sheriff, whose accounts were being rendered, at one end. On the squares of the cloth were counters, indicating the sum due from the Sheriff, and as he paid these counters were removed, or those not removed indicated by how much he was in arrears. See Inderwick, *The King's Peace,* 53 f.

pitantia. The original meaning is 'a small amount', O.F. *pitance,* from *pitet,* pity, Lat. *pietas.*

matins, nones, vespers. See p. 290.

Mysteries. Dramas dealing with biblical history. The term is often convertible with that of 'miracle-plays', i.e. dramas dealing with the legends of saints. They were first performed only in Church, afterwards in the streets. The performances are recorded as early as 1110, and lingered on after the Reformation.

PAGE 57. *as Friar Bacon's Brass Head remarked.* Roger Bacon (1214 ?-1294) is said to have made a brass head, believing that if he heard it speak, he would prosper, and if not, would fail. It spoke three times while Bacon was asleep, saying, 'Time was ', 'Time is ', and ' Time 's past '; whereupon it fell to the ground, and was shattered. See Byron, *Don Juan,* i. 217.

We are such stuff, &c. *The Tempest,* II, i. 156.

Londoners pretending . . . that they are exempt from toll. Each of the kings from Henry I to John granted London a charter to this effect. Samson, on behalf of the monastery, asserted that the King's Charter applied only to the King's own lordships, and that the right of taking toll within their demesnes was granted inalienably to the monks of St. Edmund by Edward the Confessor; but in the end he virtually ceded the point, on the mediation of the Bishop of London, by agreeing, if the Londoners paid the toll, to pay it them back.

Watch and ward. Watch by night, ward by day.

wager of battle. The right of invoking the ordeal of battle, both in civil and in criminal suits was introduced by William I. It was denounced by a decree of the Lateran Council in 1215, and Ranulf de Glanvil, Henry II's Justiciar, did his best to defeat it by his institution of the Great Assize, which offered to litigants a surer method of justice by the oaths of a jury appointed to testify to the truth of the case. Wager of battle continued to be the law of the land, however, and to be occasionally carried into effect, though generally disused, until the year 1818. In that year one Thornton, accused on apparently good grounds of murder, claimed the ordeal, and, on his accuser crying craven, was acquitted. This monstrous piece of solecism led to the abolition of the practice by statute. All the burgesses within the walls of St. Edmundsbury were exempt from the custom of the ordeal, and cleared or condemned by the oaths of the burgesses. Ketel dwelt without the walls, and was considered to be an innocent man. He was defeated in the duel, however, and hanged (*Chron.* p. 74), to the indignation of the burgesses.

vetulae exibant, &c. 'The old women came out with their distaffs, threatening and reviling.'

PAGE 58. *Jerusalem was taken,* &c. It was taken by the Crusaders under Godfrey of Bouillon in July 1099; and by Saladin in October 1187. Richard twice led his army to within eight miles of Jerusalem, once on the last day of 1191, and again in June 1192. According to a legend of the thirteenth century (Joinville, c. 108), one of the King's knights came up to him on this last occasion crying, 'Sire, sire, come hither, and I will show you Jerusalem'. 'But when the King heard these words he cast his coat of arms before his eyes. And he wept tears as he called upon our Lord : " Fair Lord God, I pray thee not to let me see Thy Holy City, if so be that I may not deliver it out of the hands of Thy enemies ".'

aver-pennies and avragiums. The *avragium* or *averagium* was the duty, owed by the tenant to his lord, of carting crops or anything else for a certain number of days in the year. The *averpenny* was a tribute into which this duty was commuted.

fodercorns. The right of a feudal lord to be supplied by his tenants with fodder for his horses, or the fodder so supplied.

PAGE 59. *Gurth, thrall of Cedric.* Characters from Scott's *Ivanhoe.* See p. 191.

Robin Hood, William Scarlet. Robin Hood, according to one version of the legend, lived as an outlaw in Sherwood Forest at the time when Jocelin wrote. Among his companions were Little John, William Scadlock (or Scarlet), and George Green the pinder (pound-keeper) of Wakefield.

Lincoln coats. Lincoln at one time dyed the best green of all England. Green was the colour of the Forester's dress.

Wilhelmus Conquestor burnt the country. See note to p. 192.

Saint Mungo, i. e. St. Kentigern, the Apostle of Cumbria in the sixth century, who lived and was buried at Glasgow. 'Mungo', in the Cumbrian tongue, meant 'dear friend', and was a name given affectionately to the Saint at St. Serf's monastery, where he spent his boyhood.

James Watt. The elaborator of the steam-engine (1736–1819). His famous Soho Engineering Works in Birmingham, carried on in partnership with Matthew Boulton (1775–1800), were the chief means of the industrial revolution.

wool 'cottons'. 'Cotton' in this sense is obsolete. It was probably derived from 'cotton' in the ordinary sense, the idea being that of down or nap. Applied to a woollen fabric of the nature of frieze.—*N. E. D.*

Lither-pool. Dr. Henry Bradley has kindly given me the following note: 'The evidence of early forms shows that Liverpool is older than Litherpool, though the corruption is of quite early date. The name originally denoted a pool (figured in early maps) formed by an overflow from the Mersey. My own view is that the original name was Welsh *llifair* = overflow, " pool " being added afterwards. Professor Wyld, in his book on Lancashire place-names, explains Liverpool as *Lēofheres-pol*, but I do not think that probable.'

Tempus ferax, Tempes edax rerum. Ovid, *Met.* xv. 234 = 'Time the bearer, Time the devourer of things.'

BOOK II. CHAPTER VI

PAGE 60. *Joe Mantons.* See note to p. 124.

an air-image fearfully emblematic. 'All visible things are emblems ; what thou seest is not there on its own account ; strictly taken is not there at all ; Matter exists only spiritually, and to represent some Idea, and *body* it forth. . . . What is Man, and his whole terrestrial life . . . but a visible garment for that divine Me of his ? '—*Sartor,* I. xi.

'pleasure of virtue'. See note to p. 123.

real Hell of a man. See p. 131.

copperas banker's ink. See note to p. 165.

PAGE 61. *reflect with Ben Jonson.* See note to p. 43.

Pitanceria. This was the room of the Pitantiarius, whose

office it was to distribute the portions or 'pittances' of food. See note to p. 56.

tacenda, i. e. 'things of which one should not speak '.

tempora minutionis. Usually four times a year—in March, April, September, October. The Infirmarius conducted the operation, and convalescence lasted four days, during which the rules of observance were considerably relaxed.

a certain Canterbury Monk. The incident is related in Eadmer's *Historia Novorum in Anglia*, ed. Rule, Rolls Series, pp. 13, 14.

clanculo, i. e. 'secretly '.

PAGE 62. *Barrator.* 'Barrator' means one who stirs up lawsuits, from O.F. *bareter*, to cheat. Sir Henry Clarke quotes from several sources to show that the men of Norfolk were famed for litigiousness. An Act was passed in 1455 to check this propensity in 'the City of Norwich and the Counties of Norfolk and Suffolk '.

has been in trouble. See note to p. 55.

PAGE 63. *preach in three languages.* See p. 61, *supra*.

like Dr. Caius, 'has had losses '. Dr. Caius is the French physician in *The Merry Wives of Windsor*. But Dogberry is the 'fellow who hath had losses' (*Much Ado*, IV. ii. 90).

Woolpit. See note to p. 55.

in the time of the Schism. Alexander III, elected Pope in September 1159, was obliged to leave Italy in 1162 on account of the power of the Anti-pope Octavian, and did not return until after his death in 1164. The bull promising St. Edmund's Abbey the reversion of Woolpit is dated January 1161.

pretended to be Scotch. Scotland sided with Octavian, England with Alexander.

PAGE 64. '*Ride, ride Rome*', &c. Arnold interprets this: 'I am riding to Rome and turning from Canterbury ', i. e. I give no allegiance to Alexander.

PAGE 65. *joint keepers of the Shrine*, i. e. officials subordinate to the Sacrist. See p. 289.

BOOK II. CHAPTER VII

PAGE 66. *Dionysius' ear.* 'On the borders of the *Latomia* [i. e. quarry] *del Paradiso* [at Syracuse] is the *Orecchio di Dionisio*, a vast excavation, in shape resembling an ear, partly no doubt natural, but certainly to a great extent artificial, with very curious acoustic properties. There is a tradition regarding it, dating, however, no further back than the sixteenth century, that it was excavated by the tyrant as a prison, and was so planned that the smallest whisper uttered in it could be heard in a chamber high in the innermost wall, where he is supposed to have sat listening to the conversation of his victims.'—Murray's *Handbook to Sicily*.

Virgil's Horn-Gate of Dreams. Vergil (*Aeneid* vi. 893) represents the true dreams as issuing through a gate of horn, and the false through a gate of ivory.

Ording. Abbot 1148–56.

as we read in Fables. See Phaedrus i. 2. The serpent (*coluber, hydra*; not the stork, as is usual in English books) is given to the frogs as a king, and devours them. This was also the version in the mediaeval paraphrases of Aesop and Phaedrus which went under the name of Romulus and are collected in *Les fabulistes latins*, vol. ii, by M. Léopold Hervieux (Paris, 1894).

PAGE 67. *Norfolk barrators.* See p. 62, and note.

' *So many men, so many minds* '. 'Quot homines, tot sententiae,' Terence, *Phormio*, ii. 4. 14.

Candlemas. The Feast of the Purification of the Blessed Virgin Mary, February 2.

sochemanni. Or 'socmanni', i. e. socage tenants, the lowest form of freehold. The tenant held his land in fee simple in return for services of an economic kind, like the payment of rent or a definite amount of agricultural work. A class of freemen of higher standing than the *ceorl* were called 'sokemen' at the close of the Anglo-Saxon period. The word *soc* in O.E. = jurisdiction or a franchise district, and the principal distinction between sokemen and villeins was that the former might obtain legal protection in the Courts.

PAGE 68. *A mountain tumbling*, &c. Horace, *Ars Poetica* 139 ' Parturiunt montes, nascetur ridiculus mus ' = 'They are big with mountains, and bear a mouse ', of those who promise great things, and perform little. The line is a translation of the Greek proverb : ὤδινεν ὄρος, εἶτα μῦν ἀπέτεκεν.

BOOK II. CHAPTER VIII

PAGE 69. *limbo.* From Lat. *limbus*, an edge, or border ; applied to a region on the border of hell reserved for unbaptized children and the just who died before Christ's coming. Hence a prison or place of duress.

a servant of servants. i. e. holding a subordinate office.

PAGE 71. *Fleam-dike and Devil's-dike.* There were several great ramparts in South Cambridgeshire, built probably before the Roman invasion across the one stretch of land where the district that was afterwards East Anglia could be easily approached from the West. The dykes consisted of a broad ditch backed by a high rampart. The Devil's Ditch, the most easterly, and the largest, but not the longest, was the boundary of the jurisdiction of St. Edmund's Abbey. It runs from north-west to south-east from the fens across Newmarket Heath to near Wood Ditton (Ditch Town). Seven miles to the west of it, and more or less parallel, was the Fleam or Balsham Ditch from Fen Ditton to Balsham. They were the boundary defences of the East Anglians against the Mercians. (C. C. Babington, *Ancient Cambridgeshire*.) The meaning of 'Fleam' is 'Fleming', and the name points to very early settlements from Flanders.

Waltham, i. e. Bishop's Waltham in Hampshire.

alb. A variety of surplice, but with close sleeves.

pallium. 'A woollen vestment worn by the Pope and conferred by him on Archbishops, this being a necessary preliminary to the special functions of their office. It is now a narrow band passing over the shoulders, with short lappets before and behind, and ornamented with crosses.'—*N. E. D.*

'*shall veil my feet*'. This is interpreted by Jocelin, ad loc.: 'he veiled the feet of the Holy Martyr when he completed the towers of the Church' (see pp. 101, 106, 107).

PAGE 72. *through the blankets of the old Night. Macbeth* I. v. 54.

Bishop of Winchester. Richard Toclive, Bishop 1173-78.

Geoffrey the Chancellor. Afterwards Archbishop of York. He quarrelled with King John, fled the kingdom, and died in Normandy in 1212.

Rosamond. Rosamond de Clifford, mistress of Henry II, or perhaps his wife by a left-handed marriage. She is said to have been poisoned by Queen Eleanor in the King's absence. See Miss Strickland's *Lives of the Queens of England.*

Tickle me, Toby, &c. A popular proverb, of which there are many versions.

PAGE 73. *law-wards.* See note to p. 174.

Prior of St. Faith's. A Benedictine Priory at Horsham in Norfolk.

PAGE 74. '*By God's eyes*', *said the King*, &c. Henry's remark is not correctly translated. He said: 'Per oculos Dei, iste electus videtur sibi dignus abbatie custodiende'; i. e. 'By God's eyes, that Abbot Elect thinks himself worthy to govern the Abbey'.

'*if we are ourselves valets*', &c. The saying 'Il n'y a point de héros pour un valet de chambre' is attributed to a Prince de Condé. Carlyle may have Hegel's observation in mind: 'Not because the master is no hero, but because the valet is a valet.'

BOOK II. CHAPTER IX

PAGE 75. *sockmen.* See note to p. 67.

PAGE 76. *allowed to possess not above two shillings.* See p. 61.

Chandos day-drudges. See note to p. 168.

PAGE 77. *Tenpound Franchisers.* See note to p. 17.

without taxes on knowledge. The reproach of being a 'tax on knowledge' was levied at the Newspaper Duty, first imposed in 1712, and raised in 1815 to 4*d.* a sheet, so that 7*d.* was the price of a newspaper. It did not apply to any publication not containing news, but all periodicals suffered at the same time under the tax on paper. In 1836 Spring Rice, the Whig Chancellor of the

Exchequer, reduced the paper tax, and fixed the Newspaper Duty at 1*d*. a sheet. The duty was finally abolished in 1855, and the paper tax in 1861.

Mr. Sale informs me, i. e. George Sale (1690–1736) in the Introduction to his famous translation of the *Koran* (1734).

to gauge ale-barrels in the Burgh of Dumfries. See note to p. 255.

PAGE 78. *Iliad in a nut-shell.* ' In nuce Ilias '—Latin proverb.

PAGE 79. *vadium et plegium.* Either word means a pledge or pawn.

the Pope appoints him Justiciary, i. e. in the Ecclesiastical Courts ; in November 1182.

his new Circuit Judges. The practice of sending the Judges of the King's Court from place to place in order to administer justice is first found under Henry I. Henry II did it occasionally in the first years of his reign, and under the Assize of Clarendon in 1166 it became a regular part of the routine of government.

official Osbert. Chron., p. 25. Osbert, son of Hervey, was an Under-Sheriff.

PAGE 80. *Mrs. Glass.* Hannah Glass (fl. 1747) wrote a book on cookery.

list-shoes. List is the selvage or border of cloth, usually of different and coarser make than the body of the cloth ; hence = the material of which such selvage is made. *N. E. D.* quotes *Jane Eyre*, ' her quiet tread muffled in a list slipper '.

BOOK II. CHAPTER X

PAGE 82. *pouncing on him like obscene harpies.* Vergil's ' obscenae volucres ' (*Aeneid* iii. 241). They were predatory monsters, daughters of Poseidon, with claws for hands and feet, the winged bodies of griffins, and the faces of maidens. They were sent by the gods to torment Phineus, on whose food they swooped as often as he made to touch it, carrying off part, and befouling the other part.

the ' eye of the master '. Cf. Aristotle, *Oeconomica* i. 6. 4 καὶ τὸ τοῦ Πέρσου . . . ἀπόφθεγμα εὖ ἂν ἔχοι· ὁ μὲν γὰρ ἐρωτηθεὶς τί μάλιστα ἵππον πιαίνει, " ὁ τοῦ δεσπότου ὀφθαλμὸς " ἔφη ('He would do well to remember the saying of the Persian, who, being asked what most fattens the horse, replied, " The eye of the master "').

The Lakenheath eels. See p. 58.

The penny of reap-silver. See p. 57.

PAGE 83. ' *Saevit ut Lupus* '. See p. 71.

Bannaleuca. Or *banleuca*, or *bannum leugae*, F. *banlieue.* The area within the jurisdiction of the Monastery. *Bannum* = an area of jurisdiction. *Leuga* or *leuca* means a league. It stands in this expression for the usual extent of the area. There was a massacre of Jews at St. Edmund's on Palm Sunday 1190. The expulsion applied to the survivors of the massacre immediately after it took place. See extract from the Chronicle of John de Taxster quoted by R. on p. 123 of his edition.

Samson hastes not, &c. Goethe's 'ohne Hast, aber ohne Rast'.

PAGE 84. *Ranulf de Glanville*. See note to p. 56.

BOOK II. CHAPTER XI

PAGE 84. *paltenerius*. Or 'paltonarius'; O.F. *pautonnier*, M.E. *pautoner*; = proud, harsh.

PAGE 85. *setting fire to the public*. Cf. p. 80.

Elmswell. See p. 101.

PAGE 86. *lodged Angels unawares*. Heb. xiii. 2.

'*a kinless loon*'. Said of the judges put into office in Scotland after the battle of Worcester. See Carlyle's *Cromwell*, 'Everyman's' Edition, ii. 281.

PAGE 87. '*Many sons I have*', &c. Ecclesiasticus vii. 24, 'Hast thou daughters; show not thyself cheerful toward them'. The *Chronicle* says: 'Filie tibi sunt multe; vultum propicium ne ostendas eis.'

PAGE 89. *Gentle Shepherd, tell me what*. This is after a line, 'Gentle shepherd, tell me where,' in a song by Dr. Samuel Howard (1710-1782), a London organist and song-composer.

BOOK II. CHAPTER XII

PAGE 89. *Double, double*, &c. *Macbeth*, IV. i.

PAGE 90. *subsannatio*. V. *subsannare*, to deride.

barrator and paltener. See notes to p. 62 and p. 84.

limbo. See notes to p. 69.

PAGE 91. '*I would have taken vengeance*', &c. Cicero, *Tusculanae Disputationes*, iv. 36. 78: Quo te modo accepissem, nisi iratus essem?'

PAGE 92. *ten knights'-fees*. Fee (med. Lat. *feodum, feudum*) = 'an estate in land (in England always an heritable estate) held on condition of homage and service to a superior lord, by whom it is granted and in whom the ownership remains; a fief'.—*N. E. D.* A 'knight's fee' usually = 'the amount of land for which the services of an armed knight were due to the sovereign' (ibid.). But the sense here is the rarer one of 'payment' or 'service'—the services of ten knights. Each of the fifty knights who held their lands of the Abbey was bound to render certain aids and services, or to pay a sum of money every year in commutation. But ten of them pleaded that they were exempt from the charge on the ground that the service they were bound to was to help the others to do theirs. Samson afterwards carried the matter to the King's Court and exacted full service from all fifty (1196). See *Chron.*, p. 48 f.

my Lord of Clare. Richard, Earl of Clare. 'The honour of

Clare was composed chiefly of the great possessions in Suffolk and Essex of Aelfric, son of Withgar or Wisgar. (Liber Domesday).' (R.) Aelfric had been steward for Queen Emma, mother of Edward the Confessor, of eight and a half hundreds in Suffolk, of which the hundred of Risebridge was one. Edward, resenting his mother's harshness to him when a boy, seized her lands after his accession, and in the year 1044 conferred the eight and a half hundreds on St. Edmund's Abbey, with all the royal rights thereto appertaining. The district, which had been in Aelfric's stewardship only, became known as the Liberty of St. Edmund. See notes by Sir Ernest Clarke on pp. 238, 241 of his translation.

a Rowland for his Oliver. Roland was a legendary nephew of Charlemagne, and celebrated in the *Chanson de Roland* and many other romances, frequently together with his comrade, Oliver. So Hall, *Chronicle, Henry VI*: ' To have a Rowland to resist an Oliver: he sent solempne ambassadors to the Kyng of Englande.' To give a Roland for an Oliver is to give like for like, or as good as one gets.

Earl Alberic. Alberic de Vere, one of the knights of St. Edmund's, first Vere, Earl of Oxford.

infeft. The past participle of the verb ' to infeft ', a variant of ' enfeoff ', ' invest with heritable property '.

the Banner of St. Edmund. There is a picture of this banner in the metrical Life of St. Edmund by John Lydgate (Harleian MS. 2278). Adam and Eve are standing on either side of the tree of knowledge; the devil, with a serpent's body, is curled round the tree; above the tree, a lamb carrying a cross (Clarke).

Roger Earl Bigot. Or Bigod. He was son of Hugh Bigod, first Earl of Norfolk, who rebelled against Stephen, and joined the Coalition against Henry II in 1173. Roger was for a time Justiciar under Richard, and joined the Barons against John in 1215.

duly seised. The usual spelling of the verb is ' seize ', to put in possession of a feudal holding; also to take possession; hence the commoner meaning of the verb; O.F. *saisir*, med. Lat. *sacire*, cognate with Teutonic *satzan*, to set. The corresponding substantive in the sense of ' possession ' is ' seisin '; as in the phrase ' to give or take seisin ' of a property.

Thomas de Mendham. Of Mendham Hall in Suffolk, and Constable of the Monastery (R).

PAGE 93. *Sochemanni.* See note to p. 67.

BOOK II. CHAPTER XIII.

PAGE 94. *Justice Errant.* See note to p. 79.

that the Commonweal take no damage. The allusion is to the formula by which the Senate extended the authority of the Consuls in time of public danger, and proclaimed martial law: ' Videant Consules ne quid respublica detrimenti capiat.'

the siege of Windleshora. Or 'Wendles ore', the *ora*, or border, of the Wendels, a name which, according to Skeat, is akin to Vandals. (Johnston, *Place-Names of England and Wales.*) Early in 1193 John, on the news of Richard's capture in Germany, proclaimed that the King was dead; but the Justiciars resisted him, and laid siege to the castles in his hands, Windsor among them. The siege was ended after a few weeks by a truce concluded in May, under which the Castle was given into the custody of Eleanor, the Queen-Mother. Samson's attitude towards John, when he became King, may be inferred from the fact that in 1205 there was a great meeting of the Barons opposed to the King at St. Edmund's Abbey, and in 1214 they again met here, and swore upon the shrine to obtain the confirmation of the Charter of Henry I (Dugdale, iii. 104).

de arduis regni. A phrase common in Parliamentary writs.

in tapinagio. Secretly, F. *en tapinois.* Ducange supposes that word may derive from Gk. ταπεινός, lowly, not rising much above the ground; or from the Lat. *talpa*, a mole.

PAGE 95. *Justiciarii ad Scaccarium.* Judges of the Court of Exchequer. The term *iusticiarius* was applied to all the Judges, the Justiciar of England, or King's Chief Minister, being distinguished from the time of Henry II onwards by the epithets *summus* and *capitalis.* The Court of Exchequer held the Sheriffs of the Counties to account for the revenues they received, and decided on all cases affecting the revenues.

BOOK II. CHAPTER XIV

A few prefatory lines to this episode in the *Chronicle* informs the reader that Jocelin had intended 'at the request of one in authority' to tell this tale 'in order to glorify the Saint'; and the writer (not Jocelin) had himself written the story out, and appended it to the *Chronicle* 'not irrelevantly, as he hoped'.

PAGE 96. *Reading Monastery.* Founded in 1121 by Henry I, who was buried here, and committed to monks of the Cluniac order (see note to p. 112), though it was an independent English Abbey, and not under the jurisdiction of Cluny.

Henry, Earl of Essex. Henry II interpreted his conduct at Consilt indulgently, and continued to treat him as a valuable minister and friend, and to place him in important commands. The challenge of Robert de Montfort, delivered six years after the event (i. e. in 1163), 'was unwelcome to the King; but once given it had to be met' (Miss Norgate, *op. cit.*, ii. 61).

PAGE 97. *St.-Vitus' tic.* See note to p. 136.

War with the Welsh. The English sovereignty in Wales, so far as it extended at the accession of Stephen, was almost completely lost during his reign, and one of Henry II's first undertakings was a war, directed principally against Owen Gwyneth,

King of North Wales, to recover and extend it. The war was
successful, and ended in Owen paying homage to Henry for his
kingdom. It began, however, with the affair at Coleshill, i. e.
Consilt, near Flint (1157), which only Henry's courage and address
prevented from turning to a disaster. It is true that Henry after
Coleshill 'got safely retreated from the Welsh War', in so far as
he never again ventured his army into the mountains, but achieved
his ends through the pressure of his fleet.

tic-douloureux. An habitual convulsive contraction of certain
muscles of the face.

PAGE 98. *Regular Habit.* i. e. of a monk. The 'regular'
clergy, or those bound by a monastic 'rule', were distinguished
from the 'secular'.

'*on the rim of the horizon*'. 'In confinio terre ac fluminis'
(*Chron.*, p. 52).

'*Infinite nature of Duty*'. See note to p. 22.

PAGE 99. *the Devil and the Dragons.* See notes to pp. 14, 20.

BOOK II. CHAPTER XV

PAGE 99. *a liberty of tourneying.* This was in 1194. The
licences were purchasable, and were, in fact, a device for raising
money (Clarke).

PAGE 100. *the Vigil of the Apostles . . . no outgate on the morrow.*
Carlyle seems to have misunderstood the *Chronicle.* The morrow
was the Vigil (June 28) ; and on that account the knights were
allowed to go about on parole, and were invited to dine with the
Abbot. (*Chron.*, p. 40.)

Christmas Mysteries. See note to p. 56.

with bell, book and candle. According to the *Encyclopaedia
Britannica* the first recorded instance of the rite is 'about 1190'
(*vid. sub* 'Excommunication'). The anathema was often added to
aggravate the major excommunication. On these occasions, when
sentence was pronounced, a bell was rung, a book closed, and
lighted candles were dashed to the ground.

PAGE 101. *Geoffrey Riddell.* Otherwise Ridel, Ridell. See
note to p. 55, and pp. 63-6.

the great tower we are building there. Samson had privily
laid by money while Sub-sacrist 'ad magnam turrim ecclesie
construendam' (*Chron.*, p. 7, and see p. 106). On *Chron.*, p. 15, we
read that he finished the towers (turres) of the Church, which had
been begun a hundred years before. 'There can be no doubt',
says R., 'that these passages refer to the great bell tower and the
lateral towers of the west end of the monastic church begun by
Abbot Baldwin.' Samson's tower was blown down a year before
his death.

Herbert the Dean. *Decanus,* i. e. a rural dean, who before the Reformation had large powers of jurisdiction over his particular division of the archdeaconry. In this case he was doubtless the *decanus Christianitatis* (Dugdale, iii. 116) whom the Abbot appointed to supervise the secular clergy of the town. All these seculars were appointed to their offices by the Abbot.

PAGE 102. *Glebe-lands at Haberdon.* 'Haburdun, within the bounds of St. Edmundsbury, lies behind the Southgate-street, extending to the river Lark, contiguous to the parish of Rougham' (R). Glebe-lands = lands which go with a benefice.

brevi manu, i. e. out of hand.

within the Liberties. A 'liberty' means in law an exceptional privilege, or the lands or domains over which the privilege extends, and especially an area in an English county exempt from the jurisdiction of the Sheriff and having a separate commission of the peace.

Adam de Cokefield. Cockfield. There is a long note by R. (p. 140 f.) on this family and on the fortunes of Nesta, the infant daughter of Adam.

PAGE 103. '*Satan with outspread wings*'. See p. 63.

worse than our armies in Flanders. The allusion is to *Tristram Shandy,* III. xi, where Walter Shandy reads out the Curse of Ermulphus: 'Our armies swore terribly in Flanders,' cried my uncle Toby,—'but nothing to this.'

Pope Innocent the Third. One of the greatest of the mediaeval Popes (b. 1160, d. 1216). He succeeded Pope Celestin in 1198 and at once brought about a truce in the war between Richard and Philip Augustus of France.

PAGE 104. *When Henry II came to St. Edmund's.* In January 1188. He took the Cross at once on hearing of the fall of Jerusalem in October 1187.

cilice. See note to p. 38.

PAGE 105. '*The Unconscious is the alone Complete*'. This is the theme of the essay on 'Characteristics': 'The healthy know not of their health, but only the sick. . . . The beginning of Inquiry is Disease; all Science originated in the feeling of something being wrong. . . . To say that we have a clear conscience is to utter a solecism; had we never sinned, we should have had no conscience. . . . The sign of right performance is Unconsciousness.'

with its eye forever turned on its own navel. 'That superstition of the Athos monks, who by fasting from all nourishment, and looking intensely for a length of time into their own navels, came to discern therein the true Apocalypse of Nature and Heaven Unveiled' (*Sartor,* III. x). Contemplation of the navel is a favourite attitude with Oriental mystics.

galvanized Dilettantisms . . . Puseyisms. See Introduction, p. xxxiii. Edward Bouverie Pusey (1800–82), Professor of Hebrew at Oxford, is often spoken of as the leader of the Anglican revival, because after Newman's secession he did his utmost to prevent others from following that example, and, while upholding the Catholicity of the English Church, distinguished her by a definite line from Rome.

BOOK II.   CHAPTER XVI

PAGE 106. '*the Hospital of Babwell*'.   ' Without the north gate of St. Edmundsbury are the ruins of St. Saviour's Hospital, which appears at first to have been called Babwell, from its situation on the borders of the fen or fields bearing that name' (R).   Pope Urban III, in a brief addressed to Samson in 1185, took under his special protection the ' Hospital of St. Saviour for the support of the sick and poor which you have constructed '.

PAGE 107. *certain dignitaries of us*.   This happened in the Church of Great Hampden in Oxfordshire, where the body rests, on July 21, 1828.   Sir Robert Pye, his son-in-law, used to relate that Hampden was killed, not by a bullet in the shoulder, but by the explosion of a pistol in his hand, the hand being shattered, and this story was accepted by various historians.   Lord Nugent committed the outrage in order to ' remove all doubt ', and, finding the bones of one hand broken, declared in favour of Pye.   Later he became convinced that he had examined somebody else's body, and said nothing of the exhumation in his *Life of Hampden*. See *Dictionary of Natural Biography*.

PAGE 108. *The Festival of St. Edmund*.   This happened in the year 1198.   The Feast Day is November 20.   The *loculus* had been undisturbed since Abbot Baldwin translated it to the Church in 1095, on which occasion he refused to open it.   But his predecessor, Abbot Leofstan (Abbot from 1044 to 1065) opened the coffin, and reclothed the body, in consequence of a dream in which St. Edmund complained that his remains were not decently preserved (Hermannus, *De Miraculis*, ed. Arnold, i. 52).

coming that night to matins.   'Cum venissemus illa nocte ad horas matutinas' (*Chron.*, p. 82).   See Introductory Note on p. 290. ' Praises ' means the office of Lauds.

commence our disciplines.   The mortification of the flesh by penance.   *N. E. D.* quotes *Monk of Evesham* (1482): 'Alle that were there ... toke disciplynys of roddys ' (disciplines of rods).

albs.   A variety of the surplice, but with close sleeves.

PAGE 109. *in the fourth holiday of the Festival*.   The Festival would last eight days, or an ' octave '.

Completorium, i. e. the office of complin, the completion of the Hours of the Day.   It is recited before retiring to rest.

Keepers of the Shrine.   *Chron.*, p. 83 ' custodes feretri '.   Presumably the subsacrist and one of his assistants, and possibly the ' two somnolent monks ' who had set fire to the shrine (p. 106). Samson as subsacrist is ' keeper of the shrine ' on p. 65.

Masters of the Vestry.   Ibid. ' magistri de vestiano '   See p. 289.

PAGE 110. *the Infirmirarius.* See p. 289.

Richard of Henham, i. e. Hingham. See note to p. 55.

John of Dice, i. e. Diss in Norfolk.

PAGE 111. *Sansculottism.* See note to p. 126.

Hubert Archbishop of Canterbury. Hubert Walter, became Archbishop in 1193 after three years in the Holy Land. Was virtual governor of England after Richard left the country in 1194. Died in 1205. He was a Norfolk man, born at West Dereham.

PAGE 112. '*Bending before men,*' *says Novalis.* See note to p. 257.

Sauerteig. See notes to pp. 25, 210.

till forty years of his Life are gone seeking it. 'At the present moment (1853) there is a suit before the Court [of Chancery] which was commenced nearly twenty years ago ; in which from thirty to forty counsel have been known to appear at one time ; in which costs have been incurred to the amount of seventy thousand pounds ; and which is no nearer to its termination now than when it was begun. There is another well-known suit in Chancery, not yet decided, which was commenced before the close of the last century, and in which more than double the amount of seventy thousand pounds has been swallowed up in costs. If I wanted other authorities for Jarndyce and Jarndyce, I could rain them on these pages.'—Dickens, Preface to *Bleak House.* The abuse was reformed by the Judicature Acts (1874).

hatchments. A shortened form of the word ' achievement ' = armorial bearings, especially ' a tablet exhibiting the armorial bearings of a deceased person, which is affixed to the front of his dwelling-place '.—*N. E. D.*

dilapidated Coventry Monks. The then Bishop of Lichfield disliked monks and replaced them by secular clergy when he could. He did this at the Monastery at Coventry in 1197 ; whereupon Pope Celestin appointed a Commission, consisting of the Archbishop of Canterbury, the Bishop of Lincoln, and the Abbot of St. Edmund's, to try the case. The monks were reinvested in the Church of Coventry in January 1198. The case was investigated at Oxford, where the *Chronicle* tells (p. 69) that the Abbot entertained fourteen of the Coventry monks and the Masters of the Schools at his inn.

City of Peeping Tom. This is clearly a mistake. The entertainment was given at Oxford. Leofric, Earl of the Mercians, laid a ruinous tax on the people of Coventry, so that they were like to starve, and when his wife Godiva interceded for them, swore in his wrath not to repeal the tax till she rode naked through the town. Thereupon she sent a herald into the town to proclaim her purpose and order the people to keep within doors, and rode unclothed through the streets. One man only looked at her through a hole in a door, and his eyes were forthwith blinded and fell out of his head. The story is first mentioned by Roger of

Wendover in the beginning of the thirteenth century; Peeping Tom was invented in the seventeenth century. See Tennyson's *Godiva*.

intrusive Bishop of Ely. Geoffrey Riddell again : see note to p. 55 on *sent me once to Acre.* With his support the monks of Ely endeavoured to set up a market at Lakenheath to the prejudice of the market at St. Edmundsbury. (*Chron.*, p. 98.)

Abbot of Cluny. This was Hugh Abbot of Cluny, who was Abbot of Reading from 1180 to 1199. He came as a guest to St. Edmund's Abbey, probably in 1200, and Samson refused to give him precedence. The Cluniacs were an offshoot of the Benedictines. In 912 Berno, Abbot of Gigny, with the assistance of the Duke of Aquitaine, built the monastery of Cluny, near Mâcon-sur-Saône, with the then novel idea of making it the Mother House of a number of dependencies in France and elsewhere. Cluniac houses were quickly founded in England, and at the time of the Dissolution there were over thirty of them.

to advise King Richard. He means King John. The Abbot's journey took place in 1203.

PAGE 113. *scissors of Destiny.* Atropos, the third of the Fates, cut the threads of men's lives with scissors.

Mirza's Vision. In Addison's allegory (*Spectator*, No. 159) Mirza, a pious Moslem, falling into a trance in the vale of Bagdad, saw a great tide flowing through a valley with a thick mist at either end. The river was the river of Time, into which a bridge or pier projected of three score and ten whole arches, and a few broken ones thereafter. The pier was full of passengers, of whom those that came to the end fell into the flood, but many fell in before the end through the trapdoors set everywhere in the floor of the bridge. At the farther end the mist lifted at one side, and Mirza saw that the tide flowed into a bright ocean full of delectable islands, but when he wished to pierce the secret behind that part of the mist which did not lift, the vision faded, and ' I saw nothing but the long hollow valley of Bagdad, with oxen, sheep, and camels grazing upon the sides of it '.

BOOK II. CHAPTER XVII

PAGE 113. *adscititious.* See note to p. 188.

callosity. i. e. a hardened skin.

PAGE 114. *Ubi homines sunt modi sunt.* 'Wherever men are there are conventions.'

PAGE 115. *the humour that thy mother gave thee.* See note to p. 44.

African Mandingo. The name of a large group or family of Negro peoples in Western Africa, and of the languages which they speak.

learned sergeants. See note to p. 9.

PAGE 116. *curable by no hellebore.* Gk. ἑλλέβορος. A name given by the ancients to certain poisonous and medicinal plants supposed to be a cure for mental disease. The best grew near two towns, one in Phocio, the other in Thessaly, both called Anticyra. So Horace, *Sat.* ii. 3. 166 ' Naviget Anticyram ', &c.

Long-Acre cabs. See note to p. 8.

white-breeched tiger. A boy-groom or footman, perhaps so called from the smart livery.

pococurantisms. Pococurante is Italian for ' caring little '.

brave men before Agamemnon.

> Vixere fortes ante Agamemnona
> Multi.　　　　　　　　Horace, *Odes*, iv. 9. 25.

Igdrasil . . . Nornas. See note to p. 34.

PAGE 117. *Dan Chaucer.* ' Dan ' is short for dominus, and is found frequently in Spenser, and in Thomson's Spenserean verse. Cf. Spenser's ' Dan Chaucer, well of English undefyled '.

Westminster Hall and its wigs. See note to p. 8.

Useful-Knowledge Societies. The tax on newspapers, raised to a prohibitive amount in 1815, aimed at suppressing the utterance of seditious or irreligious sentiment. Those who opposed the taxes argued that education was the cure; and the Useful Knowledge Society, started by Charles Knight, a liberal-minded publisher, in 1832, disseminated science and history in the *Penny Magazine* and the *Penny Cyclopaedia* to an enormous circle of subscribers. Brougham was Chairman of the Committee, which included Althorp, Russell, James Mill, and Rowland Hill.

imbroglio. See note to p. 205.

PAGE 118. *Unnameable.* See note to p. 6.

Litanias. Eccl. Gk. λιτανεία, prayer, entreaty.

Leitourgias. Gk. λειτουργία, a public service discharged voluntarily and at his own cost by a private citizen, or the public worship of the Gods; and later divine service, more especially the Eucharist.

Rotatory Calabash. See note to p. 126.

Laud at St. Catherine Creed's. On Jan. 16, 1631, Laud, as Bishop of London, consecrated the Church of St. Catherine Cree [not Creed] in London, appearing outside the gate in full canonicals and bowing to the altar. He was doing his best at the time to establish the practice of paying respect to the altar in this way. His conduct during the service of consecration, and at the celebration of the Eucharist which followed, was reported to the Long Parliament at his trial with great exaggerations, and this mendacious evidence appears in Prynne's *Canterburies Doom.* See Gardiner, *History of England*, vii. 242 f.

Robin Hood's Garland. A collection of ballads on Robin Hood appeared under this title in 1670 and was afterwards frequently reprinted.

Will Scarlet ... Wakefield Pindar. See note to p. 59.

Statute De Tallagio non concedendo. It was passed in 1297, and provided that no tallage or aid should thenceforth be levied without the consent of the lords, spiritual and temporal, and the knights and other freemen of the kingdom. The result of the struggle between Edward I and his Parliament, and the key-stone of the Parliamentary system.

Four Courts. At the beginning of the reign of Henry II there were three distinct Courts: that of the Exchequer, touching the revenue; that of Common Pleas, touching suits between subject and subject; and that of King's Bench, touching complaints against inferior courts and all matters affecting the King. During the reign of Edward III a fourth Court emerged—that of Chancery. Till then the Chancellor had merely been the executant of the King's will in equity or ' matters of grace and favour ', but at this period he became a Judge in a tribunal of his own. This was still the form of the judicial machinery when Carlyle wrote; but it was a good deal altered by the Judicature Acts of 1873-6.

Coke upon Lyttleton. Sir Edward Coke, commonly called Lord Coke (1552-1634), Chief Justice under James I, and a fearless defender of the English Law against arbitrary power. ' Coke upon Lyttleton ' is a description of the first part of his *Institutes of the Laws of England*, which appeared in 1628 (followed in subsequent years by three other parts). The first part was a reprint of Lyttleton's treatise on tenures, with a translation and a commentary. Sir Thomas de Littleton (*circa* 1417-81), one of the Judges of Common Pleas, wrote this Treatise in French, probably after he was raised to the bench in 1466. It is the chief text-book on the English law of property.

killing your man in Chancery. See note to p. 112.

PAGE 119. *like Dryden's Head in the Battle of the Books.* ' The helmet was nine times too large for the head, which appeared situate far in the hinder part ... like a mouse under a canopy of state, or a shrivelled beau within the penthouse of a modern periwig, and the voice was suited to the visage, sounding weak and remote.'

Satanic-School. Southey, in the Preface to his *Vision of Judgement*, applied this name to Byron, and it was soon extended to Shelley. The term connotes, of course, immorality and irreligion.

Cockney-School. J. G. Lockhart, in *Blackwood's Magazine*, October 1817, applied this term to Leigh Hunt, Keats, Hazlitt, Shelley. It meant sickly and sentimental.

PAGE 120. *Arachne.* See note to p. 131.

Theuth. Or Thoth, the Egyptian God mentioned in Plato, *Phaedrus*, 274 c. See note to p. 34.

Wodan. Or Odin.

She is the noisiest, &c. Cf. Vergil's description of Fame, *Aen.* iv. 173 f.

PAGE 121. *O Bobus and Company.* See p. 27.

'*small still voices*'. 1 Kings xix. 12. Gray, *Ode for Music,* v. 8 : 'the still small voice of gratitude.'

Heard are the Voices, &c. These lines are from Goethe's *Symbolum,* written in December 1815 on the occasion of August Goethe's reception into the Amalia Lodge of Freemasons in Weimar :

> Des Maurers Wandeln,
> Es gleicht dem Leben,
> Und sein Bestreben,
> Es gleicht dem Handeln
> Der Menschen auf Erden, &c.

See pp. 213, 214.

BOOK III. CHAPTER I

PAGE 123. *see the figure of him.* See p. 98.

Pleasures of Virtue and the Moral Sublime. In the eighteenth century the principal antagonists of the Utilitarian school, or of its forerunners in ethics, were the so-called ' Moral Sense Philosophers ', the third Earl of Shaftesbury (1670–1713) and Francis Hutcheson (1694–1746). Both these thinkers, Shaftesbury especially, dwell on the analogy, or rather unity, of the sense of Beauty with the sense of good, and speak of morality in aesthetic terms, as proceeding from, and attended by, a 'taste' or a 'relish'. ' The mind ', says Shaftesbury in his *Inquiry concerning Virtue or Merit,* ' observes not only things, but actions and affections. . . . It finds a foul and a fair, a harmonious and a dissonant, as really and truly here as in musical members or visible forms. It cannot withhold its admiration and ecstasies, its aversion and scorn. To deny the common and natural sense of a sublime and beautiful is mere affectation. And as this is true of the natural, so is it of the moral world.' Carlyle is prone to distrust all ethical theories which make virtue in any degree pleasant ; it is the weakness of his teaching. Cf. a passage in the Essay on Diderot : ' Shaftesbury was not only a Sceptic, but an Amateur Sceptic . . . a delicate, perfumed, gentlemanly individual, standing there in that war of Titans (hill meeting hill with all its woods), and putting out hand to it—with a pair of tweezers.'

Greatest Happiness. See Introduction, p. xliii.

Herschel-telescopes, Sir John Herschel (1792–1871), the astronomer, was the author of a great advance in the science of optics. His numerous discoveries in astronomy were only made possible by the use of new and powerful telescopes, which he began to construct in 1820.

old Jonson's dialect. See note to p. 43.

PAGE 124. *upas-boughs.* See note to p. 28.

elephantine leprosy. Elephantiasis is a name applied to various diseases which cause the skin to resemble the hide of an elephant. One such disease (*Elephantiasis Graecorum*) is often identified with leprosy.

ten years Corn-Law Debatings. See note to p. 22.

Joe-Manton Aristocracies. Joe Manton lived from 1766 to 1835, and was a famous gun-maker.

M. Jouffroy. This is probably the French philosopher Théodore Simon Jouffroy (1796–1842), the author of *Mélanges philosophiques* (in which, however, the expression here quoted is not to be found), and an example of the reconstructive Conservatism that followed the Revolution. *Avoir dans le ventre* = 'to be capable of', and, with an object of time, 'to have so much time to live'.

The old Pope of Rome. Gregory XVI, born 1765, pope from 1831 to 1846. His rule was marked by the growth of Ultramontane ideas under the Jesuit influence, and the elaboration of ceremonial, as well as by the severe repression of Young Italy, with the aid of Austrian bayonets, in the Papal States. Nine saints were canonized during his term of office, and one or two miracles were announced. Gregory lavished his revenues in patronizing men of learning, building or renovating museums and churches, carrying out great enterprises in engineering, and in keeping state. He was floated by the Rothschilds, and left a debt of 60,000,000 scudi (Nielsen, *History of the Papacy in the Nineteenth Century*). His character was naïve, jovial, and stubborn.

PAGE 125. *amphibious.* i. e. 'partaking of both lives or natures', in this case, animal and material.

Chaos first shivered and 'sneezed'. Professor Margoliouth has kindly sent me the following note: 'The "sneezing of the dawn" is taken from the Maquamah XV of Harīrī, perhaps in Rückert's translation ('bis dass der Morgen nieste,' ed. 1875, p. 129, where there is a long note). This translation was first published in 1826.'

Gregorian Chants. The sacred 'plain-song' chants of the Roman Church, regulated by Gregory the Great in the sixth century.

the late Italian Cholera. It raged in Rome, Genoa, and the Two Sicilies in the summer of 1837.

PAGE 126. *Sansculottic.* 'Culotte' is French for 'breeches'. 'Sansculotte', 'breechless', was applied in the early days of the French Revolution by the Royalists to the Revolutionaries, who adopted it as a name of honour. According to Littré, the word has reference to the disuse by the Revolutionaries of the fashionable knee-breeches in favour of pantaloons.

'*Groby Pool is thatched with pancakes.*' A Leicestershire saying, Groby Pool being a large sheet of water in that county. See *The*

Heart of Midlothian (ch. xxix, talk of the landlord at Ferry-bridge).

Squallacci. This is probably a coinage of Carlyle's own, made by affixing an Italian termination to the English word 'squall'. There may be an association with Italian *scialacquo*, meaning 'profuseness', 'lavishness'.

rotatory Calabash of the Calmucks. Carlyle was fond of this illustration. Cf. the Essay on *The Parliamentary History of the French Revolution*: 'Just so do the Kalmuck people pray; quantities of written prayers are put in some rotatory pipkin or calabash (hung on a tree, or going like the small barrel-churn of agricultural districts); this the devotee has only to whirl and churn; so long as he whirls, it is prayer; when he ceases whirling, the prayer is done.' Lowell, in an Essay, says that Carlyle read this in Richter. He may have seen a description of the prayer-wheels in Julius von Klaproth's *Travels in the Caucasus and Georgia* (Eng. translation, 1814, p. 102). A calabash is a gourd or pumpkin. 'Calmucks' is a name given by Turks and Russians to the Western Mongols who are scattered throughout Central Asia, and are nearly all adherents of Lamaism,

within the 'three hundred'. See the dictum of M. Jouffroy, quoted p. 124, and cf. *Sartor*, iii. 5: 'I have seen Solemnities linger as Ceremonies . . . to the extent of three-hundred years and more, after all life and sacredness had evaporated out of them. . . . Would Destiny offer Mankind that, after, say two centuries of convulsion and conflagration, the fire-creation [of the new Phœnix] should be accomplished, and we to find ourselves again in a Living Society,— were it not prudent in Mankind to strike the bargain?' If this be the allusion, the 'Poor Pope' of the sentence is the genus, and not an individual.

PAGE 127. *The Champion of England* . . . In former times a banquet in Westminster Hall followed the Coronation of the King in the Abbey; and at the banquet the Champion of England, an office hereditary in the Dymoke family, rode into the Hall in full armour, with the High Constable and the Earl Marshall to either side of him, while a herald in front read his challenge, to the effect that, if any one should deny the King's right, he (the Champion) would 'adventure his life against him, on what day soever he shall be appointed'. The ceremony last took place at the Coronation of George IV in 1821. The Champion, though 'a fine young man', was unable, under the weight of 70 lb. of armour, to mount his horse without some 'little assistance'. The horse was 'an old stager long accustomed to the glare of lamps' (*Times*, July 13, 1821). There is a disquisition on the incident in *Sartor Resartus*, iii. 3.

an interest of men. Cf. the expressions 'the Whig interest', the 'moneyed interest'. *N. E. D.* quotes Defoe: 'caballing and forming an interest among the men'.

'*devil's-dust*'. 'The flock to which old cloth is reduced by the machine called a devil.'—*N. E. D.* Used by dishonest manufacturers to adulterate cloth.

my friend Sauerteig. See note to pp. 25 and 210.

PAGE 128. *some old ... eight-day clock.* See note to p. 25, under *Sauerteig.*

PAGE 129. *the broad way.* St. Matt. vii. 13.

Elysian fields. The abode of the souls of the good, where they live in ease and pleasure and a vernal clime. In Homer (*Odyssey* iv. 563 f.) these fields are on the western margin of the world by the Ocean. In Vergil (*Aeneid* vi. 653 f.) they are in the lower world, but under a sky and sun of their own.

Cocker's Arithmetic. Arithmetick; composed by Edward Cocker, late practicioner in the Arts of writing, &c. London, 1688. The book went into not fewer than forty-six editions.

PAGE 130. *Manchester Insurrections.* See note to p. 13.

Sliding-scales. See Introduction, p. xiii.

consuming the way. The expression is reminiscent of the Latin 'viam (*or* campum) corripere', used, for instance, of chariots in full career.

BOOK III. CHAPTER II

PAGE 131. *Sicilian or other sulphur.* Sulphur is usually found in volcanic regions. Most of what is used in Europe comes from Sicily.

arachnes. 'Spiders.' Arachne was a maiden who challenged Athene to a contest in spinning, and, losing, was turned into a spider.

Pluto. The Ruler of the Lower World.

PAGE 132. '*Tremble intensely,' as our friend the Emperor of China says.* The 'Opium War' with China began in January, 1840 (see note to p. 240). During its progress the Chinese Emperor frequently fulminated in proclamations both against the British and against his own Generals and Ministers. Many of these proclamations, to be read in *The Times,* abound in the verb 'to tremble', but I have not found the exact expression in the text.

Cash-payment. See note to p. 30.

PAGE 133. *Courts of Requests.* This was the name of the Tribunals, both local and metropolitan, for the recovery of small debts. They were superseded in 1846 by the County Courts.

Atheistic Government. See p. 150. Carlyle thought that the Puritanism of the early seventeenth century was the last phase of earnest religion in England, that (saving the short administration of the first Pitt) Cromwell's rule was the last rule of a hero, and that atheism bore its fruit in the liberal theory of politics as truly as in other forms of moral failure. See the Introduction to *Oliver Cromwell's Letters and Speeches* on the 'last glimpse of the

God-like vanishing from this England'. 'The Age of the Puritans is not extinct only and gone away from us, but it is as if fallen beyond the capabilities of Memory herself, it is grown unintelligible. ... Not the body of heroic Puritanism only but the soul of it also, has, for the present, passed away.'

like a Clockmaker. See note to p. 25.

in spite of Bridgewater Bequests. The eighth Earl of Bridgewater (1758–1829) bequeathed £8,000, to be paid to the author of the best treatise on the 'Power, Wisdom, and Goodness of God, as manifested in the Creation'. The money was distributed among eight authors, who produced the 'Bridgewater Treatises'. Some of the titles are : *The Hand as evincing Design; The Adaptation of External Nature to the Moral and Intellectual Constitution of Man; History, Habits, and Instincts of Animals; Chemistry, Meteorology, and Digestion.* Dates of publication 1833–1840.

Unnamable god-like. See note to p. 6.

Histrionism. Histrio is Latin for 'actor'.

PAGE 134. *Valets and Varlets.* Both these words are derived from O.F. *vaslet,* and *vaslet* from med. Lat. *vassallus,* vassal. The original meaning of varlet is 'a page preparing to be a squire'.

'*Though he slay me*' ... Job xiii. 15.

Gehenna and the Pool. Gehenna, originally Ge-Hinnom, a valley to the west of Jerusalem, associated with the sacrifice of children to Molech, and accounted a sinister place (2 Kings xxiii). Here the refuse of the city and the bodies of criminals were burned, and the name became a synonym for Hell (St. Matt. v. 29 and x. 28). This Gehenna was believed to be under the earth and filled with a 'lake burning with brimstone' (Rev. xix. 26 and xx. 10).

Alison's Scotch facts. See Introduction, p. xi, and note to pp. 2–3.

PAGE 135. *as the old Spartans would have done.* Every child born of citizens in ancient Sparta was brought before the Elders of its tribe, who decided if it were strong enough to be reared. If weak or sickly, it was killed by being exposed.

two-legged animal with feathers. See note to p. 25. The parable now following has respect to the 'enchantment' of all classes in England, so continually referred to in the book. Each in spellbound isolation, the poor man dies by hunger in the sight of plenty, and the rich by surfeit. The rich man is valued only for his riches, which go to pamper others after his death.

BOOK III. CHAPTER III

PAGE 136. *Mayfair.* The rich residential district adjoining Hyde Park to the south of Oxford Street, so called from a fair formerly held on this site in May.

some other classes of creatures. He means laughing jackasses; see p. 22.

'*Incarnate Word*'. This refers to the Logos (λόγος) of the Stoics and Neo-Platonists, the Mind or Reason which permeates the world and the body of man. The Stoics distinguished between the λόγος ἐνδιάθετος and the λόγος προφορικός. 'Enclosed in the breast' it was Thought, 'issuing from the mouth' it was Word.

after the brains are quite out. See note to p. 22.

the 'knaves and dastards'. See p. 31.

the St. Vitus kind. The allusion is, of course, to St. Vitus's Dance, 'chorea' in medical parlance, so called because St. Vitus was supposed to attend to all diseases of an epileptic nature and to be able to cure them. He was a young boy martyred under Diocletian.

PAGE 137. *Johnson complained.* Perhaps a vague reminiscence of Boswell's *Life* sub 1776 (ed. Birrell, 1901, iv. 62): 'When I complained of having dined at a splendid table without hearing one sentence of conversation worthy of being remembered, he said, " Sir, there seldom is any such conversation".'

Anselm. St. Anselm (1033–1109), Archbishop of Canterbury, contended with William II and Henry I for the principle that the Bishops should be invested with their offices by the Pope or his deputy, and not by the King. St. Thomas of Canterbury (1118 ?–1170) fought with Henry II, among other causes, for the sole right of the ecclesiastical courts to deal with criminous clerks. The ultimate issue in either case was whether the government of England should or should not be a theocracy. See p. 223.

Asphaltic Lake. Large masses of asphalt are frequently cast up to the surface of the Dead Sea by earthquakes. In classical writers (e.g. Diodorus and Josephus) the sea is called the 'Asphaltic Lake' (λίμνη ἀσφαλτίτης).

BOOK III. CHAPTER IV

PAGE 138. *Our highest religion is named the 'Worship of Sorrow'.* This is from the passage, which Carlyle so often cites, in Goethe's *Wilhelm Meister's Wanderjahre*, x and xi, on the nature and grounds of Religious Belief. Three Religions are distinguished: the 'Ethnic' or Heathen, based on reverence for that which is above us; the Philosophical, on man's reverence for his equals; and the Christian, which recognizes the divine in 'humility, in mockery and despite, disgrace and wretchedness, suffering and death'. This third or highest Religion is symbolized in the story by a shrine named 'The Sanctuary of Sorrow'. See Carlyle's Essay on Goethe of 1828, and of *Sartor* II. 9: 'Small is it that thou canst trample the Earth with its injuries under thy feet, as old Greek Zeno trained thee: thou canst love the Earth while it injures thee, and even because it injures thee; for this a greater than Zeno was needed, and he too was sent. Knowest thou that "*Worship of Sorrow*"?'

PAGE 139. *The word Soul*, &c. 'If man's Soul is indeed, as in the Finnish language, a kind of *Stomach*'—*Sartor* II. 3. We say in English that a man has 'a high stomach', meaning spirit. Mr. Nevill Forbes writes: 'In Russian the word for *stomach* now is *zhivót*, but this word used to mean *life*. In Polish *zywot* means *life*, and the root is the same as qui(ck), vi(vus).'

A gifted Byron. See note to p. 31.

PAGE 140. *rest, rest perturbed spirit.* *Hamlet*, I. v. 181.

gnarring. To 'gnar' is to growl or snarl. *N. E. D.* quotes rare instances from the fifteenth century onwards to Tennyson's *In Memoriam* xxviii. Current in North Country dialect. Cf. German *knarren*, to creak.

pothering. This verb, in the intransitive, 'to make a fuss or worry', is quoted by the *N. E. D.* from 1735 (Savage) onwards. The transitive sense, 'to put into a fuss or fluster', seems to be more frequent. Pother (also pudder) does not appear before the beginning of the seventeenth century, and its origin is undetermined.

PAGE 141. '*Happiness our being's end and aim*'. Pope, *Essay on Man*, Epistle iv. 1.

eupeptic Curtis. A family of this name have been doctors and botanists for over a century. I can only guess that Carlyle is referring to some system of diet, or possibly some pill or medicine, associated with one of them.

the fattest pig of Epicurus. Horace, *Epistulae* i. 4. 15, 16:

> Me pinguem et nitidum bene curata cute vises
> cum ridere voles Epicuri de grege porcum.

Horace is speaking playfully. Epicurus (341–270 B.C.) taught that pleasure was the good, but he meant by 'pleasure' 'the freedom of the body from pain and of the soul from anxiety', and an inscription over the gate of his famous garden at Athens promised his guests no better or worse fare than barley-cakes and water. He was a native of Samos and settled in Athens in 307 B.C.

Job with potsherds. Job ii. 8: 'he took him a potsherd to scrape himself'.

Giaours. *The Giaour* (1813), one of the poetic romances by which Byron became famous between 1813 and 1816. In these poems the scene is Turkey or Greece, the hero a moody outlaw, and the heroine Lord Byron's ideal of a woman.

BOOK III.   CHAPTER V

PAGE 142. *platitudes.* See note to p. 20.

Raphael. Raphael Santi (1483–1520), the most consummate of the Italian masters. The greatest period in his career is that of the decoration of the chambers of the Vatican from 1509 onwards.

Reynolds. Sir Joshua Reynolds (1723–92), the head of 'the English School'. Not a Raphael, but generally considered to be unsurpassed in respect of the union in his portraits of delicacy and beauty with dignity and strength.

Mozart. He lived from 1756 to 1791. His finest work is in the field of opera and symphony, the operas *Don Giovanni, Figaro,* and *The Magic Flute* being his masterpieces.

a Mr. Bishop. Sir Henry Bishop (1786–1855), a conductor of the Opera at Covent Garden ; Professor of Music first at Edinburgh and afterwards at Oxford ; and a voluminous composer. His works included eighty-two operas and vaudevilles.

Goethe spoke of the Horse. I have not been able to find this.

neck clothed with thunder. Job xxxix. 19.

PAGE 143. *an epitome of the man.* 'That ideal outline of himself which a man unconsciously shadows forth in his writings, and which, rightly deciphered, will be truer than any other representation of him.'—Essay *On Richter Again.* So Milton says (*Areopagitica*) that books 'do preserve as in a vial the purest efficacy and extraction of that living intellect that bred them'.

finds a bill against you. A 'bill' means a written document, and sometimes a statement of a case at law, generally the Plaintiff's. The Grand Jury at an Assizes examines the bill of each case presented for hearing, and if there is evidence enough to justify its being heard before the Judge and an ordinary jury, 'finds it a true bill'.

PAGE 144. *Brindley.* James Brindley (1716–72) was the son of a small farmer in Derbyshire. After serving as apprentice to a millwright, he set up as a repairer of old machinery at Leek, and gained a reputation by his mechanical improvements. His chief work began in 1759, when the Duke of Bridgwater called him in to superintend the construction of canals. He was the first to carry a canal over other waterways or roads by means of aqueducts. The canal between Liverpool and Manchester and the 'Grand Trunk' between Trent and Mersey were his work. He remained to the end an illiterate and silently intuitive man, and did all his calculations and plans in his head without the use of pencil and paper.

wrestle it. The *Century Dictionary* gives this as a colloquial usage, as, e.g., in 'I'll wrestle you', i.e. with you ; and quotes the American expression to 'wrestle the cattle', i.e. to throw them down for the purpose of branding.

profound melancholy . . . is the basis of thy being. Referring,

324 NOTES

possibly, to a passage in *Dichtung und Wahrheit* (iii. 13) in which Goethe describes the melancholy that found vent in his *Sorrows of Werter*. This, he says, was fostered by 'the Literature, especially the Poetical Literature of England, the great qualities of which are accompanied by a certain earnest melancholy'. (Quoted in the Essay on Goethe of 1828.)

PAGE 145. *vis inertiae*. The power to resist external impulse.

New-Hollands. The name given to Australia by the Dutch navigators of the first half of the seventeenth century. The early exploration of the continent was mainly their work.

PAGE 146. *College Philosophies*. He means probably academic philosophers like Adam Smith and Dugald Stewart.

Fate's prophecy is fulfilled. See p. 145 : 'The Fates sing of thee that thou shalt many times be thought an ass and a dull ox.'

PAGE 147. *three years 'total stagnation of trade'*. In 1840–2.

Baconian Inductions. Francis Bacon (1561–1626) wrote his *Novum Organon* (1620), as well as other works, to advise the scientist to study Nature at first hand and to have done with the logical and metaphysical conceptions which had sterilized and entangled investigation theretofore. Induction means the method of gathering truth from the facts of experience, as opposed to Deduction, which derives it from postulates.

PAGE 148. *Berserkir-rage*. Also Berserker, -ar, Icelandic *berserkr*, = 'bear-sark' (shirt), a hero of Scandinavian mythology, who fought with praeternatural fury. Another interpretation is 'bare-sark', i.e. 'bare of shirt'. So Scott in a note to *The Pirate* : 'The Berserkars were so called from fighting without armour' (*N. E. D.*).

Bradshaw. John Bradshaw (1602–59), a successful lawyer, and one of the Parliamentarian judges; presided at the trial of Charles I ; died a member of the Council of State.

like their old Teutsch Fathers. i. e. Deutsch, German. M. Vipsanius Agrippa conducted a campaign against the Germans on the Rhine in B.C. 38. It is just possible that Carlyle is vaguely remembering a passage he had seen, or seen quoted, from Mauricius Strategicus, book x (cited in *Germania Antiqua*, ed. Karl Müllenhoff) : τὰ ξανθὰ ἔθνη θρασέα εἰσὶ καὶ ἀκατάπληκτα ἐν τοῖς πολέμοις. τολμηρά τε καὶ προπετῆ ὄντα, τὴν δειλίαν καὶ τὴν πρὸς μικρὸν ἀναχώρησιν εἰς ὄνειδος ἔχοντα, εὐκόλως θανάτου περιφρονοῦσι. 'The fair-haired nations are bold and undaunted in war. Daring and violent, they think shame of cowardice and of giving way, and make but light of death.' He may also be thinking of Caesar, *Commentarii*, iv. 7 'sese (*sc.* Germanos) unis Suebis concedere, quibus ne di quidem immortales pares esse possint'.

my Conservative friends. The term 'Conservative' had been recently introduced as a name for the extreme Tories who opposed the Reform Bill of 1832, and remained unreconciled.

PAGE 149. *Potosi*. See note to p. 3.

Golconda. Once the capital of the kingdom of that name, now a fortress, near Hyderabad. Proverbially famous for its diamonds.

Sliding-Scales. See Introduction, p. xiv.

two millions of cne's brother-men. See foot-note on p. 2.

five millions 'rejoice in potatoes'. I have not been able to trace this reference.

BOOK III. CHAPTER VI

PAGE 150. *to govern without God.* See note to p. 133.

Nell Gwyn. For many years the favourite mistress of Charles II.

Cameronian psalm-singing. At the Restoration Episcopacy was re-established in Scotland and the Solemn League and Covenant of 1643 declared an illegal oath. Goaded by long persecution, the recusant Covenanters rose in armed rebellion in 1680, and were quickly put down at Bothwell Bridge. But until the Revolution of 1688 the embers of rebellion continued to glow in the form of an armed and organized population in the south-west of Scotland, who were a perpetual menace to the Government. They were called Cameronians after Richard Cameron, one of their leaders, who fell in 1680 at the skirmish of Aird's Moss.

PAGE 151. *Cromwell's body hung on the Tyburn-gallows.* See note to p. 17.

Four Pleas of the Crown. Cf. Cowell in *The Interpreter*, a Law Dictionary, ed. 1607: 'Pleas of the Crown in Scotland be 4, robbery, rape, murder, and wilful fire. ... With us they be all suits in the King's name against offences committed against his Crown and dignity, or against his Crown and Peace.'—*N. E. D.*

Church-Extension. See Introduction, p. xxxv.

Hurd and Warburton. William Warburton (1698–1779), Bishop of Gloucester, is best known as Pope's commentator and literary executor, and for his contribution to the deistic controversy in *The Divine Legation of Moses* (1737), in which he gave so much ground to the deists as to be suspected of being one himself. He was learned, arrogant, an acute controversialist, and a shallow and legalistic thinker. Richard Hurd (1720–1808), Bishop of Worcester, now remembered for his sympathies with the romantic order of literature, as evinced in his *Letters on Chivalry and Romance* (1762), was Warburton's intimate friend, his biographer, and the editor of his Works. Carlyle is probably thinking of the controversy with Wesley and Whitefield, which Warburton opened by his *Doctrine of Grace*, and Hurd continued. It was notable for the repugnance betrayed by Warburton to any sort of 'enthusiasm'.

Paine. Thomas Paine (1737–1809) was born poor in Thetford; emigrated to Philadelphia in 1774; and became in 1775 the leading writer in the cause of American independence, especially by his two pamphlets, *Common Sense* and *The Crisis*. Returned to England in 1791, and replied to Burke's *Reflections on the French Revolution* in his *Rights of Man*. Was elected a member of the Convention in France, and narrowly escaped death as a Girondin. Returned to die in America, where he completed his deistical treatise, *The Age of Reason*. He was a master of the plain and pithy style of English prose.

the Spiritualism of England. As is clear from the use of this expression on the next page, it means the literature dealing with spiritual things, the work of the poets and philosophers.

sunk into the sere and yellow leaf. Macbeth, v. iii. 23.

'things well let alone'. i. e., of course, *laissez-faire*. It recalls Walpole's rule of *quieta non movere*.

PAGE 152. *The perennial Scriptures of Mankind have had small accession*, &c. Carlyle disparaged the English literature of his time as wanting in actuality and in the 'criticism of life'. It dealt, as a rule, with distant or fantastic scenes and times, and shirked the great conflict of the age between the scientific understanding and the religious sense. German literature, on the other hand, looked, in the main, upon the present, upon a 'real world now made holier', and 'in the new form of this century show forth the old nobleness, not consistent only with the science, the scepticism, the precision of these days, but wedded to them' (*On the State of German Literature*). Only Byron in England accepted the battle of the time, and failed to win it (Essay on Goethe, and see note on p. 31). The English poetry of the day was lacking in spontaneity (*Characteristics*), morbid, as a rule, in sentiment (Essay on Scott), violent and effusive (*Signs of the Times*), and emasculated by gentility (*Jean Paul Richter Again*). Wordsworth was 'a genuine but small diluted man' (from the Diary), Keats a man of 'weak-eyed maudlin sensibility and random tunefulness' (Essay on Burns), Scott healthy but unedifying, and Coleridge a Magian spirit, but ineffectual (see the famous description in *The Life of John Sterling*).

Philips. There were two poets of this name in the eighteenth century. The one here meant will be Ambrose Philips (1675–1749), a Fellow of St. John's College, Cambridge, later an Irish judge, and a member of Addison's circle. His 'Pastorals' (1709) excited Pope's envy, who attacked him savagely in his satires. The Pastorals and the *Epistle to the Earl of Dorset* were greatly lauded at the time, and were the most popular of Philips's writings; they are condemned, however, by the taste of to-day as frigid and artificial.

The Oracles have been dumb. Milton, 'Hymn on the Morning of Christ's Nativity,' 173.

PAGE 153. *Dilettanti by the Red Sea.* See p. 137.

Demiurgus. The δημιουργός of Plato's *Timaeus*, the Creator of the world. The word means 'a skilled workman'.

BOOK III. CHAPTER VII

PAGE 154. *Over-production.* The question whether it is possible to produce too much, i. e. whether wealth can outrun its use, was a standing topic in the Political Economy of the day. The accepted answer was that a 'general glut' is not possible, but local gluts of this or that market may arise through 'changes in the channels of trade' or over-estimates of the demand. The cure was prevision and the better regulation of industry as a whole. The distress in the cotton trade after 1836 was the result of a glut. The low price of corn in 1834-6, the flow of capital from the Joint Stock Banks, and a great boom in every market in America led to an inrush of money and a multiplication of mills. Then came the dear years, and the decline in purchasing power ; and the demand slackened as fast as the output increased. (Evidence taken by Assistant Poor Law Commissioners on distress at Stockport, 1842.)

fustian. 'Thick twilled short-napped cotton cloth.' O.F. *fustaigne,* med.Lat. *fustaneus,* perhaps = from Fostat, a suburb of Cairo (*N. E. D.*).

cassimere. The word is a variation on Cashmere. 'A thin fine twilled woollen cloth used for men's clothes ' (*N. E. D.*).

jane. Or 'jean', M.E. Gene, F. Gênes, med.Lat. Janua, Genoa. ' A twilled cotton cloth, a kind of fustian ' (*N. E. D.*).

nankeen. 'A kind of cotton cloth, originally made at Nanking from a yellow variety of cotton ' (*N. E. D.*).

the Commercial Bazaar. There is no bazaar of this name in the London Directory at the time. Owen's Labour Exchange (see note to p. 183) was sometimes called the Industrial Bazaar.

Howel-and-Jameses. Warehousemen, 9 Regent Street (*Post Office Directory*, 1843).

PAGE 155. *Two million shirtless.* See foot-note on p. 2.

Ugolino Hunger-cellars. See p. 4, and note.

'*Raise* our *rents!*' i. e. by the Corn Laws. He is alluding to the common argument of the Monopolists that the Repealer, by destroying English agriculture, will destroy his best market, and that his true policy would be to build that market up. This assumes, of course, (*a*) that other classes of the rural community beside the landlord benefited by the tax, and (*b*) that the repeal would be ruinous to the agricultural interest as a whole.

on the shores of the Dead Sea. See p. 137.

audacity at Melton Mowbray. Melton Mowbray is a hunting centre in Leicestershire.

Are not your filthy mills, &c. The whole of this paragraph is true to the mind of probably the great majority of the country gentlemen, who could see no good, and only evil, in the industries. 'The towns of Lancashire were more unfamiliar to them in those days than Denver and Omaha are in our own. . . . The whole conception of modern manufacturing industry was as horrible as it was strange in their eyes. The chief newspaper of the country party boldly declared that England would be as great and powerful, and all useful Englishmen would be as rich as they are, though all the manufacturing houses in Great Britain should be engulfed in ruin' (Morley's *Cobden*, ch. viii).

PAGE 156. *Cannot we do what we like with our own ?* See note to p. 5.

Gneiss Rock. 'Gneiss may be termed stratified or slaty granite.... When the gneiss is associated with granite it approaches to the character of that substance ; and when the two come in contact it is scarcely possible to distinguish between them.' Richardson, *Geology*, quoted in *N. E. D.*

Doggerbank. A large sand-bank situated about 100 miles from the Yorkshire coast, and a rich fishing-ground.

PAGE 157. '*retire three days to its bed* '. Brindley's practice ; see p. 144.

BOOK III. CHAPTER VIII

PAGE 157. *Land is the right basis of an Aristocracy.* See Introduction, p. xxxviii.

worth nothing ' except the labour bestowed on it '. See Introduction, p. xxxviii.

PAGE 159. *this very question, Who made the land of England ?* See quotation from Spence, Introduction, p. xxxviii.

let for seventy millions. This is above the actual land rental of the United Kingdom in 1843, which amounted to £54,590,000 (Official Return quoted in Mulhall's *Dictionary of Statistics*), but Carlyle, presumably, is thinking of the potential. On the other hand, the annual value of all kinds of Real Property assessed to the Property Tax in 1843 for England, Wales, and Scotland was £91,500,000.

sweat of Melton Mowbray. See note to p. 155.

assigns. The word is obsolete except in the legal use of one to whom a property or right is transferred.

St. Stephen's. The old chapel of St. Stephen in Westminster Palace was used as the chamber of the House of Commons from 1547 onwards, until the fire of 1834, which burnt it down.

PAGE 160. *Anti-Corn-Law Leagues.* See Introduction, p. xiv.

Ark of Deliverance. An allusion to Exodus xxxvi–xxxix, which describes the making of the Tabernacle and the Ark at the command of Moses ; or else to Noah's Ark, which was a vessel of Deliverance. This would suit better with the words : ' while hours are still granted you '.

PAGE 161. *Quarter-Sessions.* A court of Justices of the Peace held once a quarter, which deals with graver offences than those pertaining to Petty Sessions. On the administrative functions pertaining to it before the Local Government Act of 1888, see

Introduction, p. xxxi. The Justices are, or were, usually country gentlemen, and perform their duties gratuitously.

Hippocratic look. Hippocrates was a famous Greek physician, born about 460 B.C. 'Hippocratic' is applied to the 'shrunken and livid aspect of the countenance immediately before death, or in a case of exhaustion threatening death; so called because described by Hippocrates' (*N.E.D.*). A pun is perhaps intended on the meaning of the name Hippocrates = 'horse-master'.

Sliding-Scale. See Introduction, p. xiv.

Kentish-fire. 'A prolonged and ordered salvo or volley of applause, or demonstration of impatience or dissent (said to have originated in reference to meetings held in Kent in 1828–29 in opposition to the Catholic Relief Bill).'—*N.E.D.*

MENE, MENE. Daniel v. 26.

Tanneries of Meudon. During the Terror of 1794 there was 'at Meudon a Tannery of Human Skins; such of the guillotined as seemed worth flaying; of which perfectly good wash-leather was made'.—*French Revolution*, v. vii.

PAGE 162. *Game Laws.* See Introduction, p. xxxii.

Chandos Clauses. The clause in the Reform Bill under which the franchise was granted to £50 occupiers in counties, moved as an amendment to the Bill by Lord Chandos during the Committee Stage of July–September, 1831. Its object was to defeat the effect of another clause in the bill which enfranchised all free-holders of property worth forty shillings a year. The landlords worked the Chandos Clause by 'making brothers, sons, nephews, uncles—ay, down to the third generation if they happened to live upon the farm—all qualify for the same holding. . . . This they did, and successfully, and by that means gained the counties.' (Cobden, Speech at Covent Garden, Dec. 11, 1844.) On the Marquess of Chandos, afterwards Duke of Buckingham and Chandos, see note to p. 168.

Bribery Elections. See note to p. 226.

Eldorados. i.e. the 'Golden Land', a fabulous district, rich in gold beyond dreams, that existed in the imaginations of the first Spanish adventurers in S. America, and, after Orellana's voyage up the Amazon in 1540, was thought to lie somewhere near the springs of the Orinoco. Many men died in the search for it.

'*Cannot I do . . .*' See note to p. 5.

Hercules. See note to p. 17 on *Lernean Hydra-coil.*

PAGE 163. *Il faut payer de sa vie.* The expression *payer de sa personne* is quoted, with a number of examples, in Littré with the meaning 's'exposer dans une occasion dangereuse'.

Descend, O Donothing Pomp. King Lear, III. iii. 33:

> Take physic, pomp;
> Expose thyself to feel what wretches feel,
> That thou mayst shake the superflux to them,
> And show the heavens more just.

The Czar of Russia. Peter the Great (1672–1725), the pioneer of civilization in Russia. After acquiring the supreme power in 1689, Peter spent eight years in forming a trained army and developing a navy and an oversea trade. In 1697 he left Russia in disguise in the train of an Embassy to various European States, and, in order to inform himself on the art of shipbuilding, worked for some time as a common shipwright in the yards at Amsterdam and Zaandam (or Saardam), which is five miles north-west of Amsterdam.

Piepowder Court. A court held at fairs and markets for the speedy settlement of disputes between hawkers and pedlars; also called the 'Court of Dusty Foot' (O.F. *pied poudré*). Its juris diction has been transferred to Petty Sessions.

apparitor. An usher of a court.

Adamant Tablets. See note to p. 8.

Benedict the Jew. See pp. 52, 53, and notes.

thy dust, i.e. gold-dust.

anatomist-subject, i.e. not only does the deficient class or institution pay its debt by dying, but it is furthermore useful in furnishing an object-lesson in the laws of Nature.

PAGE 164. *Land-Tax Bill, Property-Tax Bill.* See note to p. 21. Both these measures were included in Peel's Income Tax of 1842, which, as Gladstone said, was 'rather a system of taxation than a single tax'.

When the brains are out . . . See note to p. 22.

Anti-Corn-Law Lecturer. A staff of travelling lecturers was employed by the Anti-Corn-Law League to expound its views throughout the country.

at a damage, as above computed, of a hundred thousand pounds an hour. The allusion is to a sentence on p. 149: 'If I were the Conservative Party, I would not for a hundred thousand pounds an hour allow these Corn-Laws to continue?'

BOOK III. CHAPTER IX

PAGE 165. *The Continental people are ' exporting our machinery . . .'* The continental nations began to reduce England's long start in industry in the 'thirties, but their competition was not for some time appreciable except in cotton and to some extent in machinery. Between 1820 and 1840 steam came into general use for the cotton industry in Alsace and the district of Lille, in Belgium, and in Switzerland; while Saxony, though not so forward as the rest in mechanical equipment, was a successful competitor in the cheaper and lower-paid articles of cotton hosiery. Whoever reads the *Authentic Report of the late important discussions in the Manchester Chamber of Commerce* (1839) will come upon familiar language about ' Britain's setting sun '. The United States had captured the market in ' Nigger clothing ', and the Germans the market in 'low fancy pantaloons'. One manufacturer had sold his goods in Saxony up to 1824, had then 'struggled on' until in 1833 he 'lost the South American Continent in every article supplied by the Saxons'. The Chamber state in a petition to Parliament that 'establishments for the making of all kinds of machinery have lately been formed in nearly all the chief towns of Europe', and that the machines were made from English models and by English artisans who were teaching the native workmen their craft. A witness before the Select Committee of the House of Commons on the export of machinery in 1841 stated that the Belgians were exporting their home-made tools all over the world. Up to this time the export of English machines for spinning cotton had been strictly prohibited, so as not to give the foreigner the secrets of the trade; but the important parts of many machines were minute, and were easily smuggled out. Most of the evidence before the Committee was to the effect that, if the prohibition of export were withdrawn, our own engineers would kill the foreign trade by the superiority of their workmanship; and that superiority was still indisputable. And in respect of cotton, many of the conclusions from the loss of local markets or the rapid growth of foreign exports were fancifully pessimistic.

copperas-fumes. 'The proto-sulphate of iron, also called *green vitriol,* used in dyeing, tanning, and making ink.'—*N.E.D.*

gnomes of Europe, slaves of the lamp. Gnomes are small and ugly spirits living in the bowels of the earth and guarding or delving its treasures. Whenever Aladdin's lamp (in the *Arabian Nights*) was rubbed its genius appeared, asked for orders, and accomplished every wish. By his aid Aladdin became exceedingly rich and prosperous.

a Hell which means, 'Failing to make money'. See pp. 131–2.

PAGE 166. *billy-rollers.* These are 'roving machines', i.e. rollers which draw out and slightly twist the rove, or sliver of cotton or wool, which is then coiled on bobbins.

PAGE 167. *'over-population'.* See Introduction, p. xlviii.

PAGE 168. *The man of Macedonia.* Acts xvi. 9.

Prize Essays, Bridgwater Bequests. See note to p. 133.

'a minimum of Four thousand five hundred a year'. See Introduction, pp. xxxiv, xxxv.

Mahometan Paradises. 'In Paradise are rivers of water without corruption, and rivers of milk, the taste whereof changes not, and rivers of wine delicious to those who drink, and rivers of honey clarified; and there shall they have all kinds of fruit, and forgiveness from their Lord.' *Koran* xlii (Palmer's translation).

Sindbads. The allusion is to the tale of 'Sinbad the Sailor' in the *Arabian Nights,* and his strange adventures in search of wealth.

Chandos Farm-Labourers. The Grenvilles succeeded to the estates of the ancient family of Chandos by marriage in 1796.

Richard Grenville, second Duke of Buckingham and Chandos
(1797–1861), succeeded to the title in 1839. He was previously
known as the Marquis of Chandos (see note to p. 162). In
September, 1841, he was made Lord Privy Seal in Sir Robert Peel's
Administration, but resigned in the following January on Sir
Robert's proposal to tamper with the Corn Law. As the stoniest
opponent of repeal he was known as 'The Farmer's Friend', and
was a butt for all manner of satire and invective in the Anti-Corn-
Law pamphlets. While the labourers on his domains lived as
poorly as man can, his prodigality involved him in a debt of
£1,000,000. In 1847 he was sold up, and retired to write books
of Memoirs on the Continent. On the agricultural population, see
Introduction, p. x.

PAGE 169. *Molière Doctors.* 'Nous avons changé tout cela':
Molière, *Le Médecin malgré lui*, ii. 6. Said by the sham doctor to
justify his mistake as to the positions of the heart and liver.

BOOK III. CHAPTER X

PAGE 170. *Destinies, Mothers of the Universe.* In Plato, *Republic*,
617 c, the Fates are 'daughters of Necessity' (θυγατέρας τῆς Ἀνάγκης
Μοίρας). But Carlyle is possibly thinking of a passage in Grimm's
Deutsche Mythologie (English translation, i. 417) on the Scandinavian Norns, the equivalents of the Μοίραι and the Parcae: 'The
weaving of the norns and the spindle of the fays gives us to
recognise *domestic motherly* divinities. Among Celts especially the
fatae (fays) seem apt to run into that sense of *matres* and *matronae.*'
The ancient cult of the *Matres* (otherwise *Matronae, Matrae*) originated in Gaul and was of Celtic origin. All that is known of it is
derived from a comparatively few sculptures and inscriptions,
which seem to show (*a*) that the Mothers were worshipped as the
genii of cities and places, since a topographical epithet is commonly
added to their names, and (*b*) that they were conceived of as
identical with the Parcae. Their number is frequently three.
See *Corpus Inscr. Lat.* vii. 927 *Matr(ibus) Parc(is)*, and article
Matres in Roscher's *Lexikon der griechischen und römischen Mythologie.* Their attributes seem further to agree with that of the
Celtic fairies; they are kind (*indulgentes*) and confer blessing and
wealth on homes and towns, and fertility on the soil.

'*wine and walnuts philosophy*'. Tennyson, *Miller's Daughter*, 31:

in after-dinner talk
Across the walnuts and the wine.

'*Soul, take thy ease . . .*' St. Luke xii. 19.

his Grace of Castle Rack-rent. *Castle Rackrent* is the title of
a novel of Maria Edgeworth's, published in 1800.

Plugson . . . in St. Dolly Undershot. The reader must try to find an affinity with Plugson in the sound of his name. 'St. Dolly Undershot' is a parody of St. Andrew Undershaft, one of the London parishes. A dolly is the name for a machine that passes strips of cloth through a detergent liquid, and then through a pair of rollers. An undershot wheel is a water-wheel that is hit by the stream of water at a point under the level of the axis. The machinery of factories was driven by water in the early days. In *Sartor* ii. 3, Teufelsdröckh says of the Professors of a University that they lived by their reputation, which, 'like a strong undershot wheel, bade fair to hold long together and of its own accord assiduously grind for them '.

Heaven's Chancery. The word Chancery may mean a Court of Law, in England the Lord Chancellor's Court; or a record office, archives.

as my Moslem friends say, 'are written on the iron leaf'. Professor Margoliouth has kindly sent me the following note: 'The reference is to the recording of men's deserts by certain angels. I do not know whence Carlyle got the idea that these leaves are of iron; as he says "my Moslem friends", perhaps he heard the phrase in conversation. I believe the record is more usually supposed to be on parchment.'

PAGE 172. *his life 'a battle and a march'.* Job vii. 1; Seneca, Epistle 36: ' vivere est militare '. Carlyle is possibly quoting his own translation of the lines in Schiller's *Wallenstein's Tod*, III. xv:

> Ein ruheloser Marsch war unser Leben,
> Und wie des Windes Sausen, heimatlos,
> Durchstürmten wir die kriegbewegte Erde.

His rendering (in *Life of Schiller*, Pt. III, p. 113, shilling edition, Chapman & Hall) is :

> Our life was but a battle and a march,
> And like the wind's blast, never-resting, homeless,
> We stormed across the war-convulsèd Earth.

All Fighting, &c. See p. 11.

Bucanier. Or buccaneers. A name given to the planters and sea-rovers of all nationalities who contested the Spanish monopoly in South America during the seventeenth century and were seated in the West Indian Islands, more especially San Domingo. From the native *boucan*, a factory for preserving meat, in which article they carried on a large illicit trade. Their power declined in the closing years of the century in consequence of the antagonism of the English and French elements, and the alliance of France and Spain in 1700 led to their extinction.

Battlefields and garments rolled in blood. Isaiah ix. 5.

PAGE 173. *Howel Davies.* Carlyle means, apparently, Edward Davis, the greatest of the buccaneer Captains and the commander of the victorious fleet which rifled the Spanish possessions on the Pacific sea-board from 1685 to 1688.

PAGE 174. *Taillefers.* The name means 'Cleaver of Iron'. The historical Taillefer was a Norman minstrel, who at Senlac obtained William's leave to strike the first stroke. He rode alone from one host to the other singing of Roland and Charlemagne, and tossing up his sword and catching it by the hilt. At the English line he pierced one man with his lance, cut down another, and died under a shower of blows.

Law-ward. The true derivation is, however, from O.E. *hláford, hláfweard,* 'keeper of the loaf'.

PAGE 175. *money,—the thing which is least of all mine.* He means, of course, that money is a social trust. Cf. the passage on land, p. 158 : 'Properly speaking, the Land belongs to these two : to the Almighty God; and to all His Children of Men '; and contrast the Duke of Newcastle's 'Have I not the right to do what I like with my own ?' (pp. 5, 156, 162).

tipstaves. The bearers of staves tipped with metal, constables or bailiffs.

Westminster Hall. See note to p. 8 on *Courts of Westminster.*

two million sitting in Bastilles, and five million pining on potatoes. See p. 149 *infra.*

PAGE 176. *our Continental friends call ' Organization of Labour',* i. e. 'l'organisation industrielle'. See Introduction, pp. lxxvii-lxxix.

' *on a minimum of four thousand five hundred'.* See Introduction, pp. xxxiv, xxxv.

BOOK III. CHAPTER XI

PAGE 177. *The latest Gospel in this world. . . .* 'Know thyself' (γνῶθι σεαυτόν) is the famous maxim of Solon, the sage and law-giver of Athens. Cf. *Sartor Resartus,* ii. 7 : ' A certain inarticulate Self-consciousness dwells dimly in us; which only our Works can render articulate and decisively discernible. Our Works are the mirror wherein the spirit first sees its natural lineaments. Hence the folly of that impossible Precept, *Know thyself*; till it be translated into this partially possible one, *Know what thou canst work at.*' This 'latest Gospel' was in the first place Goethe's, and propounded in *Wilhelm Meister* and elsewhere. Goethe was especially occupied with the case of the dilettante,—the disease of youth, the ambition to achieve ends for which the aspirant is unfit, and for which he may leave his proper path in life to wander unprofitably. It may be he will wander to the end; or it may be that, like Wilhelm, he will strike the true road while looking for the wrong one. Wilhelm began as a reformer of the German stage, and ended as a surgeon. Faust, fretting under his unsatisfied powers, and bartering his soul for boundless opportunity, is a grander version of the same case. Goethe teaches that only by working actively in a definite sphere can a man test himself and find the clue to happiness. But he must first give up many of the desires and ambitions in which the manifold factors of his nature clamour for indulgence. He must limit and deny himself (*entsagen*), subordinating the lower to the higher, preferring what is possible to what is not, and schooling himself in the 'Religion of Sorrow', or in other words of renunciation. In this search for happiness he must begin, though he will not necessarily end, with the sphere in which he finds himself. It will be as well to collect here the two or three passages in *Wilhelm Meister* which Carlyle is fond of quoting, besides that already given in a note to p. 138. *Lehrjahre*, v. 16 : ' Ere long he will feel how true it is that doubt of any sort can only be removed by activity.' Ibid.,vii. 1: ' The safe plan is always to do the task that lies nearest us.' Ibid., vii. 3: ' " In America I fancied that I might accomplish something; overseas I hoped to become useful and essential; if any task was not begirt with a thousand dangers, I considered it trivial, unworthy of me. How differently do matters now appear! How precious, how important seems the duty which is nearest me, whatever it may be ! " " I recollect the letter which you sent me from the Western world," said Jarno; " it contained the words : I will return, and in my house, amid my fields, among my people, I will say : *Here or nowhere is America !* " ' And the concluding lines of the poem ' Von den Bergen zu den Hügeln ' in *Wanderjahre*, III. i :

> Und dein Streben, sei's in Liebe,
> Und dein Leben sei die Tat.

See *Sartor* on ' The Everlasting Yea ' (ii. 9).

    old as the Prophet Ezekiel. There is no reference to the potter's wheel in Ezekiel. Carlyle is evidently thinking of Jeremiah xviii.

PAGE 178. ' *Doubt of whatever kind* ', &c. See note to p. 177 on *The Latest Gospel in this world.*

PAGE 179. *Sir Christopher.* Sir Christopher Wren (1632–1723), as Surveyor-General of the Royal Buildings, was entrusted with the public works for the restoration of London after the Fire (1666) ; and built fifty-two of the City churches besides St. Paul's. St. Paul's was begun in 1675 and substantially completed in 1716 ; during all which time Wren was the architect and the leading member of the commission in charge. His original design was in the form of a Greek cross ; but the commissioners (including several bishops), greatly to his regret, insisted on a building more after the ordinary plan of an English cathedral, and the outlines were altered to those of a Latin cross. This, the first of many disputes between Wren and the other commissioners, was no discredit to any one ; but in the other and later cases the action of the commissioners was wholly wrong in architecture and otherwise presumptuous, spiteful, and mean. The artistic defects in St. Paul's are due, each and all, to the fact that the architect was thwarted or ignored by these busybodies. It came in the end to public recriminations, and Wren had to petition Queen Anne to 'interpose her royal authority' in his favour. In 1718 the Cabal triumphed, and he was dismissed from his Surveyorship with insult. Carlyle's account requires to be corrected in two points. (a) During the years when the commission so ill-treated Wren its episcopal members were no longer active. Of its six or seven active members only the Dean of St. Paul's and one of the Chapter were of the clergy (Dean Milman's *Memorials of St. Paul's*). (b) There is no record in the *Parentalia* (the account of Wren by his son), or in Elmes's *Life*, of the architect's being hampered by lack of funds or of his appealing for subscriptions. The work was paid for by an annual tax on coal, given by Parliament, and by subscriptions from all the dioceses in England, and the account of the revenues by Dean Milman (*op. cit.*) points to their having been sufficient.

Like Gideon. Judges vi.

PAGE 180. '*It is so*', &c. I have not been able to trace this quotation.

Columbus. Christopher Columbus (? 1446–1506) set sail for the New World in 1492 in the *Santa Maria*, a small vessel, and two smaller consorts, the whole squadron comprising 120 men. His men were greatly terrified by a variation of the magnetic needle observed as they were in mid Atlantic, and on this, as on his other voyages, Columbus had to fight constantly with discouragement and mutiny. After discovering Hayti and Cuba he returned home in one of his small consorts, the flagship having been lost in a great tempest, and the other consort driven out of her course. Four other voyages followed, all of them troubled by the fears and rancours of his subordinates and superiors.

from Ursa Major, i.e. the Great Bear.

BOOK III. CHAPTER XII

PAGE 181. *Antinomians.* From the Greek ἀντί and νόμος, i.e. 'against law', a name applied to a sect represented by John Agricola, who, while embracing the principles of the Reformation, maintained that no moral law was binding on Christians, since they were justified by grace and faith and not by works. Agricola was strongly opposed by Luther from 1527 onwards, and retracted his doctrine in 1540.

Spinning Dervishes. The 'Dervishes' (from a Persian word meaning 'mendicant' or 'poor') are a large class of devotees known in all Mohammedan countries, and divided into many orders. They correspond now to Christian monks and now to friars. One of their orders, the Spinning or Dancing Dervishes (Meulevis), was founded late in the thirteenth century, the peculiar feature of their worship being an excitement under which they fall to frenzied dancing, often ended by epileptic seizures. A conical cap and wide skirts are parts of their garb.

Laborare est orare. Proverbial and mediaeval. Also current in the form, 'ora et labora'.

Talfourd-Mahon Copyrights. Sir Thomas Talfourd, a lawyer and author, who introduced the Copyright Bill of 1842. The Bill was backed and carried by Viscount Mahon, afterwards Earl Stanhope. See note to p. 34.

syllabled speech of Whirlwinds. Ezekiel i and ii.

PAGE 182. *work while it is called To-day.* St. John ix. 4.

Kepler calculations. Johann Kepler (1571–1630), besides many discoveries in general physics, was the first to discover (1619) a regular law in the movements of the planets, determined by their distance from the sun. By this he prepared the way for Newton's discovery of the law of gravitation (about 1680).

that Spartan Mother. Plutarch's *Moralia: Lacaenarum Apophthegmata* xv: ὦ τέκνοτ, ἢ τὰν ἢ ἐπὶ τᾶς (ed. Wyttenbach).

folding of the hands to sleep. Proverbs vi. 10 and xxiv. 33.

PAGE 183. '*Much of my life has been trifled away!*' This was a common reflection with Johnson; e.g. Boswell, Aug. 5, 1763: 'I have been an idle fellow all my life'; *Prayers and Meditations,* 1775 : 'Much of my life has stolen unprofitably away.'

Owen's Labour-bank. On Owen see Introduction, p. xxxviii. In 1832 he set up a 'Labour Exchange' or 'Bank of Labour' in London. The bank was a sort of co-operative bazaar, 'designed to enable artificers to exchange among themselves articles which it was thought would represent real value'. 'The shoemaker brought his pair of shoes to the bazaar, with an invoice of the cost, calculated at 6d. per hour [of work expended]. The labour note, of so many hours' value, was given to the shoemaker, who could then, or at any other time, buy with them any other deposit in the bazaar—a hat, or tea-kettle, or joint of meat, if he found what he wanted.' A commission of ½d. in the shilling was charged for expenses. After some initial success the scheme failed (G. J. Holyoake, *History of Co-operation,* i. 104 f.).

PAGE 184. *as Burns said.* Burns's poetical work after October 1787 consisted mainly in composing songs for old Scottish airs. These were published in Johnson's *Museum of Scottish Songs* and in Thomson's *Collection* ; and Burns, regarding both publications as works undertaken by the publishers for Scotland's sake, and not their own, refused to be paid for his contributions. He wrote to Thomson: 'As to my remuneration, you may think my songs either above or below price, for they shall either be the one or the other.' And again, on receiving £5 from Thomson by the post: 'You truly hurt me with your pecuniary parcel. It degrades me in my own eyes. ... As to any more traffic of that debtor and creditor kind, I swear by that honour which crowns the upright statue of Robert Burns's integrity—on the least motion of it, I will indignantly spurn the by-past transaction, and from that moment commence entire stranger to you.' Burns had reaped £20 from the Kilmarnock edition of his poems in 1786, and £500 from the second edition in the next year, but the songs were a gift to his country. See his *Epistle to James Smith* and the lines entitled *The Vision*; and for a discussion of his attitude in the matter, Lockhart's *Life*, chapter ix.

bodies forth the form of Things Unseen. Midsummer Night's Dream, v. i. 14.

PAGE 185. *descend to the Mothers, to the Manes ... Hercules-like.* Hercules twice descended to the Shades, once when he brought up Cerberus to the light of day, and again when he recovered Alcestis. The word *Manes* is connected with the adjective *manus* and means 'good'. It is most commonly used with some other word, e.g. *dii manes.* It means the spirits of the departed, the spirits of ancestors propitiated by the observances of their descendants and become the tutelary divinities of the family. They were religiously worshipped in the Roman family, and the most exalted and solemn epithets were applied to them (*casti, puri, augusti, secreti, aeterni*, &c.). In the famous passage, 'Quisque suos patimur Manes' (*Aeneid* vi. 743), the word is interpreted by Servius, who is followed by Conington, as the genius or attendant deity of a man. Thus the meaning approaches to that of the *Matres* of the Gallic cult described in a note to p. 170.

'*make thee lean for many years*'. *Paradiso*, xxv. 1-4.

'*Se tu segui tua stella!*' *Inferno*, xv. 55. Brunetto Latini is the speaker. 'If thou followest thy star thou canst not fail to reach the glorious port.'

dragons, ... Cerberuses. He is thinking of the snakes and dragons in *Inferno*, xxiv, xxv. Cerberus was the three-headed dog which guarded Hell's gate in Vergil and the third circle of the Inferno in Dante (*Inferno*, vi).

Eccovi l'uom ch'è stato all' Inferno. 'See the man who has been in Hell.' Carlyle quotes this in the Lecture on 'The Hero as Poet', as having been said by the people of Verona when Dante was in exile there. He has taken the story from a secondary source, and not from Boccaccio, Dante's first biographer, on whose word it rests. Boccaccio tells that once, when the poet was passing a gate of Verona, a woman cried out: 'Do ye see him who goes to Hell, and returns when he pleases, and brings news of those that are down there?' (Vedete colui che va nell' Inferno?) 'Which he overhearing, as if content that they should be of such an opinion, passed on, smiling a little.'

as Poet Dryden says. I have not been able to find this.

PAGE 186. *Eurydice from Tartarus.* Eurydice was the wife of

Orpheus, who, when she died, descended to Hades, and prevailed on Pluto and Persephone to release her. They promised to let her follow him, if he would not look back on her until he reached the light of day. He had almost won her when, fearing she might not be following, he looked back, and lost her.

lath and plaster hats. See p. 128.

'*Black or White Surplice*' *Controversies.* The surplice was ordered by the Second Prayer Book of King Edward VI to be used by the clergy at divine service 'at all times of their ministration'; and the injunction was upheld by Elizabeth in the Act of Uniformity and in the 'Advertisements'. Until the Anglican Revival it was the custom to substitute for it the black Geneva 'gown' during the sermon. But about 1840 the High Anglicans began to disuse the custom and retain the surplice as well during the sermon as at other times. The controversy became heated in consequence of a diocesan Charge delivered by the Bishop of London in October 1842, in which he recommended the entire retention of the surplice, at any rate during morning service, while many of the other bishops in their Charges recommended the use of the gown. See the *Quarterly Review*, May 1843, or *The Rubrics and Ritual of the Church of England*, and *A Few Thoughts on Church Subjects* by Edward Scobell (1843).

hair-and-leather Popes. See pp. 124–5.

Law-wards. See note to p. 174.

'*organising Labour*'. See Introduction, p. lxxvii.

Devil's-dust. See note to p. 127.

in a Great Taskmaster's eye. Milton, *Sonnet: On his having arrived at the age of twenty-three.*

PAGE 187. *Taillefer.* See note to p. 174.

Antaeus-like. Antaeus was a Titan, whose strength departed from him whenever he was lifted from the earth.

Goulburn-Baring Budget. Henry Goulburn was Chancellor of the Exchequer under Peel from 1841 to 1846, and Sir Francis Baring, afterwards Baron Northbrook, held the same office from 1839 to 1841.

Dilettante legislation. See Introduction, p. xxx.

'*Sinews of war*'. 'Nervos belli pecuniam infinitam' (Cicero, *Philippics*, v. 2. 5).

PAGE 188. *adscititious.* 'Supplemental', 'taken in to complete something else, though originally extrinsic'. From Lat. *adsciscere*, to accept from others. (*N. E. D.*)

'*Arms and the Man*'. Vergil's 'Arma virumque cano'. This notion of the epic of 'Tools and the Man' appears in the Essay on *Corn-Law Rhymes.*

BOOK III. CHAPTER XIII

PAGE 189. *villani, bordarii.* The villeins, by far the largest
class enumerated in the Domesday Inquest, are rustics performing
work services for their lords, and holding shares, of which however
they cannot dispose, in the lands of their villages. They were
distinct from the sokemen or freemen (see note to p. 67), for,
among other differences, a villein could not bring a suit against
his lord or claim protection from the King's courts. But they are
also distinct from a small class of personal slaves (*servi*) and from
bordarii and *cottarii.* Med.Lat. *borda* means a cottage. The *borda-
rius*, in return for his menial services to the lord, held a cottage
and a smaller plot of land than the villein; the *cottarius* merely
a cottage and croft.

sochemanni. See note to p. 67.

'*Eu Sachsen nimeth euer Sachses.* Hengist's call to his men to
attack the Britons. The first two words are an addition to the
sentence as reported in the original tale. 'The ridiculous *eu* is for
A.-S. *ge.* The phrase would be in true A.-S.: Ge Seaxan nimath
eowre [or eower] seaxas. The story is not found in the oldest
English, but occurs in Layamon's *Brut*, ed. Madden, vol. ii, p. 214,
where the sentence is: nimeth eoure sexes, take [or draw out]
your knives. In Robert of Gloucester, ed. Hearne, p. 125, it
appears as: nimeth youre saxes.'—Professor Skeat, *Notes and
Queries*, Ninth Series, xi. 158.

PAGE 190. *Fire-Chariot of Pain.* 2 Kings ii. 11.

Phalaris' Bull. Phalaris, tyrant of Agrigentum in the middle
of the sixth century B. C., built a brazen bull in which the victims of
his enmity were roasted alive, so that the roaring of the bull might
be counterfeited by their cries. He was finally overthrown and
himself roasted in his bull.

Revolts of Three Days. The Revolution that placed Louis-
Philippe on the throne of France (see note to p. 217) began on
July 26, 1830, and was master of Paris, and therewith of France,
on July 29.

Irish Widow. See p. 134.

Hlaf-díg', Benefactress. The true derivation is from O.E. *hlœf-
diʒe*, from *hláf* = loaf + root *díg*, to knead (cf. dough) = the 'loaf-
kneader'.

Mungo Park. A Scottish surgeon, who made two journeys, one
in 1796–7, and the second in 1805, in order to determine the
course of the Niger, in which he did not succeed. On the second
journey, he was drowned in the river when escaping in a crazy
canoe from a hostile force of natives. His *Travels in the Interior
of Africa* (1799) and the *Journal* of his second adventure (published
in 1815) have a high place in the literature of travel. The incident
mentioned in the text is related in chapter xv of the *Travels.*

PAGE 191. *Gurth ... Cedric.* See note to p. 19. 'The villeins had their rights as well as the lord. The lord was bound to guard them against external oppression or injury. The extent of his rights over them, no less than of their duties to him, was defined by a strict and minute code of custom, to which long presumption gave all, and more than all, the force of law. The villein's life was not harder than that of the poor free man; it was quite as secure from wrong, and more secure from want. The majority of the cultivators were indeed tied to the land; but the land was tied to them; the lord was bound to furnish each little bundle of acre strips with its proper outfit of plough-oxen, to provide each tenant with his little cottage, and to see that the heritage passed on to the next generation, just as the manor itself, and with it the tenants and their services, passed on from father to son. Even if a tenant failed in his dues the worst punishment that could befall him was the seizure of his little household goods; eviction was out of the question.'—Miss Kate Norgate, *England under the Angevin Kings*, i. 61.

The true liberty of a man, &c. This element in the doctrine of the Hero is taken almost verbally from Fichte's *Staatslehre* (*Werke*, I. iv, p. 436): 'In case of need one single man has the right and duty to compel the whole of mankind; for to that which is contrary to Right they have, as against him, no right and no freedom. For Right is an idea which they all ought to have, and which they all will have so soon as they are raised to his level. This idea, in the meantime, he has in the name of them all, as their representative, in virtue of the grace of God which works in him.' Quoted by Professor Vaughan in 'Carlyle and his German Masters', *Essays and Studies by Members of the English Association*, Oxford, 1910.

Senior, Seigneur. The French word is derived from the Latin.

PAGE 192. *Tancred of Hauteville.* Hauteville was a small castle near Coutances. Tancred, the lord of the place, and ten of his twelve sons founded the two Norman duchies of Sicily and Apulia in the first half of the eleventh century.

Champion of England. See note to p. 127.

Hereward. Hereward the Wake is a great name in legend, but little is known of him historically. He was a Lincolnshire landowner, and led the men of the Fen Country when they revolted in 1070. Their valiant resistance in the Isle of Ely attracted thither the malcontents from all over England. William bridged the marshes and stormed the camp in 1071; and Hereward, who escaped capture, was subsequently pardoned. An uncertain authority relates that the King took him with him to Normandy, and that he was there treacherously slain by Norman nobles.

Earl Waltheof. Son of Siward, and Earl of Northampton and Huntingdonshire. He submitted after Senlac, and retained his earldom; led the North in the revolt of 1069, but was restored to favour, married to the King's niece, and made Earl of Northumbria.

In 1075 Ralph of Hereford excited a revolt of malcontent Normans and English during the King's absence oversea. Waltheof, either willingly or under compulsion, promised the rebels his support, but forthwith repented of his promise, and hastened to William in Normandy to confess his guilt. William apparently forgave him; but, on returning to England to stamp out the last embers of the rebellion, had him arrested and tried before the Witan for treason. As a popular hero, and the last of the great English nobles, he was dangerous, and Norman rivals coveted his estates. William allowed himself to be persuaded. The Earl was condemned for not sooner apprising the King of Ralph's designs, and beheaded at Winchester in May 1076, to be canonized by his countrymen as martyr and saint. His beheading is regarded by historians as a judicial murder, and the greatest blot on William's record as a king.

Yorkshire and the North reduced to ashes. After Waltheof's revolt, which had its centre at York in 1069, had been put down, William ' went to and fro over points a hundred miles from one another, destroying, as far as in him lay, the life of the earth '. Domesday Book, seventeen years after, bore ' passionate witness ' to this ravaging by ' the entries of " Waste ", " Waste ", " Waste ", which we read through page after page of the Yorkshire lordships ' (Freeman).

' *A child in this William's reign* ', &c. The Anglo-Saxon (Peterborough) Chronicle under 1087 says : ' Among other things is not to be forgotten the good peace he made in this land, so that a man who was himself of any importance might fare unharmed over his kingdom with his bosom full of gold.'

PAGE 193. ' *Par la splendeur de Dieu!* ' William's favourite oath.

Joe-Manton Captains of Idleness. See note to p. 124.

PAGE 194. *Open Vestry in St. Mary Axe.* See note to p. 17.

Wahngasse of Weissnichtwo. Professor Teufelsdröckh, the mystic of *Sartor Resartus,* lived in this street, Hallucination Lane in No Man Knows Where (*Sartor*, i. 3).

Herr Ritter Kauderwälsch von Pferdefuss-Quacksalber. ' Kauderwälsch' in German means ' jargon ', ' twaddle ' ; ' Pferdefuss ', a cloven foot ; and ' Quacksalber ', a quack.

Sansculottic. See note to p. 126.

amphibium. See note, p. 125.

PAGE 195. *Antique Cheruscan.* The Cherusci were a primitive German tribe.

Your Stulz. A common German name.

The general outcome he, of what men aimed to do. On clothes as the sign of social fact and thought, see *Sartor*, i. 5.

hemmed in by Sedan and Huddersfield. Two centres of the cloth-making industry.

Sinking his taper flame-downmost, &c. In classical mythology Sleep and Death were twin brethren, children of Night (*Iliad*, xiv.

231; *Aeneid*, vi. 278). A figure of Sleep (or Death) is sometimes found on Roman tombs, leaning on, or holding, a torch reversed. Torches were usually carried reversed at Roman funerals (*Aeneid*, vi. 223 ; Lucretius, vi. 1285).

PAGE 196. *Windsor Georges.* St. George is the patron of the Order of the Garter. Two jewels in the insignia of the Order, graven with his image, are known as the Great George and the Lesser George.

walkest in a vain show. Psalms xxxix. 6.

crotchets. From F. *crochet*, a hook, or crook. The meaning here is 'a fanciful device, mechanical, artistic, or literary'. Cf. Foote's *Liar*: 'All the sighing, dying, crying crotchets that lovers have ever produced ' (*N. E. D.*).

'*fill himself with the east wind* '. Job xv. 2.

PAGE 197. *wardmotes.* Or 'moots '. O.E. *mót, gemót,* 'meeting'. The council of a ' ward ' or administrative division of a borough.

Pococurantism. A 'pococurante ' is an indifferent person, one who ' cares little ' (from the Italian).

Beau-Brummelism. George Bryan Brummell (1778–1840), the boon companion of George IV when Prince of Wales, was known as Beau Brummell. Possessed of great social gifts and a considerable fortune, he was a shining figure in society and the absolute monarch of the mode, so much so that the Prince Regent on one occasion ' began to blubber when told that Brummell did not like the cut of his coat' (Moore's *Journals*, cited in *D. N. B.*). Brummell eventually quarrelled with his patron, squandered his means in gambling, and died a bankrupt and insane.

If you go back to ' the Dead Sea '. See p. 137.

PAGE 199. '*Stuffed Clothes-suits*', &c. The saying 'nine tailors make a man' reflects the common opinion that tailors are physically feeble; it may be a corruption of ' nine tellers make one man ', a ' teller ' being a tolling bell, and the rule being that three threes are tolled at the death of a man, and three twos at the death of a woman.

succedaneum for salt. See note to p. 43.

BOOK III. CHAPTER XIV

PAGE 201. *Mr. Facing-both-Ways.* The name of one of the leading inhabitants of the City of Fair-speech in *The Pilgrim's Progress.*

Cagliostro. The self-styled Count Alessandro di Cagliostro, whose real name was Giuseppe Balsamo (1743–95), a brazen quack, who practised with extraordinary success as alchemist, freemason, and necromancer, both on the Continent and in England, until the effect of many exposures made the world too hot for him. The summit of his career was reached at Paris, where he captivated the Cardinal Rohan, figured impressively at Court, and played a part in the drama of the Diamond Necklace. He died in prison under sentence of the Inquisition for freemasonry. See his story in Carlyle's Essays, *Count Cagliostro* and *The Diamond Necklace*.

Locker of Davy Jones. ' Davy Jones, according to the mythology of sailors, is the fiend that presides over all the evil spirits of the deep' (Smollett, *Peregrine Pickle*). His locker is the ocean depths (*N. E. D.*).

prosper and get Paragraphs, i. e. in the newspapers.

PAGE 202. *extra-forensic*, i. e. ' excluded from the court where the case is tried'.

BOOK III. CHAPTER XV

PAGE 203. *Fanaticism, for any Fanum. Fanum* is Latin for temple or shrine, and the source of ' fanatic '.

PAGE 204. *Jacobinism unfolded into Saint - Simonism.* See Introduction, p. lxxvii. Jacobins were the extremists of the Revolution who became supreme under the ascendancy of Robespierre, and were defeated and discredited after his death (November 1794). They were originally members of a club which sat to debate public questions in the Jacobin (i. e. Dominican) Convent in the Rue St. Honoré.

Henry of Essex. See p. 96.

Kircherean Visual-Spectra. Athanasius Kircher (1601–80), a German Jesuit, was the inventor of the magic lantern.

PAGE 205. *infinite difference between a Good man and a Bad.* See note to p. 22.

'*All religion*', &c. I cannot find this very sentence elsewhere in Carlyle; but cf., out of many passages, *Heroes*, i : ' It [hero-worship] is to this hour the vivifying influence in man's life. Religion I find stand upon it—all religion hitherto known.'

succedaneum for salt. See note to p. 43.

though you rose from the dead. . . . St. Luke xvi. 31.

Morrison's Pill. See note to p. 20.

imbroglios. Italian *imbroglio* = ' entanglement ', from *broglio*, ' confusion '. Cf. ' broil '.

Fetishism. Fetish (Fr. *fétiche*, Lat. *facticius*, factitious) means originally ' any of the objects used by natives of the Guinea coast as amulets, or means of enchantment, or regarded by them with superstitious dread ' (*N. E. D.*).

Arkwright. Richard Arkwright (1732–92) began life as a barber at Bolton, where he became interested in cotton machinery. By the aid of a watchmaker named Kay he invented in 1767 his 'spinning frame', the first machine to turn out cotton thread strong and thin enough to be used as warp. At this time he could not afford a suit of clothes in which to appear decently in the streets. By the aid of friends he set up factories to work his invention in Derbyshire and Nottingham, the machinery being driven first by horses, then by water, and finally by steam. In spite of iniquitous invasions of his patent, and the bitter hostility of the working people, he went on improving his processes, and died enormously rich. He may be called the founder of the factory system.

Adam Smith. He lived from 1723 to 1796, and was Professor of Moral Philosophy at Glasgow. On his *Wealth of Nations* (1766), which first lifted Political Economy to the rank of a separate science, and fathered Free Trade, see Introduction, p. xlvii.

Fountain of Juturna. Juturna was an Italian goddess of fountains, and especially of a healing spring by Lavinium. There seems to be a confusion here between this spring and the pond called *Lacus Iuturnae* in the Forum at Rome. The Janiculum was one of the hills of Rome.

PAGE 206. *Salem.* Commonly identified with Jerusalem (Psalms lxxvi. 2).

Solemn before us, &c. Goethe's *Symbolum.*

Carlton Clubs. This famous Conservative Club, founded in 1832, was built close to the site of Carlton House. This house had been the residence of George IV when Prince of Wales, and was pulled down in 1826.

He will say with Faust, &c. The allusion is to Faust's Confession of Faith in Scene xvi of the drama: ' Who dare name Him ? Who profess, I believe in Him ? ... The All-enfolder, the All-preserver, enfolds He not, preserves He not thee, me, Himself ? Is not Heaven's arch over thee, and Earth firm at thy feet ? Rise not the everlasting stars with their kindly looks ? and gaze I not upon thee, eye into eye ? Comes not all this unto thee, thronging into heart and brain, and weaving its web, seen and unseen, in mystery eternal? Fill thy heart therewith, ay, through and through ; and, when the sense hath steeped thee in bliss, call it what thou wilt,—joy, heart, love, God. I have no name for it. Sense is all ; name is sound and smoke, a cloud over the sheen of Heaven.'

in the Eternal Temple. St. Paul speaks, not only of the human body (as in 1 Corinthians vi. 19), but of the human spirit also as the ' temple of God ' (1 Corinthians iii. 16, 2 Corinthians vi. 16). In *Sartor* II. 9, Carlyle speaks of ' the Holy of Holies, Man's Soul ' ; which again is a quotation from Richter, *Schmelzle's Reise* (given in the first Essay on Richter of 1827).

PAGE 207. *the rotatory calabash.* See note to p. 125.

It was said to the Prophet, &c. Ezekiel viii. 14.

thirty-two azimuths. The word is from the Arabic, meaning an arc of the heavens extending from the zenith to the horizon. Carlyle means by it simply the points of the compass.

the ' Inspiration of the Almighty '. Wisdom vii. 25. See note to p. 262 on *so says John Milton.*

PAGE 208. *tanneries at Meudon.* See note to p. 161.

Flebile Ludibrium, i.e. 'a lamentable mockery'.

PAGE 209. *Norse Odin ... did not he teach us*, &c. 'Among those shadowy Edda matters ... the main practical belief a man could have was probably not much more than this: of the *Valkyrs* and the *Hall of Odin*; of an inflexible Destiny, and that the one thing needful for a man was *to be brave.* The *Valkyrs* are Choosers of the Slain; a Destiny inexorable which it is useless trying to bend or soften. . . . The *Valkyrs*; and then that these Choosers lead the brave to a heavenly Hall of Odin, only the base and slavish being thrust elsewhither, into the realms of Hela, the Death-goddess: I take this to have been the soul of the whole Norse Belief' ('The Hero as Divinity ').

The resuscitation of old liturgies. He means, of course, the Anglican revival. Cf. pp. 105, 265; and see Introduction, p. xxxiii.

manufacture of new liturgies. An allusion, perhaps, to the religious sect of which Carlyle's friend Edward Irving was the founder in 1832, the so-called ' Catholic Apostolic Church '.

Stylitisms. St. Simeon Stylites (Gk. στῦλος, pillar) lived from 423 to 459 A.D. on the top of a pillar 60 feet high at a spot some thirty miles from Antioch. He spent most of the day praying in different postures, usually bending his head so low as almost to touch his feet, and a spectator once saw him assume this attitude 1240 times without resting. He was greatly venerated in life and after death, and an order of Stylites came into existence, who lived after his example.

PAGE 210. ' *Stars silent* ', &c. See note to p. 121.

Aesthetische Springwurzeln. 'Professor Gottfried Sauerteig's *Aesthetische Springwurzeln*; a work, perhaps, as yet new to most English readers. The Professor and Doctor is not a man whom we can praise without reservation; neither shall we say that his *Springwurzeln* (a sort of magical pick-locks as he affectedly names them) are adequate to *start* every *bolt* that locks up an aesthetic mystery: nevertheless in his crabbed one-sided way he sometimes hits masses of the truth' (Essay *On Biography*). *Springwurzel* is a magical root used by treasure-hunters. At its very touch iron doors and safes at once fly open (Grimm, *Deutsche Mythologie*, iv. 812). It is obtained by nailing up a magpie's nest; whereupon the magpie flies abroad and returns with a *Springwurzel*. So Jean Paul Richter speaks of a 'Springwurzel an das weibliche Herz', *Komische Anhänge zum Titan*, ii. 26.

The oldest Eastern Sages ... had felt it so. The ritual of the Zoroastrian Church was characterized from the first by frequent ablutions; and the sanctity of the Ganges in the religion of the Hindus, and the rite of bathing in its waters in token of the washing away of sins, are of very ancient origin.

Herr Professor Strauss. David Friedrich Strauss (1808–1874) published his *Leben Jesu* in 1835, with the purpose of proving that the gospel narrative was a collection of myths, which had grown around a few historical facts. It was the first competent attempt to apply the critical method to the New Testament, and caused great excitement both on the Continent and in England, where the book was translated by George Eliot. Strauss, at the time of the publication, was a teacher of theology at Tübingen. There is no allusion here to any personal communication between him and Carlyle. The writer is Sauerteig.

PAGE 211. *Our new friend the Emperor.* See note, p. 132.

his 'three thousand punctualities'. The elaborate ritual of the Emperor's daily life was laid down in many volumes at the 'Board of Rites' in Pekin. The coronation, the beginning of a campaign, the national sacrifices, and even unimportant actions like a tour of pleasure to Tartary could only be performed according to a code of meticulous procedure (*China*, by Samuel Kidd, 1841).

deep of Heaven, the 'Tsien'. 'Heaven, when used metaphysically, contains a very different idea from that of the firmament, with which, however, it is often confounded. Its extension as a canopy over the earth, in conjunction with which it is worshipped, is the probable reason of its alleged ubiquitous influence and its supreme honour.' The equivalent names for it, in its metaphysical sense, are 'Reason', 'Supreme Ruler' (Kidd, *op. cit.*).

PAGE 212. *Bonzes.* From Japanese *bonzo*, a religious person, used by Europeans of the members of the Buddhist religious orders in China and Japan.

Talapoins. From a Siamese word, meaning a Buddhist monk.

search and sift his whole population. 'It is the professed object of the imperial government to select ministers of state from the Hankin College according to their degrees of literary eminence. So much honour attends the acquisition of its degrees that vast efforts are made by numerous competitors to pass the examination with credit' (Kidd, *ibid.*). The title borne by the six chief ministers of state was at that time 'Great Learned Scholar'.

a Poet Goethe and German Literature. The unique worth of the German poets was to Carlyle that they did not flinch from any truth asserted by the French Freethinkers and Revolutionists, but rather took their point of view and transcended it. 'Do these foreign contemporaries of ours still exhibit, in their characters as men, something of that sterling nobleness, that union of majesty with meekness, which we must ever venerate in those our spiritual fathers [the Elizabethans]? And do their works, in the new form of this century, show forth that old nobleness, not consistent merely with science, the precision, the scepticism of these days, but wedded to them, and shining through them like their life and soul?'—Essay on *The State of German Literature.*

PAGE 213. '*The great event for the world*', &c. 'Neither is there any golden age possible, save only in this: in new arrivals among us of wise and worthy men. Such arrivals are the greatest occurrences.' (Essay on *Goethe's Works.*)

'*well selected from and burnt*'. I cannot trace this quotation.

'*the Thoughts of Thinking Souls*'. This is a saying of Carlyle's own, and occurs in the Essay on Sir Walter Scott. Cf. a passage in the Essay on Diderot: 'The taste of Literature lies in the domain of Belief.... Poetry, it will more and more come to be understood, is nothing but higher Knowledge, and the only Romance (for grown persons) Reality. The Thinker is the Poet.'

Mäson-Lodge. See note to p. 121.

BOOK IV.   CHAPTER I

PAGE 215. '*Philosophical History*'. The historians of the Voltairean school used history as a weapon in the war with the Christian Church. Bolingbroke in his essay *On the Use of History*, letter 2, had quoted the definition of it in the *Ars Rhetorica* of Dionysius of Halicarnassus xi. 2, as 'philosophy teaching by examples' (ἱστορία φιλοσοφία ἐστὶν ἐκ παραδειγμάτων); which, again, was a summary of a passage in Thucydides i. 22. The term 'la philosophie de l'histoire', first used by Voltaire in a treatise under this title in 1765, which he afterwards prefixed to his *Essai sur les Mœurs*, meant, in his mouth, the interpretation of motives and events according to his science of human nature. Thus in his essay *On Biography* Carlyle speaks of 'those modern Narrations, of the Philosophic kind, where "Philosophy teaching by Experience" has to sit, like owl on housetop, *seeing* nothing, *understanding* nothing, uttering only, with such solemnity, her most wearisome *hoo-hoo*'. In another passage, in the Essay *On History*, he deals with the same theme: Hume, and the historians of his temper, hoped to trace cause and effect in history, and gather illustrations for politics or morals. It depends, Carlyle answers, on your philosophy; for if that is sightless, there will be no light in its instances. Moreover, the facts of history are obscure, and still more the causes. Historians, therefore, should 'aim only at some picture of the things acted', and 'at most on reverent Faith, far different from that teaching of Philosophy, pause over the mysterious vestiges of Him whose path is in the great deep of Time'. The philosophical historians disliked 'enthusiasm', regarded Christianity as a myth, and preferred order at any price to violence. Thus Gibbon looked upon the end of the Antonines as the end of a golden age, and 'described the triumph of barbarism and religion'; and the judgements quoted in the text on the Norman Kings and Becket are examples of Hume's general attitude in his *History of England*, where they occur. See his character of Becket in chapter viii.

The Dog, to gain his private ends, &c. From Goldsmith's *Elegy on a Mad Dog*.

PAGE 216. '*Bible of Universal History*', &c. From *Sartor* II. 9: 'One Bible I know of whose Plenary Inspiration doubt is not so much as possible ; nay with my own eyes I saw the God's-Hand writing it ; thereof all other Bibles are but Leaves.' Quoted also, with some variation, in the Essay *On History Again*. He had the image from Richter (see a passage on History in a foot-note to the Essay *On Richter Again*.

written History . . . an Epic. 'The grand world-old Rhapsodia of Existence, page after page (generation after generation) and chapter (or epoch) after chapter. This is what someone names "the sacred Epos or Bible of World-History"' (*Count Cagliostro*. i). By the 'someone' he probably means Richter, see the quotation from *Sartor* in the note above, and the reference to the Essay *On Richter Again*.

Alexandrian Library. The largest collection of books in the ancient world, founded by the first of the Ptolemies. Of its 700,000 volumes part were lodged in the Museum, which was burnt during the siege of the city by Julius Caesar, part in the temple of Jupiter Serapis, where they were destroyed by a mob of fanatical Christians in 391 A.D.

'teaching by example'. See note to p. 215 on '*Philosophical History*'.

PAGE 217. *'the Period of Ignorance'*, i.e. the times before the coming of Mahomet.

Bourbonisms . . . Louis-Philippisms. Louis XVIII and Charles X, the first two Bourbons who were restored to the throne of France after the fall of Napoleon, were the tools or abettors of political and religious reaction. In the 'three days Revolution' of July 1830 Charles was set aside in favour of his cousin Louis-Philippe, who instituted a more liberal policy and for some time held his own by favour of the *bourgeoisie*. He was not liberal enough, however, and his opposition to electoral reform led to the Revolution of February 1848 and the Second Republic under the presidency of Louis Napoleon. In 1851 the presidency became a dictatorship, and was converted in the following year into the Second Empire.

a Governing Class and a Teaching Class. See Introduction, pp. lii, liii.

private-laws or privileges. The derivation is from L. *privus + lex*, a bill in favour of or against an individual.

PAGE 219. *'the unrealities beaten into dust'*, &c. See p. 11 on 'the dust of controversy'.

PAGE 220. *'no King in Israel . . . right in his own eyes'.* Judges xvii. 6.

'Tenpound Franchise'. See note to p. 17.

no right Aristocracy but a Land one. See Introduction, p. liv.

PAGE 221. *Fifty-two millions . . . one twenty-fourth part.* The 'peculiar burthen on land' was a phrase much in use. It was a standing argument of the landed parties, and often maintained by Sir Robert Peel, that the Corn Tax was a just compensation to the Landowners for paying by a good deal the greater part of poor-rate, church-rate, highway-rate, and tithe. The other side answered by pointing to special exemptions enjoyed by the Land, by underlining the share of the towns in the rates and taxes in question, by contending that tithe was not a tax at all, and so on (Hansard, House of Commons, March 14, 1843). Carlyle evidently takes the view of the Repealers that only the old land-tax on the assessment of 1692 (see note to p. 21) was a clear case of a 'peculiar burthen'. The revenue collected for the year ending January 5, 1842, was £52,364,000; for the following year £51,120,000. (But the expenditure exceeded these sums, in the first case by £2,000,000, and in the second by £4,000,000.) The old land-tax yielded roughly £1,200,000; but the amount redeemed under Pitt's Act has to be added, which will bring the burden to approximately £2,000,000. This gives a fraction a little smaller than one-twenty-fourth.

If we made the Holders of the Land, &c. See Introduction, p. liv.

' *on the rim of the horizon*'. p. 98.

Pandarus Dogdraught. Pandarus, a genial cynic with a cozening tongue, is the engineer of the *liaison* of the two lovers in Chaucer's *Troilus and Criseide.* The name has passed current ever since for an abettor of vice. See p. 229. Carlyle is thinking of characters such as the famous Marquis of Hertford, the original of Lord Steyne in Thackeray's *Vanity Fair.*

PAGE 222. '*peace, peace*', &c. Jeremiah vi. 14.

travelling . . . to Rome. Eadmer, a Canterbury monk, lived in the latter half of the eleventh and first half of the twelfth centuries, and was Anselm's closest friend. His *Historia Novorum,* a history of England from the Conquest to 1122, and his *De Vita et Conversatione Sancti Anselmi,* conspicuously sober and trustworthy works, were edited for the Rolls Series by Mr. Martin Rule. The story of the encounter with the Duke of Burgundy is in the first of these writings (ed. Rule, p. 89), and that of the concourse of the French people about the Archbishop in the second (ibid., p. 387 f.). Anselm was made Archbishop of Canterbury in 1093, but refused to take his pallium from William Rufus instead of the Pope. In 1097 William, with much reluctance, allowed him to go to Rome to lay the case in person before the Pontiff.

Jean-Jacques or giant-killing Voltaire, i. e. Jean-Jacques Rousseau. There may be a particular allusion here to the popularity of Rousseau in Paris after the publication of the *Nouvelle Héloïse* in 1760, and to the great ovation paid to Voltaire on his last visit to the capital a few days before his death in 1778 (see *French Revolution,* I. iv). 'Giant-killing' because of his splendid career as a paladin of religious freedom.

Schnüspel the distinguished Novelist. This is probably an allusion to Charles Dickens's triumphal first visit to America in 1842.

PAGE 223. *a European Thibet.* 'Among the Thibetans all is system and order.   A sovereign Lama is placed at the summit of their fabric.   He is esteemed the vicegerent of the only God, the mediator between mortals and the Supreme.   They view him only in the most amiable light, as perpetually absorbed in religious duty.   He is also the centre of all civil government, which derives from his authority all its influence and power.' (S. Turner, *Embassy to the Teshoo Lama.*)

Bromwicham Iron-trades.   This seems to suggest that Birmingham was originally, or alternatively, 'Bromwicham', an idea to which the popular 'Brummagem' may give some colour; and the name does appear in early documents as Brimigham and Brymecham, as well as Bermingham (Home of the Beormingas). Bromwich, in Castle Bromwich, a district of Birmingham, is the *wic* or place covered with broom (Johnston, *Place-Names of England and Wales*).

PAGE 224. *Sufficient for the day,* &c.   St. Matthew vi. 34.
   the Life-tree Igdrasil.   See p. 34 and note.
PAGE 225. *by brass-collar.*   As Gurth to Cedric; see p. 191.
PAGE 226. *imprisoned in ' Impossibility '.*   See pp. 16 and 20.

BOOK IV.   CHAPTER II

PAGE 226. *Bribery Committee.*   A Select Committee on Bribery at Elections presented a Report to the House of Commons in 1835, showing that common and open bribery and intimidation were carried on after, as well as before, the Reform of 1832, and by every class of persons with the means of influencing others.   The proportion of marketable votes in town constituencies is estimated by the witnesses at about a fifth.   In Leicester, to take an instance not much worse than many others, 600 voters out of 2,800 are reported to 'openly boast' of selling their votes and of hanging back to the last moment for bids; 400 or 500 others vote according to opinion, but expect to be paid for it; and the Corporation use the charities of the town to recruit a phalanx of burgesses whose support they sell to one or another of the candidates.   The remedy suggested is usually the ballot; but the evil is spoken of in a tone of fatalism.   Of the means of direct bribery the commonest was the 'refreshment ticket', an order on an innkeeper for food, which was saleable like a promissory note, and which the candidate redeemed for money at a safe interval after the election.   A Statute directed against the abuse was passed in 1842.

PAGE 229. *Pandarus Dogdraught.*   See note to p. 221.
   '*shun to sit' with Dogdraught.*   1 Corinthians v. 11; Psalm i. 1.

BOOK IV. CHAPTER III

PAGE 231. *King Hezekiah's Dial.* 2 Kings xx.

'*Organizing of Labour*'. See Introduction, pp. lxxvii–lxxix.

PAGE 232. *toil second to Ixion's.* Ixion slew his father-in-law, but was pardoned by Zeus, and admitted to Olympus. There he became enamoured of Hera, but by the artifice of Zeus was permitted to embrace, not Hera, but a cloud. For his sin he was bound on an ever-revolving fiery wheel, and perpetually scourged. Carlyle seems to suppose that he had to turn the wheel.

Kilkenny cats. These cats fought until nothing was left but their tails. The story arose in Ireland in the seventeenth century, and was a satire on the constant strife between Kilkenny and Irishtown, by which both places were ruined.

Spinning Dervishes. See note to p. 181.

PAGE 233. *Mother of Dead Dogs.* For a discussion of this phrase see *Notes and Queries*, tenth series, v. 509, vi. 32, 95, vii. 457. It occurs at least eight times in Carlyle's letters and books, and means either the Thames, or some limbo or welter of unfruitful sayings or doings. Thus a letter in Froude, *Life in London*, i. 196: 'I take mostly to the lanes and the fields. such as they are, "grieving by the shore of the Mother of Dead Dogs".' The quotation marks mean, probably, that he is parodying a well-known line in Homer's *Iliad* (xix. 40) or perhaps Spenser's *Prothalamion*, i. 11. In *Reminiscences*, i. 257, he says that De Quincey 'launched into the literary career of ambition and mother of dead dogs'; and in *Latter-Day Pamphlets*, No. v, the simile is beaten out in a disquisition on the Stump Orator: 'The dog that was drowned last summer, and that floats up and down the Thames with ebb and flow ever since,—is it not dead? Alas, in the hot months you meet here and there such a floating dog; and at length, if you often use the river steamers, get to know him by sight. "There he is again, still astir there in his quasi-Stygian element!" you dejectedly exclaim (perhaps reading your Morning Newspaper at the moment). Dead long since, but *not* resting; daily doing motions in that Westminster region still.'

Palace-yard. The space to the north-west of the Houses of Parliament.

A Prime-Minister, even here in England. By 1850 Carlyle had come to regard Sir Robert Peel as the one hope of the country. 'As I read the omens, there was no man in my time more authentically called to a post of difficulty, of danger, and of honour than this man. . . . He has but to lift his finger in this enterprise (of reforming the administration), and whatsoever is wise and manful in England will rally round him.'—*Latter-Day Pamphlets*, No. iv.

PAGE 234. *scaccarium-tallies.* On the word 'scaccarium' see note to p. 56. The accounts between the Exchequer and the Sheriffs were originally kept by tallies, i.e. pieces of wood notched.

PAGE 235. *William Rufus, William of Ipres.* William II was seldom or never without an army of mercenaries. William of Ypres, the confidant of King Stephen of England, and the most noxious and detested of his foreign favourites, was commander of a force of Flemish hirelings, which Stephen instituted upon his accession in 1135. King Canute and his successors, especially Harold, maintained a standing force of so-called *huscarles.* These bodies may be regarded as the forerunners of the Regular Army, and the *fyrd,* or Host of freemen, each bound to bear arms for the defence of the land, as the origin of the Militia.

Ninety thousand of such. The estimates for the Regular Army in 1842 provided for 95,600 men. There was in addition an army of 27,000 men in India, but in the pay of the Company and not the Crown.

losels. 'Wastrel', 'scoundrel'. From the now obsolete verb to 'leese' or lose, = 'one that is lost'.

PAGE 236. *brave Jean-Pauls . . . on 'water without the bread'.* Jean Paul Friedrich Richter (1763–1825), the chief of German humorists, wrote his first books in great poverty. 'The prisoner's allowance is bread and water; but I had only the latter.' Quoted in the Essay *On Richter Again* from his autobiographical reminiscences.

halberts. Or 'halberds'. A weapon in use in the fifteenth and sixteenth centuries, a combination of spear and battle-axe. It was at one time the distinctive weapon of a sergeant. 'To be brought to the halberds, to be flogged: soldiers of the infantry, when flogged, being commonly tied to three halberds, set up in a triangle, with a fourth fastened across them ' (Grose, *Dictionary of the Vulgar Tongue,* 1796, quoted in *N.E.D.*).

PAGE 237. *drummer's cat.* In the British Army it was formerly the duty of the drummer to carry out sentences of the ' cat '.

Spitalfields mob. The silk-weavers of Spitalfields in northeast London were among the most distressed of the working-classes, and riots in this quarter were frequent. A special inquiry into their condition was made by the Poor Law Commissioners in 1837.

a Fourth Estate. The ' three estates ' of the kingdom are the Lords Spiritual, the Lords Temporal, and the Commons. The ' fourth estate' is a term sometimes used of the Press.

Time Bill, Factory-Bill. See Introduction, p. xviii.

Factory-Inspectors . . . Mine-Inspectors. See Introduction, pp. xviii, xix.

seven-and-sixpence a week. See Introduction, p. x.

Sanitary Regulations. See Introduction, p. xxiii.

Aediles. Roman Magistrates, at first two, afterwards four, who, among other charges, were the sanitary police of the City.

Saint-Gileses, i. e. St. Giles's parish, Cripplegate.

PAGE 238. *There are such Mills already extant.* See p. 250, and Introduction, p. xxxix.

a hundred acres of free greenfield. The demand for open spaces in the towns was a minor element of the agitation for Public Health. In 1833 the subject was referred to a Committee of the House of Commons, who found that, with a few exceptions, the great centres of industry were altogether lacking in the means of healthy recreation, and urged that public funds should be raised, and laws enacted, for the purchase of fields near the towns and the widening of streets, so as to countervail the attractions of 'drinking-houses, dog-fights, and boxing matches'.—*Report of Committee on Public Walks.* The need was recognized again by the House of Commons Committee on the Health of Towns in 1840.

a right Education Bill. See Introduction, p. xix.

PAGE 239. *'twenty years of respite'.* See p. 231 : 'from ten to twenty years of new possibility' [after Corn Law Repeal].

'The Schoolmaster's creed', &c. See Introduction, p. xix.

'Emigration Service'. This proposal to use the ships of the Navy was made in *Chartism*, x.

a Hundred and Twenty Millions. When Carlyle wrote the year of the zenith of taxation was 1815. In that year the total amount of revenue raised in Great Britain was 68¼ millions, and in Ireland 6¼ millions, or 74½ millions in all. During the same year the funded debt of the country was increased by 54 millions.

PAGE 240. *Guiltily refused to trade.* Up to 1833 trade with China was a monopoly of the East India Company, and subject to control by the Company's officials; from 1834 onwards it was open to all British subjects, and under no control whatever from the British side. The main article sold by the Company's merchants had been opium, the import of which was forbidden by the Chinese Government in 1796. The authorities, however, connived at the traffic, which grew steadily in volume, and the Indian Government came to reckon on its annual £1,000,000 of export dues on opium as a sort of right. In 1837, whether irritated by the abuses of the now undisciplined trade, or alarmed at the effects of the drug on the Chinese people, or wishing to be rid of the foreigner, or from a mixture of these motives, the Pekin Government suddenly determined to enforce the prohibition, closed Canton, the one open port, to British ships, and called on the British merchants to surrender the opium in stock. It was surrendered, through the mediation of Sir Charles Elliot, the British Agent, and destroyed; but the (ineffective) blockade of Canton was not raised, and the Chinese now demanded of the Agent that he should hand over to them all vessels and persons thereafter detected in the illicit traffic. The demand was refused, and in 1840 the two Powers drifted into the war which ended (1842) with the cession of Hongkong and the opening of Treaty

Ports. The British Government refused to stand by Elliot in his policy of meeting the Chinese view, and connived with its subjects in the forbidden trade ; but whether it was wrong only in the letter, and not wrong on the general merits of the case, has been greatly disputed.

Mycale the Pan-Ionian rendezvous. Mycale was a promontory in ancient Ionia over against Samos. The twelve Ionian cities, of which Ephesus and Miletus were the chief, were connected by a league, religious rather than political, of which the outward mark was the Pan-Ionic Festival, celebrated in the temple of Poseidon on the northern slope of the mountain (Herodotus, i. 148).

' *Children of the Harz Rock* '. It is not clear why Carlyle, or whomever he quotes from, should call the English race by this name. The Saxons did not come originally from the Harz, and only settled in the northern parts of it in historical times. There may be an allusion in the phrase to the connexion between *Sachsen* and *saxum*. *Sachsen* is supposed to come from *sahs, seax*, a sword (see note to p. 189). These swords were originally of stone, and the name is in this way connected with *saxum*.

keep not standing, &c. From the *Wanderlied* in *Wilhelm Meister's Wanderjahre*, III. i.

PAGE 241. *Seven Sleepers.* During the persecution of the Christians by Decius in the year 250, seven of the victims, fleeing from Ephesus, took refuge in a cave. Their pursuers walled up the cave, and the seven fell into a sleep which lasted till the reign of Theodosius II, 200 years later. One of the number, on awakening, went into the city to buy bread, and was arrested for offering an obsolete coin. The Emperor Theodosius inquired into the matter, and became convinced thereby that the doctrine of the resurrection of the dead was true. The legend is related by Gregory of Tours at the end of the sixth century, but was current in the East long before that time. It is commemorated by the Roman Church on June 27.

PAGE 242. *Tailor's Hell.* ' A place under a tailor's shopboard in which shreds and pieces of cloth, cut off in the process of cutting out clothes, are thrown and looked upon as perquisites.' Cf. Green, *Upstart Courtier* : ' He can cast large shreds of such rich stuff into hell under his shopboard.' (*N. E. D.*)

BOOK IV. CHAPTER IV.

PAGE 243. *Bubble-periods with their panics.* There were commercial and financial crises in 1825 and 1836. The first of these, caused by the feverish speculation, and the facility of local banks in advancing money on feeble securities, brought about a ten days' panic which nearly drained the bullion in the Bank of England and resulted in many failures and long-continued distress. The crisis of 1836, due also to excessive speculation, was less severe and made only a temporary mark on the trade of the country.

billy-rollers. See note to p. 166.

My German friend, i.e. Sauerteig.

PAGE 244. *the stars in their courses.* Judges v. 20.

PAGE 245. *preserve game by 'bushing'.* See note to p. 47.

Sacred-Months. The name given to the month during which the Chartists proposed a 'national holiday' or general strike. The proposal was made by O'Connor and his friends in the Convention at Birmingham in July 1839; but in the following August a committee of the Convention pronounced it impracticable, and it was thereupon dropped.

'Sliding'. The reference is to the 'Sliding Scale' of the duty on wheat.

Thou art found Wanting. Daniel v. 27.

PAGE 246. *Chelsea Hospital.* Founded, as a home for old and disabled soldiers, in 1682, at the instigation of Sir Stephen Fox, Paymaster-General of the Forces.

' How is each of us ', &c. From a passage in the first chapter of Jean Paul Richter's *Siebenkäs,* quoted in the essay *On Richter Again.*

'ice-palace'. A reminiscence, probably, of the palace of ice which the Empress Anna of Russia amused herself by erecting on the banks of the Neva in 1740, and which is described by Cowper in *The Task : Winter Morning's Walk,* 122 f.

PAGE 247. *Mammon in never such gigs,* &c. At the trial of the murderer Thurtell the following dialogue took place between witness and counsel: 'I always thought him a respectable man.'—'What do you mean by respectable ?'—'He kept a gig.' Carlyle made endless play with this. So *The French Revolution,* vii. 8 : 'Imposture is in flames; one red sea of fire enwraps the world. Thrones are hurled into it, and Prebendal Stalls that drop fatness, and—ha ! what see I ?—all the *Gigs* of Creation; all, all ! '

PAGE 248. *Marsh-jötuns.* See notes to pp. 14 and 20.

Ægir. The giant Ægir, ruler of the sea, is always represented in Scandinavian mythology as good-natured, and, though a giant, lives in friendship with the gods.

Sons of the far East, i.e. Indo-Europeans.

BOOK IV. CHAPTER V

PAGE 249. *Anti-Slavery Convention . . . Exeter Hall.* See Introduction, p. xxxvi.

PAGE 250. *Model-farms, Niger Expeditions.* See Introduction, p. xxxvii.

Haiti Duke of Marmalade. The negro has had a fair chance in Haiti since the Independence of 1803; but government has always been cruel and corrupt, and little advantage is taken of an

exuberant soil. From 1804 to 1820 the country was under an
' emperor' or a king; since when it has been a republic.   The
Duke of Marmalade is a derisory title for a member of the local
nobility.

    Avec ton Être Suprême, &c. Carlyle found in Robespierre the
perfect type of the prim and narrow-minded idealist.   Under
Robespierre's ascendancy the existence of a Supreme Being was
affirmed by a decree of the Convention. At the 'Feast of the
Supreme Being', on June 8, 1794, several pasteboard figures of
Atheism, Anarchy, and the like were publicly burnt. The words
Avec ton Être Suprême, &c., were addressed to Robespierre by the
Jacobin Billaud-Varennes, who was eventually one of his accusers.
See *The French Revolution*, VI. iv.

    In a Printed Sheet of Mr. Chadwick's.   See Introduction,
p. xxiii f.

    PAGE **251**. *Mother of Dead Dogs.* See note to p. 233.

    PAGE **252**. *sick heart of a Sir Walter Scott.* See Lockhart's *Life*,
ch. lxxxii, lxxxiii. The visit to Italy lasted from December 1831
to the following May. He died at Abbotsford, September 21, 1832.

    *Vagrant Sam-Slicks.   The Clockmaker: Sayings and Doings of
Samuel Slick of Slickville*, by (Judge) Thomas Chandler Haliburton
(London, 1837). Slick is a New England pedlar, peddling clocks
in Nova Scotia, a cool and shifty fellow, who easily outwits the
heavy and gullible Nova Scotiamen.

    grant his Workers permanent interest in his enterprise. The
system of ' profit-sharing ', which has had a long history since
Carlyle wrote, was started in England in 1832 in Lord Walls-
court's works, and advocated by the mathematician and economist
Charles Babbage in his book *On the Economy of Machinery and
Manufacture*, in 1833, and subsequently by John Stuart Mill. It
was not, however, until the years 1889–91 that the idea decisively
took root. In those years it was adopted by some fifty large firms,
and in 1908, 100 firms, employing some 50,000 persons, were acting
on it. It is still regarded by many as a means to industrial peace,
but socialistic influences and the workman's habitual suspicious-
ness are against it. See the article on ' Profit-sharing' by Professor
Egerton in the *Dictionary of Political Economy*.

BOOK IV. CHAPTER VI

    PAGE **254**. *Out of the loud-piping whirlwind*, &c.   Ezekiel
i and ii.

    choke-damp. Carbonic acid gas in mines.

    Moses and all the prophets. Luke xvi. 29.

    PAGE **255**. *do nothing for Burns*, &c. Burns became suddenly
famous on the publication of his first volume of poems, the
Kilmarnock edition, in 1786; he was for some time until then
a partner with his brother in the tenancy of a small and unprofit-

able farm at Mossgiel by Ayr, and so reduced in means and reputation by the troubles connected with his marriage that it seemed his only resource to leave the country. He published his poems to acquire the passage-money to Jamaica, where he had obtained the post of overseer on an estate. His circumstances having become known to some literary men in Edinburgh, they urged him to come to the capital, to arrange for a second edition of his book and look round for help. He was 'lionised and bedinnered' by Edinburgh society in the winter of 1786–87; the tangible results being the liberal subscription to the second edition, which brought him in between £500 and £600, and an appointment as gauger on the Excise, of which the highest emolument was £70 a year. At the close of 1791, after the failure of his farm at Elliesland in Nithsdale, he was totally dependent on his work for the Excise; and his life at Dumfries, from this date to its close in July 1796, wore down his health and his peace of mind. Carlyle has delivered judgement on the whole case in his Essay on Burns.

A modern Duke of Weimar. Karl August (1757–1828). He was a mixed character, rough, coarse, imperious, but a liberal and strenuous ruler of his dukedom. See Lewes' *Life of Goethe,* IV. ii. He was on terms of intimate friendship with Goethe, who became attached to his Court in 1775, at the age of twenty-six, and continued in the service of the Duchy till his death. Schiller was made a Professor at Jena in 1788, and enjoyed besides a small pension from the duke.

Wieland. Christoph Martin Wieland (1733–1813), a kinsman of Lucian and Horace, pleaded with the German aristocracy for German literature by his wit, grace, and *bonhomie.* Of his many works the best known are *Agathon,* an educational romance (1761), and *Oberon,* a romantic epic (1781). The Duchess of Sachsen-Weimar made him tutor to her son in 1772, and he lived on a pension in or near the town until his death.

Herder. Johann Gottfried Herder (1744–1803), 'the Coleridge of Germany,' in whom the poet and the philosopher were blended in equal parts. He waked the romantic insight in Germany into the value of the primitive and popular elements in national literatures. His greatest work, *Ideen zur Menschengeschichte (Thoughts on the History of Man),* is a remarkable anticipation of later theories of evolution in idealistic terms. He was pastor of the chief church in Weimar from 1776 until his death.

Katerfeltoes. Gustavus Katerfelto (d. 1799), a native of Prussia, came to London in 1782, and made a great reputation as conjurer and quack, being especially aided by the epidemic of influenza in that year. He worked on the wonder of the ignorant with magnets, microscopes, and performing cats. Cowper mentions him in *The Task,* IV. i. 86. See *Dictionary of National Biography.* Cf. *Reminiscences,* ii. 173: 'worship as to a mere katerfelto, or thing wondered at'.

PAGE 255. *life-in-death of Poet Coleridge*. This may be a reference to Coleridge himself, to whom, as Carlyle saw him (*Life of Sterling*, I. viii), Nature had given 'a ray of empyrean light:—but imbedded in weak laxity of character, in indolences and esuriences'. He had not 'valiantly grappled with life ', but ' sought refuge in vague day-dreams, hollow compromises, in opium, in theosophic metaphysics '. Or the reference may be to *The Ancient Mariner*, iii. 51:

> The Nightmare Life-in-Death was she
> Who thicks man's blood with cold.

PAGE 256. *Honour to the name of Ashley*. See Introduction, p. xix.

Abdiel found faithful. Paradise Lost, v. 897.

' *a quiet euthanasia* ', &c. ' Absolute Monarchy is the easiest death, the true *Euthanasia* of the British Constitution.' (Hume, *Essays*, I. vii : ' Whether the British Government inclines more to an Absolute Monarchy or a Republic.')

the precept of the Prophet. Jeremiah li. 45.

Epicurus' Gods. Epicurus (see note to p. 141) taught that there were Gods, but that they could not trouble themselves with mortal things, since their life must be careless. Tennyson has presented this notion in his ' Lotos-Eaters ', after Lucretius, *De Rerum Natura*, v. 146 f.

' *Werter blowing out his existence* ', &c. The ' hero ' of Goethe's romance, *Die Tränen des jungen Werter*, is brought up against the limits of his existence by falling in love with Charlotte, another man's wife, who grants him her affection, but not her honour. Werter, unable to bear his disappointment, takes his own life by a pistol-shot.

Thersites . . . Agamemnon . . . Ulysses. Thersites was the ugliest man and most impudent talker among the Greeks before Troy. Once in an assembly he spoke insolently against Agamemnon ; whereupon Odysseus belaboured him with his sceptre, so that the weals started out under his blows (*Iliad*, ii. 212 f.).

PAGE 257. ' *one temple of the world* ', *as Novalis calls it*. Novalis is the pseudonym of Friedrich von Hardenberg (1772–1801), poet and philosopher, whose *Schriften*, in the fourth edition (1826), edited by Ludwig Tieck and Friedrich Schlegel, were reviewed by Carlyle in the *Foreign Review* in 1829. Among the Fragments in the second volume is this saying: ' There is but one Temple in the world ; and that is the body of Man. Bending before man is a reverence done to this revelation in the flesh. We touch heaven when we lay our hand on a human body.'

' *lord of the lion-heart* ', &c. From Smollett's *Ode to Independence* :

> Thy spirit, Independence, let me share !
> Lord of the lion-heart and eagle-eye,
> Thy steps I follow with my bosom bare,
> Nor heed the storm that howls along the sky.

PAGE 258. *no Brother of the Sun and Moon . . . but an Arab Man.* 'Through life we find him [Mahomet] to have been regarded as an altogether solid, brotherly, genuine man. . . . One hears of Mahomet's beauty; his fine sagacious, honest face, brown florid complexion, beaming black eyes;—I somehow like too that vein on the brow, which swelled-up black when he was in anger: like "the *horse-shoe* vein" in Scott's *Redgauntlet*. . . . Not a sensual man. . . . His household was of the frugallest. . . . They record with just pride that he would mend his own shoes, patch his own cloak.'—*Heroes*, ii. 'Brother of the Sun and Moon' was a title borne by the Emperors of China, but never, as the text would seem to imply, by the Sultans.

'Show the dullest clodpole,' &c. From *Sartor Resartus*, iii. 7.

BOOK IV. CHAPTER VII

PAGE 259. *Cliffords.* The principal branch of this great family was that whose estates were in Westmorland and Cumberland and elsewhere along the Scottish border. It was founded by Robert de Clifford, one of Edward I's greatest captains, who subsequently led the opposition to Gaveston under Edward II and fell at Bannockburn; and it played a shining part down to the Civil War.

Fitzadelms. Possibly a reference to William Fitzaldhelm, who succeeded Strongbow as governor of Ireland.

PAGE 260. *Your very Byron.* See note to p. 31.

Anaxarchus. A philosopher of the school of Democritus who was high in favour with Alexander the Great. After Alexander's death (323 B.C.) he was shipwrecked on the coast of Cyprus, and fell into the hands of Nicocreon, the king of the island, whom he had mortally offended, and who caused him to be pounded to death in a mortar. He endured his sufferings with unflinching fortitude. (Cicero, *Tusc.* ii. 21; *De Nat. Deor.* iii. 33.)

a battle and a march. See note to p. 172.

PAGE 261. *Deep calls unto Deep.* Psalms xlii. 7.

the benign Genius. The 'daemon' or guardian spirit assigned to a man at his birth; in some mythologies there is also an evil genius to counter him.

stupendous three-inch pattens. Pattens were at first a luxury for the dame and not for the maid. Thus in the popular fable the Lincolnshire blacksmith is said to have made a pair as a love-offering to the farmer's daughter, Patty. So Gay, *Trivia*, i:

> The patten now supports each frugal dame
> Which from the blue-eyed Patty takes its name.

(Brewer, *Phrase and Fable*.)

leather and prunella. Prunella (F. *prunelle*) is a strong stuff, silk or worsted, used once for clerical gowns. Pope, in the *Essay on Man*, iv. 204, says:

> Worth makes the man, and want of it the fellow;
> The rest is all but leather and prunella;

i.e. the difference between the cobbler and the parson dwindles to nothing. This has been misunderstood, and the phrase now passes for anything to which one is entirely indifferent (*N. E. D.*).

ruggedest Caliban, &c. *The Tempest*, v. i. 286; and I. ii. 325 f.

PAGE 262. *a riding in the Long-acre gig*. See notes to pp. 8 and 282.

Calmuck prayings. See note to p. 125.

dalmatics. From L. *vestis dalmatica*, robe of Dalmatia; loose long robes worn by deacons and bishops on some occasions, and by kings and emperors at their coronations.

Maecenas Twiddledee. Maecenas, the Minister of Caesar Augustus, was the patron of Horace and Vergil.

so says John Milton. 'Time serves not now to give any certain account of what the mind hath liberty to propose to herself, whether the epic form ... or whether those dramatic constitutions wherein Sophocles and Euripides reign. ... Or, if occasion shall serve, to imitate those magnific odes and hymns wherein Pindarus and Callimachus are most worthy. ... These abilities, wheresoever they be found, are the inspired gift of God, rarely bestowed, but yet to some (though most abuse) in every nation.'—*The Reason of Church-Government*, opening of Book II.

scrannel-pipes. *Lycidas*, 123:

> their lean and flashy songs
> Grate on their scrannel pipes of wretched straw.

'Scrannel' means 'meagre', 'thin' (Norwegian *skran*, 'lean').

Lands of Cockaigne. From O. F. *coquaigne*; L. *coquere*, to cook; = 'cake-land', an imaginary land of idleness and luxury.

to say with sick Saul, &c. Saul is not recorded as saying this. See 1 Samuel xviii. 10, 11.

copper shillings to be nailed on counters. An old practice. Hence the expression 'to nail a lie to the counter'.

BOOK IV. CHAPTER VIII

PAGE 263. *Bobus of Houndsditch*. See notes to pp. 26 and 27.

Friend Prudence. See p. 250.

desperate Trades' Unionism. See Introduction, p. xl.

PAGE 264. *The very Bishop informs me*, &c. See Introduction, p. xxxiv.

PAGE 265. *Demiurgus Dollar*. See note to p. 153.

Chronos. The Father and Head of the older dynasty of Gods

in the Greek mythology, who were dispossessed by Zeus and the Olympians.

St. Olaf. Olaf Haraldson (995–1030) learnt the Christian Faith on his Viking raids in England, before succeeding to the throne of Norway in 1015. His drastic suppression of heathenism alienated his subjects, who, with the aid of King Canute of Denmark and England, rebelled, drove him into exile, and made Canute king in his stead (1028). Two years later Olaf returned to Norway with an army, and fell on the field of Striklestad.

Socinian Preachers. 'Socinian' means 'Unitarian', the attitude of the modern Unitarians being very much the same as that assumed by two famous heresiarchs in the sixteenth century— Laelius Socinus or Lelio Sozzini (1525–1562), and his nephew Faustus Socinus or Fausto Sozzini (1539–1604), members of a distinguished family of Sienna. The allusion is to the Brook Farm Colony, a communistic settlement planted in 1841 on an estate eight miles from Boston, and dissolved in 1847. Its members were for the most part scholars, journalists, or ministers of religion who had resigned their charges, and its object was to combine spiritual and intellectual culture with manual labour. For the first three years it succeeded, but by and by failed to support itself. Hawthorne was a member, and drew upon its history in his *Blithesdale Romance.* Its originator, George Ripley, afterwards well known as a literary critic, was pastor of a Unitarian Church in Boston from 1826 to 1840, and during these years one of the leading spirits in what was known as the Transcendentalist Movement in New England. Emerson mentions the project in a letter to Carlyle of October 1840, in which he says: 'We are all a little wild here with numberless projects of social reform. Not a reading man but has a draft of a new community in his waistcoat pocket.'—*The Correspondence of Carlyle and Emerson,* ed. Norton, i. 309. Ripley was an admirer and correspondent of Carlyle's.

Exeter Hall. See Introduction, p. xxxvi.

Puseyisms. See Introduction, p. xxxiv, and note to p. 105.

PAGE 266. *vanishes at cock-crowing. Hamlet,* I. ii. 218.

'*bush*'. See note to p. 47.

PAGE 267. *Brindleys.* See note to p. 144.

Arkwrights. See note to p. 205.

Bath-garters. The two orders are contemptuously jumbled.

Georges. See note to p. 196.

Duke of Weimar. See note to p. 255.

The Future, &c. From Goethe's *Symbolum.* See note to p. 121.

SUMMARY

BOOK I.—PROEM

CHAP. I. MIDAS.

THE condition of England one of the most ominous ever seen in this world : Full of wealth in every kind, yet dying of inanition. Workhouses, in which no work can be done. Destitution in Scotland. Stockport Assizes (p. 1).—England's unprofitable success : Human faces glooming discordantly on one another. Midas longed for gold, and the gods gave it him (4).

CHAP. II. THE SPHINX.

The grand unnamable Sphinx-riddle, which each man is called upon to solve. Notions of the foolish concerning justice and judgment. Courts of Westminster, and the general High Court of the Universe. The one strong thing, the just thing, the true thing (p. 6).—A noble Conservatism, as well as an ignoble. In all battles of men each fighter, in the end, prospers according to his right: Wallace of Scotland (10).—Fact and Semblance. What is Justice ? As many men as there are in a Nation who can *see* Heaven's Justice, so many are there who stand between it and perdition (12).

CHAP. III. MANCHESTER INSURRECTION.

Peterloo not an unsuccessful Insurrection. Governors who wait for Insurrection to instruct them, getting into the fatallest courses. Unspeakable County Yeomanry. Poor Manchester operatives, and their huge inarticulate question : Unhappy Workers, unhappier Idlers, of this actual England ! (p. 13).—Fair day's-wages for fair day's-work: Milton's ' wages '; Cromwell's. Pay to each man what he has earned and done and deserved ; what more have we to ask ?—Some not *in*supportable approximation indispensable and inevitable (17).

CHAP. IV. MORRISON'S PILL.

A state of mind worth reflecting on. No Morrison's Pill for curing the maladies of Society: Universal alteration of regimen and way of life: Vain jargon giving place to some genuine Speech again (p. 20).—If we walk according to the Law of this Universe, the Law-Maker will befriend us; if not, not. Quacks, sham heroes, the one bane of the world. Quack and Dupe, upper side and under of the selfsame substance (22).

CHAP. V. ARISTOCRACY OF TALENT.

All misery the fruit of unwisdom: Neither with individuals nor with Nations is it fundamentally otherwise. Nature in late centuries universally supposed to be dead; but now everywhere asserting herself to be alive and miraculous. The guidance of this country not sufficiently wise (p. 24).—Aristocracy of Talent, or government by the Wisest, a dreadfully difficult affair to get started. The true *eye* for talent; and the flunkey eye for respectabilities, warm garnitures and larders dropping fatness : Bobus and Bobissimus (26).

CHAP. VI. HERO-WORSHIP.

Enlightened Egoism, never so luminous, not the rule by which man's life can be led : A *soul*, different from a stomach in any sense of the word. Hero-worship, done differently in every different epoch of the world. Reform, like Charity, must begin at home. 'Arrestment of the knaves and dastards,' beginning by arresting our own poor selves out of that fraternity (p. 29).—The present Editor's purpose to himself full of hope. A Load-star in the eternal sky : A glimmering of light, for here and there a human soul (32).

BOOK II.—THE ANCIENT MONK

CHAP. I. JOCELIN OF BRAKELOND.

How the Centuries stand lineally related to each other. The one Book not permissible, the kind that has nothing in it. Jocelin's 'Chronicle', a private Boswellean Note-book, now seven centuries old. How Jocelin, from under his monk's cowl, looked out on that narrow section of the world in a really *human* manner : A wise simplicity in him; a *veracity* that goes deeper than words. Jocelin's Monk-Latin; and Mr. Rokewood's editorial helpfulness and fidelity (p. 35).—A veritable Monk of old Bury St. Edmunds worth attending to. This England of ours, of the year 1200 : Cœur-de-Lion : King Lackland, and his thirteenpenny mass. The poorest historical Fact, and the grandest imaginative Fiction (38).

CHAP. II. ST. EDMUNDSBURY.

St. Edmund's Bury, a prosperous brisk Town; Extensive ruins of the Abbey still visible. Assiduous Pedantry, and its rubbish-heaps called 'History'. Another world it was, when those black ruins first saw the sun as walls. At lowest, O dilettante friend, let us know always that it *was* a world. No easy matter to get across the chasm of Seven Centuries: Of all helps, a Boswell, even a small Boswell, the welcomest (p. 42).

CHAP. III. LANDLORD EDMUND.

'Battle of Fornham', a fact, though a forgotten one. Edmund, Landlord of the Eastern Counties: A very singular kind of ' land lord '. How he came to be ' sainted '. Seen and felt to have done verily a man's part in this life-pilgrimage of his. How they took up the slain body of their Edmund, and reverently embalmed it (p. 45).—Pious munificence, ever growing by new pious gifts. Certain Times do crystallise themselves in a magnificent manner; others in a rather shabby one (50).

CHAP. IV. ABBOT HUGO.

All things have two faces, a light one and a dark: The Ideal has to grow in the Real, and to seek its bed and board there, often in a very sorry manner. Abbot Hugo, grown old and feeble. Jew debts, and Jew creditors. How approximate justice strives to accomplish itself (p. 51).—In the old monastic Books, almost no mention whatever of ' personal religion '. A poor Lord Abbot, all stuck-over with horse-leeches: A ' royal commission of inquiry ', to no purpose. A monk's first duty, obedience. Magister Samson, Teacher of the Novices. The Abbot's providential death (53).

CHAP. V. TWELFTH CENTURY.

Inspectors or Custodiars; the King not in any breathless haste to appoint a new Abbot. Dim and very strange looks that monk-life to us. Our venerable ancient spinning grandmothers, shriek-ing, and rushing out with their distaffs. Lakenheath eels, too slippery to be caught (p. 56).—How much is alive in England, in that Twelfth Century; how much not yet come into life. Feudal Aristocracy; Willelmus Conquestor: Not a steeple-chimney yet got on end from sea to sea (59).

CHAP. VI. MONK SAMSON.

Monk-Life and Monk-Religion: A great heaven-high Unquestionability, encompassing, interpenetrating all human Duties. Our modern Arkwright Joe-Manton ages: All human dues and reciprocities changed into one great due of ' cash-payment'. The old monks but a limited class of creatures, with a somewhat dull life of it (p. 60).— One Monk of a taciturn nature distinguishes himself among those babbling ones. A Son of poor Norfolk parents. Little Samson's awful dream ; His poor mother dedicates him to St. Edmund. He grows to be a learned man, of devout grave nature. Sent to Rome on business ; and returns *too* successful : Method of travelling thither in those days. His tribulations at home : Strange conditions under which Wisdom has sometimes to struggle with Folly (62).

CHAP. VII. THE CANVASSING.

A new Abbot to be elected. Even gossip, seven centuries off, has significance. The Prior with Twelve Monks, to wait on his Majesty at Waltham. An 'election' the one important social act : Given the Man a People choose, the worth and worthlessness of the People itself is given (p. 66).

CHAP. VIII. THE ELECTION.

Electoral methods and manipulations. Brother Samson ready oftenest with some question, some suggestion, that has wisdom in it. The Thirteen off to Waltham, to choose their Abbot: In the solitude of the Convent, Destiny thus big and in her birthtime, what gossiping, babbling, dreaming of dreams! (p. 69).— King Henry II. in his high Presence-chamber. Samson chosen Abbot : The King's royal acceptation (71).—St. Edmundsbury Monks, without express ballot-box or other winnowing machine. In every Nation and Community, there is at all times *a fittest*, wisest, bravest, best. Human Worth and human Worthlessness (74).

CHAP. IX. ABBOT SAMSON.

The Lord Abbot's arrival at St. Edmundsbury : The selfsame Samson, yesterday a poor mendicant, this day finds himself a *Dominus Abbas* and mitred Peer of Parliament (p. 75).— Depth and opulence of true social vitality in those old barbarous ages. True Governors go about under all manner of disguises now as then. Genius, Poet; what these words mean. George the Third, head charioteer of England; and Robert Burns, gauger of ale in Dumfries (76).— How Abbot Samson found a Convent all in dilapidation. His life-long harsh apprenticeship to governing, namely, obeying. First get your Man; all is got. Danger of blockheads (78).

Chap. X. Government.

Beautiful, how the chrysalis governing-soul, shaking off its dusty slough and prison, starts forth winged, a true royal soul!—One first labour, to institute a strenuous review and radical reform of his economics. Wheresoever Disorder may stand or lie, let it have a care; here is a man that has declared war with it (p. 81).—In less than four years the Convent Debts are all liquidated; and the harpy Jews banished from St. Edmundsbury. New life springs beneficent everywhere: Spiritual rubbish as little tolerated as material (83).

Chap. XI. The Abbot's Ways.

Reproaches, open and secret, of ingratitude, unsociability: Except for 'fit men' in all kinds, hard to say for whom Abbot Samson had much favour. Remembrance of benefits (p. 84).—An eloquent man, but intent more on substance than on ornament. A just clear heart the basis of all true talent. One of the justest of judges: His invaluable 'talent of silence'. The kind of people he liked worst. Hospitality and stoicism (86).—The country, in those days, still dark with noble wood and umbrage: How the old trees gradually died out, no man heeding it. Monachism itself, so rich and fruitful once, now all rotted into *peat*. Devastations of four-footed cattle and Henry-the-Eighths (88).

Chap. XII. The Abbot's Troubles.

The troubles of Abbot Samson, more than tongue can tell. Not the spoil of victory, only the glorious toil of battle, can be theirs who really govern. An insurrection of the Monks: Behave better, ye remiss Monks, and thank Heaven for such an Abbot (p. 89).— Worn down with incessant toil and tribulation: Gleams of hilarity too; little snatches of encouragement granted even to a Governor. How my Lord of Clare, coming to claim his *un*due 'debt', gets a Rowland for his Oliver. A Life of Literature; noble and ignoble (91).

Chap. XIII. In Parliament.

Confused days of Lackland's usurpation, while Cœur-de-Lion was away: Our brave Abbot took helmet himself, excommunicating all who should favour Lackland. King Richard a captive in Germany (p. 94).—St. Edmund's Shrine not meddled with: A Heavenly Awe overshadowed and encompassed, as it still ought and must, all earthly Business whatsoever (95).

Chap. XIV. Henry of Essex.

How St. Edmund punished terribly, yet with mercy : A Narrative, significant of the Time. Henry Earl of Essex, standard-bearer of England : No right reverence for the Heavenly in Man. A traitor or a coward. Solemn Duel, by the King's appointment. An evil Conscience doth make cowards of us all (p. 96).

Chap. XV. Practical-Devotional.

A Tournament proclaimed and held in the Abbot's domain, in spite of him. Roystering young dogs brought to reason. The Abbot a man that generally remains master at last : The importunate Bishop of Ely outwitted. A man that dare abide King Richard's anger, with justice on his side. Thou brave Richard, thou brave Samson ! (p. 99).—The basis of Abbot Samson's life, truly religion. His zealous interest in the Crusades. The great antique heart, like a child's in its simplicity, like a man's in its earnest solemnity and depth. His comparative silence as to his religion, precisely the healthiest sign of him and it. Methodism, Dilettantism, Puseyism (103).

Chap. XVI. St. Edmund.

Abbot Samson built many useful, many pious edifices : All ruinous, incomplete things, an eye-sorrow to him. Rebuilding the great Altar : A glimpse of the glorious Martyr's very Body. What a scene ; how far vanished from us, in these unworshipping ages of ours ! The manner of men's Hero-worship, verily the innermost fact of their existence, determining all the rest (p. 106).—On the whole, who knows how to reverence the Body of Man ?—Abbot Samson, at the culminating point of his existence : Our real-phantasmagory of St. Edmundsbury plunges into the bosom of the Twelfth Century again, and all is over (112).

Chap. XVII. The Beginnings.

Formulas, the very skin and muscular tissue of a Man's Life : Living Formulas, and dead. Habit the deepest law of human nature. A pathway through the pathless. Nationalities. Pulpy infancy, kneaded, baked into any form you choose : The Man of Business ; the hard-handed Labourer ; the genus Dandy. No mortal out of the depths of Bedlam, but lives by Formulas (p. 113).—The hosts and generations of brave men, Oblivion has swallowed : Their crumbled dust, the soil our life-fruit grows on. Invention of Speech ; Forms of Worship ; Methods of Justice. This English Land, here and now, the summary of what was wise, and noble, and accordant with God's Truth, in all the generations of English Men. The thing called 'Fame' (116).

BOOK III.—THE MODERN WORKER

CHAP. I. PHENOMENA.

How men have 'forgotten God'; taken the Fact of this Universe as it *is not*; God's Laws, become a Greatest-Happiness Principle, a Parliamentary Expediency. Man has lost the *soul* out of him, and begins to find the want of it (p. 123).—The old Pope of Rome, with his stuffed dummy to do the kneeling for him. Few men that worship by the rotatory Calabash, do it in half so great, frank or effectual a way (124).—Our Aristocracy, no longer able to *do* its work; and not in the least conscious that it has any work to do. The Champion of England 'lifted into his saddle'. The Hatter in the Strand, mounting a huge lath-and-plaster Hat. Our noble ancestors have fashioned for us, in how many thousand senses, a 'life-road'; and we their sons, are madly, literally enough, 'consuming the way' (126).

CHAP. II. GOSPEL OF MAMMONISM.

Heaven and Hell, often as the words are on our tongue, got to be fabulous or semi-fabulous for most of us. The real 'Hell' of the English. Cash-payment, *not* the sole or even chief relation of human beings. Practical Atheism, and its despicable fruits (p. 130).—One of Dr. Alison's melancholy facts: A poor Irish Widow in the Lanes of Edinburgh, *proving* her sisterhood. Until we get a human *soul* within us, all things are *im*possible: Infatuated geese, with feathers and without (134).

CHAP. III. GOSPEL OF DILETTANTISM.

Mammonism at least works; but 'Go gracefully idle in Mayfair', what does or can that mean?—Impotent, insolent Donothingism in Practice, and Saynothingism in Speech. No man now speaks a plain word: Insincere Speech, the prime material of insincere Action (p. 135).—Moslem parable of Moses and the Dwellers by the Dead Sea: The Universe *become* a Humbug, to the Apes that thought it one (137).

CHAP. IV. HAPPY.

All work, noble; and every noble crown a crown of thorns. Man's pitiful pretension to be what he calls 'happy': His Greatest-Happiness Principle fast becoming a rather unhappy one. Byron's large audience. A philosophical Doctor: A disconsolate Meat-jack, gnarring and creaking with rust and work (p. 138).—The only 'happiness' a brave man ever troubled himself much about, the happiness to get his work done (140).

Chap. V. The English.

With all thy theoretic platitudes, with a depth of practical sense in thee, great England ! A dumb people, who can do great acts, but not describe them. The noble Warhorse, and the Dog of Knowledge : The freest utterances not by any means the best (p. 142).—The done Work, much more than the spoken Word, an epitome of the man. The Man of Practice, and the Man of Theory : Ineloquent Brindley. The English, of all Nations, the stupidest in speech, the wisest in action : Sadness and seriousness : Unconsciously this great Universe is great to them. The Silent Romans. John Bull's admirable insensibility to Logic (143).—All great Peoples conservative. The English Ready-Reckoner a Solecism in Eastcheap. Berserkir-rage. Truth and Justice alone *capable* of being ' conserved '. Bitter indignation engendered by the Corn-Laws in every just English heart (147).

Chap. VI. Two Centuries.

The ' Settlement ' of the year 1660, one of the mournfullest that ever took place in this land of ours. The true end of Government, to guide men in the way they should go : The true good of this life, the portal of infinite good in the life to come. Oliver Cromwell's body hung on the Tyburn-gallows ; the type of Puritanism found futile, inexecutable, execrable. The Spiritualism of England, for two godless centuries, utterly forgettable : Her practical Material Work alone memorable (p. 150).—Bewildering obscurations and impediments : Valiant Sons of Toil enchanted, by the million, in their Poor-Law Bastille. Giant Labour, yet to be King of this Earth (153).

Chap. VII. Over-Production.

An idle Governing Class addressing its Workers with an indictment of ' Over-production '. Duty of justly apportioning the Wages of Work done. A game-preserving Aristocracy, guiltless of producing or apportioning anything. Owning the soil of England (p. 154).—The Working Aristocracy, steeped in ignoble Mammonism : The Idle Aristocracy, with its yellow parchments and pretentious futilities (156).

Chap. VIII. Unworking Aristocracy.

Our Land the *Mother* of us all : No true Aristocracy but must possess the Land. Men talk of ' selling ' Land : Whom it belongs to. Our much-*consuming* Aristocracy : By the law of their position bound to furnish guidance and governance. Mad and miserable Corn-Laws (p. 157).—The Working Aristocracy, and its terrible New-Work : The Idle Aristocracy, and its horoscope of despair (160).—A High Class without duties to do, like a tree planted on precipices. In a valiant suffering for others, not in a slothful making others suffer for us, did nobleness ever lie. The Pagan Hercules ; the Czar of Russia (162).—Parchments, venerable and not venerable. Benedict the Jew, and his usuries. No Chapter on the Corn-Laws : The Corn-Laws too mad to have a Chapter (163).

Chap. IX. Working Aristocracy.

Many things for the Working Aristocracy, in their extreme need, to consider. A National Existence supposed to depend on 'selling cheaper' than any other People. Let inventive men try to invent a little how cotton at its present cheapness could be somewhat justlier divided. Many 'impossibles' will have to become possible (p. 164).—Supply-and-demand : For what noble work was there ever yet any audible 'demand' in that poor sense? (168).

Chap. X. Plugson of Undershot.

Man's philosophies usually the 'supplement of his practice': Symptoms of social death. Cash-Payment : The Plugson Ledger, and the Tablets of Heaven's Chancery, discrepant exceedingly (p. 169).—All human things do require to have an Ideal in them. How murderous Fighting became a 'glorious Chivalry'. Noble devout-hearted Chevaliers. Ignoble Bucaniers and Chactaw Indians : Howel Davies. Napoleon flung out, at last, to St. Helena ; the latter end of him sternly compensating for the beginning (171).—The indomitable Plugson, as yet a Bucanier and Chactaw. William Conqueror and his Norman followers. Organisation of Labour : Courage, there are yet many brave men in England ! (173).

Chap. XI. Labour.

A perennial nobleness, and even sacredness in Work. Significance of the Potter's Wheel. Blessed is he who has found his Work ; let him ask no other blessedness (p. 176).—A brave Sir Christopher, and his Paul's Cathedral : Every noble work, at first 'impossible'. Columbus, royallest Sea-king of all : A depth of Silence, deeper than the Sea ; a Silence unsoundable ; known to God only (178).

Chap. XII. Reward.

Work is Worship : Labour, wide as the Earth, has its summit in
Heaven. One monster there is in the world, the idle man
(p. 181).—' Fair day's-wages for a fair day's-work ', the most unrefusable demand. The ' wages ' of every noble Work, in Heaven
or else Nowhere : The brave man has to *give* his Life away. He
that works, bodies forth the form of Things Unseen. Strange
mystic affinity of Wisdom and Insanity : All Work, in its degree,
a making of Madness sane (183).—Labour not a devil, even when
encased in Mammonism : The unredeemed ugliness, a slothful
People. The vulgarest Plugson of a Master-Worker, not a man
to strangle by Corn-Laws and Shot-belts (186).

Chap. XIII. Democracy.

Man must actually have his debts and earnings a little better
paid by man. At no time was the lot of the dumb millions of
toilers so entirely unbearable as now. Sisterhood, brotherhood,
often forgotten ; but never before so expressly denied. Mungo
Park and his poor Black Benefactress (p. 188).—Gurth born thrall
of Cedric the Saxon : Liberty, a Divine thing ; but 'liberty to die
by starvation' not so divine. Nature's Aristocracies. William
Conqueror, a resident House-Surgeon provided by Nature for her
beloved English People (191).—Democracy, the despair of finding
Heroes to govern us, and contented putting up with the want of
them. The very Tailor unconsciously symbolising the reign of
Equality. Wherever ranks do actually exist, strict division
of costumes will also be enforced (194).—Freedom from oppression,
an indispensable yet most insignificant portion of Human Liberty.
A *best path* does exist for every man ; a thing which, here and now,
it were of all things *wisest* for him to do. Mock Superiors and
Real Superiors (196).

Chap. XIV. Sir Jabesh Windbag

Oliver Cromwell, the remarkablest Governor we have had for the
last five centuries or so : No volunteer in Public Life, but plainly
a balloted soldier : The Government of England put into his
hands (p. 200).—Windbag, weak in the faith of a God ; strong
only in the faith that Paragraphs and Plausibilities bring votes.
Five years of popularity or unpopularity ; and *after* those five
years, an Eternity. Oliver has to appear before the Most High
Judge : Windbag, appealing to 'Posterity' (201).

Chap. XV. Morrison Again.

New Religions: This new stage of progress, proceeding 'to invent God', a very strange one indeed (p. 203).—Religion, the Inner Light or Moral Conscience of a man's soul. Infinite difference between a Good man and a Bad. The great Soul of the World, just and not unjust: Faithful, unspoken, but not ineffectual 'prayer'. Penalties: The French Revolution; cruellest Portent that has risen into created Space these ten centuries. Man needs no 'New Religion'; nor is like to get it: Spiritual Dastardism, and sick folly (204).—One Liturgy which does remain forever unexceptionable, that of *Praying by Working*. Sauerteig on the symbolic influences of Washing. Chinese Pontiff-Emperor and his significant 'punctualities' (209).—Goethe and German Literature. The great event for the world, now as always, the arrival in it of a new Wise Man. Goethe's *Mason-Lodge* (212).

BOOK IV.—HOROSCOPE

Chap. I. Aristocracies.

To predict the Future, to manage the Present, would not be so impossible, had not the Past been so sacrilegiously mishandled: A godless century, looking back to centuries that were godly (p. 215).—A new real Aristocracy and Priesthood. The noble Priest always a noble *Aristos* to begin with, and something more to end with. Modern Preachers, and the *real* Satanas that now is. Abbot-Samson and William-Conqueror times. The mission of a Land Aristocracy, a *sacred* one, in both senses of that old word. Truly a 'Splendour of God' did dwell in those old rude veracious ages. Old Anselm travelling to Rome, to appeal against King Rufus. Their quarrel at bottom a great quarrel (217).—The boundless Future, predestined, nay already extant though unseen. Our Epic, not *Arms and the Man*, but *Tools and the Man*; an infinitely wider kind of Epic. Important that our grand Reformation were begun (224).

Chap. II. Bribery Committee.

Our theory, perfect purity of Tenpound Franchise; our practice, irremediable bribery. Bribery, indicative not only of length of purse, but of brazen dishonesty: Proposed improvements. A Parliament, starting with a lie in its mouth, promulgates strange horoscopes of itself (p. 226).—Respect paid to those worthy of no respect: Pandarus Dogdraught. The indigent discerning Freeman; and the kind of men he is called upon to vote for (229).

Chap. III. The one Institution.

The 'Organisation of Labour', if well understood, the Problem of the whole Future. Governments of various degrees of utility. Kilkenny Cats; Spinning-Dervishes; Parliamentary Eloquence. A Prime-Minister who would dare believe the heavenly omens (p. 231).—Who can despair of Governments, that passes a Soldier's Guard-house?—Incalculable what, by arranging, commanding and regimenting, can be made of men. Organisms enough in the dim huge Future; and 'United Services' quite other than the redcoat one (234).—Legislative interference between Workers and Master-Workers increasingly indispensable. Sanitary Reform: People's Parks: A right Education Bill, and effective Teaching Service. Free bridge for Emigrants: England's sure markets, among her Colonies. London, the *All-Saxon-Home*, rendezvous of all the 'Children of the Harz-Rock' (237).—The English essentially conservative: Always the invincible instinct to hold fast by the Old, to admit the *minimum* of New. Yet new epochs do actually come; and with them new peremptory necessities. A certain Editor's stipulated work (241).

Chap. IV. Captains of Industry.

Government can do much, but it can in nowise do all. Fall of Mammon: To be a noble Master among noble Workers, will again be the first ambition with some few (p. 242).—The Leaders of Industry, virtually the Captains of the World: Doggeries and Chivalries. Isolation, the sum-total of wretchedness to man. All social growths in this world have required organising; and Work, the grandest of human interests, does now require it (243).

Chap. V. Permanence.

The 'tendency to persevere', to persist in spite of hindrances, discouragements and 'impossibilities', that which distinguishes the Species Man from the Genus Ape. Month-long contracts, and Exeter-Hall purblindness. A practical manufacturing Quaker's care for his workmen (p. 248).—Blessing of Permanent Contract: Permanence in all things, at the earliest possible moment, and to the latest possible. Vagrant Sam-Slicks. The wealth of a man the number of things he loves and blesses, which he is loved and blessed by (251).—The Worker's *interest* in the enterprise with which he is connected. How to reconcile Despotism with Freedom (252).

CHAP. VI. THE LANDED.

A man with fifty, with five hundred, with a thousand pounds a day, given him freely, without condition at all, might be a rather strong Worker: The sad reality, very ominous to look at. Will he awaken, be alive again; or is this death-fit very death?— Goethe's Duke of Weimar. Doom of Idleness (p. 253).—To sit idle aloft, like absurd Epicurus'-gods, a poor life for a man. Independence, 'lord of the lion-heart and eagle-eye': Rejection of sham Superiors, the needful preparation for obedience to *real* Superiors (256).

CHAP. VII. THE GIFTED.

Tumultuous anarchy, calmed by noble effort into fruitful sovereignty. Mammon like Fire, the usefullest of servants, if the frightfullest of masters. Souls to whom the omnipotent guinea is, on the whole, an impotent guinea: Not a May-game is this man's life; but a battle and stern pilgrimage: God's justice, human Nobleness, Veracity and Mercy, the essence of his very being (p. 258).—What a man of Genius is. The Highest 'Man of Genius'. Genius, the clearer presence of God Most High in a man. Of intrinsic Valetisms you cannot, with whole Parliaments to help you, make a Heroism (261).

CHAP. VIII. THE DIDACTIC.

One preacher who does preach with effect, and gradually persuade all persons. Repentant Captains of Industry: A Chactaw Fighter, become a Christian Fighter (p. 263).—Doomsday in the afternoon. The 'Christianity' that cannot get on without a minimum of Four-thousand-five-hundred, will give place to something better that can. Beautiful to see the brutish empire of Mammon cracking everywhere: A strange, chill, almost ghastly dayspring in Yankeeland itself. Here as there, Light is coming into the world. Whoso believes, let him begin to fulfil: 'Impossible,' where Truth and Mercy and the everlasting Voice of Nature order, can have no place in the brave man's dictionary (264).—Not on Ilion's or Latium's plains; on far other plains and places henceforth can noble deeds be done. The last Partridge of England shot and ended: Aristocracies with beards on their chins. O, it is great, and there is no other greatness: To make some nook of God's Creation a little fruitfuller; to make some human hearts a little wiser, manfuller, happier: It is work for a God! (266).

INDEX

153; Organisation of, 176, 189, 231; perennial nobleness and sacredness in, 176. *See* Chivalry, Work.

Laissez-faire, 166; general breakdown of, 166, 167.

Lakenheath eels, 58.

Landlords, past and present, 47; Land-owning, 156; who the Land belongs to, 158; the mission of a Land Aristocracy a *sacred* one, 221, 253.

Laughter, 136.

Law, gradual growth of, 118; the Maker's Laws, 207. *See* Chancery.

Legislative interference, 237.

Liberty, true meaning of, 191, 196.

Life, the, to come, 150, 209; Life never a May-game for men, 189, 260.

Literature, noble and ignoble, 93.

Liturgies, 117.

Liverpool, 59.

Loadstar, a, in the eternal sky, 33.

Logical futilities, 143, 146.

Machinery, exporting, 165.

Mahomet, 258.

Mammon, not a god at all, 61; Gospel of Mammonism, 130, 171; Working Mammonism better than Idle Dilettantism, 132, 135, 186; getting itself strangled, 164; fall of Mammon, 243, 264; Mammon like Fire, 259. *See* Economics.

Man the Missionary of Order, 82, 205; sacredness of the human Body, 112; a born Soldier, 172; a God-created Soul, 207. *See* Great Man.

Manchester Insurrection, 13; poor Manchester operatives, 13, 43; Manchester in the twelfth century, 59; even sooty Manchester built on the infinite Abysses, 206.

Marriage-contracts, 249, 251.

Master, eye of the, 82.

Meat-jack, a disconsolate, 140.

Methodism, 54, 60, 105.

Midas, 6.

Mights and Rights, 172.

Millocracy, our giant, 126.

Milton's 'wages', 17.

Misery, all, the fruit of unwisdom, 24; strength, that has not yet found its way, 260.

Monks, ancient and modern, 38, 39; the old monks not without secularity, 53, 61; insurrection of monks, 90.

Morality, 147.

Morrison's Pill, 20; men's 'Religion' a kind of, 205.

Moses and the Dwellers by the Dead-Sea, 137.

Mungo Park, 190.

National Misery the result of national misguidance, 25.

Nationality, 114.

Nature, not dead but alive and miraculous, 25.

Negro Slavery and White Nomadism, 249.

New Testament, 170-1, 261.

Nobleness, meaning of, 162.

Obedience, 79.

Oblivion a still resting-place, 121.

Organising, what may be done by, 235, 244-5.

Originality, 117. *See* Path-making.

Over-production, charge of, 154, 183.

Pandarus Dogdraught, 221, 229.

Parchments, venerable and not venerable, 156, 163.

Parliament and the Courts of Westminster, 8, 232; a Parliament starting with a lie in its mouth, 227.

Past, Present and Future, 34, 215, 224, 240.

Path-making, 114.

Pedantry, 42.

INDEX TO INTRODUCTION
AND NOTES

PRINTED IN GREAT BRITAIN AT THE UNIVERSITY PRESS, OXFORD
BY JOHN JOHNSON, PRINTER TO THE UNIVERSITY